Administration and Management in Criminal Justice

This book is dedicated to my husband, Tab, who always supports my dreams and projects, even when they require time away from home and family. It is also dedicated to my children, Bridget, Brooke, and Landon, who have brought more joy to my life than I ever thought possible.

J. A.

I would like to dedicate this book to my late father, Harivansh Lal Sawhney, a brave and honest police officer who taught me the value of treating people with respect and dignity. Recognizing his outstanding quality of service and bravery, the Government of India decorated him with the three highest honors of the land (President's Gold Medal, Police Gold Medal, and an Army medal), received by only a handful of officers in the history of India.

R. S.

Administration and Management in Criminal Justice

A Service Quality Approach

Jennifer M. Allen
University of North Georgia

Rajeev Sawhney
Western Illinois University

Los Angeles | London | New Delhi
Singapore | Washington DC

Los Angeles | London | New Delhi
Singapore | Washington DC

FOR INFORMATION:

SAGE Publications, Inc.
2455 Teller Road
Thousand Oaks, California 91320
E-mail: order@sagepub.com

SAGE Publications Ltd.
1 Oliver's Yard
55 City Road
London EC1Y 1SP
United Kingdom

SAGE Publications India Pvt. Ltd.
B 1/I 1 Mohan Cooperative Industrial Area
Mathura Road, New Delhi 110 044
India

SAGE Publications Asia-Pacific Pte. Ltd.
3 Church Street
#10-04 Samsung Hub
Singapore 049483

Printed in the United States of America

Library of Congress Cataloging-in-Publication Data

Allen, Jennifer M., author.

Administration and management in criminal justice : a service quality approach / Jennifer M. Allen, University of North Georgia, Rajeev Sawhney, Western Illinois University.—Second edition.

p. cm.
Includes bibliographical references and index.

ISBN 978-1-4833-5070-7 (pbk. : alk. paper)

1. Criminal justice, Administration of. 2. Leadership. 3. Police administration. I. Sawhney, Rajeev, author. II. Title.

K5001.A945 2014
364.068—dc23   2014008565

This book is printed on acid-free paper.

Acquisitions Editor: Jerry Westby
Publishing Associate: MaryAnn Vail
Production Editors: Brittany Bauhaus, David C. Felts
Copy Editor: Codi Bowman
Typesetter: C&M Digitals (P) Ltd.
Proofreader: Talia Greenberg
Indexer: Will Ragsdale
Cover Designer: Edgar Abarca
Marketing Manager: Terra Schultz

14 15 16 17 18 10 9 8 7 6 5 4 3 2 1

Brief Contents

Detailed Contents

Preface

We felt compelled to write this textbook because there are only a few textbooks in the area of administration and criminal justice that focus specifically on management concepts in this nonprofit, service-oriented industry. However, these handfuls of books that focus on management of criminal justice do not consider service quality. Instead, these books tend to discuss management in general without understanding the customer using the service and the role of the customer in service delivery. Since customers are part of any service delivery process, they should be an inherent part of the process that is designed to deliver the service. In criminal justice, the customer changes from call to call—sometimes it is a victim, a complainant, or a community member; other times it is an offender or another officer or agency. Thus, management and administration approaches must be customized to the environment being serviced. We hold that using a service approach to management is much more appropriate in the changing criminal justice environment. To date, and to the best of our knowledge, this is the first textbook that has adopted a service quality approach to administration in the criminal justice field. We believe this textbook is innovative and will challenge the current understandings of management in criminal justice agencies held by practitioners and researchers alike.

Approach

In this text, we question the traditional closed-system approaches often used in criminal justice and introduce the concepts used in open systems and in service quality approaches. We examine criminal justice services by focusing on who the customers are, what their demands and needs happen to be, how the changing environment can affect these services, and how criminal justice administrators can respond to the dynamic customer and environmental bases. The book also addresses the constraints placed on the field of criminal justice and how these restrictions impact the choices managers and line staff can and do make, as well as how services are provided. We acknowledge the increased pressures on criminal justice professionals to work within a global environment and in communities with heightened expectations. We also acknowledge the efforts criminal justice agencies are making to become more customer-friendly. This textbook is a forward-thinking approach to management in criminal justice, emphasizing proactive techniques for administration. We feel that training in service quality must start early in the career and in the educational process to produce effective and successful administrators in the criminal justice system. Using a service quality lens to understand and facilitate the criminal justice system provides a better learning experience in the changing U.S. and global environments for undergraduate and graduate students, who will be staffing this system in the near future. By using case studies at the end of each chapter, we provide opportunities to apply the material learned. We believe this approach will have greater meaning for the students' learning process.

The text is written with five express objectives. The first objective is to provide the theories of management. The second objective is to look at the theories through closed- and open-system approaches. The third objective is to draw attention to the issues and concerns of these two approaches in nonprofit service industries, such as criminal justice. The fourth objective is to provide a service quality lens to examine how the criminal justice field could be (and is being) redesigned to better address community needs and to respond to global and national dilemmas. We also use this time to point out how the criminal justice field is evolving and accepting the importance of quality services. Finally, we present the information in such a way that students can internalize the importance of their future role in providing high-quality and effective criminal justice services.

The text is organized in 14 chapters. The first step in improving service delivery is identifying the customers and recognizing their importance within the service delivery process, also called the customer focus, which is the primary theme presented in Chapters 1 through 3. In Chapter 4, we discuss the changing global environment and the pressures that are forcing criminal justice agencies to become more customer-oriented. In Chapters 5 through 8, we present the management principles of conflict, power, ethics, motivation, leadership, and communication in the criminal justice environment, viewed through the service quality lens. In Chapters 9 through 13, we discuss the functional knowledge of criminal justice agencies and integrate the service quality principles in these areas. In the last chapter, we provide hands-on tools to incorporate the voice of the customer in designing/modifying criminal justice services to improve the delivery of service quality. We hope the approach adopted in this textbook will better prepare the students of criminal justice to design/redesign the service delivery process to bring a greater customer orientation, thus improving the overall service quality.

Pedagogical Aids

We have included the following learning aids in every chapter:

- Chapter objectives at the beginning of each chapter to highlight the information students should master
- "In the News" boxes to help students see the practical implications of what they are reading

- "Career Highlight" boxes that describe various types of jobs in management and administration in the criminal justice field
- End-of-chapter summaries to help students prepare for exams and review in shorter form what they have learned in the chapter
- Chapter review questions to assist students in preparing for exams and to encourage them to go beyond the memorization of terms and concepts learned in the chapter
- Case studies at the end of each chapter to allow students to apply the information they have learned in a situation similar to what is likely to occur in the field of criminal justice
- Internet resources that students can use to learn more about the criminal justice field and view research in hot topics in criminal justice administration
- Lists of references and suggested readings that provide students with the primary sources for the information in these chapters

Instructor Supplement

We have also created an Instructor's Manual/Test Bank, which includes chapter outlines, discussion questions, a test bank, PowerPoint slides of each chapter, and more.

Acknowledgments

As with any endeavor of this magnitude, there are always people behind the scenes who assist in the preparation and final product. First, we would like to thank the various agencies that granted permission for us to use their policies, procedure manuals, handouts, and other documents in the text. We would also like to thank the print media and other forums for their contributions to the "In the News" inserts. We would like to offer special acknowledgments to the publishing team at Sage for their continued assistance, creativity, and hard work. As we finish the second edition, we acknowledge the contributions made by Dr. Robert Fischer, Dr. Martha Heltsley, Professor Jill J. Myers, Professor Sabita Sawhney, and Professor Jane Schmidt-Wilk. We appreciate their hard work and expertise in the first edition. We also express appreciation to our families for their constant encouragement. We welcome your comments concerning the text and look forward to writing again in this field.

Jennifer M. Allen, jennifer.allen@ung.edu

Rajeev Sawhney, R-Sawhney@wiu.edu

Defining Management and Organization

LEARNING OBJECTIVES

Upon completion of this chapter, students should be able to do the following:

- Define management, organization, and leadership
- List and discuss criminal justice organizations and the various specialties in criminal justice
- Describe nonprofit and for-profit agencies

In an era of globalization accompanied by complexity, ambiguity, rapid change, and diversity, managing any organization or agency is a difficult task. Yet good management is critical to the survival of an organization or agency. In fact, Hanson (1986) has suggested that the ability to manage is more strongly related to a firm's profitability than any other factor. Managers are challenged with making decisions, formulating goals, creating a mission, enacting policies and procedures, and uniting individuals in the organization so that completion of all of these and other related tasks can be accomplished. Despite the fact that management permeates everything that an organization does, what "the management" actually is, is not always clearly defined or identified.

Management consists of many individuals in an organization at varying levels and ranks, often classified as lower management, middle management, and upper management. Of course, people are familiar with the terms *chief executive officer, director, president, chief operating officer,* and so on. These are automatically assumed to be titles that indicate the ranks of management. We also assume that those holding the management roles work to provide the organizational mission by making decisions and setting goals for those not designated as management. But are these obvious assumptions? Hecht (1980) asserts, "Many a person who carries the title of manager is not really a manager" (p. 1). What this means is that people on the front lines may make decisions, formulate procedures, and have input into the mission and long-term goals of the organization. Individuals employed in positions considered to be at the second or third level may also have input or titles that indicate they are managers within the organization. Does this make them management? According to Hecht, "Management is an activity," and managers are "charged with a number of people working at the task of getting some activity accomplished within a set period of time" (p. 1). Research defining management has been ongoing; and, to date, there is still not a clear definition of management for all organizations. This means that each organization faces the unique task of determining how it will be managed and by whom.

This chapter will investigate the definition of management as well as tasks commonly associated with managing an organization. The term *organization* will be defined, and key aspects of organizational structures in nonprofit and for-profit agencies will be discussed. Leadership and how leaders work within organizations are discussed as well. As this book pertains to management in criminal justice, a brief summary of criminal justice agencies and their management structures is also provided in this chapter. Each chapter in the text—this one included—ends with a fictional case study and summary discussion. The case studies provide scenarios likely to be encountered in real life. Although the case studies may resemble reality, they are based on fictitious names, places, and occurrences. There are questions at the end of each case study. There are no right or wrong answers to these questions. Instead, the intent is to allow for application and processing of the information learned in the chapter.

Defining Management

As discussed earlier, *management* is a difficult term to define. It is easier to identify what a manager does or is supposed to do than to define the actual term. If one were to search for the term *management* on the Internet, words such as *supervising, directing, managing, measuring results,* and so on would display, which are all action-oriented terms. Dwan (2003) identifies management as planning goals and specifying the purpose of the agency; organizing people, finances, resources, and activities; staffing, training, and socializing employees; leading the organization and the staff; and controlling, monitoring, and sanctioning when needed (p. 44). On closer scrutiny, one will find that both the explanation proposed by Dwan and the words displayed on the Internet identify management with tasks or responsibilities, while neither provides an exact definition.

Looking in another direction, one may find that management has been defined through theory such as *scientific management,* where those in charge of an organization are to maximize productivity through selection, training, and planning of tasks and employees. Management theory has also focused on Fayol's (1949) five functions of management—planning, organizing, commanding, coordinating, and providing feedback—and bureaucratic management, where there is a clear division of labor, rules, and procedures (Weber, 1947). There are also those who see management as a "process" to be studied and analyzed through cases so that correct techniques can be taught to others (Dale, 1960). There is the human relations approach that perceives management as closely tied to sociology and the various social systems in society (Barnard, 1938; March & Simon, 1958), emphasizing a manager's understanding of workers as socio-psychological beings who need to be motivated (Tannenbaum, Weschler, & Massarik, 1961). Management has also been discussed from both decision-making and mathematical perspectives (Koontz, 1961). Although most of these will be addressed in detail in later chapters, it is important to note that they appear to be the *roles* of management and not true definitions of what it is to manage.

Koontz (1961) stated, "Most people would agree that [management] means getting things done through and with people" (p. 17). *Management,* as viewed in this book, is best defined within groups. It is an ongoing process that works toward achieving organizational goals. It may consist of multiple organizational layers, offices, people, positions, and so on. In other words, management is an ongoing process of getting things done through a variety of people with the least amount of effort, expense, and waste, ultimately resulting in the achievement of organizational goals (Moore, 1964).

CAREER HIGHLIGHT BOX
AN INTRODUCTION

Students are often interested in the types of jobs available in criminal justice, but they are not always given the chance to explore the various options during their coursework. Since this book discusses a variety of criminal justice agencies and the administration and management of those agencies, it makes sense to expose students to different career opportunities that may be available in those organizations. In each of the following chapters, look for Career Highlight Boxes, which will provide information concerning specific occupations, typical duties, pay scales, and job requirements within or related to the criminal justice system. Keep in mind that different jurisdictions have distinct requirements, so this is only a small representation of the possibilities and occupations available. In addition, students are encouraged to examine the job outlook and prospects sections in each job description with a critical eye, since demands for workers with specific skill sets changes regularly. The authors suggest that students discuss career options with faculty and advisors as they narrow down their professional goals. Students are also encouraged to contact individuals currently working in the field of criminal justice to discuss opportunities, interests, and concerns.

Identifying an Organization

Blau and Scott (1962) defined an *organization* by using categories. The first category consists of the owners or managers of the organization, and the second are the members of the rank and file. Third are the clients, or what Blau and Scott referred to as the people who are outside the organization but have regular contact with it. Fourth is the public at large, or the members of society in which the organization operates. They suggest that organizations benefit someone—either the management, the membership, the client, or the commonwealth. This definition fits well with private enterprise in that the managers or shareholders may benefit greatly from the organization's business and sales. This definition also fits well with criminal justice, since the victim and the commonwealth (public) may benefit when an offender is arrested and placed in jail. A more contemporary definition of an organization suggests that it is "an organized or cohesive group of people working together to achieve commonly agreed goals and objectives" (McGovern, 1999). In criminal justice, the typical organization is focused on identifying, deterring, preventing, and processing crime and criminal acts. It is service based. The hope of achieving goals and objectives is the same as that found in private enterprise, but the functions and activities are in contrast to private enterprise or for-profit organizations.

Members of an organization usually share common visions, missions, values, and strategic goals. A *vision* is how individuals imagine the goals of the organization will be accomplished. Each person will have a particular perception of how the organization functions. So long as the organization is working according to the vision, people perceive the organization as going well. The *mission* is the overall purpose of the organization and is used to help describe organizations to those outside of it, such as community members. The mission may be a statement or a list of goals to be accomplished (Ivancevich, Donnelly, & Gibson, 1989). A correctional institution's mission may include statements regarding protecting the public, staff members, and inmates; providing opportunities for rehabilitation; and assisting in reintegrating offenders into society once they are released. A common mission statement in police departments may include phrases that support public safety, working with citizens and the community, and reducing crime. In its 2002 annual report, the Fairfax County Police Department in Virginia stated, "The Fairfax County Police Department protects persons and property by providing essential law enforcement and public safety services, while promoting community involvement, stability, and order through service, assistance and visibility" (Fairfax County Police Department, 2002, para. 1).

The *values* held in an organization are considered priorities. They incorporate aspects of the vision and the mission to focus the activities of an organization. The values are determined by the culture of the organization. In policing, the culture tends to revolve around providing services, controlling crime, and increasing public safety. There are strict policies and procedures to be followed in carrying out the activities of the policing agency. Officers' positions are well defined, and there is a clearly identified hierarchy in the organization. Employees are expected to be honest and show integrity while completing their tasks. Again, looking at the 2002 annual report of the Fairfax County Police Department, we see that its values were identified as the following:

We believe

- The highest moral and ethical standards are the cornerstone of the agency, and all members are expected to adhere to these standards.
- The agency, through all of our employees and volunteers, strives to uphold the public trust and maintain accountability to the public.
- The employees are the most important asset of the Department, and only through teamwork, mutual respect, and cooperation can the community be best served.
- The role of the police is determined by the community it serves; through a partnership with the citizens, the Department improves the quality of life through control and reduction of crime.
- The police and the community share in the responsibility for crime control and public safety.
- The capability to accomplish our mission is determined by the dedication to public service, diversity and quality of the workforce; therefore, we seek to recruit and retain individuals who possess those qualities.
- The agency must seek to collaborate with neighborhoods to better understand the nature of local problems and to develop meaningful and cooperative strategies to solve these problems.
- The agency must enhance the skills of all personnel to ensure motivation, creativity, dedication and professionalism, while creating an atmosphere of job satisfaction, enthusiasm, security and personal career development.
- Available resources, both personnel and financial, must be expended with maximum efficiency in order to provide optimum service to the citizens of Fairfax County.
- State-of-the-art technologies and up-to-date training are essential for the maintenance and enhancement of police service delivery to the citizens of the community.
- Through the application of these commonly held values, we will achieve excellence in policing in Fairfax County. (para. 2)

It is apparent in its statements that community inclusion, integrity, and training were key aspects of its organizational culture and, in turn, its value system. Expending funds in appropriate and accountable methods was also important to the Fairfax County Police Department. In other words, these were priorities to be accomplished by this organization.

Last, organizations use *strategic goals*. Members will work toward several organizational goals to accomplish the agency's mission. The goals, also known as objectives, are the main concerns of the organization. They are generally set by the administration and passed through formal and informal messages to employees. According to Hecht (1980), objectives should filter all the way to the bottom of the agency, with each unit or department establishing and working on its own unit goals while keeping the larger organizational strategic goals in mind (p. 91). Employees may also have personal goals set for themselves. It is hoped that personal goals do not conflict with organizational goals. If this occurs, the employee may be unsuccessful with the agency, or the agency's, accomplishment of larger organizational and unit goals may be blocked. The administration at that point must step in and restate the organizational strategic goals, or retrain or terminate the employee.

The strategic goals will have "two features: a description of an intended future state and action towards achieving that future state" (Day & Tosey, 2011, p. 517). The structure and culture of the organization are reiterated in the strategic goals. Likewise, the strategic goals of an agency provide employees the opportunity to align themselves and their personal goals with the agency's stated goals. Citizens in the community can determine whether an agency is accomplishing the mission by assessing the statements made in the strategic goals and the outputs delivered by the department. Doran (1981) and Locke and Latham (2002) claim that the more specific, measurable, achievable, realistic, and time-specific (SMART) the agency's goals are, the easier it is for others to determine if an agency has actually met the strategic goals.

The better organized an organization is, the better it will be able to accomplish its goals. The term *organized* can relate to structure. Organizations are structured vertically and horizontally. They contain departments, units, specializations, work groups, jobs, and so on.

The structure is typically determined by how formal the organization is. If there is a rigid hierarchy, or what some refer to as bureaucracy, the organization is seen as centralized. *Centralized organizations* house authority positions at the top of the hierarchy, in the upper levels of the administration. Managers are responsible for most decisions in centralized organizations, and communication is sent from management to lower-level staff on how to perform tasks and on changes in policy or procedure. However, if there are few levels of authority between the top managers and the line staff (those performing the everyday tasks or jobs), the organization is seen as decentralized. *Decentralized organizations* allow for lower-level staff to make decisions on policies or procedures that directly affect the accomplishment of tasks and goals (Ivancevich et al., 1989). Delegation of authority is foremost in decentralized organizations. The structure of organizations and the impact centralization or decentralization has on how organizations function and accomplish goals will be discussed in greater detail in Chapter 2. For now, it's important to realize that the structure of an organization determines how much *autonomy,* or the power to self-govern, workers have within that organization, and may influence their individual goal setting and achievement.

The chain of command within an organization can also determine structure. A *chain of command* is the vertical line of authority that defines who supervises whom in an organization. If an organization has a well-defined, unyielding chain of command, the organization is formalized. *Formal organizations* are bureaucratic and have clearly defined rules, procedures, and policies. Those at the higher levels of the chain have the authority and power to issue commands to those at the lower level. Police departments tend to use formal chains of command, with street officers reporting to sergeants, who report to lieutenants, who report to assistant chiefs, who report to the chief of police; there may even be levels in between these. Skipping a level in the chain of command may result in formal reprimands and is highly frowned upon by coworkers and supervisors. In a formal chain of command, information will travel from the chief of police, to the assistant chiefs, to the commanders and sergeants, and finally to the street-level officers. Questions or comments regarding the information will travel up the chain of command in a similar fashion. By looking at Figure 1.1, we can see a sample of the formal structure typical of a police department. The patrol officers report to the shift sergeants, who report to the commanders in each squad. Each area of specialty has a defined chain of command within the overall chain of command or formal structure of the organization.

On the other side of the spectrum, we can see criminal justice organizations that differ greatly in formalization. Although the size of the department may make a difference, organizations such as probation have a tendency not to rely as heavily on formal chains of command. This does not mean there is no organizational structure (the larger the agency, the more formalized it may be); the structure just tends to be more loosely tied together. The organization, therefore, is less formalized. Probation officers tend to report to one individual (the deputy chief), who is directly linked to the chief probation officer. The chief probation officer, the deputy chief, and the field probation officers typically have a direct line of communication to the judge(s). In essence, this is a more *informal organizational structure.* In probation, the *line staff,* or probation officers working directly with the clients in the field, have more autonomy and input into the decision making of the organization than do those in formalized organizations. They are able to interpret policy; ask managers questions directly; and answer questions asked by offenders, family members of offenders, service providers, the judge, and so on, with little or no managerial input. Figure 1.2 demonstrates an organizational chart in a medium-sized probation department. Notice the flat horizontal structure compared to the vertical structure of the police department in Figure 1.1.

Organizations are also structured as systems (discussed in detail in Chapters 2 and 3). Basically, this means that organizations have inputs, outputs, processes, and feedback. The whole system is designed to accomplish the organizational goal(s) (McNamara, 2007). *Inputs* are taken in by the organization that include such things as resources, money, technology, people, and so forth. The inputs are used to produce a *process* whereby the people in the organization spend money and resources on activities that meet the mission of the organization in hopes that the identified goals will be accomplished. The *outputs* are the tangible results (e.g., products, services, or jobs; or, in the case of criminal justice, lowered crime rates, better protection, etc.) of the efforts produced in the process (McNamara, 2007). These are identifiable by those outside of the organization and are generally used to determine if the organization is successful. The final step in the systems approach includes feedback. This *feedback* comes from the larger environment as well as from customers, clients, stakeholders, employees, or the government, to name a few sources. In systems open to the environment, the feedback may be used to modify the inputs and processes used in accomplishing future goals (McNamara, 2007). In organizations closed to the environment, the feedback may or may not be considered in changes that are made to the organization.

The organization may have subsystems that operate within the larger system as well. Each subsystem can be thought of as a separate organization that works to accomplish its own goals while contributing to the accomplishment of the larger

NORMAL POLICE DEPARTMENT
Organizational Chart
August 1, 2008

Chief of Police

Office Associates

Assistant Chief Support Services

Vice Unit Sergeant

Vice Detectives

Record Supervisor

Office Associates

Community Services Officer

School Resource Officers

Crossing Guards

Accreditaion Manager

Crime Analyst

Youth Intervention Specialist

Investigations Unit Sergeant

CID Detectives

Evidence/Prop. Technician

Office Associate

Assistant Chief Operations

7–3 Shift Lieutenant

Shift Sergeants

Patrol Officers

Traffic Officers

Police Service Representative

Parking Enforcement

3–11 Shift Lieutenant

Shift Sergeants

Patrol Officers

K-9 Officer

Traffic Officers

Police Service Representatives

Proactive Sergeant

Proactive Officers

11–7 Shift Lieutenant

Shift Sergeants

Patrol Officers

Police Service Representative

6–4 Shift Sergeant

Patrol Officers

K-9 Officer

Figure 1.2 Organizational Chart of Medium-Sized Probation Department

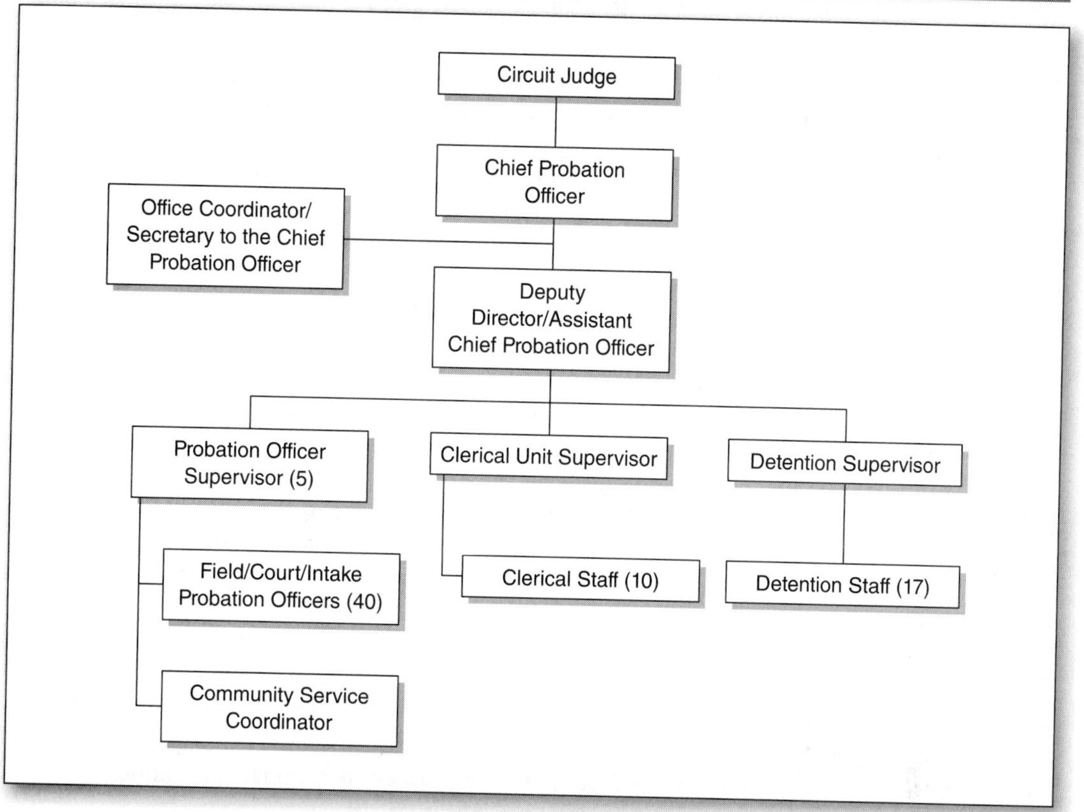

```
                          ┌──────────────────┐
                          │   Circuit Judge  │
                          └──────────────────┘
                          ┌──────────────────┐
                          │ Chief Probation  │
                          │     Officer      │
                          └──────────────────┘
┌──────────────────┐      ┌──────────────────┐
│ Office Coordinator/│    │     Deputy       │
│ Secretary to the Chief │ │ Director/Assistant│
│ Probation Officer │     │ Chief Probation Officer│
└──────────────────┘      └──────────────────┘
┌──────────────────┐  ┌──────────────────┐  ┌──────────────────┐
│ Probation Officer│  │ Clerical Unit    │  │ Detention        │
│ Supervisor (5)   │  │ Supervisor       │  │ Supervisor       │
└──────────────────┘  └──────────────────┘  └──────────────────┘
  ┌──────────────────┐  ┌──────────────────┐  ┌──────────────────┐
  │ Field/Court/Intake│ │ Clerical Staff (10)│ │ Detention Staff (17)│
  │ Probation Officers (40)│└──────────────┘  └──────────────────┘
  └──────────────────┘
  ┌──────────────────┐
  │ Community Service│
  │ Coordinator      │
  └──────────────────┘
```

SOURCE: http://webapps.chesco.org/courts/cwp/view.asp?a=3&q=606462.

organizational goal(s). The subsystems have their own boundaries, missions, and tasks, as well as their own inputs, outputs, processes, and feedback (McNamara, 2007). Detective units in police departments can be thought of as subsystems. The detectives' unit has its own mission, goals, and values, yet the detectives are working to accomplish the larger policing goals of providing services, identifying crime, and working with and protecting the public.

Groups and individual employees within an organization can also be thought of as systems with common missions, values, goals, inputs, outputs, processes, and so on. The organization can be thought of as multiple systems, all operating within multiple systems for one or more identified strategic goal(s). A simple way of considering the multiple systems approach is to think of a university campus. The individual classes offered by the Department of Criminal Justice have missions, goals, and values identified in each syllabus as course objectives and course descriptions. The courses are offered each semester by a department that also has a mission, goals, and values shared by the faculty who teach criminal justice and the students majoring in criminal justice. The Department of Criminal Justice is situated in a college or school (often called the School of Social Sciences or the College of Arts and Letters) along with other departments with similar disciplines, and they share a mission and common goals and values set by the dean. Finally, these three systems operate within the larger university setting to accomplish the mission and strategic goals and values set by the school's administration. To add to this, some universities are involved in statewide systems that include all universities within the state. In Georgia, for example, all state-funded schools belong to the University System of Georgia (USG). The USG sets a mission, goals, and values for the state educational system and passes that information down to the various systems mentioned previously. The systems approach will be investigated further in the next two chapters, but for now, suffice it to say that all organizations have systems in their structures. The impact of those systems on organizational activities, goals, and values varies greatly.

Organizations can be very complex organisms. They may operate within the confines of formal rules, regulations, and authority, or they may be more loosely based on the achievement of goals with little supervision. Organizations may also be open systems actively engaging and interacting with the environment or closed systems that accept little outside input and feedback; each is discussed in detail in Chapter 2. Either way, it is the managers who are tasked with clarifying the goals, systems, structure, and mission of the organization. Clarification of management and of goals, structure, and mission occurred in Abingdon, Illinois, in the provided news scenario. A reading of the Illinois Compiled Statutes led to questions regarding an officer's position and responsibilities in the police department. In the News 1.1 brings to light how statutory requirements may impact organizational structures, and how managers are called on to identify organizational structures and employee tasks and responsibilities.

In the News 1.1
Statute Open to Interpretation Says City of Abingdon Officials

ABINGDON—An Abingdon Police Committee meeting was held Thursday evening, July 26; a follow-up to the previous meeting held the Wednesday before. At this meeting Abingdon Chief of Police, Ed Swearingen, and Lt. Jared Hawkinson, were present as were Aldermen Jason Johnson, Ronnie Stelle, Dean Fairbank, Dale Schisler, Myron Hovind, Mike Boggs, Mayor Stephen Darmer, Treasurer Jim Davis and Abingdon City Clerk Sheila Day.

At the previous meeting the question as to whether or not specific passengers riding in Abingdon squad cars were covered by City insurance was addressed with the understanding that certain passengers would not fall under the City insurance policy. Darmer says, after speaking with the City's insurance representative, this is not the case. "He said passengers are all covered under our insurance. They're always covered. The only thing he had concerns about was the risk and this City management's call."

Johnson then addressed Illinois Compiled Statute 65 5/3.1-30-21 Sec. 3.1-30-21 regarding part-time police officers. The complete statute reads as follows: A municipality may appoint, discipline, and discharge part-time police officers. A municipality that employs part-time police officers shall, by ordinance, establish hiring standards for part-time police officers and shall submit those standards to the Illinois Law Enforcement Training and Standards Board. Part-time police officers shall be members of the regular police department, except for pension purposes. Part-time police officers shall not be assigned under any circumstances to supervise or direct full-time police officers of a police department. Part-time police officers shall not be used as permanent replacements for permanent full-time police officers. Part-time police officers shall be trained under the Intergovernmental Law Enforcement Officer's In-Service Training Act in accordance with the procedures for part-time police officers established by the Illinois Law Enforcement Training and Standards Board. A part-time police officer hired after Jan 1, 1996 who has not yet received certification under Section 8.2 of the Illinois Police Training Act shall be directly supervised. This statute was adopted Jan 1, 1996. Previously, Abingdon Police Sgt. Carl Kraemer said part-time police officer Jared Hawkinson has duties that include, but not limited to, making the schedule for the Department and Hawkinson was reported to be in charge of the Department in the absence of Swearingen, which, according to the statute, is a violation of Illinois Law. Johnson, Police Committee Chair, said that is not the case, "At the meeting it was brought up discussing an officer, Lt. Hawkinson, being in charge of the Department in absence of the Chief. According to the Illinois Compiled Statutes, it does say part-time officers shall not be assigned under any circumstances to supervise or direct full-time police officers of a police department. Now, when one reads that and when one looks at the semantics of the rank structure of the police department you see the chief, you see lieutenant and you see sergeant and being familiar with military command structure you can see where they stair-step. In fact, we have a ranking structure."

According to a hand-out passed around during the meeting Hawkinson is in charge of administrative functions: network operations, scheduling at the direction of the chief, fleet management; supervision of part-time officers: patrol officers, firearms instructor, ordinance officer and serves as the auxiliary officer liaison. Kraemer, who is a full-time officer, is the patrol supervisor and has duties including report approval, direct supervisor of departmental operation at the direction of the chief and evidence custodian. Said Johnson, "In the absence of, for whatever reason, whether it be personal vacation, whatever the occasion, in the absence of Chief Swearingen, the person who is in charge is in fact, Sgt. Kraemer. Sgt. Kraemer is the go-to-guy in place of Chief. It is not Jared Hawkinson. In stating that, going back to the Compiled Statute, in my opinion, in the way I read this, you can have five people read it and get five different opinions; Lt. Hawkinson is actually not a supervisor or directing full-time police officers in any capacity. We're trying to make sure we're not shooting ourselves in the foot with anything we do. And, like I said, five people can read the Compiled Statute and have five different interpretations. Actually, Hawkinson does not have any full-time officers reporting to him in any capacity. As far as the scheduling is concerned, the scheduling is done by the Chief and Lt. Hawkinson puts it on paper."

Swearingen noted, prior to the conclusion of the meeting, there are roadside safety checks planned for September in Abingdon to be conducted by the police department. Their focus will be on seat belt and insurance violations and those not having City Wheel Tax Stickers.

SOURCE: From "Statute Open to Interpretation Says City of Abingdon Officials," by D. Fowlks, August 2, 2007, *Argus-Sentinel, 2*(31). Copyright © 2007 *Argus-Sentinel*.

Leadership

Managers are typically considered leaders by many inside and outside of the organization. Managers are charged with leading their subordinates through the task and into completion of the job. However, the manager may or may not be good at leading. Since "leadership can arise in any situation where people have combined their efforts to accomplish a task" (Ivancevich et al., 1989, p. 296), a leader is not always a manager. In other words, management and leadership are not synonymous. An important task of *leadership* is to motivate others to accomplish organizational goals. Managers may tell subordinates what to do and how to do it, but they might not motivate subordinates to actually finish the job. Leaders inspire others not only to do the work, but also to finish it. Leaders promote change, keep an eye on the accomplishment of the job, look at long-term goals, and inspire and motivate; whereas managers maintain the status-quo, monitor the means by which the job is getting done, and solve problems as they arise in the organization. Leaders and managers can actually be at opposition in their approach to the work and accomplishment of organizational goals.

There is some debate on whether leaders are born with leadership characteristics, are taught to be good leaders, or are better able to perform leadership behaviors than others. Trait theories put forth that leaders are born with specific characteristics that make them more capable of leading others (Bass, 1981; Lippitt, 1955; Stogdill, 1974). They may be more emotionally stable; be more business-minded; or have more self-confidence, integrity, and honesty, and a constant drive to promote change and to make improvements in their environments. Contrary to this approach, it may be that the person seen as a leader is simply better able to perform the behaviors associated with leadership—being supportive of others, friendly, and approachable; able to set goals, give directions, assign tasks, inspire, and motivate—and get people in the organization to accomplish individual and organizational goals. This is a behavioral approach. Behaviorists are interested in how those perceived as leaders can motivate others to perform. In their minds, leadership can be learned (Shanahan, 1978).

The final approach to explaining leadership is situational. This approach realizes that no one behavior may be appropriate in all situations with all people and that traits alone cannot always inspire others (Fiedler, 1967). Instead, leaders should be able to adapt (and may be taught to do so) to the situation put before them in determining how best to approach the goals of the organization and the individuals being led. In this case, leadership may be a learned quality. This seems to be the approach chosen by Parke-Davis Pharmaceuticals. The company partnered with the University of Michigan Executive Education Center to develop curriculum to teach its scientists leadership skills. The curriculum required the scientists to develop an individual action plan that addressed teamwork, qualities for success and failure, self-awareness, coaching others, communication, creativity, motivation, organizational structure, setting direction, and promoting change. Parke-Davis believes that its managers have an improved sense of self-awareness, leadership behaviors, and self-confidence as a result of the program. In addition, the organization feels the program provides employees with a "clearer idea of responsibilities and values needed to lead others ... [as well as improved] communication, teambuilding, and problem solving skills" ("Making Scientists Into Leaders," 2001, p. 938). Learning how to lead, when best to lead, and in what situation leadership skills are most appropriate is the approach put forth in situational theories, as seen in the Parke-Davis curriculum.

The lack of leadership skills initially seen by Parke-Davis in the company's scientists can also appear, at times, in the criminal justice system. Managers, who are assumed to be the leaders in criminal justice agencies, are usually promoted from within and arrive at their positions because of the amount of time served with the organization, by community election, through appointment, or because of socialization skills or heroism. They do not necessarily possess the abilities to be good leaders and may not be able to adapt easily to situations that arise. Because of the way they obtained their positions, it may be more difficult for them to lead others employed by the agency, since there are relationships already formed with the community and employees. In a study of police chiefs and sheriffs, LaFrance and Allen (2010) found that sheriffs lived in the county they served for an average of 20 or more years longer than police chiefs, were more likely to have served in their current positions longer than police chiefs, and on average have worked for the agency they served for almost 6 times longer than police chiefs. Based on these findings, even though sheriffs are elected, they have obvious relationships with the community and the employees in the sheriff's office. These relationships may impact the ability to impose changes and lead the department.

In addition, employees in criminal justice agencies are not necessarily encouraged to think outside of the box, often because of constitutional and legal confines. Therefore, imagination, creativity, and long-term innovation may not be qualities valued by the agency or used by those viewed as leaders. Thinking of the sheriffs mentioned previously, we are reminded of the old saying, "There's a new sheriff in town," but even with new administration, we may see very few changes occur in the policing organization and in the providing of services. Finally, leadership in criminal justice can be constrained by environmental factors (discussed in detail in Chapter 4) that weigh into these agencies. Union contracts, budgeting constraints, legislative decisions, and court rulings may limit the amount of change a leader can accomplish inside a policing or correctional institution. They may also determine the means used and ends accomplished, so there is little a leader can do to challenge the system. Consequently, the leaders may not be inspired or motivated to accomplish the goals of the organization, and they may end up doing little for those who look to them for guidance and encouragement. Shared leadership (between managers and subordinates) and increased focus on situational leadership skills may allow criminal justice organizations to be more adaptive. Leaders need to be trained; they should not be assumed to have the abilities to lead just because they have worked for an agency for a long time. An extensive discussion on leadership is provided in Chapter 7.

For-Profit and Nonprofit Organizations

Organizations can be classified into two broad categories, namely, for-profit and nonprofit. This classification of organizations is helpful because the underlying values, objectives, visions, and mission statements that form the guiding principles in attaining organizational goals in each category are different. The inherent differences and similarities found in nonprofit criminal justice organizations and for-profit types of businesses must be understood.

For-profit organizations, such as computer manufacturers, car dealerships, restaurants, and Internet service providers, exist to generate profits from products or services (McNamara, 2007). Their goal is to make a profit by taking in more money than they spend on development, training, personnel, marketing, distribution, and sales of goods and services. For-profit businesses are organized as privately owned or publicly held corporations. They may be unincorporated sole proprietorships owned by one person or partnerships between people or organizations, and the activities of the business are viewed as taxable personal income (McNamara, 2007). The sole proprietor is liable personally for all activities and operations of the business. For-profit businesses can also be organized as corporations (known as C corporations and S corporations). A corporation is considered its own legal entity, separate from the individuals who own it or who formed the organization. Corporations can be for-profit or nonprofit (government owned, for example) (McNamara, 2007). Corporations are usually formed to limit the liability the founders will face if there are poor operations or harmful activities, and so that stock can be sold in the business. A board of directors is appointed to oversee the activities of corporations. Finally, for-profit organizations may organize as limited liability companies (LLCs). The LLC combines the advantages of the corporation with those of the sole proprietorship. The founders have minimum personal liability, unless a state or federal law is violated; they can sell stock in the business; they can retain a voice in management decisions, goals, values, and activities; and they can share in profits. This is a very popular form of for-profit organization (McGovern, 1999; McNamara, 2007).

For-profit businesses rely on a formal structure with a rigid hierarchy to accomplish their goals. A president or chief executive officer oversees the business by implementing strategic goals and objectives; working with the board of directors in governance; supporting operations; overseeing design, marketing, promotion, delivery, and quality of the product or service; managing resources; presenting a strong community image; and recruiting investors (McNamara, 2007). The hierarchy branches out from there to include vice presidents who specialize in the various aspects—marketing or promotion, human resources, operations, sales, finances, and so on—of the business. Assistants work directly under the vice presidents, and so it goes until one arrives at the employees working on the assembly line putting the product together or selling the service to consumers. In addition to the hierarchy, customers are sought after and, hopefully, retained to continuously purchase the product or use the service provided (McNamara, 2007). Investors are relied on to buy stock in the business or, in the case of sole proprietorships, to fund the business until a profit is generated. In the end, the results are the profits yielded from the sales of the product or service. These profits may be distributed among the investors or reinvested back into the organization (McGovern, 1999; McNamara, 2007).

Nonprofit agencies are created to fulfill one or more needs of a community (McGovern, 1999). Criminal justice agencies are considered nonprofit agencies that provide services to society by deterring, preventing, identifying, and processing crime and criminal acts. Even though a nonprofit organization may generate a profit, the goals of these organizations do not include generating monetary earnings, although a service or product may be provided to customers using the agency. By calling an agency "nonprofit," it can be assumed that the organization is structured in such a way that it is federally and legally forbidden to distribute profits to owners. A profit, in this case, means having more revenue than expenditures (McNamara, 2007).

All activities, goals, and values in a nonprofit organization are centered on the client. *Clients* are the consumers of the nonprofit organization's services. In criminal justice, this includes the victim, offender, community member, witness, treatment provider, and so forth. The nonprofit is designed to meet the needs of the client (McGovern, 1999; McNamara, 2007) by continually assessing the desires of the clients and determining the appropriate means of providing for them. This is a service-oriented approach and is the primary underlying theme of this textbook. Assessments may be done by the executive director or, in the case of criminal justice, the chief in charge of the agency to determine the effectiveness of the organization in meeting client needs. The executive director or chief is accountable for the work of the staff and to the public, as well as for carrying out the strategic goals of the organization. If there are failures in meeting needs—for example, crime increases instead of decreases—the chief is the one called to the carpet, so to speak, for an explanation.

The executive director or chief may also engage in fundraising to meet the needs of the nonprofit agency and, subsequently, the clientele. Fundraising is not meant to create a profit but to meet the fiscal needs of the organization (McNamara, 2007). Funds may be garnered from grants, individuals, foundations, and for-profit corporations. Grants are likely considered one of the largest fundraising initiatives in the criminal justice system (alongside forfeitures). They are given by governmental agencies (federal or state governments), foundations, and corporations to operate a specific program or initiative. Grant monies are provided up front and require an audit at the end of the grant period showing success or failure at completing the goals identified in the grant application. Individual donations may come from members of the organization or its constituents (wealthy community members, for example). They are usually small, onetime contributions of money or other assets, such as buildings or land (McGovern, 1999; McNamara, 2007). Foundations and for-profit corporations may also choose to give onetime start-up costs to nonprofit organizations on issues they identify as worthy. Microsoft founder Bill Gates and his wife, for example, give charitable donations each year to nonprofit organizations that focus on children's health, AIDS and HIV, and medical and other health issues.

Nonprofits rely heavily on staff and volunteers. The staff are hired and paid by the nonprofit. They report to the administration and work directly with the clients. Because the agency is not generating profits to pay for large numbers of employees, volunteers are commonly used to assist staff in the completion of tasks. The volunteers come from a number of sources including university intern programs, the AmeriCorps program, high school volunteer programs, civic agencies, and individuals in the community. They are not paid, but their contributions to the organization can be invaluable.

One of the key issues facing nonprofit organizations is devolution. *Devolution* is the term used to describe cutbacks in federal funding to nonprofit organizations (McNamara, 2007). Central to this issue is the fact that less money to a nonprofit means fewer services to clients. As a result of devolution, innovative staff and reliance on volunteers become even more important, as does the ability of the administration to raise funds from other outside sources (McNamara, 2007). Using fees for services is one way nonprofits can overcome the effects of devolution, but it is by no means the most popular choice. In many cases, those using the assistance of nonprofits cannot afford to purchase the services in the first place; otherwise, they would likely go to a for-profit agency for the service. When a fee is involved, the agency is concerned that those most in need of the service cannot receive it because of the fee, and clients are concerned about how to pay for the service in the first place (McNamara, 2007). As a result, assessing fees may put a hardship on the client as well as the agency. A second response to devolution is to bill an outside party for the fee. In some cases, state or county agencies are able to bill the federal government for each client who uses their service. The billed amount may not cover the full cost of the service, but it reimburses the nonprofit for some of the money spent on the client, and it does not require the federal government to make a commitment as significant as a grant (McNamara, 2007). One example of this is in court-ordered counseling services where the client receives individual mental health counseling for free from a nonprofit agency referred by the court. The agency then bills the state or federal government for each client serviced by the therapist. The therapist receives a monthly salary regardless of the number of clients counseled, and the clients receive the treatment they need regardless of the cost.

Priorities for services by nonprofits are determined by the clients, the community, and the political environment, just as the demands for goods and services in for-profit agencies are determined by many of the same individuals. In both for-profit and nonprofit agencies, administrators, as well as staff, must be aware of changes in needs and wants in the environment (McNamara, 2007). Meeting those needs and wants is highly demanding, and there are no easy answers as to how organizations should manage themselves to meet these challenges. A constant concern for progressive organizations is how to continuously improve while offering a high-quality service or product to a diverse group of customers. As discussed in Chapter 3, nonprofit organization service encounters with diverse clients can be complex.

Some of the issues facing both nonprofit and for-profit organizations include the need for good leaders who also possess the ability to manage and lead a team with vision, skill, and sufficient resources to accomplish the strategic goals identified by the agency. Setting realistic goals that are complex enough to challenge employees but not so complex that they cannot show results is also an issue. Using diversity so that all perspectives can be taken into consideration and finding people good at planning, organizing, guiding, and motivating others are keys to organizational success (McGovern, 1999; McNamara, 2007). It is also necessary to have networks in place so that administrators can seek the funds and investments needed to run a successful business. Seeking and receiving advice from experts outside of the agency is important, as well as realizing that all services, in the case of nonprofit agencies, are not going to have an immediate impact, just as all products made by for-profits are not going to be successful (McNamara, 2007). Basically, nonprofit and for-profit agencies have just as many similarities as they do differences. The most important difference to focus on is the size of the organization. "Small nonprofits are often much more similar to small for-profits than to large nonprofits. Similarly, large nonprofits are often more similar to large for-profits than small nonprofits" (McNamara, 2007).

What Are Criminal Justice Organizations?

The criminal justice system is comprised of many agencies working toward different albeit related tasks. It is important to understand these agencies, their goals and objectives, their history, and their clientele to be able to design an effective and efficient system focused on providing quality services. There are four primary areas of criminal justice—police, courts, corrections, and security (although some would not include security, since it is primarily profit-based).

The police are perhaps the most familiar part of the criminal justice system, since they are the ones called when someone becomes a victim of a crime, the ones that stop drivers who violate traffic laws, and are those seen driving around the neighborhood on patrol by community members. The police department is a highly structured agency primarily responsible for two tasks. First, the police enforce the law by responding to calls regarding law violations, arrest persons they witness or suspect to be violating the law, and make traffic or other types of stops. They rely heavily on state statutes and constitutional requirements in performing these tasks. In this role, the police are essentially gatekeepers to the criminal justice system by determining who will be arrested and brought into the system and who will be warned, let go, or otherwise ignored by the system (McCamey & Cox, 2008). Second, the police are responsible for providing services. Actual enforcement of the law is a minimal part of the police department's daily responsibilities. Using negotiation skills and mediation abilities in situations where there are disputes between parties, providing first aid, checking security alarms on buildings, investigating accidents, transporting prisoners, providing information, fingerprinting, making public speeches, handling calls about animals, and other service-related tasks are common occurrences in a police officer's day (McCamey & Cox, 2008). Strict policies and procedures are followed by the police in carrying out both law enforcement and service-related duties. Police departments typically operate in a centralized manner so that quick responses can occur when calls for assistance are made to the organization. In both enforcement and service-related circumstances, the police are largely a reactive organization that depends on public cooperation in reporting crimes, providing social control, and requesting assistance (McCamey & Cox, 2008). A detailed discussion of policing agencies is provided in Chapter 9.

The courts are depicted on television in courtroom dramas such as *Law and Order*. Most people are aware that there is a prosecuting attorney, defense counsel, a judge, and a jury in the courtroom, but they may not be aware of the court processes, rules, or procedures. Courts are also highly structured, centralized agencies reliant on formal procedures of presenting evidence and hearing cases. The major responsibility of the court system is to provide impartiality to those accused of committing criminal offenses. In court cases, both parties, the defendant and the prosecutor, are allowed to present their arguments within strict procedural guidelines, and the judge and jury are meant to act as decision makers in determining guilt or innocence. Yet this is not the only function of the courts. The courts also determine bail, conduct preliminary hearings, rule on admissibility of evidence, interpret the law, and determine the appropriate sentences for offenders. Constitutional guarantees are the backbone of the court system. By using formal procedures and structures, the court is better able to guarantee objective treatment of those coming before it and to more closely apply the law and constitutional requirements. Without such structure, the court would be full of bias and inconsistency. A detailed discussion of the courts is provided in Chapter 10.

Probation, parole, and treatment programs are not typically as structured as are police departments and courts. Employees in these specialties are tasked with making decisions on rehabilitation alternatives that best meet the needs of each individual client. In this case, a strict policy or procedure explaining what to do or what program to use if the client consumes drugs, for example, may not be appropriate. The procedure described in the agency's policy manual may actually encourage additional drug use in one person while discouraging it in another. Consequently, probation and parole officers and treatment providers must have the ability to choose from numerous alternatives, to weigh the costs and benefits of each against the client's unique situation, and to make the decision on which alternative the client will benefit from the most. In probation and parole offices and treatment programs, the administration uses a hands-off approach as long as the employees are meeting the overall goals of the organization. (It should again be noted that the size of the organization will make a difference, so the ability to generalize structure is limited.) The means used to achieve the goals are less important than the end result of rehabilitation in most probation, parole, and treatment agencies. Probation and parole are discussed in Chapter 11.

As noted in Figure 1.3, corrections is the end result of the criminal justice system. Corrections is another area where individuals may have some experiences (in driving past a prison, knowing someone who was jailed, hearing descriptions of the experiences of jailed celebrities, or watching a prison drama on television) but may not have experienced firsthand the spectrum of correctional alternatives. Thinking of corrections, one tends to think of prisons with fences, correctional officers, and uniformed inmates; however, corrections also includes probation, parole, treatment, diversion, and prevention programs. In this textbook, we discuss correctional institutions, like prisons, in a chapter on prisons, jails, and detention centers (see Chapter 12). Correctional institutions are found at both the state and federal levels. They have paramilitary structures, although there is autonomy in that the states can make decisions about their institutions separately from the federal system. The primary differences in the institutions may include the gender being housed, the age of the inmates, the types of offenses committed by the inmates, and the treatment programs provided. But there are stark similarities in formalization regarding policies and procedures, training of employees, security, and control (McCamey & Cox, 2008). Employees in correctional institutions tend to follow strict policies, often explained in extensive policy manuals and academies, and to work within a highly structured chain of command.

Security is the last area of specialty in criminal justice. Security agencies have seen increased attention through Homeland Security (antiterrorism) initiatives since the terrorist attacks in New York City and Washington, DC, in 2001. The field of security includes many aspects such as private security (guards, protection services, loss prevention, and investigations), cybersecurity (computer-based crime), corporate security (finances, workplace violence, legal liability, health care issues, and risk assessment), as well as governmental security (executive security, investigations, and reporting). Security agencies differ greatly in their organizational structures. As discussed previously, what works for one organization may be unworkable for another. Since the security industry is one of the areas in criminal justice that can be in both private and public sectors, labeling this field as having only formal or informal organizational structure is impossible. Someone who works for a university campus security program may find a highly formalized organization similar to that of the police department in a local town or municipality. Another individual working as a private investigator with a firm may find that there is little structure and much more autonomy in this position. This person is able to decide when to work, how long to work in a day, and how to perform surveillance needed to get the information required. Both parties may have the exact same training and be involved in similar types of tasks, even though the organizational structure differs greatly, impacting the way in which they do their jobs. The security industry is discussed in detail in Chapter 13.

Chapter Summary

- Identifying management in an organization may be difficult because policies, procedures, goals, values, and the mission can be influenced by line staff as well as top administrators.
- Many theoretical attempts have been made to identify who management is and the responsibilities of management in an organization. In this text, management is viewed as efficient and effective in meeting organizational goals while using the least amount of resources possible.
- Organizations differ greatly in size, structure, values, goals, and mission. Organizations can be formal or informal, centralized or decentralized. They may have defined chains of command and vertical communication or loosely identified chains of command and horizontal communication. The overall purpose of any organization is to achieve agreed-on goals and objectives.
- Organizations have a vision of how work should be accomplished by the line staff. They identify a mission statement so that those outside of the organization are aware of their purpose. Organizations create value structures that depend on the people working in the organization and the culture of the organization. Values are considered the priorities of the organization. In addition, organizations use strategic goals to guide their efforts and to accomplish their stated missions. The goals are measurable outcomes used to assess the overall effectiveness of the organization. The more specific, measurable, achievable, realistic, and time-specific (SMART) goals are, the easier they are to identify and achieve.

Figure 1.3 The Criminal Justice System

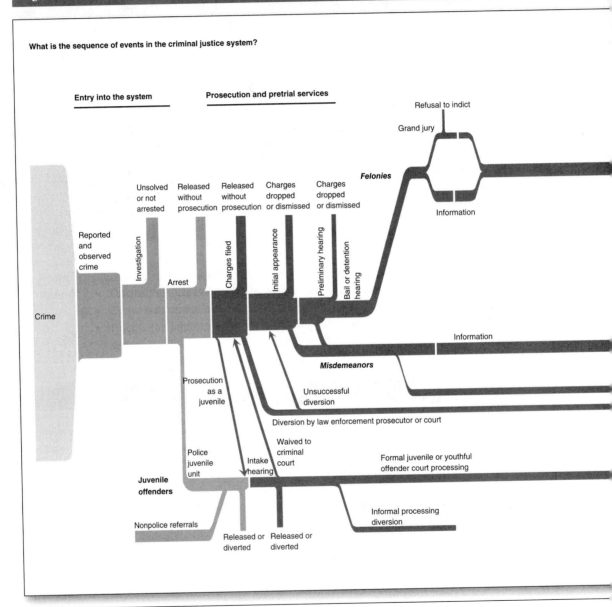

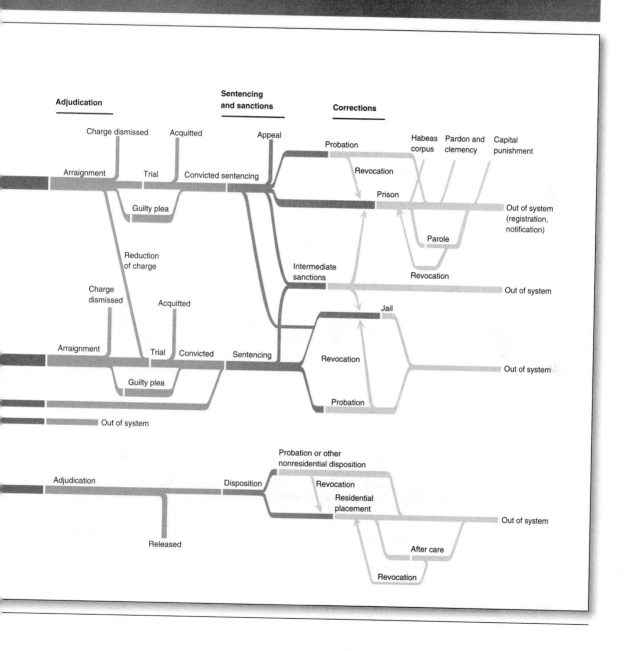

Adjudication

Charge dismissed   Acquitted

Arraignment   Trial   Convicted sentencing

Guilty plea

Reduction
of charge

Charge
dismissed   Acquitted

Arraignment   Trial   Convicted

Guilty plea

Out of system

Sentencing
and sanctions

Appeal

Corrections

Probation   Habeas   Pardon and   Capital
corpus   clemency   punishment

Revocation

Prison

Out of system
(registration,
notification)

Parole

Intermediate
sanctions   Revocation

Out of system

Jail

Sentencing   Revocation

Probation

Out of system

Adjudication   Disposition

Probation or other
nonresidential disposition

Revocation

Residential
placement

Out of system

Released

After care

Revocation

- Organizations can be considered systems consisting of inputs, processes, outputs, and feedback. Each organization is made of smaller subsystems operating within the larger organizational system—a multiple systems approach. Employees and managers can also be considered systems operating within subsystems.
- Leaders motivate others to accomplish organizational goals. They may or may not be identified as managers within an organization. Being able to lead is not the same as being a manager. Managers may or may not be good leaders. Theoretical attempts to explain leadership have focused on those born with qualities that make them able to lead others, those taught to be leaders, and those who learn to rely on situations to determine the best way to lead.
- For-profit agencies are designed to develop and deliver products or services that generate income. They may be organized as sole proprietorships, corporations, or LLCs. For-profit organizations tend to be structured formally, with ends being more important than means in accomplishing strategic goals.
- Nonprofit organizations are created to fulfill community and client needs. They are not concerned with generating earnings and rely heavily on fundraising through grants, corporations, individuals, foundations, and governmental agencies to meet budgetary needs. Line staff and volunteers are employed to accomplish strategic goals. One of the biggest issues facing nonprofit organizations is devolution.
- For-profit and nonprofit agencies are similar in that they both require inputs and feedback from the environment. They also rely on good leadership, sufficient resources, achievable goals, diverse staff, and planning for future activities to succeed.
- The biggest difference between nonprofit and for-profit agencies is the size of the organization.
- There are four areas of specialty in criminal justice—policing, courts, corrections, and security. Each area consists of agencies that are organized differently depending on their size, clientele, and strategic goals. All of them work together to accomplish the larger system's goals of upholding the laws, deterring criminal acts, and rehabilitating offenders.

Chapter Review Questions

1. How is management identified in an organization?

2. Think of an organization in which you are involved. What is the mission of the organization? Identify one or two of its strategic goals. How does it accomplish its goals? Would you consider it successful or unsuccessful in accomplishing the goals identified? Is the organization centralized or decentralized? On what information are you basing your response?

3. Identify potential inputs, processes, outputs, and feedback that may be found in a probation department.

4. What qualities do criminal justice agencies share? How are they different? What determines the organizational structure in criminal justice organizations? Describe multiple systems that may exist in a correctional facility.

5. What are the similarities and differences in nonprofit and for-profit agencies? Identify a for-profit agency in your community. Identify a nonprofit agency in your community. What are the differences and similarities between these two agencies? What types of products or services do they provide?

CASE STUDY

Patowonk is a small county in Missouri with a population of 28,000. The Patowonk County Sheriff's Department has approximately 20 officers and 7 part-time auxiliary officers. The department has 3 officers dedicated to drug investigations. The officers primarily handle crimes related to marijuana distribution and manufacturing. Most other crimes in Patowonk are property offenses, juvenile delinquency, and domestic violence. Tom Beasley is the sheriff in Patowonk County. He has worked for the department for 28 years, beginning as a deputy patrol officer and working his way through the ranks. He has a high school diploma and no college education. He is 49 and has held his current position for the previous 2 years. When assuming the sheriff's position, he made very few changes to the department and did not plan to make any future changes since he believed it to be operating well. Sheriff Beasley gets along well with the city council, city police chief, the media, and the mayor. Community members have been supportive of the department, and everyone appears to be doing what is expected. Turnover and complaints within and about the department have been low.

Patowonk County is situated along Interstate 55 between St. Louis, Missouri, and Memphis, Tennessee. Although the interstate has not contributed to problems in Patowonk County in previous years, there has been an increase in drug arrests for transportation and distribution by federal agencies operating in the area. Most of the arrests have not involved citizens of Patowonk County and have not garnered media or citizen attention.

In July 2012, an 85-mph high-speed chase of three individuals transporting 30 pounds of cocaine through Patowonk County to the border of Illinois led to the death of two people and the injury of four others.

Steven Scott, 21 years of age, was driving a 2002 Jeep Grand Cherokee through downtown Macon, the county seat, when he failed to yield to oncoming traffic at an intersection. A deputy police officer, John Sims, witnessed the incident and attempted to stop the jeep at the intersection of Franklin and Meadowbrook. The jeep fled, reaching speeds of 85 mph within city limits. The chase lasted four minutes.

Scott went west on Fountain Street and made a sharp left turn at Macon High School. Students were exiting the school for the day and there was considerable foot and vehicle traffic in the parking lot of the school. The jeep hit a book depository for the library, went airborne, and struck two students and a vehicle parked in the handicapped parking area for the building.

One of the students, Amanda Ben, struck by the jeep on the school parking lot, was killed instantly. The other student struck by the jeep, Susan Knight, recovered, but required extensive reconstructive surgery and hospitalization. A third student, Jack Harris, who was getting into a vehicle parked in the handicapped parking area, was hospitalized briefly and fully recovered from non-life-threatening injuries. Steven Scott received minor injuries in the crash. A teenage passenger in the jeep, whose name was withheld from the media, was thrown from the vehicle and died at the scene. A second passenger in the vehicle, Michael Lane, received several broken bones as a result of the crash. Deputy Sims's vehicle did not strike any pedestrians or vehicles in the parking lot. Deputy Sims was unharmed in the accident.

Although the suspects in the high-speed chase cannot sue the police department, the parents of Ben are suing for wrongful death of their daughter. They allege that the deputy should have ceased the chase once the jeep turned toward the school. In their argument, continued pursuit of the jeep led to Scott increasing speed and driving recklessly through school pedestrian traffic, causing the unnecessary death of Ben and injuries to Harris and Knight. The families of Harris and Knight have filed separate suits for medical expenses incurred as a result of the accident. Each has named the Patowonk County Sheriff's Department, Sheriff Beasley, several supervising officers, and Deputy Sims as defendants in the lawsuits.

(Continued)

(Continued)

Police departments have differing standards governing high-speed chases of vehicles because of the potential dangers associated with excessive speeds. In some jurisdictions, high-speed chases are discouraged and are only used as a last resort. A high-speed chase is considered a form of deadly force and has resulted in the injury and death of many offenders as well as innocent motorists and pedestrians. Patowonk County Sheriff's Department's policy on high-speed chases mirrored the requirements of the U.S. Supreme Court, which states that to use deadly force, an officer must show that a suspect poses a significant threat of death or serious injury to the officer or others.

Questions for Discussion

1. Should police officers pursue, at high speeds, motorists who violate traffic laws? Is the Patowonk County Sheriff's Department's policy on high-speed chases thorough enough? If so, why do you think that is the case? If not, what would you add to the policy?

2. Is the Patowonk County Sheriff's Department responsible for the death of Amanda Ben and/or the injuries of Knight and Harris? Is Deputy Sims? Is Sheriff Beasley? Why or why not? Would you place responsibility on another person(s)? If so, who and why? Who can be considered the "management" in this situation? Who are the line staff? Is the "management" responsible for what occurred, or is the line staff?

3. Do the police department involved or the officer involved need additional training in high-speed pursuit situations?

4. In your opinion, did leadership fail in this occurrence, and if so, how? What was the service that was being offered in this case? Was the service successful or unsuccessful? Why?

Internet Resources

Administrative Office of U.S. Courts—http://www.uscourts.gov/adminoff.html

FEDSTATS—http://www.fedstats.gov/aboutfedstats.html

U.S. Department of Justice—http://www.usdoj.gov

References and Suggested Readings

Barnard, C. (1938). *The functions of the executive.* Cambridge, MA: Harvard University Press.

Bass, B. M. (1981). *Stogdill's handbook of leadership.* New York, NY: Free Press.

Blau, P. M., & Scott, W. R. (1962). *Formal organizations: A comparative approach.* Scranton, PA: Chandler.

Dale, E. (1960). *The great organizers.* New York, NY: McGraw-Hill.

Day, T., & Tosey, P. (2011). Beyond SMART? A new framework for goal setting. *Curriculum Journal, 22*(4), 515–534. doi:10.1080/09585176.2011.627213

Doran, G. T. (1981). There's a S.M.A.R.T. way to write management's goals and objectives. *Management Review, 70*(11), 35–36.

Duncan, W. J. (1983). *Management: Progressive responsibility in administration.* New York, NY: Random House.

Dwan, S. (2003). Juggling management basics. *NZ Business, 17*(5), 44.

Fairfax County Police Department. (2002). *Mission—Police Department.* Retrieved from http://www.fairfax county.gov/police/inside-fcpd/pdf/annualreport2002.pdf.

Fayol, H. (1949). *General and industrial management.* London, England: Sir Isaac Pitman.

Fiedler, F. E. (1967). *A theory of leadership effectiveness.* New York, NY: McGraw-Hill.

Hanson, G. (1986). *Determinants of firm performance: An integration of economic and organizational factors.* Unpublished doctoral dissertation, University of Michigan Business School, Ann Arbor, MI.

Hecht, M. R. (1980). *What happens in management: Principles and practices.* New York, NY: AMACOM.

Internet Center for Management and Business Administration, Inc. (n.d.). *Frederick Taylor and scientific management.* Retrieved from http://www.netmba.com/mgmt/scientific.

Ivancevich, J. M., Donnelly, J. H., Jr., & J. L. Gibson. (1989). *Management: Principles and functions* (4th ed.). Boston, MA: BPI Irwin.

Koontz, H. (1961). The management theory jungle. *Journal of the Academy of Management, 4*(3), 174–188.

LaFrance, C., & Allen, J. (2010, January). An exploration of the juxtaposition of professional and political accountability in local law enforcement management. *International Journal of Police Science and Management, 12*(1), 90–118.

Lippitt, G. H. (1955). What do we know about leadership? *National Education Association Journal, 15,* 556–557.

Locke, E. A., & G. P. Latham. (2002). Building a practically useful theory of goal setting and task motivation: A 35-year odyssey. *American Psychologist, 57*(9), 705–717.

Making scientists into leaders at Parke-Davis Research. (2001). *Training and management development methods, 15*(3), 937–939.

March, J., & Simon, H. (1958). *Organizations.* New York, NY: John Wiley.

McCamey, W. P., & Cox, Steven M. (2008). The criminal justice network: Exploring the system (5th ed.). Dunham, NC: Carolina Academic Press.

McGovern, G. (1999). *The revolution inside.* Retrieved from http://www.gerrymcgovern.com/ nt/1999/nt_ 1999_12_06_revolution_inside.htm.

McNamara, C. (2007). *Basic overview of nonprofit organizations.* Retrieved from http:// managementhelp .org/org_thry/np_thry/np_intro.htm.

Moore, F. G. (1964). *Management: Organization and practice.* New York, NY: Harper & Row.

Shanahan, D. T. (1978). *Patrol administration: Management by objectives* (2nd ed.). Boston, MA: Allyn & Bacon.

Stogdill, R. M. (1974). *Handbook of leadership: A survey of theory and research.* New York, NY: Free Press.

Tannenbaum, R., Weschler, I. R., & Massarik, F. (1961). *Leadership and organization.* New York, NY: McGraw-Hill.

Taylor, F. W. (1911). *The principles of scientific management.* New York, NY: Harper & Row.

Weber, M. (1947). *The theory of social and economic organization.* New York, NY: Free Press.

2

Open Versus
Closed Systems

LEARNING OBJECTIVES

Upon completion of this chapter, students should be able to do the following:

- Define closed-system models—scientific management, administrative management, and bureaucratic management
- Define open-system models—total quality management model and supply chain/ synergy model
- Describe how the environment is changing and the need for a learning organization
- Explain how the criminal justice system can become a learning organization

Organization design and management practices have transformed over time in response to changes in society. New organizations emerge when fresh needs are discovered or new technologies are available. Alternatively, organizations die or are transformed when the needs satisfied by them no longer exist or have been replaced by other needs (Katz & Kahn, 1966; Mitroff, Mason, & Pearson, 1994). *Organizational theory* is a way to examine and analyze organizations more precisely and intensely based on patterns and trends in organizational design and behavior, which otherwise may not have been done (Daft, 2001). The purpose of this chapter is to explore the nature of organizations and organizational theory. Scholars have provided various models to characterize organizations to view them more scientifically. These models become the basis for explanations of organizational events, and they can be broadly classified as closed systems or open systems depending on their starting presumption (Thompson, 1967). The *closed-system models* tend to focus on internal events when explaining organizational actions and behavior, while *open-system models* focus on events occurring externaly to the organization that influence changes within the organization. A *systems view* considers an organization as a set of interacting functions that acquire inputs from the environment, process them, and then release the outputs back to the external environment (Daft, 2001). At the outset, it needs to be clarified that the words *model* and *theory* will be used interchangeably in this chapter, though at a more subtle level it could be argued that they have fine differences in their implications.

The rest of the chapter is loosely divided into three sections. The first provides a discussion on the closed-system models, where the three main subfields of the classical perspective are presented—namely, scientific management, administrative management, and bureaucratic management. Within each subfield, the advantages and disadvantages in managing the criminal justice system are examined. In the second section, the open-system models are reported, where the humanistic and behavioral perspectives are introduced. This section provides a discussion on the total quality management model and the supply chain/synergy model, which introduces a new concept of including the customer's perspective in designing open systems. Within each model, the advantages and disadvantages in managing the criminal justice system are examined. The third section examines the changing face of the criminal justice system, making a strong argument for building learning organizations. Such organizations, which are more effective and better suited to the criminal justice system, can only be developed on the foundations of an open system.

Closed-System Models: The Classical Perspective

Closed-system models consider the external environment (technological advancements, the cultural and demographic characteristics of the community, legal decisions, political decisions, etc.—described in detail in Chapter 4) to be stable and predictable, and they assume that it does not intervene in or cause problems for the functioning of an organization. Therefore, the closed-system models do not depend on the external environment for explanations or solutions to managerial issues; instead, they are enclosed and sealed off from the outside world (Daft, 2001). These models rely primarily on internal organizational processes and dynamics to account for organizational, group, and individual behaviors. The central management objective addressed in these models is the efficient running of the organization. Closed systems are easier to deal with theoretically than open systems, and they are preferred, despite their limitations. For example, if abuse of prisoners took place in a certain prison, a closed-system approach would look for explanations for the abuse within the prison itself and then adopt correctional procedures. The prison would examine the prison policies, prison warden, correctional officers, prison culture, officer–inmate interaction, inmate–inmate interaction, and other organizational components of the prison. It would not pay attention to the external environment to identify the causes of the problems. In other words, the external environment would not be blamed for the abuse. The prison and its officials would assume that something within the facility led to these issues.

The closed-system models, some of which may seem unrealistic in the present circumstances, were the products of the problems and subsequent changes that emerged during the Industrial Revolution. At the beginning of industrialization in the mid-1800s, the early factories were highly inefficient. There were no documented correct ways of doing work. Organizations were constantly thinking of ways to design and manage work to increase productivity, with the focus primarily being internal. The theories and models that emerged as a result are often termed *machine models,* also popularly known as *classical models* or *traditional models.* These models sought to make organizations run like efficient, well-oiled machines by correcting the internal functioning of the organizations.

The three main subfields of the classical perspective are scientific management, administrative management, and bureaucratic management. As will be examined, *scientific management* focuses on the productivity of the individual worker, *administrative management* focuses on the functions of the management, and *bureaucratic management* focuses on the overall organizational system within which the workers and management interact. Though each subfield has a somewhat different focus, they contain some overlapping elements and components. All of these models assume that people are *rational beings,* who act logically and correctly when faced by a given situation. In other words, these models assume that labor is homogenous and that workers behave and act the same way every time they face a similar situation. According to these models, the correctional officer, the police officer, and the jury will all behave the same way when presented with similar situations at different times and in different places.

Scientific Management

In scientific management, the focus was on improving individual productivity. Frederick Winslow Taylor (1856–1915), the father of scientific management, believed that poor management practices and procedures were the primary problems. While employed at Midvale Steel Company in Philadelphia, Pennsylvania, he began experimenting with methods that focused on the worker–machine relationship in manufacturing plants. Based on his observations, he formulated opinions in the areas of task performance, supervision, and motivation that are discussed here (Locke, 1982; Taylor, 1911).

Task performance. Taylor (1911) was convinced that decisions about organizations and job design should be based on precise, scientific study of individual situations. He believed that there was one right way of doing each task, and he attempted to define and document those optimal procedures through systematic study. Taylor calculated that with correct movements, tools, and sequencing, each man was capable of loading 47.5 tons of steel per day instead of the typical 12.5 tons, and Midvale Steel would be able to reduce the number of shovelers needed from 600 to 140.

These types of observations are examples of *time and motion studies,* which identify and measure a worker's physical movements and record the time of activity to determine how to do an activity through the smallest amount of effort. To implement these scientific principles, it was expected that management would do the following:

- Develop standard procedures for performing each job
- Select workers with appropriate abilities and skills to do each job
- Train workers in the standard procedures
- Support workers through careful planning of their work

Supervision. Taylor felt that a single supervisor could not be an expert in all of the tasks on the shop floor. Since the supervisors were promoted after demonstrating high skills in performing a particular function, they should be considered an authority only in that area of expertise. Therefore, each first-level supervisor—called *foremen* on the shop floor of a manufacturing plant—should be responsible only for workers who performed a common function familiar to the supervisor. Several of these supervisors would be assigned to each work area, with each having separate responsibility for planning, production scheduling, time and motion studies, material handling, and so forth in their area of expertise.

Motivation. Taylor believed that workers could be motivated to work at their fullest capabilities through monetary incentives. Therefore, he advocated a piecework system, in which the workers' pay was tied to their output. Workers who met a standard level of production were paid a standard wage rate; higher rates were paid for higher production. He also worked out an incentive system that paid each employee $1.85 per day for meeting the new standard, an increase from the previous rate of $1.15. Productivity at Midvale Steel shot up overnight.

Besides Taylor's contribution to scientific management, the husband-and-wife team of Frank and Lillian Gilbreth also made significant contributions to the field. Frank Gilbreth specialized in time and motion studies (Gilbreth, 1970; Locke, 1982). He identified the most efficient ways to perform tasks in 17 work elements (such as lifting, grasping, hammering, etc.) and called them *therbligs.* In one of his studies, he used motion picture film to record and examine the work of bricklayers; he then restructured the tasks in a way that reduced the number of motions from 18 to 5, resulting in a 200% productivity increase (Lewis, Goodman, & Fandt, 2001). Lillian Gilbreth focused on the human aspects of industrial engineering for improving efficiency and productivity. She favored standard days, safer working conditions, scheduled lunch breaks and rest periods, and abolition of child labor.

Contemporary industrial engineers still use time and motion studies and the principles of scientific management to design jobs for greatest efficiency. These methods are also employed in sports. Coaches take their players through hours of videotapes along with commentary on how to perform an action correctly with the least amount of energy and maximum effect. The positions the players are recruited to play have been carefully matched to individual strengths. In law enforcement, the principles of scientific management are greatly emphasized when designing physical strength–building routines and in training officers to deal with uncooperative and dangerous offenders. Hours of videotapes and hands-on training are used to train law enforcement officers in physically handling uncooperative offenders and in the use of force. Every move is carefully planned and simulated by law enforcement officers using task performance and the time and motion studies.

Although the traditional model of organizational design for the police department derives from changes made during the Industrial Revolution (Batts, Smoot, & Scrivner, 2012), these departments sometimes fail in correctly applying the scientific management principles in administration. Supervisors are considered an authority in their area of proficiency; however, in policing, they are often also considered an authority in other areas where they may not have experience. Such an attitude of presumed expertise by the supervisor is a growing problem, as the field is becoming more specialized and complex. In line with the argument presented by Taylor (1911), rising specialization can be better handled by requiring several different supervisors to work as a team. The team members may have separate responsibilities for planning, training, and so forth in their areas of expertise, which will result in better preparedness of the officers being supervised and in good, quality service.

The strongest criticism that comes against scientific management involves the treatment of the worker as a machine. It is hard to imagine that workers, who have emotions, unlike machines, would always act in a predictable way, like machines. For example, two law enforcement officers will not act the same way in dealing with a similar situation; in fact, the same law enforcement officer will not deal in exactly the same way when confronted with a similar situation every time. This difference in action will emerge despite the best of training given to the officers. An officer called to the shopping mall for a juvenile shoplifting incident may not make an arrest the first time he or she responds to the scene. However, on a second response, the officer may take custody of the juvenile and transport the child to the police station. In both instances, the amount of property stolen may be the same, but the officer makes a different decision.

A second criticism brought forth against Taylor (1911) and Gilbreth's (1970) research is their consideration that workers are hired for their physical ability and not for using their mind. Their work establishes that the role of management is to maintain stability and efficiency, with top managers doing the thinking and workers doing what they are told. As mentioned in Chapter 1, innovative or creative thinking is not always a valued characteristic in criminal justice. One would assume that such an assumption would be insulting to any worker in any given organization, but it is at times a reality in criminal justice. In law enforcement, officers are faced with numerous situations that they may be experiencing for the first time, in which they have to react immediately before the situation becomes a catastrophe. Given such demands, it is hard to envision managing the criminal justice system effectively by having first-line officers always referring back to their senior officers for directions; however, this is close to what occurs. Batts et al. (2012) suggest, "Like the auto assembly plants of Henry Ford, traditional police agencies are characterized by a hierarchical authority structure that clearly distinguishes decision-makers from line staff, emphasizes adherence to principles of structure over flexibility, and prizes uniform operations" (p. 2). This is grossly apparent in the police policy manuals that cover just about any action and situation an officer will experience. Consequently, officers are limited, in many cases, in their responses to everyday calls for service. It is not uncommon for officers to spend the first or second eight-hour day of their training with an agency doing nothing but reading the policy manual.

Administrative Management

Scientific management focused primarily on the technical core—that is, the work performed on the shop floor by the frontline workers. In contrast, *administrative management* focuses on managers and the functions they perform. Henri Fayol (1841–1925), a French mining engineer, gained popularity when he revitalized a struggling mining company and turned it into a financial success. Based on this successful experience, he identified management functions as planning, organizing, commanding/leading, coordinating, and controlling. He proposed 14 general principles of management, which formed the foundation for modern practice and organizational design (Fayol, 1949), and are discussed below.

Fayol's General Principles of Management

1. *Division of work.* Efficiency and productivity could be improved by dividing the work into smaller work elements called tasks and assigning them to the workers. High repetition of tasks improves the learning, thus increasing the efficiency and productivity of employees.

2. *Authority.* To carry out managerial responsibilities, the managers should have the authority to issue commands to their staff.

3. *Discipline.* The staff should be disciplined to obey the issued commands and the rules of the organization for its smooth functioning.

4. *Unity of command.* Each worker should get orders from one boss to whom he or she reports. This clear line of command will avoid conflicts and confusion.

5. *Unity of direction.* All similar and related activities should be organized and directed under one manager. Such an arrangement will also facilitate unity of command.

6. *Subordination of individual interest to the general interest.* The goals of the organization should supersede the interests of individual employees.

7. *Remuneration of personnel.* The financial compensation for the work done should be based on the principle of fairness to both the employees and the organization.

8. *Centralization.* Power and authority should be concentrated at upper levels of the organization. However, the middle management and their subordinates should be given sufficient authority to perform their jobs properly.

9. *Scalar chain.* A single, continuous line of authority should extend from the top level to the lowest frontline worker in the organization.

10. *Order.* An organization should provide a work environment where the policies, rules, instructions, and so forth are clear and easily understood, resulting in both material

and social order. Worker productivity improves when the system ensures that materials are in the right place at the right time, and that the right workers are assigned to the jobs best suited to their skills.

11. *Equity.* Management should display equity, fairness, and a sense of justice toward subordinates.

12. *Stability of personnel tenure.* Employees learn with experience, making them more productive and efficient with tenure and job security. Therefore, employee turnover should be prevented as much as possible.

13. *Initiative.* The general work environment should provide the subordinates sufficient freedom to take initiative in carrying out their day-to-day work.

14. *Esprit de corps.* Management should foster worker morale, team spirit, and harmony among workers to create a sense of organizational unity.

Many of the principles proposed by Fayol, such as division of work, authority and responsibility, unity of direction, remuneration of personnel, and order (Fayol, 1949), are compatible with the views of scientific management and apply well to the criminal justice system. Fayol favors division of labor, a principle that is implemented in criminal justice agencies. There are line personnel (police officers, correctional officers, probation officers, juvenile officers) who are frontline workers implementing the organizational goals and objectives. Specialized staff members work behind the scenes, supporting the frontline officers by providing advice in such areas as planning, research, legal issues, and so forth. Auxiliary functions provide logistical support, including record keeping, communications, operations, map directions, coordination, and so on (Wren, 1994). Specialization and division of labor bring efficiency by focusing on understanding the law and mastering the technicalities of work. Specialization allows workers to develop greater expertise, thus enabling them to perform the work more efficiently. Fayol also favors centralization of power and authority at upper levels of the organization.

Furthermore, Fayol (1949) proposes subordination of individual interests to the goals of the organization. Such centralized authority is observed in policing and corrections. Most decisions are vested in the hands of the administration and are delivered from the top down. Work is often designed and assigned to criminal justice officers with efficiency and productivity in mind. Authority resides with the supervisors to enable them to give orders and get the work done. There is strict discipline, making it essential that members of the criminal justice system respect the rules that govern it. There is unity of command, unity of direction, and adherence to the uninterrupted chain of authority in law enforcement, corrections, and security agencies. There is also emphasis placed on equipment being well maintained and put in the right place to be available at the right time, since numerous situations that arise in criminal justice require very fast response times.

Mismanagement of Fayol's organizational elements can lead to breakdown and disorganization (Dias & Vaughn, 2006; Wren, 1994). For example, when unity of direction is not strictly adhered to, the criminal justice system fails. Dias and Vaughn cite the example of administrative breakdown during the riots of May 1992 in Los Angeles after the acquittal of the officers who were charged with the beating of Rodney King. It was reported that no specific senior officer of the Los Angeles Police Department (LAPD) could be identified from whom the frontline officers were to receive orders or to whom they were to report (Police Foundation, 1992). Similarly, the abuses at Abu Ghraib prison in Iraq were attributed to the unclear dissemination of procedures, goals, and objectives, which resulted from conflicting directions that soldiers got from multiple senior officers. There was a lack of unity of command that led to administrative failure (Hersh, 2004).

Though Fayol's (1949) managerial functions of planning, organizing, leading, and controlling are routinely used in criminal justice agencies, some of the principles are not compatible with those of contemporary management. For example, centralization of power and authority at upper levels of the organization is not considered to be a favored practice. Instead, modern management principles allow frontline workers more autonomy and authority for making and carrying out decisions. Modern management places much more emphasis on good training that will enable the officers to make appropriate decisions rather than always reverting back to the centralized power hub to get directions. Training improves officers' skills, making them more aware of the demands of the environment in which they are working, and thus enabling them to provide superior service to all of their customers (e.g., citizens, clients, offenders, arrestees, detainees, etc.). By definition, anybody to whom an agency provides a professional service is the customer. Contemporary management views employees as valuable assets whose interests must be considered at all times (Lewis et al., 2001).

Bureaucratic Management

Whereas scientific management focuses on the productivity of the individual worker, and administrative management focuses on the functions of the manager, bureaucratic management focuses on the overall organizational system in which both the workers and the managers interact. The *bureaucratic model* was developed by Max Weber (1947), and it emphasizes designing and managing organizations based on five principles:

1. *Impersonal social relations.* Weber did not favor employees relating on a social basis in the workplace. He felt such interactions led to *nepotism* (favoritism based on social connections), which compromised productivity and efficiency. Therefore, he said that organizations should operate according to laws, which would eliminate such favoritism. According to him, performance should be the sole measure of performance. He emphasized distance between supervisors and workers and felt there was no place for emotions in rule enforcement. Maintaining personal distance was considered a strong defense against the potential loss of power in the event that a supervisor was required to reprimand the subordinate. In application to criminal justice, correctional officers in prisons are trained to maintain social distance with the inmates to prevent a loss of control and to heighten their ability to reprimand inmates.

2. *Employee selection and promotion.* Weber emphasized that employees should be selected based on their skills and technical competence, and that they should be promoted based on performance and not on whom they know. He felt that nepotism had no place in a bureaucratic setup. Though that may be true for most big organizations, there is still nepotism in personnel policies of smaller organizations, including law enforcement agencies.

3. *Hierarchy of authority and spheres of competence.* According to Weber, within an organization, job positions should be ranked according to the amount of power and authority each possesses. In the resulting pyramid-shaped hierarchical structure, power and authority increase as the levels get higher, and each lower-level position is under the direct control of one higher-level position. Weber believed that authority and responsibility should rest in a position and not be based on who is holding that position. For example, if the written rules state certain expectations of duties from a supervisor, then these obligations cannot change when different individuals hold that same supervisory job. Adapting this Weberian tenet to law enforcement, there is continuous innovation in designing new aptitude-assessing tools followed by more rigorous and creative training methods. More thorough background checks and better oral tests are also being employed for screening purposes. An emphasis on professionalism and community policing is encouraging autonomy among police officers. Various law enforcement agencies have raised their requirements for recruitment and promotion to improve the sphere of competence in their officers. Hiring and promotions are not always based on education. Police officers in most states are not required to have a bachelor's degree. A high school diploma or GED is sufficient. As a result of increased professionalism, some departments are implementing promotion standards that include degree requirements, although it is not standard throughout the United States (McFall, 2006). In areas requiring degrees, the advanced degree weighs into the promotion process.

4. *System of rules and procedures.* Weber emphasized the need to provide clear formal rules and guidelines for performing all organizational duties, to which employees must strictly adhere. He believed that provision of a comprehensive set of rules and procedures enabled people to make decisions that are more objective, without allowing their personal judgments to interfere. Moreover, rules and procedures help maintain continuity when people retire or leave.

Organizations at national, state, and local levels (such as the International Association of Chiefs of Police, Police Executive Research Forum, the National Sheriffs' Association, and the National Organization of Black Law Enforcement Executives) have invested much time and effort in writing standards and rules by which to regulate employee behavior in law enforcement agencies. Although there are no national mandates on police departments, outside of laws, there is an accrediting body called the Commission on Accreditation of Law Enforcement Agencies that works with departments to standardize rules and expectations for employees. In this way, a police department seeking accreditation can better identify hiring, promotion, evaluation, and supervision standards while clarifying standards on which agency and individual performance can be measured. Not every department is accredited (an issue that is also discussed in Chapter 9), but all departments set minimum standards and policies for their officers. In some cases, the standards for hiring and supervision may also come from the state and federal levels, depending on whether the officer works for a state or federal agency. For example, in Illinois, police departments face mandates on the reporting of offenses charged against police officers, on newly hired police officers, and on weapons and training requirements. According to the mandates, a new police officer must complete the Law Enforcement Basic Training Course within the first six months of hire, sheriffs and deputy sheriffs must complete 20 training hours per calendar year, and all law enforcement officers must complete the Mandatory Firearms Training Course and requalify annually in firearms training. Agencies must report to the Illinois Law Enforcement Training and Standards Board (2008) any arrest or conviction of a law enforcement officer.

5. *Task specialization.* Weber believed that task specialization provides greater efficiency. He emphasized that the duties should be divided into simpler, more specialized tasks to enable an organization to use its workers more efficiently. Such division of work leads to less interference, and allocates responsibility with each job. Task specialization is used today in all criminal justice agencies. In policing, for example, officers may be assigned to units such as community policing, juvenile divisions, homicide divisions, special victims divisions, or detectives units. Probation officers are trained to work with specific types of offenders. They may work with those offenders on low-risk probation in which the offender is referred to many treatment and rehabilitation programs and the probation officer is simply a liaison and coordinator for the offender. Other probation officers may work specifically with unique populations of offenders such as those on electronic monitoring, those placed inside facilities such as boot camps or drug rehabilitation centers, or sexual offenders. In either case, the employees are able to work more efficiently, since they are responsible for just one part of the overall agency's population.

The advantages of Weber's bureaucratic principles include the following:

- Productivity is increased by matching personal competence with job requirements.
- Efficiency is enhanced through the adoption of task specialization. Furthermore, employees are selected and promoted based on their skills and competence, which ensures the best available person for the job.
- Duplication of work is eliminated by strictly allocating designated spheres of work activity to individuals, thus creating clear lines of control.
- With the given procedures and rules, employees can predict the effort required to earn rewards, and they are more clear on the career progress path, which results in greater loyalty.
- Rules and procedures eliminate impartiality, and allow greater standardization and continuity through easy replacement of employees.

The bureaucratic model can best be applied in a very structured work environment characterized by a well-defined chain of command, a rigid hierarchy, and strict formal rules. These conditions are best adapted to a system providing standardized services. However, there is much criticism against the bureaucratic and machine models when applied to the criminal justice system, where every encounter is believed to be different.

As mentioned before, machines do not have feelings like human beings, and can provide the same outcome when operating under similar conditions. However, human beings have emotions that can change during interactions with other human beings, even when the conditions may be the same as in other encounters. Since criminal justice services are highly labor-intensive and involve a high degree of contact between the officer and the other person (e.g., offender, victim, citizen, complainant, etc.), there is a significant scope of human emotions and feelings surfacing during decision making, which may lead to different outcomes even under similar conditions. Consequently, principles of Weber's management model that are embedded in the unrealistic assumption of treating people as machines have limitations when applied to the criminal justice system. According to the machine and bureaucratic models, given procedures and rules, anyone can take the supervisory role effectively. However, as will be discussed in Chapter 7, personality traits of individuals can confound their leadership abilities and can introduce inconsistency between what they are supposed to do and what they actually do.

One can see the impact of human emotions and feelings that play out in the courtroom. Judges working in juvenile court often adopt parent figure or lawgiver roles when listening to cases and determining what is in the best interest of the juvenile. Judges acting as parent figures are most concerned with the overall well-being of the youth and less concerned about the formalities of due process in the court and the courtroom. In this case, the judge may allow the youth or the youth's family to present information and to show remorse. Once that occurs, the judge weighs the information and emotion in the final determination of adjudication and disposition. Instead of a standard punishment, the judge may provide continuances so that a resolution outside of court can be determined, or the judge may place the child on supervision for an undetermined amount of time while problems are resolved. Lawgiver judges are just the opposite. These judges are primarily concerned with procedural requirements. This type of judge holds the child's total well-being and personality to be less important than due process. Even if the child is in need of care and rehabilitation, the judge may dismiss a case if the prosecutor cannot prove beyond a reasonable doubt that the youth committed the act alleged in the petition. Treatment or identification of problems in the child's life is secondary to statutory requirements. The personalities of both types of judges influence how they function in the courtroom (Cox, Allen, Hanser, & Conrad, 2014). Therefore, it is hard to imagine comprehensive coverage of all situations by extensive rules and procedures.

Often, situations will emerge that are fuzzy and not clearly under the command of any single department. This phenomenon is truer for service industries, where new situations emerge all the time that had not been thought of by the management. Especially in criminal justice, unique situations emerge constantly and require innovativeness to address. The same set of rules cannot be enforced in the exact same fashion in all situations. In juvenile justice, some detention centers operate under a policy that forces youth who commit felony offenses to remain in detention for a minimum time. Although this provides ammunition for increased funding at the end of the budget year, it is not always feasible—nor is it necessary—to hold every felony offender in detention. Incarceration is supposed to be reserved for those who pose the most threat to society. If one looks at shoplifting statutes, for example, a child who steals an HDTV from a retail store in Missouri can be charged with a felony offense if the television is worth more than $500 (Missouri Revised Statutes, 2007). A person must ask if this child is really a threat to society. Does this child really belong in detention with others who might have committed much more serious offenses, such as robbery or rape? In this case, a generalized rule regarding detention of youth may not be appropriate for all.

Rulification, emphasizing the rules and policies of the organization that best meet the needs of every situation, consistent with Weber's principles of management, is impossible in the criminal justice system. Rulification gives rise to bureaucratic *red tape,* a term often used for strict adherence to procedures and rules. Bureaucratic red-tapism works against organizational innovativeness and progress, leading to a sharp decline in service quality. Strict adherence to procedures and rules and an unwieldy chain of command in a bureaucratic structure slow the pace of change, adversely influencing flexibility and innovativeness. Everything has to be done in accordance with the rules, with no place for innovative approaches to deal with new situations that are emerging from changes in the environment (discussed in detail in Chapter 4). Nowhere is this seen more obviously than in the war on drugs. Policies have been enacted to control drug distribution and manufacturing. The United States has spent billions of dollars fighting the war on drugs, only to see a drug raid occur one hour and the drug market flourishing in the same neighborhood within the next hour. Statutes require the incarceration of drug offenders, even though other approaches to preventing continued drug involvement may be more effective. Little creative thought has traditionally existed in this approach to crime control (although we may be seeing changes with the use of drug courts).

Furthermore, because of strict vertical lines of command and multiple layers of hierarchy, bureaucratic structures stifle communication, often giving rise to the *grapevine.* This informal communication may not provide entirely true information, but it becomes a powerful source for filling the void created by formal communication. It may also give rise to informal leaders, who can interfere with the authority of the formal leaders and adversely affect the employees' attitude toward their work. Consequently, the formal leaders may face difficulty enforcing procedures and rules. Therefore, criminal justice agencies must pay special attention to combat the negative influence of grapevines through innovative structural changes. For example, detention centers often use *linking pins,* or individuals who convey information from one shift to another, thus maintaining continuity. In one detention center familiar to the authors, one employee was hired to work four hours of his shift with the day staff and four hours with the evening staff. He was able to provide informal information from one shift to the other. Since he was the only employee in this position, the organization held him accountable for the information shared. In other words, there was a single, identifiable source for informal communications between the two shifts. This was beneficial for both the employees and the agency because formal and informal communication could be passed in a somewhat controlled manner.

Another tenet of Weber's (1947) theory is specialization of tasks, which brings efficiency. However, it is now seen that specialization up to a point improves efficiency, but then it acts detrimentally to the very same cause. As employees get more and more specialized, they start losing perspective on the full picture of the organization, and they start working in silos. These workers lose flexibility to accommodate any variability in a situation that does not fit into their rigid job definitions. An accompanying implication of specialization is resistance to change. Furthermore, too much specialization promotes suboptimal use of resources, adversely impacting organizational capacity. For example, visiting a bank that operates on specialization, one will typically find long lines in front of some customer service representatives and none in front of others. This is because of the nature of customer needs, which are not equally divided on any given day among all employees specializing in different areas. This bank obviously is unable to fully use all of its employees, some being overworked and some having very little work. On the other hand, another bank where the employees are cross-trained will be better able to fully use all of its personnel. In this bank, customers with different needs can stand in any line and can be served by any customer service representative, thus leading to almost equal lines in front of all employees. Similarly, in law enforcement there should be some amount of specialization, which should be integrated with cross-training for officers to handle a broad spectrum of functions.

The bureaucratic and machine models do not give much attention to the interdependence between various subsystems of an organization. Instead, they promote specialization that breeds the *departmentalization mentality,* where the department becomes more important than the organization. This isolation defeats the overall efficiency of the organization because departmental excellence supersedes the organizational goals. For example, consider a travel department in an organization that flies the sales associates for business purposes on red-eye flights. The express objective is to curb travel costs, an important measure used to evaluate the performance of the travel department. However, the sales associates complain that they are very tired and unproductive the next day after having traveled the previous night. Consequently, they cannot procure much business for the organization, the very objective for which they traveled. In this example, interdependence between the two subsystems (travel and marketing) has been ignored, and the travel department's performance goals have superseded the organizational performance goals.

Although there is the positive argument that specialization brings ownership, ownership can cause agendas to shift (Braiden, 1992) and personal interests to become more important than organizational interests. If one were to look at the organizational chart of a police department today, one would notice that there are many more divisions than there were 30 years ago. There are traffic, drug, vice, fraud, crime prevention, juvenile, homicide, special victims, and detective divisions, and the list goes on and on. It is easy for detectives from several of the divisions to work cases involving the same suspects, yet not collaborate because their specialties keep them from doing so (Braiden, 1992). Although this may be efficient in solving a particular incident, it is not efficient for the overall accomplishment of the goal of law enforcement, or to provide high customer satisfaction.

According to the Weberian principles, employees have to fit a role definition stated in rules and procedures. Individual creativity has no place in a bureaucratic structure. This inflexibility is in direct conflict with the changing face of modern organizations. In today's organizations, managers are required to display greater creativity and innovation to make decisions that solve problems as they work toward achieving the organization's goals. Employee creativity and innovativeness are of special significance in service industries, where customers desire customization to their specific needs. Failing to allow frontline officers to voice concerns or adopt productive approaches to solving the problems they face is a recipe for disaster. Such an approach produces a demoralized officer who checks out of the job by doing only what is minimally required to get by and to stay out of trouble. In an article on the demoralization of employees, Braiden (1992) states,

> They are the inevitable product of the drudgery of routine labor that ultimately dulls the brain and saps the spirit. . . . Sadly, bright people literally chain their brain at the gate coming in, function through their shift, and pick it up again on the way out. We go out of our way to hire the brightest people we can find, and then we teach them to follow orders like soldiers. (p. 96)

This is clearly a part of the bureaucratic mind-set of controlling and managing each aspect of the employee's day. Breaking tasks into the smallest pieces possible is key in a bureaucracy to allow for accountability, efficiency, and standardization of tasks, even though it may not be the best way to handle the job at hand. Despite the several negative characteristics, bureaucracy remains the dominant model within criminal justice organizations (although it can be argued that community policing initiatives have worked to change this approach). Consequently, there is great reluctance within the criminal justice system to open up and accommodate changes to meet the shifting needs of the society it serves.

CAREER HIGHLIGHT BOX
POLICE AND DETECTIVES

Nature of the Work

Police officers protect lives and property. Detectives and criminal investigators, who sometimes are called agents or special agents, gather facts and collect evidence of possible crimes. Law enforcement officers' duties depend on the size and type of their organizations.

(Continued)

(Continued)

Duties

Uniformed police officers typically do the following:

- Enforce laws
- Respond to calls for service
- Patrol assigned areas
- Conduct traffic stops and issue citations
- Arrest suspects
- Write detailed reports and fill out forms
- Prepare cases and testify in court

Detectives and criminal investigators typically do the following:

- Investigate crimes
- Collect evidence of crimes
- Conduct interviews with suspects and witnesses
- Observe the activities of suspects
- Arrest suspects
- Write detailed reports and fill out forms
- Prepare cases and testify in court

Police officers pursue and apprehend people who break the law and then warn them, cite them, or arrest them. Most police officers patrol their jurisdictions and investigate any suspicious activity they notice. They also respond to calls, issue traffic tickets, investigate domestic issues, and give first aid to accident victims.

Detectives perform investigative duties such as gathering facts and collecting evidence.

The daily activities of police and detectives vary with their occupational specialty and whether they are working for a local, state, or federal agency. Duties also differ among federal agencies, which enforce different aspects of the law. Regardless of job duties or location, police officers and detectives at all levels must write reports and keep detailed records that will be needed if they testify in court.

The following are examples of types of police and detectives who work in state and local law enforcement and in federal law enforcement.

State and Local Law Enforcement

Uniformed police officers have general law enforcement duties. They wear uniforms that allow the public to easily recognize them as police officers. They have regular patrols and also respond to calls for service.

Police agencies are usually organized into geographic districts, with uniformed officers assigned to patrol a specific area. Officers in large agencies often patrol with a partner. During patrols, officers look for any signs of criminal activity and may conduct searches or arrest suspected criminals. They may also respond to emergency calls, investigate complaints, and enforce traffic laws.

Some police officers work only on a specific type of crime, such as narcotics. Officers, especially those working in large departments, may also work in special units, such as horseback, motorcycle, canine corps, or special weapons and tactics (SWAT) teams. Typically, officers must work as patrol officers for a certain number of years before they may be appointed to one of these units.

Many city police agencies are involved in community policing, a philosophy of bringing police and members of the community together to prevent crime. A neighborhood watch program is one type of community policing.

Some agencies have special geographic and enforcement responsibilities. Examples include public college and university police forces, public school district police, and transit police. Most law enforcement workers in special agencies are uniformed officers.

State police officers, sometimes called *state troopers* or *highway patrol officers*, have many of the same duties as other police officers, but they may spend more time enforcing traffic laws and issuing traffic citations. State police officers have authority to work anywhere in the state and are frequently called on to help other law enforcement agencies, especially those in rural areas or small towns. State highway patrols operate in every state except Hawaii.

Transit and railroad police patrol railroad yards and transit stations. They protect property, employees, and passengers from crimes such as thefts and robberies. They remove trespassers from railroad and transit properties and check the IDs of people who try to enter secure areas.

Sheriffs and deputy sheriffs enforce the law on the county level. Sheriffs' departments tend to be relatively small. Sheriffs usually are elected by the public and do the same work as a local or county police chief. Some sheriffs' departments do the same work as officers in urban police departments. Others mainly operate the county jails and provide services in the local courts. Police and sheriffs' deputies who provide security in city and county courts are sometimes called bailiffs.

Detectives and criminal investigators are plainclothes investigators who gather facts and collect evidence for criminal cases. They conduct interviews, examine records, observe the activities of suspects, and participate in raids or arrests. Detectives usually specialize in investigating one type of crime, such as homicide or fraud. Detectives are typically assigned cases on a rotating basis and work on them until an arrest and conviction are made or until the case is dropped.

Fish and game wardens enforce fishing, hunting, and boating laws. They patrol hunting and fishing areas, conduct search and rescue operations, investigate complaints and accidents, and educate the public about laws pertaining to their environment.

Federal Law Enforcement

Federal law enforcement officials carry out many of the same duties that other police officers do; however, they have jurisdiction over the entire country. Many federal agents

(Continued)

(Continued)

are highly specialized. The following are examples of federal agencies in which officers and agents enforce particular types of laws.

- *Federal Bureau of Investigation (FBI) agents* are the federal government's principal investigators, responsible for enforcing more than 300 federal statutes and conducting sensitive national security investigations.
- *U.S. Drug Enforcement Administration (DEA) agents* enforce laws and regulations relating to illegal drugs.
- *U.S. Secret Service uniformed officers* protect the President, the Vice President, their immediate families, and other public officials.
- *Federal Air Marshals* provide air security by guarding against attacks targeting U.S. aircraft, passengers, and crews.
- *U.S. Border Patrol agents* protect international land and water boundaries.

Training, Other Qualifications, and Advancement

Education requirements range from a high school diploma to a college or higher degree. Most police and detectives must graduate from their agency's training academy before completing a period of on-the-job training. Candidates must be U.S. citizens, usually at least 21 years old, and meet rigorous physical and personal qualifications.

Important Qualities

Ability to multitask. Officers and detectives may find that the demands of their job vary from day to day. But multiple tasks and extensive paperwork must be completed on time.

Communication skills. Police and detectives must be able to speak with people when gathering facts about a crime and to then express details about a given incident in writing.

Empathetic personality. Police officers need to understand the perspectives of a wide variety of people in their jurisdiction and have a willingness to help the public.

Good judgment. Police and detectives must be able to determine the best way to solve a wide array of problems quickly.

Leadership skills. Police officers must be comfortable with being a highly visible member of their community, as the public looks to them for assistance in emergency situations.

Perceptiveness. Officers must be able to anticipate another person's reactions and understand why people act a certain way.

Strength and stamina. Officers and detectives must be in good physical shape both to pass required tests for entry into the field and to keep up with the daily rigors of the job.

Education and Training

Police and detective applicants usually must have at least a high school education or GED and be a graduate of their agency's training academy. Many agencies require some college coursework or a college degree. Knowledge of a foreign language is an asset in many federal agencies and urban departments.

Candidates must be U.S. citizens, must usually be at least 21 years old, have a driver's license, and must meet specific physical qualifications. Applicants may have to pass physical exams of vision, hearing, strength, and agility as well as competitive written exams. Previous work or military experience is often seen as a plus. Candidates typically go through a series of interviews and may be asked to take lie detector and drug tests. A felony conviction may disqualify a candidate.

Applicants usually have recruit training before becoming an officer. In state and large local police departments, recruits get training in their agency's police academy. In small agencies, recruits often attend a regional or state academy. Training includes classroom instruction in constitutional law, civil rights, state laws and local ordinances, and police ethics. Recruits also receive training and supervised experience in areas such as patrol, traffic control, use of firearms, self-defense, first aid, and emergency response.

Some police departments have cadet programs for people interested in a career in law enforcement who do not yet meet age requirements for becoming an officer. These cadets do clerical work and attend classes until they reach the minimum age requirement and can apply for a position with the regular force.

Detectives normally begin their career as police officers before being promoted to detective.

State and local agencies encourage applicants to continue their education after high school by taking courses or training related to law enforcement. Many applicants for entry-level police jobs have taken some college classes, and a significant number are college graduates. Many junior colleges, colleges, and universities offer programs in law enforcement or criminal justice. Many agencies offer financial assistance to officers who pursue these or related degrees.

Fish and game wardens also must meet specific requirements; however, these vary. Candidates applying for federal jobs with the U.S. Fish and Wildlife Service typically need a college degree, and those applying to work for state departments often need a high school diploma or some college study in a related field such as biology or natural resources management. Military or police experience may be considered an advantage. Once hired, fish and game wardens attend a training academy and sometimes get additional training in the field.

Although similar to state and local requirements, the requirements for federal law enforcement agencies, such as with the FBI or Secret Service, are generally stricter. Federal agencies require a bachelor's degree, related work experience, or a combination of the two. For example, FBI special agent applicants typically must be college graduates with at least three years of professional work experience. There are lie detector tests as

(Continued)

(Continued)

well as interviews with references. Jobs that require security clearances have additional requirements.

Federal law enforcement agents undergo extensive training, usually at the U.S. Marine Corps base in Quantico, Virginia, or the Federal Law Enforcement Training Center in Glynco, Georgia. Furthermore, some federal positions have a maximum age for applicants. The specific educational requirements, qualifications, and training information for a particular federal agency are available on its website. (See the Contacts for More Info section for links to various federal agencies, http://www.bls.gov/ooh/Protective-Service/Police-and-detectives.htm#tab-8.)

Advancement

Police officers usually become eligible for promotion after a probationary period. Promotions to corporal, sergeant, lieutenant, and captain usually are made according to a candidate's position on a promotion list, as determined by scores on a written examination and on-the-job performance. In large departments, promotion may enable an officer to become a detective or to specialize in one type of police work, such as working with juveniles.

Federal agents often are on the General Services (GS) pay scale. Most begin at the GS-5 or GS-7 level. As agents meet time-in-grade and knowledge and skills requirements, they move up the GS scale. Jobs at and above GS-13 are often managerial positions. Many agencies hire internally for these supervisory positions. A few agents may be able to enter the senior executive service ranks of upper management.

Employment

Police and detectives held about 794,300 jobs in 2010.

Police and detective work can be physically demanding, stressful, and dangerous. Police officers have one of the highest rates of on-the-job injuries and fatalities.

In addition to confrontations with criminals, police officers and detectives need to be constantly alert and ready to deal appropriately with a number of other threatening scenarios. Officers regularly work at crime or accident scenes and other traumatic events as well as deal with the death and suffering that they encounter. Although a career in law enforcement may take a toll on their private lives, many officers find it rewarding to help members of their communities.

The jobs of some federal agents, such as U.S. Secret Service and DEA special agents, require extensive travel, often on short notice. These agents may relocate a number of times over the course of their careers. Some special agents, such as those in the U.S. Border Patrol, may work outdoors in rugged terrain and in all kinds of weather.

Injuries

Police and detectives have a higher rate of injuries and illness than the national average. They may face physical injury when conflicts with criminals occur, during motor-vehicle pursuits, when exposure to communicable diseases occurs, or through many other high-risk situations. Police work can be both physically and mentally demanding as officers must be alert and ready to react throughout their entire shift. Police and detectives may minimize these risks by following proper procedures.

Work Schedules

Uniformed officers, detectives, agents, and inspectors usually are scheduled to work full time. Paid overtime is common. Shift work is necessary because protection must be provided around the clock. Because more experienced employees typically receive preference, junior officers frequently work weekends, holidays, and nights. Some police officers chose to work off duty as security for restaurants, retail stores, and other establishments.

Job Outlook

Employment of police and detectives is expected to grow by 7 percent from 2010 to 2020, slower than the average for all occupations. Continued demand for public safety will lead to new openings for officers in local departments; however, both state and federal jobs may be more competitive.

Because they typically offer low salaries, many local departments face high turnover rates, making opportunities more plentiful for qualified applicants. However, some smaller departments may have fewer opportunities as budgets limit the ability to hire additional officers.

Jobs in state and federal agencies will remain more competitive as they often offer high pay and more opportunities for both promotions and inter-agency transfers. Bilingual applicants with a bachelor's degree and law enforcement or military experience, especially investigative experience, should have the best opportunities in federal agencies.

The level of government spending determines the level of employment for police and detectives. The number of job opportunities, therefore, can vary from year to year and from place to place. Layoffs are rare because retirements enable most staffing cuts to be handled through attrition. Trained law enforcement officers who lose their jobs because of budget cuts usually have little difficulty finding jobs with other agencies.

Earnings

The median annual wage of police and detectives was $55,010 in May 2010. The median wage is the wage at which half the workers in an occupation earned more than that amount and half earned less. The lowest 10 percent earned less than $32,440, and the top 10 percent earned more than $88,870.

(Continued)

(Continued)

The median wages for police and detectives occupations in May 2010 were as follows:

- $68,820 for detectives and criminal investigators
- $54,330 for transit and railroad police
- $53,540 for police and sheriff's patrol officers
- $49,730 for fish and game wardens

Many agencies provide officers with an allowance for uniforms as well as extensive benefits and the option to retire at an age that is younger than a more typical retirement age.

SOURCE: Bureau of Labor Statistics, U.S. Department of Labor, *Occupational Outlook Handbook, 2012– 13 Edition*, Police and Detectives, on the Internet at http://www.bls.gov/ooh/protective-service/ police-and-detectives.htm.

Open-System Models: The Humanistic Perspective

Classical thinkers made significant contributions to the theory and practice of management. However, their theories did not always achieve the desired results because they did not include the behavioral perspective of management. During the early 20th century, the industrialized nations of the world were experiencing social and cultural changes. Their standards of living and working conditions were improving. Under these changing conditions, it was increasingly noted that the actions of management were not necessarily consistent with the ones predicted by the closed-system models. More and more, human behavior was being seen as an important factor in shaping managerial style and worker actions (Daft, 2001).

In 1924, various studies were being performed at Western Electric Company's plant in Hawthorne, Illinois, trying to understand how different factors would increase productivity (Rieger, 1995; Roethlisberger & Dickson, 1956). One such study (Parson, 1974) examined the impact of levels of lighting on productivity. Two groups were formed; the test group was subjected to different levels of light, and the control group was subjected to the same level of light. The results demonstrated that the productivity of the test group went up when the light was increased, when the light remained the same, and when the light decreased; however, the productivity of the control group went up as well, even though the lighting level remained the same. These were rather confusing results.

Elton Mayo, a Harvard professor, was invited with his team to study this phenomenon in greater depth. They found that the increase in productivity was being caused by the human behavior, which they called the *Hawthorne effect* (Parson, 1974). They explained that workers in both groups perceived that special attention was being given to them within their organization because they were chosen for the study, causing them to develop a sense of pride, which in turn motivated them to improve their performance. The so-called Hawthorne studies also revealed that organizations work as social systems, which promote the formation of informal groups that operate parallel to the formal structure within an organization. These informal groups are formed on the basis of the social relations that members may develop inside and outside of the organization. Mayo believed that work attitudes and sentiments of the members of a group are important motivating factors that determine their productivity. The Hawthorne studies introduced the human element to management thinking that had been missing from the closed-system models. Though the Hawthorne studies were conducted between 1924 and 1933, their influence on management thinking was not felt until the 1950s due to the Great Depression and World War II.

Workers are members of social groups and work organizations, both of which play important roles in shaping worker behaviors and actions. As the workers move back and forth between the workplace and their social groups, they inadvertently bring external influences into the organization in the form of values and behaviors, impacting the internal functioning of an organization. This realization that organizations cannot be isolated from the external environment and should be integrated into the management principles led to the birth of open-system models. These models are embedded in human relations theory, which comprises the research of scholars such as Elton Mayo, Abraham Maslow, and David McGregor (see detailed discussion in Chapter 6). The primary theme of these human relations models favors the designing of jobs so that the workers are allowed to use their full potential. The four basic characteristics that flow from human relations theory, which differentiate the open-system models from the closed-system models, are as follows:

1. *Individual differences.* Management must recognize that people are different and will react differently to similar situations. Therefore, management must not assume employees to be homogenous when designing and allocating tasks. However, greater standardization among employees can be achieved through good training.

2. *Motivation.* Individuals can be motivated to work toward achieving organizational goals. Therefore, it is essential for the managers to be constantly designing and creating schemes to stimulate the interests and desires of the employees toward planned goals of the organization (see detailed discussion in Chapter 6).

3. *Mutual interest.* Employees have an inherent need to socialize at their work, which drives them to pursue membership in informal groups that have common interests. The management must recognize that these needs cannot be satisfied by formal groups. Therefore, the management must facilitate the formation of informal groups, which brings employees together to pursue common interests. Having a lounge where officers can have lunch or a coffee break or an in-house gym facility where officers can work out allows for the creation of informal socialization among those who take advantage of the opportunities.

4. *Human dignity.* Employees like to be treated with respect. Their individuality needs to be respected for them to love their job and work toward organizational goals.

In *open-system models,* the principal starting assumption is that the external variables or events play a significant role in explaining what is happening within an organization. Revisiting the example of prisoner abuse that was discussed earlier under the closed-system model, an open-system approach would look for external reasons to explain the problem. Researchers may discover that the problem started two years ago when the governor visited the state prison. In his speech, the governor mentioned reducing the budget for the prisons, which was not well received among the inmates. The conditions at that prison were already appalling. Any further cut in the budget was perceived by the inmates as implying a worsening of inmate privileges and security, making them angry and confrontational. Such defiant inmate behavior led to more hours of work for the correctional officers, who were already underpaid due to restrictive budgets. The officers became angry and resorted to dealing with the prisoners heavy-handedly, thus leading to abuse. Close examination of this example shows the interaction among an external stimulus, officers' responses, and inmates' (customer) reactions, all collectively interacting to create the chaos.

Yet another open-system example is that of the brutality and discrimination scandals that were rampant in the late 1980s among police departments in Los Angeles and Milwaukee (Skolnick & Fyfe, 1993) and the new accusations of discrimination of law enforcement arising from the George Zimmerman and Trayvon Martin case. In Los Angeles and Milwaukee, the researchers found that these communities, especially the minority populations, were apprehensive because of a lack of adequate representation in the local police force. Consequently, they would not be cooperative with the local police force. As a result, the local police force was not friendly and helpful to the minority community, and often would look at its members suspiciously. The actions of the local police force seemed discriminatory. In this example, to get a clearer perspective of the existing problem, one has to include the role played by the employees and the customers, who are a part of the external social system.

The previous examples illustrate that the open-system models are definitely more realistic in identifying workable solutions as compared to closed-system models, but they are extremely difficult to interpret because of dynamic interactions among the external variables. These external influences can be experienced by organizations from the actions of the existing competitors, potential competitors, suppliers, customers, and government. The influence of these external factors has been amplified in recent years due to a changing environment as reflected in growing globalization, increased diversity, rising ethical standards, and rapid advances in technology accompanied by rising e-commerce. Next, we discuss two popular open-system models that have express implications for improving service quality in the criminal justice systems.

Total Quality Management (TQM) Model

In the 1970s and 1980s, Japanese organizations made a significant impact throughout the world with their extremely high product quality. The success of the Japanese companies was attributed to their prevention-oriented quality approach through employee involvement, which was different from the American model that was based on an inspection-oriented quality approach. The Japanese companies incorporated the suggestions from their employees in improving the manufacturing process to prevent errors from occurring. They also introduced the *voice of the customer* in designing the product and modifying the process to provide higher quality because they realized that the customer is the final judge of product quality. A product that is well made but that does not satisfy the needs of the customer will not be highly rated by the customer. Four important elements of this model, dubbed *total quality management (TQM),* were the following:

1. *Employee involvement.* This means companywide participation of the workers in quality control and quality improvement. It also means active thinking on the part of all employees on how to improve the system. This radical thinking was a significant departure from the classical management models in which the workers were hired for their physical work and the thinking was to be left to the management.

2. *Customer focus.* Instead of focusing on product attributes that management thinks are important, which was the dominant paradigm for the classical management models, the TQM companies consult on these attributes with their customers, who are the final judges of quality. The TQM companies then try to meet or exceed the needs and expectations of their customers.

3. *Continuous improvement.* The TQM companies are not satisfied with their performance, but are constantly striving to do better. They are constantly making incremental improvements in all areas of the organization, which are typically suggested by the employees. Employee involvement is a paradigm shift as compared to the classical models, where the improvement was initiated by the management. These small changes are easy to implement because they have been identified and approved by the employees, who feel involved, and because these modifications do not require drastic changes to the existing work conditions.

4. *Benchmarking.* The TQM companies are constantly studying the best companies in the business to identify areas where improvements can be made and to find the best method of incorporating improvements. Benchmarking is outward looking, which is again a paradigm shift in comparison to the classical models, that were inward looking for making any changes and improvements.

The previous concepts, which are universally accepted in improving service quality in most industries, are very difficult to accept and implement by most criminal justice officers, who are deeply entrenched in the Weberian model of bureaucracy. However, more recently, there has been a change in philosophy in allowing victims and offenders, seen as customers who assess the quality of the justice they receive, more of a say in their cases and in sentencing decisions. In 2004, victims were given new and expanded rights in the courtroom, as discussed in In the News 2.1. Not only can they now appear and be seen in court, but they also can provide victim impact statements, and they are given much more information on the processing of the offenders in their cases. This change may raise the bar in how cases are handled when a victim is involved by providing more quality services to the victim and offender (concepts proposed by TQM). In the News 2.1, however, shows how court personnel, especially defense attorneys, have concerns about the victim's involvement in court sentencing and bail hearings because it has the possibility of bringing about biased consequences.

In the News 2.1
Giving Crime Victims More of Their Say:
A Federal Law Has Created Tensions in the Legal System

W. Patrick Kenna felt cheated. In 2000, he invested $20,000 with a currency trading company, hoping to earn enough to start a new business. Instead, he lost nearly the entire sum, defrauded along with dozens of other investors. A Los Angeles businessman, Kenna took some comfort in knowing that the two men responsible—father and son owners of the company—would spend significant time behind bars, but he wanted to make sure the judge knew just how much trouble they had caused.

Kenna made his anger clear during the father's 2005 sentencing, but when the son's day in court arrived three months later, the federal judge denied Kenna's request to speak. "I listened to the victims the last time," Judge John Walter said. "There just isn't anything else that could possibly be said." Kenna was furious. "We didn't feel that the judge was taking into consideration the victims in the case," he says. So he turned to the U.S. Court of Appeals for the Ninth Circuit, which ordered the judge to let Kenna speak at a new hearing.

The reversal in Kenna's case reflects the growing influence of crime victims since the passage in 2004 of landmark federal legislation granting them new and expanded rights. Three years later, the changes are beginning to have an impact, shifting the balance of a legal system that historically has been solely a two-party affair. One result is tension between legal parties and concern among defense attorneys who fear that a greater role for victims conflicts with the right of defendants to a fair trial.

Historically, the adversarial legal system has carved out roles in criminal cases only for the prosecutor and the accused. Victims have been relegated to the sidelines unless they were testifying. Although the interests of prosecutors usually align with those of victims, they are not always the same: for instance, when victims want tougher sentences than prosecutors do. Victims' rights advocates hope the changes are just the start and are pushing to put victims on an equal footing with defendants and prosecutors. "What our goal should be is to put the victim back into the position as if no crime had been committed," says Paul Cassell, a former federal judge who resigned this year to advocate for victims.

Crime victims began winning rights at the state level decades ago, but the 2004 legislation brought the protections to the federal level for the first time. Victims now must be notified about court developments. They must be allowed to speak during bail and sentencing hearings. And most important, the law gives them the ability to appeal rulings when they think their rights are being violated, as Kenna did. The Justice Department is even funding three legal clinics, in Maryland, Arizona, and South Carolina, to help victims assert these rights in court.

Bias. But defense attorneys say that changing the adversarial system further would have dangerous consequences. Most problematic, they say, would be allowing victims more control over prosecutorial decisions. Victims can be biased, attorneys say, and they sometimes fail to understand how their case fits into the system as a whole.

It's often hard to define a victim in the first place. For instance, is a woman a victim in a marijuana-dealing case because her boyfriend beat her while he was high on drugs he bought from the dealer? A court said no. Could an Arizonan tell the judge he opposed the death penalty at the sentencing hearing for the man who killed his wife? That judge, too, said no.

Defense attorneys are also wary of the influence that victims may have on plea agreements. And they point out that a victim's testimony, in bail or sentencing hearings, is not subject to the same cross-examination as is the testimony of other witnesses. Overall, they worry that inserting victims more broadly into the process pits the defendant against not one, but two, adversaries.

Victims' rights advocates make just the opposite argument. They say the victims' rights laws are not uniformly enforced on a federal level—and are almost nonexistent in many states. Instead, they say, victims often get little guidance from the government. Mindful of such problems, a small group of advocates is helping victims with appeals and other legal issues through the federally funded clinics. "Having the attorney there is starting to turn the rights into more than rhetoric," says Meg Garvin, a lawyer at Lewis and Clark Law School who coordinates the clinics.

One satisfied client of the clinic is Marylander Tracy Palmer, a 41-year-old mother of two who had been trying to escape her ex-husband since 1994, when he first was convicted of assaulting her. In 2001 he was sentenced to 15 years in jail, but it was only by chance that Palmer found that a judge was about to release him after just four years. She protested that she was not notified of the hearing. A judge rebuffed her, but the federal clinic helped her win another review of her ex-husband's release, a decision now on appeal.

The victims' rights laws are changing the system for prosecutors like Trey Gowdy in Spartanburg, S.C. He now may have to make an extra phone call to keep victims' lawyers in the loop, but Gowdy says he's never had a major conflict. Still, he thinks the best service for victims—as for defendants—is the government doing its job well. "The better the prosecutors," says Gowdy, "the less you will feel victims having needs."

SOURCE: "Giving Crime Victims More of Their Say: A Federal Law Has Created Tensions in the Legal System," by E. Schwartz, December 13, 2007, *U.S. News and World Report.* Copyright © 2007 U.S. News & World Report, L.P. All rights reserved. Reprinted with permission.

Supply Chain/Synergy Model

Most complex organizations are often viewed as a collection of interrelated systems, where changes in one subsystem will impact the functioning of the other system. Therefore, promoting coordination and cooperation among different subsystems, known as a *supply chain* perspective, will accomplish more than when the subsystems are working in isolation. This property, in which the whole is greater than the sum of its parts, is referred to as *synergy* (Lewis et al., 2001).

The supply chain phenomenon works very well in the criminal justice system, which is comprised of different agencies. For example, when a crime is committed, a law enforcement agency responds. Once the criminal suspects are apprehended, they are screened for prosecution by the state's prosecutors. Once the offenders are charged, they are entitled to a trial, which is presided over by a judge. If the defendants are found guilty of the crime(s), they are sentenced. At this point, the corrections department supervises offenders in various ways. As the offender passes from one agency to the next in this chain of activities, the agency that hands over the offender is the supplier, and the agency that receives the offender is the customer. In this supply chain approach, at each stage of the criminal justice system there is a *supplier* and a *customer*. As the offender moves to the next stage, the agency that was a customer in receiving the offender now becomes the supplier to the next agency. For the criminal justice system to work efficiently and effectively, there needs to be a high degree of coordination among different agencies involved in its processes. So one can understand how problems arise in the criminal justice system when police officers apprehend criminals and the court system lets them go with lesser charges or a softer penalty by striking a plea bargain. The law enforcement officer (acting as supplier) may not fully understand why the court system (acting as customer) operated the way it did. The police may have expected a harsher penalty and may be disappointed when this does not happen. Consequently, when faced with the same-case scenario again, the police may handle the situation in a different fashion by not making an arrest, knowing that the court will not proceed as the police had hoped.

In the business world, to benefit from the synergy among different entities working in the supply chain network, one of the latest trends is the adoption of *enterprise resource planning (ERP)*, which is a complex information system that collects, processes, and provides information about an organization's entire activities, leaving no blind spots. It integrates the different functions of the organization, allowing the managers and employees to use the information to adjust plans and respond to opportunities and threats in real time. Lack of integration of different agencies involved in security functions was an essential problem in the response to the terrorist attacks of September 11, 2001. Law enforcement did not have the systems necessary to integrate the information they were receiving from various sources and agencies to identify the potential threat to the United States. They could not connect the dots to prevent the terrorist activities. Now, 12 years later, there are still issues with information system planning. Even though systems have been put in place for the Central Intelligence Agency, the Federal Bureau of Investigation, and other agencies to share information, they are restricted in what they can share with one another. They have not developed clear-cut plans for emergencies in each U.S. city, and the upper-level management has experienced turnover so many times that policies and procedures in homeland security are ambiguous at best. In the News 2.2 discusses some of the issues still faced by the U.S. government in the fight against terrorism on American soil and abroad.

The supply chain model discussed previously includes the role of employees, customers, and suppliers in introducing outside influences into the workings of an organization, thus making the solutions to the existing problems more realistic. This model mandates that managers focus on relationship building with customers, suppliers, and other partners in their attempt to create modern organizations. In criminal justice, one can see this application in probation offices, where officers within probation are commonly brought together to informally staff or discuss cases as a group. This allows for the officers to address any issues or concerns they may have about a particular case as well as potential ideas they may have about processing the case, that are not traditionally used. When looking at a single case, for example, and if a probation officer allows it to be staffed, the officer working the case may receive multiple suggestions on how best to handle the case from others in the office. This shows that not all officers would respond to the situation in the same manner. The probation officers can also bring up a program or treatment opportunity that they are aware of but that is not commonly used by the agency. Comments or information can be gathered from others in the group on whether the program or opportunity would work well in this situation. Support can also be given to the probation officer to assist in the decisions being made. All involved feel more valued at having contributed to the case and to the decision-making process while also having worked toward the organizational goal of treatment and rehabilitation of offenders. Adoption of such integrated practices in other areas of the criminal justice system will only add value.

In the News 2.2
Are We Safer Today?

Two years ago, we and our colleagues issued a report card to assess the U.S. government's progress on the bipartisan recommendations in the 9/11 Commission report. We concluded that the nation was not safe enough. Our judgment remains the same today: We still lack a sense of urgency in the face of grave danger.

The U.S. homeland confronts a "persistent and evolving terrorist threat," especially from al Qaeda, according to a National Intelligence Estimate in July. Six years after the attacks, in the wake of a series of ambitious reforms carried out by dedicated officials, how is it possible that the threat remains so dire?

The answer stems from a mixed record of reform, a lack of focus and a resilient foe. Progress at home—in our ability to detect, prevent and respond to terrorist attacks—has been difficult, incomplete and slow, but it has been real. Outside our borders, however, the threat of failure looms. We face a rising tide of radicalization and rage in the Muslim world—a trend to which our own actions have contributed. The enduring threat is not Osama bin Laden but young Muslims with no jobs and no hope, who are angry with their own governments and increasingly see the United States as an enemy of Islam.

Four years ago, then–Defense Secretary Donald Rumsfeld famously asked his advisors: "Are we capturing, killing or deterring and dissuading more terrorists every day than the madrassas and the radical clerics are recruiting, training and deploying against us?"

The answer is "no."

U.S. foreign policy has not stemmed the rising tide of extremism in the Muslim world. In July 2004, the commission recommended putting foreign policy at the center of our counterterrorism efforts. Instead, we have lost ground.

(Continued)

(Continued)

Our report warned that it was imperative to eliminate terrorist sanctuaries. But inside Pakistan, al Qaeda "has protected or regenerated key elements of its homeland attack capability," according to the National Intelligence Estimate. The chief threat to Afghanistan's young democracy comes from across the Pakistani border, from the resurgent Taliban. Pakistan should take the lead in closing Taliban camps and rooting out al Qaeda. But the United States must act if Pakistan will not.

We are also failing in the struggle of ideas. We have not been persuasive in enlisting the energy and sympathy of the world's 1.3 billion Muslims against the extremist threat. That is not because of who we are: Polling data consistently show strong support in the Muslim world for American values, including our political system and respect for human rights, liberty and equality. Rather, U.S. policy choices have undermined support.

No word is more poisonous to the reputation of the United States than Guantanamo. Fundamental justice requires a fair legal process before the U.S. government detains people for significant periods of time, and the president and Congress have not provided one. Guantanamo Bay should be closed now. The 9/11 Commission recommended developing a "coalition approach" for the detention and treatment of terrorists—a policy that would be legally sustainable, internationally viable and far better for U.S. credibility.

Moreover, no question inflames public opinion in the Muslim world more than the Arab–Israeli dispute. To empower Muslim moderates, we must take away the extremists' most potent grievance: the charge that the United States does not care about the Palestinians. A vigorous diplomatic effort, with the visible, active support of the president, would bolster America's prestige and influence—and offer the best prospect for Israel's long-term security.

And finally, no conflict drains more time, attention, blood, treasure and support from our worldwide counterterrorism efforts than the war in Iraq. It has become a powerful recruiting and training tool for al Qaeda.

Beyond all our problems in the Muslim world, we must not neglect the most dangerous threat of all. The 9/11 Commission urged a "maximum effort" to prevent the nightmare scenario: a nuclear weapon in the hands of terrorists. The recent National Intelligence Estimate says that al Qaeda will continue to try to acquire weapons of mass destruction and that it would not hesitate to use them. But our response to the threat of nuclear terrorism has been lip service and little action. The fiscal 2008 budget request for programs to control nuclear warheads, materials and expertise is a 15 percent real cut from the levels two years ago. We are in dire need of leadership, resources and sustained diplomacy to secure the world's loose nuclear materials. President Bush needs to knock heads and force action.

Military power is essential to our security, but if the only tool is a hammer, pretty soon every problem looks like a nail. We must use all the tools of U.S. power—including foreign aid, educational assistance and vigorous public diplomacy that emphasizes scholarship, libraries and exchange programs—to shape a Middle East and a Muslim world that are less hostile to our interests and values. America's long-term security relies on being viewed not as a threat but as a source of opportunity and hope.

At home, the situation is less dire, but progress has been limited. Some badly needed structures have been built. In 2004, Congress created a director of national intelligence to unify the efforts of the 16 agencies that make up the U.S. intelligence community. The new DNI, Mike McConnell, must now take charge and become the dynamic, bold leader whom the commission envisioned, rather than just another bureaucratic layer. He has recognized the importance of sharing intelligence, of moving from a culture based on the "need to know" to one based on the need to share, as we recommended in our report. But he is still struggling to gain control of budgets and personnel. No DNI will be able to make reform last without significant time in the job and strong support from the president.

Congress also created the National Counterterrorism Center, where CIA analysts, FBI agents and other experts from across the government sit side by side and share intelligence continuously. This is a clear improvement over the pre-9/11 way of doing business, but those inside the center still face restrictions on what they can share with their home agency—a disturbing echo of failed practices. State and local officials also complain that they are not getting the information they need.

In 2004, George Tenet, then the director of central intelligence, testified that it would take five years to fix the CIA. Three years later, we have seen signs of progress, but it is not fixed yet. Flush with resources, the CIA is investing heavily in the training of intelligence analysts and improving its ability to collect information on terrorist targets, particularly by agents on the ground. Disappointingly, despite recruitment drives, only 8 percent of the CIA's new hires have the ethnic backgrounds and language skills most needed for counterterrorism.

A wider problem is that, because of intelligence failures (notably involving Iraq and 9/11) and controversial policies (notably about abuse and interrogation), the public lacks confidence in the CIA. That is not good for the agency or the country. We recognize that intelligence agencies must keep many secrets, but more candor and openness are the only ways to win sustained public support for the reforms we still need.

The FBI, the agency responsible for domestic intelligence, also has much more to do. The number of bureau intelligence analysts has more than doubled since 9/11 (to about 2,100), but they are still second-class citizens in the FBI's law enforcement culture. Modern 21st-century information systems are not yet in place, and top positions are turning over too often. Six years after 9/11, the FBI's essential unit on weapons of mass destruction is just beginning its work.

When it comes to transportation security—the failure so basic to 9/11—we have seen some successes. For example, the Terrorist Screening Center, a football-field-size room filled with a giant electronic board and dozens of experts, tracks the flight manifests of 2,500 international flights arriving in the United States each day. But the prescreening of passengers is still left to the airlines, which lack access to complete watch lists of suspected terrorists. Congress mandated national standards for secure driver's licenses but has not given states the money to make it happen. Moreover, technological improvement has been far too slow. A pilot program of high-tech explosive-detecting "puffer devices" at airports is of doubtful effectiveness and has been delayed indefinitely. Advanced baggage-screening systems will not be in place until 2024. That timeline might work for our grandchildren, but it won't work for us.

Nor will the pace of efforts to prepare the country to respond to future attacks. Congress passed a better formula for distributing federal homeland-security grants to the states on the basis of risk and vulnerability, rather than pork and politics. But the new law still allows the broadcast industry until February 2009 to hand over the prime slice of the broadcast spectrum that police and firefighters need to beam radio messages through concrete and steel. Disaster could well strike before then.

(Continued)

(Continued)

We also lack a legal framework for fighting terrorism without sacrificing civil liberties. The Privacy and Civil Liberties Oversight Board created in response to our recommendations has been missing in action. The board has raised no objections to wiretaps without warrants and to troubling detention and interrogation practices. It even let the White House edit its annual report. Now strengthened by a new law, the board must become a firm, public voice in support of civil liberties.

Finally, there's the question of Congress. Three years ago, we said that strengthening congressional oversight of counterterrorism was among the most difficult and important of our recommendations. Congressional oversight of homeland security and intelligence must be robust and effective. It is not. Three years ago, the 9/11 Commission noted that the Department of Homeland Security reported to 88 congressional committees and subcommittees—a major drain on senior management and a source of contradictory guidance. After halfhearted reforms followed by steps backward, that number is now 86.

Those are just the main items on our list of concerns. Six years later, we are safer in a narrow sense: We have not been attacked, and our defenses are better. But we have become distracted and complacent. We call on the presidential candidates to spell out how they would organize their administrations and act urgently to address the threat. And we call on ordinary citizens to demand more leadership from our elected representatives. The terrible losses our country suffered on 9/11 should have catalyzed efforts to create an America that is safer, stronger and wiser. We still have a long way to go.

SOURCE: From "Are We Safer Today," September 9, 2007, by T. H. Kean & L. H. Hamilton, Woodrow Wilson International Center for Scholars.

NOTE: Thomas H. Kean and Lee H. Hamilton are the former chair and vice chair of the 9/11 Commission.

Changing Face of the Criminal Justice System— Need for a Learning Organization

With globalization, the Internet, and rapid technological changes, the environment for all organizations is becoming unpredictable, characterized by complexity and surprises. In this highly volatile environment, managers are working to redesign their companies toward *learning organizations,* which are highly flexible and adaptable in embodying the tenets of the open-system model (Daft & Lewin, 1993). The attention in these companies is on problem solving (Gebert & Boerner, 1999). These organizations value open communication and cooperation, engaging everyone in identifying and solving problems. Such progressive organizations are based on little hierarchy and a culture that promotes employee and customer participation.

These rapid changes in the environment have also provided different sets of challenges for the criminal justice system, each of which is briefly discussed next.

1. Significant changes have occurred in the last 50 years that have altered the demographics of criminal activities. The traditional family of the 1950s, which consisted of a

husband, a housewife, and two children, is fast being replaced by the two-income family. For this new family unit, time is at a premium, resulting in children spending greater amounts of time without adult supervision, watching television, and surfing the Internet. The children are easily influenced by violence that is being propagated through television and the Internet.

2. In the United States, immigrants accounted for a major share of the increase in the labor force in the 1990s, and they are expected to provide a growing share of the workforce in the 21st century. By the year 2020, it is estimated that Asian Americans, African Americans, and Hispanics will comprise more than 35% of the U.S. population and will form 30% of the U.S. workforce. Also by the year 2020, it is forecasted that women will comprise 50% of the U.S. workforce (Judy & D'Amico, 1997). The growing diversity in the U.S. workforce, also true for criminal justice services, is bringing a variety of challenges to the workplace in the form of supporting diversity, balancing work and family concerns, and coping with the conflict brought by different cultural styles. Another trend is the change in prisoner demographics, with a greater number of immigrants or second-generation immigrants and women becoming involved in criminal activities. This change has introduced challenges for criminal justice agencies to deal with gender and cultural issues.

3. Technology, especially information technology including the Internet, is playing a primary role in knowledge management and the sharing of information. Companies today assume that ideas can emerge from everyone, and the role of the manager is to facilitate open channels of communication to allow ideas, information, and knowledge to flow throughout the organization. An emphasis on knowledge management and information sharing has led to flattening of organizational structures and greater empowerment and involvement of employees. This technology age has created more white-collar jobs, a direct consequence of which is the increase in intricate white-collar crimes, thus adding another layer of complexity to the jobs in the criminal justice system.

4. Over the last several years, the confidence of the American public in businesses has reached a new low. Consequently, there is a resurgence in the public's expectations toward corporate responsibility, as they demand higher standards related to business ethics, corporate governance, regulation of business, and other stakeholder considerations. The American public is pushing the corporations to maintain higher socially responsible behavior and to fulfill their economic, legal, ethical, and philanthropic responsibilities toward their stakeholders. These public expectations of higher ethical and moral responsibilities from corporations have created new duties for the criminal justice system. In addition, the standards the public holds for corporate responsibility and accountability also apply to criminal justice agencies and employees.

5. As mobility and communication have become cheaper and faster, law and order problems are acquiring a unified global field. The Internet has torn down the boundaries of time and space, providing terrorists with a far-reaching global network, reaching people they could not have reached before. In the 21st century, law-enforcing agencies will have to learn to work in cooperation with agencies in other parts of the world because the planning of terrorist activities may be done in one country or a nexus of countries and the recruiting of terrorists in other countries and implementation of terrorist activities in still another country. For example, there is evidence that the masterminds of the al Qaeda organization, Osama bin Laden and Ayman al-Zawahiri, were located in the

mountains of Afghanistan and later moved to the heart of Pakistan; the terrorists are being recruited in the Middle East; and terrorists' activities are being carried out in the United States and Europe. Pakistan has become somewhat of a safe haven for al Qaeda, even though the United States has assisted Pakistan in the past.

In the News 2.3
Planning for Attack Done Outside of U.S.

The 19 terrorists suspected in the Sept. 11 attacks spent about $500,000 preparing an operation that was planned and launched from overseas, beginning several years ago in Germany with support in Britain, the United Arab Emirates and Afghanistan, senior government officials have tentatively concluded.

U.S. investigators have determined that four hijackers were trained in camps in Afghanistan run by Osama bin Laden—whose al-Qaeda network is believed responsible for the assaults on New York and Washington—and have developed tentative links to the terrorist mastermind for most of the others, according to preliminary conclusions reached by the Justice Department, the FBI and the CIA. Government investigators are becoming increasingly convinced that one or two other hijackings were in the works, officials said, and are focusing on three men in U.S. custody who received flight training. One was detained while seeking flight simulator training in Minnesota before the hijackings, and two others were arrested on a train in Texas after departing a jet that was grounded after the attacks, sources said.

Government officials said other people in the United States may have provided minor assistance or had knowledge that a terrorist operation was underway. But the FBI has found little evidence so far that the teams of hijackers received much support here, sources said.

"There seems to be no U.S. mastermind," one official said.

The Justice Department has cast a global dragnet over the last two weeks in a hunt for accomplices. It is narrowing its criminal investigation to a number of individuals and is beginning to formulate criminal charges that could be filed against them, sources said. But a senior Justice official declined to predict when the first indictment might be handed down.

"We are past the first phase, and we are beginning to sharpen and focus the investigation," one Justice official said. "You don't get smoking guns in a case like this. The key is going to be in the details, in putting together the pieces, and we've gone a long way to doing that. . . . We're looking with particularity at a number of people."

The disclosures provide the fullest picture yet of the direction and scope of the U.S. investigation into the deadliest terror attack in American history, which have left 6,500 people missing or dead in New York, Washington and Pennsylvania. The hijackings have led to arrests on every continent but Antarctica.

In tracing $500,000 flowing into U.S. bank accounts used by Mohamed Atta and other members of the hijacking teams, the FBI has documented numerous large cash withdrawals and a long trail of hotels, rental cars and airplane trips that largely dispel any notion of an austere plot, a senior government official said. Previous reports have said the attacks cost no more than $200,000.

Some of the money used to prepare the attack has already been linked to accounts in the Middle East, the source said, and investigators have documented instances of simultaneous withdrawals from the same account in different cities.

"This was not a low-budget operation," the official said. "There is quite a bit of money coming in, and they are spending quite a bit of money."

Investigators are now convinced that the details of the terror plot were hatched in Hamburg, Germany, where Atta and two other suspected hijackers, Marwan Al-Shehhi and Ziad Jarrahi, are believed to have run a terrorist cell out of a second-floor student apartment.

In the hours following the Sept. 11 terror attacks, German intelligence agents intercepted a phone conversation between jubilant followers of Osama bin Laden that led the FBI to search frantically for two more teams of suicide hijackers, according to officials in both countries.

The Germans overheard the terrorists refer to "the 30 people traveling for the operation." The FBI already knew that 19 suspected hijackers had died on four planes, and started scouring flight manifests and any other clues for 11 more people still at large, who might have been part of the plot.

The FBI is doubling its contingent of agents working on the investigation in Germany, in the belief that the trail will lead from there to the Middle East, one official said. The initial concept for the Sept. 11 attacks likely came from Afghanistan, where bin Laden is believed to be hiding, another official said.

Investigators have found that the leaders in the plot moved in and out of the United States beginning at least 18 months ago, with lower-level hijackers not arriving until this year. Atta returned to Germany at least twice after arriving in the United States, a source said.

"There were two groups on each plane," one senior official said. "You've got the brains, who are the pilots and the leaders, and then you have the muscle coming in later on. They were the ones who held the passengers at bay."

The FBI is deeply suspicious of the circumstances surrounding three key men who have been detained in the case. Zacarias Moussaoui was taken into custody in Minnesota in August after he attempted to pay cash to learn how to steer, but not take off or land, in a jumbo jet.

One official said Moussaoui was in Norman, Okla., at the same time that Atta and several other hijackers were.

Moussaoui is not cooperating with authorities.

Two others, Mohammed Jaweed Azmath and Ayub Ali Khan, were detained on an Amtrak train Sept. 12 in Fort Worth, Texas, with hair dye, large amounts of cash and box-cutters like the ones used in the hijackings. The men, who had lived in Jersey City, N.J., had flown on a plane from Newark to St. Louis that was grounded after the attacks. Both men were flight-trained, one source said.

FBI agents have combed the passenger manifest on that flight and have not found anyone else who is believed to be a potential hijacker, an official said.

Adding another important element to the global investigation, British authorities Friday accused an Algerian pilot of training four of the hijackers, including the apparent pilot of the jet that crashed into the Pentagon.

During an extradition hearing in London, British prosecutor Arvinda Sambir suggested that Lotfi Raissi, 27, may have been a knowing participant in the terrorist plot, and that U.S. authorities might charge him with conspiracy to murder.

"The hope is that he will be able to tell us who planned what and when," added one senior U.S. official.

As the world becomes more connected through modern communication and information technologies, the environment for criminal justice agencies is becoming extremely complex. Criminal justice organizations have to learn to cross lines of time, culture, and geography to be successful. Law enforcement officers today, for example, need to know a second and third language and develop cross-cultural understanding. The mind-set needed by officers in criminal justice is to expect the unexpected and be prepared for constant change. Moreover, the increase in white-collar crimes, the rising number of female offenders and juvenile offenders, and increased international terrorism have created greater awareness and involvement of the general public in the criminal justice system. As a result, there is greater scrutiny by citizens of the existing criminal justice system to examine the quality and effectiveness of the service being delivered. As administrators of the criminal justice system struggle to create customer-oriented learning organizations, they are finding that specific dimensions of their organizations, entrenched in Weber's bureaucratic model, have to be changed: "The learning organization is incompatible with the bureaucratic configuration of police organizations" (Oettmeier, 1992, p. 52). The five areas of organization design that need to be revisited in the criminal justice system are structure, tasks, systems, culture, and attitude. They require change in the following ways:

1. *From vertical to horizontal structure.* Traditionally, the most common organizational structure has been functional, in which activities are grouped together by common work (function). A chain of command flows within each function from the top to the bottom, with decision-making authority residing with upper-level management. Typically, communication across different functions takes place only at the top level. Therefore, to communicate across functions, information has to flow from the bottom to the top within a function and then be communicated to the other functional head, who then passes the information down within his or her function. This strict chain of command slows the flow of information, which may be crucial in this rapidly changing environment. Even now, it is being debated whether, if the information had flowed faster between different law enforcement agencies, they could have prevented the September 11, 2001, terrorist acts.

In a learning criminal justice organization, the vertical structure that creates distance between the administrator at the top and the staff is a mantra for failure. Therefore, the vertical hierarchy must be drastically reduced. Flatter organizations that reduce the distance between different ranks should be designed to promote faster information flow and greater coordination. Moreover, Daft (2001) asserts that departmental functions ought to be eliminated and structures should be created that promote horizontal workflows. Self-directed teams with members from several functional areas are the fundamental work unit in a learning organization.

2. *From routine tasks to empowered roles.* Scientific management advocates precisely defined jobs and the exact steps to perform them. Each job is defined as a sequence of narrowly distinct tasks, which are done in a sequence of steps like a machine. Knowledge and control of these tasks resides with the senior management, and employees are

expected to do as they are told. However, in this volatile environment, the requirements for each job change so rapidly that officers in criminal justice organizations need to use their discretion and responsibility to solve the problem rather than be guided strictly by the rules of the task. Historical limitations on discretionary decisions need to be readdressed as the implementation of a learning organization is analyzed. In a learning organization in criminal justice, officers need to play a role in the team or department, which is constantly redefined or modified. The officers need to be trained extremely well and then encouraged to work with one another to find solutions rather than be constantly looking at the supervisors or senior officers for directions.

3. *From formal control systems to shared information.* In large organizations such as the criminal justice system, information processing is centralized at the top. Formal systems are often implemented to manage the growing amount of complex information and to help identify any variation from accepted norms and measures (Hurst, 1995). However, such formal procedures also increase the distance between leaders and their workers, thus slowing the processing of information and further adding to the complexity.

In a learning criminal justice organization, information needs to be widely shared, and officers often must be entrusted with complete information to enable them to react quickly. Information control should not be used as a means for power, but rather, senior officers should find ways of disseminating information and keeping lines of communication open. Communication should be maintained with all stakeholders, including other agencies involved in criminal justice and society at large, to enhance the learning capability.

4. *From rigid to competitive to adaptive culture.* In traditional organizations, strategy is formulated by senior officers and imposed on the organization, leaving little scope for swift adjustments to external environmental changes. These organizations become victims of their own system when the environment changes dramatically.

In a learning criminal justice organization, each officer is a valued contributor, and the organization thrives on creating relationships that allow officers to develop their full potential. Consequently, the officers are aware of the big picture and how various parts fit together. The empowered workforce is fully involved in contributing to strategy development, making it more realistic and amenable to environmental changes. Since officers are in touch with a diverse group of stakeholders, the strategy emerges from the input of all stakeholders. Such a culture encourages openness and equality, and is geared toward continuous improvement.

5. *From confrontational to collaborative.* In traditional organizations, the customers and suppliers are not considered partners, but rather competitors who need to be kept at arm's length. However, the learning organizations approach their customers and suppliers as partners who can provide important information to allow improvements (Daft, 2001). Instead of using the "us against them" mentality, criminal justice agencies can (and have, in some cases) survey offenders, victims, and the community about procedures, policies, and processes that work or fail to work effectively in the processing of cases.

The previous discussion suggests that in this highly uncertain environment, criminal justice agencies need to be modified and redesigned toward becoming learning organizations, which supports the line of thinking presented earlier in the open-system models. We acknowledge that criminal justice agencies may be limited in how far they can go in becoming learning organizations (because of laws, mandates from courts, etc.); however, the adoption of some learning approaches is better than none. Numerous criminal justice organizations fail in providing superior service because they close themselves from external influences and are primarily guided by their agency subcultures, which may not conform to the external environment. Without input from external environments, criminal justice agencies are shortsighted regarding the changing political, economic, social, and legal realities; consequently, they are unable to meet the demands of society. Often, when criminal justice agencies shut themselves off from the external environment and public scrutiny, they become insular and function with impunity until they are revealed through scandals, judicial intervention, government intervention, government investigation, or commission reports (Dias & Vaughn, 2006). To move in the direction of creating flexible and adaptable learning organizations, there is a need for criminal justice officers to adopt the human relations approach propagated in the open-system models. In addition, there is need to reduce hierarchy, promote open communication and cooperation, and encourage greater employee and customer participation, so that organizations can continually align themselves with the changing needs of the external environment. Although this has been accomplished in some areas of criminal justice (e.g., community policing, probation, parole, etc.), there is much work to be done to the system as a whole in terms of greater employee and customer participation. Identification and involvement of the customers is crucial in improving service quality because the customer is viewed as an input to which value is added by the service process in the criminal justice system. Chapter 3 will include a discussion on service quality and identification of all of the customers of criminal justice services.

Chapter Summary

- Organizations continually confront the uncertainty of new challenges and problems that they have to address in a timely, efficient, and effective manner for their survival. Therefore, organizations die or are transformed when the needs satisfied by them no longer exist or have been replaced by other needs.
- Organizational theory is a way to examine and analyze organizations more precisely and intensely based on patterns and trends in organizational design and behavior.
- A systems view considers an organization as a set of interacting functions that acquire inputs from the environment, processes them, and then releases the outputs back to the external environment.
- Closed-system models consider the external environment to be stable and predictable and assume that it does not intervene with or cause problems to the functioning of an organization. These models rely primarily on internal organizational processes and dynamics to account for organizational, group, and individual behaviors. The central management objective addressed in these models is the efficient running of the organization.

- The theories and models that emerged from closed systems are often called machine models; they are also popularly known as classical models or traditional models. These models sought to make organizations run like efficient, well-oiled machines by correcting the internal functioning of the organizations.
- The three main subfields of the classical perspective are scientific management, administrative management, and bureaucratic management. Scientific management focuses on the productivity of the individual worker, administrative management focuses on the functions of the management, and bureaucratic management focuses on the overall organizational system within which the workers and management interact.
- During the early 20th century, the industrialized nations experienced better standards of living and improved working conditions. Simultaneously, it was being observed that effective managers were not necessarily following all of the principles laid down in the classical closed-system models. Human behavior was an important factor in shaping the managerial style and worker actions.
- Acknowledging that human behavior could influence the working of an organization was an acceptance that factors external to an organization had to be considered in the management principles, giving birth to the open-system models. In open-system models, the principal starting assumption is that the external variables or events play a significant role in explaining what is happening within an organization.
- Since most work is done by teams in direct contact with customers, the open-system models (total quality management model and supply chain/synergy model) include customers in an attempt to create modern organizations.
- The total quality management (TQM) model supports the inclusion of the voice of the customer in designing the product/service and modifying the process to provide higher quality. Four important elements of the total quality management model are employee involvement, customer focus, benchmarking, and continuous improvement.
- For the criminal justice system to work efficiently and effectively, there needs to be a high degree of coordination among different agencies involved in its enforcement. In this supply chain relationship, at each stage of the criminal justice system there is a supplier and a customer. Therefore, promoting coordination and cooperation among different subsystems, known as a supply chain perspective, will accomplish more than when the subsystems are working in isolation. This property, in which the whole is greater than the sum of its parts, is referred to as synergy.
- The environment facing the criminal justice system is rapidly changing because of globalization, demographics, the Internet, and rapid technological changes. In this highly volatile environment, managers of the criminal justice system need to redesign and modify their agencies to become learning organizations, which are highly flexible and adaptable. In an attempt to create learning organizations in the criminal justice system, the five areas of organization design that need to be revisited are structure, tasks, systems, culture, and attitude. In each of these areas, the emphasis should be on problem solving by promoting a culture of employee and customer participation.

Chapter Review Questions

1. Describe the primary differences in closed-system and open-system models.

2. If you were to apply closed-system models to criminal justice agencies, which areas of criminal justice would they best fit? What about open-system models?

3. Describe how the principles of the bureaucratic model apply to law enforcement.

4. How are probation and parole officers specialized in the tasks they perform? What about police officers and corrections officers?

5. Explain how criminal justice agencies can become learning organizations.

The city of Smithville has a population of 38,500 people. On any given day, approximately 97,000 people visit the city for work, shopping, school, and recreational activities. The Smithville Police Department handles about 51,000 calls for service per year. There is a chief of police, 4 lieutenants, 7 corporals, 12 sergeants, and 47 patrol officers on staff. The chain of command and organizational structure of the department mirror other police departments in the area. The closed system allows for a top-down structure, with those in command determining the policies and procedures to be followed by the lower-level employees. The department has many of the traditional specialized units seen in other policing agencies—traffic, detectives, homicide, special victims, community policing, juvenile, and so forth. Officers are assigned to divisions depending on their area of expertise. Patrol officers work very closely with state police officers, who investigate all traffic accidents that occur in the state.

In May 2012, the department received a call about a car accident on Highway 17 on the outer edge of town. Patrol Officer Mike Brady was dispatched to the accident. Upon arrival, he found three teenagers, two adult males, and one adult female assisting what appeared to be an unconscious girl on the side of the road. Josie Carmen, a 16-year-old passenger of a crashed Jeep Liberty was lying in a ditch on the side of the road. The 16-year-old driver of the wrecked vehicle was hysterical and was being comforted by two of the teenagers and the adult female. Upon closer inspection, Officer Brady found that Carmen had succumbed to her injuries. He moved everyone away from the body. When Carmen was pronounced dead at the scene of the accident. No one else was injured or transported to the hospital.

Officer Brady secured the scene as he waited for the state police to arrive to investigate the accident. Some of the individuals at the scene gave him spontaneous statements about what happened. State police officers arrived within the hour and started interviewing witnesses and bystanders as well as setting up traffic scene equipment to recreate and investigate the accident.

Officer Brady filed a report on the traffic accident that indicated the vehicle was traveling at a high rate of speed and lost control. According to his report, the vehicle swerved across the road and hit a culvert. Carmen had been thrown from the vehicle. His report was based on spontaneous statements made while he secured the scene and on comments he overheard others saying when he arrived at the scene. Officer Brady did not claim to be the investigating officer or to have interviewed witnesses or bystanders.

In another report, the state police claimed that Carmen had been "playing chicken" with the oncoming car. In the game of chicken, a teenager would stand in the road while the car sped toward him or her. At the last minute, either the car would turn or the teenager would jump out of the way to avoid being hit. When Carmen was standing in the road, the oncoming vehicle lost control, swerved across the road, and hit a culvert. Carmen was hit by the out-of-control car and sustained head injuries and internal injuries that led to her death. According to the report, each teenager, with the exception of the driver, had taken a turn playing chicken with the car. The two adult males and the adult female lived in homes located near the accident, had heard the collision and kids screaming, and had run to the scene to assist. At least one of the adult males claimed not to have seen anyone on the road in front of the car, and the other adult male claimed to have seen a car speeding back and forth down the road but did not see anyone standing in the road.

Immediately following the accident, Carmen's parents were in constant contact with the Smithville Police Department. The Smithville police provided the family with a copy of the traffic accident report filed by Officer Brady. The family also received a copy of the traffic accident investigation report from the state police. After that, no additional information was provided to the family even though the family had asked for another investigation to determine if their daughter was actually standing in the road in front of the car. The family claimed that witness accounts were inconsistent and that their daughter had not been playing chicken with the car.

Carmen's family sent Officer Brady, who had secured the accident, an e-mail on August 24 asking about the follow-up investigation. Officer Brady responded on September 1 with the following note: "I have forwarded this information to the state patrol and they will be in touch soon. Thank you."

After three weeks of no response, the family e-mailed Brady again. Again, Brady's response on October 7 was that the inquiry had been forwarded to the state patrol.

In December 2012, the family received a call from Officer Adams, a traffic investigator with the state police, who stated that no new information was available. According to Officer Adams, the state police still believed that Carmen had been playing chicken with the car on the day of the accident and that no follow-up investigation was occurring. The investigation apparently ended there.

No charges were filed against the driver of the vehicle, even though some considered it negligence on her part to have been speeding toward a person standing in the road. A spokesperson for the Smithville Police Department stated that they could not say for sure that Carmen was playing chicken with the car since they did not investigate the accident. The spokesperson also said the department did not feel that there was any other substantial information to show that Carmen was not involved in a game of chicken prior to the accident. The family claims that the driver of the car should be charged if there was wrongdoing and that by not charging the driver the police are admitting that Carmen was not playing chicken.

Carmen's family would like the police to reopen the investigation since "there have been mixed eyewitness statements about what occurred." The spokesperson for the Smithville Police Department claims that the investigation is not within their jurisdiction since all traffic accidents are investigated by the state police. The state police claim that no additional investigation is necessary since there is no evidence contrary to their findings. The prosecutor has stated that the case is a sad situation but there is not a strong enough case to demonstrate evidence of wrongdoing by a particular person. The prosecutor claims that the investigation did not yield enough evidence for an arrest.

Questions for Discussion

1. How has task specialization played a role in this case? Has it been successful in increasing efficiency or customer satisfaction? Why or why not?

2. What should the family do now that the state police department has closed the investigation? Should the state police department reopen the investigation? Why or why not? What role, if any, does the Smithville Police Department have in the investigation or in opening a new investigation?

3. How does this case and the actions of Officers Brady and Adams resemble an assembly-line production?

4. How could the organizational structure of police departments be modified to better serve Carmen's family and the community at large in these types of incidents?

Internet Resources

International Association of Chiefs of Police—http://www.theiacp.org

Office of Juvenile Justice and Delinquency Prevention—http://www.ojjdp.ncjrs.gov

U.S. Department of Homeland Security—http://www.dhs.gov

References and Suggested Readings

Batts, A. W., Smoot, S. M., & Scrivner, E. (2012). Police leadership challenges in a changing world. *New Perspectives in Policing Bulletin.* Washington, DC: U.S. Department of Justice, National Institute of Justice. NCJ 238338.

Braiden, C. R. (1992). Enriching traditional roles. In L. T. Hoover (Ed.), *Police management: Issues and perspectives.* Washington, DC: Police Executive Research Forum.

Child, J. (1973). Predicting and understanding organizational structure. *Administrative Science Quarterly, 18,* 168–185.

Cox, S. M., Allen, J. M., Hanser, R., & Conrad, J. C. (2014). *Juvenile justice: A guide to theory, policy, and practice* (6th ed.). Thousand Oaks, CA: Sage.

Daft, R. L. (2001). *Organization theory and design* (7th ed.). South-Western College: Florence, KY.

Daft, R. L., & Lewin, A. Y. (1993). Where are the theories for the new organizational forms? An editorial essay. *Organizational Science, 4,* i–v.

Dias, C. F., & Vaughn, M. S. (2006). Bureaucracy, managerial disorganization, and administrative breakdown in criminal justice agencies. *Journal of Criminal Justice, 34,* 543–555.

Fairholm, G. W. (1994). *Leadership and the culture of trust.* Westport, CT: Praeger.

Fayol, H. (1949). *General and industrial management.* London, England: Sir Isaac Pitman.

Gebert, D., & Boerner, S. (1999). The open and the closed corporation as conflicting form of organization. *Journal of Applied Behavioral Science, 35*(3), 341–359.

Gilbreth, F. B. (1970). Science in management for the one best way to do work. In H. F. Merrill (Ed.), *Classics in management* (pp. 217–263). New York, NY: American Management Association. (Original work published 1923.)

Guillen, M. F. (1997). Scientific management's lost aesthetic: Architecture, organization, and the Taylorized beauty of the mechanical. *Administrative Science Quarterly, 42,* 682–715.

Gulick, L., & Urwick, L. (Eds.). (1937). *Papers on the science of administration.* New York, NY: Institute of Public Administration, Columbia University.

Hersh, S. M. (2004). *Chain of command: The road from 9/11 to Abu Ghraib.* London, England: Allen Lane.

Hurst, D. K. (1995). *Crisis and renewal: Meeting the challenge of organizational change.* Boston, MA: Harvard Business School Press.

Illinois Law Enforcement Training and Standards Board. (2008). *Mandates.* Retrieved from http://www.ptb .state.il.us/mandates/mandates_main.htm.

Jones, D. (1997, April 4). Doing the wrong things. *USA Today,* 1–2.

Judy, R. W., & D'Amico, C. (1997). *Workforce 2020: Work and workers in the 21st century.* Indianapolis, IN: Hudson Institute.

Katz, D., & Kahn, R. L. (1966). *The social psychology of organizations.* New York, NY: Wiley.

Lewis, P. S., Goodman, S. H., & Fandt, P. M. (2001). *Management challenges in the 21st century* (3rd ed.). Mason, OH: Thomson South-Western.

Locke, E. A. (1982). The ideas of Frederick W. Taylor: An evaluation. *Academy of Management Review, 7,* 14–24.

Longmire, D. R. (1992). Activity trap. In L. T. Hoover (Ed.), *Police management: Issues and perspectives.* Washington, DC: Police Executive Research Forum.

McGregor, D. (1960). *The human side of enterprise.* New York, NY: McGraw-Hill.

McFall, E. (2006). Changing profession requires new level of education. *The Police Chief, 73*(8), Retrieved from http://policechiefmagazine.org/magazine/index.cfm?fuseaction=display&article_ id=972&issue_ id=82006.

Mintzberg, H. (1979). *The structuring of organizations.* Englewood Cliffs, NJ: Prentice Hall.

Missouri Revised Statutes. (2007). *Stealing and related offenses,* Chap. 570. Sec. 570.030. Retrieved from http://www.moga.mo.gov/statutes/C500-599/5700000030.HTM.

Mitroff, I. I., Mason, R. O., & Pearson, C. M. (1994). Radical surgery: What will tomorrow's organizations look like? *Academy of Management Executive, 8*(2), 11–21.

Morin, W. J. (1995, July 1). Silent sabotage: Mending the crisis in corporate values. *Management Review,* 10–14.

Oettmeier, T. (1992). Matching structure to objectives. In L. T. Hoover (Ed.), *Police management: Issues and perspectives.* Washington, DC: Police Executive Research Forum.

Parson, H. M. (1974). What happened at Hawthorne? *Science, 183,* 922–932.

Pennings, J. M. (1992). Structural contingency theory: A reappraisal. *Research in Organizational Behavior, 14,* 267–309.

Police Foundation. (1992). *The city in crisis: A report by the special advisor to the Board of Police Commissioners on the civil disorder in Los Angeles.* Washington, DC: Author.

Rice, G. H., Jr., & Bishoprick, D. W. (1971). *Conceptual models of organization.* New York, NY: Appleton-Century-Crofts.

Rieger, B. J. (1995, October). Lessons in productivity and people. *Training and Development, 49*(10).

Roethlisberger, F. J., & Dickson, W. J. (1956). *Management and the worker.* Cambridge, MA: Harvard University Press. (Original work published 1939.)

Skolnick, J. H., & Fyfe, J. J. (1993). *Above the law.* New York, NY: Free Press.

Stern, R. N., & Barley, S. R. (1996). Organizations and social systems: Organization theory's neglected mandate. *Administrative Science Quarterly, 41,* 146–162.

Taylor, F. W. (1911). *The principles of scientific management.* New York, NY: Harper.

Thompson, J. D. (1967). *Organizations in action.* New York, NY: McGraw-Hill.

Weber, M. (1947). *The theory of social and economic organization.* New York, NY: Oxford University Press.

Wren, D. A. (1994). *The evolution of management thought* (4th ed.). New York, NY: Wiley.

3

Service Quality Approach

LEARNING OBJECTIVES

Upon completion of this chapter, students should be able to do the following:

- Discuss the increasing role of services in a growing economy
- Define service and explain the distinguishing characteristics of service quality
- Discuss the importance of involving the customer in designing the criminal justice system
- Explain the potential problems in not considering an offender as a customer of criminal justice services
- Describe the "symptom versus cause" approach to examining the criminal justice system
- Describe service quality and explain how to measure it
- Identify and explain Gap 1 to Gap 5 in service quality
- Explain the scope of service quality in the criminal justice system

In the United States, the criminal justice system is currently under tremendous pressure to promote an environment of continuous improvement in both quality and productivity. The increasing prison population, the failures apparent in the current "get tough on crime" philosophy, and the skyrocketing cost of corrections are indicators that there is a significant opportunity to improve the existing criminal justice system. According to Zager, McGaha, and Garcia (2001), the cost of confining inmates in the United States is more than $50 billion annually, or $33,334 per inmate per year (p. 223). More recently, an editorial in the *New York Times* (November 10, 2012) puts this estimate at $52 billion a year. These statistics make one wonder why the cost of locking up a criminal is more than the average salary that some students will earn after graduating from a university with a bachelor's degree. It is hard for any progressive society to justify such an outrageous cost for incarceration. Consequently, the efficiency and quality of criminal justice services are routinely debated in professional and academic environments across the United States, with the intention of improving their deliverability.

There are two glaring problems in the existing criminal justice system that need to be addressed in order to improve productivity and reduce cost. First, existing criminal justice services have been designed and delivered solely from the service providers' perspectives, despite the fact that criminal justice services are consumed directly and indirectly by multiple stakeholders in a society. Although citizens are included in some aspects of criminal justice, for the most part, they are secondary considerations in determining how the system will operate. The primary justification for excluding the consumers from the discussion has been embedded in an argument—though a rather weak one—that there are special conditions and circumstances in the administration of criminal justice services that do not warrant customer inclusion. Second, multiple agencies are involved in providing different components of criminal justice services, with a high amount of interdependence among them. Yet these agencies often ignore the codependence that exists and continue to work in isolation, losing the benefits that close interaction would have provided in improving the criminal justice system. This philosophy can lead to duplication in services, higher costs in providing services, mismanagement of services, and a failure to service stakeholders. The mind-sets of isolationism among different criminal justice agencies are reinforced by the fact that all of these agencies are designed from the service providers' perspective and fail to properly identify and involve all of the stakeholders. Much of the existing literature in criminal justice discusses a predominantly service provider's perspective. Consequently, the prescriptive solutions offered to improve the criminal justice system are less insightful and more restrictive in applicability. Such an approach has not effectively served the needs of our society. To many experts who have also been trained in other fields of management, the noninclusion of customers and a lack of integration among different interdependent agencies when designing and delivering criminal justice services belie the principles of good management. It may be asked, How can the quality and effectiveness of a complex service like the criminal justice system, which involves multiple agencies and multiple stakeholders, be improved without identifying and involving the customers of that service and without integrating the multiple agencies?

This chapter places the criminal justice system in the realm of a service quality environment. First, a discussion is provided on the growing importance of services in the current economy, including how criminal justice services have grown over the years. The second section defines what constitutes a service and places the criminal justice system in proper perspective. The third section provides a discussion on the characteristics of services—including criminal justice services—to understand why customers are such an intricate part of the service design and delivery system. The fourth section identifies different customers of the criminal justice system, and examines why a bias may exist toward noninclusion of certain stakeholders as customers of criminal justice services. Finally, a new perspective is presented that considers both the service providers and the multiple stakeholders in designing and managing services. We believe this new approach will better prepare students in identifying more robust and innovative solutions to improving the quality and effectiveness of the criminal justice system.

The Role of Services in an Economy

Think of the importance of different services in one's daily life. Food services, banking services, retail services, health services, law enforcement services—to name a few—are all forms of services that one enjoys every day. It would be hard to imagine an existence without these and other services. Thus, it is important to realize that services are an integral part of a society.

As an economy progresses, the sophistication and level of services improve and new services are provided. Almost six decades ago, Clark (1957) argued that as nations develop, there is a shift of the labor force from agriculture to manufacturing to services. This phenomenon is often described as a *transformation of an economy* from an agrarian to an industrial to a postindustrial society. The United States is considered a postindustrial society in which the standard of living is not defined by the quantity of goods available, but by the sophistication and quality of services available. Today, more than 80% of the workforce in the United States is employed in the service sector, contributing more than 70% to the nation's income (Fitzsimmons & Fitzsimmons, 2006).

According to the *Bureau of Justice Statistics Bulletin* (Kyckelhahn, 2011), "In 2007, federal, state, and local government spent $228 billion and employed 2.5 million people for police protection, corrections, and judicial and legal services. Local police protection represented the largest share of both total justice expenditures (32%) and employment (36%), followed by state corrections (19% of expenditures and employment)" (p. 1). Between 1982 and 2002, the expenditures increased at the federal 276%; state, 208%; and local, 132% levels, after adjusting for inflation. But between 2002 and 2007, federal expenditures increased 7% and local expenditures increased 1%, while state expenditures declined 5%. The per-capita justice expenditures went up from $158 in 1982, to $586 in 2001, to $755 in 2007 per U.S. resident. Over the same period, the police protection per-capita expenditure per U.S. resident went up from $84, to $254, to $344; the corrections expenditure went up from $39, to $200, to $246; and the judicial and legal services expenditure went up from $34, to $132, to $165 (Bauer & Owens, 2004, p. 2; Kyckelhahn, 2011).

Definition of Service

What constitutes a service? If that question were asked of a handful of people, there would be many different answers. Haywood-Farmer and Nollet (1991) summarize this problem very aptly:

> Despite more than 25 years of study, scholars in the field of service management do not agree on what a service is. Indeed, instead of coming closer to a definition they seem to be less certain. . . . [T]he problem is trying in a few words to describe 75 percent of the economic activity of developed nations. Is it any wonder that there are exceptions for all definitions? (p. 11)

There are several definitions of service, which can be found in service operations and service marketing books. The following definition by Gronroos (1990) applies well in the present context of the criminal justice system:

> A service is an activity or series of activities of more or less intangible nature that normally, but not necessarily, take place in interactions between customer and service employees and/or physical resources or goods and/or systems of the service provider, which are provided as solutions to customer problems. (p. 27)

Some of the terms used in this definition may not be clear at first. The definition will become clearer as one reads the rest of the chapter. The reader is advised to revisit this definition after having gone through the entire chapter.

Think of all of the services that an individual enjoys in a typical day, while in school, at work, or while socializing. There is a wide range of services with varying degrees of *bundling with the goods;* that is, goods are integrated with a sale of the service. The services can be classified on a continuum ranging from pure services to various degrees of mixed services. For easy reference, services can be grouped in three categories, described here.

1. *Services that come with purchased goods.* For example, a prison may buy photocopy machines and computers for use in doing paperwork in the offices. This equipment will have to be serviced by the company that sold the photocopier to the prison from time to time for maintenance and when it breaks down. Here, the service accompanies the purchase of the goods. Often, the quality of after-sales service is an important deciding factor in the purchase of a particular brand of photocopier or computer.

2. *Services that facilitate the purchase of goods.* For example, consider taking a police car to the mechanic for servicing. The mechanic services the car and changes the tires that need to be replaced due to regular wear and tear. In this case, the service is facilitating the selling of goods (tires).

3. *Services that are pure.* Probation or law enforcement services provided in a community are an example. Here, typically, the service provided does not involve any accompanying goods. A probation officer who monitors a probationer is providing a service to the offender and the community; there is no exchange of goods between any of the parties. A police officer who responds to a call of domestic violence provides a service to both the victim and perpetrator who are on the scene when the officer arrives. The officer does not give or sell a good to either party.

Another important distinction that needs to be made up front is between commercial services (Categories 1 and 2) and noncommercial services (Categories 3 and 4). Commercial services tend to be driven by profit motive, whereas noncommercial services have other motives for existence.

1. *Business-to-consumer services* (e.g., retail services). These services are purchased by individuals for themselves or on behalf of someone else. For example, an individual may buy a plane ticket for himself or herself or for someone else. In this case, the major challenge for the airline is to deal with many different customers every day, each of whom may have different needs and expectations.

2. *Business-to-business services* (e.g., consulting services). An example of this type of service would be if John Deere is buying logistics services through UPS to ship parts to customers who have John Deere equipment. Here, the main challenge comes in dealing with multiple contacts in the client organization, generating a complex set of relationships. Often, the users of services from the John Deere company may not directly be involved in the purchase of services from UPS. In another example, private security agencies engage in business-to-business services when they contract security officers to large companies. The security officers are actually employed by the private agency, but they work at the company paying for their services. The other employees and the customers of the company are not involved in the contractual agreement between the private security agency and the larger company.

3. *Public services* (e.g., criminal justice services). These services are provided by federal, state, or local governments for the community. There is generally no direct payment for the services, but funding comes through taxes. The biggest challenges for these service providers are the multiple stakeholders. Often, the direct recipient of the service, an individual, has little power to influence the agency or the service. Some public services, like law enforcement, are provided for the good of society and are not necessarily welcomed by those who have to deal with the police, courts, or corrections.

4. *Not-for-profit services* (e.g., charities). The challenges faced by these organizations concern the managing of the workforce of volunteers, who might not follow organizational procedures because of a lack of training.

Given such variations, it is difficult to make general statements about service management without understanding the unique characteristics of services that introduce a challenge in their design and management.

Characteristics of Services

This section will examine the distinctive features of services and explore how they relate specifically to the field of criminal justice. A clear understanding of such features will help in designing and delivering a more customer-friendly and open-systems-based criminal justice system.

Customer involvement in the service process. In services, it is important to maintain the distinction between inputs and resources. While the *inputs* are the customers themselves, the *resources* are the facilitating infrastructure, employees, gadgets, equipment, and capital used in the process of service delivery (Fitzsimmons & Fitzsimmons, 2006). Consequently, the service system must interact with the customers, as they are a part of the service delivery process.

Since the customer is a dynamic being whose behavior is volatile and unpredictable, the service quality experience can change from moment to moment. Think of a situation in which a customer was enjoying an evening with friends at an upscale restaurant. Everything was going fine until the customer ordered a refill for her drink. The wait staff had to be reminded again, and by the time the drink was served, the customer was almost done with her food and did not need the drink. That little extra wait to get a refill changed the entire experience that the customer had been enjoying. Consider this same concept in criminal justice. If a person calls the police department because he is disturbed by loud music coming from the neighbor's apartment, the complainant expects the police to come immediately and address the situation. If time elapses with no police response, the complainant may choose to address the situation himself or call the police again (ignoring the third option of giving up on the issue). If the complainant has to go to the apartment and address the neighbor personally, a larger and potentially more violent encounter may occur. If the complainant has to call the police again, he may regard the police as uncaring and indifferent. Depending on the response time for the second call, the complainant may lodge a grievance against the police. This single event can change the complainant's view of the police and the department more generally. Therefore, the service provider has to be extremely careful and sensitive in dealing with the customer. Because the police are the first responders in criminal justice, they have to be constantly alert in their interactions with customers (the general public, victims, complainants, and suspected offenders) to ensure a good service quality experience.

Simultaneous production and consumption. Typically, services are created and consumed simultaneously. For example, consumption of a haircut service and the delivery of the haircut service take place at the same time. If the service provider takes off more hair than the customer wanted, there is no remedy to correct the error. Similarly, if a law enforcement officer does not remind a criminal suspect of his or her Miranda rights before interrogation, then service quality has been compromised and nothing can be done to undo the service error. In other words, in a service environment, the simultaneous production and consumption of services puts tremendous pressure on the service provider to understand the customer needs, communicate clearly, and then provide the correct service the first time. Good training is extremely important because there is very little recourse to undo service errors.

Perishability. A service is a perishable commodity, which if not consumed at the time of its offering cannot be inventoried for later use. In other words, unused service capacity is lost forever because it cannot be stored. For example, a vacant room in a hotel on a given night or an unsold seat on a flight is lost revenue. Therefore, marketing has to play a major role in matching supply with demand through advertising and the use of dynamic pricing. There are no inventories or buffers to rely on to absorb the fluctuations in demand for services. In other words, the full impact of demand variations (external variations) is transmitted to the system, which the service manager then has to manage. For example, because of demand variation, a customer may experience different wait times at the haircutting salon depending on the time of the day and the day of the week. Of course, for simplification it is assumed that there are no call-in reservations for haircut services. In contrast, a manufacturing business can hold the inventory of finished goods from the market to prevent the external variations from influencing the internal operations of a firm.

Perishability has important implications in the criminal justice system. A county sheriff has to examine the past data to forecast the expected incidents on a given weeknight and decide how many officers to schedule for duty. If too many officers are put on duty on a certain night and no incidents occur, then the police officers are idle, resulting in low capacity use and, hence, wasted capacity. The sheriff cannot tell his or her officers to work longer hours on another night to make up for no work on the previous night. In contrast, if too few officers are scheduled on a given night, then there could be delayed responses to 911 calls if several law-and-order problems occurred at the same time. A delayed response to 911 calls is parallel to increased customer wait time or queuing that has resulted from demand fluctuations. Note that in law enforcement there is always an uncertainty as to what may happen at any given time on any given day. In addition, there is no provision for making a reservation for most of the services provided by law enforcement agencies, which makes the management of capacity extremely challenging. In a service environment, a manager is constantly required to strike a balance among service capacity, facility use, and customer wait time/queuing to cope with the demand and supply fluctuations.

Intangibility. Services are ideas and concepts that are not patentable and that can be replicated. However, the service delivery process of a given company is typically hard for competitors to replicate. In addition, a company should continuously improve its service delivery process to stay ahead of its competitors. For example, McDonald's food has been imitated by many fast-food chains. However, most of the competitors have not been very successful in replicating the service delivery process of McDonald's to offer the same standard of service.

On the other hand, intangibility characteristics of a service present a problem for the customer to be able to see, feel, or test the performance before purchase. Therefore, customers rely primarily on the service provider's reputation to gauge the quality of services that they will be purchasing. As an example, customers may visit one hair salon rather than another because they have heard good things about the stylists. In many service areas, the government has to intervene to guarantee acceptable service quality. The intangibility characteristic of service has important implications for the criminal justice system. The supposed fairness of a trial may be dependent on the public's perception of the judge's reputation. Likewise, the apparent fairness of the police officers' handling of a case involving a minority offender depends on the public's perception of the city's police force. All efforts are made by the government in the form of laws and procedures to guarantee acceptable service quality in criminal justice. Once offenders are arrested, how they are processed through the justice system is predetermined by procedural law. This is to prevent any perceptions of bias or prejudice in the delivery of services. As long as the system progresses as the public believes it should, the perception of the system delivering quality services is positive. However, when something happens with which the public does not agree (a highly publicized case is dismissed, there is a case of police brutality, or a parolee commits a new criminal offense), the criminal justice system's reputation is challenged and questions arise about the services being provided. The most recent case of George Zimmerman, who was charged with murdering Trayvon Martin, is a prime example of the public's perception that poor services were provided.

Heterogeneity. The customers' involvement in the service delivery process, along with the intangible nature of services, results in large variation of service from customer to customer. The variation in service delivery is greater in more labor-intensive services and those with high customer contact because of increased interaction between customer and employee. Variation in services by itself is not bad, but how it is interpreted and perceived by the customer is important—which, in turn, depends on the customer's expectation. For example, consider a dining experience at a fancy restaurant, keeping in mind that the restaurant industry is very labor intensive and involves high customer contact. If a handful of students sat down to discuss their dining experiences, one would hear many different stories of their encounters, even when they may all have visited the same restaurant. The variation resulting from customization of service in a fancy restaurant is acceptable because that is in sync with customer expectation. On the other hand, variation in service from McDonald's would be unacceptable to the customers because they have come to expect (through advertisements) that McDonald's offers a standardized service. Similarly, in criminal justice services there is a high level of labor intensity and high customer–employee contact, thus introducing the possibility for high variation in service delivery. In some areas of criminal justice, variation may be acceptable—for example, when dealing with juvenile crime. However, variation of service in the criminal justice system is often considered unacceptable because it is interpreted as a lack of consistency, or is perceived to involve bias or prejudice. Therefore, it is extremely important for the criminal justice system to educate citizens about the delivery of its services and the special circumstances in which it operates that may result in service variation so that the system's actions are not always misinterpreted or misunderstood by the public. Even though services may vary, criminal justice services are closely monitored by various governmental and nongovernmental interest groups for fairness of treatment. There are also clear and detailed guidelines and standards. Combining these with good employee training in following proper procedures is necessary for higher consistency in providing quality criminal justice services.

CAREER HIGHLIGHT BOX
JUDGES, MAGISTRATES, AND OTHER JUDICIAL WORKERS

Nature of the Work

Judges, mediators, and hearing officers apply the law to court cases and oversee the legal process in courts. They also resolve administrative disputes and facilitate negotiations between opposing parties.

Duties

Judges, mediators, and hearing officers typically do the following:

- Research legal issues
- Read and evaluate information from documents such as motions, claim applications, or records

(Continued)

(Continued)

- Preside over hearings and listen to or read arguments by opposing parties
- Determine if the information presented supports the charge, claim, or dispute
- Decide if the procedure is being conducted according to the rules and law
- Analyze, research, and apply laws, regulations, or precedents to reach judgments, conclusions, or agreements
- Write opinions, decisions, or instructions regarding the case, claim, or dispute

Judges commonly preside over trials or hearings of cases regarding nearly every aspect of society, from individual traffic offenses to issues concerning the rights of large corporations. Judges listen to arguments and determine whether the evidence presented deserves a trial. In criminal cases, judges may decide that people charged with crimes should be held in jail until the trial, or they may set conditions for their release. They also approve search and arrest warrants.

Judges interpret the law to determine how a trial will proceed, which is particularly important when unusual circumstances arise for which standard procedures have not been established. They ensure that hearings and trials are conducted fairly and the legal rights of all involved parties are protected.

In trials in which juries are selected to decide the case, judges instruct jurors on applicable laws and direct them to consider the facts from the evidence. For other trials, judges decide the case. A judge who determines guilt in criminal cases may impose a sentence or penalty on the guilty party. In civil cases, the judge may award relief, such as compensation for damages, to the parties who win the lawsuit.

Some judges, such as appellate court judges, review decisions and records made by lower courts, and make decisions based on lawyers' written and oral arguments.

Judges use various forms of technology, such as electronic databases and software, to manage cases and prepare for trials. In some cases, a judge also may manage the court's administrative and clerical staff.

The following are examples of types of judges, mediators, and hearing officers:

Judges, magistrate judges, and magistrates preside over trials or hearings. They typically work in local, state, and federal courts.

In local and state court systems, they have a variety of titles, such as *municipal court judge, county court judge, magistrate,* and *justice of the peace*. Traffic violations, misdemeanors, small-claims cases, and pretrial hearings make up the bulk of these judges' work.

In federal and state court systems, *general trial court judges* have authority over any case in their system. *Appellate court judges* rule on a small number of cases by reviewing decisions of the lower courts and lawyers' written and oral arguments.

Hearing officers, also known as *administrative law judges* or *adjudicators*, usually work for government agencies. They decide many issues, such as if a person is eligible for workers' compensation benefits, or if employment discrimination occurred.

Arbitrators, mediators, or *conciliators* help opposing parties settle disputes outside of court. They hold private, confidential hearings, which are less formal than a court trial.

Arbitrators are usually attorneys or business people with expertise in a particular field. They hear and decide disputes between opposing parties as an impartial third party. When arbitration is required, if one side is not happy with the decision, they can still take the matter to court. Arbitration may also be voluntary, in which the opposing sides agree that whatever the arbitrator decides will be a final, binding decision.

Mediators are neutral parties who help people resolve their disputes. Mediators suggest solutions, but they do not make binding decisions. If the opposing sides cannot reach a settlement with the mediator's help, they are free to pursue other options.

Conciliators are similar to mediators. Their role is to help guide opposing sides to a settlement. The opposing sides must decide in advance if they will be bound by the conciliator's recommendations.

Judges, mediators, and hearing officers held about 62,700 jobs in 2010, and most were employed by local, state, and federal governments. Some arbitrators, mediators, and conciliators work for state and local governments. The following industries employed the most judges, mediators, and hearing officers in 2010:

State government, excluding education and hospitals	36%
Local government, excluding education and hospitals	28
Federal government, excluding postal service	7
Professional, scientific, and technical services	3

Judges, mediators, and hearing officers do most of their work in offices and courtrooms. Their jobs can be demanding because they must sit in the same position in the court or hearing room for long periods and give undivided attention to the process.

Arbitrators, mediators, and conciliators usually work in private offices or meeting rooms. They may travel to a neutral site chosen for negotiations.

Work Schedules

Most judges, mediators, and hearing officers work full time, but many often work longer hours to prepare for hearings. Some judges work part time and divide their time between their judicial responsibilities and other careers.

Training, Other Qualifications, and Advancement

Judges, magistrate judges, magistrates, and administrative law judges are often required to have a law degree and work experience as a lawyer. Additionally, most judges and magistrates must be either appointed or elected into judge positions, a procedure that often takes political support. Many local and state judges are appointed to serve fixed renewable terms, ranging from 4 years to 14 years. A few judges, such as appellate court judges, are appointed for life. Judicial nominating commissions screen candidates for

(Continued)

(Continued)

judgeships in many states and for some federal judgeships. Some local and state judges are elected to a specific term, commonly four years, in an election process.

Arbitrators, mediators, and conciliators learn their skills through education, training, or work experience.

Education

For most jobs as a local, state, or federal judge, a law degree is necessary. Getting a law degree usually takes seven years of full-time study after high school—four years of undergraduate study, followed by three years of law school. Law degree programs include courses such as constitutional law, contracts, property law, civil procedure, and legal writing.

In some states, administrative law judges and other hearing officials do not have to be lawyers. However, federal administrative law judges must be lawyers and must pass a competitive exam from the U.S. Office of Personnel Management.

For mediators, arbitrators, and conciliators, education is one pathway. They can take a certificate program in conflict resolution at a college or university, a two-year master's degree in dispute resolution or conflict management, or get a doctoral degree through a four-year or five-year program. Many mediators have a law degree, but master's degrees in public policy, law, and related fields also provide good backgrounds.

Work Experience

Most judges, mediators, and hearing officers get their skills through years of experience as practicing lawyers. About 40 states allow those who are not lawyers to hold limited-jurisdiction judgeships, but opportunities are better for those with law experience.

Arbitrators, mediators, and conciliators are usually lawyers or business professionals with expertise in a particular field, such as construction or insurance. They need to have knowledge of that industry and be able to relate well to people from different cultures and backgrounds.

Training

All states have some type of orientation for newly elected or appointed judges. The Federal Judicial Center, American Bar Association, National Judicial College, and National Center for State Courts provide judicial education and training for judges and other judicial branch personnel.

More than half of all states, as well as Puerto Rico, require judges to take continuing education courses while serving on the bench. General and continuing education courses usually last from a few days to three weeks.

Training for arbitrators, mediators, and conciliators is available through independent mediation programs, national and local mediation membership organizations, and postsecondary schools. To practice in state-funded or court-funded mediation programs, mediators must usually meet specific training or experience standards, which vary by state and court. Most mediators complete a 40-hour basic course and a 20-hour advanced training course. Some people get training by volunteering at a community mediation center or by comediating cases with an experienced mediator.

Licenses

Judges who are lawyers already hold a license.

Federal administrative law judges must be licensed to practice law.

For mediators, arbitrators, and conciliators, no national license exists. State requirements vary widely. Some states require arbitrators to be experienced lawyers.

Advancement

Advancement for some judicial workers means moving to courts with a broader jurisdiction. Advancement for various hearing officers includes taking on more complex cases, starting businesses, practicing law, or becoming district court judges.

Important Qualities

Critical-reasoning skills. Judges, mediators, and hearing officers must apply rules of law. They cannot let their personal assumptions interfere with the proceedings. For example, they must base their decisions on specific meanings of the law when evaluating and deciding whether a person is a threat to others and must be sent to jail.

Decision-making skills. Judges, mediators, and hearing officers must be able to weigh the facts, apply the law or rules, and make a decision relatively quickly.

Listening skills. Judges, mediators, and hearing officers must pay close attention to what is being said to evaluate information.

Reading comprehension. Judges, mediators, and hearing officers must be able to evaluate and distinguish the important facts from large amounts of complex information.

Writing skills. Judges, mediators, and hearing officers write recommendations or decisions on appeals or disputes. They must be able to write their decisions clearly so that all sides understand the decision.

Job Outlook

Employment of judges, mediators, and hearing officers is expected to grow by 7% from 2010 to 2020, slower than the average for all occupations. The number of federal and state judgeships is expected to experience little to no change because nearly every new position for a judge must be authorized and approved by legislature.

(Continued)

(Continued)

Budgetary constraints in federal, state, and local governments are expected to limit the employment growth of judges, magistrates, and administrative law judges, despite the continued need for these workers to settle disputes.

Arbitration and other alternatives to litigation are often faster and less expensive than trials. However, employment growth of arbitrators, mediators, and conciliators is expected to be moderate. This is primarily because conflicting parties often opt for court proceedings or try to resolve the problem on their own without a judge or mediator.

Job Prospects

The prestige associated with becoming a judge will ensure continued competition for these positions. Most job openings will arise as a result of judges, mediators, and hearing officers leaving the occupations because of retirement, teaching, or expiration of elected term.

As with judges, turnover is low for arbitrators, mediators, and conciliators, so opportunities may be limited. Those who specialize in one or more areas of arbitration, mediation, or conciliation should have the best job opportunities.

Earnings

The median annual wage of judges, mediators, and hearing officers was $91,880 in May 2010. The median wage is the wage at which half the workers in an occupation earned more than that amount and half earned less. The lowest 10% earned less than $35,400, and the top 10% earned more than $164,510.

The median wages for judges, mediators, and hearing officer occupations in May 2010 were the following:

- $119,270 for judges, magistrate judges, and magistrates
- $85,500 for administrative law judges, adjudicators, and hearing officers
- $55,800 for arbitrators, mediators, and conciliators

According to the Administrative Office of the U.S. Courts, in the federal court system, the Chief Justice of the U.S. Supreme Court earned $223,500, and the Associate Justices averaged $213,900. Federal circuit judges earned an average of $184,500 a year. District court judges and judges in the Court of Federal Claims and the Court of International Trade had average salaries of $174,000.

Although federal judges' pay has not changed since January 2009, the average pay for state judges has increased.

According to a 2011 survey by the National Center for State Courts, the median annual wage of chief justices of the states' highest courts was $152,500 and ranged from $115,160 to $228,856. The median annual wage of associate justices of the states' highest courts was $146,917 and ranged from $112,530 to $218,237. The median annual wage of state intermediate appellate court judges was $140,732 and ranged from $105,050 to $204,599. The median annual wage of state judges of general jurisdiction trial courts was $132,500 and ranged from $104,170 to $178,835.

Most judges, mediators, and hearing officers work full time, and many often work longer hours to prepare for case hearings. Some judges work part time and divide their time between their judicial responsibilities and other careers.

SOURCE: Bureau of Labor Statistics, U.S. Department of Labor, *Occupational Outlook Handbook, 2012– 13 Edition*, Judges, Mediators, and Hearing Officers, on the Internet at http://www.bls.gov/ooh/legal/judges-mediators-and-hearing-officers.htm.

Customer Involvement in the Criminal Justice System[1]

The previous discussion on the characteristics of services suggests the importance of identifying and involving the customers in designing and delivering an effective and efficient service. However, identifying all of the direct and indirect customers of any public service is not easy, and the task becomes even more challenging when it involves the criminal justice system. In this section, the challenges faced in criminal justice services and in identifying all of the customers of its services are explored.

Who are the customers of criminal justice services? If one posed this question to several people, one may find that different people will give different answers. However, it can be put forth that the victim is the direct customer and the offender and society are the indirect customers of criminal justice services. In support of this, it can be argued that by apprehending and charging an offender, a service is provided by law enforcement agencies to the victim, and by keeping the criminals off the street, criminal justice agencies provide safety to the citizens of a community, thus rendering a service to them. However, on numerous occasions the providers of criminal justice services have not recognized the victim and society as their customers. Many incidents are reported in the media when the victims of a crime complain about the ill treatment they received from law enforcement agencies. Victims may not be taken seriously, may not be questioned about the incident, or may be kept in the dark as to how the investigation is going. Aside from the frustrations felt by victims, this type of treatment also promotes a negative view of the agency and the services it provides. As was noted in In the News 2.1 (Chapter 2), efforts are being made to allow victims more say in the services they receive from the criminal justice system. However, this issue is far from being resolved.

It is not easy to consider the offenders as customers, because they have violated a person or the property of another. However, to fully service all parties involved in a criminal act, an offender should also be considered a customer. It can be argued that

---

[1]The words *goods* and *services* will be used interchangeably.

offenders are important indirect customers of the criminal justice system. They are considered indirect customers because they do not volunteer for criminal justice services, but they consume them once involved in the system. The rest of this section examines the confusion around this topic and presents the fallacy of the various arguments that are given to justify the noninclusion of the offender as one of the customers. Alternative arguments will be presented to support the case that an offender, in addition to the victim and society, should be considered a customer in the designing of criminal justice services. The inclusion of the offender as a customer in designing and delivering criminal justice services contributes to a robust, efficient, and effective criminal justice system. This is well illustrated in In the News 3.1. The article discusses the needs of a typical offender in adjusting to life after prison, and how the prison or other agencies working closely with the prison can prepare the offender. For such changes to occur in the criminal justice system, it is important that offenders are viewed as customers, whose needs have to be satisfied.

In the News 3.1
Federal Court Program Focuses on Life After Prison

For Rhonda Tigney, the hardest part about adjusting to life after federal prison was checking the box on job applications that indicated she had been convicted of a felony.

The former accountant and mother of four had once earned between $20 and $30 an hour. But after pleading guilty to bank fraud and serving nearly three years in a federal prison in Connecticut, the best she could get at first was an $8-an-hour job at Panera Bread Co.

"I have a degree in finance. Finding a job had never been a problem," she said. "But now, all employers focus on that one box."

As one of about a dozen participants in a new federal court program designed to help certain kinds of offenders succeed after their release from prison, Tigney found a group of people who understood what obstacles lay ahead and how to navigate them.

The Middle District of Pennsylvania—which spans 33 counties, including Lackawanna and Luzerne—is one of 10 federal court systems to implement a program like this, according to Len Bogart, chief U.S. probation officer in Scranton. Together with the federal probation department, U.S. District Judges Yvette Kane in Harrisburg and Thomas I. Vanaskie in Scranton started the Court-Assisted Re-entry Program in March with the hope that it will cut down on the likelihood that participants will re-offend.

"These people come out and they have no job, no driver's license, no place to stay," Kane said. "All that makes it hard to succeed."

The program is a lot like drug court programs across the nation, in which participants have regular, frequent contact with judges and probation officers to ensure they stay on track. In the new federal court program, Kane and Vanaskie meet once a month with offenders to get a report on how each participant is doing and to set goals for the next month.

"One offender came before me and said he was having trouble getting a job," Kane said. "So the goal for him was to apply for five jobs a week, and to show me proof that he was doing it."

Other goals could include attending drug or alcohol treatment, paying fines and restitution and finding suitable housing, Bogart said.

Offenders who meet all the goals set for them, continually test negative for drugs and alcohol and attend all required meetings with the judge and their probation officer will be able to finish their supervised release in two years, Bogart said. Participants in the program must have been sentenced to at least three years of supervised release after completing their prison sentence.

Not just any offender can participate in the program, though.

The judges and Bogart have put together a stringent list of criteria meant to weed out those least and most likely to re-offend. They look at everything from a defendant's addiction and criminal history to whether they have a stable home life and a supportive family.

Tigney said she was nervous at first about going back in front of a judge. But now, she credits the program with helping her succeed. When she was finally released from prison, she came home to Harrisburg with nothing. She has since moved to a better-paying job.

So far, the program seems like a success, the judges and Bogart said.

Eventually, the judges and Bogart plan to have criminal justice professors and students at Shippensburg University measure the success of the re-entry program by comparing participants and non-participants, with a focus on the number of people in each category to re-offend. That information will figure largely in the decision by the judges as to whether to continue the program.

There are three sources of confusion, which are intricately intertwined and collectively work to create the fuzziness in recognizing offenders as customers of criminal justice services. These sources of confusion are discussed next.

1. *Public service.* Criminal justice services are considered public services. There are two primary differences between private and public services, each of which contributes to the confusion in identifying all of the customers of public services.

a. *Direct and indirect customers due to externalities.* In private goods and services, a customer is the direct beneficiary of the service, with little or no indirect benefit to others (i.e., the customer is the one getting the haircut); in public goods and services, besides the direct consumption, there is a significant indirect consumption enjoyed by other stakeholders. These indirect benefits arise from *positive externalities* that emerge. For example, education brings a direct benefit to the students and their families, but it also brings a significant indirect benefit to the neighborhood in terms of a decrease in juvenile crimes (see Greenwood, 2008; Sabates, 2008; Vacca, 2008). Similarly, in the criminal justice system, the direct beneficiary is the victim, but the offender can also benefit from going through the correctional process. However, citizens are so accustomed to seeing only the direct customer because of their interaction in the market for private goods and services that the indirect customers are often overlooked when identifying all of the customers of public goods and services.

b. *Purchaser versus consumer.* Is the entity who *pays* for a service the customer, or is the entity who *consumes* the service the customer, or are both customers? Private goods and services are bought and sold through the market. Predominantly, the purchaser and the consumer are the same for private goods and services, and they are called the customer. For example, when John buys an airline ticket for himself, he is the purchaser as well as the consumer of the service. Adding a level of complexity to this example, consider the case in which John's mother buys an airline ticket for him. In this situation, John is the direct consumer of services, and his mother is the purchaser. Even in this latter case, where the purchaser and the direct consumer are not the same, it is easy to identify both of them as being the customers of the airlines. Furthermore, the payment for private goods is made immediately before or after consumption and is directly related to the amount of goods and services consumed. These characteristics allow the provider of private services to recognize the customers (both consumer and purchaser) easily. Sometimes, the payment may be postponed to a future time that is mutually agreed upon by both the seller and the buyer (e.g., a person buys furniture and both the buyer and seller agree that the buyer may make no payments for 12 months).

The previous criteria for judging who is a customer are ingrained in the minds of individuals to such a large extent that when these conditions are not evident, individuals and agencies may sometimes find it difficult to identify the customers. However, the previous conditions generally do not hold true for public goods and services, thus making the task of identifying all of the customers extremely difficult. For example, when an individual is stopped for a speeding violation, the individual typically does not immediately make a payment to the law enforcement officer for the services rendered—the service being traffic enforcement. Instead, the individual may be paying taxes at a predetermined time of the year, a part of which goes toward supporting law enforcement services. This disconnection between service delivery and the indirect method of payment may obscure a law enforcement officer's ability to recognize the speed violator as a customer. To continue, the previous thought is developed in greater depth using an example from public education, after which the criminal justice system will be revisited.

In the U.S. public education system, the majority of financial support to the public schools comes from local property taxes. A small part of the financial support comes from the school fee that is paid by the students (if there is one required). In the identification of the purchaser and consumer of education services, the following four scenarios are possible, each increasing in its level of complexity: (i) A family owns a house and pays property taxes. The family also has young kids who go to the public school. Here, the family is the purchaser and the direct consumer; (ii) a family owns no property and lives in subsidized housing due to low income, and pays no property taxes. The family has kids who go to school. This family is clearly a consumer but not a purchaser; (iii) a family owns a house and pays property taxes, but has no kids who attend the local schools. This family is a purchaser but not a direct consumer of the school education. Nevertheless, this family is an indirect consumer of education because its members enjoy the benefits of potentially lower juvenile crime rates and increased education of the local children (positive externalities); (iv) a family does not own a house and pays no property taxes, and has no school-aged kids. This family is neither a purchaser nor a direct consumer of school education. Nevertheless, this family is an indirect consumer of education because its members may realize the potential for lower juvenile crime rates and increased education of the local children (see Greenwood, 2008; Sabates, 2008; Vacca, 2008) (positive externalities).

Continuing with the example, the school board members want to revise the school curriculum for the year 2014. They want to invite their customers to the school board meeting, but must determine whom should they invite. If the school board considers families with school-going kids as their customers and only invites them, then the board is ignoring the interests of families who are financially supporting the school system (the purchasers). If the school board decides to invite only the tax-paying families (the purchasers), then the board is ignoring the interests of families who are the immediate consumers of school services. Therefore, the school board must invite all families, which include (i) families who pay property taxes and have school-going kids (purchasers and direct consumers), (ii) families who do not pay property taxes but have school-going kids (direct consumers but not purchasers), (iii) families who pay property taxes but have no school-going kids (purchasers and indirect consumers), and (iv) families who pay no property taxes and have no school-aged kids (indirect consumers but not purchasers). Similarly, this logic can be applied to the criminal justice system. The system must consider the victims (direct customer and purchaser), complainants (direct customer and purchaser), and society (purchaser) as its customers, as well as the offenders (indirect customer and purchaser), who are all a part of society and pay taxes.

From the previous discussion, it may be concluded that identifying customers based on whether they pay for the service (purchaser) or whether they directly benefit from the service (direct customer) occurs for private goods and services only. For public goods and services, there are numerous indirect customers in addition to direct customers; both the direct and the indirect customers do not pay directly to the service provider, and often the time between consumption and the payment for consuming the public service is indeterminate. Therefore, application of private sector criteria in the identification of customers for public goods and services will lead to incomplete identification of all customers. For example, the budget for public services is determined by politicians who represent the views and interests of their constituents, but they are funded by taxpayer money. The citizens of a county are the purchasers of criminal justice services because they contribute to the taxes, but not all of them may be direct beneficiaries (that is, they are not involved in an incident in which the police respond); some may be indirect beneficiaries (if they see crime rates lowered in their communities or they commit an offense). Therefore, it is important to identify indirect beneficiaries of public services and consider them as customers, too. Consequently, if the traditional business approach is used in identifying customers, there will be confusion in identifying both direct and indirect customers of criminal justice services and in treating them fairly.

2. *Criminal justice system as a monopoly.* The second source of confusion in recognizing offenders as customers of criminal justice services is that the criminal justice system, like any public service, operates as a type of monopoly. A monopoly is

a market where there exists only one seller and no closely related alternatives for that seller. In terms of schools, for example, public schools may be the only option for children living in certain communities. The public police department may be the only option for law enforcement protection in a city or community. Typically, *monopolies* are less sensitive to customers and their needs. Therefore, it may be that a part of the behavior of the agents of the criminal justice system in not attempting to identify all of the customers and understand their needs originates from the fact that they are part of a monopoly. In addition, there is an enormous amount of power vested in the officers of the criminal justice system in comparison to the various consumers of these services, which could put blinders on the service providers in considering the sentiments of all of the stakeholders of their services. We acknowledge that there is a private policing industry as well as private correctional agencies and private security. However, as will be discussed in the chapters addressing the public policing and correctional agencies (Chapters 9–13), private firms do not share the same powers as publicly employed officers. These groups have not been given the same respect as public officers, as they are often seen as security guards or police-for-hire. Privatized policing agencies also fall into the business industry since they are for-profit groups and, in most cases, are directly paid by their consumers. A private policing agency may patrol a gated community of wealthy individuals, for example. The individuals pay the officers, or the private policing agency, directly for their services. The same thing occurs for private prisons, which are typically paid a daily rate by the state to house offenders who cannot fit in public facilities because of overcrowding.

3. *Noncooperation by the offender.* In the delivery of private services, the customer cooperates with the service provider. However, public services like the criminal justice system are provided for the good of society and are not necessarily loved by those who have to deal with them, often resulting in noncooperative behavior of the offender. The noncooperative attitude of the offender, for example, may confuse the officers in criminal justice and cause them not to view the offender as a customer. To provide a better perspective, the uncooperative behavior of the customer is discussed in the context of two different services, after which the criminal justice system is revisited.

In the first example, there may be noncooperative and disruptive students in a class because they perceive, correctly or incorrectly, that material in a particular course is irrelevant to their career goals. The students are unhappy and feel that they have been forced by the university to take particular courses that will not add any value to their careers. However, it is not uncommon for instructors to get e-mails or phone calls from such students, a few years after they have graduated, stating how they are benefiting at their workplace from the material that was taught.

The students' noncooperative behavior may be because of a lack of information, a lack of maturity, or miscommunication about the course's relevance to their future endeavors. Instead of taking the initiative of establishing the connection between the material taught and the career aspiration of students, the instructor might leave it to the student to find the relevance of the material taught. The instructors may feel that they are providing an important service for the future well-being of the students, who should be thankful and should not question the instructor's intention. This attitude is generally prevalent when the instructors feel that they are right and are not accountable to anyone. Such a mind-set serves the interests of neither the customer nor the service provider. If there were promotional material put together by the school, supplemented by the instructors' initiative of relating the course material to the students' future goals, the service quality would have improved significantly. Left to themselves, the students find the relevance of the material much later, when their overall awareness and maturity have increased. If students' noncooperative attitudes are taken seriously by the instructor as a reason to exclude them from being treated as a customer of knowledge provided in class, that will only reinforce the nonlearning attitude of the students. Such a mind-set of the instructor would be misplaced and could be considered as reacting to a *symptom,* which in this case is the noncooperative behavior of the student. This behavior on the part of the instructors emerges when they act from a position of power, presuming that they are right and the student is wrong, and thus believing that the fault lies with the student and that the instructors are doing everything correctly.

However, if the instructors are farsighted, then they will treat all of the students as customers, even the noncooperative and disruptive students. The instructor should find the *cause* of the disruptive behavior of the students and then fine-tune their course material and teaching method so that more students can immediately relate the course to their career goals and become cooperative. Such an attitude is only possible if the instructors view all of the students as their customers. Of course, this recommended cause-based approach would be far more time-consuming and often may be difficult for the frontline worker (the instructors, in this case) to adopt due to workload pressures. For example, in education, the pressures from research and assigned committee duties may leave little or no time for the instructor to adopt a more time-consuming, cause-based approach. In other words, the increased sensitivity toward the customer through the adoption of a cause-based approach by frontline workers has to be supported from the top. A cause-based approach calls for different management style, requiring the top management to provide for time, training, and performance measures to promote such an approach. In this example, the university administration would have to acknowledge that instructors need more time to focus on course preparation and material development by lowering the requirements for instructor service on committees and article or book publications.

Using another example of a noncooperative attitude from a customer, this time in the airline industry—a service with which most are familiar—a symptom-based approach to service is described. Sometimes, passengers have been reported to become agitated and behave in an uncooperative manner, even becoming dangerous to fellow passengers. Such behavior is often dealt with by the aircrew by repeatedly asking the passenger to sit down calmly in a seat. On refusal to cooperate, the passenger is blacklisted, prosecuted for endangering the lives of other passengers, fined and jailed, and so on. Is that the correct resolution to the problem? The answer is no because the airline is focusing on the symptom, which in this case is the uncooperative behavior of the passenger. Such uncooperative and unsettled behavior of a passenger can be explained in one of two ways: Either the passenger is mentally imbalanced, or there is something troubling the passenger, which is leading to the agitated and uncooperative behavior. If the passenger has mental problems, then medical attention is needed and not jail time. Alternatively, if the passenger's uncooperative attitude is because of issues troubling the passenger, then the airline should find a solution and not prosecute. An action of prosecuting the passenger by the airline is embedded in an assumption that the airline is right and the passenger is wrong. Furthermore, it is reflective of an attitude that the airline does not consider this uncooperative passenger as its customer. However, a service is about solving customer problems. The right approach should be that the airline identifies the cause that has led to the noncooperative behavior of the passenger and tries to remove that cause from future occurrences. Such a productive step will not only resolve the current problem, but also prevent it from happening in the future, thus improving the overall quality of the service. Take a look at In the News 3.2 to see how the criminal justice system is implementing a cause-based approach to offender treatment.

In the News 3.2
Mental-Health Court for Re-Entering Prisoners "Long Overdue"

City and state officials yesterday announced the launch of a special mental-health court that is intended to reduce recidivism by helping mentally ill prison inmates transition back to society.

Mayor Nutter praised the program as another in a long list of innovative and successful First Judicial District specialty courts, which also include Drug Court, DUI Court and the former Eagles Court at Veterans Stadium.

"Some folks make some bad decisions or have challenges in their lives and find themselves in the criminal justice system," Nutter said. "That doesn't mean that they don't need and deserve treatment with the utmost dignity and respect."

Participants will be assigned a parole officer and given a course of behavioral and mental-health treatment upon their release from prison.

There are about a dozen other mental-health courts in the state, but Philadelphia's is the first to focus on inmates' re-entry into the community.

Sheila Woods-Skipper, the Common Pleas Criminal Supervising judge, said that the court aims to treat the underlying problems afflicting mentally ill offenders in hopes of keeping them out of the criminal justice system.

"We want to stop the revolving door of recidivism," said Woods-Skipper, who will preside over the new court.

To enter the program, inmates must meet certain requirements that include eligibility for Medicaid, being deemed medically suited for the program and having no more than five previous incarcerations. Violent offenders will not be considered for the program.

"Carefully screened mentally ill offenders will enter the program and will receive intensive mental-health treatment and counseling, along with intensive court supervision," Woods-Skipper said.

Treatment plans for the offenders will be determined on an individual basis by the Department of Behavioral Health and Mental Retardation Services' Philadelphia Forensic Assertive Community Treatment Team.

Participants must follow the rules of their parole and will be required to adhere to their treatment plans. Offenders will be under strict court supervision and will be required to appear in court before Woods-Skipper at various points during their treatment.

For many who spoke yesterday after the announcement at the Criminal Justice Center, the Mental Health Court is a long overdue response to mental illness in the criminal-justice system.

State Supreme Court Justice Seamus P. McCaffery and District Attorney Lynne Abraham likened the prevalence of mental illness in today's prisons to that of state-run mental hospitals of the 1950s.

"Right now, according to our estimates, over 30 percent of the people currently incarcerated in our jails are there because they suffer from mental illness," McCaffery said.

"There are around 1,900 inmates in our prison system who could be benefiting from this," Abraham said.

What is the difference between a cause and a symptom? To help understand the difference, consider an example of a patient developing a fever. Here, the *symptom* is the fever, which can be measured and felt; however, the *cause* may be some infection, which is not apparent but requires more analysis before it can be identified. When the patient visits a medical doctor, if the doctor treats only for the fever, then it is a *symptom-based treatment*. Such an approach may lead the fever to go away temporarily, but it will resurface because the infection (cause) has not been treated. Alternatively, if the doctor runs some tests to identify the reason for the fever, and then treats both the fever and the infection, it is a *cause-based treatment*. Obviously, a cause-based treatment requires more work on the part of the doctor, but it is better for the long-term health of the sick patient.

Using the previous lens of *symptom versus cause,* the uncooperative behavior of the offenders in criminal justice services is reexamined. The uncooperative behavior is a symptom. It may have stemmed from some misinformation or a past experience of the offender in dealing with criminal justice agencies, or the offender may simply be mentally unbalanced (as discussed in In the News 3.2). Added to this complexity is the fact that criminal justice services have a negative stigma attached to them because of the way they have been presented in various media. For example, to be seen with the police raises questions of blame and guilt in the mind of the community. Given such negative stigmatization—particularly if the offender is falsely accused—it is not hard to imagine why an offender might not cooperate with law enforcement. Consider the case of the bombing at the Atlanta, Georgia, 1996 Summer Olympics. Richard Jewell, who first spotted the bomb and informed authorities, was widely publicized as the bomber but was later found to be completely innocent. It was a case of being in the wrong place at the wrong time. In addition, the suspected offender often may not see the actions of law enforcement agencies as a benefit. This unhappiness and unwillingness of the participant (suspect) to cooperate with the service provider can be challenging to law enforcement. However, if the offender's uncooperative behavior leads the police to deal with the situation heavy-handedly, then the original premise is reinforced in the mind of the suspect and other onlookers. Therefore, noncooperative behavior of a suspect presents a very delicate situation for law enforcement agencies. It requires the agencies foremost to identify and examine the causes that lead suspects to be noncooperative, and modify the delivery of the law enforcement service to remove such causes.

Perhaps the suspect is uncooperative because the suspect does not see the benefit provided by the police during the encounter. Take a domestic violence incident, for example. Some states now require the police to make an arrest at a domestic violence scene. Of course, the person arrested at the scene is not going to see this as beneficial. However, the removal of this person from the situation allows tempers to decrease and potentially blocks additional offenses (murders, shootings, stabbings, etc.) from occurring. In actuality, this is beneficial for the domestic violence offender if the offender is kept from committing additional offenses. Yet most people involved in domestic violence do not see the benefit of the arrest and are noncooperative when the police initiate their service (the arrest). One way the police can prevent potential uncooperativeness is by disseminating information to citizens on their policies and practices. How many advertisements or feature programs have educated the community about law enforcement services? Or how many programs have shown how the offenders benefited in improving their lives after correctional services? These are rare in the media, while what is shown most often is how law enforcement agencies catch the criminals, which brings negative stigmatization to their services.

The treatment of offenders is an important component in their reform process. Therefore, officers in the criminal justice system need to treat offenders as customers; otherwise, their method will regress to a symptom-based approach. In a symptom-based approach, the criminal justice system may improve its efficiency in bringing to justice those who break the law, but the problems will resurface over and over again since the root cause of the failure has not been identified and treated. On the other hand, if the criminal justice system includes the offender as a customer and focuses on addressing the individual offender's needs, circumstances, and social environment, agencies will be more likely to find the root cause of the problem and deal with it, making it a cause-based approach. Besides addressing the victim's complaint, attention can be focused on trying to understand why the crime was committed by the offender and trying to prevent it from happening in the future. Some components of the criminal justice system have already adopted this approach. Corrections—specifically, probation and parole—focuses on the causes of offender actions. Similarly, agencies that work with juvenile offenders focus on cause-based approaches that benefit young criminals. Restorative justice programs are using this philosophy in their approach to crime, criminals, victims, and the community. Specialized courts, which are becoming very popular, focus on the cause of drug use or truancy. In addition, community policing subscribes to this philosophy of treating everyone—citizens, victims, complainants, and offenders—as customers, and working with them to better serve their needs so as to deter criminal activity or help integrate offenders back into society.

Unfortunately, not all policing practices have adopted a cause-based approach. In addition, the courts attempt to understand the cause of the criminal act in some cases but not in others. The use of mandatory sentences and other determinate sentencing practices severely limits the criminal justice system's ability to view offenders as customers. If service quality concepts were greatly enhanced in criminal justice and more focus placed on the adoption of a cause-based approach, there may be improvement in the quality of criminal justice services. One result may be the reinstitution of indeterminate sentences and practices that are more discretionary. In doing so, focus can be redirected to the true issues causing crime, whether they be physical, mental, emotional, social, or environmental. Focus can also be placed on preventing crime at the front end of the system (policing) instead of just detecting violations and enforcing the law. If the same message is carried throughout the criminal justice system—that is, identify the cause of the offensive behavior and assist in fixing it—the chances for success in reducing crime, in general, and for deterrence may be higher. Adoption of such a cause-based approach leading to superior service quality requires changes in the mind-set of the leadership, changes in training methods, changes in performance evaluation and motivation, and changes in communication styles—all of which are discussed in subsequent chapters. This would also require a change in the current societal approach to crime and criminal justice—from punitive philosophies to treatment philosophies. The positive note here is that efforts toward this approach are being made, as mentioned earlier and as will be discussed in detail in later chapters.

As concluding advice, any time there is doubt about whether a particular stakeholder is a customer, ask a simple question: If this individual/group/organization did not exist, would it adversely impact the business? If the answer is yes, then that individual/group/organization is a customer. According to this rule of thumb, the victim, the offender, the complainant, and society are all customers of the criminal justice system and should be considered in its design and delivery of services.

Defining Service Quality

As discussed earlier, customers are part of the service delivery process. Therefore, in judging the quality of the service, the customers not only look at the outcome of the service, but also view the process of which they are an intricate part. For example, the quality of a dining service at a restaurant is judged not only by the quality of the food that was served, but also by how the restaurant took the customer through the entire experience of dining, from the time the customer entered the restaurant to the time he or she left. Complainants in policing incidents judge the entire experience as well, from the time of the initial call to the reaction and response of the police. In addition, the intangibility characteristic of services makes it difficult to provide an objective measure of service quality; instead, it introduces into play the role of customers' perceptions and expectations in measuring service quality. Perceived quality results from a comparison of expectations with perceptions of performance. It is a form of attitude based on the consumer's judgment, which may be related but not necessarily equivalent to satisfaction. For example, based on many factors (stories from friends, dining magazine reviews, etc.), a customer forms a certain impression about the kind of experience he or she should have in a particular upscale restaurant. Finally, one night the customer goes there for dinner with a friend. The customer comes out saying the restaurant's service quality was substandard because his or her perception of the restaurant's performance fell short of the expectation that he or she had formed about it. In other words, the gap between expected and perceived service becomes the measure of service quality, resulting in either a positive or negative experience.

Parasuraman, Zeithaml, and Berry (1988) have identified and defined five dimensions on which they measure the gap between customers' perceptions of service received and expectations of service desired. These five dimensions are described next.

1. *Reliability* is defined as the "ability to perform the promised service dependably and accurately" (Parasuraman et al., 1988, p. 23). Customers expect the service will be performed in the same manner every time without any errors. For example, customers expect their bank and credit card statements to be accurate and delivered around the same date of the month. When there are errors or delays in these statements, it adversely impacts the customers' perception of the service delivery. Similarly, when there is a burglary in a house, the victim expects the police officer to make an accurate report. If there is a delayed response to the victim's call for assistance, or it appears that the officer is not taking the situation seriously and is not asking the right types of questions, it may be perceived by the victim that the service is unreliable. The victim may be left with some doubt that anything will happen with the burglary investigation.

2. *Responsiveness* is defined as the "willingness to help customers and provide prompt service" (Parasuraman et al., 1988, p. 23). For example, when customers call for a clarification on a credit card billing statement, they expect to be attended by a service representative in a reasonable amount of time who will answer all queries. Similarly, when a distress call is placed to 911, callers expect an immediate response from the emergency operator. Getting a busy signal or no response to the call goes against what is perceived to be the expected service. In addition, once an officer is dispatched to the crime scene, it is perceived by the victim that the officer should be there in a reasonable amount of time. Any delay in this service could allow for additional harm to the victim(s) or for the offender to escape detection and apprehension.

3. *Assurance* is defined as the "knowledge and courtesy of employees and their ability to inspire trust and confidence" (Parasuraman et al., 1988, p. 23). Embedded in this dimension are features involving politeness, respect, and consideration toward the customer; effective communication; competence to perform the service; and the general attitude that convinces the customers that the server has their best interest at heart. For example, the respect, consideration, and knowledge in answering questions demonstrated by the juvenile detention officer in dealing with parents about their

daughter's alleged offense will impact the parents' perception about service performance. Calming the fears of parents whose children have been recently detained, whether for short or long periods, is part of the responsibility of a juvenile detention officer. Possessing the ability to explain what will happen in the near future in their child's case is imperative in conveying a sense of professionalism and responsibility to the parents.

4. *Tangibles* are defined as the "physical facilities, equipment, and appearance of personnel" (Parasuraman et al., 1988, p. 23). The condition of the physical infrastructure and the professional appearance of employees indirectly impact the customer's perception of service quality. A customer uses them as tangible evidence to form impressions about service performance. For example, when customers dining in a fancy restaurant visit its washroom, which is unclean, they come out feeling that the restaurant must not be keeping very high standards of hygiene in its kitchen area too, and that immediately lowers the customer's perception of the food quality. Similarly, a law enforcement officer attired in a grungy uniform and with unkept hair does not lend much credibility to the professional handling of the crime report. There are certain expectations by the public that police officers will arrive in crisp policing uniforms, looking sharp and clean, just as there are expectations that the judge will wear a black robe and inmates will wear prison uniforms. Without these standards, questions of professionalism and safety are aroused.

5. *Empathy* is defined as "caring, individualized attention the firm provides its customers" (Parasuraman et al., 1988, p. 23). Empathy is felt by the customer when a firm takes the customer's problem as its own and tries to help—for example, when a customer onboard a plane realizes that he or she has left his or her driver's license at the airline ticket counter while checking in luggage, and the flight attendant takes responsibility to contact the ground crew at the airport to arrange for safe delivery of the license to the customer's residence. Similarly, when a police officer gives a victim his or her personal business card with a contact number, the victim feels better about the interaction. The victim believes that the officer is available for further discussion and assistance. This behavior increases the victim's perception that he or she received individualized care and assistance.

Measuring Service Quality

As noted earlier, it is important for organizations to know if they are measuring up to the customer's expectations when performing services. The gaps between expected and perceived service are routinely measured by companies to gauge their service quality. Customer feedback surveys or brief telephone interviews are common measures used by businesses to assess their services and customer satisfaction. Parasuraman, Zeithaml, and Berry (1985) define the gap between customer expectations and perceptions as Gap 5 (see Figure 3.1), which in turn depends on the size and direction of the four gaps that are associated with the delivery of the service.

Figure 3.1 Service Quality Model

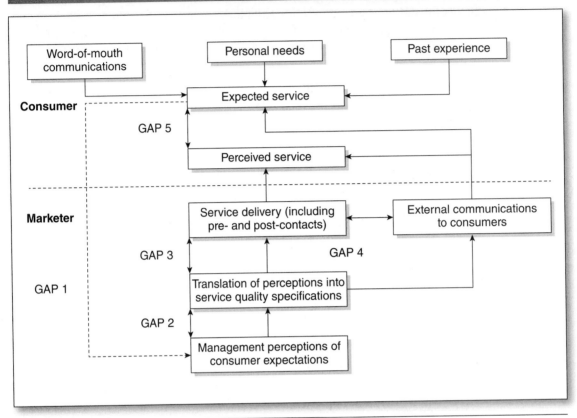

SOURCE: From "A Conceptual Model of Service Quality and Its Implications for Future Research," by A. Parasuraman, V. A. Zeithaml, and L. L. Berry, Fall 1985, *Journal of Marketing, 45,* pp. 41–50. Published by the American Marketing Association, reprinted with permission.

Gap I: Consumer Expectation—Management Perception Gap

According to Parasuraman et al. (1985), the first gap measures the variance between customer expectations and management's perception of these expectations. This gap arises because management does not have a full and proper understanding about how numerous information sources, like advertising, past experience with the firm and its competitors, personal needs, and communications with friends, are used by customers to formulate their expectations. Therefore, this gap can be closed by improving market research, and by improving internal communications between management and employees as well as externally with customers. This gap is significant in the area of criminal justice services, where there is very little market research done to understand how society perceives the services provided by the various agencies in the system or how the needs of society may have changed over time. Only occasionally will a police department measure the community's perception of its policing effectiveness. It is unheard of for a prison to survey the local community on its current or past experiences with the facility. In addition, the communication within criminal justice agencies is highly bureaucratic and complex, missing a lot of subtle information that has grave implications. Communication among different agencies involved in administering the criminal justice system is, in most cases, minimal, with everyone closely guarding their territory and exercising power through withholding information rather than sharing information. Communication with the community can be almost nonexistent, with the exception of formal responses to citizen complaints, media inquiries, and calls for service. Later, in Chapter 8, a more detailed discussion on communication is provided.

Gap 2: Management Perception—Service Quality Specification Gap

The second gap arises when management is unable both to formulate target levels of service quality to meet perceptions of customer expectations and to translate these targets into workable specifications. There may be a lack of management commitment to service quality or a perception that meeting customers' expectations is unfeasible, thus resulting in Gap 2. To close this gap, management has to set quality improvement goals and standardize service delivery tasks. Community policing, found in various forms throughout the United States, has mostly been an attempt to meet customer expectations through goals and service delivery. As officers become engaged in communities, they can better identify what is expected from the police in those areas, and they can set goals to close the gaps that may exist between perceived and expected police activities.

Gap 3: Service Quality Specifications—Service Delivery Gap

The third gap is called the service performance gap, which results from the inability of the actual service delivery to meet the specifications set by management. For example, after extensive research, a luxury hotel may identify that from the time a guest calls the housekeeping department, it should take three minutes for housekeeping to be knocking on the guest's door to deliver the item or service requested. However, the real data show that housekeeping staff typically do not meet the target of three minutes, but takes longer. Similarly, research may show that from the time a citizen places a 911 call, it should take three minutes for a law enforcement officer to be at the site. However, the data show that the officers typically do not meet the target and take longer than three minutes to arrive. This gap may arise due to numerous reasons, including unsatisfactory teamwork, imperfect employee selection, a lack of adequate staff on hand, inadequate training, and poor job design. When budgets are low, agencies in criminal justice may not be as choosy in their pick of candidates for positions because they fear losing the funding for the position if they do not hire someone right away. In this case, people may be hired who cannot, or choose not to, adequately perform the duties. Moreover, the training budgets may be inadequate, resulting in officers who are not fully trained.

In such a case, unethical practices or abuse of power may become issues for the system. Additionally, a manager may underestimate staffing needs on a particular shift on a given day. Even though management may be sending messages that these are unacceptable behaviors, the mediocre level of the employees can create a disparity in services provided to society.

Gap 4: Service Delivery—External Communications Gap

The fourth gap is called the external communications gap, and it results from exaggerated promises given by media advertising and other external communications, which raise customer expectations that cannot be met by the service delivery. This gap can be closed by bringing about greater communication between operations people responsible for the firm's service capability and marketing and advertising people responsible for communicating with customers. Policing systems have struggled with this issue for years. Countless numbers of off-record or poorly worded comments have made it into the media circuit. Tapes of police brutality and unethical behaviors have been played on television stations over and over until this seems to be ordinary and accepted behavior in the criminal justice system. However, recently an expansion and hiring of officers skilled in answering media questions and in providing information to the public has been the trend. Now, there are police officers specifically appointed to prevent external communications gaps. Line staff are also warned about acting inappropriately in public since there are numerous ways citizens can record the activities of the system (over cell phones, with digital cameras, etc.).

As mentioned earlier, Gap 5 depends on the size and direction of the four gaps that are associated with delivery of the service. The authors of the service quality gap model have developed an instrument called SERVQUAL for measuring Gap 5 (Parasuraman et al., 1988). They use multiple items to measure the five dimensions of service quality (i.e., reliability, responsiveness, assurance, empathy, and tangibles) that comprise Gap 5. This instrument involves two parts—one to record customer expectations for a service, followed by a second section to record the customer's perceptions of the service delivered by the organization.

Scope of Service Quality in the Criminal Justice System

In this section, a comprehensive view of the criminal justice system is provided from five perspectives (content, process, structure, outcome, and impact), with the express goal of identifying possible measures of service quality. For criminal justice services, the scope of service quality extends beyond the quality of service that is provided for the offender; it also includes the impact on the family, community, and the victim.

Content. Are standard procedures being followed in the service delivery? For example, is the police officer following accepted interrogation practices when questioning the suspect? For routine services, standard operating procedures are generally developed, and service personnel are expected to follow these procedures. Informing suspects of their constitutional rights prior to questioning them about the offense and during processing is an established practice in the criminal justice system. It was determined by the U.S. Supreme Court that constitutional rights applied to all individuals accused of a crime. Officers who fail to allow for due process jeopardize their cases and their careers.

Process. Is the sequence of steps in the service delivery process accurate, well coordinated, and logically correct? The express objective here is to bring an efficient use of service resources to create the maximum impact. The customer interaction with the service provider and the interaction and communications among service personnel are closely monitored. Based on the entire process, check sheets are developed for use as common measurement devices. Simulated exercises can be done within the existing process to identify problems with coordination and activity sequencing, which can then be corrected. Disaster drills in realistic settings are regular features for emergency services (such as police, fire, ambulance, etc.) to test a unit's performance and to identify problems and correct them. After the school shootings in the 1990s, school safety became a major concern. Emergency plans for evacuation were created by police departments and the federal government. Many hours of training were provided to the officers, school employees, students, and parents to ensure that everyone was well aware of the tactics should an emergency occur. Fortunately, very few plans have had to be used in real-life situations. But this means evaluation of the effectiveness of the devised process is still largely unknown. Only in a true emergency situation can the success of the strategy be measured.

Structure. The physical infrastructure, support equipment, competence of the personnel, and the organizational design are important for improved service quality, and need to be examined regularly. Typically, the quality conformance standards set within an industry are used to compare or benchmark the adequacy of an agency's physical facilities and equipment. Police officials are required to maintain certain standards for their equipment. Similarly, standards are enforced in the areas of personnel qualifications for hiring, promotion, and merit increases. Mostly, service agencies administer self-evaluation procedures and peer performance appraisals for promoting organizational effectiveness in controlling quality, although these may vary greatly from agency to agency.

Outcome. Another measure of service quality is consumer satisfaction. The concept of monitoring customer satisfaction by tracking measurements should be widely used. Innovative approaches to measuring outcome quality should be employed. For example, the quality of service response can be documented by examining how many rings occur before the phone is answered by service personnel in a credit card company. In addition, satisfaction of service personnel with their performance can be an important measure of quality outcome, which is often not used by agencies in their evaluation procedures. Sometimes for public services, an assumption, though erroneous, is made that the status quo is acceptable unless the level of complaints begins to rise. Criminal justice agencies may rely on the "if it ain't broke, don't fix it" philosophy, although it can lead to questionable practices by personnel who believe no one is watching their activities. This atmosphere does not conform well to the ever-changing political, national, international, and technological landscapes, so it is important that criminal justice agencies develop techniques to measure the outcome of their services.

Impact. What is the long-term effect of the service on the consumer? Do the residents of a town feel safe when walking the streets? The response to such questions would be a good measure of the impact of police performance. Similarly, infant mortality and life expectancy are often used as measures of health care performance, while literacy rates and scores on nationally standardized tests are used as measures of the performance of education. Accessibility of service to the greater population is another important measure of impact, which is typically quoted as the population served per unit area. Recidivism rates are by far the most widely used performance measures in criminal justice. Unfortunately, they do not tell the full story of what accomplishments are actually made in this field. Other measures, such as increased educational levels, lowered abuse and neglect rates, improved public relations, and greater professionalism and accountability, to name only a few, are also performance measures in criminal justice.

Based on the discussion, it is suggested that if an open-systems approach to criminal justice were adopted with more frequency, where the offenders and victims are also treated as customers, there would be a better understanding of crime causation and deterrence. Such understanding will allow for installation of proper service designs and methodologies. It may be difficult for a number of people trained in the conventional criminal justice system to accept the inclusion of service quality approaches and the direct and indirect customers, but until that attitude changes, it will be challenging to design a more effective and efficient criminal justice system. Given that criminal justice agencies are in a service business, where they process the customer, if the definition of customer is incorrect, it is hard to imagine that the service will be beneficial for society as a whole.

In the chapters that follow, various management concepts are presented that would be necessary in designing an effective and friendly service delivery system; these are followed by presentation of the content knowledge of the various fields of the criminal justice system in which the management concepts need to be applied. In the last chapter, service quality is revisited. A hands-on tool called the *quality function deployment* is provided that can be used specifically to incorporate the voice of the customers in designing an effective and efficient criminal justice system that delivers the highest level of service quality.

Chapter Summary

- There are two glaring problems in the existing criminal justice system that need to be addressed to improve productivity and reduce cost. First, existing criminal justice services have been designed and delivered solely from the service provider's perspective, despite the fact that criminal justice services are consumed directly and indirectly by multiple stakeholders in society. Second, multiple agencies are involved in providing different components of criminal justice services with a high amount of interdependence among them. Yet these agencies ignore this codependence and work in isolation, thus losing the benefits that close interaction would have provided in improving the criminal justice system. The noninclusion of customers and a lack of integration among different interdependent agencies when designing and delivering criminal justice services belie the principles of good management.

- Services can be classified on a continuum ranging from pure services to various degrees of mixed services. Services are also commercial (business-to-consumer services and business-to-business services) or noncommercial (public services and not-for-profit services) in nature.

- There are five distinctive features of services, namely, (i) customer involvement in the service process, (ii) simultaneous production and consumption, (iii) perishability, (iv) intangibility, and (v) heterogeneity. These characteristics of services suggest the importance of identifying and involving the customers in designing and delivering an effective and efficient service.

- The offender is an important indirect customer of the criminal justice system. The inclusion of the offender as a customer in designing and delivering criminal justice services will better address crime and crime causation.

- There are three sources of confusion in identifying offenders as customers in criminal justice: (i) It can be hard to recognize indirect customers; (ii) being basically a monopoly, the criminal justice system is less sensitive to customers and their needs; and (iii) noncooperative behavior of the offender may confuse the officers of the criminal justice agencies.

- Using a symptom-based approach to criminal justice allows problems to continue to arise because it does not address the root causes of crime. In contrast, a cause-based approach focuses on trying to understand why the crime was committed by the offender and trying to prevent it from happening in the future.

- Any time there is doubt about whether a particular stakeholder is a customer, ask a simple question: If this individual/group/organization did not exist, would it adversely impact the business? If the answer is yes, then that individual/group/organization is a customer.

- Parasuraman et al. (1988) identified reliability, responsiveness, assurance, tangibles, and empathy as the five dimensions on which to measure the gap between customers' expectations of service desired and their perception of service received. Using these dimensions, they go on to measure the gap between expected service and perceived service (Gap 5), which is a sum of four other gaps. Gap 1 is defined as the consumer expectation–management perception gap. Gap 2 is defined as the management perception–service quality specification gap. Gap 3 is defined as the service quality specifications–service delivery gap. Gap 4 is defined as the service delivery–external communications gap.

- In the criminal justice system, the scope of service quality extends beyond the quality of service that is provided for the offender; it also includes the impact on the family, community, and the victim (and the victim's family).

Chapter Review Questions

1. What is the role of services in an economy? How has the role of the criminal justice system changed in the U.S. economy?

2. How would you define criminal justice services? Name some of the services provided to offenders, victims, and society in general.

3. Discuss how the five characteristics of service apply to different agencies in the criminal justice system.

4. Who are the customers of the criminal justice system? Do you agree that the offender should be included as a customer of the criminal justice system? Why or why not?

5. Provide an example of a symptom-based approach in treatment of offenders in criminal justice. Provide an example of a cause-based approach in treatment of offenders. Which approach would you use, and why?

6. What are the five dimensions of service quality? Define them in the context of criminal justice services.

7. How would you measure service quality in criminal justice services using the five-gap approach defined in the chapter?

CASE STUDY

The Richmond Correctional Center is a large-sized prison in the Midwest. The prison houses 1,530 inmates and employs 306 correctional officers as well as administrative and counseling staff. The prison's population primarily consists of young African American males between the ages of 18 and 29. The most common offense committed by the offenders is drug possession and manufacturing. The average sentence is six years.

On September 22, an incident report was filed regarding an altercation between an inmate, 54-year-old Matthew Ross, and a correctional officer, 31-year-old Andre Brown. The incident report was accompanied by a number of supplemental reports from other inmates and officers who witnessed the altercation. According to the report written by Officer Brown, inmate Ross refused to return his lunch tray to the kitchen when told to do so. Ross then became irate and attacked Officer Brown.

The report filed by Ross claims a completely different scenario. According to Ross, he was eating his lunch when Officer Brown approached him. Officer Brown said something that Ross did not hear. When Ross asked him to repeat the comment, Officer Brown screamed at him, sprayed him with pepper spray and hit him until he fell to the ground. Witness reports on the incident support the claim that Officer Brown was not provoked.

Criminal charges were immediately filed against inmate Ross for assault against a correctional officer. No charges were filed against Officer Brown.

Ross went to court on the assault charges in February. The case was dismissed after a bench trial with Judge Madison Lamb for lack of sufficient evidence.

Ross then filed a federal civil suit against the Richmond Correctional Center, the Department of Corrections, the warden, and Officer Brown. The federal court ruled that Ross was entitled to a $275,000 settlement for brutality and excessive force. Officer Brown has left the facility and currently works at a different institution in Nebraska.

Questions for Review

1. In your opinion, is this a case of excessive force and brutality? Why or why not?

2. How could the incident have been handled better? What should the prison do to avoid similar situations in the future?

3. Are inmates customers? Explain why you think they are or are not.

4. Was inmate Ross treated as a customer of the prison? Using what you have learned in this chapter, how should Ross have been treated? What does it mean to treat him as a customer? Apply the five-gap approach to this scenario.

5. What would be a symptom-based approach in resolving this situation? What would be a cause-based approach?

Internet Resources

American Bar Association—http://www.abanet.org

American Correctional Association—http://www.aca.org

Office for Victims of Crime—http://www.ojp.usdoj.gov/ovc

References and Suggested Readings

Aragon, R. (1993). Positive organizational culture: A practical approach. *FBI Law Enforcement Bulletin, 62*(12), 10.

Bauer, L., & Owens, S. D. (2004, May). Justice expenditures and employment in the United States, 2001. *Bureau of Justice Statistics Bulletin* (NCJ 202792).

Clark, C. (1957). *The conditions of economic progress* (3rd ed.). London, England: Macmillan.

Cole, A. W. (1993). Better customer focus: TQM and law enforcement. *The Police Chief, 60*(12), 23–26.

Corsentino, D., & Bue, P. T. (1993). Employee involvement: Implementing quality change. *FBI Law Enforcement Bulletin, 62*(11), 10–11.

Fitzsimmons, J. A., & Fitzsimmons, M. J. (2006). *Service management: Operations, strategy, information technology* (5th ed.). New York, NY: McGraw-Hill/Irwin.

Gondles, J. A., Jr. (1993). Excellence in corrections: Moving beyond buzzwords. *Corrections Today, 55*(3).

Greenwood, P. (2008). Prevention and intervention programs for juvenile offenders. *Future of Children, 18*(2), 185–210.

Gronroos, C. (1990). *Service management and marketing.* Lexington, MA: Lexington Books.

Haksever, C., Render, B., Russell, R. S., & Murdick, R. G. (2000). *Service management and operations* (2nd ed.). Upper Saddle River, NJ: Prentice Hall.

Haywood-Farmer, J., & Nollet, J. (1991). *Services plus: Effective service management.* Quebec, Ont., Canada: Morrin Boucherville.

Johnston, R., & Clark, G. (2005). *Service operations management: Improving service delivery* (2nd ed.). Upper Saddle River, NJ: Prentice Hall.

Kyckelhahn, T. (2011). *Justice expenditures and employment,* FY 1982–2007—statistical tables. Bureau of Justice Statistics

Metters, R., King-Metters, K., Pullman, M., & Walton, S. (2006). *Successful service operations management* (2nd ed.). Mason, OH: Thomson South-Western.

Parasuraman, A., Zeithaml, V. A., & Berry, L. L. (1985, Fall). A conceptual model of service quality and its implications for future research. *Journal of Marketing, 49,* 41–50.

Parasuraman, A., Zeithaml, V. A., & Berry, L. L. (1988). SERVQUAL: A multiple-item scale for measuring consumer perceptions of service quality. *Journal of Retailing, 64*(1), 12–40.

Sabates, R. (2008). Educational attainment and juvenile crime. *British Journal of Criminology, 48*(3), 395–409.

Sasser, W. E., Olsen, R. P., & Wyckoff, D. D. (1978). *Management of service operations.* Boston, MA: Allyn & Bacon.

Simonsen, C. E., & Arnold, D. (1993). TQM: Is it right for law enforcement? *The Police Chief, 60*(12), 20–22.

Stevens, D. J. (2000). Improving community policing. *Law & Order, 48*(10), 197–204.

Vacca, J. S. (2008). Crime can be prevented if schools teach juvenile offenders to read. *Children & Youth Services Review, 30*(9), 1055–1062.

Zager, M. A., McGaha, J., & Garcia, L. (2001). Symposium: Prison privatization and public budgeting: A meta-analysis of the literature. *Journal of Public Budgeting, Accounting & Financial Management, 13*(2), 222–244.

Environmental Influences

LEARNING OBJECTIVES

Upon completion of this chapter, students should be able to do the following:

- Identify funding sources in criminal justice and describe how funding impacts the criminal justice system
- Discuss how the use of technology by criminal justice professionals and offenders influences organizations in criminal justice
- Explain how cultural and demographic factors affect criminal justice services
- Identify the types of laws involved in criminal justice and how the system is altered as a result of legal changes
- Describe how unions impact criminal justice agencies and personnel issues
- State how politics influences decision making, funding, technology, legal decisions, union negotiations, and other resources in criminal justice

Organizations in criminal justice identify their organizational structures, missions, goals, policies, and procedures to assist them in carrying out tasks; however, organizations do not operate within a vacuum. They must take into account many different environmental influences. A few of these, such as funding opportunities, technological advancements, the cultural and demographic characteristics of the community, legal decisions, political decisions, and unions and union negotiations, will be addressed in this chapter. Although U.S. Supreme Court decisions and the media are also environmental factors that greatly impact criminal justice, these two issues will not be discussed in detail here. Students can understand their importance, however, by recalling information learned in other courses.

First of all, funding sources will be addressed. Funding is perhaps one of the most critical issues in criminal justice. Without funds, the police cannot be proactive in their approach to crime, probation cannot treat and rehabilitate offenders, and correctional institutions cannot alleviate many of the problems they face. One example of how important funding is can be seen in 1992, when the Criminal Justice Act, which provided compensation and expense reimbursement to more than 10,000 attorneys who represented indigent federal offenders in court, ran out of money. The result was that cases were suspended and there were worries that if additional supplemental funding were not found, cases would not proceed to trial (violating the defendants' constitutional rights) and charges would have to be dropped (McMillion, 1993). Most recently, we have seen states struggling to support their criminal justice systems, as federal funding has declined and block grants have disappeared or "zeroed out." North Carolina has claimed to have seen a 43% decline in federal funding in just five years (Yearwood, 2009, pp. 672–673).

Second, the chapter will discuss the tremendous impact technology has had on criminal justice. As services become more efficient and effective due to improved technology, they also become harder to provide because of a lack of training and skilled employees in technology and the inability of criminal justice to afford the newest technology available, along with the invention of new offenses—like cyberbullying, Internet fraud, and identity theft. Consequently, technology has created a standard for crime prevention and control that the criminal justice system has a difficult time accomplishing.

Just as technology is changing, so is the cultural and demographic makeup of American society. Immigrants have moved to the United States in greater numbers than ever before. As they do so, the demands on the social structure change and the abilities of the criminal justice system to handle the needs and desires of the new population are challenged. Sometimes, laws are able to ease a few of the burdens placed on the system as a result of cultural, demographic, and technological changes. However, this is not always the case. Laws themselves can initiate problems for the system. Reading the case study at the end of this chapter may make it clearer how laws can conflict at federal, state, and local levels, at times putting unrealistic expectations on the criminal justice system and its employees. Unions can add input to laws and attempt to make them more applicable to the jobs criminal justice employees perform, although union membership and support have declined over the last several years. Finally, politics and political pressures are never-ending. Simple elections or appointments of new administrators have staggering effects on the processes, procedures, and job performance of those working in criminal justice. Politics also influences organizational effectiveness.

Funding in Criminal Justice

In the context of this book, *funding,* usually defined as payment or interest on a debt or an investment in a program or agency, refers to different methods of financially supporting the criminal justice system. Funding determines the programs that will continue or cease to exist and the new programs that will be offered. The annual budgets of criminal justice agencies rely most heavily on public funds (taxes), and they are highly influenced by political and social concerns. If, for example, politicians are concerned about smoking in public places, laws may be enacted to ban smoking. If this is the case, the police must comply with the new statute and develop ways in which enforcement of the new smoking ban will be effective. The ban could require a change in, and increased cost of, policing tactics, including driving by bars and restaurants or actually entering them to detect smokers and increasing patrol in and around public buildings. Police administrators and the courts must be concerned with what the law means for their agencies, how to monitor the behavior, and how best to use already stretched resources to enforce the new law. The recent decision by Washington and Colorado to legalize marijuana is another example of how laws change the way the criminal justice system operates. In the News 4.1 demonstrates how police practices have changed in response to the new marijuana laws.

In the News 4.1
K-9 Dogs Are Retrained or Retired
After Marijuana Legalized

K-9 units are often highly skilled to assist officers in performing certain tasks of policing, such as drug identification, suspect location, bomb identification, etc. K-9 units undergo months of training in order to develop the skills they need to be successful on the job. But, dogs in Washington State and Colorado are finding that their particular skill sets may not be as useful as they once were. Since Washington State and Colorado legalized recreational marijuana, police dogs trained to sniff-out drugs in cars, buildings, and on people have to learn a new trick. Some police agencies in these states are training K-9's not to alert on pot while other agencies are phasing out marijuana sniffing K-9 units altogether by allowing the dogs to retire.

In both states, possession of one ounce or less of marijuana is legal, and concerns exist that K-9 alerts, and the resulting searches by police, will violate citizen rights. There's also concern that evidence of other crimes found during a search from a K-9 alert could lead to cases being dismissed in court.

There hasn't been agreement about how to respond to the new laws. There's some debate on responses since possession of marijuana by minors is still illegal in both states, and marijuana possession by anyone is illegal under the laws of the U.S. federal government. Possessing large amounts of marijuana is also illegal, so there may still be a need for drug dogs in Washington and Colorado. What actions police agencies eventually take in these states may depend on Supreme Court interpretations of search and seizure.

Paraphrased from "Police Under Pressure to Retrain Drug Dogs After Marijuana Legalized in 2 States," by Dan Springer, June 9, 2013, FoxNews.com. Retrieved from http://www.foxnews.com/politics/2013/06/09/police-forced-to-retrain-drug- dogs-after-marijuana-legalized/#ixzz2XR76aiTa.

Although these opportunities have declined during the recent economic issues experienced by the United States, each year the Department of Justice and many other governmental offices announce grant opportunities for programming in criminal justice. Criminal justice agencies are encouraged to apply for and use grant funds to supplement the budgets they get from state and local governments. In addition to the grants, county and city boards and state legislators sit down and hash out how tax dollars will be distributed among the various agencies requesting public funds from the city, state, and county. This is a daunting task, but they are the only true *funding sources*—entities that provide funding through monetary or material goods—available to law enforcement, corrections, probation, parole, courts, juvenile systems, and public security agencies. Each of these groups has to develop budgets identifying their potential needs and wants for an entire year, and they hope that those holding the purse strings will see the agency's priorities as important enough to fund. All of the agencies are in competition with one another to secure funds and other resources, yet they are expected to work with one another in accomplishing the similar goals of deterring and preventing crime. This rather unique relationship sets up a type of rivalry that can, in some cases, carry over into other aspects of crime fighting. Known as *territorial jealousy,* agencies are often afraid to collaborate with one another because they do not want other agencies invading the "territory" they have staked out for themselves (Cox, Allen, Hanser, & Conrad, 2014). They consider themselves experts and resent involvement from outside agencies and people. Even if they have a good idea for programming or services, they might not share it or ask for funding for fear that another agency will steal the concept. As expected, this inhibits creative and innovative programming. If they do ask for funding for the idea and do not receive it, they may blame other agencies that were given funding for new programs or services, or may hold a grudge throughout the budget year toward agencies that got more money than they did. The costs of territorial jealousy can be very serious, especially if agencies fail to cooperate with one another and fail to create necessary programs and ask for funding for them (Cox et al., 2014).

Innovative administrators may be able to identify additional funding sources for their individual agencies, as often occurs when an agency wants to implement a program without asking the county or state for tax dollars. Still, with the enormous number of responsibilities the manager has in running the agency, dedicating time to fundraising can be difficult. If an administrator dedicates too much time to raising funds and not enough time to managing and guiding employees, the agency may suffer. If the administrator focuses on management duties and fails to participate in fundraising, the agency may be unsuccessful in monetarily meeting its needs. A balance between the two must be met. Basically, the manager of the agency is asked to run a second business, which is raising money to support the first business (McNamara, 2007). Unfortunately, as is often the case in criminal justice, managers may come from nonmanagerial ranks within the agency. They may not have the skills necessary to accomplish both managing and fundraising, and they may not be experts in planning, marketing, implementing, financing, fundraising, and evaluating programs on top of guiding and leading the employees and organization. Agencies that already struggle to meet their monetary needs might hesitate to spend money on the administrative overhead needed to attract and retain managers that have the skills to appeal to funding sources (McNamara, 2007).

Of course, big businesses and for-profit agencies would suggest hiring outside consultants to aid in creating and marketing programs provided by the agency. But criminal justice agencies are not always able to rely on the expertise of outside consultants because, in most cases, they do not have enough money to hire these consultants. The fees paid to private consultants are seen, at times by the public and the media, as frivolous spending, taking valuable dollars away from the services provided to the agencies' clients (McNamara, 2007). Consequently, criminal justice agencies commonly rely on low-cost or volunteer-based assistance, which leads to a lack of research and comprehensive strategic planning—both of which are necessary in sustaining an organization. This brings the issue full circle—back to the initial dilemma faced by managers in these agencies. If managers want to research and support developmental activities for new programs, they must convince potential funders that there is a low risk of loss and a high chance for success (McNamara, 2007). To do this, the managers, using the little time available, must be experienced and skilled enough to strategically plan and implement a program that warrants additional and continued funding. Perhaps most important, the managers must be able to market the program.

Potential external funding sources for criminal justice agencies include state and federal grant programs; foundations; individual donors; in-kind donations of equipment, land, or buildings; religious or other civic groups and agencies; and private businesses. In some states, fees for services such as probation and parole and for electronic monitoring have been authorized by legislation. State and federal legislators have also authorized forfeitures of money and property that can be shown to have been the result of criminal activity. Fines and restitution are other ways that agencies can finance services and programs for clients. All of the money or property gained through supplemental resources is funneled back into the agency.

Federal and state governments use public funds collected through taxes to sponsor criminal justice agencies in two ways. First, they set annual budgets for payroll, travel, upkeep of the facility, office and inmate supplies, employee benefits, and new hires, to name a few expenses. The budget is designed to cover the basic needs of the agency for the fiscal year. Second, they provide grants. *Grants* are monies that support the unique programs and services offered by the agency, the employees who work with these programs, and any new ideas for programs and services (McNamara, 2007). One such grant is a *research grant,* which gives funds for the discovery of facts or theories, or the application of theories, in programs. If an agency wanted to study the effects of a victim impact panel on offender recidivism and empathy, it may apply to the state or federal government for a research grant. The government also provides *demonstration grants,* which assess the feasibility of a particular theory or approach in treating, diverting, capturing, or rehabilitating offenders (McNamara, 2007). In a recent demonstration grant, the National Institute of Justice found that orders of protection for teenage victims of dating violence may make a difference in future reoffending but require the accompanying "network of supportive adults, including parents and school personnel" (Klein et al., 2013, p. 4).

Project grants are provided to agencies that wish to implement particular individual projects that comply with legislation enacted by the states (McNamara, 2007). Referring back to the smoking ban example, we are likely to see an increase in smoking cessation programs and support groups for smokers as a result. Agencies in criminal justice could apply for project grants to develop and implement such programs. *Block grants* come directly from the federal government in the form of large sums of money given to states for a particular purpose. The states may then distribute the money to various agencies working on issues related to the specified purpose (McNamara, 2007). Drug Abuse Resistance Education (D.A.R.E.) programs, gang diversion programs, and programs aimed at ending methamphetamine use and distribution are usually funded through block grants.

Last are the *formula grants*. These grants provide funding to specific agencies by using a statistically based process (McNamara, 2007). The government looks at indicators defined by legislation or regulations to determine if the agency is eligible for the money. Indicators may include per-capita income, if poverty is the issue being addressed; mortality, if there are concerns about elderly abuse or infant deaths; or unemployment rates, if crime has increased dramatically as the economic climate has changed in a particular city (perhaps a large business closed). The funding source will then determine statistically whether the agency can best use the money to address the issue of concern (McNamara, 2007).

Criminal justice agencies can also rely on private funds. These come from organizations or people involved in charitable giving, such as foundations, businesses, private individuals, and community groups. *Foundations,* such as the Bill and Melinda Gates Foundation, the Annie E. Casey Foundation, and others, provide funds to criminal justice agencies for programs that meet the foundation's areas of priority. For example, the Bill and Melinda Gates Foundation gives priority to funding related to diseases, public education, public libraries, and at-risk families. The Gates Foundation considers funding for programs that increase the number of children that graduate from high school on time, improve access to the Internet and other technological resources for public libraries that serve low-income and at-risk families, and provide housing resources to families who are currently homeless (see the Bill and Melinda Gates Foundation website at http://www.gatesfoundation.org/ for more information). In the case of juvenile courts that deal with abuse and neglect issues, funding from this source might create programming that encourages better housing and living conditions for children. *Corporate foundations* are private, for-profit businesses that provide funding or in-kind donations to criminal justice agencies. The corporation might donate land or a building to the agency to use for programming (McNamara, 2007). This would be considered an *in-kind donation* of material goods. No cash is exchanged. Walmart and JCPenney have been known to make in-kind donations of clothing and food to children in foster-care programs. Corporate foundations also provide monetary funds to agencies for programs and services.

Private individuals who are interested in programs or services in their communities also are sources of funds for criminal justice agencies. Private individuals may take on the challenge of creating the program and funding it in consultation with the criminal justice agency, or they may provide start-up or continuing funds to the agency (McNamara, 2007). Private individuals can also be involved with civic or community organizations that give funds to agencies. In this case, the Rotary Club or Kiwanis group might sell sandwiches as their annual fundraiser and donate the money collected to the agency. Religious organizations are commonly involved in this type of donation as well. During the U.S. government shutdown in October 2013, Head Start programs, which have been instrumental in providing educational, health, economic, and law enforcement benefits to 3- and 4-year-olds (National Head Start Association, n.d.) throughout the nation, were affected by the loss of funding. Yet a Head Start program in Georgia was able to remain open because of private funding. In the News 4.2 demonstrates how private groups and individuals are interested in specific types of programs and are willing to fund those programs when necessary.

In the News 4.2
Head Start Reopens: Preschool Program Secures Private Funding

The Ninth District Head Start program was open Tuesday, thanks to private funding.

Staff and parents were notified Monday that the preschool program was reopening, said Kay Laws, Head Start director for Ninth District Opportunity.

The program closed Monday due to the government shutdown, which coincided with the beginning of the federal program's grant cycle.

Ninth District Opportunity's Head Start covers 20 Georgia counties, including Dawson.

Before the word on reopening had come down, teachers at the local Head Start program, located off of Allen Street across from the library, were initially worried that students would suffer.

Teacher Bethany Goines said staff had been "just telling the kids we're having a fall break."

"The kids that struggle with separation anxiety have gotten to where they don't cry anymore in the mornings," Goines said. "Now, with this . . . [we were] afraid they [were] going to regress and have that anxiety all over again."

The primary concern for officials was the ability for parents to be able to find and afford child care on such short notice, which was given on Oct. 2.

"If you're needing someone to watch your children for a day or two, you might could locate family, friends, whatever," Laws said at the time. "But if you're having to plan for three or four weeks, then you'll have to look at different options."

After hearing about the Head Start dilemma, Houston philanthropists Laura and John Arnold donated $10 million to the National Head Start Association, temporarily funding programs across six states, including Georgia.

Laura Arnold is an ex-oil company executive and John Arnold is an investor. They chair The Arnold Foundation, a philanthropic organization established in 2008.

The annual grant for Ninth District's is $19.8 million alone.

According to a news release, if the government funds Head Start for the full year when the shutdown is over, the local programs will repay the funds made available by the national association at no interest.

The funding should keep Head Start programs open through the end of October.

"We are hopeful that the federal government will have worked out the budget by this time, and our grant funds will be available once again," Laws said. "In the meantime, we will be only making purchases that are necessary."

Margie Nichols, the grandparent of a child who attends the local Head Start program, said she thought it was "sad that the kids have to suffer."

"It's very hard for children this age to make adjustments," she said last week.

Nichols' grandchild is one of the special needs students at Head Start.

"Margie's grandchild receives services from us and from the board of education through the special needs program," said Barbara Padgett, Head Start Center Director.

Padgett had worked out arrangements with the school system to service their special needs students at Riverview Elementary.

The pre-K program run at Riverview Elementary continued to operate on a normal basis, according to Dawson County superintendent Keith Porter.

"There will be no cessation of pre-K services at Riverview Elementary," he said. "We've been waiting for any kind of word and, based on not hearing anything, we've found it safe to assume the funding for those programs is fine."

Unlike some students, the teachers didn't have much of an alternative plan until Head Start opened again.

"I've been working with children for 21 years and I've never seen anything like this," said Theresa Mitchell, a teacher.

Staff writer David Renner contributed to this report.

Source: From "Head Start Reopens: Preschool Program Secures Private Funding, by Carley Sharec, October 9, 2013, *Dawson Community News*. Retrieved from http://www.dawsonnews.com/archives/13050.

For the agencies, each funding source carries with it the advantage of receiving necessary resources to complete or implement a program. However, audits, reviews, mandated results, matching funds, and short-term funding opportunities (as noted in In the News 4.2) are distinct disadvantages (McNamara, 2007) of using these resources.

Management must be aware of what the funding source may or may not provide, as well as whether the source is interested in the program. Using resources from several funding agencies might be necessary to fully fund the desired program.

Agencies may run into the issue of not receiving funding at all, even though the service or program is required by state or local legislators. In the war on terrorism, for example, the federal government has been encouraging more cooperation and preparation among state and local police and fire departments to counter terrorist attacks. It has also initiated the First Responders programs, to identify and train those who will be the first on the scene of a major catastrophe. However, encouraging preparation is very different from paying for the preparation to occur. After the September 11, 2001, attacks on the World Trade Center and the Pentagon, the federal government provided grant dollars for emergency preparedness. Yet two years later, Kady (2003) reported that the Council on Foreign Relations had found that fire departments, for the most part, only had enough radios for half of their employees and enough breathing apparatuses for a third of those employed. Police departments did not have enough protective gear to secure a site after an attack that uses weapons of mass destruction, and public health laboratories were still without the basic equipment and the expertise to respond to a crisis involving biological or chemical weapons. Similar problems were found to persist even in 2007, as discussed by Thomas H. Kean and Lee H. Hamilton (the former chair and vice chair of the 9/11 Commission) in In the News 2.2 provided in Chapter 2. As a final note on funding issues, this textbook would be remiss if it did not mention that agencies that get funding from places other than tax dollars can become resource dependent and unable to provide services without the supplemental aid. In this case, the agency may actually focus its efforts in ways that support the initiatives of those providing the funding. In support of this argument, Alexander and Wells (2008) found that substance abuse providers may make referrals to agencies on the basis of funding strategies and potential. If the agency is likely to monetarily support the substance abuse provider agency, the provider agency is likely to use the supporting agency's services again and again. This type of referral-based strategy affects overall treatment comprehensiveness for the offender because the offender may fail to get the services needed as a result of the agency's narrowly focused goal of securing funding from one or two key funding sources.

Technology in Criminal Justice

It could be argued that technology has impacted criminal justice more than any other field. The invention of the car, cellular phone, desktop and laptop computer, computer-assisted dispatching (CAD), Global Positioning System (GPS), Internet, and other technological advances have changed the way crime occurs, how law enforcement polices society, how criminals are detained, how crime is detected, and how offenders are supervised. The 911 emergency system with which the public is so familiar uses computer technology to dispatch officers and other emergency personnel to addresses that appear on the dispatcher's screen. CAD can also assist in officer roll calls, in lookout calls to street officers, and with officer assessments. Courts now even rely on technological systems like computerized dockets and public access to computer records. No longer is there a reliance on keys for prison cell doors, which can now be opened remotely by the push of a button. Probation and parole officers do not have to spend hours driving around checking on offenders' whereabouts because they can track them with electronic monitoring and GPS units. The security field can watch entire interiors of stores and can follow suspicious people on camera without ever leaving a main security control booth. The security industry, particularly in Las Vegas, can even identify people with facial recognition technology as they walk through a casino. The satellite imagery used to take photographs during the inauguration ceremony of President-elect Barack Obama on January 20, 2009, which was attended by more than 1.8 million people, could also identify each person in the audience and on the stage—yet another technological wonder that will help law enforcement agencies.

As one can imagine, technology sets the bar very high for criminal justice. Society expects the system to use technology to enforce, detect, and reduce crime and its effects. Not only does society want police and the courts to have instant access to information on offenders and case law, but it also wants the correctional and probation/parole systems to closely monitor offenders living in society through technological tracking systems. The increased expectations for the use of technology can be detrimental to the system, as those involved become overwhelmed by the information or bogged down while trying to interpret or access the information. Messages through technology can also be confusing. No one can forget how failed communications over radios contributed to the deaths of firefighters and police officers in the collapse of the World Trade Center in 2001. In addition, images taken with video cameras or phones, such as those of the Rodney King beating in 1991, can bolster negative responses to the actions of criminal justice personnel. The simple taping or photographing of an incident by a third party and broadcasting of it without knowledge of the full story can impact the criminal justice system greatly by raising the demands it faces. As society uses technology to increase activities and information sharing, criminal justice struggles to undertake the increased workloads, education requirements, understandings, and training necessitated by technological advancements. The truth is that technology progresses much more quickly than the criminal justice system does.

One difficulty is finding employees who understand and can use the technology available to detect and reduce crime. New employees may not have been introduced to the type of technology used in criminal justice. A new worker in a prison facility must spend several hours in the control booth learning to use the equipment to manipulate cameras, open the doors with the correct sequence of buttons, and answer and transfer phone calls to the appropriate units and people. They are also expected to monitor the yards, dayrooms, cafeteria, school, and treatment offices, all while answering questions over the intercom or face-to-face from employees and inmates outside of the booth. These employees must learn the procedures as well as statutory and case law guidelines governing the technology while they become familiar with the gadget. As soon as workers are trained in the current technology, new software programs, gadgets, or upgrades are introduced. The agency is then right back to square one in training employees and remaining current in the technology. Understandably, current employees may demonstrate resistance to learning new technology. An employee who has worked for an agency for an extended time might not be willing to change from a paper-and-pencil method to a computerized format to complete the same task. What basically happens is that new technology brings with it new skill requirements for some while deskilling others (Manning, 1992).

A second difficulty in using technology in crime fighting is the enormous cost associated with it. Gadgets, computers, and training employees to work with technology all cost money. As discussed at the beginning of this chapter, criminal justice agencies do not always have the money to spend. Thus, if employees need to be retrained, the agency may send one or two workers to the training and expect them to return and train the others left behind. Although this sounds like a good idea, a significant amount of knowledge is lost in the transfer from trained employees to their colleagues who did not attend the training workshops. To highlight another issue, the agency might not be able to afford the technological upgrade or training and might have to make do with the technology already in use. This may not at first appear to be a problem, but if offenders are using the new technology to commit crimes while criminal justice agencies are not able to use it to *stop* crimes, the offenders are a step ahead.

Technology also creates new types of crime. In an age of information technology, people are sharing personal and financial information on the Internet. This has created a new market for fraud called identity theft. *Identify theft* occurs when someone wrongfully obtains and uses another person's personal information for purposes of fraud or deception. Identity theft usually results in economic gain on the part of the offender. The Federal Trade Commission reported more than 350,000 identity theft complaints in 2012 (Federal Trade Commission, 2013).

Cyberbullying is another offense we have heard a lot about in recent years. As we move to quickly embrace the Internet and other communication devices, we open the door for those with cruel intentions to more easily attack us in our homes and in our private lives. *Cyberbullying* is a form of bullying that relies on technological programs such as e-mail, instant messaging, websites, social networking sites, and chat or bash boards to intimidate, shame, and inflict "unwarranted hurt and embarrassment on its unsuspecting victims" (Beale & Hall, 2007, p. 9). Data available on cyberbullying show an increase in recent years (Chu, 2005; Hinduja & Patchin, 2008; Wolak, Mitchell, & Finkelhor, 2006).

Domestic and international terrorism pose new kinds of technological worry for the criminal justice system. *Cyberterrorism* is a form of terrorism that uses highly sophisticated technology—specifically, computers and the Internet—to plan and carry out terrorist attacks. Cyberterrorism can be used to damage the nation's economic, business, and military infrastructures (Schmalleger, 2008, p. 68). Terrorist groups are easily able to use the Internet to meet, organize, train, and convey messages among their members. As long as technology continues to advance, so will the efforts and abilities of groups that are antagonistic toward Americans as well as the laws that govern the United States. Another issue is the fact that any U.S. laws put in place to limit terrorist access to technology do not apply, and therefore cannot change behaviors outside of American borders (Schmalleger, 2008).

Judith Collins (2006) points out in her book how ill-equipped police are to handle identity theft (and probably the other Internet-based crimes discussed previously). According to her, identity theft continues to increase in frequency and severity, while law enforcement is having to learn how to track Internet provider addresses nationally and internationally, verify URLs (web addresses), and trace e-mails. These are the same police who may have been accustomed to chasing down leads with notebooks and interviews. Now, they must understand and be savvy about working with the internal programming of the computer and the Internet. Other crimes, such as theft of goods, cyberstalking, malicious/hate-crime communications, child pornography, copyright infringement, and many more, have dominated the Internet as well (Collins, 2006). As politicians and the criminal justice system address one offense and try to get a handle on how best to prevent it, a new offense pops up. Even though the access to technology increases the criminal justice system's efficiency, effectiveness, and information sharing, the problems it creates are overwhelming to an already overly burdened system.

Cultural and Demographic Issues

A society's shared attitudes, values, purpose, and routines define its *culture*. That culture affects what laws are created and determines socially acceptable and unacceptable behaviors. The legislators support the cultural norms and values by passing laws, while the criminal justice system upholds the culture by enforcing the laws. Consequently, it is important for all people to understand the culture of a community and to actively participate in it. Basically, all social structures are tied into the defined culture. It is only when the norms (shared cultural expectations) become confused that conflicts occur and we are likely to see law violations.

As an example of cultural conflicts, consider the current debate on marijuana legalization mentioned earlier. In recent years, a new argument has emerged regarding how the U.S. government should approach drug enforcement. Of course, there are many individuals supporting harsher sentences, strict enforcement, and renewed efforts to eradicate drugs as the only options in preventing a drug epidemic (French, 2005). But the fact that by 2005, a total of 10 states, including California, Arizona, Washington, Alaska, and others, had legalized marijuana for medicinal purposes through popular vote, and 2 states—Washington and Colorado—legalized recreational marijuana use in 2012–2013, cannot be ignored. This represents a change in philosophy regarding drugs, specifically marijuana, among U.S. citizens. The legalization and decriminalization movement has also garnered support in other states. New York, for example, has worked to reform the "Rockefeller Drug Laws," and 10 other states have adopted laws that greatly reduce the penalties associated with the possession, use, and sale of small amounts of drugs (French, 2005). So cultural acceptance of marijuana is in transition. Legal and political approaches have to keep pace with what society holds as collectively acceptable; otherwise, a cultural gap occurs, creating difficulties for the criminal justice system in that the expectations are no longer clear, and following one set of expectations (legal and political) generates discord among the people holding the second set of expectations (citizens).

One challenge to the cultural agreements in American society is caused by immigration. Immigration is an ongoing political and social debate. Immigration influences the norms and values of the members of a community because new individuals bring with them from other countries their own understandings of the law and what constitutes acceptable and unacceptable behaviors. As In the News 4.3 points out, cultural and demographic changes in a community's makeup shape how the criminal justice system functions. For instance, as more Spanish-speaking immigrants move into the Midwest, police officers are finding themselves in need of second-language skills. Of course, this has a trickle-down effect once there are arrests of Spanish-speaking suspects. Workers in the prosecutor's office, the court, the probation office, the prison, and the parole office will also experience a need for Spanish-speaking employees.

In the News 4.3
Hablas Español? Police Are Learning—Officers
Who Breach Language Barrier Increase in Value

PEORIA—A few months ago, Scott Schraeder, a deputy with the Peoria [Illinois] County Sheriff's office, came across a man drifting around the parking lot of a Bellevue gas station with no identification and no idea where he was. Avoiding eye contact and fidgeting with his pockets, the man first answered Schraeder's questions with silence.

And to make a tricky situation even worse, the little that he did say was all in Spanish. Though not fluent in the language, Schraeder began probing for answers in the stranger's native tongue.

"I just established the basics with him. What's your name? What's your age? Where are you going?" said Schraeder, who took two years of Spanish in high school and has maintained his skill ever since.

He eventually gathered that the man was from Chicago in search of work downstate and had been abandoned by his fellow travelers. He was taken to a local homeless shelter for the night and ended up disappearing the next day with another group of Hispanic men.

"Who knows where they wandered off to?" Schraeder said.

While law enforcement officials state these types of encounters in central Illinois are infrequent, if not rare, the steady change in demographics has increased the appreciation for bilingual officers.

"We're fortunate to have him with us," Deputy Chief Joe Needham said.

Practically nonexistent 20 years ago, the Hispanic population has gained a foothold in mid- to small-sized towns throughout the Midwest. In the Tri-County Area alone, the Hispanic population grew from 3,642 to 5,399—a 48.2 percent increase—from 1990 to 2000, according to data from the U.S. Census Bureau. The latest figures peg Peoria's share at 3,895 residents—or about 3.5 percent.

Drawn to the region by manufacturing and agricultural jobs, Hispanics are moving here in greater numbers that show no signs of stopping.

"I don't want to say it happens every day, but I know a half a dozen times or more a month I'm called upon to translate," said Javier Grow, a Spanish-speaking traffic officer with the Peoria Police Department. "It kind of goes in spurts."

Though some authorities may privately bristle at learning a second language to do their job, experts say open and clear lines of communication are crucial in crime-fighting. Waiting for translations can lengthen response time and misunderstanding could lead to fatal mistakes.

"Officer Friendly needs to be able to speak with everyone if [he or she wants] to work effectively," said Virginia Martinez, an attorney with the Mexican American Legal Defense and Educational Fund, a civil rights organization for Latinos living in the United States. "In the meantime, you don't want to put the general population at risk."

Aside from the lack of communication, culture issues can further complicate police–Hispanic relations. Most immigrants lack a firm grasp of American laws and customs and can harbor suspicion toward law enforcement because of corrupt police forces in their home countries.

"A lot of the community distrusts police. The Hispanic community is very sensitive, you need to earn their trust," said Catalina Zavala, director of Hispanic services at Peoria's Friendship House. "I talk to them and say the police are there to help them not hurt them."

The hot button issue of illegal immigration also can cast a long shadow.

"Because of their immigration status, many of these Hispanics try to stay away from police," said Leigh Culver, a police officer in Omaha, Neb., who researched language barriers in law enforcement. A reluctance to contact police often makes them ideal victims, Culver added.

Even so, many agencies said language and cultural barriers between police and the Hispanic community haven't reached a boiling point. In fact, the majority said they make do with just a few or no bilingual officers or borrow ones from large departments.

"I've been to Marquette Heights, I've been to East Peoria, I've been up to Chillicothe, Morton," said Grow, who grew up learning the language from his Spanish mother. "I've been called at one, two o'clock in the morning. When I'm at work, when I've just gotten off, whenever."

Some get creative and utilize friends, family members or others to help.

The village of Bartonville has two auxiliary officers who can speak the language as well as emergency dispatchers trained in basic Spanish, Police Chief Brian Fengel said. If they're not available, his wife can translate after learning Spanish during a stint as a missionary nurse in Chile.

Morton Police Chief Nick Graff said until recently his department counted one fluent officer among its ranks. "Unfortunately," Graff added, "he got hired away by corporate security with Caterpillar." Patrol officers there now rely on seasonal workers from Mexico at the nearby Nestlé pumpkin canning plant to help translate.

Chillicothe resident Bennie Razo, who sits on the city's police commission, has been interpreting for officers there about 35 years. "They call me and say I can't understand what's going on," he said. "Most of the time they can handle it on their own."

To aid small police departments in netting and keeping bilingual officers, state and federal agencies offer an array of courses in survivor Spanish.

For example, Illinois State Police and the Police Training Institute at the University of Illinois have a course at their academy that teaches cadets basic words and key phrases to help them communicate in a crisis situation, according to Trooper Juan Valenzuela.

(Continued)

(Continued)

Although pressure to adapt in the Tri-County Area remains low, in other parts of the state, fluency in Spanish has become indispensable. Once a graying hamlet of 6,000 on the banks of the Illinois River, Beardstown is now home to more than 1,000 Hispanics. Beardstown's Mayor Bob Walters estimated the city's Hispanic population jumped over the years from zero to about 35 percent.

The flood of new residents, mainly from Mexico, came to Beardstown looking for jobs at the large Excel pork processing plant.

As a result, an officer encountering a Spanish-speaking person is now an everyday occurrence, Police Chief Tom Schlueter said. To bridge the language gap, almost all of the full-time officers have gone through a basic Spanish course for law enforcement, and city ordinances are now printed in Spanish, he said. The department still uses translators to help with investigations or questionings.

Though influx of immigrants and their families has been a boom for business, the changes have stressed the town and department's limited resources.

"It's been a strain on us financially," Schlueter said. "I wouldn't say we're getting used to it. But, we're getting through it."

Demographic factors such as age, race, gender, and socioeconomic class have also been identified to affect crime rates. Erickson (quoted in Lipke, 2000) stated that 90% of all violent crimes are committed by men, and one-half by people under the age of 25. Therefore, in areas where there are large numbers of males and young people, the crime rates are higher. In Louisiana prior to Hurricane Katrina, citizens had a higher-than-average chance of being victimized. Young males between the ages of 18 and 24 made up 5.2% of the overall Louisiana population. This was the seventh-highest percentage in the United States (Lipke, 2000). An excellent example of how age contributes to criminal behavior can be found in areas of the country that host spring breakers. Police departments in these areas face the same concerns as those with youthful populations. From March 1 through April 3, 2013, the Panama City Police Department, the Florida Highway Patrol, and the Florida Division of Alcoholic Beverages and Tobacco issued 5,676 traffic citations and made 3,438 arrests, including booking 657 offenders through a mobile beach booking system and 1922 people into county jail (Garmen, 2013). Other areas, such as the Midwest, have lower overall populations and crime rates. One potential explanation for this is that people living in the Midwest primarily reside in suburban and rural areas, which have less crime than cities.

Analysis of official arrest statistics has traditionally shown a disproportionate number of blacks and indicates that males are arrested three to four times more often than are females (Cox, Allen, Hanser, & Conrad, 2008). Lipke (2000) has suggested that the factors leading to the social disorder of a neighborhood (i.e., average income of the residents, transience of the population, housing conditions, educational levels, and family structure) can increase crime and greatly impact the criminal justice system. Cox et al. (2008) argue that few direct connections to criminal behavior can be drawn by looking only at gender, race, and age without also looking at the social-environmental factors that contribute to crime. The truth is that none of the characteristics mentioned in this section can be identified as a direct cause of crime. They may be contributory and should be considered in prevention and diversion approaches, but they are best viewed as indicators of problem areas where police and other criminal justice agencies should focus their resources.

Legal Pressures

As was pointed out in the previous section, laws are supposed to be reflective of the culture. In the United States, laws are based on *common law,* or customs, traditions, and precedents. Adopted from the British tradition, the common beliefs and values held by U.S. citizens are allowed to dictate what should and should not be illegal. Once an action is determined as collectively unacceptable and forbidden by written legislation, it is considered a *statutory* or *criminal law.* Statutory laws provide the legal definition of crime and its subsequent punishment. Such laws apply to everyone regardless of their status in society—this includes police officers and others in the criminal justice system. Consider as an example a statutory law stating that people in vehicles must wear seat belts. This law is required to be enforced by traffic patrol officers who also have to wear seat belts while patrolling. Punishments for violating statutory laws are indicated in the law itself. Hence, patrol officers will issue citations to those violating the seat belt ordinance.

CAREER HIGHLIGHT BOX
PSYCHOLOGISTS

Nature of the Work

Psychologists study mental processes and human behavior by observing, interpreting, and recording how people and other animals relate to one another and the environment.

Duties

Psychologists typically do the following:

- Conduct scientific studies to study behavior and brain function
- Collect information through observations, interviews, surveys, tests, and other methods
- Find patterns that will help them understand and predict behavior

(Continued)

(Continued)

- Use their knowledge to increase understanding among individuals and groups
- Develop programs that improve schools and workplaces by addressing psychological issues
- Work with individuals, couples, and families to help them make desired changes to behaviors
- Identify and diagnose mental, behavioral, or emotional disorders
- Develop and carry out treatment plans
- Collaborate with physicians or social workers to help treat patients

Psychology seeks to understand and explain thoughts, emotions, feelings, and behavior. Depending on the topic of study, psychologists use techniques such as observation, assessment, and experimentation to develop theories about the beliefs and feelings that influence a person's actions.

Psychologists often gather information and evaluate behavior through controlled laboratory experiments, psychoanalysis, or psychotherapy. They also may administer personality, performance, aptitude, or intelligence tests. They look for patterns of behavior or cause-and-effect relationships between events, and use this information when testing theories in their research or treating patients.

The following are common occupational specialties:

Clinical psychologists assess, diagnose, and treat mental, emotional, and behavioral disorders. Clinical psychologists help people deal with problems ranging from short-term personal issues to severe, chronic conditions.

Clinical psychologists are trained to use a variety of approaches to help individuals. Although strategies generally differ by specialty, psychologists often interview patients, give diagnostic tests, and provide individual, family, or group psychotherapy. They also design behavior modification programs and help patients implement their particular program.

Some clinical psychologists focus on certain populations, such as children or the elderly, or certain specialties, such as the following:

Health psychologists study how psychological factors affect health and illness. They educate both patients and medical staff about psychological issues, and promote healthy-living strategies. They also investigate health issues, such as substance abuse or teenage pregnancy, and develop programs to address the problems.

Neuropsychologists study the relation between the brain and behavior. They typically work with patients who have sustained a brain injury.

Clinical psychologists often consult with other medical personnel regarding the best treatment for patients, especially treatment that includes medication. Two states, Louisiana and New Mexico, currently allow clinical psychologists to prescribe medication to patients. In most states, however, only psychiatrists and medical doctors may prescribe medication for treatment. For more information, see the profile on physicians and surgeons.

Counseling psychologists advise people on how to deal with their problems. They help patients understand their problems, including issues in the home, workplace, or community. Through counseling, they work with patients to identify the strengths or resources they can use to manage problems. For information on similar workers, see the profiles on mental health counselors and marriage and family therapists, substance abuse and behavioral disorder counselors, and social workers.

Developmental psychologists study the psychological progress and development that take place throughout life. Many focus on children and adolescents. Developmental psychologists also increasingly study aging and problems faced by the elderly.

Forensic psychologists use psychological principles in the legal and criminal justice system to help judges, attorneys, and other legal specialists understand the psychological findings of a particular case. They often appear in court as expert witnesses. They typically specialize in family court, civil court, or criminal court.

Industrial-organizational psychologists apply psychology to the workplace by using psychological principles and research methods to solve problems and improve the quality of work life. They study issues such as workplace productivity, management or employee working styles, and morale. They also work with management on matters such as policy planning, employee screening or training, and organizational development.

School psychologists apply psychological principles and techniques to education-related issues. For example, they may address students' learning and behavioral problems, evaluate students' performances, and counsel students and families. They also may consult with other school-based professionals to suggest improvements to teaching, learning, and administrative strategies.

Social psychologists study how people's mindsets and behavior are shaped by social interactions. They examine both individual and group interactions and may investigate ways to improve negative interactions.

Some psychologists become professors or combine research with teaching. For more information, see the profiles on postsecondary teachers and high school teachers.

Work Environment

Psychologists held about 174,000 jobs in 2010. About 34 percent of psychologists were self-employed, 29 percent worked in educational services, and 20 percent worked in healthcare settings.

Some psychologists work alone, which may include independent research or individually counseling patients. Others work as part of a healthcare team, collaborating with physicians, social workers, and others to treat illness and promote overall wellness.

Many clinical and counseling psychologists in private practice have their own offices and can set their own schedules. Other typical workplaces include clinics, hospitals, rehabilitation facilities, and community and mental health centers.

Most research psychologists work in colleges and universities, government agencies, or private research organizations.

Most school psychologists work in public schools, ranging in level from nursery school through college. They also work in private schools, universities, hospitals and clinics, community treatment centers, and independent practice.

(Continued)

(Continued)

Work Schedules

Psychologists in private practice can often set their own hours, and many work part time as independent consultants. However, they often offer evening or weekend hours to accommodate clients. Those employed in hospitals, nursing homes, or other healthcare facilities also may have evening or weekend shifts. Most psychologists working in clinics, government, industry, or schools work full-time schedules during regular business hours.

Training, Other Qualifications, and Advancements

Psychologists need a master's, specialist, or doctoral degree in psychology. Practicing psychologists also need a license or certification.

Education

Most clinical, counseling, and research psychologists need a doctoral degree. Psychologists can complete a Ph.D. in psychology or a Doctor of Psychology (Psy.D.) degree. A Ph.D. in psychology is a research degree that culminates in a comprehensive exam and a dissertation based on original research. In clinical, counseling, school, or health service settings, students usually complete a 1-year internship as part of the doctoral program. The Psy.D. is a clinical degree and is often based on practical work and examinations rather than a dissertation.

School psychologists need a master's, specialist (Ed. S. degree, which requires a minimum of 60 graduate semester hours), or doctoral degree in school psychology. Because their work addresses education and mental health components of students' development, school psychologists' training includes coursework in both education and psychology.

Graduates with a master's degree in psychology can work as industrial-organizational psychologists. When working under the supervision of a doctoral psychologist, master's graduates also can work as psychological assistants in clinical, counseling, or research settings. Master's degree programs typically include courses in industrial-organizational psychology, statistics, and research design.

Entry into psychology graduate programs is competitive. Most master's degree programs do not require an undergraduate major in psychology, but do require coursework in introductory psychology, experimental psychology, and statistics. Some doctoral degree programs require applicants to have a master's degree in psychology, while others will accept applicants with a bachelor's degree and a major in psychology.

Most graduates with a bachelor's degree in psychology find work in other fields such as business administration, sales, or education.

Licenses and Certification

In most states, practicing psychology or using the title of "psychologist" requires licensure or certification.

In all states and the District of Columbia, psychologists who practice independently must be licensed. Licensing laws vary by state and type of position. Most clinical and counseling psychologists need a doctorate in psychology, an internship, at least 1 to 2 years of professional experience, and to pass the Examination for Professional Practice in Psychology. Information on specific requirements by state can be found from the Association of State and Provincial Licensing Boards. In many states, licensed psychologists must complete continuing education courses to keep their licenses.

School psychologists must be licensed or certified to practice in schools. This credential varies by state and is usually obtained through the state's department of education. Information on specific requirements by state can be found from the National Association of School Psychologists (NASP).

In addition, NASP awards the Nationally Certified School Psychologist (NCSP) designation, which is a nationally recognized certification. Currently, 30 states accept the NCSP as a route to licensing or certification. To become nationally certified, candidates need a minimum of 60 graduate semester hours in a school psychology program, a 1,200-hour supervised internship, and to pass the National School Psychology Examination.

The American Board of Professional Psychology awards specialty certification in 13 areas of psychology, such as clinical health, couple and family, psychoanalysis, or rehabilitation. Although board certification is not required for most psychologists, it can demonstrate professional expertise in a specialty area. Some hospitals and clinics do require certification. In those cases, candidates must have a doctoral degree in psychology, state license or certification, and any additional criteria of the specialty field.

Training

Psychologists typically need previous related work experience. To become licensed, for example, psychologists must have completed one or more of the following: predoctoral or postdoctoral supervised experience, an internship, or a residency program. School psychologists also must complete a yearlong supervised internship program to become licensed or certified.

Important Qualities

Analytical skills. Analytical skills are important when performing psychological research. Psychologists must be able to examine the information they collect and draw logical conclusions from them.

Communication skills. Psychologists must have strong communications skills because they spend much of their time listening to and speaking with patients.

Observational skills. Psychologists study attitude and behavior. They must be able to watch people and understand the possible meanings of people's facial expressions, body positions, actions, and interactions.

(Continued)

(Continued)

Patience. Because research or treatment of patients may take a long time, psychologists must be able to demonstrate patience. They also must be patient when dealing with people who have mental or behavioral disorders.

People skills. Psychologists study people and help people. They must be able to work well with their clients, patients, and other medical professionals.

Problem-solving skills. Psychologists need problem-solving skills to find treatments or solutions for mental and behavioral problems.

Trustworthiness. Patients must be able to trust their psychologists. Psychologists also must keep patients' problems in confidence, and patients must be able to trust psychologists' expertise in treating sensitive problems.

Employment

The median annual wage of psychologists was $68,640 in May 2010. The median wage is the wage at which half of the workers in an occupation earned more than that amount and half earned less. The lowest 10 percent earned less than $39,200, and the top 10 percent earned more than $111,810.

The median annual wages of psychologist occupations in May 2010 were the following:

- $87,330 for industrial-organizational psychologists
- $66,810 for clinical, counseling, and school psychologists
- $89,900 for psychologists, all other

Psychologists in private practice can often set their own hours, and many work part time as independent consultants. However, they often offer evening or weekend hours to accommodate clients. Those employed in hospitals, nursing homes, or other healthcare facilities may also have evening or weekend shifts. Most psychologists working in clinics, government, industry, or schools work full-time schedules during regular business hours.

Job Outlook

Overall employment of psychologists is expected to grow 22 percent from 2010 to 2020, faster than the average for all occupations. Employment growth will vary by specialty.

Employment of clinical, counseling, and school psychologists is expected to grow 22 percent, faster than the average for all occupations. Greater demand for psychological services in schools, hospitals, mental health centers, and social services agencies should drive employment growth.

Demand for clinical and counseling psychologists will increase as people continue to turn to psychologists to help solve or manage their problems. More psychologists will be needed to help people deal with issues such as depression and other mental disorders, marriage and family problems, job stress, and addiction. Psychologists also will be needed to provide services to an aging population, helping people deal with the mental and physical changes that happen as they grow older. Through both research and practice, psychologists are also helping other special groups, such as veterans suffering from war trauma, other trauma survivors, and individuals with autism.

Demand for psychologists in the health care industry is also expected to increase, because their work on teams with doctors, social workers, and other [health care] professionals provides patients with comprehensive, interdisciplinary treatments. In addition to treating mental and behavioral health issues, psychologists work on teams to develop or administer prevention or wellness programs.

As the overall number of students grows, more school psychologists will be needed to work with students, particularly those with special needs, learning disabilities, and behavioral issues. Schools also rely on school psychologists to assess and counsel students. Additionally, school psychologists will be needed to study how both in-school and out-of-school factors affect learning, which teachers and administrators can use to improve education.

Employment of industrial-organizational psychologists is expected to grow 35 percent, much faster than the average for all occupations, as organizations use these psychologists to help select and keep employees, increase productivity, and identify potential workplace improvements. However, because it is a small occupation, the fast employment growth will result in only about 800 new jobs over the 10-year period.

Job Prospects

Job prospects should be best for those who have a doctoral degree in an applied specialty and those with a specialist or doctoral degree in school psychology. Because admission to psychology graduate programs is so selective, job opportunities for doctoral graduates are expected to be fair.

Employment of school psychologists will grow to accommodate the increasing number of children in schools, and many will also be needed to replace workers who retire. Because of the limited number of graduates in this specialty, school psychologists are expected to have good job opportunities.

Candidates with a master's degree will face competition for positions, and many master's degree holders will find jobs in a related field outside of psychology. Even industrial-organizational psychologists, despite much faster than average employment growth, are expected to face competition for positions due to the large number of qualified graduates. Industrial-organizational psychologists with extensive training in quantitative research methods and computer science may have a competitive edge.

SOURCE: Bureau of Labor Statistics, U.S. Department of Labor, *Occupational Outlook Handbook, 2012–13 Edition*, Psychologists, on the Internet at http://www.bls.gov/ooh/life-physical-and-social-science/psychologists.htm.

Procedural law, another type of statutory law, is a set of rules that regulates how an offender is processed by the criminal justice system. Rules on search and seizure, gathering and submission of evidence, arrest procedures, and waivers to adult court from juvenile courts are specified processes contained in procedural law. Procedural laws can change because of court decisions or legislative enactments. Individuals working in the criminal justice system have to stay abreast of new decisions that change the processes they use to perform their duties.

Case law also impacts the criminal justice system. This type of law is created by the courts when they review actions that come before them. The decisions made by the court form a precedent and are written down. Other courts take into consideration the reasoning behind precedents when settling future cases. Traditionally, decisions made by the U.S. Supreme Court have the most impact on the daily operations of the criminal justice system, although precedence can come from appellate courts as well. *In re Gault* (1967), for example, provided constitutional rights to juveniles appearing in juvenile court, while *Furman v. Georgia* (1972) forbade the use of capital punishment for anyone for more than a decade in U.S. history. Punishments for crimes that had customarily allowed for a death sentence had to be adjusted as a result of *Furman.* This decision has been overturned, though there is currently some ongoing debate within state legislatures and courts on the death penalty. Even the U.S. Supreme Court has revisited the issue by limiting habeas corpus challenges by death row inmates (*McCleskey v. Zant,* 1991), barring the death penalty for the mentally challenged (*Atkins v. Virginia,* 2002), and deciding in *Roper v. Simmons* (2005) that juveniles—those under the age of 18—cannot receive capital punishment. These decisions and others like them greatly influence the choices made, operations, policies, and procedures of those working in the criminal justice system.

Civil laws and the liabilities they bring are constantly on the minds of criminal justice personnel. *Civil laws* are focused on relationships among people, businesses, organizations, and governmental agencies. Civil laws specify rules for contracts, libel, unfair practices, divorce, child custody, the manufacture and sale of goods and services, as well as other contractual issues (Schmalleger, 2008). If someone or some organization violates a civil law, a lawsuit that seeks a monetary award, not a punishment, may follow. Civil suits can be filed with the state or federal courts. Violations of civil law are considered wrongful acts but not a crime. Criminal justice personnel can be held liable for civil violations if it is found by the court that they acted in gross negligence or in an unfair or unjust manner. Consider racial profiling, for example. A 2000 article by Jost reported that 59% of those individuals surveyed in a Gallup poll felt that racial profiling was widespread, while 81% said they disapproved of the practice. Claims that the police are profiling and pulling over drivers based on race have ignited many civil lawsuits in numerous states. Damages for cases proven to show racial profiling by police have cost taxpayers and policing agencies thousands of dollars in addition to forcing new data collection and statistical procedures onto police departments. New York City is one such police department that started collecting data and analyzing it with an independent auditor and civil rights groups as a result of a civil settlement involving racial profiling in 2003 (Wood, 2006).

Administrative laws have also been used in preventing racial profiling and discrimination. These laws are created by the government to control the activities of industry, businesses, and individuals (Schmalleger, 2008). Civil rights in hiring, for example, have been controlled through administrative laws. Agencies cannot systematically pass over candidates with equal or greater qualifications in favor of a particular race or class. If it can be proven that an organization is doing so, the agency is subject to criminal sanctions as well as civil litigations.

Administrative laws, like other laws, are not always as obvious as one would hope. In past practice, the 1964 Civil Rights Act has primarily resulted in a focus on disparities in minority hiring, promotions, and other equal opportunities in the workplace. But the recently determined case of *Ricci v. DeStafano* (2009) may alter traditional administrative practices. In a question of reverse discrimination in New Haven, Connecticut, the U.S. Supreme Court decided that the city of New Haven could not arbitrarily throw out firefighters' promotional exam scores because no minorities qualified for promotion based on the results. The 5–4 ruling stated that a fear of litigation because of disparate impact—when an action unintentionally favors one group over another—is not an appropriate reason to throw out the test scores. To ignore the scores, the city had to demonstrate that by allowing the scores to result in promotions, there was a disparate impact on a particular race or class, or they had ignored other assessment procedures that would have reduced the adverse impact on a particular race or class. The plaintiffs argued that by failing to certify and promote the individuals scoring highest on the exam, the city had violated Title VII of the 1964 Civil Rights Act through disparate treatment of a particular group or individual based on race. In this case, all qualified firefighters, regardless of race or class, had the opportunity to prepare for and take the promotional exams, and the test was viewed by the Supreme Court as open and fair (*Ricci v. DeStafano*, 2009). In another case, *Fisher v. University of Texas at Austin* (2013), Abigail Fisher, a white student, claimed she was denied admission to the University of Texas at Austin because of her race. The Supreme Court vacated the lower court's decision and remanded the case back to the lower court for additional consideration. The Supreme Court did not side with either party but claimed that, as previously decided in *Grutter v. Bollinger* (2003), the university can establish a goal of diversity as long as the goal meets strict scrutiny in its implementation (meaning the university's admissions policy uses race as only a single element considered in conjunction with a broad array of qualifications and characteristics of applicants). As of October 2013, the Supreme Court faces another civil rights challenge involving race and university admissions policies in *Schuette v. Coalition to Defend Affirmative Action, Integration, and Immigrant Rights and Fight for Equality by Any Means Necessary* (12-682). These rulings demonstrate the difficulties that exist for agencies in interpreting and following administrative, civil, procedural, and criminal laws while still developing a diverse environment and servicing their clients.

Laws change daily, and this has incalculable impact on the criminal justice system. Agencies often wait anxiously for rulings from the U.S. Supreme Court on constitutional interpretations. How a police officer should handle an arrest one day may vary the next. Whether correctional institutions can deny privileges or operate over capacity can change with a single court decision. Politicians can enact new laws that significantly transform the goals and mission of a single criminal justice agency. As shown in *Ricci v. DeStefano* (2009), even established directives and understandings of the law can be overturned. Basically, laws create a complex environment within which the criminal justice system and its many facets must operate.

Unions

Even though there has been a gradual decline in union membership overall, in 2012, a total of 14.4 million U.S. workers still belonged to unions. Unions are now included in every type of professional and blue-collar industry in the United States and currently constitute 11.3% of the total makeup of the workforce (Bureau of Labor Statistics, 2013):

> In 2012, 7.3 million employees in the public sector belonged to a union, compared with 7.0 million union workers in the private sector. The union membership rate for public-sector workers (35.9 percent) was substantially higher than the rate for private-sector workers (6.6 percent). Within the public sector, local government workers had the highest union membership rate, 41.7 percent. This group includes workers in heavily unionized occupations, such as teachers, police officers, and firefighters. (Bureau of Labor Statistics, 2013, para. 4)

Trade and labor unions are deeply embedded in American history. As early as the 1700s, groups of workers would refuse to perform their jobs until working conditions were improved or their demands for benefits, such as shorter working days, were met. As time went on, formal unions (sometimes called federations) were created. *Unions* include groups of employees who decide to bargain collectively through majority vote for improvements in their jobs such as increases in wages, benefits, and better working conditions (American Federation of Labor, 2008). Collective bargaining units have been very successful in increasing wages for those belonging to the union. In a 2003 Bureau of Labor Statistics study, workers in the public protection sectors—firefighters; police, detectives, and public servants; sheriffs, bailiffs, and other law enforcement officers; and correctional institution officers—were found to make $13.07 an hour as compared to $10.26 for those working in the same occupations but not involved in a union. Guards and police in the private sector were paid an average wage of $11.10 an hour as compared to $7.76 an hour for their nonunion counterparts (Foster, 2003). As they have done throughout history, unions use their legal rights to independently change employer treatment of employees and rely on political and legislative acts to create laws governing the workplace.

In businesses where unions are present, the company is required to negotiate and work within a union contract that governs the actions of both the management and employees. Once negotiated and accepted, a union contract lasts somewhere between three and five years. The contract covers a number of issues, including due process provisions on suspension and termination; nondiscrimination policies; seniority systems; wages; medical, health, and retirement benefits; grievance procedures to resolve conflicts between management and employees; working hours, breaks, and overtime;

union membership requirements and fair share obligations; and identification of union and management representatives. The contract will also state when the union can and cannot strike, as well as when and if employees can be locked out of the workplace by the management (American Federation of Labor, 2008). In most instances, salary increases, vacation time, shift differential issues, and paid holidays are also identified in the union contract. Each contract is tailored to the specific needs of the agency and its employees, and it may vary from negotiation period to negotiation period. There are no guarantees of what may appear in a new contract once an old contract expires and negotiations take place.

The police were one of the first organizations to unionize in criminal justice. The International Union of Police Associations (IUPA) was founded in 1954 as the National Conference of Police Associations (NCPA) (IUPA, 2013). It currently includes policing unions in the United States and Canada and is chartered by the American Federation of Labor and Congress of International Organizations (AFL-CIO), a 55-member federation of national and international labor unions. Another nationwide policing union is the National Association of Police Organizations (NAPO), which was created in 1978 (NAPO, 2013). These unions have been very influential in securing benefits for law enforcement officers at the local, state, and national levels. The IUPA played pivotal roles in passing the National Police Officers Bill of Rights, the Fair Labor Standards Act (FLSA), and several amendments to the FLSA. Efforts on behalf of this union limited the number of hours police officers could work in a week without compensation and ensured that overtime was paid at time-and-a-half rates by policing organizations (IUPA, 2013). In addition, NAPO (2013) supported the Medal of Valor for Public Safety Officers; the Police, Fire, and Emergency Officers Educational Assistance Fund of 1998; and the Bulletproof Vest Partnership Grant Act of 1998, as well as many other legislative initiatives related to violent crimes, family leave and compensation, and death benefits for officers killed in the line of duty. There is no doubt that policing unions have benefited law enforcement officers by creating legislation that benefits police officers while defeating efforts that undermine the interests of law enforcement (NAPO, 2013).

Although not as powerful as policing unions, correctional officers and probation officers have unionized in various parts of the country typically by state or county. These associations tend to be less political and legislatively driven at the federal level than the policing unions, working only to maximize the benefits of their membership within specific agencies and geographical areas. Membership in these labor unions is meager when compared to other unionized fields. The only national union servicing these groups is the American Federation of State, County & Municipal Employees, which includes many types of public employees including teachers, child care providers, nurses, and correctional personnel (American Federation of State, County, and Municipal Employees, 2013). Although unions have made positive changes in policing and other fields in criminal justice, collective bargaining groups still have their critics. Literature on policing unions, in particular, points to the belief that collective bargaining changes the nature of the employee's relationship with the police department. Critics claim that bargaining allows for reduced police chief authority in setting policy and making policy decisions. Traditionally, the police chief had the ability to change policy without consulting with union leaders. Some collective bargaining contracts now require consultation on policy changes regardless of whether they directly impact working conditions and employees or traditional managerial responsibilities (Kadleck, 2003, p. 342; see also Hewitt, 1978; Salerno, 1981; Sylvia, 1994). Other critics have argued that unions are indicative of bad management practices by police chiefs and demonstrate a failure by the agency to effectively respond to the police officers' needs (Kadleck, 2003, p. 344; see also Bolinger, 1981; International Association of Chiefs of Police [IACP], 1977; Sirene, 1985). Finally, the accountability of policing unions has been questioned. In this case, critics argue that since unions have a hand in making government policy and in potentially setting budget priorities but are not elected or appointed by the public, they are not truly accountable to the public (Adams, 2008; Kadleck, 2003, p. 345; see also IACP, 1977; Kearney, 1995; Levi, 1977).

Politics

The political environment surrounding criminal justice is complex and multifaceted. The simple election of a prosecuting attorney can change the way court procedures are handled and the types of cases heard in courts. An appointment of a chief to a police department can change the expectations of the law enforcement officers in a town and can impact the types of offenders arrested. Political pressures are inherent in the system because criminal justice administrators are appointed or elected. Political activities get judges onto the bench, police chiefs appointed, and legislators who decide the law elected. If those criminal justice professionals who are elected or appointed do not pay attention to the public's wants, they can easily lose their positions. In an article discussing politics in criminal justice, Jost (2009) recalls a 1980s election where three liberal California Supreme Court judges failed to capture the public's vote because of their past decisions not to uphold death sentences from state courts. This resulted in the governor appointing Republican justices to the previously all-Democratic Supreme Court.

Political changes made before, during, and after elections have enormous impact on both the formal and informal processes of the criminal justice system. The direct and indirect effects of political decisions are realized throughout the entire criminal justice system. Legislative decisions made before or after an election, or during a politician's tenure in office, can indirectly impact budgets, agency operations, organizational effectiveness, and job duties. Court decisions by elected judges can change the way crimes are processed and which crimes result in arrest. For example, if it is commonplace for a newly elected judge to throw out cases involving small amounts of illegal substances, then the police will eventually stop making arrests for those crimes. Judges may also have limited discretion in the courtroom regarding sentencing as a result of legislative requirements on punishment. Legislators may pass sentencing guidelines because of pressures from the public to get tough on crime. Budgetary constraints enacted at the national level, through budget decisions by the House and

Senate, will also change the programming provided at local probation offices and in correctional centers since government funding filters from the top down.

Pressures by special interest groups in the community or at the national level directly impact criminal justice. Victim advocate groups, for example, have forced tremendous changes in how police respond to domestic violence calls. As a result of their demands for change, it is routine for officers to arrest at least one of the parties involved in the domestic violence incident. Not only does this limit autonomy in policing domestic violence, but it also increases the prosecutor's and court's caseloads. In addition, it results in higher costs of incarceration as the offender sits in jail awaiting court or bail or is sentenced to an anger management program or institution. Even single individuals can lobby the legislation for legal changes that impact how line staff in criminal justice do their jobs. Megan's Law is one example of how a single person or family can change the requirements of agencies. Megan's Law is the result of a New Jersey case involving 7-year-old Megan Kanka, who was raped and killed by a child molester who had moved across the street from the Kanka family. After her death, her family lobbied New Jersey legislators to pass a law requiring states to warn the public about known sex offenders. In 1994, New Jersey implemented the statute, which was followed in 1996 by federal legislation. Now, all states have some form of Megan's Law (Zgoba, Witt, Dalessandro, & Veysey, 2008). The implementation of the law has increased responsibilities for those in criminal justice, as the police are required to register sex offenders and to update registries when necessary. Essentially, the communities in which the local police, prosecutor, judge, and sheriff work can apply pressure to these individuals and change the way jobs are done.

Indirect pressures and direct pressures can come from all avenues. As a result, the criminal justice system may have a difficult time navigating its way through the various political agendas. Enforcing the wants of one group may create an issue for another. Using fair enforcement and consistent application of the law is the only way the criminal justice system can operate within a highly political environment. Of course, this assumes that the law is written clearly.

Chapter Summary

- Funding is one of the biggest issues in criminal justice. Not having enough money to effectively provide the services expected by society can create issues related to time, initiative, and ability for the management of the agency. Seeking out additional funding sources, aside from public tax dollars, is an alternative available to criminal justice agencies.
- Agencies in criminal justice may decide to pursue grants, in-kind donations, private funds, or goods and money from foundations to subsidize newly developed programs and services, continuing programs and services, or agendas not fully funded by the annual fiscal budget.
- Technology has perhaps had the biggest impact on criminal justice. On the one hand, it creates issues, such as insufficient training, unskilled employees, budgetary constraints, and new crimes, for the criminal justice system. On the other hand, it provides faster and more professional service to the public and the customers of criminal justice.

- There have been a number of technology-based crimes created by technology. It is complicated for the criminal justice system to track and eventually arrest and prosecute offenders who use technology to commit their crimes.
- As the demographics of the United States change, so does the role of criminal justice. Officers need additional skills to work with the increased numbers of immigrants. Demographics such as age, race, gender, and ethnicity can impact crime rates and policing and correctional strategies. Where people live, whether it is rural or urban, shapes the likelihood that they will be victimized. Although the list of factors that may contribute to crime is extensive, family structure, income level, housing conditions, schools, and transience have been identified in research as major concerns.
- The culture of a society includes its norms, values, behaviors, and expectations. The culture defines what is or is not socially acceptable. It also contributes to the creation of laws. Social structures within society are tied together through cultural understandings. When there is a misunderstanding of culture, conflicts may occur. This creates work for the criminal justice system, as it is responsible for upholding the collective culture. Agencies are struggling with programs designed to handle differing cultural views. In addition, what society deems as acceptable and unacceptable behavior is changing.
- Laws in the United States are based on common law. This concept was adopted from England and means that laws are derived from commonly held beliefs, customs, traditions, and values. Essentially, the law is culturally based. Laws are not static. They may be changed at the federal, state, and local levels. These laws greatly impact the decisions made and the procedures used in criminal justice.
- There are numerous types of laws in the United States. Statutory laws or criminal laws provide the definitions of crime. Procedural laws explain how a person is processed once arrested and brought into the criminal justice system. Case law is determined through decisions made by the court. Civil laws focus on individual relationships, not criminal interactions, by specifying rules for contracts. Verdicts in civil cases result in monetary awards or procedural changes. Finally, there are administrative laws, which are created by the government to control business, industry, and individuals' activities.
- The majority of policing agencies are unionized. Unions are groups of employees that collectively bargain to gain increases in pay, better working conditions, and benefits. Unions create contracts that manage the actions of both employees and administrators. The criminal justice system has seen its workers using unions since 1954. Currently, correctional personnel and probation officers are becoming more active in collective bargaining, although mainly within their own states and agencies.
- Political pressures can come from direct and indirect sources. Altering laws at the national or state level manipulates the criminal justice system indirectly. Budgets, procedures, or organizational effectiveness may change as a result of indirect pressures. Community members and special interest groups have a more direct impact on the inner workings of the criminal justice system.

Chapter Review Questions

1. How has funding in the criminal justice system been affected since the terrorist attacks of 9/11? Have policing initiatives changed? Court initiatives? Probation or corrections initiatives? Do you think congressional and presidential elections change the funding priorities? If so, how? If not, why not?

2. In your opinion, what technological advancement has created the most problems for criminal justice? What has been the most beneficial? Explain why you believe this.

3. Identify some of the characteristics of the culture at your school. What behaviors or actions are culturally acceptable and what ones are unacceptable? Has that changed since you first arrived at school? What about within your community (at home)? What is the culture there? What is the demographic makeup of your school and community? Does your school use race in determining admissions?

4. If you were working in a police department as a detective, what employee issues would matter most to you? Higher salaries? More time off? Compensation time? Health, disability, or life insurance? What other important issues can you think of? Why do these matter to you? How would you convince the union representatives and the administration that these were important to employees?

5. Identify two or three recent changes to policing as a result of politics. Identify some changes to corrections. Were these good changes? Why or why not?

6. How are services provided to victims, offenders, and the general public influenced by the environmental factors discussed in this chapter?

CASE STUDY

The New Berlin Probation Office in Missouri handles juvenile delinquency and abuse/neglect cases. The office works approximately 315 cases of abuse and neglect each year. They are handled by three deputy juvenile officers in collaboration with the Division of Family Services (DFS) and its assigned caseworkers. The cases proceed through court in the usual manner—the child is taken into custody by a doctor, the police, or the probation officer; the case goes to court for a protective custody hearing to determine if the child is being held away from the parents for a valid reason; jurisdiction is established; an adjudication hearing is held and it is determined if the child and parents need further separation and monitoring; and a disposition is handed down in the case. If the child is kept out of the family home, the disposition includes a permanency planning case meeting with the probation officer, the parents, service providers, and the caseworker from DFS. The meeting is held to establish guidelines for the parents and DFS in working toward reunification with the child. The probation officer monitors the case plan and reports to the court on successes or failures every six months. The guidelines for the parents normally involve drug counseling and testing, parenting classes, budgeting classes, supervised visits, home visits, and so forth. DFS requirements include monitoring visits; providing for the child's mental, physical, educational, and emotional well-being; counseling; doing home visits; and working with the parents, probation office, and other service providers. The goal in every Permanency Planning Case Plan is to reunify the child with the parents.

In Missouri state law and in policy written by the juvenile probation office, cases involving abuse and neglect have 18 months to reach a resolution. At the conclusion of the 18 months, the probation office, in consult with DFS, makes a determination on whether to reunite the child with the family or to pursue a termination of parental rights. In cases of termination, the case will proceed to court and the judge will determine if reunification is a possibility. If not, the court will rule that the parents no longer have a legal right to the child. Basically, this frees the child up for adoption through the state's adoption system and the child becomes a permanent ward of the state. This approach has worked well for the New Berlin Probation Office. Only about nine cases a year have resulted in termination of parental rights, although many cases have neared the 18-month cutoff.

At this point in time, New Berlin has approximately 32 cases (encompassing 96 total children) that have been active for 14–17 months. The probation officers are working to reunify the children with their parents and have made considerable accomplishments with most of the families, although there is still work to be done to ensure that the children are not returned to abusive or neglectful environments. Only 4 of the 32 cases are expected to result in the termination of parental rights.

(Continued)

(Continued)

As the work week begins, a call is received from the Missouri State Court Administrators Office. The clerk alerts the chief probation officer of a new federal law. On Wednesday of the week before, the federal government determined that cases of abuse and neglect must meet a resolution within 13 months of the date of disposition. Any case over the 13-month limit is subject to a termination of parental rights hearing, effective immediately. Since federal law overrides state laws, states and local jurisdictions failing to come into compliance with the new federal statute will risk losing federal and state tax dollars. According to the clerk, failure to meet the statute is not an option. The clerk informs the chief that his office is expected to comply with the statute within the next 120 days. Missouri legislators are already negotiating new wording for the Missouri state law. The chief is told to modify his office's policy on abuse/neglect cases to align with the federal directive.

Questions for Discussion

1. Imagine you are the chief probation officer. Considering the fact that your officers are working 32 cases that qualify for termination of parental rights under the new federal statute, what do you advise them to do? How are you taking into consideration the success that has been accomplished among some families? What consideration are you giving to the number of children now facing permanent removal from their parents?

2. How do you rewrite your office policy? What do you include in it?

3. Are there any alternatives to the new law? What else might you be able to do to bring as many of the cases into compliance as possible while still following the statute? What role might the judge play in this? Are these decisions ethical and in the best interest of the child?

4. How often do you think this type of incident occurs in criminal justice? What unique challenges do these incidents place on the system that we may not see in other industries?

Internet Resources

Administrative Office of U.S. Courts—http://www.uscourts.gov

Federal Bureau of Prisons—http://www.bop.gov

National Association of Police Organizations—http://www.napo.org

References and Suggested Readings

Adams, R. J. (2008). The human right of police to organize and bargain collectively. *Police Practice & Research, 9*(2), 165–172. doi:10.1080/15614260802081329

Alexander, J. A., & Wells, R. (2008). How do resource dependencies affect treatment practices? The case of outpatient substance abuse treatment programs. *Medical Care Research and Review, 65*(6), 729–747.

American Federation of Labor. (2008). *Industry*. Retrieved from http://www.aflcio.org/joinaunion/why/uniondifference/uniondiff10.cfm.

American Federation of State, County, and Municipal Employees. (2013). About AFSCME. Retrieved from http://www.afscme.org/union/about.

Atkins v. Virginia, 122 S. Ct. 2242, 153 L. Ed. 2d 355 (2002).

Beale, A.V., & K. R. Hall. (2007). Cyber bullying: What school administrators (and parents) can do. *The Clearing House, 18*, 8–12.

Bolinger, H. E. (1981). Police officers' views on collective bargaining and use of sanctions. In A. H. More (Ed.), *Critical issues in law enforcement* (pp. 165–174). Cincinnati, OH: Anderson.

Bureau of Labor Statistics. (2013, January). News release: Union members—2012. Retrieved from http://www.bls.gov/news.release/pdf/union2.pdf.

Chu, J. (8 August, 2005). You wanna take this online? Cyberspace is the 21st century bully's playground where girls play rougher than boys. *Time.* Retrieved from http://www.time.com/time/magazine/article/0,9171,1088698,00.html.

Collins, J. M. (2006). *Investigating identify theft: A guide for businesses, law enforcement, and victims.* Hoboken, NJ: Wiley.

Cox, S., Allen, J., Hanser, R., & Conrad, J. (2014). *Juvenile justice: A guide to policy, practice, and theory* (8th ed.). Thousand Oaks, CA: Sage.

Federal Trade Commission. (2013, February). *Consumer sentinel network data book, January–December 2012.* Retrieved from http://ftc.gov/sentinel/reports/sentinel-annual-reports/sentinel-cy2012.pdf.

French, T. W. (2005). Free trade and illegal drugs: Will NAFTA transform the United States into the Netherlands? *Vanderbilt Journal of Transnational Law, 38*(2), 501–540.

Fisher v. University of Texas at Austin, 631 F. 3d 213—Court of Appeals, 5th Circuit 2011.

Fisher v. University of Texas, No. 11-345, slip op. (2013).

Foster, A. C. (2003). Differences in union and nonunion earnings in blue-collar and service occupations. Retrieved from http://www.bls.gov/opub/cwc/cm20030623ar01p1.htm.

Furman v. Georgia, 408 U.S. 238 (1972).

Garmen, V. (2013, April). Officials mull spring break successes, challenges. *The News Herald.* Retrieved from http://www.newsherald.com/news/officials-mull-spring-break-successes-challenges-1.123482?page=2.

Grutter v. Bollinger, (02-241). 539 U.S. 306 (2003).

Hewitt, W. H. (1978). Current issues in police collective bargaining. In A. W. Cohn (Ed.), *The future of policing* (pp. 207–223). Beverly Hills, CA: Sage.

Hinduja, S., & Patchin, J. W. (2008). Cyberbullying: An exploratory analysis of factors related to offending and victimization. *Deviant Behavior, 29*(2), 129–156.

In re Gault, 387 U.S. 1 (1967).

International Association of Chiefs of Police. (1977). *Critical issues in police labor relations.* Gaithersburg, MD: Author.

International Union of Police Associations. (2008). *IUPA history timeline.* Retrieved from http://www.iupa.org/index.php?option=com_content&task=view&id=7&Itemid=16.

Jost, K. (2000, March 17). Policing the police. *CQ Researcher, 10*, 209–240.

Jost, K. (2009, April 24). Judicial elections. *CQ Researcher, 19*, 373–396.

Kadleck, C. (2003). Police employee organizations. *Policing: An International Journal of Police Strategies & Management, 26*(2), 341–352.

Kady, M., II. (2003, September 12). Homeland security. *CQ Researcher, 13*, 749–772.

Kearney, R. C. (1995). Unions in government: Where do they go from here? In S. W. Hays & R. C. Kearney (Eds.), *Public personnel administration: Problems and prospects* (3rd ed.). Englewood Cliffs, NJ: Prentice Hall.

Klein, A., Salomon, A., Elwyn, L., Barasch, A., Powers, J., & Maley, M., et al. (2013). Exploratory study of juvenile orders of protection as a remedy for dating violence. National Institute of Justice, U.S. Department of Justice, Office of Justice Programs. Retrieved from https://www.ncjrs.gov/pdffiles1/nij/grants/242131.pdf.

Levi, M. (1977). *Bureaucratic insurgency*. Lexington, MA: Lexington Books.

Lipke, D. J. (2000). Take a bite out of crime. *American Demographics, 22*(12), 46–47.

Manning, P. K. (1992). Technological and material resource issues. In L. T. Hoover (Ed.), *Police management: Issues and perspectives*. Washington, DC: Police Executive Research Forum.

McCleskey v. Zant, 499 U.S. 467, 493–494 (1991).

McMillion, R. (1993). Cash crunch. *ABA Journal, 79*(5), 122.

McNamara, C. (2007). *Basic overview of nonprofit organizations*. Retrieved from http://managementhelp .org/org_thry/np_thry/np_intro.htm.

National Agricultural Library Rural Information Center. (2007). *A guide to funding resources*. Retrieved from http://www.nal.usda.gov/ric/ricpubs/fundguide.html.

National Head Start Association. (n.d.). *Benefits of Head Start and Early Head Start programs*. Retrieved from http://www.nhsa.org/files/static_page_files/399E0881-1D09-3519-AD56452FC44941C3/Benefits ofHSandEHS.pdf.

National Association of Police Organizations. (2013). *What is NAPO?* Retrieved from http://www.napo.org.

Ricci v. DeStefano, 129 S. Ct. 2658– 2009

Ricci v. DeStefano, 530 F.3d 87 (2d Cir 2008), cert granted, 129 S. Ct. 894 (2009).

Roper v. Simmons, 543 U.S. 551 (2005).

Salerno, C. A. (1981). *Police at the bargaining table*. Springfield, IL: Charles C. Thomas.

Schmalleger, F. (2001). *Criminal justice today: An introductory text for the twenty-first century* (6th ed.). Upper Saddle River, NJ: Prentice Hall.

Schmalleger, F. (2008). *Criminal justice: A brief introduction* (7th ed.). Upper Saddle River, NJ: Prentice Hall.

Sirene, W. H. (1985). Management: Labor's most effective organizer. In J. J. Fyfe (Ed.), *Police management today: Issues and case studies*. Washington, DC: International City Management Association.

Sylvia, R. D. (1994). *Public personnel administration*. Belmont, CA: Wadsworth.

Unions.org. (2008). *Unions: What are they and what do they do?* Retrieved from http://www.unions.org/ resources/AllAboutUnions.pdf.

Wolak, J., Mitchell, K., & Finkelhor, D. (2006). *Online victimization of youth: Five years later*. National Center for Missing & Exploited Children.

Wood, M. (2006). Data on racial profiling leads to police reform, Garrett says. *Virginia Law*. Retrieved from http://www.law.virginia.edu/html/news/2006_spr/garrett.htm.

Yearwood, D. L. (2009). Criminal justice funding in North Carolina: A system in crisis. *Journal of Alternative Perspectives in the Social Sciences, 1*(3), 672–686.

Zgoba, K., Witt, P., Dalessandro, M., & Veysey, B. (2008). *Megan's Law: Assessing the practical and monetary efficacy*. Washington, DC: U.S. Department of Justice. Retrieved from http://www.ncjrs.gov/pdffiles1/ nij/grants/225370.pdf.

5

Conflict, Power, and Ethical Issues ❖

LEARNING OBJECTIVES

Upon completion of this chapter, students should be able to do the following:

- Describe organizational conflicts and identify their causes
- Explain Pondy's model of organizational conflict
- Describe personality defect theory
- Identify five styles of conflict management
- Explain different approaches to conflict resolution
- Describe the attributes of personal power
- Describe the characteristics of position power
- Explain the different tactics for increasing power
- Explain organizational politics and how it is influenced by power
- Explain the ethical problems in various criminal justice agencies
- Explain the organizational code of ethics and the different factors that influence it
- Explain corporate social responsibility and whistle-blowing

There are numerous Senate committee debates over issues facing the United States that are regularly featured on the C-SPAN cable channel. In these debates, different solutions are offered to resolve a problem. For example, the Iraq problem had Congress divided on how to tackle the ongoing issues. The Democrats strongly felt that the solution to continued violence in Iraq was to pull out U.S. troops and allow the Iraqi forces to deal with the sectarian violence. In contrast, the Republicans felt that U.S. troops should stay in Iraq to stabilize the situation and work alongside the Iraqi forces. Both parties took their solutions to their constituents to seek approval and backing for their suggested course of action. This issue was used as a platform for elections of various officials, elections that would change the power structure in the Senate and the Oval Office.

Similarly, in day-to-day functioning, organizations are faced with decision making that typically involves more than one possible solution. Choosing one alternative over another may benefit some people and adversely impact others within the agency—causing conflict. Consequently, individuals use power, acquired or vested, to influence the adoption of their favored alternative, which will result in accomplishing their desired final outcome. The success of managers or administrators will depend on their ability to deal effectively with conflicts and sources of power. If these are not managed ethically, they create uncertainty, chaos, and stress, which ultimately lead to devastatingly negative consequences. In contrast, ethically managed conflicts can contribute positively to the development and growth of an organization.

In this chapter, conflict, power, and ethics are discussed, as well as how they overlap in the field of criminal justice. First, the prevalence of conflict at many levels of community, governmental, and bureaucratic operation and interaction among various agencies of criminal justice is examined. Organizational conflict is defined, followed by a discussion on various types of conflicts seen in organizations as a result of structural and personal relationships. Conflict management techniques and selecting appropriate conflict management strategies are also examined. Second, there is an examination of the role and parameters of power within the context of improving the administration of criminal justice by integrating quality and greater cooperation among subsystems. The chapter also provides a discussion of the various sources of power that are primarily reflected within the different agencies of criminal justice and the bureaucracy itself. How power is employed and manipulated as a tool for maintaining the system, enhancing individual and departmental status, and protecting vested occupational interest is also explored. In addition, another source of power is examined, bestowed on the officers of criminal justice as directed and implied by their positions and roles, which is reflected between the enforcers and the violators of law and order. Within this power relationship, ethical decision making becomes critical in the promotion of service quality in criminal justice. Third, there is an examination of ethics and an explanation of how organizations form the code of ethics that guides their decision making. Social responsibility in the changing environment is also addressed in this discussion.

Organizational Conflict

Conflicts and disagreements are normal in human relationships and occur naturally in the day-to-day functioning of an organization. Conflicts can be a source of motivation for organizations to arrive at innovative ways of solving problems. Progressive organizations provide a workplace environment that recognizes the differences of opinion and encourages a broader worldview by allowing all parties to learn and improve in an effort to continuously evolve (Pascale, 1990; Wanous & Youtz, 1986; Whetten & Cameron, 2002). Such organizations provide their workforce with training and skills to expand their perspectives in solving problems, resulting in improved communication, trust, and productivity. A well-trained manager will direct conflict toward productive outcomes, while striving to maintain an optimal balance (Kelly, 1970; Robbins, 1974; Thomas, 1976). Alternatively, conflicts can be a source of destruction when not handled effectively by managers. Personality conflicts and arguments can generate a negative spiral that can poison the entire environment of an organization, resulting in chaos, miscommunication, lack of trust, and falling productivity. Typically, such organizations do not succeed in a competitive environment. Therefore, how managers deal with conflicts is an important determinant of organizational success (Seybolt, Derr, & Nielson, 1996; Tjosvold, 1991).

Effective conflict management requires managers to be proficient in three areas of skill development. First, managers should understand the different stages through which conflict evolves so that they can identify and rectify it in earlier stages. Second, they should be able to identify the types of conflict and their cause(s) so that they can develop workable strategies to reduce dysfunctional conflict. Third, they should examine the different strategies available to them and choose the one most appropriate for dealing with the given situation so that the relationships between disputing parties are not damaged.

Five Stages of Organizational Conflict

One of the most widely accepted models of organizational conflict was proposed by Pondy (1967). According to this model, conflict is a dynamic process that passes through five stages:

Stage 1, described as *latent conflict,* is when there is no actual conflict, but the conditions are right for a conflict to develop. The conditions could be influenced by the aftereffects of preceding conflict and by environmental factors discussed in the next section, such as scarcity of resources, incompatible goals, differentiation, and so forth.

Stage 2, described as *perceived conflict,* is when there is awareness in one entity, individual, or group that its goals are being frustrated by the actions of another individual or group. Consequently, at this stage disagreements between different departments escalate and hostile conditions begin to emerge in day-to-day exchanges.

Stage 3, described as *felt conflict,* is when the groups involved in conflict feel the discomfort and tension, which may be amplified by certain other conditions inside or outside the organization. As the disagreements increase, cooperation among the groups declines and the blaming of one another starts increasing, generating a negative environment of distrust. The perceived conflict and felt conflict are mutually reinforcing because when there is perceived tension, individuals act accordingly and start feeling tension around them. Likewise, when individuals feel conflict, they start perceiving an environment that is tense and uncomfortable.

Stage 4, described as *manifest conflict,* is when the conflict comes out into the open and is manifested in different forms. In Los Angeles in 1992, for example, the manifest conflict felt between the public and the police was expressed in the rioting and property damage that ensued after a jury acquitted four police officers accused in the Rodney King beating. Manifest conflict can also be demonstrated through a lack of cooperation, ignoring another party, or verbal or written attacks.

Stage 5, described as *conflict aftermath,* is when the conflict has been addressed in one way or another and the general environment is still tense. Even when the conflict is resolved amicably between the involved parties, the heated arguments that may have taken place during the conflict resolution process produce scars that hang on for some time. Time is a healer, but it can take a while before relationships get back to normal between the conflicting parties. During this intervening period, called the conflict aftermath period, it is easy for other conflicts to emerge.

Causes of Conflict

Conflicts can be classified broadly into two categories, namely, people-focused and issue-focused (Amason, Hochwarter, Thompson, & Harrison, 1995; Eisenhardt, Kahwajy, & Bourgeois, 1997; Guetzkow & Gyr, 1954). Conflict can arise between employees because of clashes in their personalities. Typically, these *people-focused conflicts* are emotional disputes that are more difficult to resolve and that threaten relationships. Conflicts can also arise from disagreements over issues. *Issue-focused conflicts* typically involve disagreements over negotiable matters. If managed properly, this type of conflict can enhance relationships and provide for continuous development and growth. For example, a probation employee who works an on-call rotation may want to trade rotations with another individual in the agency so that the first employee can attend a family event. If the management is able to persuade another probation officer to volunteer to trade rotations, the employee may feel better about the situation, his or her colleagues, and the agency overall. If no one steps forward to voluntarily exchange rotations and the management does not play a role in resolving the conflict, the employee may feel disgruntled and experience a loss of morale.

According to *personality defect theory,* conflicts emerge because of personality imperfections. Managers who adopt this theory believe that people who are involved in conflicts are inherently bad people and troublemakers. Researchers say this theory accounts for only a small percentage of organizational conflicts (Hines, 1980; Schmidt & Tannenbaum, 1960). Alternatively, people may not be inherently bad, but they may also not be properly trained to resolve their disagreements—leading to conflict. As discussed next, aggressive and abrasive behavior leading to organizational conflicts is often a reflection of employee frustration arising from the work environment. Some of the more common factors observed in the work environment that lead to conflict are personal differences arising from disparity in assumptions, perceptions, and expectations; lack of complete information or misinformation; task and team interdependence and goal incompatibility; and scarcity of resources.

Because of differences in family upbringing, values, education, culture, and past experiences, people see the world differently from one another. These are known as *personal differences*. For example, it may be difficult for the head of a police department who is recruited from another region and is embedded deeply in variant political and cultural values to agree about routine operational issues within the police department. Such differences are reflected in a person's assumptions, perceptions, and expectations (Adler, 1991; Hocker & Wilmot, 1991; Sillars & Weisberg, 1987; Trompenaars, 1996; Weldon & Jehn, 1995). O'Leary and Newman (1970) argue, "It is likely that different types of persons with identifiably different value orientations are attracted to police work than to probation and parole work" (p. 103). Emerging from these differences is a tendency in most to think that their view is correct, which inevitably leads to conflict and disagreement. In an empirical study, O'Leary and Newman found that there were not only differences in values, but also differences in personal esteem and perceived status among probation and police officials. They argue that when people are uncertain about their status within an organization, they become uneasy and tense in their interactions, resulting in conflicts. Resolving such preexisting differences is difficult, though not impossible. If proper training is not provided to workers to handle such differences amicably, they become emotional issues and take on moral overtones. Consequently, conflicts based on personal differences may often seem like people-focused conflicts. These personal differences can get projected in the form of unreasonable personalities, especially in organizations characterized by wide-ranging demographic diversity. In law enforcement, officers may be seen as unreasonable for any number of actions. The tendency to fall into a philosophy that the police are always right is easy for law enforcement officers and may gravely impact their approach to situations and to citizens, potentially leading to conflict.

Conflict may rise between different parties when they operate with *incomplete or incorrect information*. Such information gaps are a potential source of misunderstanding and can lead to disagreement and conflict. This type of conflict is common in organizations but is simple to resolve. Obtaining more information and sharing of information sources generally resolves such conflicts. In the top-down structure and shift work used in policing and corrections, it is plausible for bottom-level line staff to receive incomplete information or misinformation on their job duties. For instance, a corrections officer might believe that the practice of allowing inmates to congregate at or near the telephone is still acceptable. This may not be the case, however, if the administration has identified a problem with the inmates congregating and has issued a command not to allow it to happen. If the officer did not receive the memo, the individual may experience a conflict between what the officer believed to be acceptable and what the administration considers so (and the officer could possibly be reprimanded for not enforcing the new command).

Within an organization, there are numerous areas where the *tasks are interdependent*. The tasks are said to be interdependent when resources, both equipment and people, may be shared between different departments. For example, a piece of equipment such as a photocopier may be shared by several departments, creating potential scheduling conflicts regarding which department uses it at what time. The interdependence between departments may also occur in the form of input–output relationships, where one task forms an input to the next, like that seen in assembly-line functioning. If the department responsible for providing the input does not meet the needs of the department accepting these inputs, then there is a conflict. For example, often students arrive in higher-level elective courses without properly being exposed to the material in the basic courses. This lack of preparation of the students causes a conflict between the instructors teaching the elective courses and those who were responsible for teaching basic courses. Similarly, a link is formed between different agencies in the criminal justice system as an individual is processed through the system, from suspect to defendant to offender to inmate to parolee. For example, the arrest practices of the police impact the number and types of defendants in courts, and the sentencing practices of the courts impact the number and types of inmates who populate the correctional facilities (Forst, 1977).

Despite the interdependence between different agencies, the criminal justice system does not operate like an organization in a typical sense, often providing fertile ground for conflicts. It has many sources of authority and power relationships, and its decision network is composed of innumerable complex subprocesses that do not follow a linear chain of command. The formal relationships among police, prosecutors, prisons, probation officers, parole boards, trial and appellate courts, satellite services such as welfare agencies, child protective services, and consultant professions like psychology and psychiatry are loose and amorphous, despite structural interdependence (O'Leary & Newman, 1970). Despite the fact that the activities of the police have a direct influence on court calendars and eventually affect prison populations, there is no line and staff relationship between police and prosecutors, or between these positions and courts and correctional personnel. Highlighting such problems, Forst (1977) cites an anecdote from when he worked as a researcher for a local trial court jurisdiction. He observed,

> The sheriff and his staff were unhappy with the judges' inconsistency in granting telephone calls to defendants awaiting trial in jail; this evidently caused dissension and unrest among the jail population. The sheriff was also displeased with the wide variety of commitment forms the judges were using for the same types of commitment. (p. 409)

> At the same time, the judges complained about the late delivery of defendants coming from jail to trial. Normally, trial time is at 9.00 a.m. and the judges want to start promptly so that the assembled jurors do not waste their time and the criminal cases can be disposed of as quickly as possible. However, the deputy sheriffs frequently brought the defendants to court late. It was finally discovered that the deputies were late because of particular security measures and unnecessarily circuitous routes to the courtrooms. (p. 409)

Another area for potential conflict is *team interdependency*, which emerges when teams comprising individuals from different departments work on a project. The greater the interdependence is among units, the higher the potential for conflict. For example, a county sheriff may bring task forces together from a number of agencies, all with their own training, expertise, equipment, and experience, to work on a drug-related problem. As they come together, they may realize that the failures of one task force cause problems for one or more of the other task forces. If the group from Agency A is not sharing information with the other groups or is not correctly documenting its activities, it could result in a ruined case for the other agencies.

Conflict may emerge when two or more departments or functions have an *overlapping authority* for the same task. Such confusion often emerges when an organization is undergoing transformation in its structure and has not clearly expressed relationships between different groups. In the case of treatment providers, there is commonly an overlap in programs. One or more departments in an agency may be able to refer youth into a program without the consent or knowledge of another department. This can result in overcrowding of the program and difficulty in fully accomplishing the goals set forth in treatment. Similarly, probation and police officers have responsibility for executing tasks that intersect at certain points (O'Leary & Newman, 1970). Yet these agencies do not share the same objectives or use the same techniques or methods. They are separated from one another by differences in tradition, staffing patterns, budget, status, and sometimes even by distance. "While all are part of the same system and often deal with many of the same people, they are indeed specialized agencies with different demands and loyalties" (O'Leary & Newman, 1970, p. 101), which often results in conflict.

Goal incompatibility among different individuals, units, or departments may lead to conflicts. In this case, the goals of one group may directly contradict the goals of another group. For example, given the present global threat of terrorism, airport security may want to install stringent checkpoints for protection, which sometimes may result in flight delays. At the same time, personnel in control towers responsible for safe takeoff and landing are interested in timely departures. When the delays are caused by security, it becomes a headache for tower control people to reschedule flight departures and arrivals, often leading to conflict between the two groups. Similarly, conflict may occur between agencies of criminal justice because of disagreements about the purpose of law enforcement, sentencing, or community treatment. Supporting this notion, O'Leary and Newman (1970) note,

> For example, in achieving their enforcement goals, the police may well see a need for means of identifying probationers and parolees, perhaps subjecting them to be more readily accessible to interrogation or search than suspects not under sentence. At the same time, probation and parole field agents may see such police objectives and techniques as counter-productive to their mandate to help offenders adjust in the community. (p. 102)

Closely related to goal compatibility is the issue of *differentiation*, whereby different functions develop different orientations toward how to attain organizational goals and improve performance. Since their tasks differ, their views often may not match, resulting in conflict. For example, manufacturing believes that organizational profits can be increased by cutting costs through greater standardization. In contrast, marketing believes that organizational profits can be improved by increasing revenue through increased sales by providing greater customization. Thus, manufacturing sees the solutions to profitability (standardizing the product for all) very differently from marketing (customizing the product for individuals). This results in conflict. In criminal justice, one can experience similar conflicts when looking at practice and the law. The laws, especially those mandating sentences, are designed to standardize punishments for offenders committing the same types of crime. However, from a treatment perspective, there may be different reasons for the commission of the crime depending on the individual, and addressing the reasons with contrary sentences may be a better solution than standardized punishment. This creates a conflict between what is best for the treatment and rehabilitation of the offender and what the law says must occur.

Overlapping authority resulting in ambiguous responsibilities between different agencies, *uncertainties* and *resource scarcity* collectively act as catalysts to the previous conditions in bringing about conflicts within an organization. When organizations are working under a constraint of uncertainty and scarce resources, the allocation of these resources becomes a contentious issue resulting in conflicts. For example, each year when the annual agency budgets are determined by U.S. counties, criminal justice agencies experience conflicts and tension with one another. They are each interested in gaining the largest portion of the money available for their programs, employees, training, and equipment.

Organizational *rewarding systems* are based on various criteria. When the rewarding criterion is tied to the attainment of organizational goals, typically it will encourage cooperation among employees. Alternatively, if the rewards are tied to attainment of individual goals without any consideration to the overall objective of the organization, the emergence of conflicts is a very real possibility. For example, if pay raises were given based on the number of traffic tickets written in a month, officers may see the incentive as a competition with one another. Instead of only stopping vehicles that blatantly violate traffic laws, officers may pursue very minor infractions just to ensure that they write more tickets than someone else in the department. This could result in not accomplishing the other goals of the policing agency at all because officers are more concerned with the individual goal of receiving an incentive raise while competing with others in the department.

Conflict Management Strategies

Ruble and Thomas (1976) offer a two-by-two matrix with five strategies to address conflict. Each strategy reflects different degrees of cooperativeness and assertiveness. A cooperative attitude reflects the importance of relationships and focuses deeply on the needs of the interacting party, whereas an assertive position focuses predominantly on an individual's needs.

When the position taken is both assertive and uncooperative, it is an attempt to focus on the satisfaction of one's needs at the expense of the other party. This approach is known as *competing* and generates antagonism and resentment. Though such an approach may appear to accomplish a lot in the short run, it sacrifices relationship building and typically produces a backlash that is counterproductive in the long run. A competing approach may be recommended if, from past experience, the belief is that the other party would take undue advantage of a more collaborative approach. Attorneys in a civil case, for example, adopt a competing approach when presenting a case to a jury. The goal is to resolve the conflict in a fashion that maximizes their client's interests by placing their concerns above the concerns of the other parties. In the end, the plaintiff's attorney wants to win a settlement for the client.

Then again, the position taken in a conflict may be uncooperative but unassertive, where the conflict is avoided or a solution is postponed. In this case, the individual is said to be exhibiting *avoiding* behaviors. Some managers are not emotionally prepared to cope with the stress arising from confrontations and try to avoid such situations. Repeated use of this strategy is unproductive because the issues do not get resolved. It may, however, be useful to adopt an avoiding stance if the issues in the conflict are very trivial. This tactic may also be practical as a temporary postponing strategy to allow conflicting parties to cool off and come to the table with rational alternatives rather than approach the issue on the basis of emotions.

The *accommodating* position implies adopting a cooperative and unassertive attitude, which may be focused on relationship building by sacrificing one's interest. Unfortunately, this position does not result in long-term relationships because one always feels others are taking advantage, which lessens the satisfaction gained from the sacrifice. A person may also find that others are making more progress and feel as though he or she is failing to accomplish personal objectives, thus resulting in a lowered self-esteem. Appeasement can sometimes reflect a sign of weakness and may encourage the other party to make unreasonable demands. However, this position can be appropriate when the issue is not really important to the individual, or the other party has significantly more power.

The *compromising* approach involves finding a middle ground by adopting intermediate assertiveness and cooperativeness to obtain partial satisfaction for both parties. Such a position requires both parties to make a sacrifice to obtain an equitable agreement. This approach of compromising may serve as a solution when an agreement has low probability. However, using this approach too often sends a message that the manager is more interested in resolving disputes than solving problems. Once the workers get such a feeling, they will always adopt a higher beginning position so that the split-the-difference approach will work in their favor.

In *collaboration,* a person is assertive but cooperative in an attempt to resolve the problem with a win-win solution. By framing the issue positively, the aim here is to find a solution to the problem rather than finding faults with one another. This approach facilitates a long-term, trust-based relationship among involved parties by focusing their disagreements on problems and not on people.

Each of the five positions discussed here can work appropriately in a given situation. However, the most suitable approach to most conflict situations is considered to be the collaborative style, which is longer lasting and provides the best joint outcome. In the process of conflict management, it becomes important for the manager to ensure that the relationships between the disputing parties are not damaged, by tactfully enabling them to settle their interpersonal disputes. An important task of a successful manager is to frame the conflict appropriately for it to be resolved amicably between disagreeing parties. Three important principles of promoting cooperative strategy are the following:

1. *Focus on bigger goals.* Sometimes, focusing on larger goals that involve the interests of both parties can shift the focus from conflict to cooperation. Typically, police satisfaction comes from crimes cleared by arrest, prosecutors and courts are satisfied with conviction results, and correctional authorities are satisfied by low rates of recidivism and high offender compliance. Yet crime reduction, promotion of quality of life, and citizen satisfaction may be superior shared goals for all of the agencies to agree on, which will promote cooperation rather than competitive interaction.

2. *Improve communications.* As discussed earlier, often conflict arises from a lack of communication or from miscommunication, which, if improved, can help reduce or prevent conflicts. Communicating properly during the conflict resolution stage is also critical. New and effective means are being designed to facilitate communication among different agencies of the criminal justice system. The most visible evidence is the computerized management information systems, which allow real-time communication and information exchange among the police departments, the courts, and the jails. Furthermore, bringing together representatives from different agencies and the use of role-reversal techniques can improve communication. For example, having a police officer work with probation officers on particular cases, and vice versa, will educate them on the operational perspectives of each role and promote awareness of the features of the other's viewpoint. Also, various applications of game theory techniques allow the participants to understand the benefits of improved communication and cooperation as compared to dysfunctional competition emerging from an arms-length, isolated approach. In addition, feedback and leadership roles are important in improving the overall communication within an organization, which is discussed in detail in Chapter 8.

3. *Develop negotiating skills of employees.* Organizations can teach skills to employees to help them negotiate for win-win outcomes to difficult problems. Sometimes, using a neutral third party in mediation can help reduce conflict. Third parties are extremely helpful when trust between conflicting parties is low. Police departments are keenly aware of the need for officers to have negotiation skills when working with the public and offenders. They provide training to officers regularly to promote these skills.

Power

Power and its use are reflected in the day-to-day activities pertinent to the administration of criminal justice, such as police power, discretionary power, the sentencing power of the court, the absolute power of correctional officers over inmates, and the revocation power of probation and parole officers (Robin, 1974). These various types of power are primarily reflected in two kinds of relationships: (1) those within the different agencies and the bureaucracy itself; and (2) those between the enforcers and violators of law and order, which are unique to criminal justice. Most of the discussion in this section pertains to the first power relationship, which is typical of any organization. The second power relationship is discussed in the next section, on ethics.

Power is defined as the ability of an individual or a group to influence the behavior or action of another individual or group to do something they would not have done otherwise (French & Raven, 1959). In the workplace, power is used as the primary means for directing and controlling people's behaviors or actions toward attaining desired outcomes (both personal and organizational). This role of power is called *dominance*. However, power may sometimes be used to empower someone, thus playing an *empowerment* role. Alternatively, it may be used to resist others' power, thus playing the *resistance* role. *Organizational power* is a broader concept and can be exercised upward, downward, and horizontally in organizations. There are two basic sources of power within an organization, namely, *personal attributes* and *position characteristics*. Embedded within these are the five forms of power defined by French and Raven: coercive, reward, legitimate, referent, and expert. People may acquire power based on their personal characteristics, or power may be embedded in the position they are holding within the organization. Neither of these power bases is truly independent. For example, people at higher positions in an organization are likely to concurrently have power originating from legitimate, expert, discretion, centrality, and a host of other sources, each of which is discussed later in this section. These power bases may also be interdependent because each power source may reinforce the other power source. Consequently, it is hard to disaggregate power in these two sources because both of the sources feed into each other.

Authority is associated with power but is limited in scope. Authority emanates from a formal position held within an organization and flows down the *vertical hierarchy*. It is the position to which power is conferred by the organization. Consequently, subordinates accept authority of the position holder because they believe it is vested legitimately. People in organizations may sometimes have authority without power, and they may sometimes have power without authority. Charismatic, experienced policing officers may receive considerable respect and power from younger officers even though they are not afforded legitimate power within the agency. Their charisma and time invested in the job allow them authority over (or the ability to influence) others.

Attributes of Personal Power

Individuals derive power within organizations from four personal characteristics, namely, expertise, personal attraction, effort, and legitimacy (French & Raven, 1959). In this knowledge-based era, power is less likely to come from one's formal position within an organization, and more likely to come from one's ability to perform. Recognizing that *expertise* is an important source of power, considerable time and effort need to be spent to upgrade one's expertise to avoid obsolescence. Embedded in the knowledge and capabilities of an individual, expertise can be acquired through formal education, self-directed learning, on-the-job learning, or work experience. Expertise is identified with rational and objective decision making, a quality that is greatly valued within organizations. Individuals with such expertise are deemed more reliable and trustworthy and are much sought after, giving them power. Alternatively, if individuals get typecast as a specialist, it may hurt their interest of moving into general management positions, which typically control power at the higher levels within organizations. Sometimes, the expertise of subordinates can become problematic if they do not skillfully make that knowledge available to a superior without threatening the boss's decision-making authority.

Personal attraction is reflected in physical characteristics, pleasing and comforting behavior, and a charismatic or charming personality. People with these traits of personal attraction gain power because others are drawn to them. Attractive people are deemed by others to be more trustworthy and intelligent (Dion & Dion, 1987). Numerous studies and surveys have found that individuals with attractive physical appearances are judged by others to have socially likable personality characteristics. Surveys show that the work of attractive people is considered of higher quality, they receive higher performance appraisals, and they earn higher salaries (Moore, Graziano, & Millar, 1987; Ross & Ferris, 1981). Typically, attractive workers have greater social acceptance and are more successful. Dressing and grooming have been found to contribute to attractiveness (Thompson, 2001). Another source of attractiveness is *charisma*, referred to as a magnetic personality, an attractive aura or charm. It is defined as an innate gift or a mystical quality in an individual that cannot be acquired in a skill-development workshop. Individuals with charisma are more easily accepted as leaders, which empowers them. Similarly, individuals with pleasing and agreeable behaviors are more influential and effective. Pleasing and agreeable behaviors are typically linked with friendships and puts fellow colleagues at ease. Individuals with such behavior are highly likable and are viewed as more trustworthy, evoking less resistance to their viewpoint. People with disagreeable personalities seem insensitive, threatening, and less credible, putting them at a disadvantage in attaining power among their peers.

Personal effort may be mirrored in hard work, commitment, dedication, and discipline—traits that are commonly appreciated in the workplace because they indicate employee reliability. Such workers are known to do whatever it takes to get the work done, earning them the trust of coworkers and supervisors. In a short amount of time, such individuals tend to become more knowledgeable about workplace activities and are generally sought out by their bosses for advice. These workers earn greater responsibility and are asked to do sensitive jobs that are critical to organizational goals. Their performance is a reflection on the boss's ability, putting the workers in a position of power to gain favors from their supervisors.

Yet another trait of personal power is *legitimacy,* which is bestowed on actions that are harmonious with the existing organizational culture and value system. Primarily, such acts are not investigated or contested, but rather are easily accepted, as they echo the core organizational values. Individuals perceived as having legitimacy are trusted by supervisors because their actions communicate a consistent set of priorities valued by the organization. This reduces any uncertainty. These individuals are sought out by organizational leaders, who see mirror images of their values and beliefs in them. Consequently, these workers are handpicked by the bosses and groomed to be their successors to carry on the traditions of the organization. Trust and approval from senior members provide power to these individuals within the organization.

So far, this chapter has discussed how personal traits (expertise, personal attraction, effort, and legitimacy) may increase the influence of an individual in the workplace. These personal traits provide supervisors and peers with the confidence that the individual can be trusted, making the person a likely candidate for positions of power and influence.

Characteristics of Position Power

Power may also originate from task assignments and the position held within an organization. Within the given organizational structure, employees holding higher positions in the vertical hierarchy typically have greater access to power—think in terms of policing sergeants, corporals, or chiefs. In other words, a vice president will have more power than a manager within the same department, due to vertical seniority. On the other hand, horizontal power pertains to relationships across departments. It examines the power hierarchy among the vice presidents of different departments, knowing that all vice presidents are not equal. Researchers (Kanter, 1979; Pfeffer, 1992) have found four important characteristics associated with a position that provides power; namely, formal position, discretion, centrality, and relevance, each of which is discussed here. Among these four characteristics of power, formal position and discretion describe the relationships in the context of hierarchal power, while centrality and relevance discuss the relationships in the context of horizontal power.

Formal position within an organizational structure not only provides legitimate power associated with the higher position, but also access to other key contacts and resources that further enhance one's power. It provides *visibility*, which is defined as the number of influential people an individual knows and with whom he or she is seen. Access to powerful and influential people increases one's *power by association*. Such linkages offer the opportunity to share accomplishments directly with people who control resources within the organization, and can provide desirable assignments and promotions. For similar reasons, *people-oriented positions* within an organization come with more power than *task-oriented positions*. People-oriented positions allow regular contact and face-to-face communication with senior officials, decision makers, union leaders, and other informal leaders through participation in meetings, conferences, and other programs. Sometimes, the position itself may be low in the hierarchy, but it may give access to high-level people, allowing for increased power. For example, secretaries to the vice presidents or presidents have a lot more power than formally provided by their position because they have direct access to the senior executive and everyone has to go through them. This works in a similar way in criminal justice. The administrative assistant working directly for the prison warden, chief probation officer, or police chief has considerable power in determining what information gets to the warden or chief and who has access to the warden. In the court system, the circuit clerk exercises this power. The clerk determines what the judge knows and does not know about paperwork; court documents; and communications from attorneys, witnesses, offenders, and other officers of the court.

Discretion refers to the flexibility and freedom to exercise one's decision. Organizations can rarely keep pace, in changing their rules to standardize tasks, to match the needs of the rapidly changing internal and external environments, often bringing inconsistencies and disruptions. Few rules and established routines govern flexible positions, so power is given to these executives to adopt unique and often creative solutions to resolve the non-routine challenges. Often such discretion, or flexibility of decision making, is embedded in positions that deal with work assignments that have high variety and novelty (Hinings, Hickson, Pennings, & Schneck, 1974). One good measure of the discretionary power in a position may be the maximum dollar amount to which an employee can make an independent decision without consulting the boss. Distribution of resources for rewards and punishments is another indicator of discretionary power, which is also referred to as *reward power* and *coercive power*. Police officers who respond to calls for service have enormous amounts of discretion in most situations. It would be impossible for legislators, the courts, and agencies to determine directives for every possible scenario an officer may face in a typical day. Since the requirements on an officer fluctuate greatly each day, most of the decisions made at the scene are left to the officer as long as the officer operates within the confines of the law and agency policy and procedure.

Centrality refers to the central position held in a network of functional and social relationships within an organization, which provides access to information and resources critical to the organization's success. While horizontal networks link positions at similar levels of authority, the vertical networks link positions along the chain of command at different levels. The old adage "information is power" implies that the more one knows, the more power one has. Typically, senior executives have greater access to information, giving them more power. By holding an important place in a communication network, a person is better informed about what is happening within the organization. Since information is spread between different people and different positions, being an important part of the information network not only satisfies their information needs, but it can also satisfy the information needs of others. Similarly, greater centrality in workflow networks allows an executive to tap into the resources of more people. Availability of diverse resources is found to be an important distinguishing factor of high performers, providing them greater power. Looking at the hierarchies found in typical criminal justice agencies, one can see that lieutenants or sergeants hold central spots in communication networks. Therefore, they are able to exercise great power in determining which and what type of information flows downward as well as upward in the hierarchy.

Relevance of the activities performed by an administrator to the overall objectives of an organization is an indicator of position power. The importance of these activities may change from time to time. For example, if an organization is facing a lawsuit, the attorney retained for legal advice and counsel becomes important. If law enforcement is involved in a questionable activity, such as abuse or intimidation, legal or ethical questions may arise from the community about the appropriateness of the actions. As this occurs, the media specialists become essential to the organization. They possess the position and power to create a larger issue or to appease the community and the media in their pursuit of answers.

Tactics for Increasing Power

Typically, power in organizations is not an individual phenomenon, but is related to the role departments play in the organization, the resources they control, and the environmental contingencies with which departments cope. For example, as mentioned earlier, all vice presidents do not enjoy the same power within an organization. Their power is contingent on the contribution made by their respective departments to the organizational goals. Researchers (Boeker, 1989; Saunders, 1990) have proposed five factors, discussed next, that determine the power of a department in the horizontal context of other departments within an organization. By strengthening each of these five factors, executives leverage their departments within the organization, resulting in greater power for themselves.

One of these factors is *dependency*. Organizations are a complex web of interdependencies between different departments. If Department B depends more on the outcome of Department A than vice versa, Department A has more power than Department B. In criminal justice, federal agencies have more jurisdictional latitude when it comes to processing and investigating cases in the United States. State agencies and local departments may have to depend on the federal agencies for information, transportation, and evidence, just to name a few issues. This affords federal agencies more power than the state and local agencies.

Control of resources is another factor in determining power within departments. Typically, departments that control the distribution of financial resources or who are more directly involved in generating revenue for the organization have more power.

Centrality reflects the importance of the activity performed by the department in the overall goal of the organization. The greater the perceived role of the contribution made by the department, the greater the power afforded to it. For example, a probation officer will work with an offender before and after sentencing. When provided the opportunity to recommend a sentence for the offender, the probation officer has a greater understanding of what may work best for this particular wrongdoer. Judges who view probation officers and their work as important will provide them with greater power in influencing sentences for offenders.

Nonsubstitutability implies that a department's task cannot be performed easily by someone else. In juvenile probation, departments can be highly specialized in the types of cases they handle. Some departments may focus specifically on abused/neglected youth, while others may focus on delinquents sentenced to intensive probation. The officers are not asked to work across departments, thus allowing for specialization in one particular aspect of juvenile justice.

The final aspect of determining power is *coping with uncertainty*. By helping reduce uncertainties, departments are better able to predict future changes. This gives them power. Similarly, departments with better absorption capacity can reduce the negative consequences of uncertainties and increase their power (Hickson, Hinings, Lee, Schneck, & Pennings, 1971). Although this is somewhat difficult to accomplish in the ever-changing environment of criminal justice, statistics and research departments within agencies and those hired by agencies are helping to reduce uncertainties by maintaining various types of statistics specific to agency and community needs.

In summary, power exists in all organizations and gets used during interactions between people and between groups. Personal power is significantly derived from the role departments play in an organization. By leveraging the role of one's department, one's individual power tends to be enhanced within the organization.

CAREER HIGHLIGHT BOX
PROBATION OFFICERS AND CORRECTIONAL TREATMENT SPECIALISTS

Nature of the Work

Many people who are convicted of crimes are placed on probation, instead of being sent to prison. People who have served time in prison are often released on parole. During probation and parole—and while they are in prison—offenders must stay out of trouble and meet other requirements. Probation officers and correctional treatment specialists work with and monitor offenders to prevent them from committing new crimes.

Duties

Probation officers and correctional treatment specialists typically do the following:

- Evaluate offenders to determine the best course of treatment
- Provide offenders with resources to aid in rehabilitation
- Discuss treatment options with offenders
- Arrange treatment programs
- Supervise offenders and monitor their progress
- Conduct meetings with offenders as well as their family and friends
- Write reports on the progress of offenders

Probation officers and correctional treatment specialists work with offenders who are given probation instead of jail time, who are still in prison, or who have been released from prison. The following are types of probation officers and correctional treatment specialists:

Probation officers, who are called **community supervision officers** in some states, supervise people who have been placed on probation. They work to ensure that the offender is not a danger to the community and to help in their rehabilitation. Probation officers write reports that detail each offender's treatment plans and their progress since they were put on probation. Most probation officers work with either adults or juveniles. Only in small, mostly rural, jurisdictions do probation officers counsel both adults and juveniles.

Pretrial services officers investigate an offender's background to determine if that offender can safely be allowed back into the community before his or her trial date. They must assess the risk and make a recommendation to a judge who decides on the appropriate sentencing or bond amount. When offenders are allowed back into the community, pretrial officers supervise them to make sure that they stay with the terms of their release and appear at their trials.

Parole officers work with people who have been released from jail and are serving parole to help them re-enter society. Parole officers monitor post-release offenders and provide them with various resources, such as substance abuse counseling or job training, to aid in their rehabilitation. By doing so, the officers try to change the offenders' behavior and thus reduce the risk of that person committing another crime and having to return to jail or prison.

Both probation and parole officers supervise offenders though personal contact with the offenders and their families. Probation and patrol officers require regularly scheduled contact with offenders by telephone or through office visits, and they may also check on offenders at their homes or places of work. Probation and parole officers also oversee drug testing and electronic monitoring of offenders. In some states, officers do the jobs of both probation and parole officers.

Correctional treatment specialists, who also may be known as **case managers** or **correctional counselors**, counsel offenders and develop rehabilitation plans for them to follow when they are no longer in prison or on parole. They may evaluate inmates using questionnaires and psychological tests. They also work with inmates, probation officers, and staff of other agencies to develop parole and release plans. For example, they may plan education and training programs to improve offenders' job skills.

Correctional treatment specialists write case reports that cover the inmate's history and the likelihood that he or she will commit another crime. When their clients are eligible for release, the case reports are given to the appropriate parole board. The specialist may help set up counseling for the offenders and their families, find substance-abuse or mental health treatment options, aid in job placement, and find housing.

Correctional treatment specialists also explain the terms and conditions of the prisoner's release, write reports, and keep detailed written accounts of each offender's progress. Specialists who work in parole and probation agencies have many of the same duties as their counterparts in correctional institutions.

The number of cases a probation officer or correctional treatment specialist handles at one time depends on the needs of offenders and the risks associated with each individual. Higher risk offenders usually command more of the officer's time and resources. Caseload size also varies by agency.

Technological advancements—such as improved tests for screening drug use, electronic devices to monitor clients, and kiosks that allow clients to check in remotely—help probation officers and correctional treatment specialists supervise and counsel offenders.

Probation officers and correctional treatment specialists held about 93,200 jobs in 2010. They work with criminal offenders, some of whom may be dangerous. While

(Continued)

(Continued)

supervising offenders, they may interact with others, such as family members and friends of their clients, who may be upset or difficult to work with. Workers may be assigned to fieldwork in high-crime areas or in institutions where there is a risk of violence or communicable disease.

In 2010, nearly all probation officers and correctional treatment specialists worked for either state or local governments:

State government, excluding education and hospitals	56%
Local government, excluding education and hospitals	41
Social assistance	2
Nursing and residential care facilities	1

Probation officers and correctional treatment specialists must meet many court-imposed deadlines, which contributes to heavy workloads and extensive paperwork. Many officers travel to do home and employment checks and property searches, especially in rural areas. Because of the hostile environments probation officers may encounter, some must carry a firearm or other weapon for protection.

All of these factors, as well as the frustration some officers and specialists feel in dealing with offenders who violate the terms of their release, contribute to a stressful work environment. Although the high stress levels can make the job difficult at times, this work also can be rewarding. Many officers and specialists receive personal satisfaction from counseling members of their community and helping them become productive citizens.

Work Schedules

Although many officers and specialists work full time, the demands of the job often lead to their working much longer hours. For example, many agencies rotate an on-call officer position. When these workers are on-call, they must respond to any issues with offenders or law enforcement 24 hours a day. Extensive travel and paperwork can also contribute to their having to work longer hours.

Training, Other Qualifications, and Advancement

Qualifications vary by agency, but a bachelor's degree is usually required. Most employers require candidates to pass oral, written, and psychological exams.

Important Qualities

Communication skills. Probation officers and correctional treatment specialists must be able to effectively interact and communicate with a wide range of people.

Critical-thinking skills. Probation officers and correctional treatment specialists must be able to assess the needs of individual offenders before determining the best resources for helping them.

Decision-making skills. Probation officers and correctional treatment specialists must consider the relative costs and benefits of potential actions and be able to choose appropriately.

Emotional stability. Probation officers and correctional treatment specialists must cope with hostile or otherwise upsetting situations, as well as with other stresses on the job.

Organizational skills. Probation officers and correctional treatment specialists must be able to manage multiple case files at one time.

Writing skills. Probation officers and correctional treatment specialists interpret training materials and write detailed reports on a regular basis.

Education and Training

A bachelor's degree in social work, criminal justice, psychology, or a related field is usually required. Some employers require a master's degree in a related field for candidates who do not have previous related work experience.

Although job requirements may vary, related work may include work in probation, pretrial services, parole, corrections, criminal investigations, substance abuse treatment, social work, or counseling. Work in any of these fields is typically considered a plus in the hiring process.

Most probation officers and correctional treatment specialists must complete a training program sponsored by their state government or the federal government, after which they may have to pass a certification test. In addition, they may be required to work as trainees or on a probationary period for up to 1 year before being offered a permanent position.

Some probation officers go on to specialize in a certain type of casework. For example, an officer may work only with domestic violence offenders or deal only with substance-abuse cases. Officers receive training specific to the group that they are working with so that they are better prepared to help that type of offender.

Most agencies require applicants to be at least 21 years old and, for federal employment, not older than 37 years of age. In addition, most departments require candidates to have a record free of felony convictions and to submit to drug testing. A valid driver's license is often required.

Advancement

Advancement to supervisory positions is primarily based on experience and performance. A graduate degree, such as a master's degree in criminal justice, social work, or psychology, may be helpful or required for advancement.

Job Outlook

Employment of probation officers and correctional treatment specialists is expected to grow by 18 percent from 2010 to 2020, about as fast as average for all occupations.

(Continued)

(Continued)

Continued growth in the demand for probation and parole services will lead to new openings for officers.

Mandatory sentencing guidelines in the 1980s and 1990s called for longer sentences and reduced parole for some offenses, resulting in an increase in the prison population. However, these guidelines are being reconsidered at both the federal and state levels due to budgetary constraints, court decisions, prison overcrowding, and doubts about the guidelines' effectiveness.

As guidelines are reduced or repealed, judges have more flexibility in sentencing offenders for each case. For offenders who are deemed to be a lower risk, this may result in less prison time, more community-based corrections, or some combination of the two.

As alternative forms of punishment, such as probation, become more widely used, the demand for probation and parole officers will grow. There also will be a need for parole and probation officers to supervise the large number of people who are now in prison when they are released.

Employment growth depends primarily on the amount of government funding for corrections, especially how much there is for probation and parole systems. Although community supervision is far less expensive than keeping offenders in prison, a change in political and social trends toward more imprisonment and away from community supervision could result in reduced employment opportunities.

Job Prospects

In addition to openings resulting from growth, many openings will be created by the need to replace large numbers of these workers expected to retire in the coming years. This occupation is not attractive to some potential entrants because of relatively low earnings, heavy workloads, and high stress. For these reasons, job opportunities should be excellent for those who qualify.

Earnings

The median annual wage of probation officers and correctional treatment specialists was $47,200 in May 2010. The median wage is the wage at which half of the workers in an occupation earned more than that amount and half earned less. The lowest 10 percent earned less than $30,920, and the top 10 percent earned more than $80,750.

Although many officers and specialists work full time, the demands of the job often lead to their working much longer hours. For example, many agencies rotate an on-call officer position. When these workers are on-call, they must respond to any issues with offenders or law enforcement 24 hours a day. Extensive travel and paperwork can also contribute to their having to work longer hours.

SOURCE: Bureau of Labor Statistics, U.S. Department of Labor, *Occupational Outlook Handbook, 2012–13 Edition*, Probation Officers and Correctional Treatment Specialists, on the Internet at http://www.bls .gov/ooh/community-and-social-service/probation-officers-and-correctional-treatment-specialists.htm.

Use of Power and Politics

A surge in information technology compounded by an increasing use of flatter organizational structures has precipitated a change in the role of a typical manager from authoritative to one of mentoring and coaching. Nevertheless, managers engage in *organizational politics,* a process of bargaining and negotiation, to increase their power. Such behavior allows them to influence decision making to obtain preferred outcomes, especially at times of uncertainty. Pfeffer, author of the book *Managing With Power* (1992), argues that managers who want to succeed must learn the art of politics. He writes, "To get things done, you need power—more power than those whose opposition you must overcome—and thus it is imperative to understand where power comes from and how these sources of power can be developed."

The domain of political activity typically applies to influencing decisions regarding structural changes, managing promotions, and managing scarce resource allocation. From time to time, organizations experience *structural change* by altering their organizational configuration to meet the needs of a changing environment. This reorganization can change the power and authority vested in different positions. Executives use politics to maneuver structural changes to put their people in central positions, which in turn provides them greater power and authority. A few years ago, Missouri created a State Court Administrators office. During this time, probation offices were asked to restructure their workers to better allocate their time and positions for pay and promotion evaluation. Each office determined the importance of all workers by identifying their duties and their perceived place on the pay scale. In doing this, power and authority that had been afforded to certain employees was adjusted and diverted to other positions. Workers were concerned about losses of power and authority, while administrators were focused on maneuvering particular individuals into central and key positions.

Executives use politics to manipulate a greater share of scarce resources. This is called *managing promotions.* Resources are vital for good performance, which is an important factor in determining a person's power in the organization.

Managing scarce resource allocation is another way that executives use politics to influence hiring, transfers, and promotions to place their people in important positions. Such maneuvering strengthens their network and alliances, affording them greater power. When politics involves deception and dishonesty to promote individual self-interest, it is considered an *abuse of power.* Such behavior leads to conflict and disharmony in the workplace. Research (Ferris & Kacmar, 1992) has shown that employees who perceive inappropriate use of power within an organization tend to experience job dissatisfaction and low morale, resulting in inferior organizational performance.

Ethical Decision Making

Earlier, it was mentioned that in criminal justice there is another source of power that emerges between the enforcers and the violators of law and order. For example, police are empowered with the use of force. Within this context are the much-publicized cases of the "video-taped Rodney King beating in Los Angeles, the torture of a Haitian immigrant with a plunger in New York, the Diallo shooting in New York, and the widespread corruption in New Orleans" (Raines, 2006, p. 2) that draw attention to questionable police ethics resulting from the abuse of discretionary power. These and other such cases reported in the media from time to time reflect unfavorable attitudes of the police based on race, ethnicity, and socioeconomic conditions. Numerous studies using data collected from different parts of the United States suggest that the previous issues are systemic and pervasive throughout the country (Jang, Joo, & Zhang, 2010). Today, black men are imprisoned at 6.5 times the rate of white men, although we could argue many points as to why this is the case (Forman, 2012).

Although unethical acts may not be the norm for most employees in the criminal justice system, there are those who work in positions of power within the system who choose to abuse that power. These acts have to be addressed. Adverse publicity from such incidents and other controversial practices erodes public confidence toward police and other criminal justice agencies. However, in a democratic society the criminal justice agencies want to be considered legitimate in a community and need the support from citizens. Failure to gain legitimacy can have serious consequences. For example, if the public has no confidence in law enforcement agencies, they are less likely to report crimes or call for services and assistance (Goudriaan, Wittebrood, & Nieuwbeerta, 2006). In fact, research shows that people in economically disadvantaged communities are less likely to report their victimization to the police (Baumer, 2002). However, such information from victims and witnesses is important to the successful resolution of crimes. In addition, lack of confidence in law enforcement agencies leads to unwillingness of the residents to abide by the law and a greater likelihood to challenge the authority of law enforcement agencies. Moreover, the level of public confidence in law enforcement agencies has a significant influence on citizens' perceptions of personal safety and fear of crime, which may be used as a proxy for quality of life. Consequently, people may start moving out from such areas with high crime and low confidence, thus dropping the value of businesses and real estate in these areas.

Similarly, ethical issues surface sometimes when the crime lab reports circumvent true scientific investigation methods for the sake of prosecuting an offender. Though such misreporting is not the norm, it does happen. The *Journal of Forensic Sciences* published a symposium on the ethical responsibilities of forensic scientists in 1989, where an article discussed a number of unacceptable lab reporting practices, including (1) preparation of reports containing minimum information with the express purpose of not giving the other side ammunition for cross-examination, (2) omitting some significant point from a report, and (3) falsifying the results (Giannelli, 2012). The failure to sometimes report accurate information or provide misleading information in the crime lab report suggests that the expected impartiality is replaced by a viewpoint tainted with prosecutorial bias, thus undermining the purpose. To most of us whose knowledge of crime labs comes from television shows such as *CSI*, the forensic experts seem like infallible scientists out to find the truth, regardless of where it leads. However, this can be far from accurate. In unscrupulous cases, lab reports hide or obscure the negative confirmatory tests, while positive presumptive and confirmatory test results are included in final lab reports with the express purpose of strengthening the pro-prosecution platform. In some cases, the police may share their suspicion regarding suspects with the lab workers before the forensic examinations are conducted, thus prejudicing them toward the desired outcome. On numerous occasions it is found that the lab examiners perceive themselves to be part of the prosecution team, with the express objective to help the police and the prosecutors convict the suspect—thus lying about the test results or withholding important information. For example, one of the most notorious cases involved Fred Zain, the chief serologist in the West Virginia State Police Crime Lab, who falsified test results from 1979 to 1989 (Giannelli, 2012). Similarly, the North Carolina crime lab scandal is reported by Giannelli, where the FBI investigation found that the lab provided information favorable to the prosecution, often misrepresenting the results. It has also been found that some forensic examiners may provide "dry-lab" results—that is, fabricate results without performing the necessary lab tests. It has also been found that the forensic workers may lie about their academic credentials or accreditation to get a job, which may compromise the lab test results due to lack of expertise.

> These types of problems have led to scandals at dozens of crime labs across the nation, resulting in full or partial closures, reorganizations, investigations or firings at city or county labs in Baltimore; Boston; Chicago; Colorado Springs, Colorado; Dallas; Detroit; Erie County, New York; Houston; Los Angeles; Monroe County, New York; Oklahoma City; San Antonio, Texas; San Diego; San Francisco; San Joaquin County, California; New York City; Nashville, Tennessee; and Tucson, Arizona, as well as at state-run crime labs in Illinois, Montana, Maryland, New Jersey, New York, Oregon, Pennsylvania, Virginia, Washington, North Carolina, West Virginia and Wisconsin, plus the federally-run FBI and U.S. Army crime labs. (Clarke, 2010, p. 1)

Judges are another very important part of the entire criminal justice system. Of all the public officials involved in the justice system, including the police, prosecutors, correctional officers, and parole officers, judges exercise the most influence and power. Therefore, society would expect judges to be law-abiding citizens who would conduct themselves ethically and professionally at all times. Unfortunately, this is not always the case, as demonstrated by numerous cases involving judicial misconduct reported by Hunter and Friedman (2009). Hunter and Friedman reported on instances where bribes and sexual favors are given in place of lighter sentences to convicted offenders. If the judges are caught, they may not be disciplined because the disciplinary councils or other investigative bodies are usually composed of judges who are their peers. Moreover, there is no public oversight, and often the decisions are passed in secrecy. This suggests that complaints against judges are not taken seriously, a case supported by statistical facts. For example,

> 1,163 complaints were filed against federal judges from October 1, 2007, through September 30, 2008, and 759 complaints were concluded during that time period. The vast majority of the concluded complaints—742—were dismissed, nine were withdrawn, and only four resulted in any type of disciplinary action. The statistics in state courts are similar.

In California, 909 judicial complaints were filed in 2008 and 892 were concluded. Of the concluded complaints, only 34 (3.8%) resulted in punishment—ranging from advisory letters to removal from the bench. New York's Commission on Judicial Conduct received 1,923 complaints last year, a record number. Of those, around 3% led to discipline, including 33 letters of caution and 26 formal charges. (Hunter and Friedmann, 2009, p. 7)

Interestingly, discipline can be imposed by commissions that oversee judicial complaints only on sitting judges. However, while facing misconduct charges if the judges resign or retire, then they can avoid disciplinary sanctions altogether, and sometimes, they can even retain full retirement benefits (Hunter & Friedmann, 2009).

Once incarcerated, correctional staff members have complete power over incarcerated offenders and, in some cases, over their release from prison, which has led to abuse of power resulting in sexual assault and rape. A *Prison Legal News* (August, 2006) cover story by Hunter profiles examples of sexual abuse by correctional officers and other employees in 26 states. Another report published by the Bureau of Justice Statistics (Beck & Harrison, 2007), stated that 60% of allegations of sexual abuse involved staff members rather than other prisoners. Furthermore, this report estimated that 38,600 state and federal prisoners had self-reported sexual abuse or misconduct by prison employees. This is not even a complete picture, as a vast number of cases go unreported because it is very difficult to prove misconduct by prison staff when the incarcerated victims are often considered untrustworthy. Moreover, in most correctional settings, the coworkers may be unwilling to report the unethical behavior of the involved prison staff members. Using the information from a 2005 U.S. Department of Justice report, Hunter (2013) noted, "In many cases where there was sufficient evidence to prove that a staff member had sexually abused an inmate, the OIG has found that some prosecutors are reluctant to prosecute prison staff who do not use force or overt threats to obtain sex with inmates, often because the penalty is only a misdemeanor." And when they are caught for sexually abusing prisoners, many prison and jail workers are not prosecuted. According to the Bureau of Justice Statistics report, in 2006 only 56% of staff members involved in substantiated incidents of sexual abuse were referred to prosecution. And even the ones who were prosecuted were often released on low bonds, pleaded to lesser charges that may not involve sex crimes, and received short sentences or probation. These data insinuate that rape is less serious when the victim is a prisoner and the predators are government employees (Hunter, 2013).

In the News 5.1
Why Police Lie Under Oath

Why Police Lie Under Oath

Thousands of people plead guilty to crimes every year in the United States because they know that the odds of a jury believing their word over a police officer's word are slim to none. As a juror, whom are you likely to believe: the alleged criminal in an orange jumpsuit or two well-groomed police officers in uniforms who just swore to God they're telling the truth, the whole truth and nothing but? As one of my colleagues recently put it, "Everyone knows you have to be crazy to accuse the police of lying."

But are police officers necessarily more trustworthy than alleged criminals? I think not. Not just because the police have a special inclination toward confabulation, but because, disturbingly, they have an incentive to lie. In this era of mass incarceration, the police shouldn't be trusted any more than any other witness, perhaps less so.

That may sound harsh, but numerous law enforcement officials have put the matter more bluntly. Peter Keane, a former San Francisco Police commissioner, wrote an article in The San Francisco Chronicle decrying a police culture that treats lying as the norm: "Police officer perjury in court to justify illegal dope searches is commonplace. One of the dirty little not-so-secret secrets of the criminal justice system is undercover narcotics officers intentionally lying under oath. It is a perversion of the American justice system that strikes directly at the rule of law. Yet it is the routine way of doing business in courtrooms everywhere in America."

The New York City Police Department is not exempt from this critique. In 2011, hundreds of drug cases were dismissed after several police officers were accused of mishandling evidence. That year, Justice Gustin L. Reichbach of the State Supreme Court in Brooklyn condemned a widespread culture of lying and corruption in the department's drug enforcement units. "I thought I was not naïve," he said when announcing a guilty verdict involving a police detective who had planted crack cocaine on a pair of suspects. "But even this court was shocked, not only by the seeming pervasive scope of misconduct but even more distressingly by the seeming casualness by which such conduct is employed."

Remarkably, New York City officers have been found to engage in patterns of deceit in cases involving charges as minor as trespass. In September it was reported that the Bronx district attorney's office was so alarmed by police lying that it decided to stop prosecuting people who were stopped and arrested for trespassing at public housing projects, unless prosecutors first interviewed the arresting officer to ensure the arrest was actually warranted. Jeannette Rucker, the chief of arraignments for the Bronx district attorney, explained in a letter that it had become apparent that the police were arresting people even when there was convincing evidence that they were innocent. To justify the arrests, Ms. Rucker claimed, police officers provided false written statements, and in depositions, the arresting officers gave false testimony.

Mr. Keane, in his Chronicle article, offered two major reasons the police lie so much. First, because they can. Police officers "know that in a swearing match between a drug defendant and a police officer, the judge always rules in favor of the officer." At worst, the case will be dismissed, but the officer is free to continue business as usual. Second, criminal defendants are typically poor and uneducated, often belong to a racial minority, and often have a criminal record. "Police know that no one cares about these people," Mr. Keane explained.

All true, but there is more to the story than that.

Police departments have been rewarded in recent years for the sheer numbers of stops, searches and arrests. In the war on drugs, federal grant programs like the Edward Byrne Memorial Justice Assistance Grant Program have encouraged state and local law enforcement agencies to boost drug arrests in order to compete for millions of dollars in funding. Agencies receive cash rewards for arresting high numbers of people for drug offenses, no matter how minor the offenses or how weak the

(Continued)

(Continued)

evidence. Law enforcement has increasingly become a numbers game. And as it has, police officers' tendency to regard procedural rules as optional and to lie and distort the facts has grown as well. Numerous scandals involving police officers lying or planting drugs—in Tulia, Tex. and Oakland, Calif., for example—have been linked to federally funded drug task forces eager to keep the cash rolling in.

The pressure to boost arrest numbers is not limited to drug law enforcement. Even where no clear financial incentives exist, the "get tough" movement has warped police culture to such a degree that police chiefs and individual officers feel pressured to meet stop-and-frisk or arrest quotas in order to prove their "productivity."

For the record, the New York City police commissioner, Raymond W. Kelly, denies that his department has arrest quotas. Such denials are mandatory, given that quotas are illegal under state law. But as the Urban Justice Center's Police Reform Organizing Project has documented, numerous officers have contradicted Mr. Kelly. In 2010, a New York City police officer named Adil Polanco told a local ABC News reporter that "our primary job is not to help anybody, our primary job is not to assist anybody, our primary job is to get those numbers and come back with them." He continued: "At the end of the night you have to come back with something. You have to write somebody, you have to arrest somebody, even if the crime is not committed, the number's there. So our choice is to come up with the number."

Exposing police lying is difficult largely because it is rare for the police to admit their own lies or to acknowledge the lies of other officers. This reluctance derives partly from the code of silence that governs police practice and from the ways in which the system of mass incarceration is structured to reward dishonesty. But it's also because police officers are human.

Research shows that ordinary human beings lie a lot—multiple times a day—even when there's no clear benefit to lying. Generally, humans lie about relatively minor things like "I lost your phone number; that's why I didn't call" or "No, really, you don't look fat." But humans can also be persuaded to lie about far more important matters, especially if the lie will enhance or protect their reputation or standing in a group.

The natural tendency to lie makes quota systems and financial incentives that reward the police for the sheer numbers of people stopped, frisked or arrested especially dangerous. One lie can destroy a life, resulting in the loss of employment, a prison term and relegation to permanent second-class status. The fact that our legal system has become so tolerant of police lying indicates how corrupted our criminal justice system has become by declarations of war, "get tough" mantras, and a seemingly insatiable appetite for locking up and locking out the poorest and darkest among us.

And, no, I'm not crazy for thinking so.

SOURCE: From "Why Police Lie Under Oath" by Michelle Alexander, *The New York Times*, February 2, 2013.

Besides abuse of discretionary power, there is a host of other day-to-day work scenarios that put criminal justice officers in the midst of ethical dilemmas. Sometimes, situations arise that require officers to weigh the laws they are sworn to uphold against the life of an innocent victim. Harrison (1999) cites an example:

> Imagine working as a police officer assigned to investigate the kidnapping of an 11-year-old girl. Officers have arrested a suspect who may know of the girl's whereabouts. Unless they elicit a quick confession, the girl may die. Under the law, the suspect has an absolute right against self-incrimination. Officers may adhere to the law and respect the rights of the suspect, or use extralegal measures to coerce the information they need to save a life. The dilemma becomes which course of action better serves the concept of Jeffersonian Happiness—that of respecting the individual arrestee's rights or that of serving the greater good by using formal authority to ensure safety for the community. (p. 3)

Such incidents force officers to confront the "noble cause" corruption dilemma of violating fundamental laws to serve a greater moral good (Harrison, 1999). Similarly, police executives and officers are often subjected to ethical situations when they have to be responsive to local political power while pursuing their professional task of law enforcement (Nelligan & Taylor, 1994). Likewise, community policing officers who are mandated to establish close relationships with community members are often presented with ethical challenges in the exercise of their discretionary power. As they become more socially integrated, they run the risk of information overload, which puts them in an ethical quandary as to what incidents to process and what to ignore.

Ethical issues also emerge when officers are involved in the recruitment and management of informants. Dunningham and Norris (1998) ask,

> Is it appropriate to practice deceptive techniques to recruit an informer? Should an informer, in the pursuit of intelligence, be permitted to commit criminal offences? Is it correct to use an informer who is known to have been involved in serious crime and ignore past offending? (p. 21)

For informants to be used on more than one occasion there has to be reciprocity, which implies mutuality of advantage. This is at the heart of many of the ethical dilemmas faced by officers in the area of policing. In addition, police officers are constantly exposed to dangerous environments, unusual working hours, and inconsistent sleep habits, all of which add to the stress of the job and may blur their judgment of right and wrong when decisions have to be made in split seconds.

Steps Taken to Address Ethical Issues

Such difficult and often unique situations and scenarios embedded in ethics are a focus of a number of forums arranged throughout the country where academics and practitioners regularly get together. One can see by the sheer number of discussions that it can be extremely difficult for employees to distinguish between ethical and unethical behaviors. Consequently, the impact of ethical versus unethical behavior on agency performance has been hard to study because of disagreement over what behaviors are considered ethical or unethical. For example, the practice of accepting cups of coffee at the local McDonald's was widely held as ethical and acceptable until recent years (as discussed in In the News 5.2). Various arguments have been given by officers to explain their unethical behavior, such as basic stupidity; not realizing it was against the law; believing corruption is part of the job and is required to survive their job; or believing that they are doing the right thing, that they are doing what the agency requires; that they are simply following orders; or that this was the best way to help out a friend; or to feed their ego, to satisfy their greed and achieve personal gains, or as a type of revenge (Steinberg & Austern, 1990).

In response to problems that arise due to unregulated discretionary power, reforms are continuously being made in the emerging new criminal justice system (ENCJS) to provide checks and balances. For example, there has been bail reform

> in which documentation of a defendant's social ties in the community becomes the basis for unconditional and unsecured pretrial release. This procedure replaces the discretionary practice of the courts, which have traditionally used bail unnecessarily, with undue harshness, in violation of constitutional guarantees, and in a way that prejudices the defendant's chances for acquittal. (Robin, 1974, p. 354)

Similarly, the National Prison Rape Elimination Commission has issued proposed standards to reduce sexual abuse behind bars. All 50 states have enacted laws criminalizing sex between prisoners and prison staff; thus, employees who engage in sexual misconduct can no longer claim consent as a defense. Another important change in criminal justice is the use of scientific diagnosis and classification to match the personality type of the providers of service to those being treated, which improves the quality of service. Furthermore, the application of an advocacy principle has led to the creation of the office of ombudsman in the prison community, which acts on prisoner complaints and grievances. Greater control of police discretionary power has been maintained by having the police complete citizen contact forms for each encounter with the public regardless of circumstances. In addition, there now has to be an onsite arrest review by assistant district attorneys to assess the legality, appropriateness, and value of police arrests of particular categories of suspects (Robin, 1974).

In the News 5.2
Free Coffee? Thanks, but No Thanks

Hello, Fairbanks! An article a few weeks ago in the *News-Miner* caught my eye, in which a Chicago police officer was accused of flashing her badge and screaming at Starbucks employees, demanding free coffee and baked goods. The officer was suspended for 15 months and ordered to undergo counseling. According to the article, the officer's attorney maintained that "she never used her job to demand coffee—but that some stores gave it to her for free because she was an officer."

When should a police officer accept a free cup of coffee or a discounted meal? The bottom-line answer: Never. At the Fairbanks Police Department, we have a strict personnel policy that prohibits the receipt of gratuities—this includes coffee and discounted meals at restaurants. Surprisingly, this is not the case in many areas of the country. When I attended the FBI National Academy in Quantico, Va., I had the opportunity to interact with more than 220 law enforcement administrators from every region of the United States. I have to admit that I was somewhat taken aback by the "gradient of tolerance" that was expressed regarding the acceptance of such gratuities.

In general, cultural acceptance of such practices was strong around the East Coast regions of the United States, diminishing as one moved westward. By the time one looked to standard police policies in the Northwest states and Alaska, complete prohibitions regarding the acceptance of any type of gratuity was the norm.

How did such practices originate? I suspect that the biggest factor lies in the evolution of modern, professional policing, and the accompanying changes in wages and benefits that occurred. In the "early days" of the late 1800s and early 1900s, police officers received little training and were paid poorly. As a result, many citizens and shopkeepers sympathized with the long hours and poor benefits experienced by these officers, and wished to "help them out" by offering free meals, coffee, etc. Additionally, savvy business owners realized it was beneficial to have police officers spending their break and meal times at their establishments, thus obtaining a "supplemental security force" for the price of a few meals and cups of coffee.

Thankfully, policing has evolved and today's highly trained police professional is likely to earn a respectable wage and benefits package. As such, there is simply no need or necessity to accept offers of free goods or services. Furthermore, if one were to start accepting such offers, it can pose ethical dilemmas in a number of areas:

- What is the expectation of the store owner? If a restaurant was providing free meals to officers, and the business is then burglarized, is the owner going to expect "special attention" from the police regarding the case?
- Is it fair to other merchants? If police are frequenting certain establishments because of offered gratuities, would other merchants suffer from a correspondingly reduced police presence at their own locations? Would neglected merchants then feel pressure to "compete" by offering similar gratuities, just to ensure a comparable police presence?
- Where does the officer "draw the line"? If a simple cup of coffee is OK, how much worse is a free breakfast? Discounted merchandise?

Thankfully, we don't need to head down that road and make such value judgments. The fairest, simplest and most ethical approach to the issue is to simply prohibit all such practices. Our officers receive a comprehensive wage and benefits package, and can afford to pay for the goods and services they receive in the same manner as the other hard-working residents of our community.

The reason that I feel compelled to address this issue lies in one problem area that we sometimes encounter. We have a lot of generous, well-meaning merchants in this community, many of whom have relocated from other locales where the culture of providing minor gratuities to police officers was considered perfectly acceptable. Most of these folks are offering a cup of coffee or a meal out of simple appreciation, and are certainly not expecting any kind of "payback."

I hope these folks realize that, when we politely refuse their offers, we do not mean to offend them or show disdain for their generosity. We are simply letting them know that it is our duty and pleasure to serve them, and nothing more is expected (or accepted) in return.

SOURCE: From "Free Coffee? Thanks, but No Thanks," by D. Hoffman, chief of the Fairbanks (AK) Police Department, December 21, 2008, *Fairbanks Daily News-Miner.*

As changes are incorporated and behaviors are questioned, an environment of uncertainty and confusion prevails. It is here that the agency has to identify the policies on acceptable and unacceptable behaviors. Research suggests that six spheres of influence impact an individual when confronted with ethical choices—the workplace, family, religion, legal system, community, and profession (Ferrell, Fraedrich, & Ferrell 2008). Typically, people learn these values and principles through the socialization process with family members, social groups, and workplace. The level of importance of each of these factors will vary depending on the importance the decision maker perceives the issue to be. For some employees, ethical issues may not reach the level of critical awareness if supervisors fail to identify and educate employees about specific problem areas. Top-level managers have to mirror those desirable behaviors to create a culture built on ethical values. These top managers and supervisors provide blueprints for the corporate culture of the organization, failure of which can result in a corporate culture evolving on its own that may reflect part of the values of the company. Leaders play a crucial role in influencing the organizational culture and ethical posture. Leaders, by their ability to motivate others and by having the power to enforce rules and policies, can guide and direct others toward achievement of goals (Ferrell et al., 2008). Raines (2006) argues that the reasons influencing the ethical conduct of police officers emerge from certain basic factors, such as a code of silence and personal loyalty, hiring practices, the demands of the profession, socialization, personal morality, character, and supervision. The fact that police officers typically do not report fellow officers for misconduct is known as the code of silence and is well documented in policing literature (Klockars, Ivkovic, & Haberfeld, 2004). More discussion on officers' willingness to overlook fellow officers' unethical behaviors appears in Chapter 9.

Generally, ethical dilemmas involve situations in which decision rules are often vague or in conflict. And there are no magic formulas or computer software that will provide for a solution. A significant factor in ethical decision making is the ethical component of corporate culture. If the corporate culture encourages or rewards unethical behavior, then its employees may act unethically (Ferrell et al., 2008). This behavior will further translate into hiring practices, whereby hiring people with similar values becomes more probable, thus reinforcing the unethical environment. In addition, lack of proper screening may allow individuals with questionable ethical standards to join the police force. Another possibility is that the minimum requirements for hiring new recruits may be inadequate, which could be attracting young individuals at a stage of moral development that is not appropriate to a policing job that demands the highest moral character (Raines, 2006). Alternatively, the recruits may be hired with high moral values and good intentions, but after joining the workforce, the socialization process may adversely impact their moral reasoning. They could be influenced by the group values and established behaviors of their peers, who may have become disillusioned and hardened by conditions they encountered on the force (Raines, 2006). Training and supervisor attitudes toward misconduct, which are embedded in the same system, may also be reinforcing the established behavior of the recruit. If the organizational norms of an agency support unethical behavior, eventually the officers will either adopt the undesirable behavior or quit the organization (Hirschman, 1970).

Typically, issues that are communicated as being high in ethical importance have a strong influence on employees' ethical behavior. Consequently, identification of ethical issues that employees may encounter in their day-to-day work is a significant step toward developing their ability to make ethical decisions. Therefore, good training programs and communication systems to educate employees about the organization's ethical standards are important in developing effective ethics programs. Training can educate employees about the organizational policies and expectations, relevant laws, and regulations–to maintain ethical standards within the organization. Training can also make employees aware of the available resources and the support system to assist in ethical decision making.

A variety of resources can also be deployed to monitor the efficacy of an ethics program. Observing employees, internal audits, surveys, reporting systems, and investigations can assess compliance with the organization's ethical code and standards (Ferrell et al., 2008). Organizations can monitor employees' ethical decision-making capabilities by observing how they handle an ethically charged situation or use role-playing exercises in training. Questionnaires can be used to gauge the benchmark of ethical performance by surveying the employees on their understanding on a broad set of issues and gaining their perceptions on the ethical and unethical practices within the organization. Analysis of this information will provide a better understanding of what type of unethical practices may be occurring and why, which may help develop more effective training programs. In addition, the existence of internal systems by which employees can report unethical practices is useful for monitoring and evaluating ethical practices. Help lines and ethics officers are two such sources that organizations have used.

Most organizations begin the process of establishing organizational ethics programs by developing codes of conduct, which are formal statements that describe the expectations of an organization from its employees (Ferrell et al., 2008). It is a statement that is comprehensive and serves as the basis for rules of conduct. The code of ethics typically specifies acceptable and unacceptable types of behavior, and states the methods for reporting violations, disciplinary action for violations, and a structure of due process. Through the enforcement of formal codes, policies, and rules by the management, the opportunity that employees have for unethical behavior in an organization can be eliminated. Research shows that organizational codes of ethics often contain six core values, namely, trustworthiness, respect, responsibility, fairness, caring, and citizenship. These values will not be effective without training and the support of top management in making them a part of the corporate culture. For example, financial companies such as banks or savings and loan companies have developed detailed sets of rules and procedures to avoid the opportunity for employees to take advantage of their trusted positions.

A deeper understanding of the previous factors in the context of personal ethics and organizational culture is required to identify solutions to eradicate the abuse of power and unethical behaviors in criminal justice. When faced with ethical issues, people base their decisions on their values and the principles of right or wrong, most of which are learned by individuals through their socialization process. Every individual has an ethical decision framework, or *personal ethics,* that guides the person's behavior in day-to-day decision making. The set of personal beliefs and values that individuals bring to the workplace guides their moral reasoning to take any action. Many theories associated with moral philosophies refer to value orientation and such things as economics, idealism, and relativism. The economic value orientation theory is associated with values that can be quantified in monetary terms. According to this theory, people may justify their action as ethical if an act produces more monetary value than its effort. Alternatively, idealism is a moral philosophy that places value on ideals as products of the mind. For some individuals, these ethical principles may simply be in line with the good behavior defined and expected by colleagues and society; for others, these codes of ethics may be an internal set of standards that are self-chosen rather than forced by external expectations. The difference here is between the use of ethical absolutism and ethical relativism. *Ethical absolutism* suggests that "objective standards of truth exist independently of us" (Harris, 1997, p. 103), implying that there "exists an eternal and unchanging moral code that transcends the physical world and is the same for all people at all times and places" (Holmes, 1998, p. 165). Officers driven by ethical absolutism will not be influenced by the culture of the organization and the values of peers and colleagues in conducting themselves. On the other hand, *ethical relativism* maintains that ethical dimensions of right and wrong vary from person to person and from place to place (Holmes, 1998; Rachels, 1999). Consequently, personal values and perspectives rather than universal ethical principles influence the appraisal of any situation. Officers driven by ethical relativism may be more easily influenced by organizational culture and the values that they are subjected to in their day-to-day work environment.

Using the previous framework, Catlin and Maupin (2004) examined two cohorts of police officers in a state police organization. The first cohort was studied during the recruit academy and after one year on the job, and the second cohort was studied at one and two years on the job. They observed that the ethical orientation of the officers changed from high absolutism to high relativism and from high idealism to low idealism. In discussing these results with the training commanders of this police organization, they found that this change may have occurred because of many training and acculturation factors. They conclude,

> From the first day of the academy, there is significant emphasis on the necessity to protect oneself physically and emotionally. Firearms training, defensive tactics, as well as arrest tactics focus on self-protection. In addition, the police subculture is rife with themes of protecting oneself from the scrutiny of the public, administration and management or the brass, and from other officers. (p. 297)

Another possible explanation could be that a large number of officers with the moral absolutism orientation may have self-selected out of the profession because of conflict with the ambiguity inherent in the police role. Moral absolutism may be in conflict with the broad range of discretion that officers must use in dealing with their day-to-day duties as a law enforcement agent on the street. Such discretion is amplified by the fact that the officer is dealing with nonvoluntary clients in an environment of limited resources as well as ambiguous goals and performance measures. Another possible explanation of the observed results could be provided by the socialization theories, which maintain that the beliefs, attitudes, and values possessed by officers are developed as a direct result of occupational experiences rather than from previously learned behavior (Lyman, 1999).

If a large number of police officers are going to experience major challenges to their ethical framework, then training should prepare them for such challenges. However, there is very little evidence that current police training focuses on identification of personal ethical orientations and preparing officers to deal with the ramifications of their personal ethics (Raines, 2006). For example, in California (Harrison, 1999), "of the 800 hours a new recruit spends in basic academy training, only a fraction deals with issues beyond basic skills. Most police training academies devote little classwork to the broader understanding of the police role in society at a philosophical level" (p. 5).

Training in ethics is imperative in creating an ethical environment and ethical employees and is no different from training in other areas. A policing agency would not assign guns to new officers without first training them in the proper way to use and carry the weapon. Similarly, agencies must train employees on what is and is not expected of them before giving them the discretionary power to serve and protect citizens. It is unacceptable to believe that individuals only learn right and wrong behaviors from their parents, schools, teachers, peers, and religious affiliations. Criminal justice agencies must take responsibility for introducing and reinforcing right and wrong behaviors through training (Allen, Mhlanga, & Khan, 2006). Without such training, individuals may not make reliable and correct decisions, allowing for unethical, unprofessional, or improper actions. Providing the skills necessary to make ethical and professional decisions ensures that criminal justice personnel will react as desired when confronted with a situation that could allow for unacceptable behavior (Allen et al., 2006).

A fundamental change has been seen in the promotion of increased education of criminal justice personnel, which had been conspicuously absent, even at the higher levels of the pyramid (Robin, 1974). Consequently, there has been subsidization of "the pre-service university education of individuals planning careers in law enforcement and the education of in-service practitioners enrolled in relevant college curricula" (Robin, 1974, p. 357). It is felt that higher education will make the officers more aware and will also encourage and reinforce a sense of commitment to the procedures and goals, which will prevent abuse of discretionary power that results in unethical decisions. In addition, proper screening during recruitment can reduce the number of individuals with misplaced personal morality entering the police force.

In addition, to control the behavior and actions of its employees, an organization can outline rules and regulations, which offer a foundation for its organizational culture. *Organizational culture* nurtures and shapes the overall frameworks of values within which individuals operate and that are reflected in everyday practices. These organizational values guide the decisions and behaviors of employees regarding whether they are right or wrong in a moral sense, as well as promote fairness and justice when dealing with one another and with those outside of the organization. To prevent the abuse of power and other ethical violations, such as taking bribes or kickbacks and various other forms of corruption, organizations can explicitly adopt a *code of ethics* that defines the principles of morality or rules of conduct. Law enforcement has a separate code of ethics and code of conduct. The police code of conduct was originally passed in 1957 at the annual International Association of Chiefs of Police (IACP) conference. This document was revised in 1989, creating two documents—a code of ethics and a police code of conduct, which were approved by the IACP in 1991 at their annual conference. The code of ethics is used more like an oath of office at police academy graduation ceremonies, and the police code of conduct is the ethical mandate that provides guidance to the officers in performing their jobs (Raines, 2006).

Correctional agencies tend to create their own codes of ethics for specific institutions. For example, the Nevada Department of Corrections (2006) states the following in its code of ethics for correctional institution staff:

> The Nevada Department of Corrections is committed to a code of ethics that will guide the performance, conduct, and behavior of its employees. This code will ensure that our professionalism is reflected in the operation and activities of the Department and is recognized by all interested parties. In this light, the following principles are practiced:
>
> - Employees shall maintain high standards of honesty, integrity, and impartiality, free from any personal considerations, favoritism, or partisan demands.
> - Employees shall be courteous, considerate, and prompt when dealing with the public, realizing that we serve the public.
> - Employees shall maintain mutual respect and professional cooperation in their relationships with other staff members of the Department of Corrections.
> - Employees shall be firm, fair, and consistent in the performance of their duties. Employees shall treat others with dignity, respect, and compassion and provide humane custody and care, void of all retribution, harassment, or abuse.
> - Employees shall uphold the tenets of the United States Constitution, its amendments, the Nevada Constitution, federal and State laws, rules and regulations, and policies of the Department.
> - Whether on or off duty, in uniform or not, employees shall conduct themselves in a manner that will not bring discredit or embarrassment to the Department of Corrections and the State of Nevada.
> - Employees shall report without reservation any corrupt or unethical behavior that could affect either inmates, employees, or the integrity of the Department of Corrections.
> - Employees shall not use their position for personal gain.
> - Employees shall maintain confidentiality of information that has been entrusted to them and designated as such.
> - Employees shall not permit themselves to be placed under any kind of personal obligation that could lead any person to expect official favors.
> - Employees shall not accept or solicit from anyone, either directly or indirectly, anything of economic value, such as a gift, gratuity, favor, entertainment, or loan which is, or may appear to be, designed to influence their official conduct.

- Employees will not discriminate against any inmate, employee, or any member of the public on the basis of race, gender, creed, or national origin.
- Employees will not sexually harass or condone sexual harassment with or against any person.
- Employees shall maintain the highest standards of personal hygiene, grooming, and neatness while on duty or otherwise representing the Department. (n.p.)

These ethical values can be incorporated in policies and rules that guide the organization's decision-making system, which determines rewards, promotions, selection, and training of employees. These efforts at the organizational level help reinforce the personal and ethical standards of employees. Both private and public sector organizations nowadays are spending a lot of money in establishing formal ethics programs. Significant measures are being taken by progressive organizations in providing comprehensive training to their employees to bring standardization in adopting ethical measures in everyday decision making. Ethics hotlines have been set up in some organizations to answer any questions that employees may face in ethical decision making.

Within the context of organizational culture, employees learn about values, beliefs, and behavior from watching their superiors. Therefore, leadership plays a crucial role in influencing the ethical standards that will be adopted within an organization. Through their personal example, the top leaders can create and sustain a culture of high ethical behavior among their employees. When the senior executives engage in unethical practices or overlook such behavior by failing to take firm and decisive action against their colleagues, they are encouraging this behavior to filter down through the organization. Murphy and Caplan (1991) suggest that in a police department, integrity begins with the police chief. The chief must

> make clear to the force that corruption will not be tolerated . . . [and] in formulating the message, the chief must take care not to attack all personnel. An anticorruption program should not offend those who have maintained standards. The chief's statements condemning corrupt officers should offer comfort to the honest and dedicated ones, as well as counsel and support to dishonest officers who are still redeemable. Finally, in defending a moral ideal, the chief should not be perceived as expressing meanness, envy, or moral superiority. (p. 313)

They go on to say that the chief must set an example by not accepting gratuities, taking gifts, or assisting friends and family with traffic tickets, as well as refraining from other behaviors identified as improper. Development of a code of ethics may be easier said than done, but the task should be taken on by those in positions of power in criminal justice agencies. Formal codes of ethics and training programs become worthless in instilling high ethical standards among employees when the leaders cannot demonstrate these values through their personal actions and behaviors.

Similarly, the organizational goals should not be so unreasonable that instead of motivating employees to perform better, they force workers to adopt unethical behaviors and abuse power. As noted by Murphy and Caplan (1991), policy manuals, especially in criminal justice, can become so specific that it is unrealistic for officers to follow every policy without taking the chance of violating another:

> The existence of so many prohibitions can have an effect opposite to that intended. Officers will come to view the rules as a public relations ploy, as pious announcements not to be taken seriously. If the manual makes it seem as if everyone is eligible for disciplinary action, the threat of punishment loses much of its significance; when discipline does occur, it therefore seems arbitrary and unfair. (p. 317)

Murphy and Caplan (1991) also point out that overmanaging through policy can create the belief that even honest mistakes may be sanctioned, so minor rule violations must be hidden. This perception facilitates corruption.

Often, it becomes difficult to report internally the unethical behavior of senior executives because of the fear of retribution. However, by going outside the organization to report the unethical action, the employee is said to be *blowing the whistle*. The action may be reported to the government, press, or special interest groups. More and more U.S. states are now enacting laws to protect whistle-blowers (Costa-Clarke, 1994). In addition, the federal False Claims Act allows whistle-blowers to file a case against government wrongdoers in the name of the United States. In 1986, the government strengthened the False Claims Act, providing greater protection to whistle-blowers, which has helped the government recover billions of dollars in false claim cases (Jackson, 1999). The government has also enacted the Foreign Corrupt Practices Act of 1977 to report against organizations that are paying bribes to high government officials in foreign countries in an attempt to get contracts and sell products and services. In addition, Congress created a U.S. Sentencing Commission to issue new guidelines for white-collar crimes, which are on the rise as the knowledge-based economy continues to grow.

In the last decade, the external stakeholders have started to play a major role in influencing organizations to adopt more stringent ethical standards in guiding their decision making. Important stakeholders include government agencies, customers, and special interest groups. Government agencies draw limits in the form of health and safety laws, environmental protection requirements, and other such social requirements with which organizations have to comply. Similarly, special interest groups lobby for the interests of factions in society in various forums. Mothers Against Drunk Driving (MADD) is an important interest group that is working with law enforcement on a campaign to increase the use of sobriety checkpoints, which research has shown to reduce alcohol-related fatal crashes by at least 20%. MADD is also pushing Congress to use part of a billion-dollar federal antidrug advertising campaign to persuade underage drinkers to stop consuming alcohol (McDonald & Dewey-Kollen, 2006).

An extension of managerial ethics is the notion of *corporate social responsibility*, which refers to the management's obligation to make decisions and take actions that promote the welfare of society. As U.S. citizens are becoming more educated and affluent, their expectations of ethical responsibilities from agencies are also increasing. In addition, over the years many stories have emerged from the business world and the criminal justice arena that have brought countless social and ethical issues to the attention of the public. The scandals involving Enron, Arthur Andersen, WorldCom, Tyco, the Los Angeles Police Department and Rodney King, and prison beatings, to name a few, breached the public trust. In these and other such cases, the public believes that organizations have done something wrong or treated individuals or groups unfairly. In other words, the simple question being debated is whether these agencies behaved ethically or in a socially responsible way. The standards for socially responsible conduct are especially important for criminal justice agencies whose roles are intricately intertwined with the welfare of society.

In summary, power should be used in ethical ways that ensure people are treated fairly. For example, reward power should not be used to discriminate against certain people and to favor others but should be based on true merit. Similarly, people should be punished consistently and promptly when they violate the organizational rules and regulations. Treating corruption and unethical behaviors as agency failures and not individual failures allows for the creation of traditions, policies, or practices that foster ethical behaviors (Murphy & Caplan, 1991). Rules established to deal with unacceptable behavior should be made known to employees ahead of time and should be easily available for reference. Continuous focus on what is expected, increasing accountability, and open discussions on misconduct and ethical violations should be common practices and embedded in organizational culture (Allen et al., 2006). The Association of Certified Fraud Examiners estimates that because of unethical and criminal behavior, U.S. industry loses around $400 billion annually (McClenahen, 1999). Recently, one study found that organizations that had an ethical commitment, as reflected by a formal inclusion of a code of ethics in the management reports, outperformed organizations that did not include a code of ethics (Verschoor, 1998). The costs to society when employees in criminal justice behave unethically may be much more difficult to measure but may result in similar, if not increased, losses for those using criminal justice services, those relying on criminal justice for safety, and those working in the system in ethical ways, as the public loses faith in the ability of the system to act in a just and fair manner.

Chapter Summary

- Disagreement is normal in human relationships and occurs naturally in the day-to-day functioning of an organization. Individuals use power, acquired or vested, to influence the final outcome of disagreements. Since there are others within organizations who are adversely impacted by the adoption of a particular decision, there is often a conflict.
- Power, politics, and conflict exist in every organization. If not managed ethically, they will create uncertainty, chaos, and stress, leading to devastatingly negative consequences. In contrast, ethically managed conflicts can contribute positively to the development and growth of an organization.
- Effective conflict management requires managers to be proficient in three areas of skill development. First, they should be able to identify the types of conflict and their cause(s). Second, they should examine

the different strategies available to them and choose the one most appropriate for dealing with the given situation. Third, managers should ensure that the relationships between the disputing parties are not damaged, by tactfully enabling them to settle their interpersonal disputes. A successful manager can frame the conflict appropriately for it to be resolved amicably between disagreeing parties.

- Conflicts can be classified broadly into two categories—people-focused and issue-focused.
- According to personality defect theory, conflicts emerge because of personality imperfections. Managers who adopt this theory believe that people who are involved in conflicts are inherently bad people and troublemakers.
- Some of the more common factors observed in work environments that lead to conflict are (i) personal differences arising from disparity in assumptions, perceptions, and expectations; (ii) lack of complete information or misinformation; (iii) task and team interdependence and goal incompatibility; and (iv) scarcity of resources.
- Pondy's (1967) model of organizational conflict states that conflict is a dynamic process that passes through five stages—latent conflict, perceived conflict, felt conflict, manifest conflict, and conflict aftermath.
- Ruble and Thomas (1976) offer a two-by-two matrix with five styles to address conflict—competing, avoiding, accommodating, compromising, and collaboration. Each style reflects a different degree of cooperativeness and assertiveness. Each of the five positions can work, depending on the situation at hand. However, the most appropriate approach is considered the collaborative style, which is longer lasting and results in the best joint outcome.
- Conflict resolution approaches include focusing on bigger goals, improving communications, and developing negotiating skills of employees.
- Power is defined as the ability of an individual or a group to influence the behavior or action of another individual or group to do something they would not have done otherwise. In the workplace, power is used as the primary means for directing and controlling people's behaviors or actions toward attaining desired outcomes, which may be personal or organizational goals.
- Authority is associated with power but is limited in scope. Authority emanates from a formal position held within an organization and flows down the vertical hierarchy.
- There are two basic sources of power within an organization, namely, personal attributes and position characteristics.
- Typically, power in organizations is not an individual phenomenon, but is related to the role departments play in the organization, the resources they control, and the environmental contingencies with which departments cope.
- Managers engage in organizational politics, a process of bargaining and negotiation, to increase their power. The domain of political activity typically applies to influencing decisions regarding structural changes, managing promotions, and managing scarce resource allocation. Such maneuvering strengthens their network and alliances, providing them with greater power.
- When politics involves deception and dishonesty to promote individual self-interest, it is considered an abuse of power. Such behavior leads to conflict and disharmony in the workplace.
- To prevent the abuse of power and other ethical violations such as taking bribes, kickbacks, and various other forms of corruption, organizations adopt a code of ethics that defines the principles of morality or rules of conduct. These principles are shaped by personal ethics of the employees, organizational culture, and external stakeholders.
- Employees learn about values, beliefs, and behavior from watching their superiors. Therefore, leadership plays a crucial role in influencing the ethical standards that will be adopted within an organization. Also, the organizational goals should not be so unreasonable that instead of motivating employees to perform better, they force workers to adopt unethical behavior and abuse power. Numerous studies using data collected from different parts of the United States suggest that questionable, unethical

practices in different criminal justice agencies are systemic and pervasive throughout the country, and we need to address them urgently.

- Often, it becomes difficult to report internally the unethical behavior of senior executives because of the fear of retribution. By going outside the organization to report the unethical action, the employee is said to be "blowing the whistle." In recent years, federal legislation has been passed to give whistle-blowers more legal protection. States are also adopting legislation to protect whistle-blowers.
- An extension of managerial ethics is the notion of corporate social responsibility, which refers to the management's obligation to make decisions and take actions that promote the welfare of society. Social goals should not be seen as competition for profits; instead, innovative policies should be adopted that concurrently promote both the profits and the social goals.

Chapter Review Questions

1. Some conflicts are considered beneficial for organizations. Discuss how and why this is the case.

2. What is the difference between people-focused conflicts and issue-focused conflicts? Give an example of each of these in a criminal justice agency.

3. How does personality defect theory explain conflicts?

4. Provide an example of conflict that may occur in criminal justice. Describe how it would proceed according to Pondy's (1967) model of conflict.

5. Explain the difference(s) between power and authority.

6. What do you understand the term *organizational politics* to mean? How do individuals in criminal justice use politics to increase their power within an organization?

7. What might be included in a policing code of ethics? What factors impact the code of ethics in an organization?

CASE STUDY

Lisa Camper is a fairly new hire at the Icuza Juvenile Probation Office. She is 27 years old and a single mom. Her duties at the probation office are to work with male and female youth who have been abused or neglected. She works closely with the parents of the youth to reunite them with their children and with the Division of Family and Youth Services to ensure that the children are well cared for while under the court's supervision.

Camper has done well in the 14 months she has been employed by the department. She gets along with other probation officers and with the detention and family services workers. Her work has been exemplary in court, and it appears that she has helped several children return home to safer environments.

Camper has stated in conversations that she is interested in adopting another child. She doesn't want to remarry but would like a sibling for her current child.

(Continued)

(Continued)

Today, Camper came into your office. She informed you that there was an impending case scheduled for termination of parental rights. She stated that she has been talking to child protective services about fostering and then, potentially, adopting the child in the case. She said that she feels a real connection to the child and wants to provide him a permanent home. She went on to say that she isn't pursuing a termination of parental rights for this reason but truly believes she would be a better parent to the child than his biological parents.

Once Camper was finished, you asked her for the case file and decided to further investigate the information. Upon review of the case in question, you found that Camper has not followed all policies leading to termination of parent rights. The child was having supervised visitation with the biological parents three times a week until 5 months ago. Camper recommended that the visitation be reduced to once a week. Additionally, the biological mother was attending drug rehabilitation but had missed a few appointments. Rather than meet with the mother and CPS worker, Camper held a hearing with the judge to report the missed appointments and to recommend reduced contact with the child. You also noticed a letter to the CPS worker from Camper 7 months ago that discussed termination of parental rights. By law, a termination of parental rights cannot be recommended until after the 13th month of continued custody. It appears to you that Camper has been attempting to sabotage the reunification of the child with the biological parents.

Questions for Discussion

1. In your opinion, has Camper's behavior jeopardized her case or the reputation of the Icuza Juvenile Probation Office? Why or why not?

2. Have Camper's actions been ethical? Defend your answer.

3. If you believe that Camper was unethical, identify the point at which she crossed the line. How might this type of behavior impact the delivery of services to both the current client and his mother, as well as to Camper's other clients?

4. What should the manager do in this situation?

5. What steps should be taken to ensure this does not happen in the future?

6. Why are ethics so important in criminal justice? How should managers ensure that employees understand and exhibit ethical behaviors?

Internet Resources

American Civil Liberties Union—http://www.aclu.org

National Sheriff's Association—http://www.sheriffs.org

Office of Justice Programs—http://www.ojp.usdoj.gov

References and Suggested Readings

Adler, N. J. (1991). *International dimensions of organizational behavior* (2nd ed.). Boston, MA: PWS-Kent.

Aldag, R. J., & Kuzuhara, L. W. (2002). *Organizational behavior and management: An integrated skills approach.* Mason, OH: South-Western/Thomson Learning.

Allen, J. M., Mhlanga, B., & Khan, E. (2006). Education, training, and ethical dilemmas: Responses of criminal justice practitioners regarding professional ethical issues. *Professional Issues in Criminal Justice, 1*(1), 3–28.

Amason, A. C., Hochwarter, W. A., Thompson, K. R., & Harrison, A. W. (1995). Conflict: An important dimension in successful management teams. *Organizational Dynamics, 24*(2), 20–34.

Baumer, E. P. (2002). Neighborhood disadvantage and police notification by victims of violence. *Criminology,* 579–617.

Beck, A. J., & Harrison, P. M. (2007, December). *Sexual victimization in state and federal prisons reported by inmates.* Bureau of Justice Statistics. Special Report.

Boeker, W. (1989). The development and institutionalization of subunit power in organizations. *Administrative Science Quarterly, 34*(3), 388–410.

Catlin, D. W., & Maupin, J. R. (2004). A two cohort study of the ethical orientations of state police officers. *Policing: An International Journal of Police Strategies & Management, 27*(3), 289–301.

Clarke, M. (2010). Crime labs in crisis: Shoddy forensics used to secure convictions. *Prison Legal News, 21*(10), 1–22.

Costa-Clarke, R. J. (1994, Winter). The costly implications of terminating whistleblowers. *Employment Relations Today, 21*(8), 447–454.

Daft, R. L. (2001). *Organization theory and design* (7th ed.). Florence, KY: South-Western College.

Dion, K. L., & Dion, K. K. (1987). Belief in a just world and physical attractiveness stereotyping. *Journal of Personality and Social Psychology, 52*(45), 775–780.

Dunningham, C., & Norris, C. (1998, January–March). Some ethical dilemmas in the handling of police informers. *Public Money and Management, 18,* 21–25.

Eisenhardt, K. M., Kahwajy, J. L., & Bourgeois, L. J., III (1997, July/August). How management teams can have a good fight. *Harvard Business Review, 75*(9), 77–85.

Ferrell, O. C., Fraedrich, J., & Ferrell, L. (2008). *Business ethics: Ethical decision making and cases* (7th ed.). Boston, MA: Houghton Mifflin Company.

Ferris, G. R., & Kacmar, K. M. (1992). Perceptions of organizational politics. *Journal of Management, 18*(1), 93–116.

Forman, J., Jr. (2012). Racial critiques of mass incarceration: Beyond the new Jim Crow. *Prison Legal News, July, 23*(7), 1–16.

Forst, M. L. (1977). To what extent should the criminal justice system by a "system"? *Crime & Delinquency, 23,* 403–416.

French, J. R. P., & Raven, B. (1959). Bases for social power. In D. Cartwright (Ed.), *Studies in social power* (pp. 150–167). Ann Arbor: University of Michigan Institute for Social Research.

Gianelli, P. C. (2012). The North Carolina crime lab scandal. *Criminal Justice, 27*(1).

Goudriaan, H., Wittebrood, K., & Nieuwbeerta, P. (2006). Neighborhood characteristics and reporting crime: Effects of social cohesion, confidence in police effectiveness and socio-economic disadvantage. *British Journal of Criminology, 46,* 719–742.

Guetzkow, H., & Gyr, J. (1954). An analysis of conflict in decision-making groups. *Human Relations, 7,* 367–381.

Harris, C. E. (1997). *Applying moral theories.* Boston, MA: Wadsworth.

Harrison, B. (1999). Noble cause corruption and the police ethic. *FBI Law Enforcement Bulletin, 68*(8), 1–7.

Hickson, D. J., Hinings, C. R., Lee, C. A., Schneck, R. E., & Pennings, J. M. (1971). A strategic contingencies theory of intraorganizational power. *Administrative Science Quarterly, 6,* 216–229.

Hines, J. S. (1980). *Conflict and conflict management.* Athens: University of Georgia Press.

Hinings, C. R., Hickson, D. J., Pennings, J. M., & Schneck, R. E. (1974). Structural conditions of intraorganizational power. *Administrative Science Quarterly, 21,* 22–44.

Hirschman, A. O. (Ed.). (1970). *Exit, voice, and loyalty: Responses to decline in firms, organizations, and states.* Boston, MA: Harvard University Press.

Hocker, J. L., & Wilmot, W. W. (1991). *Interpersonal conflict.* Dubuque, IA: W. C. Brown.

Holmes, R. L. (1998). *Basic moral philosophy.* Boston, MA: Wadsworth.

Hunter, G. (2006, August). Guards' rape of prisoners rampant, no solution in sight. *Prison Legal News, 17*(8).

Hunter, G. (2013, February). Sexual abuse by prison and jail staff proves persistent, pandemic. *Prison Legal News.*

Hunter, G., & Friedmann, A. (2009). Judge not: Judges benched for personal misconduct. *Prison Legal News, 20*(8), 1–8.

Jackson, P. (1999, April). Whistles and safety valves. *CA Magazine, 132*(3), 43–44.

Jang, H., Joo, H., & Zhang, J. (2010). Determinants of public confidence in police: An international perspective. *Journal of Criminal Justice, 38,* 57–68.

Kanter, R. (1979, July–August). Power failure in management circuits. *Harvard Business Review, 57*(4), 65–75.

Kelly, J. (1970, July/August). Make conflict work for you. *Harvard Business Review, 48,* 103–113.

Klockars, C. B., Ivkovic, S. K., & Haberfeld, M. (Eds.). (2004). *The contours of police integrity.* Thousand Oaks, CA: Sage.

Lyman, M. D. (1999). *The police: An introduction.* Upper Saddle River, NJ: Prentice Hall.

McClenahen, J. S. (1999, March 1). Your employees know better: Companies can't get away with bad ethics programs. *Industry Week, 248*(5), 12–13.

McDonald, C. J., & Dewey-Kollen, J. (2006, November). DUI deterrence. *Law Officer Magazine, 2*(9), 52–55.

Moore, J. S., Graziano, W. G., & Millar, M. G. (1987). Physical attractiveness, sex role orientation, and the evaluation of adults and children. *Journal of Personality and Social Psychology, 13*(1), 95–102.

Murphy, P. V., & Caplan, D. G. (1991). Fostering integrity. In R. Dunham & G. Alpert (Eds.), *Critical issues in policing* (pp. 304–324). Prospect Heights, IL: Waveland Press.

Nelligan, P. J., & Taylor, R. W. (1994). Ethical issues in community policing. *Journal of Contemporary Criminal Justice, 10*(1), 59–66.

Nevada Department of Corrections. (2006). *Code of ethics.* Retrieved from http://www.doc.nv.gov/about/codeofethics.php.

O'Leary, V., & Newman, D. J. (1970). Conflict resolution in criminal justice. *Journal of Research in Crime and Delinquency, 7*(2), 99–119.

Pascale, R. (1990, February). Creating contention without causing conflict. *Business Month,* 69–71.

Pfeffer, J. (1992). *Managing with power: Politics and influence in organizations.* Boston, MA: Harvard Business School Press.

Pondy, L. R. (1967). Organizational conflict: Concepts and models. *Administrative Science Quarterly, 12*(2), 296–320.

Rachels, J. (1999). *The elements of moral philosophy.* Boston, MA: McGraw-Hill.

Raines, J. B. (2006). *Ethics, integrity, and policy misconduct: Analyzing ethical awareness, standards, and action of law enforcement officers in the United States.* Unpublished doctoral dissertation, North Carolina State University.

Robbins, S. P. (1974). *Managing organizational conflict: A nontraditional approach.* Englewood Cliffs, NJ: Prentice Hall.

Robin, G. D. (1974). The emerging new criminal justice system. *Journal of Applied Behavioral Science, 10*(3), 347–360.

Ross, J., & Ferris, K. R. (1981). Interpersonal attraction and organizational outcomes: A field examination. *Administrative Science Quarterly, 26,* 617–632.

Ruble, T., & Thomas, K. (1976). Support for a two-dimensional model of conflict behavior. *Organizational Behavior and Human Performance, 16,* 143–155.

Saunders, C. S. (1990). The strategic contingencies theory of power: Multiple perspectives. *Journal of Management Studies, 27,* 1–18.

Schmidt, W. H., & Tannenbaum, R. (1960, November/December). Management of differences. *Harvard Business Review, 38*(6), 107–115.

Seybolt, P. M., Derr, C. B., & Nielson, T. R. (1996). *Linkages between national culture, gender, and conflict management styles* (Working Paper). University of Utah.

Sillars, A., & Weisberg, J. (1987). Conflict as a social skill. In M. E. Roloff & G. R. Miller (Eds.), *Interpersonal processes: New directions in communication research.* Beverly Hills, CA: Sage.

Steinberg, S. S., & Austern, D. T. (1990). *Government, ethics, and managers: A guide to solving ethical dilemmas in the public sector.* Westport, CT: Praeger.

Thomas, K. (1976). Conflict and conflict management. In M. D. Dunnette (Ed.), *Handbook of industrial organizational psychology* (pp. 889–935). London, England: Routledge/Kegan Paul.

Thompson, L. (2001). *The mind and heart of the negotiator* (2nd ed.). Upper Saddle River, NJ: Prentice Hall.

Tjosvold, D. (1991). *The conflict positive organization.* Reading, MA: Addison-Wesley.

Trompenaars, F. (1996). Resolving international conflict: Culture and business strategy. *Business Strategy Review, 7,* 51–68.

Verschoor, C. C. (1998). A study of the link between a corporation's financial performance and its commitment ethics. *Journal of Business Ethics, 17,* 1509–1516.

Wah, L. (1999). Ethics linked to financial performance. *Management Review, 88*(7), 7.

Wanous, J. P., & Youtz, A. (1986). Solution diversity and the quality of group decisions. *Academy of Management Journal, 1,* 149–159.

Weldon, E., & Jehn, K. A. (1995). Examining cross-cultural differences in conflict management behavior: Strategy for future research. *International Journal of Conflict Management, 6,* 387–403.

Whetten, D. A., & Cameron, K. S. (2002). *Developing management skills* (5th ed.). Upper Saddle River, NJ: Prentice Hall.

Motivation

The word *motivation* comes from the Latin *movere,* which means to move. It is a complex construct with more than 140 definitions (Landy & Becker, 1987). Most simply, motivation can be defined as a set of all forces, both within the individuals and in the surrounding environments, that drive people's behavior to satisfy their unmet needs. Internal forces are embedded in the psychological being of an individual; therefore, personality, values, culture, attitudes, and so forth are relevant in understanding individual motivation.

Work motivation pertains to meeting the needs at the workplace by motivating employees to behave in a certain manner. Workers are constantly seeking to satisfy *intrinsic needs* through accomplishments and achievements, and *extrinsic needs* through pay, job security, and promotion (Richer & Vallerand, 1995). A highly motivated workforce is able to contribute at the uppermost level, leading to superior organizational performance. Therefore, excellence in service quality demands that management understand the concepts of worker motivation and human needs and manage them effectively to retain highly motivated workers (Grant, 1998). Often, one reads anecdotes describing high-quality customer interaction with employees from Federal Express, Disney, Marriott, and Southwest Airlines, just to name a few, all of which express pride in their company's highly motivated and well-trained employees. Management in each of these organizations understands the contribution that a motivated worker can make toward organizational success:

> J. W. "Bill" Marriott, Jr., chairman and chief executive officer of Marriott says, "The cornerstone of our corporate culture has always been—take care of your employees, and they will take care of your customers." (Marriott & Brown, 1997)

> Herb Kelleher, CEO of Southwest Airlines, explains, "It used to be a business conundrum: who comes first: the employees, customers, or shareholders? . . . That's never been an issue to me. The employees come first. If they're happy, satisfied, dedicated, and energetic, they'll take real good care of the customers. When the customers are happy, they come back. And that makes the shareholders happy." (Godsey, 1996)

It is, thus, important for organizations to understand why employees behave the way they do, what motivates them, how they continue to stay motivated, and how organizations can motivate their employees toward the behavior desired for organizational success. These primary issues facing both managers and workers are at the core of motivation theory. An understanding of these concepts of work motivation and human needs is necessary for the officers and administrators in the criminal justice system to be effective in accomplishing organizational goals. It is hard to imagine that an unmotivated law enforcement officer would provide the highest level of customer service to the victim, suspect, or society.

Various motivation theories proposed over the years have been classified broadly into needs theories and process theories. This chapter will first examine the *needs theories* of motivation (those of Maslow, Alderfer, Herzberg, and McClelland), which primarily define the various inherent needs of an individual and examine why people behave the way they do. Next, the *process theories* of motivation (expectancy, equity, procedural justice, and reinforcement) are examined, which focus on how to enhance an individual's motivation. Subsequently, a discussion on the relationship between motivation and performance is provided, which examines ways to improve individual abilities through motivation. Last, a discussion is offered on how to promote a motivating work environment in the criminal justice system by incorporating elements of a successful motivation program.

Content/Needs Theories

The motivation models described in this section consider innate or primary human needs, which are theorized to motivate individuals to behave in a specific manner. They help in the understanding of what people want. Collectively, these theories focus on workers' needs, which are considered the sources of motivation that result in specific worker behavior. Often, these theories are also referred to as *content theories,* as their primary focus is on the content of needs.

Maslow's Needs Hierarchy

The oldest and probably most well-known needs theory of human motivation was proposed by psychologist Abraham Maslow, who developed the concept of the *hierarchy of needs*. Maslow (1954) theorized that all human beings share a set of fundamental needs that motivate behavior. Maslow identified and ranked these needs in a hierarchy of five categories, from lower physical needs to higher psychological needs:

1. *Physiological needs.* The basic requirements for survival, including food, air, water, warmth (clothing), and shelter.

2. *Safety needs.* The need for a secure and stable environment; absence of pain, threat, or illness; and protection against loss of the basic survival needs. Violence and danger are often considered as stress-related factors in law enforcement. Therefore, personal safety is a primary need for law enforcement officers, which drives their day-to-day behavior at the workplace. By constantly updating the protective gear, ammunition, and safety training provided to officers, the administrators can cater to their safety needs. Consequently, law enforcement officers will feel safer and more motivated to deal with potential danger in serving the public, thus improving the service quality.

3. *Belonging needs.* A person's desire for love, affection, affiliation, and interaction with other people, including social acceptance and approval from others, especially from those who are significant in their lives. Acceptability within the ranks of other officers, which is considered by most as the immediate family, is an important need felt by most law enforcement officers. Therefore, supervisors must improve their supervising skills to provide a more supportive environment for the officers to keep them motivated. Empirical studies have shown that social support within the community of law enforcement officers can reduce job stress, thus promoting physical and mental well-being and improving the officers' motivation. (Gove, 2005).

4. *Esteem needs.* The human desire for self-esteem; developing a positive self-image through one's achievements; and social esteem, being recognized and respected by others. Esteem needs are fulfilled by gaining status in the eyes of others and attaining good reputations or high rankings in groups. In an empirical study, Gove (2005) found praise had a significant positive motivational effect on law enforcement officers because it increased their personal esteem. Consequently, it led to improved morale, productivity, and retention.

5. *Self-actualization needs.* The need for self-fulfillment—a desire to fulfill one's potential and to do what the individual is capable of doing. Self-actualizers display these important positive characteristics: "increased acceptance of self, of others and of nature; increased spontaneity; superior perception of reality; greatly increased creativeness" (Maslow, 1970, p. 26). Maslow suggested that self-actualizing individuals focus more on the needs and well-being of others, rather than their own needs and well-being. Some argue that self-actualization needs of law enforcement officers are higher than those of an average citizen, which motivates them to risk their lives for the well-being of others. Therefore, it is important for administrators to constantly keep their officers challenged in the workplace so that they have the opportunity to continuously satisfy their self-actualization needs.

Maslow recognized that individuals are motivated by multiple needs, and he theorized that these needs change over time. In his theory, behavior is motivated primarily by the lowest unsatisfied need. Thus, higher-order needs (belonging, esteem, and self-actualization) will not be important until the lower-order needs (physiological and safety) are at least partially satisfied. The *satisfaction-progression process* illustrates that as a person satisfies a lower-level need, the next-higher level of need becomes that person's primary motivator. For example, when basic physiological needs are met, people will be concerned with needs for safety and security. Then, once safety needs are satisfied, belonging needs motivate behavior; once these needs have been gratified, people's attention turns to esteem needs; and so forth. This process describes how people seek to move up the hierarchy of needs. The one exception to this satisfaction-progression process is self-actualization: As people experience self-actualization, they desire more, not less, of this need. Based on the paucity of people reporting experiences of self-actualization, Maslow (1970) suggested that only about 10% of the population reach the stage of becoming self-actualizing individuals.

Maslow developed his theory inductively based on his clinical observations, not from empirical research conducted in work organizations. Although the categories he identified provide a useful framework for understanding what motivates human behavior, research has found that individual needs do not cluster neatly around these five categories. In addition, over the years, there has been little evidence that supports his notion that these categories form a hierarchical sequence.

Alderfer's Existence-Relatedness-Growth (ERG) Theory

Clayton Alderfer (1972) developed the ERG theory in response to problems with Maslow's hierarchy. *ERG theory* was one of the earliest empirically developed models that attempted to conceptualize human needs in a way that was relevant to organizational settings. Based on his research, Alderfer argued that Maslow's five categories could be grouped into three broad categories of needs:

1. *Existence needs.* Physiological and security needs for material things, corresponding to Maslow's physiological and some of his security needs. As discussed earlier, safety needs are very important among law enforcement officers (Glazier & Chapman, 2005), as well as officers working in other areas of criminal justice.

2. *Relatedness needs.* Interpersonal needs in the workplace, including needs for interpersonal security, correspond to Maslow's belongingness needs and some of his safety and esteem needs. Barnes, Sheley, Logsdon, and Sutherland (2003) found that job satisfaction of law enforcement officers is highly influenced by positive support from their immediate family and the community.

3. *Growth needs.* Development of human potential, corresponding to Maslow's self-esteem and self-actualization needs. You may have seen the U.S. Army's slogan of "Be all that you can be," which is pushing an individual to achieve his or her maximum potential.

Alderfer agreed with Maslow that people tend to move through the categories, from existence to relatedness to growth, as the needs in each category are satisfied. However, his theory differs on two other points. Alderfer (1972) argued that in addition to the *satisfaction-progression process,* there is also a *frustration-regression sequence.* If individuals are consistently frustrated in their attempts to satisfy higher needs, then the next-lower category will become the primary driver of behavior. For example, for an individual who is consistently frustrated in attempts to satisfy growth needs, relatedness needs will dominate behavior. Alderfer also disagreed with Maslow's idea that only one need dominates behavior; instead, he argued that more than one need may be operating in a given individual at any time.

ERG theory has not been empirically verified; however, the studies conducted to date show stronger support for Alderfer's model than for Maslow's hierarchy (Schneider & Alderfer, 1973).

Herzberg's Motivation-Hygiene Theory

The need theories offered by Maslow and Alderfer are helpful in identifying the different categories of needs that may motivate people. However, these theories do not specify how to address employee needs, which is important since different needs may be addressed in different ways.

Frederick Herzberg (1966), a scholar in the field of organizational behavior, developed another content theory that simplifies the categorization of needs into two factors, namely, motivators and hygiene. *Motivators* are factors that promote motivation and, therefore, job satisfaction; *hygiene* factors reduce job dissatisfaction but do not promote motivation.

According to Herzberg (1966), *motivator factors* satisfy growth and esteem needs, leading to employee job satisfaction and motivation. Also referred to as *growth factors,* they are related to the content of the job including the work itself, recognition for work well done, responsibility, achievement, personal growth, advancement possibilities, and feedback. These factors are intrinsically rewarding and lead to the experience of job satisfaction. When these factors are present, people put forth more effort. Herzberg (1966) suggested that for employees to be truly motivated to perform their work, growth factors must be built into the job. Of interest, though, is that if these factors are absent, most people will not experience dissatisfaction.

Nelson (1996) conducted a study of 1,500 employees in various work settings to find that instant recognition from managers served as the most powerful motivator of the 65 potential incentives evaluated. Discussing employee retention, Nelson found limited job praise and recognition to be a primary reason why employees leave. Furthermore, this study found that in research dating as far back as the 1940s, recognition and appreciation have always outranked salaries as prime motivators. In criminal justice services, specifically, giving praise and recognition opens the lines of communication and builds trust, which promotes motivation and creates a supportive workplace (Gove, 2005; Sunoo, 1999). However, administering praise and recognition requires supervisors to publicly talk about feelings, which is hard for most police officers who have been trained over the years to hide their emotions to be effective in their jobs (Davidson, 1999). Therefore, it is important for those training police at all levels to consider it necessary for officers to learn and then practice giving praise and recognition (Gove, 2005).

> Gone are the days when a majority of police applicants held prior military experience, accustomed to taking orders without question. Agency leaders now utilize coaching and mentoring programs better served to influence desired behavior. This manner of leading requires praise to build self-esteem within the developing officer. (Gove, 2005, pp. 15–16)

According to this two-factor theory, job dissatisfaction arises from the absence of hygiene factors and factors related to the context of the job that address lower-level needs. *Hygiene factors* include working conditions, coworker relations, supervision and supervisor relations, salary, status, job security, company policy, and administration. When hygiene factors are absent, it results in job dissatisfaction. When hygiene factors are improved, dissatisfaction is less, but motivation is not necessarily higher. According to Herzberg (1966), improving working conditions and the work environment, providing fringe benefits, or providing good benefit plans serve mainly to reduce job dissatisfaction and to retain people in the organization, but none of these promotes motivation, job satisfaction, or job performance. Studies have found that workers in strenuous jobs with high demands and low controls, such as a police force, when subjected to lower levels of social support within the workplace, suffered a higher prevalence of cardiovascular disease, indicating high stress. The supervisors in the police force are more prone to stress because of their additional administrative duties (Gove, 2005; Johnson & Hall, 1988). Police officers in general experience obesity, stress, physical inactivity, and increased tobacco use, which have all been linked to cardiovascular disease (Franke, Cox, Schultz, & Anderson, 1997; Ramey, 2003).

The two-factor theory proposed by Herzberg helps in reinforcing an understanding that some factors in a workplace tend to motivate employees, and others have little impact on worker motivation and productivity. However, an important thought to consider is that the manager's perception of motivational and hygiene factors may be different from an employee's perception. This difference in perceptions may result in a continued gap because of no corrective action being taken by the management. In the News 6.1 discusses how police work can motivate police officers. The work itself can be used to address motivational and hygiene factors.

In the News 6.1
Police Practice: The Work Itself as a Motivator

For decades, management and leadership theorists have proposed the concept that employee motivation is based upon several factors, including interpersonal relationships, organizational effects, and

(Continued)

(Continued)

the work itself. Such theories have deemphasized the importance of other, longer-held theories about employee motivation, such as salary, benefits, and working conditions. From a motivational standpoint, viewing the work itself as a motivational device usually has depended on internal motives (intrinsic rewards) concerning the type of work employees engage in and their personal beliefs about the work they perform. Amid all material published concerning the phenomenon of motivating employees in the workplace, very little addresses how managers can use employees' work to enhance their professional confidence or how managers can use that work experience to help motivate employees toward better quality work or productivity.

Some individuals believe that police work requires personal motivation, self-pride, professional satisfaction, and individual expectations. By capturing these effects of personal motivations, officers could promote a deeper commitment to their organization and possibly enhance their career. Douglas McGregor's X and Y theories view employees as either self-motivated and hard working (Theory Y) or mindless, lazy employees who must be coerced into doing their jobs (Theory X).[1] These theories persuaded managers at the Pulaski, Tennessee, Police Department that something that glorified employees at their daily work, while performing routine activities, would serve as a powerful internal motivational force that the department could capitalize upon for wide-spread, long-term organizational benefit. However, the methodology used to accomplish this feat proved the most difficult part of the concept to create.

In educational sessions, leadership theorists cite the intrinsic value of work as one of the significant motivational features of an employment environment, but they provide very little, if anything, to guide managers to successfully accomplish this. How can managers take the work itself and use it as a motivational tool? Traditionally, most theorists suggest using rewards or some type of accolade. This approach has given rise to the dramatic increase in performance and excellence awards. However, managers often encounter problems when implementing these types of approaches. Albeit powerful motivational tools, they contain many drawbacks inherent in their application. For example, equity issues occur in a variety of forms complicating the process, such as commonly held values prove difficult to define, organizational concerns may arise, and personality-based issues sometimes make recognition awards impractical. Some employee merit systems even praise undeserving employees for substandard efforts—at least in the eyes of the recipient's peers. Reward/recognition programs of these types usually suffer reversals of intended effect via employee cynicism and a host of creative work reversals.

Police managers should avoid these pitfalls to positively influence employees within their organization. How can a manager use the work employees perform to laud its inherent values, use it to help reinforce the organizational values, and provide first-rate service to the community? The answer to this complex question lies within a single concept—that managers could harness the initial motivations that brought their employees into the service of law enforcement and, thus, provide a continual motivational drive.

The Pulaski Experience

The Pulaski Police Department tried a unique attempt to take "work itself" at face value, capture it on video, and produce it in a valorous presentation to help increase employee motivation. In the past, the media has used sporting events to glamorize certain events and people with great impact.

Department managers believed that if portraying sporting-event figures and participants in such dramatic postures, relating to their employment, has such an effect on the participants and those viewing the presentations, then using the same premise in relation to law enforcement personnel should have an equally beneficial result.

Production

Over a 9-month period, a reserve officer made candid videotapes of department personnel during their routine workdays. These videos ranged from field events to office work, from actual operations to organized events of fellowship. Additionally, the officer captured video of a regularly scheduled department meeting, which focused on different individuals as they participated in the meeting.

The photographer also took video of the city and used it for the introductory portion of the tape, accompanied by inspirational background music. The video presentation was divided into segments of each shift depicting a freeze-frame of officers with a caption of their rank and date of service. Following the still-shot segment, the producer included several vignettes of each officer involved in normal work activities. The videotape ended with a list of all employees, their assignments, and an inspiring message on life.

Presentation

The video made its debut at the end of the year at an annual holiday party for all of the employees and their families. Managers noticed the effect from the outset; department personnel displayed markedly visible emotional reactions as the tape played. Managers presented all officers with a personal copy of the "video yearbook" and told them that it served as tangible proof of their significance and importance to the agency.

Evaluation

The film achieved more than being merely a video yearbook. Taken at its face value, the video serves as a historical document and has accomplished its mission of increasing employee motivation as well. Initially, the tape reaffirmed the employees' importance to the agency. The fact that the department used resources to make the video not only served as a silent testimony of the officers' importance to the agency, but it also dramatized their individual role in helping the agency attain its overall mission and sustaining the overall prestige of the law enforcement profession. Both of these factors serve as strong inspirations to employees about who they are and their value to the agency. Such a strong visual presentation becomes a public recognition of the intrinsic value these employees hold in their work. The video allows officers to see themselves through the eyes of others; realize how important their work appears to others; understand how integral their contribution is to accomplishing the goals of the agency; and recognize how vital they are to the everyday operations of the department.

On a far deeper level, the tape may serve as a personal motivator over an extended period of time. As the employees view the tape in the future, they may reinforce their own importance to the organization. Similarly, viewing the tape with friends and family members can serve to enhance

(Continued)

(Continued)

the motivational effects to a much greater extent than viewing it with colleagues. Those involved in producing the video believed it would serve as a long-term motivator by reminding employees why they originally began service with the organization, or in law enforcement in general. This reminder may instill a renewed vigor to employees and to the work they perform and help maintain the highest level of professional expertise in daily operations.

Although the idea may appear very simple in concept, numerous employees have proven its impact by asking for a second copy of the tape. This was exactly the reaction that department managers had hoped to accomplish. Each time employees view the video they reinforce their initial reason for becoming police officers, as well as build loyalty to the department they serve.

For other agencies, the cost of producing a similar video cannot be valued in terms of its relationship to the potential benefits it may provide because those benefits are impossible to quantify. An agency merely needs the services of an individual with the technical skills to create such a motivational tool and to have managers who care enough about their employees to arrange the production. Even if the film does not achieve anticipated motivational goals, it can still serve as an expression of gratitude to employees from their managers. That factor itself should prove a worthy reason to create the video.

Conclusion

Because each employee is motivated by different stimuli, a motivational video may not benefit all employees. However, for many people working in modern organizations, such recognition of the work they perform, presented in a positive light, can serve as a beneficial, long-term motivational stimulus.

As with any profession, law enforcement officers need motivational support from their managers as well. To this end, the Pulaski, Tennessee, Police Department created a motivational video for its employees as a way to recognize their contributions to the success of the department and their value to the community they serve. The overwhelmingly positive reaction to the video justified the department's efforts. Other police managers may discover that they have little to lose from producing such a video for their departments and much to gain. In the interest of their employees, police managers should examine new ways to motivate their officers and, more important, highlight the value of the often-seemingly unappreciated profession these men and women have chosen.

1. For further information, see Douglas McGregor, *The Professional Manager* (New York, NY: McGraw-Hill, 1967).

SOURCE: "Police Practice: The Work Itself as a *Motivator*," by J. L. White, February 2001, *FBI Law Enforcement Bulletin*, *70*(2), pp. 7–10.

NOTE: Dr. White recently retired as the assistant chief of the Pulaski, TN, Police Department.

McClelland's Theory of Learned Needs

The motivation models previously described consider innate or primary human needs. However, people may also be motivated by factors that are learned and reinforced through life experiences. American psychologist David McClelland (1961; 1971) theorized that individuals from childhood onward learn certain needs from the culture and social norms of their society and environment. McClelland studied three secondary, or learned, needs that he considered important sources of motivation. They include the need for achievement, the need for power, and the need for affiliation. He theorized that although individuals may be motivated by different learned needs at different times, for each individual, one of these needs is likely to dominate in influencing behavior.

The *need for achievement* is defined as the extent to which a person values success. People with high needs for achievement derive satisfaction from good performance. They desire success through their efforts, rather than teamwork or luck; from a moderate level of risk; and from unambiguous feedback and recognition for their success. Examples of people with high needs for achievement are entrepreneurs who establish challenging goals for themselves and thrive on competition. They rely on themselves and know that if successful or not, they are responsible, accountable, and in charge. This need may be a major driving force for most law enforcement officers and criminal justice professionals, for whom success may be experienced through apprehending law-breaking suspects or helping an offender reintegrate into the community. The need for achievement may also come from a feeling that one is making a difference in the lives of others. Barnes et al. (2003) found that "the involvement in COP [community-oriented policing] is more highly correlated with aspects of job satisfaction among patrol officers than it is among corrections officers and detectives" (p. vi).

The *need for power* is the need to have an influence on one's environment, including other people and material resources. It is the need to establish, maintain, or restore personal prestige or power. McClelland (1961) discovered that many top-level executives do not have a high need for achievement, but rather have a high need for power. This need is displayed in a variety of behaviors:

- Strong, aggressive actions toward others
- Attempts to help, control, persuade, or impress others
- Actions that result in strong emotions in others
- Behavior that tries to enhance or preserve the doer's reputation

McClelland (1961) noted that the need for power may be a need for personalized power or for socialized power. *Personalized power* is the enjoyment of power for its own sake, as a symbol of status. People who have a personalized orientation to power see power as adversarial, in a win-lose context, and use it to advance their careers and interests. In contrast, *socialized power* is the need to have an influence for the good of others, improve society, or increase organizational effectiveness. These individuals tend to have high self-control, are careful about exercising personal power, and plan carefully for conflict with others. They recognize that in a win-lose environment, one person's gain is another's loss. People with a high need for power tend to be superior performers, hold supervisor positions, have above-average attendance records, and are rated by others as having good leadership abilities. Tremendous power is vested in the officers of the criminal justice system. Some of the officers enjoy this power as a symbol of status, while others perceive it as a means to improve society. In a sample of 278 academy recruits in the New York Police Department, Raganella and White (2004) found personalized and socialized powers were important motivators for both the male and female recruits.

The *need for affiliation* refers to the desire to establish and maintain friendly and warm relationships with others. McClelland (1961) identified characteristics of individuals with high needs for affiliation as follows:

- A strong desire for approval and reassurance from others
- A tendency to conform to the wishes and norms of others when pressured by people whose friendship they value
- A sincere interest in the feelings of others

Since people with high needs for affiliation prefer to work with others than alone, they often take jobs involving greater levels of interpersonal contact. Supporting the role of belongingness in motivating employees, Barnes et al. (2003) found that respondents are more frustrated when they feel that public perception is not favorable. The study found that community-oriented policing (COP) produced positive impacts on officer job satisfaction, and the performance level among police officers increased when there was greater community support and recognition of their work. The increase in job satisfaction may have been due to a more positive interaction between officers and community members, resulting in officers' changing feelings about their jobs. The study also discusses the role of family in reducing stress among the various ranks of law enforcement officers. Barnes et al. found that among their respondents, divorce rates increase correspondingly with age and are higher for women, officers in higher ranks, and those without a college degree. They found that the strength of employee relationships mitigates some of the stress often associated with law enforcement occupations.

McClelland's (1961) theory expands on the needs theories that only considered workers' internal needs with which they are born. It suggests that through appropriate training, organizations may actually develop workers' needs in ways that benefit their careers and the organization. Furthermore, it identifies different characteristics of people to match them with particular kinds of jobs in organizations, resulting in higher productivity. Selective hiring practices combined with McClelland's (1961) work on needs may result in better matching of criminal justice employees with positions in the criminal justice field. It would be interesting to consider whether this combination would lead to lower levels of burnout among criminal justice workers.

Main Message of the Content Theories

The principal message of the previous theories is that workers have both internal needs and acquired/learned needs, which they are constantly trying to satisfy. Fulfillment of the needs results in contentment, but unmet needs trigger motivation. Knowledge of these unsatisfied worker needs will help managers determine which outcomes motivate employees. The manager can then control (administer, facilitate, or withhold) the outcomes that satisfy the worker's needs and communicate to the worker that receiving the outcomes will depend on performing desired behaviors. This process will allow the satisfaction of worker needs while contributing to organizational performance. However, one significant weakness of content theories is that it assumes that managers will be able to identify accurately a worker's internal needs and expected outcomes. This assumption may not always hold true because the intensity of needs and perceived outcomes varies widely among people. In criminal justice, it may be even more difficult to identify internal needs and outcomes since the situations and work environments of these employees vary greatly from day to day and month to month. Talking with and involving employees in the overall organizational development and goal creation is one way that managers can identify motivators and needs.

The content theories have been extensively examined in criminal justice to understand the motivation differences related to gender and race. Similar motivations among men and women who become police officers have been reported in most research (Raganella & White, 2004). Meagher and Yentes (1986) note, "The reasons expressed by male and female police officers for career selection do not markedly differ" (p. 321). The most commonly cited reasons for females entering policing were job security and helping others (Charles, 1982). Salary was the major attraction for policewomen in other studies (Ermer, 1978; Milton, 1972). Bridges (1989) found that males and females ranked salary and advancement opportunities equally. Alternatively, other research found minor differences in motivators for male and female police officers. Raganella and White (2004), for example, found that females ranked opportunities for career advancement significantly higher than did men. Lester (1983) found that the decision to join a police force for males was more heavily influenced by having friends and relatives who were officers. In contrast, females were attracted to the police force out of a desire to help people (Perlstein, 1972; Raganella & White, 2004).

Studies have found job security to be an important motivator for both black and white officers (Reiss, 1967). Alex (1969) found that minority officers were attracted to the job because of the benefits of government service, such as secure income, low probability of layoffs, and decent opportunity for advancement, rather than for police work itself. In contrast, Lester (1983) concluded that white males found the military structure of the police force and job security to be less important than did minority recruits, but having friends and relatives in the field were more important factors for joining. In a more recent study in the New York City Police Department, Raganella and White (2004) found that the overall motivations for becoming a police officer were very similar among white, black, and Hispanic recruits. The researchers further found that the rankings and mean scores on various motivating factors for Hispanic recruits mirrored those of black recruits. Both black and Hispanic recruits rated the opportunity to help people as significantly higher as a motivating factor than did white recruits. In contrast, the white recruits rated good companionship with coworkers as significantly more influential than the rating given by black or Hispanic recruits.

Clearly, recruitment strategies in criminal justice can be more successful if they target the specific motivations of females and minorities (Raganella & White, 2004). An analysis of the factors motivating such target groups will help in designing recruitment strategies and identifying program changes that would attract a larger applicant pool of qualified women and minorities from which to choose. An application of the principles of content theories can also be seen in Murphy's (2006) research where he examines the motivation of rank-and-file police officers to become executives and to improve the next generation of leaders. The findings of the study identify the needs of the rank-and-file officers that should be addressed if the executive development program hopes to increase the depth of the talent pool.

Process Theories

The second set of motivation theories is called the process theories. These examine the motivation process by linking the content variables (human needs, effort, and outcomes) to particular actions of the individual. Process theories include expectancy, equity, procedural justice, and reinforcement theories.

Expectancy Theory

Expectancy theory, developed by Victor Vroom (1964), explains that people put forth effort (work) to accomplish those things that they *believe* will lead to the results (outcomes) they desire. This theory assumes that people make conscious and rational choices by weighing the costs and benefits of different options available to them and then selecting the behavior that yields the most desirable results. In other words, expectancy theory links effort to outcomes in explaining how workers make choices among available alternatives and the levels of efforts required.

The key variable in the model is *effort,* which is an individual's actual expenditure of energy. According to the model, an individual's level of effort depends on three factors:

1. *Valence.* This refers to the extent to which anticipated outcomes appear attractive or unattractive to an individual. These outcomes could be pay, job security, recognition, feelings of accomplishment, good relationships with coworkers, and so on. In the model, valence can range from –1.0 (a very undesirable outcome) to +1.0 (a very desirable outcome).

2. *Instrumentality.* This refers to the workers' expectations that certain job performances and work behaviors will lead to particular outcomes. These *outcomes* refer to the anticipated consequences that are relevant to an individual. Workers should have a clear knowledge of what work behavior and actions will result in achieving rewards from the organization. Not all work-related outcomes are equally attractive to any one person. Just like valence, instrumentality can vary in size and can be negative or positive, ranging from –1.0 (worker perceives that job performance will not result in obtaining the desired outcome) to +1.0 (worker perceives that job performance will result in obtaining the desired outcome). An instrumentality of zero means that a worker perceives that there is no relationship between job performance and desired outcome.

3. *Expectancy.* This refers to the workers' expectations that they have the ability and the opportunity to achieve the desired level of job performance. Expectancy refers to an

individual's estimate or judgment of the likelihood of some event or outcome occurring. It is a perceived probability and can range from 0 (impossible) to 1 (certain). An expectancy of zero means that the workers believe that it is impossible for their effort to result in the expected level of performance. An expectancy of 1 implies that workers are absolutely certain that their effort will result in the expected level of performance.

The model identifies two types of expectations or probabilities:

1. The *effort-to-performance (E➔P) expectation* is the person's belief or subjective probability that putting forth the effort will actually result in the performance or accomplishment of some job or task.

2. The *performance-outcome (P➔O) expectation,* also known as instrumentality, is the person's belief that a particular level of performance (accomplishment) in a given situation will result in a particular set of outcomes.

According to the theory, E➔P expectations, P➔O expectations, and the valences of various outcomes considered by the employee, together influence a person's level of motivation. These factors are assumed to operate in a multiplicative fashion; hence, all three of them need to occur together. For example, if a pay raise appears very attractive to an officer (valence = 1.0), the officer is fairly confident that increasing effort will improve performance (E➔P = 0.8), and the officer also strongly believes that improved performance will result in the desired outcome (a pay raise) (P➔O = 0.9), then the officer appears to have a relatively high level of motivation: (1.0 × 0.8 × 0.9 = 0.72). However, if the officer does not believe that improved performance will lead to the desired outcome (the pay raise) (P➔O = 0.1), then the level of motivation or motivational force will not be so high (1.0 × 0.8 × 0.1 = .08). Because of the multiplication factor in the model, all three factors must be high for an officer's motivational level to be high. If any one of the three factors is zero, then according to expectancy theory, the officer's motivation level will be zero.

The assessment of each factor is based on officers' perceptions, which drive their behaviors. Therefore, management must be cognizant that there could be a gap between employee and management perceptions. This gap should be identified and closed by management by taking various actions, such as disseminating information to rectify the perceptions, changing the reward system to align with a system that may be perceived more positively by the employees, and so forth.

Researchers have focused extensively on the expectancy theory of motivation, examining it in a variety of settings (military, nursing, educational institutions, and private corporations), with some studies supporting the theory and others not finding support (Campbell & Pritchard, 1976; Mitchell, 1982a, 1982b; Stahl & Harrell, 1981). Using criminal justice as an example, expectancy theory may be challenging to apply. Several researchers (Guyot, 1991; Reuss-Ianni, 1983; Rubinstein, 1973) have argued that police organizations would offer a difficult environment to test expectancy theory because their work culture undercuts the capacity of the management initiatives to change workers' habits. For example, police officers may expect that identifying, apprehending, and arresting a drug offender will reduce the number of drugs and drug offenses in a particular neighborhood. However, in reality, once one drug offender is arrested, another steps into his or her place. So even though the officers put forth the effort to investigate and arrest one offender, the desired outcome was not achieved. In other cases, though, officers may feel the success of expectancy theory. For example, police officers may want to reduce the speeds of drivers traveling through highway construction zones. They may sit in the zone, monitoring and ticketing those who exceed the speed limit in that area. After several days of effort, the officers may find that drivers are more cautious and compliant with the speed limit in the construction zone. The effort put forth in this situation resulted in the desired outcome. Assuming that a pay raise is attractive to the officers, and that the senior management aligns the decline in speeding with rewarding the officers, these officers will remain highly motivated according to expectancy theory.

Expectancy motivation theory was used by Mastrofski, Ritti, and Snipes (1994) to account for variation in officers' DUI (driving under the influence) arrest rates in 19 Pennsylvania police departments. They found that effort–performance expectancy variables (opportunity and ability) exerted the greatest influence on officers' behavior. Capability (experience and training) and opportunity (work shift and nonsupervisory responsibilities) were the strongest predictors of officers' productivity. They also found that the reward–cost balance variables were less powerful. The personal feelings of the officers about the seriousness of drunk driving had no effect. Furthermore, personal commitment to a legalistic style was significant but not a powerful intrinsic reinforcement for making arrests. The instrumentality variables showed weak effects that were opposite of what expectancy theory predicted; the arrest productivity was lowest among the officers most inclined to perceive that the department provided incentives for drunk-driving arrests. A few officers (8%), considered to be mavericks, made most (44%) of the arrests, flouting the department's incentive system. These officers were alienated from their peers and management, and their performance was decoupled (separate) from their agencies' extrinsic rewards system. The personal beliefs of these maverick officers were a strong motivator.

An interesting question to ask would be whether the previous results would hold for community policing, where the police officers serve as clinicians who engage in problem solving with the clientele they serve (DeJong, Mastrofski, & Parks, 2001; Mastrofski, 1998). To answer this question, DeJong, Mastrofski, and Parks used expectancy theory to explain the variation in police officers' problem-solving behavior in the context of community policing. The researchers collected data from ride-alongs with the police officers. They found that "officers who engage in more problem-solving are motivated by potential recognition of such behavior" (p. 31). They also found that "expectancy motivation theory provides a more likely explanation for the behavior of the community police officers than that of traditional 'beat' officers" (p. 31).

Equity Theory

Besides satisfying needs, employees are also interested in being treated fairly in the way workloads are assigned and rewards are distributed, which is sometimes referred to as *distributive fairness*. In 1963, J. Stacy Adams proposed the equity theory of motivation, which theorizes that individuals are motivated by the perceived comparison of their outcome/input ratio to the outcome/input ratio of another person or group of workers perceived to be similar to the individuals. Input is defined as the workers' expectation of the effort required to do the job, and outcome is defined as the workers' expectation of what they will receive in exchange for the effort. As with expectancy theory, equity theory is also based on workers' expectations of their outcome/input ratio compared to their coworkers and not any objective measure of actual outcome/input ratio. Also, the comparison is of ratios and not absolute values of outcomes and inputs.

Equity is said to exist between individuals A and B if A perceives that the outcomes/inputs ratio for A equals the outcomes/inputs ratio for B. *Overpayment inequity* for A exists if A perceives that the outcomes/inputs ratio for A is greater than the outcomes/inputs ratio for B. *Underpayment inequity* for A exists if A perceives that the outcomes/inputs ratio for A is less than the outcomes/inputs ratio for B. Equity is impacted if workers change their inputs or outcomes, workers try to change the inputs or outcomes of the individuals with whom they are comparing themselves, workers change the individual with whom they are comparing themselves, workers change their perceptions of outcome/input ratio for themselves or the person with whom they are comparing themselves, or workers move to another job. Typically, motivation is the highest when workers perceive that distribution equity exists in the organization. Both underpayment inequity and overpayment inequity are nonproductive for organizations. In the case of overpayment, typically the workers are motivated to change their perceptions of inputs or outcomes to restore equity, thus resulting in no productive gain for the organization. They are less likely to be motivated to increase their inputs to restore equity. On the other hand, in the case of underpayment, the workers may feel frustrated and unmotivated, resulting in their reducing inputs, and sometimes leaving the organization, both of which reduce the productivity and the service quality of the organization.

Generally held as a popular theory, equity theory has been extensively researched by scholars to understand race and gender differences in criminal justice. Mounting pressure has come from community groups, professional organizations, and other social groups on policing and corrections to have adequate representation of female and minority officers, in addition to pay parity across the genders and different ethnic groups. Barnes et al. (2003) identify several areas in which male and female officers appear to experience inequity in corrections and patrol work environments. Male officers may view female officers as unable to accomplish some of the tasks required to complete the job. They may even hold the perception that female officers receive special treatment as a result of their gender (separate shower rooms, maternity leave, not having to work with certain offenders, etc.). In the case of male officers, the men may believe they are "overpaying" for the perceived inabilities of females to carry the workload and may not contribute to or assist in situations where female officers are present. Female officers generally feel underestimated and labeled as weaker employees. This leads to frustration. In some instances, the female officer may leave the criminal justice organization. In cases where leaving is not an option, female officers may transfer to positions more commonly dominated by (and perceived to be better suited for) females. Clearly, recruitment strategies in criminal justice can be more successful if they introduce greater equity (Raganella & White, 2004). A more detailed discussion of gender issues in corrections is presented in Chapter 12.

Procedural Justice Theory

While equity theory focuses on the fair distribution of outcomes to encourage high levels of motivation, procedural justice theory focuses on the *fairness of the procedures* used in arriving at various decisions impacting the distribution of outcomes (Folger & Konovsky, 1989; Greenberg, 1990; Tyler, 1988). Workers will have higher motivation when they perceive that the processes of assessing their performance, grievances, disputes, and allocation of outcomes are fair.

Like the other process theories, procedural justice theory is premised on the workers' perceptions about the procedures rather than what these procedures may be in reality. According to the theory, two important factors that impact workers' perceptions of the fairness of procedures are (i) treatment of workers by managers who are typically the distributors of outcomes—honesty, courtesy, respect for workers' opinions and viewpoints, and timely and detailed feedback all contribute favorably in impacting the workers' perception about procedural fairness; and (ii) transparency, objectiveness, and depth of explanation given by management in assessing performance. In simple words, it is important how the management assesses inputs, including time, effort, education, skills, and so forth; how the management evaluates performance; and how the management distributes outcomes across workers. DeAngelis and Kupchik (2007) conducted an empirical study to examine the factors that shape police officers' satisfaction with their city's system for investigating and resolving citizen complaints alleging officer misconduct. The data collected from 373 officers of a large urban police department in a western U.S. city support the importance of procedural justice in shaping officers' satisfaction more than the actual outcomes reached in the cases.

Research shows that workers' perceptions of procedural justice may be significant when outcomes such as promotions, pay, and benefits are relatively few. Research also suggests that individuals who receive medium or high levels of outcomes generally perceive the procedural outcomes as fair regardless of the fairness of procedures (Greenberg, 1987). In the policing environment where promotions may rarely occur, a perception of procedural unfairness may take place if the person promoted is not viewed as the best person for the job. Procedural justice theory may be of vital importance, particularly if the promoted person is seen as having received the position as a result of a "good ol' boy" system instead of as an earned position through time, effort, education, and skill level. In an empirical study, Maeder and Wiener (2008) found that procedural justice played a primary role in acceptance of agreements reached through bilateral negotiation. In addition, they found that negotiations characterized by greater procedural justice resulted in higher potential for integrative bargaining. In another study, Lambert, Hogan, and Griffin (2007) examined the impact of procedural justice on correctional staff job stress, job satisfaction, and organizational commitment. Using multivariate models, the researchers found that procedural justice reduced job stress and improved job satisfaction among correctional workers.

Reinforcement Theory

Often, people repeat behavior that provides pleasure and avoid behavior that is unpleasant. This behavior pattern is the basis for the *reinforcement theory* of motivation proposed by B. F. Skinner (1969), a well-known behavioral psychologist. The four principal techniques of reinforcement theory are as follows:

1. Positive reinforcement involves giving a reward when desired behavior occurs, reinforcing the likelihood of similar behaviors being repeated. Shows that use animals to perform, such as those at Sea World, are prime examples of positive reinforcement. The dolphin or whale is rewarded with a treat every time the act is performed during the show. This rewarding system is designed to reinforce the behavior pattern. Similarly, as mentioned before, Gove (2005) argues the importance of police supervisors giving praise to their officers to reinforce desired behavior.

2. Escape or avoidance reinforcement involves removing some unpleasant consequences or conditions when desired behavior occurs, thus motivating the individual to repeat the behavior. For example, in prison administration, there may be some jobs that an officer feels are very good and others that he or she considers bad. The jail warden can tell the officers that if they perform well in the job, they will be promoted to the desired position within a year. Consequently, the officers will be motivated to do a good job to avoid or escape the position they prefer not to have.

3. Repeated nonreinforcement causes extinction of motivation for undesired behaviors. For example, if an inmate or client constantly makes unwarranted demands, then not rewarding these demands consistently over a period will stop this behavior.

4. Punishment is a stronger way of reducing undesired behavior. It presents an unpleasant consequence or leads to removal of a desired consequence, whenever an undesired behavior occurs. Research has provided mixed results on using punishment as a negative reinforcement technique. Studies have shown that punishment may strengthen undesired behavior as a rebellion by the worker who is punished, and it may also create a demotivating working environment accompanied by hostility toward the superiors who handed down the punishment (Frimary & Poling, 1995).

Reinforcement theory is popular in organizations. Praise for good work can be an effective reinforcer. An employee's job satisfaction is directly related to individual recognition and positive reinforcement for work well done. However, extending praises or positive comments to employees who perform admirably is an elusive quality among police supervisors (Leonard, 1997). Some supervisors do not praise employees because they fear they would be committed to giving those employees favorable annual evaluations, which may also translate into a lot of extra paperwork (Leonard, 1997). This is a misplaced fear because individual acts deserving of praise make up only a small part of an employee's total performance. Many other supervisors reserve praise for spectacular acts done beyond the call of duty, and some supervisors simply are afraid to praise certain individuals because they feel threatened by them. Closely related to fear of competition is the feeling of jealousy that may influence a supervisor's decision not to praise, even if it is truly deserved. As a result, a culture of lack of praise gets reinforced, and when the frontline workers themselves become supervisors, they are unable to communicate praise to their subordinates. Besides, the very nature of the police work is such that rarely will citizens call to tell officers how much their services are appreciated. In agencies like policing, where minor occurrences can result in physical, mental, or emotional harm to victims, suspects, or bystanders, and liability is of the utmost importance, applying reinforcements in the proper manner is imperative. However, when the reward and punishment system within an organization is used to manipulate or control workers, the impact may be negative, resulting in distrust. In an article on ethics in policing, Allen, Mhlanga, and Khan (2006) suggest the creation of ethical policies that motivate employees to practice acceptable behaviors.

Motivation and Performance

Performance is often defined as a measure of individuals' accomplishments of their assigned tasks. According to motivation theories, a more motivated worker performs better than a less motivated worker, if all else is assumed equal. Work behavior may be *intrinsically motivated,* in which case a worker is motivated by the satisfaction derived from accomplishing the task itself. In such situations, the workers should be offered challenging projects, assigned to work that allows them to reach their full potential, and provided with the opportunity to make significant contributions to their work and the organization. As college degrees in criminal justice become more popular, new recruits taking jobs in the system expect positions that are more challenging. In contrast, a worker may be *extrinsically motivated,* in which case the worker's behavior is performed with the expectation of acquiring materialistic awards or to avoid penalty. The reinforcement theory discussed earlier deals with how positive and negative stimuli can be used to generate or alter extrinsically motivated behavior. Materialistic awards in the form of monetary incentives are important in the community because of what they represent. They are a means to multiple ends.

In addition to motivation, the level of performance may be impacted by several other factors such as personality, skills, training, ability, resource availability, working conditions, and so forth. Therefore, high performance may not necessarily be because of high motivation, just as low performance cannot automatically be ascribed to low motivation. Assuming a one-to-one relationship between motivation and performance may lead the manager away from identifying the real causes of poor performance, and thus fail to address the appropriate actions to correct the situation to improve performance. Nevertheless, improving performance is important, as it reinforces motivation. As an individual's performance improves, it results in greater happiness and satisfaction, thus motivating the employee to provide greater input.

In an empirical study (Glazier & Chapman, 2005) involving probation officers employed by the Harris County Community Supervision and Corrections Department (HCCSCD) in Houston, Texas, the researchers found that these officers not only faced safety issues but also emotional strain from long-term contact with offenders. It was found that officers assigned to fieldwork as a part of their regular job experienced more stressful situations from working in unsafe communities. The stress factor of the probation officers increased when external factors such as public scrutiny, financial limitations, and role ambiguity resulting from departmental policies and procedures were present. The officers demonstrated negative outcomes of stress in the form of increased levels of absenteeism, reduced attention to the details of the job, increased health problems, and emotional problems. The researchers found that the majority of the officers in the study appeared to be highly burned out: 64% of the officers were in emotional exhaustion, 64% were high in depersonalization, and 46% felt they lacked a feeling of personal accomplishment. The employee assistance program (EAP) was used to reduce stress among the HCCSCD officers and staff. All three of the pretests-posttests used to study the impact of the EAP demonstrated lower levels of burnout following the intervention. One interesting finding in this study was that the officers reported higher levels of depersonalization than emotional exhaustion as a consequence of work-related stress. A similar pattern was observed in an earlier study done with police officers (Glazier, 1996). These results may suggest that the professionals who work directly with offenders in criminal justice services may attempt to alleviate burnout by depersonalizing the individuals they serve (Glazier & Chapman, 2005). In other words, lack of motivation and high stress have a direct impact on the service quality of the criminal justice system.

In another study, Barnes et al. (2003) examined the differences in job-related stress and job satisfaction among corrections officers, patrol officers, and detectives, and the relationship between job satisfaction and stress in an urban sheriff's department. This research measured job-related stress through self-reported feelings of difficulty and frustrations associated with features of a law enforcement career. The sample was composed of 844 officers with an average of 11.5 years of experience with the Sacramento Sheriff's Department. This study measured job satisfaction on eight dimensions, namely, structure of job, policies and resources, compensation, diversity of tasks, supervision, promotions, training, and employee relationships—each of which has been discussed earlier in the context of motivation theories. It was found that the respondents were very satisfied with the structure of the job and employee relationships. The responses showed mild satisfaction with diversity of tasks and supervision. However, compensation, training, promotions, and policies and resources were areas of concern. Consistent with the previous research, they found that "respondents are more frustrated with public perceptions, the department and courts, and more concerned with job-related risks than stressed by the challenges of the job" (p. ii).

Barnes et al. (2003) found that corrections officers became less satisfied with some aspects of their job the longer they worked for the department. As examined earlier in the motivation theories, lower satisfaction may be because of the routine nature of the job and the fact that it offers less diversity and challenge over time. The study also identified several areas in which male and female officers experienced the corrections and patrol work environment very differently. Supporting the notion of inequity examined in motivation theories, the study found that the perceptions of the difficulty of meeting the challenges in criminal justice cut across assignment and gender lines. Female patrol officers and male corrections officers perceived that they were assigned to challenges that are more difficult. The study also found that detectives were more satisfied than other corrections workers, which supports the various motivation theories stated earlier because detectives are given greater autonomy and have higher task variety, more challenges, and greater pay compensation.

Workplace Design to Promote Motivation

Based on the findings, the focus must turn to the various elements of workplace design, such as job design, training, goal setting, performance appraisal, pay, career development, and promotions that advance organizational performance directly and indirectly by motivating workers to provide greater input. While job design and goal-setting exercises focus primarily on how to motivate workers to contribute their inputs to their jobs and to organizational goals, the other tools of performance appraisal, pay, career development, and performance focus on feedback loops that motivate individuals to improve to meet their goals.

Job Design

Job design is the process of breaking a job into smaller tasks and integrating it with the appropriate techniques, procedures, training, and equipment with the intent to improve productivity. It allows an opportunity to match workers with specific tasks based on their natural abilities. Effective job design can make a job less stressful and more enjoyable, thus motivating the worker to contribute higher levels of inputs.

Scientific Management

In 1911, Frederick W. Taylor (1911) proposed the *principles of scientific management* by claiming that there was one best way to perform a task. He stressed that management should use the principles of job simplification and job specialization to identify this "one best way" to perform a job. Proponents of scientific management use time and motion studies to determine the single best way to perform a task. Such studies reveal the minimum time it takes to perform a task and the motions that mimic the least amount of effort. Workers are then provided clear guidance on exactly what they need to do, accompanied by training to practice these moves again and again until they master the task. These principles of scientific management can be used very effectively in training law enforcement and corrections officers to deal with offenders.

The premise of scientific management is that by using less effort to accomplish the same task, the workers will be able to enjoy greater outcomes and hence will be motivated to provide higher input. Such work behavior that is guided by external rewarding systems caters only to extrinsic motivation, ignoring the important role of intrinsic motivation. The strict adherence to the specified time and motion standards takes away all room for creativity of individual workers, leaving them with a feeling that they have no control over their workspace. In addition, specialization that may increase productivity in the short run, due to learning, becomes a curse in the long run, when workers find the work monotonous and repetitive. Consequently, the workers' motivation level drops and the quality of work life diminishes, often leading to absenteeism and turnover.

Job Enlargement

In light of the learning acquired from the principles of scientific management, a new philosophy of work design was adopted that was based on increasing the number of tasks performed by a worker—that is, *horizontal job loading*. Around the 1950s, scholars and practitioners thought that by expanding the content of a job but keeping the same level of responsibility and difficulty, it might increase the intrinsic motivation (Griffin, 1982). Mixed results were observed in different companies that experimented with job enlargement (Filley, House, & Kerr, 1976). Some companies reported success in the form of increased worker productivity and satisfaction, while others did not experience any long-term changes. It was observed that by allocating more tasks of a simple nature, the boredom set in after a longer period as compared to when the workers did one simple task. In these companies, the workers still did not feel much control or variety in their jobs that would challenge their intelligence and provide them a sense of accomplishment and satisfaction.

Job Enrichment

The previous results made scholars and practitioners think about increasing the variety and complexity of the tasks, which would provide intrinsic motivation to workers (Griffin, 1982). Workers feel more motivated when they are allowed control over their work behaviors. Experimenting with this idea in the 1960s, companies began giving their workers some of the responsibilities that earlier were resting with their supervisors, resulting in *vertical job loading*. Research evidence was mixed (Griffin, 1982), supporting the increase in productivity because of job enrichment in some companies, but showing no significant impact in others. It is still not clear whether workers with enriched jobs are actually more motivated and perform at a higher level. Not all workers welcome the increased responsibility that comes with job enrichment.

Job Characteristics Model

The principles of scientific management were used in job design with a belief that job simplification and specialization would bring efficiency, which would be motivating to an individual. The negative impact of scientific management on intrinsic motivation was eliminated in job design by adopting job enlargement and job enrichment. The idea here was that jobs that are more interesting and meaning-ful will provide greater motivation to workers to perform at higher levels. In the 1970s, Hackman and Oldham (1976; 1980) proposed the *job characteristics model* that built on these early approaches. In this model, performance is seen as a self-reinforcing factor in influencing intrinsic motivation; thus, good performance pro-vides higher satisfaction, which in turn motivates workers to continue to perform at a higher level.

According to the job characteristics model, there are five core dimensions in a job: skill variety, task identity, task significance, autonomy, and feedback. The workers' intrinsic motivation is affected by their perception of these dimensions. Higher job scores on each dimension imply higher levels of intrinsic motivation.

1. **Skill variety** is the degree to which a job requires a worker to use different skills in performing a wide range of tasks or in operating different equipment. For example, a scientist working in a research lab has higher skill variety than someone working in a fast-food restaurant.

2. **Task identity** is the degree to which a job requires a worker to perform the entire job from the beginning to the end. Higher task identity allows workers to link the results with their efforts.

3. **Task significance** is the extent to which a job has an impact on the lives or work of other people inside and outside the organization.

4. **Autonomy** is the extent to which a job provides a worker the liberty to schedule work and decide the procedure to complete it.

5. **Feedback** is the extent to which workers are provided information on the effectiveness of their performance.

Once again, it is the workers' *perception* of the five core dimensions that impacts their intrinsic motivation. Hackman and Oldham (1980) have developed the *job diag-nostic survey* to measure the five dimensions. The survey computes the *motivating potential score (MPS),* which is calculated by taking the average of the first three core dimensions (skill variety, task identity, task significance) multiplied by autonomy and feedback. Each of the core dimensions is measured on a scale of 1 to 7, with 1 being the lowest and 7 being the highest. Since there are three variables measured to derive the MPS, the lowest score possible is 1 and the highest possible is 343 (7 ′ 7 ′ 7). The survey is a good tool to identify the core dimensions that need to be redesigned to increase a job's MPS and, thus increase workers' intrinsic motivation.

The earlier models were intended to simplify jobs and make them more interesting and meaningful to motivate workers to contribute their inputs to their individual jobs and organizational goals. One study (Hochstedler & Dunning, 1983) found that police officers had low job satisfaction and low performance when they felt uninvolved in the information flow in their police agencies. The lack of involvement made the jobs less interesting and less meaningful to the police officers. Alternatively, in another study involving 2,733 police officers, it was found that regardless of the county studied, the officers in smaller police departments tended to enjoy higher job satisfaction compared to officers in larger police departments. One of the main factors associated with these results was the fact that smaller departments were able to involve their officers in decision-making processes, thus making their jobs more interesting and meaningful (Dantzker, 1997). Departments may be able to increase officers' skills by supporting education and training. Departments may also assist officers in better identifying with their positions and with the good they do for society, and they may provide adequate amounts of feedback to officers. However, little can be done to increase officer autonomy when politicians limit discretion through legislative controls, as mentioned in Chapter 4.

Goal Setting

Research shows that individuals are intrinsically motivated to meet the challenge of accomplishing their goals, even when there may be no rewards attached to the goals themselves. However, if there are extrinsic awards involved with attaining the goals, then the effect on performance is even more powerful. Therefore, goal setting can be used to promote both the intrinsic and extrinsic motivation (Locke & Latham, 1990).

A *goal* is a target or a desired end result accomplished through one's behavior and actions. According to the goal-setting theory, individuals' motivation and performance are significantly influenced by the goals that they try to attain at the workplace (O'Leary-Kelly, Martocchio, & Frink, 1994). *Specificity* and *difficulty* are the two major characteristics of goals that lead to higher levels of motivation and performance. Specific goals are often quantifiable and can be measured objectively. For example, the probation department may have a specific goal of reducing juvenile crime by 5% within six months. Difficult goals are harder to reach but not impossible to attain. Harder goals cause workers to focus greater attention on goal-attaining activities and exert higher levels of effort (Wood, Mento, & Locke, 1987). Nevertheless, it is important to ensure that workers have requisite skills and resources to attain the goals. If workers lack appropriate skills and adequate resources, they may feel frustrated about not attaining their goals, and this may cause demotivation.

CAREER HIGHLIGHT BOX
STATISTICIANS

Nature of the Work

Statisticians use mathematical techniques to analyze and interpret data and draw conclusions. Many economic, social, political, and military decisions rely on the work of statisticians.

(Continued)

(Continued)

Duties

Statisticians typically do the following:

- Determine the questions or problems to be addressed
- Decide what data are needed to answer the questions or problems
- Determine methods for finding or collecting data
- Design surveys or experiments or opinion polls to collect data
- Collect data or train others to do so
- Analyze and interpret data
- Report conclusions from their analysis

Statisticians design surveys, experiments, and opinion polls to collect data. Some surveys, such as the U.S. Census, include data from nearly everyone. For most surveys and opinion polls, however, statisticians use sampling to collect data from some people in a particular group. Statisticians determine the type and size of the sample to be surveyed or polled.

Statisticians develop survey questionnaires or reporting forms for collecting the data they need. They also often write instructions for workers who collect and tabulate the data. Surveys may be mailed, conducted over the phone, or collected online or through some other means. Statisticians analyze the data that are collected. In their analysis, statisticians calculate averages, reliability, and other specifics of the data. They also choose and conduct tests to find out the data's reliability and validity.

Statisticians explain the limitations of the data to prevent inaccurate conclusions from being drawn, and they identify trends and relationships. Statisticians use computers with specialized statistical software to analyze data. Some statisticians help to create new statistical software packages to analyze data more accurately and efficiently.

Statisticians write reports to explain their findings and the data's limitations. They may present their reports to other team members and to clients with tables, charts, and graphs. Statisticians also recommend how to improve the design of future surveys or experiments.

Statisticians work in many fields, such as education, marketing, psychology, and sports: any field that requires collection and analysis of large amounts of data. In particular, government, health, and manufacturing employ many statisticians:

Government. Nearly every agency in the federal government employs statisticians. Some government statisticians develop and analyze surveys that measure unemployment, wages, and other estimates of jobs and workers. Other statisticians help to figure out the average level of pesticides in drinking water, the number of endangered species living in a particular area, or the number of people who have a certain disease, for example. At national defense agencies, statisticians use computer programs to test the likely outcomes of different defense strategies.

Health. Statisticians known as biostatisticians or biometricians work in pharmaceutical companies, public health, and medicine. They design studies that test whether drugs successfully treat diseases or conditions. They also work for hospitals and public health agencies, where they help identify the sources of outbreaks of illnesses in humans and animals.

Manufacturing. Statisticians design experiments for product testing and development. For instance, they help to design experiments to see how car engines perform when exposed to extreme weather conditions. Statisticians also contribute to the design of marketing strategies and prices for final goods.

Statisticians held about 25,100 jobs in 2010. About a third of statisticians work for government, mostly at the federal level. Most federal statisticians are employed at the Bureau of the Census, the Bureau of Economic Analysis, the National Agricultural Statistical Service, or the Bureau of Labor Statistics. Many statisticians hired by the federal government are known as mathematical statisticians. These workers develop advanced statistical models for several purposes, such as filling in gaps from non-responses to surveys.

Many statisticians work for private businesses, such as pharmaceutical and insurance companies, and often work in teams with other professionals. For example, in pharmaceutical companies, statisticians may work with scientists to test drugs for government approval. In insurance companies, they may work with actuaries to calculate the risks of insuring different situations. Because statisticians in business provide advice on research projects or oversee the gathering of data, they travel occasionally for face-to-face meetings with team members.

The following tabulation includes selected industries which employed statisticians in 2010:

Federal government, excluding postal service	20%
Scientific research and development services	12
Colleges, universities, and professional schools; state, local, and private	9
State government, excluding education and hospitals	8
Insurance carriers	7

Work Schedules

Statisticians generally work full time. Overtime may be needed to meet deadlines.

Training, Other Qualifications, and Advancement

Most statisticians enter the occupation with a master's degree in statistics, mathematics, or survey methodology, although a bachelor's degree is sufficient for some entry-level jobs. Research and academic jobs generally require a Ph.D.

(Continued)

(Continued)

Education

Many colleges and universities offer undergraduate and graduate degree programs in statistics. A bachelor's degree in statistics is not needed to enter a graduate program, although significant training in mathematics is essential. Required subjects for a bachelor's degree in statistics include differential and integral calculus, statistical methods, mathematical modeling, and probability theory.

Because statisticians use and write computer programs for many calculations, a strong background in computer science is helpful. Training in engineering or physical science is useful for statisticians working in manufacturing on quality control or productivity improvement. A background in biology, chemistry, or health sciences is useful for work involving testing pharmaceutical or agricultural products.

Important Qualities

Critical-thinking skills. Statisticians use logic and reasoning to identify the strengths and weaknesses of alternative solutions, conclusions, or approaches to problems.

Problem-solving skills. Statisticians must develop techniques to overcome problems in data collection and analysis, such as high nonresponse rates, so that they can draw meaningful conclusions.

Speaking skills. Because statisticians often work in teams, they must be able to orally communicate statistical information and ideas so that others will understand.

Writing skills. Good writing skills are important for statisticians because they need to explain technical matters to people without their level of statistical expertise.

Advancement

Opportunities for promotion are greater for people with master's degrees or Ph.D.s. Statisticians with a master's degree or a Ph.D. usually can design their own work. They may develop new statistical methods. They may become independent consultants.

Job Outlook

Employment of statisticians is projected to grow 14 percent from 2010 to 2020, about as fast as the average for all occupations. Growth will result from more widespread use of statistical analysis to make informed decisions. In addition, the large increase in available data from the Internet will open up new areas for analysis.

Government agencies will employ more statisticians to improve the quality of the data available for policy analysis. This occupation will also see growth in research and development in the physical, engineering, and life sciences, where statisticians' skills in designing tests and assessing results prove highly useful.

Statisticians will continue to be needed in the pharmaceutical industry. As pharmaceutical companies develop new treatments and medical technologies, biostatisticians will be needed to do research and conduct clinical trials. Research and testing are necessary to help companies obtain approval for their products from the Food and Drug Administration.

A large amount of data [are] generated from Internet searching. Businesses will need statisticians to organize, analyze, and sort through the data for commercial reasons.

Job Prospects

Job prospects for statisticians will be very good. Graduates with a master's degree in statistics and with a strong background in an allied related field, such as finance, biology, engineering, or computer science, should have the best prospects of finding jobs related to their field of study.

Earnings

The median annual wage of statisticians was $72,830 in May 2010. The median wage is the wage at which half the workers in an occupation earned more than that amount and half earned less. The lowest 10 percent earned less than $39,090 and the top 10 percent earned more than $119,100.

In March 2011, the average annual salary in the federal government was $95,695 for statisticians and $108,868 for mathematical statisticians.

As shown in the tabulation below, statisticians working for the federal government had the highest median annual wage in May 2010:

Federal government, excluding postal service	$94,970
Scientific research and development services	83,140
Insurance carriers	66,050
Colleges, universities, and professional schools; state, local, and private	65,020
State government, excluding education and hospitals	45,370

Statisticians generally work full time. Overtime may be needed to meet deadlines. Some employers offer tuition reimbursement.

SOURCE: Bureau of Labor Statistics, U.S. Department of Labor, *Occupational Outlook Handbook, 2012–13 Edition*, Statisticians, on the Internet at http://www.bls.gov/ooh/math/statisticians.htm.

Managers may set goals for their subordinates, but these goals should be accepted by the subordinates so they have a sense of ownership and are motivated to achieve them. Goals that are forced onto the subordinates may not lead to motivation and high performance. Some organizations practice a formal goal-setting process called *management by objectives (MBO)* in which managers periodically meet with their superior to set goals and to evaluate the attainment of previously set goals (Carroll & Tosi, 1973). The manager is given the autonomy to decide how to meet the goals. Progress toward the targets may be periodically reviewed by the managers with their superiors. During the review, if it is felt that the managers require additional resources or lack certain skills, then they are made available to them. On the other hand, if it is felt that the goals were unattainable during the given period, then the goals are modified or the time is extended. The success of the MBO program depends on the difficulty and appropriateness of the goals that are set. Dexterity in the goal-setting process by superiors can not only provide motivated workers but also contribute to organizational goals. Originally, MBO programs were devised for managers, but in many companies they are also being used for nonmanagers.

Goal setting in the MBO program was targeted toward making individuals take ownership of what they do care about in their work, so that they feel motivated to contribute their highest inputs to their jobs and to attaining organizational goals. This concept is not new in policing. In 1995, Paul Robinson implemented a similar program in the Merseyside Police Department in England. When Robinson became the new human resources director, he quickly devolved the main police department into area offices with a core board remaining at the headquarters. Each area office set its own goals, controlled its own budget, and adapted its policing strategies to its community's needs. The staff was required to identify their goals and to work out strategies for improving performance. The overall goal of Robinson's plan was to turn the police department into a performance-oriented organization.

Performance Appraisal

Most officers want to do a good job for their supervisors, coworkers, and agencies because they want to advance within their organizations. To accomplish these objectives, officers need a clear understanding of their roles and continuous feedback on their performance. Once the input has been offered by the workers, their performance needs to be evaluated to allocate desired outcomes to sustain high levels of motivation and performance (George & Jones, 2002). Supervisors can solve this issue by communicating openly and honestly with their officers. The basic assumption here is that supervisors can accurately appraise the contribution of their subordinates. When supervisors fail to communicate their expectations and objectives clearly, leading to a hurtful experience for the officer, it may create a negative emotional attitude that may be difficult to change.

- According to expectancy theory, examined earlier, workers will have higher motivation when valence, instrumentality, and expectations are all high. Both expectancy and instrumentality are dependent on accurate appraisal of performance.
- Equity theory suggests that workers are motivated to perform at a high level if they perceive that in comparison to their peers they are receiving outcomes that are in proportion to their contribution to their jobs and the organization. Therefore, accurate appraisal of workers' performance is an important prerequisite for the existence of equity.

- According to procedural justice theory, workers will have higher motivation when they perceive that the processes of assessing their performance, grievances, disputes, and allocation of outcomes are fair.

The three process theories of motivation emphasize the importance of accurate performance appraisals for higher motivation and performance. Through accurate feedback in the form of performance appraisal, two express objectives can be met: the workers know whether they are contributing the required amount of inputs to their jobs and to the organization, and the workers find out whether their input is directed on the right path. A positive performance appraisal is a reward in itself, providing satisfaction and happiness to the workers and reinforcing their motivation to keep up their level of contribution. On the other hand, if the performance appraisal is disapproving, then it signals three possible problem areas—lack of motivation on behalf of the worker to contribute the required input, lack of skills that prevents a worker from contributing certain inputs, or the inputs are misdirected and thus not resulting in the desired performance. Deeper probing allows the management to identify the exact cause of unacceptable performance and enables them to work with the employees to correct it. This corrective action motivates workers because it improves their performance and results in higher outcomes like pay raises and promotions. Performance appraisals also allow the management to identify special talents in the workers and match them more effectively with the organizational requirements. In developing a performance appraisal, managers need to think of the following:

Formal versus informal appraisals. Formal appraisals have a fixed schedule and are determined in advance (Fisher, Schoenfeldt, & Shaw, 1990). Typically, they are provided in writing. In contrast, informal feedback may be provided more frequently, is less detailed, and focuses on the immediate issues on which the worker is interested in getting feedback. For example, workers may want feedback on a more frequent basis than that provided by the formal system. Alternatively, supervisors may want to use feedback to motivate officers on a day-to-day basis. Informal appraisals may vary from a supervisor commending a worker for doing an outstanding job on a special assignment to criticizing an officer for slacking off and missing a court date. Since informal performance appraisals take place right after desired or undesired behaviors, they are very effective and beneficial. Ideally, an organization should rely on both formal and informal performance appraisals to motivate its members to perform at a high level (George & Jones, 2002).

Factors to be evaluated. The evaluation process and the performance rating instrument are important pieces of information that should be provided to all workers prior to their first day at work for them to work toward obtaining a good rating. Assessment can be based on *traits, behaviors,* and *results,* each providing some advantages and disadvantages (Fisher et al., 1990; Latham & Wexley, 1982).

Traits tell what workers are like, but cannot accurately predict what they will do on the job. Since performance is impacted by both traits/abilities and the situational factors, consideration of only traits may provide an inaccurate prediction of performance. Trait-based performance appraisals can potentially be challenged by a worker in a court of law on charges of employment discrimination. For example, favoring the performance of police officer A over B simply because A is bigger and more muscular would be considered a trait-based performance appraisal, and can potentially be challenged in court on charges of employment discrimination.

Focusing on the *behavior* to assess performance implies focusing on the actions that a worker exhibits at the workplace and not on what the worker is like as a person. Adopting this appraisal method is suitable when the worker is trained to follow the prescribed process of doing a job. For example, telling police officers that they should explain the Miranda rights to a suspect before interrogating, answer any questions calmly, avoid using excessive force, and be respectful when apprehending a suspect who has broken the law, and then assessing officers on their performance of these tasks would be a behavior-focused assessment. The common criteria on which behavior is evaluated are attitude, compatibility, dependability, knowledge, efficiency, and organization (Drafke & Kossen, 2002). *Attitude*, a bad one, may be judged as one that is negative with regard to work, the employer, coworkers, and others. *Compatibility,* defined as the ability to work well with others, is extremely important in an era of teams, work groups, and matrix organizations. *Dependability* is an extremely important criterion, especially in the criminal justice environment because of the sensitive nature of the work in which officers are involved in their daily routine and where secrecy and timeliness are of great significance. Maintaining current *knowledge* is important for criminal justice employees as they work in this volatile and dynamic world, where new threats arise every day. Efficiency and organization reflect an individual's behavior toward keeping the work environment clean and organized for smooth functioning of the overall process.

In *result-oriented* performance appraisals, the focus is simply on the actual output. If there are many parallel ways of reaching the end result, then result-oriented performance appraisal may be advantageous. However, often the workers have control over their behavior but not on the end product because many other factors may be impacting the results. In such cases, it would be unfair to evaluate the performance of a worker based on results. Result-oriented performance appraisal has sometimes been seen to motivate individuals to take shortcuts or push them to adopt unethical means to enhance their immediate performance, which may be counterproductive to the long-term interest of the organization. The use of quota systems in traffic enforcement is a result-oriented approach to appraising the performance of patrol officers. If officers are rewarded for reaching or exceeding a traffic ticket quota, the officers may write tickets to individuals who are not warranted. This could result in more challenges to officer performance in traffic courts as well as negative community feedback. Instead of allowing officers to use discretion in enforcing traffic laws, result-oriented appraisals may remove the decision making from officers and create an atmosphere of competition.

Methods of appraisal can be objective or subjective. *Objective measures* are typically quantifiable and specific and are not dependent on the perception of the person interpreting the performance. For example, decreasing crime by 3% within one year is a specific target. In contrast, *subjective measures* are based on the evaluator's perceptions of the performance on various measures included in the evaluative scale (DeCotiis, 1977). Since perceptions can be distorted, subjective measures are vulnerable to many of the biases and problems that can distort perceptions. To overcome this problem, researchers and managers have put considerable attention in constructing subjective measures of performance.

Typically, when subjective measures are used, supervisors identify specific dimensions of performance (traits, behaviors, or results) directly related to the job. To assess an individual's performance on each of these dimensions, a rating scale is developed. Though there are numerous rating scales, the three more popular types are graphic rating scales, behaviorally anchored rating scales, and behavioral observation scales (George & Jones, 2002). While graphic rating scales can be used to assess traits, behaviors, or results, the behaviorally anchored scales and behavior observation scales focus exclusively on behaviors.

A graphing rating scale comprises of one of more continuum with clearly specified intervals to assess the performance of an officer. As shown in Figure 6.1a, level of service may be assessed by rating officers on their helpfulness toward a citizen filing a complaint on a five-point scale ranging from "very unhelpful" to "very helpful." Because of the ease of use, these scales are popular in organizations. However, a major disadvantage of these scales is that not all raters interpret the scale points as same. For example, what may be "very unhelpful" behavior to one rater may be only "unhelpful" to another rater because we have not defined the meaning of "unhelpful."

A behaviorally anchored rating scale (BARS) tries to overcome this shortcoming by carefully defining the meaning of each scale point in Figure 6.1a. For example, in Figure 6.1b, "very unhelpful" as asked earlier has been better defined as meaning "ignores citizens filing complaints who need help." Similarly, "unhelpful" as stated earlier has been better defined as "keeps citizens filing complaints waiting unnecessarily." Likewise, other scale points in Figure 6.1a have been defined in Figure 6.1b. However, sometimes the behavior may not be captured on a single point but may overlap on more than one point on the scale. For example, an officer may greet a complainant but otherwise tend to keep them waiting for a long time to register their statement. Also, these scales require considerable amount of time to develop.

A behavioral observation scale (BOS) tries to overcome the BARS problem of officers exhibiting behaviors corresponding to more than one point on the scale by describing each scale point along with asking raters to indicate the frequency with which the officer performs the behaviors, as shown in Figure. 6.1c. However, BOS is very time-consuming to construct and for raters to complete.

Who appraises performance varies from organization to organization. Typically, a supervisor under whom an individual works is the most knowledgeable on a day-to-day basis of the subordinate's performance on all three levels—trait, behavior, and

Figure 6.1 Examples of Subjective Measures of Performance

A. Graphic Rating Scale

How helpful is this officer towards citizens filing complaints?

Very unhelpful	Somewhat unhelpful	Neither unhelpful nor helpful	Somewhat helpful	Very helpful

B. Behaviorally Anchored Rating Scale

1	2	3	4	5
Ignores citizens filing complaints who need help	Keeps citizens filing complaints waiting unnecessarily	Promptly answers questions when asked by citizens filing complaints	Completes transactions in a timely manner	Pleasantly greets and offers assistance to citizens coming in to file complaints

C. Behavioral Observation Scale

	Almost never				Almost always
Pleasantly greets citizens filing complaints	1	2	3	4	5
Answers questions promptly					
Completes transactions in a timely manner					

results (George & Jones, 2002; Lancaster, 1996). There may also be other forms of appraisal such as the following:

A. Self-appraisals are those in which workers are asked to evaluate themselves on certain elements related to work, of which it may be otherwise difficult for supervisors to get an accurate picture. However, the self-appraisal may be exaggerated because of the worker knowing that outcomes are related to performance. At other times, the self-appraisal may be understated because the worker has poor self-esteem and has no knowledge of how other peers are performing to make a knowledgeable estimation of one's own performance.

B. Peer appraisals are done by coworkers who work with the individual. Sometimes, because of social relationships, coworkers' judgments may be biased favorably or unfavorably toward the worker who is being evaluated. Nevertheless, peer rating is important, as it is an indicator of whether a worker is a team player, which is an important characteristic of an officer of the criminal justice system. Since team performance depends on the members being motivated to perform at a high level, it is expected that everyone will show due diligence in peer ratings. By accurately appraising one another's performance, team members can help motivate one another to perform well.

C. Subordinate appraisal is when supervisors are evaluated by the people working under them. These evaluations are especially useful to gauge the leadership or managerial qualities of a worker. For the subordinates to give an accurate appraisal (especially if it is a negative one), it is very desirable that the appraisals be anonymous so that subordinates do not fear retaliation from the supervisor.

D. Customer/client appraisal is when outsiders who deal with the organization are asked to evaluate the person with whom they have contact. These evaluations are useful as they provide the perception of the organization by outsiders who are removed from the day-to-day politics of that organization.

E. In a 360-degree appraisal, a worker's performance is evaluated by several sources discussed here, and these data are then aggregated. Receiving feedback based on evaluations from multiple sources has the potential of providing officers with a more complete picture of their strengths and weaknesses and areas for improvement. However, one potential downside of a 360-degree appraisal is that it may turn into a popularity contest, with officers who are well liked being rated higher than those who may be less popular but produce better results. Another fear is that supervisors may be reluctant to make unpopular but correct decisions, as this may have a negative effect on how their subordinates evaluate them, especially when appraisals are anonymous. Scholars believe that the most advantageous form of 360-degree appraisals is one that is based on behavioral evaluation and not on traits or results. These appraisals should be anonymous, to allow greater honesty. Care should be taken in selecting the set of evaluators rather than asking the individuals who are most conveniently available. Training provided to evaluators may be useful in bringing greater standardization to the evaluation.

Besides carrying out evaluation and appraisal, supervisors and managers must become facilitators, coaches, and mentors to their workers. In each of these roles, the managers can motivate their workers to perform at a higher level. The evaluation should not only be tied to the past actions, but should constantly be future-oriented. Too often, evaluations are judgments on the past, with no plans for the future. It is important to identify the causes for poor performance, to be followed with an action plan on how some of the mistakes can be overcome, what new training needs to be instituted for the officers to help improve. It is important to remember that a mistake is doing something wrong once, and a failure is doing that thing wrong twice. It is not bad to make some mistakes, but it is bad not to learn from your mistakes. And the role of the supervisor is to help an officer learn, help the officer achieve progress and improvement. Raters should also acknowledge the areas where an officer has improved and identify the causes for superior performances in those areas. This exercise should help the officers learn and adapt from their experience to areas that have been identified as needing improvement. In addition, the supervisor should help the officers identify and introduce growth and expansion into new areas and introduce new responsibilities into their goals with the intention to aid the officer in advancing their career. Administrators in criminal justice are expected to lead by example. If police chiefs want officers to work at higher levels of performance, the chiefs must do so themselves, and must give officers the tools and feedback to complete the job as expected.

Appraisal threats resulting from conscious or subconscious rater-biases are a very natural part of any evaluation process. Accuracy of an evaluation is significantly decreased because of these biases, often robbing the officer of compensation, recognition, advancement, or the chance to correct deficiencies before being fired. These biases are the halo effect, the Hawthorne effect, recency error, uniformity error, contrast error, conflict avoidance error, distance error, trait measurement error, personal bias, and cost concerns (Drafke & Kossen, 2002), each of which is described next.

The halo effect. This bias results from a situation where an officer may be given a good rating solely because all previous evaluations have been good. Instead of spending time and doing due-diligence in conducting the evaluation process of the work done by the officer over this last period, the supervisor gives a good evaluation on the faith and the hope that the previous good work has continued. It is also possible that this halo effect may work in reverse, where an officer who has received a series of poor ratings in the past is given a poor evaluation without truly evaluating the performance over this last period. In both of these instances, it is possible that the officer broke the pattern. Therefore, everyone should be evaluated on the merits of the performance in this period as if the current period is the first evaluation (Drafke & Kossen, 2002).

The Hawthorne effect. In a very famous study done at Hawthorne, it was found that workers' productivity improved when they found that they were being observed. Therefore, it is argued that if you observe to evaluate workers, they will change their behavior. Because people change their behavior when observed, an evaluator does not observe typical performance, thus bringing an element of bias in the evaluation process.

Recency error. Typically, the evaluation process is annual, implying that the performance of the entire 12 months should be accounted for in the evaluation process. However, often the officer may be more closely observed in the last month before the appraisal report is due. If the officers are good, they will receive a good rating, even if the performance during the other 11 months was mediocre. Alternatively, if the work during this last month is bad, they will get a low rating, even if the performance during the rest of the year was excellent. If officers know that the supervisor is prone to this method of evaluation, they may increase their efforts just before the anniversary date so that they receive a better rating (Drafke & Kossen, 2002).

Uniformity error. This threat arises when everyone in a team or department is given the same evaluation (superior, mediocre, or low), regardless of their effort. In any of these cases, the evaluations are inaccurate and adversely impact the motivation. The better performers may give up trying to excel. In addition, if managers rate everyone high or average, then later they may have a problem firing someone who deserves to be released. When upper management sees that everyone in the department is rated average or below, these officers may be overlooked for advancement or raises. Furthermore, when the current manager is replaced by a new manager who does not do uniformity rating but starts accurate evaluations, those officers who were high or average may see a sudden drop in their ratings. This may cause confusion and other related problems (Drafke & Kossen, 2002).

Contrast error. This threat arises when the rater evaluates employees relative to one another rather than to performance standards. If everyone in a group is doing a mediocre job, then an employee performing somewhat better may be rated as excellent because of the contrast effect. This same individual would be rated average or poor in a higher performing group. Although it may be appropriate to compare the staff at times, performance appraisal ratings are an evaluation of an employee's performance against job requirements rather than a comparison with other fellow employees (Lewis, Goodman, & Fandt, 2001).

Conflict avoidance error. There may be a conscious decision on the part of the supervisor to give an evaluation that is higher than the officer deserves to avoid a confrontation. Some officers are very bold and will go on offensive during an evaluation if they perceive it will be low. Some other officers can be very argumentative and will scrutinize every word, thus lengthening the evaluation process and resulting in much wasted time. Knowing this history, a supervisor may not feel it is worth the stress or time and a low evaluation will not change this officer anyway, thus giving the officer a higher rating that the officer can live with (Drafke & Kossen, 2002).

Distance error. Sometimes, the immediate supervisor may not be the evaluator; rather, it is someone who does not directly work with the officer and does not have firsthand knowledge of the officer's performance. This distance between the rater and the officer may cause accuracy problems in the evaluation process.

Trait measurement error. It is the evaluation of one's personality and not of one's work, thus giving higher rating to extroverts than introverts; higher rating to tall officers as compared to short officers; higher rating to attractive people as compared to less attractive or obese officers; and so on. Performance evaluation is of the work done and not of the personality or physical traits.

Personal bias error. Despite the fact that all of us have personal biases, good evaluators do not let their personal likes and dislikes impact their appraisal. Personal bias may involve a difference of opinion over what is important on the job. For example, one supervisor may weigh heavily toward punctuality, while another supervisor may favor organizational abilities. So the first supervisor will rate high on everything for an officer who is always punctual, while the second supervisor will rate high on everything for an officer who has good organizational abilities and is neat. Other biases may result from attitudes toward gender, race, color, religion, age, politics, and the like (Drafke & Kossen, 2002).

Cost concerns error. This bias leads to lower rating than what officers deserve because the supervisor wants to save money by not giving merit raises.

The appraisals that are inaccurate, not necessarily negative, require a response from an officer. However, it is difficult for officers to evaluate objectively their appraisal for inaccuracy without bringing in one's emotions, if it is a negative report. If the poor evaluation is accurate, but the officer wants to improve, then the situation needs to be analyzed to identify the causes for poor performance. If poor performance is because of a lack of training and ability deficit, then ask for more training and education that will improve skills. If the performance has been compromised because of poor communication, then prepare a written list of confusing points and meet with the evaluator to discuss and clarify these issues. If the performance was hampered because of misunderstanding resulting from an unclear job description, then request a revised job description and/or meet with the supervisor to clarify. If the poor performance is a result of criteria used that is unknown to the officers, then they should ask for a copy of the performance appraisal and clarify the specific behavior that will earn a higher evaluation. If the poor performance resulted from personal problems, then the officers should discuss their plan to resolve these issues with the supervisor, giving some commitment that they will deliver better performance in the immediate future. If the poor performance is a result of rater error, then the officers have to look deeper into identifying whether this is an inadvertent error or a conscious error made because of bias against them. If it is an inadvertent error, then do not accuse but gently question the supervisor. However, if the error is resulting from a bias, then weigh the political cost with the benefits and the likelihood of success before deciding to appeal against it. An informal protest of an evaluation is less risky than a formal one; therefore, it is always better to try an informal protest first, as one can always make a formal protest later if it does not work (Drafke and Kossen, 2002).

Distribution of Financial and Nonfinancial Outcomes

Performance appraisal is followed by outcomes, where some form of incentive is related to good performance. The various content and process theories of motivation discussed earlier suggest the importance of financial and nonfinancial outcomes in motivating workers. While financial outcomes may be primarily in the form of pay increases, bonuses, and monetary rewards, the nonfinancial outcomes may come as vacations, perks, promotions, and other career opportunities.

Pay is an important financial incentive, which may be based on merit, job description, tenure, or a combination of all three (Lawler, 1981). Of these, merit pay will provide the most drive to improve and sustain motivation (Bennett, 1991). It is typically used at the upper levels in organizations, though performance-based pay would serve well even at the lower levels. Merit pay may be based on individual or group performance. Though *individual-based merit pay* provides the maximum motivational impetus, often workers are highly interdependent and their performance is impacted by the performance of others. In this case of interdependence, group merit pay is more appropriate than individual merit pay. Sometimes, these incentives may be given as *group bonuses* or group monetary incentives rather than increases in salary. Such an incentive system maintains pay parity based on tenure and job description, but also introduces merit-based incentives to create the difference and sustain motivation. The organizations must create innovative incentive and rewarding systems that reflect both individual and team performance.

One issue with bonuses being connected to performance is the traditional view of women in policing. In studies on women in policing, researchers have found that male officers and supervisors (who are also mainly male) tend to hold negative attitudes toward women officers. They found that women were less aggressive, made fewer arrests, issued fewer traffic tickets, and were less likely to be involved in conduct unbecoming a police officer (Morash & Greene, 1986). Male supervisors, according to the study, tend to rate women as less effective in comparison to their male counterparts in handling violent situations. This is problematic if merit pay is linked to performance perceptions and subsequent supervisory evaluations. What was not addressed in the studies on women in policing were the situations in which these actions occurred.

> For example, the women's lower arrest rates may mean that the women were not taking enough initiative. Alternatively, it might indicate that the women handled the situations better than the male officers, if the latter caused incidents to escalate into confrontations which resulted in unnecessary arrests. A third explanation is that when a more experienced male patrolled with a female rookie, he tended to take charge of the situation and take credit for arrests more frequently than with female rookies. Thus, it is necessary to look beyond the numbers to an interpretation of their meanings. (Martin, 1993, p. 332)

Career opportunities such as fast-track management programs, special training opportunities, working on special projects, or simply getting a promotion are all forms of nonfinancial incentives. Good career progress can provide both intrinsic and extrinsic motivation. The economic gains that come with career progress provide extrinsic motivation, while personal fulfillment and a sense of achievement that come with being promoted cater to intrinsic motivation.

Chapter Summary

- Motivation can be defined as a set of all forces within the surrounding environment that drive individuals' behavior to satisfy their unmet needs. Personality, values, culture, attitudes, and so forth are relevant in understanding individual motivation.

- Excellence in service quality demands that management understand the concepts of worker motivation and human needs and manage them effectively to retain highly motivated workers. It is hard to imagine that an unmotivated officer would provide the highest level of customer service.
- An understanding of the concepts of work motivation and human needs is necessary for the officers and administrators in the criminal justice system for them to be effective in accomplishing the organizational goals with and through their subordinate officers.
- Content theories of motivation consider innate or primary human needs, which help us understand what people want. Collectively, these theories focus on workers' needs, which are considered the sources of motivation that result in specific worker behavior.
- The principal message of the need/content theories is that workers have internal needs and acquired/learned needs, which they are constantly trying to satisfy. Fulfillment of needs results in contentment, but unmet needs trigger motivation. Knowledge of these unsatisfied worker needs helps managers determine which outcomes will motivate workers. The manager can then control (administer, facilitate, or withhold) the outcomes that satisfy the workers' needs and communicate to the workers that receiving the outcomes will depend on performing desired behaviors. This process will allow the satisfaction of worker needs while contributing to the organizational performance.
- The second set of motivation theories is called the process theories. These theories examine the motivation process by linking the content variables (human needs, effort, and outcomes) to particular actions of the individual. These are expectancy, equity, procedural justice, and reinforcement theories.
- According to motivation theories, a more motivated worker performs better than a less motivated worker, if all else is assumed equal. Work behavior may be intrinsically motivated, in which case workers are motivated by the satisfaction derived from accomplishing the task itself. In such situations, the workers should be offered challenging projects, and assigned to work that allows them to reach their full potential, and the workers should be provided with the opportunity to make significant contributions to their work and the organization. In contrast, workers may be extrinsically motivated, in which case worker behavior is performed with the expectation of acquiring materialistic rewards or to avoid penalty. The reinforcement theory discussed earlier deals with how positive and negative stimuli can be used to generate or alter extrinsically motivated behavior. Materialistic rewards in the form of monetary incentives are important in society because of what they represent.
- Besides motivation, the level of performance may be impacted by several other factors, such as personality, skills, training, ability, resource availability, working conditions, and so forth.
- Various elements of workplace design such as job design, training, goal setting, performance appraisal, pay, career development, and promotions all help in advancing organizational performance directly and indirectly by motivating workers to provide greater input.

Chapter Review Questions

1. Explain the five needs in Maslow's needs hierarchy, and identify how they compare with the three needs in Alderfer's ERG theory and the three needs in McClelland's theory.

2. Explain the differences between the various types of reinforcement techniques. In your opinion, which one works the best in a law enforcement agency?

3. What are the differences between content/needs theories and process theories of motivation?

4. Explain expectancy theory. How can you improve the motivation in law enforcement services by using the principles of this theory?

5. Why are the perceptions important in equity theory? What are the problems in implementing this theory in law enforcement services? As an employee in a law enforcement office, what sort of equity do you want? What about in a probation office? How would equity theory apply to probation officers?

6. Explain why goals are important in motivating people. Provide some methods of effective goal setting.

7. Why should administrative officers in correctional institutions be concerned about job design? How can job characteristics theory help in designing good jobs?

8. Discuss the impact of motivation on service delivery and quality in policing, probation, and the courts.

CASE STUDY

You are the supervisor of a small inmate transportation office in Kentucky. You have one assistant manager and 14 officers working in your office. You are the chief supervisory officer and are tasked with keeping the budget, doing performance appraisals, training, handling disciplinary issues, and recommending promotions. You have one officer in your department who has been with the company for three years. The officer is slow at the job but works hard, rarely asks for days off, and is friendly to the other staff. No one complains about this particular officer.

Two years ago this officer applied for a promotion. He took the promotion exam and passed. You coached him on his interview skills and provided him with the materials he needed to understand the job. Even though you did all of this, you did not formally recommend him to the corporate headquarters for promotion. That year, he was not promoted.

Last year, he again applied for promotion to sergeant. He took the exam and passed, was provided the material to understand the job, and participated in an interview with people from the corporate headquarters. Again, you failed to support his application for promotion. Corporate headquarters did not promote him.

After his second attempt, he visited with you in the office for advice. You told him why you didn't recommend him and gave him feedback on improving his interview skills and performing the job required. He stated that he would apply again if a position opened up.

This year a sergeant's position is available and the officer has expressed an interest in the position. You informed him that his performance overall had improved and you felt comfortable recommending him for promotion.

The officer again took the promotion exam and passed. You met with him to discuss the interview and provided informational materials to him, just as you had done in the past. After you worked with him a third time but prior to writing your recommendation for promotion, you were informed by the corporate human resources department that this officer filed a grievance against you for discrimination and complained that he had never received feedback on his prior promotion attempts. He claimed that you had failed to recommend him for promotion because of his age, not because of performance. An investigator from the corporate office will be coming to meet with you next week as a result of the complaint.

(Continued)

(Continued)

Questions for Review

1. What issues are you facing as a result of the complaint? Does this affect your recommendation for promotion? Why or why not?

2. What is the driving force for the complaint? Will the complaint impact the motivational levels in the department? Or with this officer? How about your level of motivation?

3. What motivation theory may have contributed to the filing of the complaint?

4. Is there a better way to determine promotions? Explain your answer.

5. How might the quality of services change as a result of the complaint?

Internet Resources

American Bar Association—http://www.abanet.org

Supreme Court of the United States—http://www.supremecourtus.gov

United States Secret Service—http://www.secretservice.gov

References and Suggested Readings

Adams, J. S. (1963). Towards an understanding of inequity. *Journal of Abnormal and Social Psychology, 67,* 422–436.

Aldag, R. J., & Kuzuhara, L. W. (2002). *Organizational behavior and management: An integrated skill.* Mason, OH: Thomson South-Western.

Alderfer, C. P. (1972). *Existence, relatedness, and growth: Human needs in organizational settings.* New York, NY: Free Press.

Alex, N. (1969). *Black in blue: A study of the Negro policeman.* New York, NY: Appleton-Century-Crofts.

Allen, J. M., Mhlanga, B. M., & Khan, E. (2006). Education, training, and ethical dilemmas: Responses of criminal justice practitioners regarding professional and ethical issues. *Professional Issues in Criminal Justice: A Professional Journal, 1*(1), 3–28.

Barnes, C., Sheley, J., Logsdon, V., & Sutherland, S. (2003). *Stress and job satisfaction in an urban sheriff's department: Contributions of work and family history, community oriented policing, and job assignment.* Sacramento: Institute of Social Research, California State University.

Bennett, A. (1991, September 10). Paying workers to meet goals spreads, but gauging performance proves tough. *Wall Street Journal,* pp. B1, B8.

Bridges, J. (1989). Sex differences in occupational values. *Sex Roles, 3*(4), 205–211.

Burke, R. J., Shearer, J., & Deszca, G. (1984). Burnout among men and women in police work: An examination of the Cherniss model. *Journal of Health and Human Resources Administration, 7,* 162–188.

Campbell, J. P., & Pritchard, R. D. (1976). Motivation theory in industrial and organizational psychology. In M. D. Dunnett (Ed.), *Handbook of industrial and organizational psychology* (pp. 63–130). Chicago, IL: Rand McNally.

Carroll, S. J., & Tosi, H. L. (1973). *Management by objectives: Applications and research.* New York, NY: Macmillan.

Charles, M. T. (1982). Women in policing: The physical aspect. *Journal of Police Science and Administration, 10*(2), 194–205.

Dantzker, M. L. (1997). Police officer job satisfaction: Does agency size make a difference? *Criminal Justice Policy Review, 8,* 309–322.

Davidson, L. (1999). The power of personal recognition. *Workforce, 78*(7), 44–49.

DeAngelis, J., & Kupchik, A. (2007). Citizen oversight, procedural justice, and officer perceptions of the complaint investigation process. *Policing, 30*(4), 651.

DeCotiis, T. A. (1977). An analysis of the external validity and applied relevance of three rating formats. *Organizational Behavior and Human Performance, 19,* 247–266.

DeJong, C., Mastrofski, S. D., & Parks, R. B. (2001). Patrol officers and problem solving: An application of expectancy theory. *Justice Quarterly, 18*(1), 31–61.

Drafke, M. W., & Kossen, S. (2002). *The human side of organizations* (8th ed.). Upper Saddle River, NJ: Prentice Hall/Pearson Education.

Ermer, V. B. (1978). Recruitment of female police officers in New York City. *Journal of Criminal Justice, 6,* 233–246.

Filley, A. C., House, R. J., & Kerr, S. (1976). *Managerial process and organizational behavior.* Glenview, IL: Pearson Scott Foresman.

Fisher, C. D., Schoenfeldt, L. F., & Shaw, J. B. (1990). *Human resource management.* Boston, MA: Houghton Mifflin.

Folger, R., & Konovsky, M. A. (1989). Effects of procedural and distributive justice on reactions to pay raise decisions. *Academy of Management Journal, 32,* 115–130.

Franke, W. D., Cox, D. F., Schultz, D. P., & Anderson, D. F. (1997). Coronary heart disease risk factors in employees of Iowa's Department of Public Safety compared to a cohort of the general population. *American Journal of Industrial Medicine, 31*(6), 733–737.

Frimary, P., & Poling, A. (1995, Winter). Making life easier with effort: Basic findings and applied research on response effort. *Journal of Applied Behavioral Analysis, 28*(4), 583–591.

George, J. M., & Jones, G. R. (2002). *Organizational behavior* (3rd ed.). Upper Saddle River, NJ: Prentice Hall.

Glazier, B., & Chapman, B. (2005, December). *Stomp out stress.* Harris County Supervision and Corrections Department. Final report to the National Institute of Justice Corrections and Law Enforcement Family Support Program (NCJRS document number 212419). Washington, DC: U.S. Department of Justice.

Glazier, C. R. (1996). *Assessment of burnout: The development of a behavioral rating scale.* Unpublished doctoral dissertation, University of Houston, Houston, TX.

Godsey, K. D. (1996, October 20). Slow climb to new heights. *Success,* 20–26.

Gove, T. G. (2005, October). Praise and recognition. *FBI Law Enforcement Bulletin, 74,* 10.

Grant, L. (1998, January 12). Happy workers, high returns. *Fortune,* p. 81.

Greenberg, J. (1982). Approaching equity and avoiding inequity in groups and organizations. In J. Greenberg & R. L. Cohen (Eds.), *Equity and justice in social behavior* (pp. 389–435). New York, NY: Academic Press.

Greenberg, J. (1987). Reactions to procedural injustice in payment distributions: Do the means justify the ends? *Journal of Applied Psychology, 72,* 55–61.

Greenberg, J. (1990). Organizational justice: Yesterday, today, and tomorrow. *Journal of Management, 16,* 399–432.

Griffin, R. W. (1982). *Task design: An integrative approach.* Glenview, IL: Pearson Scott Foresman.

Guyot, D. (1991). *Policing as though people matter.* Philadelphia, PA: Temple University Press.

Hackman, R. J., & Oldham, G. R. (1976). Motivation through the design of work: Test of a theory. *Organizational Behavior and Human Performance, 16,* 250–279.

Hackman, R. J., & Oldham, G. R. (1980). *Work design.* Reading, MA: Addison-Wesley.

Hellriegel, D., Slocum, J. W., Jr., & Woodman, R. W. (2001). *Organizational behavior* (9th ed.). Mason, OH: Thomson South-Western.

Herzberg, F. (1966). *Work and the nature of man.* Cleveland, OH: World Publishing.

Hochstedler, E., & Dunning, C. M. (1983). Communication and motivation in a police department. *Criminal Justice and Behavior, 10,* 47–69.

Johnson, J., & Hall, E. (1988). Job strain, workplace social support, and cardiovascular disease: A cross-sectional study of a random sample of the Swedish working population. *American Journal of Public Health, 78*(10), 1336–1342.

Lambert, E. G., Hogan, N. L., & Griffin, M. L. (2007). The impact of distributive and procedural justice on correctional staff job stress, job satisfaction, and organizational commitment. *Journal of Criminal Justice, 35*(6), 644.

Lancaster, H. (1996, July 9). Performance reviews are more valuable when more join in. *Wall Street Journal,* p. B1

Landy, F. J., & Becker, W. S. (1987). Motivation theory reconsidered. *Research in Organizational Behavior, 9,* 1–38.

Latham, G. P., & Wexley, K. N. (1982). *Increasing productivity through performance appraisal.* Reading, MA: Addison-Wesley.

Lawler, E. E., III. (1981). *Pay and organization development.* Reading, MA: Addison-Wesley.

Lester, D. (1983). Why do people become police officers: A study of reasons and their predictions of success. *Journal of Police Science and Administration, 11*(2), 170–174.

Lewis, P. S., Goodman, S. H., & Fandt, P. M. (2001). *Management challenges in the 21st century* (3rd ed.). Cincinnati, OH: South-Western College.

Locke, E. A., & Latham, G. P. (1990). *A theory of goal setting and task performance.* Upper Saddle River, NJ: Prentice Hall.

Maeder, E. M., & Wiener, R. L. (2008, September/October). Likelihood of using drug courts: Predictions using procedural justice and the theory of planned behavior. *Behavioral Sciences & the Law, 26*(5), 543.

Marriott, J. W., Jr., & Brown, K. A. (1997). *The spirit to serve: Marriott's way.* New York, NY: Harper Business.

Martin, S. E. (1993). Female officers on the move? A status report on women in policing. In R. G. Dunham & G. P. Alpert (Eds.), *Critical issues in policing: Contemporary readings* (pp. 327–347). Prospect Heights, IL: Waveland Press.

Maslow, A. H. (1954). *Motivation and personality.* New York, NY: Harper & Row.

Maslow, A. H. (1970). *Motivation and personality* (2nd ed.). New York, NY: Harper & Row.

Mastrofski, S. D. (1998). Community policing and police organization structure. In J. Brodeur (Ed.), *How to recognize good policing: Problems and issues* (pp. 161–189). Thousand Oaks, CA: Sage.

Mastrofski, S. D., Ritti, R. R., & Snipes, J. B. (1994). Expectancy theory and police productivity in DUI enforcement. *Law & Society Review, 28,* 101–136.

McClelland, D. C. (1961). *The achieving society.* New York, NY: Van Nostrand.

McClelland, D. C. (1971). *Motivating trends in society.* Morristown, NJ: General Learning Press.

Meagher, S., & Yentes, N. (1986). Choosing a career in policing: A comparison of male and female perceptions. *Journal of Police Science and Administration, 14*(40), 320–327.

Milton, C. (1972). *Women in policing.* Washington, DC: The Police Foundation.

Mitchell, T. R. (1982a). Expectancy-value models in organizational psychology. In N. T. Feather (Ed.), *Expectations and actions: Expectancy value models in psychology* (pp. 293–312). Hillsdale, NJ: Lawrence Erlbaum.

Mitchell, T. R. (1982b). Motivation: New directions for research, theory and practice. *Academy of Management Review, 7,* 80–88.

Morash, M., & Greene, J. (1986). Evaluating women on patrol: A critique of contemporary wisdom. *Evaluation Review, 10,* 230–255.

Murphy, P. V., & Caplan, D. G. (1991). Fostering integrity. In R. Dunham & G. Alpert (Eds.), *Critical issues in policing* (pp. 304–324). Prospect Heights, IL: Waveland Press.

Murphy, S. A. (2006). Executive motivation: From the front lines to the boardroom? *International Journal of Police Science & Management, 8*(3), 232–245.

Nelson, B. (1996). Dump the cash, load on the praise. *Personnel Journal, 75*(7), 65–70.

Nelson, B. (1999, January/February). The ten ironies of motivation. *Strategy and Leadership, 27,* 26–31.

O'Leary-Kelly, A. M., Martocchio, J. J., & Frink, D. D. (1994). A review of the influence of group performance. *Academy of Management Journal, 37,* 1285–1301.

Perlstein, G. (1972). Policewomen and policemen: A comparative look. *Police Chief, 39,* 72–74.

Raganella, A. J., & White, M. D. (2004). Race, gender, and motivation for becoming a police officer: Implications for building a representative police department. *Journal of Criminal Justice, 32,* 501–513.

Ramey, S. L. (2003). Cardiovascular disease risk factors and the perception of general health among male law enforcement officers: Encouraging behavioural change. *AAOHN Journal, 51*(5), 219–226.

Reiss, A. J., Jr. (1967). Career orientations, job satisfactions and the assessment of law enforcement problems by police officers. In the President's Commission on Law Enforcement and Administration of Justice (Ed.), *Studies in crime and law enforcement in major metropolitan areas: Field surveys III (Vol. 2).* Washington, DC: U.S. Government Printing Office.

Reuss-Ianni, E. (1983). *The two cultures of policing.* New Brunswick, NJ: Transaction Books.

Richer, S., & Vallerand, R. (1995). Supervisors' interactional styles and subordinates' intrinsic and extrinsic motivation. *Journal of Social Psychology, 135*(6), 707–722.

Robinson, P. (1995). Blue thunder. *People Management, 1*(9), 26–27.

Rubinstein, J. (1973). *City police.* New York, NY: Farrar, Straus & Giroux.

Schneider, B., & Alderfer, C. P. (1973). Three studies of measures of needs satisfaction in organizations. *Administrative Science Quarterly, 18*(4), 489–505.

Skinner, B. F. (1969). *Contingencies of reinforcement: A theoretical analysis.* East Norwalk, CT: Appleton-Century-Crofts.

Stahl, M. J., & Harrell, A. M. (1981). Modeling effort decisions with behavioral decision theory: Toward an individual differences model of expectancy theory. *Organizational Behavior and Human Performance, 27,* 303–325.

Sunoo, B. P. (1999, April). Praise and thanks: You can't give enough. *Workforce,* 56–58, 60.

Taylor, F. W. (1911). *The principles of scientific management.* New York, NY: Harper.

Tyler, T. R. (1988). What is procedural justice? *Law and Society Review, 22,* 301–335.

Vroom, V. H. (1964). *Work and motivation.* New York, NY: Wiley.

Whetten, D. A., & Cameron, K. S. (2002). *Developing management skills* (5th ed.). Upper Saddle River, NJ: Prentice Hall.

White, J. L. (2001, February). Police practice: The work itself as a motivator. *FBI Law Enforcement Bulletin, 70*(2), 7–10.

Wood, R. E., Mento, A. J., & Locke, E. A. (1987). Task complexity as a moderator of goal effects: A meta-analysis. *Journal of Applied Psychology, 72,* 416–425.

7

Leadership

After having an exceptionally successful record of accomplishment with Boston Police District D-4 (1977–1982), Massachusetts Bay Transit Authority (1983–1986), and Boston Metropolitan Police (1986–1990), William Bratton was invited to lead the New York Transit Police from 1990 to 1992. His effective leadership resulted in reducing felony crimes by 22% and robberies by 40%. Subsequently, he was invited to head the New York Police Department (NYPD), where his superior leadership led to greater public confidence in the NYPD. Between 1994 and 1996, the overall crime rate fell by 17%, felony crime fell by 39%, murders fell by 50%, theft fell by 35%, and the NYPD had a 73% positive rating up from 37% four years earlier (Kim & Mauborgne, 2003). This is one of the many anecdotes that provide evidence of the importance of effective leadership in improving service quality in criminal justice agencies. Suggesting the importance of leadership as a primary characteristic in criminal justice agencies, Wright (1999) notes, "The organizational climate which is directly influenced by the leadership of the agency determines how much unethical behavior will be present in a criminal justice agency or, for that matter, any organization" (p. 67). Wright goes on to say,

> Employees pay attention to what the bosses care about. It is the positive duty of criminal justice agency heads to ensure that ethical practice is attended to. This requires the chief executive to define and set a standard of ethical practice, and to maintain that standard with diligence and constancy. (p. 67)

If one examines all great business companies or nonprofit organizations, the common characteristic observed is that they have all benefited from the contributions of great leaders. Jack Welch at General Electric, Bill Gates at Microsoft, Steve Jobs at Apple, Meg Whitman at eBay, Anne Mulcahy at Xerox, Rudolph Giuliani as mayor of New York, and William Bratton as police chief of the LAPD are all leaders, visionaries, and motivators; they inspire individuals, groups, and organizations to perform at a higher level and achieve their goals. They prompt their organizations to provide excellent product and service quality leading to increased customer satisfaction, which is the primary goal of all for-profit and nonprofit organizations. Similarly, in the criminal justice system, the idea that leaders and managers have an important role to play in improving service quality is now more deeply entrenched within current debates about organizational change. Pagon (2003) notes, "Different times call for different people.... Not only has police work changed; so have the public and the communities into which it is separated.... Police leaders have to change themselves, their organizations, and their people" (pp. 167–168). In other words, to increase the quality of service provided by an organization, a strong leader is a necessity, making the topic of leadership very important in the criminal justice field.

Leadership Versus Management

Leadership has been a topic of philosophical debate for centuries. Discussions relating to leadership and leadership effectiveness date from the Indian, Greek, and Latin classics, and continue today to be subjects of study. Given such a far-reaching history, it would seem that there should be a clear and consistent definition of leadership. However, despite the fact that numerous researchers and theorists have described and explained the same phenomenon, there has been no consistent definition of leadership. It has been noted (Stogdill, 1974) that each individual researcher seems to have a unique definition of leadership. However, there is a general agreement on two characteristics: Leadership involves influencing other members of the group, and it involves directing the group's effort toward achieving its goals (George & Jones, 2002).

Whenever people are placed in a group comprising more than one person with the express objective of attaining a goal, there is a natural tendency for somebody to take the leadership role. The individual who is most likely to be able to influence the other group members in certain ways to attain the goal will be the one to take on this *informal leadership* role. However, the informal leaders have no formal authority but only their persona to influence others. Alternatively, individuals can be placed in a position within an organization that bestows on them a *formal leadership* role that gives them formal authority in directing their subordinates toward achieving the targets set for the organization. For example, managers, police chiefs, prison wardens, and judges play a formal leadership role within their respective organizations. The formal leaders can easily be discovered by looking at the organizational chart, which provides a view of the overall authority relationships established within an organization. However, effective leaders within an organization are the ones who not only have a formal platform to influence others, but also have the ability to influence them outside of their formal authority. In other words, these individuals integrate both the formal and informal aspects of leadership in influencing their subordinates to accomplish organizational goals.

Sometimes, the discussion is addressed under the topic of leadership versus management. Management is discussed in the context of formal leadership, a platform that individuals are provided within an organization, which provide them with power to influence others. (A detailed discussion on power is presented in Chapter 5, and management is discussed in Chapter 1.) On the other hand, leadership is discussed outside of the scope of formal authority, more in the context of one's informal ability to influence others. The main idea being presented in this discussion is that effective managers have to be leaders, too. To avoid confusion, the authors of this textbook use the term *leadership* to encompass both leadership and management functions.

The questions that come to mind related to the topic of leadership are these: Can it be predicted among a group who is the most likely candidate to become a leader? Can people acquire the skills to become a leader? How does one stay a leader? The answers to such questions are addressed by a large volume of literature written about leadership, which will be presented under the different leadership theories.

Introduction to Leadership Theories

Leadership has been variously characterized as personality, the art of inducing compliance, the exercise of influence, a power relation, an instrument of goal achievement (Stogdill, 1974), behavior change (Petrillo & Bass, 1961), the need to overcome resistance to change (Bass, 1985), the "influential increment over and above mechanical compliance with routine directives" (Katz & Kahn, 1978, p. 528), and integration of ideas, resources, and people (Lawrence & Lorsch, 1967), just to cite a few examples. There have been five dominant paradigms of leadership advanced in the 20th century, within which many theories of leadership have been proposed. To a large extent, each approach has been an extension of and response to the criticisms of the previously dominant paradigm. Individually, each approach lends some valuable insights toward leadership but fails to provide a universal perfect theory to aid in the understanding of the term. Collectively, the approaches provide a multifaceted view of leadership while conceptually challenging the assumptions of each theory.

Traits Approach

The first approach to explaining leadership involved studying *traits* or *characteristics* by assuming that there are certain traits that an individual must possess to become a leader. The various types of traits examined by researchers included physical characteristics, personality characteristics, social characteristics, and personal abilities and skills (House & Podaskoff, 1994). The research concluded that successful leaders are more ambitious, have a higher sense of achievement and responsibility, are more motivated, demonstrate higher levels of honesty and integrity, have more self-confidence, and have better people skills (Lewis, Goodman, & Fandt, 2001). More recent research on other traits has concluded that "energy level and stress tolerance, self-confidence, internal control orientation, emotional maturity, and integrity" (Yukl, 1981, p. 280) are highly relevant to the effectiveness of a leader. "These characteristics were seen to be fixed, largely inborn, and applicable across situations" (Hollander & Offerman, 1990, p. 179). Traits theory was largely designed to try to predict whether an individual would manifest leadership abilities. Premised on the assumption that leadership traits were inborn, this theory encouraged finding individuals with the prerequisite traits to place them as leaders rather than developing leaders through training.

Traits theory was in vogue for the first four decades of the 20th century. However, a group of influential reviews published in the late 1940s (Gibb, 1947; Jenkins, 1947) reported a lack of consistent relationships between individual traits and leadership. Consequently, they encouraged researchers to explore alternative paradigms.

More recently, there has been a renewed interest in traits theory, where the researchers have examined how the existence of traits may be perceived by peers and subordinates. This literature stream concludes that existence of certain traits in individuals may be perceived by their peers and subordinates as leadership qualities. Such perceptions in the minds of employees may place individuals in the leadership role (House & Podsakoff, 1994), even though these traits fail to distinguish effective from ineffective leaders. For example, officers in law enforcement may look at someone with a good height and physique and regard this person as a leader. However, a good height and physique do not necessarily correlate with this individual being a successful leader. In addition, detectives are sometimes viewed as leaders within departments because they exhibit personality characteristics that are desirable to others (charismatic, laid-back, knowledgeable, and calm, etc.). However, becoming a detective does not necessarily require leadership skills. Officers can be promoted through merit exams, length of service, friendships with those in power, and so forth. So being a detective does not necessarily mean the person is a good leader; it just means the person holds a higher position in the department and displays characteristics often associated with leadership (whether effective or not).

Behavioral Approach

The criticisms of traits theory shifted studies of leadership to focus on an examination of observable behaviors of leaders. The natural thought here was to examine what leaders actually do and how they do it. This approach, which was dominant in the 1950s and 1960s, focused on how subordinates reacted to a leader's behavior. The main goal of the various behavioral theories was to try to prescribe how leaders should behave.

Major studies of *behavioral leadership* were conducted at Ohio State University (Halpin & Winer, 1957) and focused on two different dimensions of leader behavior. The first was *consideration*, which revolves around a leader's concern for people, with an emphasis on satisfying employee needs. It is reflected in mutual trust, two-way communication, respect for employees' ideas, and empathy for their feelings. These leaders are typically open and friendly, willing to listen to employee needs and make changes to address them, and thus bring employees closer to their subordinates. The second was *initiating structure*, which revolves around a leader's concern for productivity. These leaders set performance goals, set standards, and provide resources and guidance toward attaining the goals. The assessment of these two types of behaviors and their resultant outcomes found no consistent patterns between leader behavior and outcomes. However, there were some consistencies between leader behavior and success within certain types of situations, which suggested that the situation or context of the leadership process might impact a leader's effectiveness. It was also observed that one behavior did not occur at the expense of the other. These behaviors are *independent* because one behavior does not exclude the leader from adopting the other behavior. These behaviors could be *complementary* to the extent that leaders can engage in both types of behavior. For example, officers working as hostage negotiators may display both the behaviors at one point or another and perhaps at the same time. The negotiator better understands the current situation and is prepared, through training, practice, and previous experiences, to act as an effective leader during hostage situations. These leaders will display consideration for the hostages and employees while working with the Special Weapons and Tactics (SWAT) teams, as well as a heightened concern to enhance productivity to resolve the situation quickly and end the standoff.

In addition to the two leadership behaviors discussed already (consideration versus initiating structure), leaders also behave in other ways that have important effects on their followers. Leaders have the *power* to both reward and punish their subordinates to increase the likelihood of favorable behavior and decrease the occurrence of undesirable behaviors, implying leadership success. To understand the influence of power, it is important to understand different types of power and to consider whether the source of power is prescribed by the leader's position or is a result of the leader's personality attributes. A detailed discussion on the topic of power is provided in Chapter 5. Students are strongly encouraged to reread that discussion to better understand the relationships and differences between power and leadership.

Similar studies of leader behavior at the University of Michigan (Kahn & Katz, 1953; Katz, Maccoby, & Morse, 1950) also failed to produce significant consistent evidence of any relationship between leader behavior and outcomes. No leadership style was found to be universally superior to others. However, despite the fact that the behavioral approaches were not able to fulfill their mission and determine the one best leadership style, they did further leadership knowledge, ascertaining that behavior was a factor that explained leadership effectiveness within a given context or setting.

Contingency Theories of Leadership (Situational Leadership Models)

The trait approach focused on what effective leaders are like and the behavioral approach examined what leaders do. However, both of these leadership approaches ignored the impact of situations in which leadership takes place. The situation moderates the impact of the leader's traits and the leader's behavior. Therefore, a superior comprehension of leadership can be gained by understanding the moderating impact of situation on leadership.

The proponents of *situational leadership* assert that there is no one best leadership style, but that different situations require different leadership styles. The situational analysis of leadership was popular from the late 1960s to the late 1970s. Building on the fact that leadership effectiveness appeared to be tied to contextual factors, the *situational or contingency approaches* focused on the moderating effect that certain situational variables would have on the relationship between leader traits, and behaviors and outcomes. Four elements frequently cited as having an influence on a leader's behavior are the nature of the task or activity, resource availability, the history of the task, and the history of the people involved. These elements do not act independently but interact to influence the leader's effectiveness. The four most popular contingency models are Fiedler's contingency model, Hersey and Blanchard's model, House's path-goal model, and Vroom and Yetton's model.

Fiedler's contingency model (1967) assumes that leaders will be relationship-oriented or task-oriented and cannot easily change between different situations. He devised a unique scale to measure leader style called the *least-preferred coworker scale*. Fiedler asked leaders to describe their experience in dealing with their least-preferred coworker (LPC)—that is, the one with whom they had the most difficult working relationship. The leader was asked to rate the LPC on a number of dimensions. *Relationship-oriented leaders* (also called the high LPC leaders) described their LPC in relatively positive terms. These leaders were able to look beyond the difficult working relationship and appreciate the human aspect of the coworker in making positive comments. Alternatively, the *task-oriented leaders* (also called the low LPC leaders) described their LPC negatively, focusing more on the inability to get the task accomplished. Fiedler suggested that the way leaders describe their LPC provided good insight into their approach to leading. Furthermore, Fiedler maintained that leaders' performances are dependent on their motivational system and the degree to which the leaders are able to control and influence the situation. The three contingency variables considered in this model are as follows:

1. *Group atmosphere.* It defines the leader–member relationship, thus capturing the degree of acceptance of the leader by the team. Higher leader acceptance, trust, and loyalty make it easy for the leader to get the team to commit to a task. Thinking of a SWAT team, the leader is clearly defined, and the group atmosphere pushes the leader up in the minds of others, making them more willing to listen and contribute to the team's purpose and goals.

2. *Task structure.* This defines the complexity of the task. Compared to a nonroutine task, a routine task will be well-defined and have clear guidelines and procedures, thus making it easier for the leader to accomplish goals. Again, SWAT teams may face nonroutine situations, but they are well-versed through training and practice, and they can perform their tasks using clear guidelines and procedures. The team leader is easily able to guide the SWAT team through the situation, even though it may be unique, because the tasks they perform are routine regardless of the circumstances surrounding their involvement.

3. *Position power.* This is the extent to which a leader has reward, coercive, and legitimate power (Hellriegel, Slocum, & Woodman, 2001). The SWAT team leaders are clearly identified as having legitimate power, since they earned the position through experience, training, and service. Officers involved with the SWAT team often become members because it is a reward given to them for length of service, expertise, specialties, or excellence in job performance.

Combining the three contingency variables with the least-preferred coworker scale, Fiedler (1994) created an eight-point leader effectiveness scale, which suggests that both relationship-oriented and task-oriented leaders perform successfully in certain situations and not in others. According to Fiedler's model, task-oriented leaders are most effective in extreme situations that are highly favorable or unfavorable, and relationship-oriented leaders are most effective in moderately favorable situations. The most favorable situation presented to a leader is when the team supports the leader, the leader's power position is high, and the task is well structured (like that described in the SWAT or tactical units discussed earlier). In this situation, the leader can involve everyone, improve relationships with team members, and get the task accomplished; thus, the satisfaction and performance remain high. Similarly, when the situation is highly unfavorable, a task-oriented leader can define task structure and establish authority over subordinates to accomplish the goals. Because leader–member relations are poor anyway, strong task-oriented leaders will not be concerned about their popularity when making decisions to accomplish the task.

Other researchers have questioned Fiedler's model on the use of the LPC ratings to measure leader style, suggesting that better measures of a leader's behavior are needed. The LPC scale developed by Fiedler is a one-dimensional concept, suggesting that a leader who is high on relationships will be low on task. This assumes that the LPC score is a trait of a leader and does not change over time, thus suggesting that leadership style is fixed. In other words,

> leaders cannot be taught to be relationship oriented or task oriented in responding to a particular situation, nor can a leader alter his or her style according to the situation. Instead, leaders must be assigned to situations in which they will be effective because of their style, or situations must be changed to fit the leader. (George & Jones, 2002, p. 403)

However, successful leaders are known to change their leadership style with the situation presented to them, rather than adapting the same leadership style to all situations.

Hersey and Blanchard's contingency model (1977) assumes that leadership style is not static, but can be changed to match the readiness level of the employees. They propose *four different leadership styles* that a leader can adopt depending on the level of readiness of the subordinates on task ability and psychological preparedness. In the *low-readiness level,* where workers have poor ability and skills or are psychologically unwilling to perform the task, a *telling style* of leadership is appropriate. This leadership style is very directive and shows little concern for people. It involves giving explicit directions about how to accomplish the task. Probation officers may use a telling leadership style with probationers when instructing them on how to meet the court's orders.

In the *moderate-readiness level,* where the workers may have low ability because of a lack of education or experience but demonstrate high levels of willingness to learn, a *selling style* of leadership is more appropriate. This leadership style is based on a high concern for both people and productivity; the leaders "sell" their directions by involving people and giving them a chance to get clarity and understanding through two-way communication. For example, during training sessions in the police academy, police recruits are able to ask questions and garner additional information from the trainers to better understand the type of work they are about to pursue.

In the *high-readiness level,* where the subordinates have the necessary education, experience, and skills but are not fully confident of their ability to perform their tasks and *participating style* of leadership is most appropriate. In this leadership style, the leaders have a high concern for people and a low concern for production. The leaders share their ideas with subordinates, encourage them to participate, and facilitate decision making by providing some guidance. Within criminal justice, this can be seen occurring in annual training sessions where probation, police, and corrections officers come together to learn about topics and to discuss their personal experiences in the field. Facilitators in the training, sessions may have material they want to cover in the training but they allow for input and participation from the trainees.

In the *very-high-readiness level,* where the subordinates are well prepared and confident and are ready to accept responsibility, a *delegating style* of leadership is most appropriate. This leadership style is represented by leaders' low concern for both people and production. The leader provides little direction and support because the followers are highly prepared to take on the responsibility. Looking at probation again, one can see that probation officers work with little micromanagement and supervise their cases in ways they believe are most appropriate. Thanks to socialization in the field, training, and good leadership at other points, they are able to follow the directions of the administration and the court while working on their own.

Though Hersey and Blanchard's model is an advancement over Fiedler's model because it incorporates the characteristics of followers, its weakness is that it does not consider the situation faced by the leader. Making this amendment, House (1971) proposed a *path-goal theory* that takes into account the situational contingencies as well as the leadership style and the use of rewards. Here, the leader's main purpose is to increase the subordinates' motivation to attain both personal and organizational goals by performing at a high level. This increased motivation is attained by determining the needs, goals, and outcomes that subordinates are trying to achieve at the workplace; developing an incentive system that rewards subordinates for performing at a high level, while achieving their goals; and helping and guiding subordinates and clearing obstacles from their path to ensure that they can perform at a high level and attain their work goals.

House identified four types of behavior that leaders can engage in to motivate their subordinates (cited in Yukl, 1981). *Supportive leadership behavior* is open, friendly, and approachable, thus showing concern for the workers' well-being and personal needs. This style is very effective when the subordinate lacks self-confidence. New trainees and hires may experience supportive leadership during their probationary period with a criminal justice agency. *Directive leadership behavior* is reflected when the leader is more involved in telling workers what to do, planning, directing, setting performance goals, and emphasizing rules and regulations. This style is very effective when the subordinate faces an ambiguous job and cannot operate effectively. Police departments tend to use directive leadership by specifying the beat an officer will patrol; directing the officer's job duties; providing performance measures for shifts or annual goals; and stressing policies, procedures, and standard operating procedures for handling evidence, servicing citizens, and answering calls for criminal incidents (to name only a few). Policy manuals can sometimes be hundreds of pages long, directing every behavior of a police officer. *Participative leadership behavior* is demonstrated when the leaders consult their subordinates and encourage them to participate in decision making. This style is very effective when the subordinate is unchallenged by the task and needs higher goals. *Achievement-oriented leadership behavior* involves having trust in the ability and willingness of the workers to be highly productive. These leaders set challenging goals for their workers, and provide them with continuous guidance and learning opportunities to perform at high levels.

The two situational contingencies considered in path-goal theory are the following: (1) *personal characteristics of the group members* such as their skill, ability, willingness, and needs. If the workers have low ability and willingness, then the leader may need to act as a coach and motivator to help the workers improve their performance. If the subordinates have high skill, willingness, and are focused, then the leader can use rewards to direct their behavior to attain high performance; and (2) the *work environment* is reflected by the degree of clarity provided in the task structure and the formal line of authority giving legitimate power. Path-goal theory offers a better understanding of how leadership can become more effective by specifying how to motivate the subordinates. Unfortunately, criminal justice agencies are not always able to provide rewards because of the nature of their business (public agencies), even when the workers are highly skilled, willing to perform, and focused on the job. Leaders in this case may have to use creativity by looking for other means to motivate workers. At a probation office where one of the authors of this book was employed, the leadership would often allow for flexibility in work schedules so subordinates could attend graduate education programs or other events the subordinate believed to be important. In addition, it is not uncommon in the criminal justice field for the state or county to reimburse tuition fees to subordinates who pursue higher education. Although it is not perceived as a bonus (like those given in for-profit organizations), tuition reimbursement programs can be looked at as ways to motivate employees, increase professionalism in the field, and develop critical and analytical thinking skills in employees. Higher education may even promote increased leadership skills.

Developed in the 1970s, *Vroom and Yetton's model* (1973) recognizes that one of the most important tasks of a leader is decision making; good decisions help an organization realize its goals, while bad decisions obstruct the attainment of goals. The Vroom and Yetton model discusses the different ways in which leaders can make decisions and how subordinates can be involved in this decision-making process (see Table 7.1).

Table 7.1 Decision Methods for Group and Individual Problems

Group Problems	Individual Problems
AI. You solve the problem or make the decision by yourself, using information available to you at the time.	AI. You solve the problem or make the decision by yourself, using information available to you at the time.
AII. You obtain the necessary information from your subordinates, and then decide on the solution to the problem yourself. You may or may not tell your subordinates what the problem is in getting the information from them. The role played by your subordinates in making the decision is clearly one of providing the necessary information to you, rather than generating or evaluating alternative solutions.	AII. You obtain the necessary information from your subordinate, and then decide on the solution to the problem yourself. You may or may not tell the subordinate what the problem is in getting the information from him. His or her role in making the decision is clearly one of providing the necessary information to you, rather than generating or evaluating alternative solutions.
CI. You share the problem with the relevant subordinates individually, getting their ideas and suggestions without bringing them together as a group. Then you make the decision, which may or may not reflect your subordinates' influence.	CI. You share the problem with your subordinate, getting his or her ideas and suggestions. Then you make a decision, which may or may not reflect your subordinate's influence.
CII. You share the problem with your subordinates as a group, obtaining their collective ideas and suggestions. Then you make the decision, which may or may not reflect your subordinates' influence.	GI. You share the problem with your subordinate, and together you analyze the problem and arrive at a mutually agreeable solution.
GII. You share the problem with your subordinates as a group. Together you generate and evaluate alternatives and attempt to reach agreement (consensus) on a solution. Your role is much like that of chairman. You do not try to influence the group to adopt "your" solution, and you are willing to accept and implement any solution that has the support of the entire group.	DI. You delegate the problem to your subordinate, providing him or her with any relevant information that you possess, but giving the subordinate responsibility for solving the problem by him- or herself. You may or may not request the subordinate to tell you what solution he or she has reached.

SOURCE: From *Leadership and Decision Making*, by V. H. Vroom and P. W. Yetton, © 1973, Pittsburgh, PA: University of Pittsburgh Press. Reprinted by permission of the University of Pittsburgh Press.

Participation by subordinates in decision making and problem solving ensures that they will accept and support the decision. This ownership of the decisions by the subordinates makes the implementation of changes easy, thus enhancing leadership effectiveness. Sometimes, subordinates may have information that is more accurate because of their position within an organization, resulting in a superior decision because of their involvement. However, involvement of subordinates can make the decision-making process longer. At times, subordinates may push for decisions that benefit them personally but may not be the best for the organization, thus putting the leader in an awkward position to reject the subordinate's suggestion. Given that involvement of subordinates in decision making can be both beneficial and detrimental to leadership effectiveness, the Vroom and Yetton model identifies when and how much to involve the subordinates.

In the process of deciding the optimal amount of subordinate involvement, Vroom and Yetton (1973) recommend first identifying if it is an individual or a group decision. Subsequently, there are five decision-making styles, ranging from least participative to most participative, from which a leader can choose. Next are the different participative styles from which to choose.

To narrow down the appropriate decision-making style, the model provides a list of questions concerning the specific characteristics of the decision that is pending, the distinguishing features of the subordinates involved, and the extent to which the leader has the required information to make a sound decision. These questions are arranged in a decision tree. Answering each question methodically on the decision tree directs the leader toward the problem type that characterizes the decision that needs to be made. For each problem type, there will be a set of appropriate leadership styles. Of these multiple feasible styles, one style is recommended to minimize the time required to make the decision (time being measured by the number of people involved, multiplied by the number of hours spent by each person), which is the least participative style. The other styles are recommended to promote subordinates' development and growth, which are premised on higher levels of participation.

Thinking outside of the typical employer–employee relationship and considering how police officers use leadership and decision making in the course of their jobs, one can see that a street cop may use both the least participative style of decision making as well as the most participative style during a typical day in the field. For example, an officer who arrives on the scene of a domestic violence incident may arrest the person viewed as the offender. The officer relies on information available at the time (from victim, witness, or offender statements and/or legal guidelines) to make the decision. In this case, the officer may decide that removal of the offender is the best alternative to allow emotions to decrease in intensity and to protect the victim or children that may be involved. Here there is the least participation of the victim, witness, or offender, as they are only information providers.

In another call, the officer may be involved in community policing initiatives. In community policing, the police collaborate with the community on programs, decisions, activities, and so forth that are aimed at lowering crime rates in a particular area and increasing the quality of life for residents. By allowing community members input into the process of policing and the problems facing the community, the police and the community attempt to identify resolutions to those problems. In this case, the officer works with the community to identify a resolution, and works to implement that resolution in policing practices in that geographical area. Here the community is highly participative in the decision-making process of how policing will occur and how the community will respond to crime.

Transactional Leadership Theory

Transactional leadership theory focuses on the process of interaction between a leader and the followers rather than the character of the people (trait theory) or the situation (contingency theory). Transactional leaders work through the given system and conform to organizational norms and values. The leader–follower relationships are based on a set of past interactions and exchanges between leaders and followers. The effectiveness of these leaders depends on the extent to which they clarify expectations and goals. Bass (1985) identified two main interaction processes that comprise transactional leadership—contingent reward leadership and management by exception. *Contingent reward leadership* allows leaders to interact with followers by clarifying the role and task requirements expected of their subordinates; by providing proper guidelines and structure; and by initiating proper rewards and meeting the social needs of the subordinates, resulting in improved productivity (Yammarino & Bass, 1990). These transactions are focused toward helping subordinates attain their goals through positive reinforcement, sometimes referred to as contingent reward leadership. Police departments may clearly identify the path to promotion for officers wishing to pursue higher positions. In this case, the officers would be informed of their current job expectations as well as the guidelines and structure in place to apply for promotion. Officers could then work toward accomplishing the guidelines to fulfill their desire of being promoted. *Management by exception* allows leaders to interact with subordinates only when they deviate from expectations by giving them negative feedback, suggesting failure to meet standards. Management by exception may be classified as passive or active, depending on the timing of the leader's intervention (Bass & Avolio, 1993; Lievens, VanGeit, & Coetsier, 1997). When leaders intervene after standards are not met, then it is classified as *passive* management by exception. For example, providing negative feedback to correctional officers only during times of performance evaluations is considered passive feedback. Alternatively, if the leader tries to anticipate mistakes or problems, then it is termed as *active* management by exception. Transactional leadership focuses on simple exchange processes and does not set challenging expectations to achieve higher levels of performance. These leaders typically neglect to focus on developing the long-term potential of workers.

New Wave of Change Leadership Theories

Since the mid-1970s, researchers have offered macrofocused studies of leadership that have moved away from individual and small-group aspects of leadership and instead have focused on how leaders impact the working culture within an entire organization, leading them beyond the normal levels of performance. The theories advanced in this current wave have been called *charismatic leadership theory* (Conger & Kanungo, 1987; 1988; House, 1971), *transformational leadership theory* (Bass, 1985; Burns, 1978), and *visionary leadership theory* (Sashkin, 1988). Despite the different names, the common thread weaving these theories together is that they infuse ideological values and moral purpose into organizations that induce commitment and organizational citizenship among workers, resulting in change. More recently, these theories have been grouped together under the label *outstanding leadership theory* (House & Podsakoff, 1994). Outstanding leaders are those who accomplish outstanding achievement and corporate turnaround in direct contrast to fulfilling normal requirements of positions and everyday responsibilities. Outstanding leadership theory is based heavily on the belief that stress (either individual or organizational) is key to facilitating the leadership dynamics (Pillai & Meindl, 1998). This group of theories extends the transactional theories; as Hollander and Offerman (1990) note, "Transformational leadership can be seen as an extension of transactional leadership, but with greater leader intensity and follower arousal" (p. 182).

Charismatic leadership theory. Charismatic leaders create an environment of change around them and attract people by their personality to work toward accomplishing these changes. These leaders have an innate quality of relating with people and inspiring and motivating them to perform beyond their normal level. Researchers (Conger & Kanungo, 1987; Gardner & Avolio, 1998) believe that charismatic leaders make an impact at the organizational level by identifying an ambitious vision of the perceived future for both the organization and the employees. These leaders elevate individuals to higher levels on Maslow's (1954) needs hierarchy chart by determining and influencing the corporate value system and by earning the complete trust and loyalty of the subordinates by displaying self-confidence, determination, optimism, and courage. Charismatic leaders tend to obtain power through their followers' identification with them. As mentioned before, William Bratton, who was invited to head the NYPD in the early 1990s, used charismatic leadership, which inspired and motivated the police force and resulted in a significant decline in crime and increased public confidence from 37% to 73% within four years (Kim & Mauborgne, 2003). Burtell Morris Jefferson, the first African American chief of the Metropolitan Police Department of Washington, is another individual who falls into the category of charismatic leaders. Despite all odds against him as a black officer, he pushed forward in his career. Not only could he convey his values and virtues to bring out the best in others, but he also created a positive environment that made possible the development of other minority law enforcement officers (Williams & Kellough, 2006).

Transformational leadership theory. Transformational leaders do not accept the status quo but recognize the need to challenge the existing standards and operating procedures and enable others to achieve higher levels of performance. Transformational leaders do not rely solely on formal rules and regulations, but integrate features of the transactional and charismatic models of leadership. Several researchers have focused on transformational leadership; the main difference between them is the process they propose to elevate subordinates to higher levels on Maslow's (1954) needs hierarchy chart, so that these individuals can perform at high levels and can be instrumental in organizational change. Bass (1985) proposes three ways in which transformational leaders inspire their subordinates to higher levels of performance and in accomplishing organizational goals. These include increasing the subordinates' awareness of the importance of tasks and the importance of doing them well; increasing the subordinates' realization of their need for personal growth, development, and achievements; and motivating the subordinates to fulfill their dreams and contribute to the success of the organization.

The four primary dimensions of transformational leadership are inspirational motivation, intellectual stimulation, idealized influence, and individualized consideration (Bass, 1998; Sosik, Kahai, & Avolio, 1998; Sosik & Megerian, 1999). *Inspirational motivation* refers to the leader fostering among the followers a sense of change through a vision of a better future that is significantly different from the present. Such leaders get followers involved and eventually committed to making a change. John Augustus, the father of modern probation, is a prime example of an inspirational motivator. Augustus attended court in Massachusetts in the mid-1800s and was the first individual to offer his home to selected offenders so they could avoid prison (which was the most commonly used punishment). He assured the court that he would monitor the offenders and return them to court when demanded. After participating in this process several times, Augustus also created forms to assist in the investigation, treatment, and rehabilitation of offenders. Over time, other volunteers stepped forward to monitor offenders in the community. Consequently, his vision of punishment as extending beyond just prison was the impetus for modern-day probation. *Intellectual stimulation* is demonstrated by the leaders when they inspire workers to question the existing paradigm and assumptions. The leaders encourage the workers to be innovative and creative in defining the new paradigm, to explore new ideas and methods, and to provide creative solutions. (Restorative justice proponents were very successful at intellectual stimulation during the late 20th and early 21st centuries.) Community policing is another initiative that allows for innovation and creativity in the policing of citizens. Officers are provided the freedom to use new methods and ideas to develop relationships with the community. Of course, not all of these approaches are successful, but transformational leaders focus on how to correct the problem rather than find whom to blame. They have relatively high levels of tolerance toward mistakes made by conscientious workers, and they are ready to help these workers learn from mistakes and be more productive. Followers are encouraged to ask their leader for direction and guidance to improve themselves. *Idealized influence* refers to the behaviors and values of a transformational leader, such as high standards of ethics and moral conduct, that followers like to emulate. To earn such idealized influence, the transformational leaders often consider the needs and interests of their followers over their own needs (Hellriegel et al., 2001). Such leaders are admired, respected, and trusted by the followers, who feel free to question what is being advocated. The followers can identify easily with the goals because of consistency with their own self-concept and being. *Individualized consideration* arises when the leader acts as a coach, mentor, teacher, facilitator, confidant, and counselor to help followers successfully achieve higher levels of their potential capability. Continuous improvement through involvement is standard practice.

It is important to note that sometimes the terms *charisma* and *transformational leadership* are used interchangeably. Bass (1985; Bass & Avolio, 1993) makes a distinction between them by suggesting that charisma forms a subdimension of transformational leadership. Probation officers are adept at practicing individualized consideration with clients on their caseloads. As officers get to know clients and better understand their personal needs and weaknesses, they can coach and mentor the client into better behaviors and making better choices. As a former juvenile probation officer, one of the authors of this text can strongly relate to this approach because she acted as a confidante, a facilitator of treatment and rehabilitation services, and a counselor to many juveniles assigned to her caseload. Individualized case plans were made in each instance so that the client's problems could be addressed in the best manner, and client input and relationship building were key components in the interactions she had with the youth.

CAREER HIGHLIGHT BOX
FIRE FIGHTING OCCUPATIONS

Nature of the Work

Every year, fires and other emergencies take thousands of lives and destroy property worth billions of dollars. Fire fighters help protect the public against these dangers by responding to fires and a variety of other emergencies. In addition to putting out fires, they are frequently the first emergency personnel at the scene of a traffic accident or medical emergency and may be called upon to treat injuries or perform other vital functions.

During duty hours, fire fighters must be prepared to respond immediately to a fire or others [sic] emergency. Fighting fires is dangerous and complex, [and] therefore requires organization and teamwork. At every emergency scene, fire fighters perform specific duties assigned by a superior officer. At fires, they connect hose lines to hydrants and operate a pump to send water to high-pressure hoses. Some carry hoses, climb ladders, and enter burning buildings—using systematic and careful procedures—to put out fires. At times, they may need to use tools, like an ax, to make their way through doors, walls, and debris, sometimes with the aid of information about a building's floor plan. Some find and rescue occupants who are unable to safely leave the building without assistance. They also provide emergency medical attention, ventilate smoke-filled areas, and attempt to salvage the contents of buildings. Fire fighters' duties may change several times while the company is in action. Sometimes they remain at the site of a disaster for days at a time, rescuing trapped survivors, and assisting with medical treatment.

Fire fighters work in a variety of settings, including metropolitan areas, rural areas with grasslands and forests, airports, chemical plants and other industrial sites. They have also assumed a range of responsibilities, including emergency medical services. In fact, most calls to which fire fighters respond involve medical emergencies. In addition, some fire fighters work in hazardous materials units that are specially trained for the control, prevention, and cleanup of hazardous materials, such as oil spills or accidents involving the transport of chemicals. (For more information, see the *Handbook* section on hazardous material removal workers.)

Workers specializing [in] forest fires utilize different methods and equipment than other fire fighters. In national forests and parks, *forest fire inspectors and prevention specialists* spot fires from watchtowers and report the fires to headquarters by telephone or radio. Forest rangers also patrol to ensure that travelers and campers comply with fire regulations. When fires break out, crews of fire fighters are brought in to suppress the blaze with heavy equipment and water hoses. Fighting forest fires, like fighting urban fires, is rigorous work. One of the most effective means of fighting a forest fire is creating fire lines—cutting down trees and digging out grass and all other combustible vegetation in the path of the fire—to deprive it of fuel. Elite fire fighters called smoke jumpers parachute from airplanes to reach otherwise inaccessible areas. This tactic, however, can be extremely hazardous.

When they aren't responding to fires and other emergencies, fire fighters clean and maintain equipment, study fire science and fire fighting techniques, conduct practice drills and fire inspections, and participate in physical fitness activities. They also prepare written reports on fire incidents and review fire science literature to stay informed about technological developments and changing administrative practices and policies.

Most fire departments have a fire prevention division, usually headed by a fire marshal and staffed by *fire inspectors*. Workers in this division conduct inspections of structures to prevent fires by ensuring compliance with fire codes. These inspectors also work with developers and planners to check and approve plans for new buildings and inspect buildings under construction.

Some fire fighters become *fire investigators*, who determine the causes of fires. They collect evidence, interview witnesses, and prepare reports on fires in cases where the cause may be arson or criminal negligence. They often are asked to testify in court. In some cities, these investigators work in police departments, and some are employed by insurance companies.

Work environment. Fire fighters spend much of their time at fire stations, which are usually similar to dormitories. When an alarm sounds, fire fighters respond, regardless of the weather or hour. Fire fighting involves the risk of death or injury from floors caving in, walls toppling, traffic accidents, and exposure to flames and smoke. Fire fighters also may come into contact with poisonous, flammable, or explosive gases and chemicals and radioactive materials, which may have immediate or long-term effects on their health. For these reasons, they must wear protective gear that can be very heavy and hot.

Work hours of fire fighters are longer and more varied than the hours of most other workers. Many fire fighters work more than 50 hours a week, and sometimes they may work longer. In some agencies, fire fighters are on duty for 24 hours, then off for 48 hours, and receive an extra day off at intervals. In others, they work a day shift of 10 hours for 3 or 4 days, a night shift of 14 hours for 3 or 4 nights, have 3 or 4 days off, and then

(Continued)

(Continued)

repeat the cycle. In addition, fire fighters often work extra hours at fires and other emergencies and are regularly assigned to work on holidays. Fire lieutenants and fire captains often work the same hours as the fire fighters they supervise.

Training, Other Qualifications, and Advancement

Applicants for fire fighting jobs are usually required to have at least a high school diploma, but candidates with some education after high school are increasingly preferred. Most municipal jobs require passing written and physical tests. All fire fighters receive extensive training after being hired.

Education and training. Most fire fighters have a high school diploma; however, the completion of community college courses, or in some cases, an associate degree, in fire science may improve an applicant's chances for a job. A number of colleges and universities offer courses leading to 2- or 4-year degrees in fire engineering or fire science. In recent years, an increasing proportion of new fire fighters have had some education after high school.

As a rule, entry-level workers in large fire departments are trained for several weeks at the department's training center or academy. Through classroom instruction and practical training, the recruits study fire fighting techniques, fire prevention, hazardous materials control, local building codes, and emergency medical procedures, including first aid and cardiopulmonary resuscitation (CPR). They also learn how to use axes, chain saws, fire extinguishers, ladders, and other fire fighting and rescue equipment. After successfully completing this training, the recruits are assigned to a fire company, where they undergo a period of probation.

Many fire departments have accredited apprenticeship programs lasting up to 4 years. These programs combine formal instruction with on-the-job training under the supervision of experienced fire fighters.

Almost all departments require fire fighters to be certified as emergency medical technicians. (For more information, see the section of the *Handbook* on emergency medical technicians and paramedics.) Although most fire departments require the lowest level of certification, Emergency Medical Technician-Basic (EMT-Basic), larger departments in major metropolitan areas increasingly require paramedic certification. Some departments include this training in the fire academy, whereas others prefer that recruits earn EMT certification on their own but will give them up to 1 year to do it.

In addition to participating in training programs conducted by local fire departments, some fire fighters attend training sessions sponsored by the U.S. National Fire Academy. These training sessions cover topics such as executive development, anti-arson techniques, disaster preparedness, hazardous materials control, and public fire safety and education. Some States also have either voluntary or mandatory fire fighter training and certification programs. Many fire departments offer fire fighters incentives such as tuition reimbursement or higher pay for completing advanced training.

Other qualifications. Applicants for municipal fire fighting jobs usually must pass a written exam; tests of strength, physical stamina, coordination, and agility; and a medical examination that includes a drug screening. Workers may be monitored on a random basis for drug use after accepting employment. Examinations are generally open to people who are at least 18 years of age and have a high school education or its equivalent. Those who receive the highest scores in all phases of testing have the best chances of being hired.

Among the personal qualities fire fighters need are mental alertness, self-discipline, courage, mechanical aptitude, endurance, strength, and a sense of public service. Initiative and good judgment also are extremely important because fire fighters make quick decisions in emergencies. Members of a crew live and work closely together under conditions of stress and danger for extended periods, so they must be dependable and able to get along well with others. Leadership qualities are necessary for officers, who must establish and maintain discipline and efficiency, as well as direct the activities of the fire fighters in their companies.

Advancement. Most experienced fire fighters continue studying to improve their job performance and prepare for promotion examinations. To progress to higher level positions, they acquire expertise in advanced fire fighting equipment and techniques, building construction, emergency medical technology, writing, public speaking, management and budgeting procedures, and public relations.

Opportunities for promotion depend upon the results of written examinations, as well as job performance, interviews, and seniority. Hands-on tests that simulate real-world job situations are also used by some fire departments.

Usually, fire fighters are first promoted to engineer, then lieutenant, captain, battalion chief, assistant chief, deputy chief, and, finally, chief. For promotion to positions higher than battalion chief, many fire departments now require a bachelor's degree, preferably in fire science, public administration, or a related field. An associate degree is required for executive fire officer certification from the National Fire Academy.

Employment

In 2010, total paid employment in firefighting occupations was about 310,400. These employment figures include only paid career fire fighters—they do not cover volunteer fire fighters, who perform the same duties and may constitute the majority of fire fighters in a residential area.

About 91 percent of paid firefighters were employed by local governments in 2010. Some large cities have thousands of career fire fighters, while many small towns have only a few. Most of the remainder worked in fire departments on Federal and State installations, including airports, chemical plants, and other industrial sites. Private fire fighting companies employ a small number of fire fighters.

In response to the expanding role of fire fighters, some municipalities have combined fire prevention, public fire education, safety, and emergency medical services into a

(Continued)

(Continued)

single organization commonly referred to as a public safety organization. Some local and regional fire departments are being consolidated into countywide establishments to reduce administrative staffs, cut costs, and establish consistent training standards and work procedures.

Job Outlook

Although employment is expected to grow as fast as the average for all jobs, candidates for these positions are expected to face keen competition as these positions are highly attractive and sought after.

Employment change. Employment of workers in fire fighting occupations is expected to grow by 9 percent over the 2010–2020 decade, which is slower than the average for all occupations. Continued population growth will increase the number of emergency calls requiring firefighter responses. The majority of situations that firefighters respond to are medical—rather than fire—emergencies, and the aging of the population will lead to an increased demand for emergency responders. In addition, jobs will be created as volunteer firefighters are converted to paid positions in areas where population growth creates the need for a full-time workforce. An increase in urban populations, where full-time firefighters are more common, also is expected to increase the demand for firefighters.

Job prospects. Prospective fire fighters are expected to face keen competition for available job openings. Many people are attracted to fire fighting because it is challenging and provides the opportunity to perform an essential public service; a high school education is usually sufficient for entry; and a pension is usually guaranteed after 25 years work. Consequently, the number of qualified applicants in most areas far exceeds the number of job openings, even though the written examination and physical requirements eliminate many applicants. This situation is expected to persist in coming years. Applicants with the best chances are those who are physically fit and score the highest on physical conditioning and mechanical aptitude exams. Those who have completed some fire fighter education at a community college and have EMT or paramedic certification will have an additional advantage.

Earnings

The median annual wage of firefighters was $45,250 in May 2010. The median wage is the wage at which half the workers in an occupation earned more than that amount and half earned less. The lowest 10 percent earned less than $23,050, and the top 10 percent earned more than $75,390.The median annual earnings were $ 36,600 for other protective services, and median annual earnings for all occupations were $33,840 in 2010.

Median annual earnings of first-line supervisors/managers of fire fighting and prevention workers were $62,900 in May 2006. The middle 50 percent earned between $50,180 and $79,060. The lowest 10 percent earned less than $36,820, and the highest 10 percent earned more than $97,820. First-line supervisors/managers of fire fighting and prevention workers employed in local government earned a median of about $64,070 a year.

Median annual earnings of fire inspectors and investigators were $48,050 in May 2006. The middle 50 percent earned between $36,960 and $61,160 a year. The lowest 10 percent earned less than $29,840, and the highest 10 percent earned more than $74,930. Fire inspectors and investigators employed in local government earned a median of about $49,690 a year.

According to the International City-County Management Association, average salaries in 2006 for sworn full-time positions were as follows:

	Minimum annual base salary	Maximum annual base salary
Fire chief	$73,435	$95,271
Deputy chief	66,420	84,284
Assistant fire chief	61,887	78,914
Battalion chief	62,199	78,611
Fire captain	51,808	62,785
Fire lieutenant	47,469	56,511
Fire prevention/code inspector	45,951	58,349
Engineer	43,232	56,045

Fire fighters who average more than a certain number of work hours per week are required to be paid overtime. The hours threshold is determined by the department. Fire fighters often earn overtime for working extra shifts to maintain minimum staffing levels or during special emergencies.

Fire fighters receive benefits that usually include medical and liability insurance, vacation and sick leave, and some paid holidays. Almost all fire departments provide protective clothing (helmets, boots, and coats) and breathing apparatus, and many also provide dress uniforms. Fire fighters generally are covered by pension plans, often providing retirement at half pay after 25 years of service or if the individual is disabled in the line of duty.

SOURCE: From the *Occupational Outlook Handbook, 2008–09 Edition* and 2012–13 Edition, by the U.S. Department of Labor, Bureau of Labor Statistics. Available online at http://www.bls.gov/oco/ocos158.htm.

Styles of Leadership

People may be promoted or transferred to a position within an organization that places them in a formal leadership role. However, titles are not enough to function as a leader. These individuals must also have some appeal and connection that inspires other people to follow them. According to DuBrin (1995), the characteristics present in many leaders that instill in others the desire to follow these individuals include confidence, honesty, assertiveness, enthusiasm, self-awareness, extroversion, intelligence, initiative, achievement, and decisiveness.

Leadership styles are influenced by the philosophy of the leaders, which results in two distinct styles—namely, autocratic versus participative—and a number of combinations of both of these styles. *Autocratic leaders* have a lot of confidence in their decision-making ability and are very clear about the process in which they want things done; they have little confidence in the decision-making ability of their workers. Consequently, autocratic leaders keep decisions and controls to themselves and express what they want and how they want it directly to their subordinates, who simply follow orders. To instill confidence in the subordinates and to be successful, an autocratic leader must have broad and diversified knowledge and should be able to demonstrate it. In addition, the employees should feel uncomfortable in planning and decision making and instead want their leader to give strong directions. The situation sometimes may demand the leader to act in an autocratic style. For example, during an emergency or crisis, there is not enough time to gather a group of people and involve them in collective decision making. Instead, the police sergeant will quickly assess the situation at hand and pass directives on what role is expected from each team member to address the crisis. When the situation involves time pressures and physical danger, the subordinates typically view the leader's autocratic initiatives as acceptable.

Some leaders are benevolent autocrats. These leaders maintain absolute decision-making power, but they are also concerned about the well-being of their subordinates. Therefore, they will reward the employees who follow their directives. One major drawback of autocratic leadership is that the leader misses the thinking capabilities of the subordinates to provide constructive and innovative solutions. Often, the workers may shut their minds at the workplace and become indifferent and less committed to contributing to the betterment of the workplace. The workers may lose morale, become very unsure of their capabilities, and be fearful in using their initiative in their work. It becomes very difficult to replace the autocratic leaders when they leave because the subordinates have not been mentally trained for the independent thinking required to take on the position of a leader. One may be able to apply autocratic leadership to modern policing, as a result of the organizational structure of traditional police organizations. The leaders in policing organizations make all of the decisions, sending them from the top of the hierarchy to the bottom. Those at the bottom have to do very little thinking about job expectations, duties, and methods of policing. Those decisions have already been made and, in most cases, have been recorded in policy manuals. Initiatives such as community policing are changing this approach, but the autocratic leadership style is still present in many policing organizations across the United States.

Another approach to leadership is termed *participative*, sometimes also called *behavioral* or *democratic*. *Participative leaders* tend to understand the mission and core values of the organization, educate their subordinates on the needs and objectives, and involve people by drawing on their knowledge in day-to-day functioning and problem solving. Of course, when workers sense their voice being heard, they feel more committed to change and decision making. Typically, the self-esteem of workers increases when they feel that they have been trusted to make competent decisions. In addition, the collective thinking of the leader and the group members is likely to produce more innovative solutions than if only the leader were involved in active thinking. Probation officers will commonly "staff" cases with other officers in formal meetings to help make decisions on the best approach for a particular client. In this situation, the officers are not suggesting that they cannot develop a case plan on their own, but rather, that they see the opportunity for additional input from other officers as beneficial. Using the "more heads are better than one" philosophy, the officers may receive suggestions for treatment, rehabilitation, and reintegration that they would not have thought of without additional input. For success under participative leadership, the employees should be receptive to the participative approach. The workers should have the necessary knowledge and skill to participate in decision-making processes. They should feel a sense of ownership and a desire to grow, and they should be willing to contribute to planning and decision making. Sometimes, involving workers in decision making may be perceived by the employees as a sign of weakness, a lack of qualification, and an inability of their leader to lead them. Furthermore, if the general environment in an organization is one of low trust and confidence, the workers may provide input and say things that they feel the leader wants to hear rather than saying or doing what is right and best for the organization.

The Ohio State and University of Michigan studies investigated the behavior of leaders along two dimensions, the first being the concern of the leader for the people and the second being the concern of the leader for the task outcomes. Blake and Mouton (1978) created a grid that measures the concern for people on one axis and the concern for outcomes along the other. Blake and Mouton also took into account whether the motivation of the leader was positive or negative. The *Blake-Mouton Managerial Grid* was introduced as a tool to gain knowledge about one's managerial style. In an extensive survey done by the National Industrial Conference Board, the grid was mentioned as one of the most frequently identified behavioral science approaches to management.

The grid (Figure 7.1) provides a visual framework for understanding various approaches to leadership. The two axes describe *concern for production* and *concern for people*, measured on a scale from 1 (low) to 9 (high). The grid presents a conceptual frame of reference for guiding the organizational development process through various

Figure 7.1   Black and Mouton's Managerial Grid

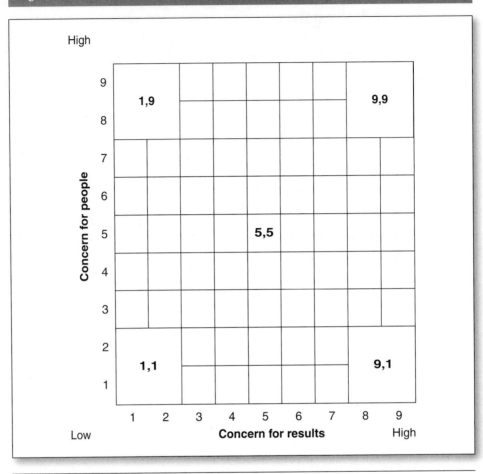

SOURCE: From *The New Managerial Grid,* by R. Blake and J. Mouton, 1978, Houston, TX: Gulf Publishing.

states—team building, interface conflict solving, ideal strategic corporate modeling, tactical implementation of the model, and stabilization. This widely known grid concept focuses on five fundamental leadership styles.

1. **9, 9: Contribute and Commit (Team Management):** This is the most sound leadership style. Work accomplishment is from committed people, and interdependence is achieved through a common stake in the organization. This common purpose leads to relationships of trust and respect.

2. **9, 1: Control and Dominate:** This is a dictatorial style of leadership where the focus is entirely on results. Operational efficiency results from arranging working conditions so that human elements interface only minimally.

3. **1, 9: Yield and Comply:** This is an accommodating style of leadership where the concern for people is placed above the concern for results. With this leadership style, thoughtful attention to people's needs for satisfying relationships leads to a comfortable, friendly organization atmosphere and work tempo.

4. **5, 5: Balance and Compromise:** This style of leadership aims for maintaining the status quo, focusing neither on people nor on results. Adequate organization performance is possible by balancing the necessity to get out work with maintaining a satisfactory level of morale.

5. **1, 1: Evade and Elude:** This fifth fundamental style of leadership is indifferent to both people and results. The leader exerts only the minimal effort to get required work done that is necessary to sustain organizational membership (Blake & Mouton, 1978).

From the previous discussion, it may be concluded that there is no one best style of leadership. Ultimately, the right leadership style is dependent on a combination of the situation, the type of followers, and the strengths of the leader. To be an effective leader, one should customize the leadership approach to these three variables, and one should be flexible to change the leadership style when required. This approach to leadership was discussed earlier under contingency leadership theory.

Leadership as a Skill

Leadership is a skill that can be developed through training. Quinn and Rohrbaugh (1983) provide the Competing Values Framework that examines leadership and managerial skills (see Figure 7.2). A database of more than 40,000 managers has also been compiled (Cameron & Quinn, 2000) to understand and improve management and leadership skills. This research has shown that leadership and management skills fall into four categories (Whetten & Cameron, 2002):

1. **Clan skills**—These include the skills required to develop effective interpersonal skills, such as building teamwork or communicating supportively;

2. **Adhocracy skills**—These skills are required to manage the future and promote changes, like solving problems creatively or articulating an energizing vision;

3. **Market skills**—These skills are required to manage external relationships to compete effectively such as motivating others or using power and influence;

4. **Hierarchy skills**—These skills are required to sustain control and stability while managing personal stress and time or solving problems rationally (p. 16).

The two top quadrants, representing clan and adhocracy skills, are usually associated with leadership by describing what individuals do under conditions of change. In other words, people at the top are expected to display leadership when organizations are dynamic and undergoing transformation. They are said to "focus on setting the direction, articulating a vision, transforming individuals and organizations, and

Figure 7.2 Leadership and Management Skills Organized by the Competing Values Framework

	Flexibility change		
Internal maintenance	**CLAN SKILLS** • Communicating supportively • Building teams and teamwork • Empowering	**ADHOCRACY SKILLS** • Solving problems creatively • Articulating a vision • Fostering innovation	**External positioning**
	HIERARCHY SKILLS • Managing personal stress • Managing time • Maintaining self-awareness • Analytical problem solving	**MARKET SKILLS** • Motivating others • Gaining power and influences • Managing conflict	
	Stability control		

SOURCE: From *Developing Management Skills,* 5th Edition, © 2002, pg. 16, by D. A. Whetten and K. S. Cameron, 2002, Upper Saddle River, NJ: Prentice Hall. Reprinted by permission of Pearson Education Inc., Upper Saddle River, New Jersey.

creating something new" (Whetten & Cameron, 2002, p. 15). The two bottom quadrants, hierarchy and market skills, are typically associated with management by describing what individuals do under conditions of stability. They have been said to "focus on monitoring, directing, and refining current performance" (Whetten and Cameron, 2002, p. 15). Furthermore, Whetten and Cameron note,

> Managers cannot be successful without being good leaders, and leaders cannot be successful without being good managers. No longer do organizations have the luxury of holding on to the status quo, worrying about doing things right but failing to do the right things; keeping the system stable instead of leading change and improvement; monitoring current performance instead of formulating a vision of the future; concentrating on equilibrium and control instead of vibrancy and charisma. (p. 16)

Therefore, the researchers conclude that competencies of both a manager and a leader need to be developed in this dynamic environment to lead successfully.

Daft and Marcic (2004) suggest two different sets of qualities and skills for leaders and managers, which may overlap within a single individual. They suggest a leader should be able to demonstrate qualities such as vision, passion, creativity, flexibility, inspiration, innovativeness, courage, and imaginativeness, as well as be experimental, able to initiate change, and personally powerful. Alternatively, managers must be rational, consultative, persistent, problem solvers, tough-minded, analytical, structured, deliberate, authoritative, and be stabilizers and have position power.

In general, people with aspirations to become successful managers and leaders should attempt to develop several types of skills. *Technical skills* pertain to the knowledge and ability that are necessary to perform the job. *Human resource management skills* are behavioral skills required to work effectively with other people. Some of the skills considered here are communication, listening, and motivational skills. *Conceptual skills* pertain to the ability to see relationships that may seem to be hidden and to be able to sense clearly the abstract and seemingly disparate entities. Within criminal justice, employees, leaders, and managers have to possess a clear understanding of their jobs to meet the numerous requirements placed on them while working with offenders, complainants, victims, and the public. In addition, they must be able to work well with other people to provide quality services to those with whom they come in contact. Finally, inherent or learned skills that allow them to see the hidden or ambiguous relationships among pieces of evidence, cases, causes of crime, and so forth are everyday necessities in the criminal justice profession. A lack in any of these areas adds strain to an already demanding position.

Supporting the leadership skills, French and Stewart (2001) identify five leadership practices that managers in a law enforcement environment should follow:

1. *They should challenge the process.* Search out challenging opportunities to change, grow, innovate, and improve; experiment; take risks; and learn from mistakes.

2. *They should inspire a shared vision.* Envision an uplifting and enabling future; enlist others in a common vision by appealing to their values, interests, hopes, and dreams.

3. *They should enable others to act.* Foster collaboration by promoting cooperative goals and building trust; strengthen people by giving power away and providing choice; develop competence, assign critical tasks, and offer visible support.

4. *They should model the way.* Set an example by behaving in ways consistent with shared values; achieve small "wins" that promote consistent progress and build commitment.

5. *They should encourage the heart.* Recognize the contributions to the success of every project; celebrate team accomplishments regularly.

Managerial and leadership skills can be developed by proper education, training, and practice. Formal education can amplify one's learning from personal experiences and help one rely less on trial-and-error practices. On-the-job training and learning from the experiences of other, more successful colleagues can help tremendously in improving leadership and management skills. More recently, leadership development workshops and programs are being offered. These programs incorporate the various aspects proposed in different leadership models examined earlier, thus developing a more optimal and balanced use of the full range of leadership styles. In addition, a *multifactor leadership questionnaire* (MLQ) can be distributed to the subordinates and coworkers of the target leaders. The responses help identify the strengths and weaknesses of the target leader, thus providing a base profile (Avolio & Bass, 1991; 1995).

This profile can be complemented by collecting more information gathered through systematic observation of the leader's behavior and by administering a personality-based questionnaire to the target leader. Based on the profile generated using these integrated approaches, the target leader can identify areas for improvement. Developmental coursework and learning objectives can be ascertained for improvement, which can then be acquired by attending leadership development workshops and programs.

In the News 7.1
Leadership in a Correctional Environment

The need for sound leadership in the management of prisons is evident after a cursory examination of recent court interventions, media and legislative scrutiny, and escalating budgets. Leadership is essential to good public service, because legislators often provide missions that are vague, if not conflicting, and may fail to provide the necessary resources to carry out the missions. Indeed, according to Dilulio "the quality of prison life depends far more on management practices than on any other single variable....If most prisons have failed, it is because they have been ill-managed, under-managed or not managed at all."

Competencies of Effective Leaders

Seiter encourages transformational leadership to meet the challenges and changing missions of modern corrections. Transformational leadership brings about changes in people and organizations by the leaders having holistic awareness of themselves so that thoughts, feelings and actions are consistent. He believes leaders and followers must meet new challenges together, requiring an empowered and inspired staff that can exercise creativity for problem solving and help the organization learn. This article presents 10 competencies of effective correctional management that the author developed during his 30 years of public and private correctional service. Using the acronym CORRECTION, he explains that correctional leaders must strive to practice the following ideals:

- Concentrate on the big picture;
- Observe their areas of responsibility frequently;
- Resolve problems quickly;
- Respond to every inquiry;
- Enhance their abilities;
- Communicate with people internal and external to the organization;
- Think outside the box, but not too far;
- Integrity is everything;
- Offer their skills to resolve problems; and
- Nurture their staff.

Concentrate on the big picture. This means establishing a clear vision for the organization and focusing on what is important. This function is central to the leadership role and is a primary determinant of the effectiveness of a leader. Denhardt describes this ability as "creating a vision of the future that already exists in the minds of others." Leaders develop a vision for the organization and provide the strategies for producing the changes needed to accomplish the vision. Kotter explains that establishing a vision does not have to be brilliantly creative and certainly is not mysterious. It is an exhaustive process of gathering and analyzing data. More succinctly, it requires the ability not only to meet the next situation but to make the next situation.

Creating a vision and communicating that vision to all staff is only part of this competency. Correctional leaders must also be highly observant and cognizant of the interests and desires of stakeholders external to the correctional environment, in other words, "seeing the big picture." Today's correctional leader must be acutely aware of both the internal and external environmental factors affecting the correctional system. These external factors may be citizen groups, the courts, legal-aid agencies, media sources, unions, public-health organizations, legislative actors, private correctional companies, and other interested groups or individuals. This competency relates to what Rowe describes as foresight, or "the ability to foresee the likely outcome of a situation." This ability may be partly intuitive but can be enhanced with knowledge and experience. Senge adds that creating a shared vision is an ongoing process; that is, there may be a predominant image of the future, but that image will eventually evolve into a new vision.

Effective leaders will observe their areas of responsibility frequently. One of the truisms in corrections or other public services is that in times of crises, the leaders will be held accountable. Too often, correctional leaders convince themselves that they are too busy and tied to the office and, therefore, are forced to delegate the inspection or observation of internal operations to management staff. Time and again, this attitude has proved disastrous. Even with the most experienced management staff performing the observation role, staff and management still want to see leaders acting as a check and balance to verify their good labor. Simply stated, the staff want leaders in the facility to praise good work, criticize poor performance, reassure that operations are being performed correctly and to simply see their presence. Boin and Hart provide some wisdom for commissioners, directors, wardens and sheriffs in their statement on expectations for such leaders: "It is assumed they are well-prepared for any crisis that may occur and will take effective measures to protect the public, limit harm and compensate damages. Any event or behavior that deviates from these standards increases public unease and is likely to elicit strong criticism."

Correctional leaders will resolve problems quickly. This competency involves concerted listening to learn of impending problems, frequent observation of areas of responsibility, developing strategies to resolve problems, being tenacious about the resolution of problems, implementing a plan for resolution developed by as many staff as reasonable, and evaluating and altering the plan if necessary. It is with this competency that effective leaders must display their talents for leadership. Cooper noted that leaders of public enterprises "should exercise their best technical judgment when tackling complex problems. Their technical knowledge and skills are tools for which they are being paid; they are the specific justification for the fiduciary role on behalf of the people." Staff are often aware of most problems. And problems that do not receive attention indicate to them that the leaders do not care. Leaders who believe a problem will resolve itself with the passage of time are often wrong and find the problem to have escalated into a serious situation. This is particularly true with personnel problems.

(Continued)

(Continued)

Respond to every inquiry. Leaders of correctional organizations receive many inquiries during the course of a day. Effective leaders will see that every inquiry, both from internal and external sources, receives a response. By their nature, correctional systems are complex and generally closed to the public. When perplexed or disgruntled citizens do not get a satisfactory response to a question, they want to speak to the person in charge. Some of the inquirers are angry, some are confused, some are frustrated, and others may be desperate, but all need an answer to their issues. To avoid a timely reply or to deny a reply by simply not responding is not in the best interests of the leader or the organization.

Enhance their abilities. Effective leaders are continuously learning about themselves, their organization, their discipline or industry, their followers, and new ways to benefit and build value to each of these. Taking courses, reading books, attending workshops and conferences, building coalitions with colleagues to exchange ideas, and subscribing to journals related to corrections are all ways to increase one's knowledge about this complex field. The correctional environment is continuously changing, and leaders must adapt to these changes. "Hour to hour, day to day, week to week, executives must play their leadership styles like a pro—using the right one at just the right time and in the right measure. The payoff is in the results," according to Goleman. Leaders recognize the value of knowledge, skills and experience to all employees of an organization but often overlook themselves as needing further development. With the advancement of technology in modern corrections, leaders need an understanding of the benefits and pitfalls of the many new technological applications related to their industry. Leaders are intimately aware of their strengths and weaknesses and work diligently on exploiting each to the best advantage of the organization. This may require that leaders surround themselves with people of superb abilities as compensation or enhancement. Genuine leaders never develop an attitude that they already know enough to get the job done. Kellerman believes that leaders must be reflective in that they should emphasize the importance of self-knowledge, self-control and good habits.

Communicate with people internal and external to the organization. Great correctional leaders use every opportunity to convey their vision and values to staff, visitors, volunteers and entities external to the organization in every manner possible. In today's work environment, persuasion can work as effectively (and in most cases, more effectively) as preaching from positional authority. One mark of an effective leader is the ability to convey sincerity and dedication to the organization's mission in a manner that causes followers and citizens willingly to choose to attach themselves to the purposes of the mission. How leaders communicate to staff and citizens with their actions has greater impact than communicating either verbally or in writing. According to Rowe, "Effective leadership is demonstrated minute by minute in the things we do and say, every day. People see, note and feel every action, and word that we utter. Any incongruity in what they see, hear and feel dissipates trust." Trust is "the cornerstone of the servant leader model of leadership, in that collegiate relationships are based on mutual respect and feedback, and direct in-the-field access to leaders." Servant leadership focuses on the philosophy of supporting people who desire to serve first, and then lead, as a method of providing service to individuals and organizations.

Listening is an important element in communications as well. Denhardt believes that leaders practice empathetic listening, described as "listening for and comprehending the subtle nuances of sound and movement that reflect a person's inner state," and evocative speaking, which is "skillfully using image-based words and metaphors that evoke a sensory or emotional response in those who hear you." For example, an endeavor may be described evocatively as a journey.

Think outside the box, but not too far. It goes without saying that today's correctional leaders must use all the creativity and innovativeness they can muster to meet the challenges of a constantly changing system. There are countless ways in which leaders can express creative solutions to problems without usurping rigid policies and procedures. All creative ideas are not likely to emanate solely from the leader. The leader must establish an environment by which all staff and citizens can freely submit ideas and proposals for problems or simply to increase effectiveness or efficiency. The corrections field is not a profession that particularly rewards creativity too far removed from traditional practice. Before launching a radical departure from standard practice, a leader would be wise to engage in some serious thought about the possible outcomes of such an action.

Integrity is everything in correctional leadership. While the citizenry has devout expectations of public leaders in general, those expectations for public officials working in the criminal justice system are even higher. Some would argue that choosing an ethical path in life is often difficult, because the right choice to take is not clear, given the many choices human beings encounter. Stohr et al. argue that in the workplace, especially in corrections, the right choice is understood and doable but may not be the easiest course to take. Cooper asserts that leaders' "ethical identity emerges incrementally from the pattern of decisions that they make over the course of a career." Practitioner associations such as the American Correctional Association and the American Jail Association have well-established codes of ethics, as do most correctional departments and sheriff's offices. However, these ethics codes cannot and are not intended to cover every possible situation to be encountered by a correctional employee. Consequently, it is the correctional leader's responsibility to establish an atmosphere in which employees desire to…make a concerted effort to do the right thing. This is accomplished by providing a shining example of how professional correctional employees should behave and conduct the organization's business. Setting a good example on and off duty, establishing and communicating positive values, and recognizing that all stakeholders are scrutinizing every behavior exhibited by the leader are ways to convey the unwavering ethical behavior expected of all employees. This includes disciplining, in an equal fashion, all those who fall outside the acceptable norms, and praising those who exhibit extraordinary ethical behavior. Training for preservice and in-service should cover this topic thoroughly and be reinforced at every occasion by management and the leader.

Offer their skills to resolve problems. The leader is expected to have knowledge and skills beyond most employees and should offer them to staff on occasions when it is appropriate. Good leaders will make an effort to expand the knowledge base and experiential level of promising employees by providing new work tasks. Appropriate delegation of new tasks to select employees can serve to develop future managers and leaders. Leaders should stifle their desire to perform tasks, which subordinates could perform to enhance their career potential. However, in times of crisis or other extraordinary occasions, leaders should offer their skills and knowledge to resolve issues. This

(Continued)

(Continued)

reaffirms the staff's confidence in the abilities of the leader and sends a message that no job is beyond the performance of the leader and instills the team concept.

Nurture their staff. This is one of the primary roles of leaders. True leaders are completely committed to the growth of others and believe that they have value that exceeds their tangible contribution as employees. Leaders cherish their employees and will go to great lengths to retain them. McCormack offered a good rule of thumb for leaders, "There's no mystery to holding on to good employees. Give them a lot of responsibility, don't insult them with their paycheck, and tell them once in awhile how they're doing."

Summary

This article has provided some information on the topic of correctional leadership. Regrettably, there is a scarcity of literature on this specific topic of great importance and impact on the public. While this article presents no empirical data on correctional leadership, it provides areas in which empirical analysis could be conducted to build knowledge on the leadership needs of correctional systems. There is no question that the complexities of leading in the corrections field are increasing. As the expense of incarceration increases and the public becomes aware of the impact of that expense, correctional leaders will, by force, become even more accountable to the public and their elected representatives. Tomorrow's leaders will have to be more creative in matters of correctional effectiveness and efficiency in providing for the safety of the public. California's Proposition 36, which curtails incarceration for nonviolent drug offenses, is just the beginning of this effort by a critical public. Academics and practitioners will have to examine the best methods of developing and recognizing effective leaders and determining what leadership styles or theories will be beneficial for different classifications of prisons.

SOURCE: From "Leadership in a Correctional Environment," by M. Montgomery (pp. 38–42), *Corrections Today*, August 2006. Reprinted with permission of the American Correctional Association, Alexandria, VA.

EDITOR'S NOTE: This article is a shortened version of an article that was published in the May/June issue of *Corrections Compendium*.

Leadership and the Criminal Justice System

Few would disagree that effective leadership is central to the process of organizational change. Connection between poor leadership and corruption, mistreatment, discrimination, and abuse of power often threatens to delegitimize the different agencies of the criminal justice system. Therefore, one of the most critical questions confronting the various agencies in criminal justice is how to integrate leadership and the delivery of an ethical, effective, and value-based service that protects society and its key principles. Extensive work has been done in this regard in British policing, which includes changes that can be mimicked in the United States for improving service quality. Given the concern over police corruption and racism following the Macpherson inquiry in

1999 (which was an investigation focused on the racially driven murder of Steven Lawrence in 1993 and the institutionalized racism prevalent in the police department), the Home Office in England initiated an examination of existing recruitment, training, and promotion practices, with special emphasis on the selection of senior officers. Subsequently, in 2001 National Police Leadership Faculty and the Police Leadership Development Board (PLDB) were created to emphasize the importance of the quality of police leadership.

A primary characteristic that distinguishes police and correctional organizations from most other public institutions is the paramilitary structure. This structure encourages the adoption of an authoritarian approach to leadership (Bruns & Shuman, 1988), premised on the old models of bureaucratic design with power centered at the top. A common belief is that because of training and experiences, the officers in law enforcement and corrections would be more supportive of an autocratic and transactional style of leadership instead of a participative leadership style. However, increasingly a consensus is building among organizational theorists (Bruns & Shuman, 1988) that suggests that the autocratic and transactional style of leadership is outdated and inconsistent with long-term development and changes desired by progressive organizations. In its place, the transformational leadership style, which encourages participation and open communication, is on the rise. Research shows that the participative style of management in which managers and subordinates work together as equals is more productive (Bruns & Shuman, 1988).

Like other organizations, criminal justice agencies must balance constancy and predictability with adaptation and change. As they strive to standardize operations to improve service quality, most leaders in criminal justice agencies must recognize the fluid context in which their agencies operate. The changing environment for the criminal justice system includes the rise of terrorism, new patterns of immigration, and increased accountability because of Internet-promoted social media—factors to which the leaders must adapt and evolve to remain effective. Furthermore, the biggest change is coming from the contemporary employees, called Generation Y, employees who are described as savvy in technology use, conscientious, unselfish, and independent in their thinking, while also more tolerant of differences than those of other generations (Beck & Wade, 2004). These employees are described as altruistic, wanting to make the world a better place, and interested in making a positive impact in their world. Batts, Smoot, & Scrivner (2012) examined studies from the Pew Research Center (2007) and concluded that "groups born in the 1980s and early 1990s are more accepting than their elders of issues such as affirmative action, immigration and the appropriate scope of government, as well as far more supportive of an ethnically diverse workforce and responsive to concerns of diverse communities. These characteristics are extremely desirable for police officers but the challenge is whether current police organizations can capitalize on these attributes" (p. 4). Despite desirable attributes, both research and practice describe contemporary employees as often lacking certain essential work attributes that require the leader to play the role of a mentor and coach to help these young officers meet their personal goals and objectives (Batts et al., 2012). Besides differences in personal characteristics, the contemporary officer also brings lifestyle changes to the workplace that may conflict with traditional law enforcement practices and leadership. "These changes include: placing a greater value on balancing work and family, experiencing comfort with questioning authority and challenging the traditional chain of command, demanding ongoing performance feedback, expecting transparency and timely outcome measures that show what is working, and relying on instant feedback from electronic communication and social networking" (Batts et al., 2012, p. 4). Symbols of modern life such as social media, instant messaging and blogs, along with Twitter, YouTube, MySpace, and Facebook—all supported by the handheld, portable, web-connected devices that the contemporary employees are comfortable, in using. These most recent changes in technology have been an integral part of the lives of contemporary officers entering the criminal justice system. All these factors set the contemporary employees apart from those who grew up or accepted the paramilitary organizational model characterized by a hierarchical authority structure.

The current officers who are in leadership positions were influenced by norms established by traditionalist and Baby Boomer cultures (Batts et al., 2012). They apply traditional work standards and have divergent viewpoints about autonomy and supervision. Effective leaders will need to provide autonomy and opportunities to be creative. The mentality of "do as I say," which once worked in the paramilitary model, will no longer resonate with the current officers who seek in their leader a mentor and a coach. Thus, future leaders will need to develop persuasion methods with strong oral and written communication skills that allow developing logical dialogue. Current-generation officers are coming into the criminal justice system with more degrees than their supervisors and have a strong interest in problem solving. They expect their leaders to give them dignity, authority, and discretion to solve problems. Future executives will need to move away from micromanaging and become "big picture" executives. It is clear that current-generational issues not only involve absorbing new employees with different values, but motivating and leading them. In a survey conducted by the Center for Creative Leadership (CCL) of those in leadership positions, 74% believed that the currently entering workforce will place unique demands on their organizations. The survey findings strongly suggest that the businesses will have to go beyond current organizational norms and will have to develop innovational cultures and changes to business practices that are compatible with changing communication patterns and skills developed in the technology sector (Criswell & Martin, 2007). For example, IBM, Accenture, Ernst & Young, and Google all have developed feedback systems where employees can request feedback at any time. They have developed training programs focused on interactive dialogue as part of critiquing skills. Google has provided online "office hours" where any employee can put new ideas (Batts et al., 2012). Criminal justice agencies can benefit by adopting some of these progressive ideas, particularly those relating to supervisor training and communication skills. Some police departments now conduct virtual roll calls where officers obtain preshift briefing information via e-mail or mobile data transfer. The Los Angeles Police Protective League (LAPPL), the Union for Los Angeles Police Department's rank-and-file officers pioneered a web-based communication system that enabled the union to hold virtual meetings (Batts et al., 2012). A number of supervisors have assigned their contemporary officers to help manage social media for the department, a phenomenon that becomes critical at times of large demonstrations and major events. Therefore, participatory forms of management and leadership have been proposed for bringing any real change in police organizations. In England, the PLDB has already acknowledged the need for transformational leadership throughout the service (Silvestri, 2007) and has instituted training and selection methods that promote the principles of transformational leadership. Such behavior is important to police leaders to influence directly the rank-and-file officers and the overall process of change (Tang & Hammontree, 1992).

Likert (1981) cited studies conducted by the United States Army, Navy, and Air Force, which have a highly regimented hierarchical structure similar to some criminal justice agencies. These studies found that as the administrators and supervisors moved their managerial behavior closer to a participative style, there was a corresponding improvement in satisfaction among officers, accompanied by an increase in organizational productivity. In another study, the results indicated that "law enforcement supervisors and middle managers in the state of Arizona strongly support a leadership style that is highly participative" (Bruns & Shuman, 1988, p. 156). Similarly, Steinheider, Wuestewald, and Bayerl (2006) found that involvement in decision making fostered "employee perceptions of organizational support, organizational commitment, and better labor management relations. It also suggests that inclusion promotes communication at all levels and helps bridge the typical schism between police management and line officers" (p. L5). According to Stevens (2000), senior police officers "can no longer take comfort in the traditional response of a punishment centered organizational bureaucracy accentuated through a reactive policy" (p. 198). Therefore, a critical issue for law enforcement organizations in planning and implementing organizational change is how to lead senior police officers through involvement and participation.

Supporting the tenets of the participative leadership style, other empirical studies (Deluga, 1988, 1989; Deluga & Souza, 1991) found that within the law enforcement environment, the transformational leadership style appeared to work the best in encouraging more activities that are rational. Dobby, Anscombe, and Tuffin (2004) found that police leaders who displayed transformational behavior had a range of positive effects on their subordinates' attitudes toward their work, promoting both their job satisfaction and their commitment to the organization. According to Bass (1985), leaders use transformational leadership behaviors to try to advance the awareness of subordinates by appealing to higher morals and values such as liberty, justice, equality, and humanitarianism.

Support for transformational leadership was found by Murphy and Drodge (2004) in a case study based on interviews with 28 police officers and participant observations at case study sites. They concluded, "transformational leaders have particular relational strengths that serve to elevate levels of commitment, work satisfaction, and motivation" (p. 1). The researchers further elaborated on the four dimensions of transformational leadership in a law enforcement environment: (1) *Individualized consideration* is used by transformational leaders to motivate followers to work toward both personal and organizational goals. The case study revealed, "an essential component of individualized consideration is ensuring that the right people are placed in jobs with opportunities to ignite their passion. This individual attention to placing the right person in the right job, was evident in both formal and informal leaders" (p. 8). Respondents placed a strong emphasis on the importance of such supportive and caring leaders who inspired and encouraged them to develop and then recognized and rewarded their achievements. (2) *Idealized influence* concerns the fostering of trust and respect in the relationship between leader and follower. The respondents placed a strong emphasis on the role of ethics and core values in their leader's life for him or her to be valued and respected. Based on the data analysis, Murphy and Drodge concluded that "a police organization's explicit values must reflect the core values of the broader society which the organization serves, and that police leaders must demonstrate the utmost respect for those values both personally and professionally to be truly transformational" (p. 10). They also found that the subordinates valued knowledge and experience in their formal and informal leaders. (3) *Inspirational motivation* relates to the leadership quality of uniting people around a common tangible benefit that is more than what the subordinates expected to accomplish. Murphy and Drodge found the "key ingredient of inspirational motivation at the case site involved communicating the vision to all officers and reiterating it often" (p. 11). Such a unifying vision is presented to the police officers by giving them an understanding of how they fit into the grand scheme of the organization. There is a paradigm shift in the vision when one considers the community-based policing model, which requires a proactive community involvement in contrast to reactive police enforcement. Community-based policing calls for building relationships with key community stakeholders, in comparison to reinforcing cultural norms of detached emotional distance from the community propagated in the professional model of policing. In community-based policing, police leaders work to inspire and encourage individual officers "towards goals that have value in society beyond the rather narrow constraints provided by typical police work" (p. 12). Finally, (4) *intellectual motivation* involves engaging the minds of the subordinates, exposing them to thought-provoking issues that force them to think outside of the box to identify creative solutions. For example, in community policing, the leader's intellectual stimulation initiatives are reflected in training, coaching, and mentoring the subordinates to question assumptions and find new approaches to performing some fundamental duties. The discussion suggests that transformational leadership theory is a useful model for raising the level of service quality in policing beyond its current prosaic usage (Murphy & Drodge, 2004). Other criminal justice organizations can apply transformational leadership theory as well, though they are beyond the focus of this discussion.

In conclusion, over the last decade there has been a renewed interest in the role of leadership in driving organizational changes in the criminal justice system. More specifically, participatory forms of management and leadership have been recognized as vital to effecting any real change in criminal justice organizations. Reflective and creative thinking promoted among rank-and-file officers through participative leadership is now deeply rooted within current debates (Silvestri, 2007). Optimism in change can be seen in the findings of Dobby et al. (2004), who surveyed more than 1,000 senior police officers and found that most felt that effective leadership corresponds closely to transformational leadership. It is increasingly felt that such a participative approach promotes better relationships among officers within an organization. In addition, it improves external relationships with the customers served. Emphasizing this point, Marks and Fleming (2004) argue, "External democratization on the part of the police can only be expected to come to light if internal organizational democratization is manifest" (p. 800).

Chapter Summary

- There is no consistent definition of leadership; however, there is a general agreement on two characteristics—leadership involves influencing other members of the group, and leadership involves directing the group's effort toward achieving its goals.
- Informal leaders have no formal authority but only their persona to influence others. Alternatively, individuals can be placed in a position within an organization that bestows on them a formal leadership role. The formal leaders can easily be discovered by looking at the organizational chart. Effective leaders integrate both the formal and informal aspects of leadership in influencing their subordinates to accomplish organizational goals.
- Leadership has been variously characterized as personality, the art of inducing compliance, the exercise of influence, a power relationship, an instrument of goal achievement, behavior change, the need to overcome resistance to change, and integrating, just to cite a few examples.
- There have been five dominant paradigms of leadership advanced in the 20th century, within which many theories of leadership have been proposed. To a large extent, each approach has been an extension of and response to the criticisms of the previously dominant paradigm. The first approach (traits approach) involved studying traits or characteristics, assuming that there are certain traits that an individual must possess to become a leader. The second approach (behavioral approach) focused on an examination of observable behaviors of leaders.
- The proponents of the third approach (situational leadership) assert that there is no one best leadership style but that different situations require different leadership styles. The most popular contingency models are Fiedler's contingency model, Hersey and Blanchard's model, the path-goal model, and Vroom and Yetton's model.
- The fourth approach is the transactional leadership theory, which focuses on the process of interaction between a leader and the followers rather than the character of the people (trait theory), behavior, or the situation (contingency theory). The two main interaction processes that comprise transactional leadership are contingent reward leadership and management by exception. The fifth approach is composed of the macrofocused studies of leadership, which have moved away from individual and small-group aspects of leadership and instead have focused on how leaders impact the working culture within an entire organization, leading them beyond the normal levels of performance. The theories advanced in this current wave have been called charismatic leadership theory, transformational leadership theory, and visionary leadership theory. More recently, these theories have been grouped together under the label outstanding leadership theory.
- Leadership styles are influenced by the philosophy of the leaders, resulting in two distinct styles: autocratic and participative. Autocratic leaders keep decisions and controls to themselves and express what they want and how they want it directly to their subordinates, who simply follow orders. Participative leaders tend to understand the mission and core values of the organization, communicate the needs and

objectives to their subordinates, and then involve the employees to draw on their knowledge in day-to-day functioning and problem solving.

- Blake and Mouton created a grid that measures the concern for people on one axis and the concern for productivity on the other axis. The Managerial Grid provides a visual framework for understanding five fundamental leadership styles.

- It may be concluded that there is no one best style of leadership. Ultimately, the right leadership style is dependent on a combination of the situation, the type of followers, and the strengths of the leader. To be an effective leader, one should customize the leadership approach to these three variables, and one should be flexible to change the leadership style as required. Managerial and leadership skills can be developed by proper education, training, and practice.

- Effective leadership is important for all branches of the criminal justice system. Connection between poor leadership and corruption, mistreatment, discrimination, and abuse of power threatens to delegitimize the different agencies of the criminal justice system.

- Leadership in the criminal justice system is not essentially different from all other forms of leadership found in other organizations, prompting employees to garner learning from wherever it exists and imbue it into the criminal justice system. Transformational leadership theory is a useful model for raising the level of service quality in policing beyond the current prosaic usage.

Chapter Review Questions

1. What are the differences between formal and informal leaders? Think of a boss for whom you have worked. Was this boss also a leader?

2. What are the traits and behavior approaches to leadership? How are these approaches different?

3. Explain the contingency theory of leadership. Is it an advancement over the traits and behavioral approaches to leadership?

4. What are the similarities and dissimilarities among Fiedler's model, the Hersey and Blanchard model, the path-goal model, and the Vroom-Yetton model?

5. What is a transactional theory of leadership? In what different ways did a boss for whom you have worked follow a transactional leadership model?

6. Think of your previous bosses who may have exhibited the broad concept of charismatic leadership. Describe all of the different behaviors of these people that are consistent with those of a charismatic leader.

7. What are the different competencies that you need to develop most to become a transformational leader?

8. Think of all of your previous bosses and categorize their leadership styles as either autocratic or participative. How was their interaction different with their subordinates?

9. What are the different skills required to become an effective leader?

10. What is the role of leadership in improving service quality in the criminal justice system?

11. What are the different characteristics that a leader should demonstrate to be effective in the criminal justice system?

CASE STUDY

Brown County School District consists of 49 schools from prekindergarten to high school. With a student population of more than 15,000, the district is one of the largest in the state. This year, the school suspended 5,697 students and expelled 394. That is enough students to empty five of the schools completely. A new zero-tolerance policy is being blamed for the high numbers of suspensions and expulsions.

History

Schools in Brown County have experienced an increase in on-campus violence and rule infractions in the past two years. Violations include vandalism to the bathrooms, lockers, hallways, and classrooms; fights; bullying; gang activity; and sexual activity as well as minor infractions such as bringing cell phones to school, tardiness, absenteeism, and disrespect to teachers and administrators. Four months into the 2008–2009 school year, videos of students bullying others, fighting, and engaging in sex acts on the school property appeared on YouTube. In addition, reports of other behaviors that violate school policy and the law were documented on MySpace and Facebook.

During a recent altercation, an assistant principal was knocked to the ground and a teacher was punched in the face while attempting to break up a fight among several students. Superintendent William Jones decided this was enough. In a board meeting, a new policy of zero tolerance was passed. Accordingly, any child determined to have engaged in disruptive behavior faced an investigation and hearing to determine suspension or expulsion. Each month, parents were required to sign a code of conduct manual, which outlined the zero-tolerance policies and included rules and regulations for behavior. Parent/teacher meetings were held to explain expectations within the school and the risk to students if they participated in a rule violation. It was made clear that defending yourself, your friends, and your property were not exceptions to the rules. Superintendent Jones stated on the news that there were no loopholes to the zero-tolerance policy and that the school would do whatever was necessary to teach students that there are consequences to their behaviors.

The Results

Aside from the high numbers of expulsions and suspensions, other results of the zero-tolerance policy include increased numbers of students in the Alternative School; increased need for staffing of the Alternative School and traditional classrooms; overtime for staff who worked double-time and on the weekends to process the cases; and increased tensions among students, parents, teachers, and administrators. There were also complaints from the community about the expulsion of students who had not been in trouble previously and who were active participants in the school environment.

Matthew Sikes is one student who found himself expelled, even though he had never been in trouble at school before. He had a physical altercation with a boy he did not know after someone

(Continued)

(Continued)

had posted insulting comments about him on the Internet. Sikes was told by others that the boy had done it. When he confronted the boy, the boy threw a punch and Sikes responded with his own punch. Both boys were expelled. Sikes has since attended the Alternative School, where he has met students who have drug addictions, criminal records, and are consistently disruptive in class. His grades have dropped significantly, and he claims that he does not learn anything in the alternative school environment.

Suzanna Heart is another student who was expelled after bringing her cell phone to school and using it to call her mother for a ride home. According to Heart, "I normally ride with a friend, but she went home sick. I had to call my mom to see if she would pick me up before she left for work. I was using the phone when a teacher saw me. I tried to tell her why but she took the phone and wouldn't give it back." Heart started yelling and cursing at the teacher when the phone was confiscated. As a result, she was sent to the principal's office and promptly suspended. At her hearing, it was determined that expulsion was necessary. Heart's mother has moved her into a private school instead of enrolling her in the Alternative School.

Some of the parents of students who have been expelled or suspended have tried to speak with the school board, superintendent, and principals about the zero-tolerance policy. They have been told to seek remediation in the court system instead of through the school system. Attorneys for the parents have been making public statements defending the actions of the youth based on the school's environment and culture as well as reminding the public of the emotional immaturity of children and their inability to sometimes resolve conflicts by themselves.

In recent statements, the school district continues to support the zero-tolerance policy and claims it has no plans to back down on the enforcement of the policy. Administrators have asked for parental support during the transition and hope that the community understands that the schools are trying to fulfill their commitment to educating youth in a safe environment.

Questions for Review

1. What is a zero-tolerance policy? Is it a good way to manage behavior in organizations? Why or why not?

2. How else could the school district deal with the behaviors of students? Are you surprised by the approach taken in Brown County? Why or why not?

3. What leadership style is the school district using in this approach to managing students and teachers? What leadership style is most appropriate in dealing with student infractions in the school?

4. Has the school district taken time to work with the community, students, parents, teachers, and so forth to determine what services are necessary in this case? What should the district do to provide better services to the involved parties?

5. How does this approach impact the culture, environment, and motivation of people within the school organization? (Consider all people, not only students.)

Internet Resources

American Society of Criminology—http://www.asc41.com

Federal Bureau of Investigation: The FBI Training Academy—http://www.fbi.gov/about-us/training

National Association for Court Management—http://www.nacmnet.org

References and Suggested Readings

Adlam, R., & Villiers, P. (Eds.). (2003). *Police leadership in the twenty-first century: Philosophy, doctrine and developments.* Winchester, England: Waterside Press.

Avolio, B. J., & Bass, B. M. (1991). *The full range of leadership development.* Binghamton, NY: Bass, Avolio & Associates.

Avolio, B. J., & Bass, B. M. (1995). Individual consideration viewed at multiple levels of analysis: A multi-level framework for examining the diffusion of transformational leadership. *Leadership Quarterly, 6,* 199–218.

Bass, B. M. (1985). *Leadership and performance beyond expectations.* New York, NY: Free Press.

Bass, B. M. (1990, Winter). From transactional to transformational leadership: Learning to share the vision. *Organizational Dynamics, 18,* 19–31.

Bass, B. M. (1996). *A new paradigm of leadership: An inquiry into transformational leadership.* Alexandria, VA: U.S. Army Research Institute for the Behavioral and Social Sciences.

Bass, B. M. (1998). *Transformational leadership: Industrial, military, and educational impact.* Mahwah, NJ: Lawrence Erlbaum.

Bass, B. M., & Avolio, B. J. (1993). Transformational leadership: A response to critiques. In M. M. Chemers & R. Ayman (Eds.), *Leadership theory and research: Perspectives and direction* (pp. 49–88). San Diego, CA: Academic Press.

Batts, A. W., Smoot, S. M., & Scrivner, E. (2012). Police leadership challenges in a changing world. *New Perspectives in Policing Bulletin,* Washington DC Department of Justice, 1–20.

Beck, J., & Wade, M. (2004). *Got game: How the gamer generation is reshaping business forever.* Boston, MA: Harvard Business School Press.

Blake, R., & Mouton, J. (1978). *The new managerial grid.* Houston, TX: Gulf.

Brief, A. P., Aldag, R. J., & Wallden, R. A. (1976). Correlates of supervisory styles among policemen. *Criminal Justice and Behavior, 3,* 263–271.

Bruns, G. H., & Shuman, I. G. (1988). Police managers' perception of organizational leadership styles. *Public Personnel Management, 17*(2), 145–157.

Burns, J. M. (1978). *Leadership.* New York, NY: Harper & Row.

Cameron, K. S., & Quinn, R. E. (2000). *Diagnosing and changing organizational culture.* Reading, MA: Addison-Wesley.

Charman, S., Savage, S., & Cope, S. (1999). Getting to the top: Selection and training for senior managers in the police service. *Social Policy and Administration, 33*(3), 281–301.

Conger, J. A., & Kanungo, R. N. (1987). Toward a behavioral theory of charismatic leadership in organizational settings. *Academy of Management Review, 12,* 637–647.

Conger, J. A., & Kanungo, R. N. (1988). Behavioral dimensions of charismatic leadership. In J. A. Conger, R. N. Kanungo, & Associates (Eds.), *Charismatic leadership: The elusive factor in organizational effectiveness* (pp. 78–97). San Francisco, CA: Jossey-Bass.

Conger, J. A., & Kanungo, R. N. (1998). *Charismatic leadership in organizations.* Thousand Oaks, CA: Sage.

Criswell, C., & Martin, A. (2007). 10 Trends: A study of senior executives' views on the future. *ACCL Research White Paper,* Greensboro, NC., Center for Creative Leadership.

Daft, R. L., & Marcic, D. (2004). *Understanding management* (4th ed.). Mason, OH: Thomson South-Western.

Deluga, R. J. (1988). Relationship of transformational and transactional leadership with employee influencing strategies. *Group and Organizational Studies, 13*(4), 456–467.

Deluga, R. J. (1989). The effects of transformational, transactional, and laissez-faire leadership characteristics on subordinate influencing behavior. *Basic and Applied Social Psychology, 11*(2), 191–203.

Deluga, R. J., & Souza, J. (1991). The effect of transformational and transactional leadership style on the influencing behavior of subordinate police officers. *Journal of Occupational Psychology, 64*(1), 49–55.

Densten, I. L. (2003). Senior police leadership: Does rank matter? *Policing: An International Journal of Police Strategies and Management, 26*(3), 400–418.

Dobby, J., Anscombe, J., & Tuffin, R. (2004). *Police leadership: Expectations and impact* (Home Office Online Report 20/04). London, England: Home Office.

Dubrin, A. J. (1995). *Leadership: Research findings, practice, and skills.* Boston, MA: Houghton Mifflin.

Fiedler, F. E. (1967). *A theory of leadership effectiveness.* New York, NY: McGraw-Hill.

Fiedler, F. E. (1971). Validation and extension of the contingency model of leadership effectiveness: A review of empirical findings. *Psychological Bulletin, 76,* 128–148.

Fiedler, F. E. (1994). *Leadership experience and leadership performance.* Alexandria, VA: U.S. Army Research Institute.

French, B., & Stewart, J. (2001, September). Organizational development in a law enforcement environment. *FBI Law Enforcement Bulletin,* 14–19.

Gardner, W. L., & Avolio, B. J. (1998). The charismatic relationship: A dramaturgical perspective. *Academy of Management Review, 23*(1), 32–58.

George, J. M., & Jones, G. R. (2002). *Organizational behavior* (3rd ed.). Upper Saddle River, NJ: Prentice Hall.

Gibb, C. A. (1947). The principles and traits of leadership. *Journal of Abnormal and Social Psychology, 42*(3), 267–284.

Halpin, A. W., & Winer, B. J. (1957). *A factorial study of the leader behavior descriptions.* In R. M. Stogdill & A. E. Coons (Eds.), *Leader behavior: Its description and measurement.* Columbus: Ohio State University, Bureau of Business Research.

Hellriegel, D., Slocum, J. W., Jr., & Woodman, R. W. (2001). *Organizational behavior* (9th ed.). Cincinnati, OH: South-Western College.

Hersey, P., & Blanchard, K. H. (1977). *Management of organizational behavior.* Englewood Cliffs, NJ: Prentice Hall.

Hollander, E. P., & Offermann, L. R. (1990). Power and leadership in organizations. *American Psychologist, 45*(2), 179–189.

House, R. J. (1971). A path-goal theory of leader effectiveness. *Administrative Science Quarterly, 16,* 321–339.

House, R. J., & Podsakoff, P. M. (1994). Leadership effectiveness: Past perspectives and future directions for research. In J. Greenberg (Ed.), *Organizational behavior: The state of the science* (pp. 45–82). Hillsdale, NJ: Lawrence Erlbaum.

House, R. J., Spangler, D. W., & Woycke, J. (1991, September). Personality and charisma in the U.S. presidency: A psychological theory of leader effectiveness. *Administrative Science Quarterly, 36,* 364–396.

Jenkins, W. O. (1947). A review of leadership studies with particular reference to military problems. *Psychological Bulletin, 44,* 54–79.

Kahn, R. L., & Katz, D. (1953). Leadership practices in relation to productivity and morale. In D. Cartwright & A. Zander (Eds.), *Group dynamics* (pp. 554–571). New York, NY: Harper & Row.

Katz, D., & Kahn, R. L. (1978). *The social psychology of organizations* (Rev. ed.). New York, NY: Wiley.

Katz, D., Maccoby, N., & Morse, N. (1950). *Productivity, supervision, and morale among railroad workers.* Ann Arbor: University of Michigan, Survey Research Center.

Kelloway, E. K., & Barling, J. (2000). What we have learned about developing transformational leaders. *Leadership and Organizational Development Journal, 21,* 355–362.

Kim, W. C., & Mauborgne, R. (2003, April). Tipping point leadership. *Harvard Business Review, 81*(4), 60–69.

Lawrence, P. R., & Lorsch, J. W. (1967). *Organization and environment*. Cambridge, MA: Harvard University Press.

Lewis, P. S., Goodman, S. H., & Fandt, P. M. (2001). *Management challenges in the 21st century* (3rd ed.). Cincinnati, OH: South-Western College.

Lievens, F., VanGeit, P., & Coetsier, P. (1997). Identification of transformational leadership qualities: An examination of potential biases. *European Journal of Work and Organizational Psychology, 6*(4), 415–430.

Likert, R. (1981, November/December). System 4: A resource for improving public administration. *Public Management Review, 41*(6), 674–678.

Marks, M., & Fleming, J. (2004). As unremarkable as the air they breathe? Reforming police management in South Africa. *Current Sociology, 52*(5), 784–808.

Maslow, A. H. (1954). *Motivation and personality*. New York, NY: Harper & Row.

Montgomery, M. (2006, August). Leadership in a correctional environment. *Corrections Today*, 38–42.

Murphy, S. A., & Drodge, E. N. (2004). The four I's of police leadership: A case study heuristic. *International Journal of Police Science and Management, 6*(1), 1–15.

Pagon, M. (2003). The need for paradigm shift. In R. Adlam & P. Villiers (Eds.), *Leadership in the twenty-first century: Philosophy, doctrine and developments*, Winchester, England: Waterside Press.

Petrillo, L., & Bass, B. M. (Eds.). (1961). *Leadership and interpersonal behavior*. New York, NY: Holt, Rinehart and Winston.

Pew Research Center (2007). How young people view their lives, futures, and politics: A portrait of generation next. Washington, DC: Pew Research Center.

Pillai, R., & Meindl, J. R. (1991). The effects of a crisis on the emergence of charismatic leadership: A laboratory study. *Best Paper Proceedings: Annual Meeting of the Academy of Management, Miami*, 420–425.

Pillai, R., & Meindl, J. R. (1998). Context and charisma: A "meso" level examination of the relationship of organic structure, collectivism, and crisis to charismatic leadership. *Journal of Management, 24*(5), 643–671.

Potts, L. W. (1982). Police leadership: Challenges for the eighties. *Journal of Police Science and Administration, 10*(2), 181–187.

Quinn, R. E., & Rohrbaugh, J. (1983). A special model of effectiveness criteria: Towards a competing values approach to organizational analysis. *Management Science, 29*, 363–377.

Sashkin, M. (1988). The visionary leader. In J. A. Conger, R. N. Kanango, & Associates (Eds.), *Charismatic leadership: The elusive factor in organizational effectiveness* (pp. 122–160). San Francisco, CA: Jossey-Bass.

Silvestri, M. (2007). Doing police leadership: Enter the "new smart" macho. *Policing & Society, 17*(1), 38–58.

Sosik, J. J., Kahai, S., & Avolio, B. J. (1998). Transformational leadership and dimensions of creativity: Motivating idea generation in computer-mediated groups. *Creativity Research Journal, 11*, 111–121.

Sosik, J., & Megerian, J. (1999). Understanding leader emotional intelligence and performance: The role of self-other agreement of transformational leadership perceptions. *Group and Organization Management, 24*, 367–390.

Steinheider, B., Wuestewald, T., & Bayerl, P. S. (2006). When twelve heads are better than one: Implementing a shared leadership concept in a police agency. *Academy of Management Best Papers Proceedings*, Academy of Management Conference, Atlanta, GA.

Stevens, D. J. (2000, October). Improving community policing: Using management styles and total quality management. *Law and Order*, 197–204.

Stogdill, R. M. (1948). Personal factors associated with leadership: A survey of the literature. *Journal of Psychology, 25*, 35–71.

Stogdill, R. M. (1974). *Handbook of leadership: A survey of the literature*. New York, NY: Free Press.

Sullivan, B. (2004). Police supervision in the 21st century: Can traditional work standards and the contemporary employee coexist? *Police Chief, 71*(10).

Tang, T. L., & Hammontree, M. L. (1992). The effects of hardiness, police stress, and life stress on police officers' illness and absenteeism. *Public Personnel Management, 21*(4), 493–510.

Vroom, V. H., & Yetton, P. W. (1973). *Leadership and decision making*. Pittsburgh, PA: University of Pittsburgh Press.

Whetten, D. A., & Cameron, K. S. (2002). *Developing management skills* (5th ed.). Upper Saddle River, NJ: Prentice Hall.

Williams, B. N., & Kellough, J. E. (2006, November/December). Leadership with an enduring impact: The legacy of Chief Burtell Jefferson of the Metropolitan Police Department of Washington, DC. *Public Administration Review, 66*(6), 813–822.

Wright, K. N. (1999, Summer/Fall). Leadership is the key to ethical practice in criminal justice agencies. *Criminal Justice Ethics,* 67–69.

Yammarino, F. J., & Bass, B. M. (1990). Long-term forecasting of transformational leadership and its effects among naval officers: Some preliminary findings. In K. E. Clark & M. B. Clark (Eds.), *Measures of leadership* (pp. 151–171). West Orange, NJ: Leadership Library of America.

Yukl, G. A. (1981). *Leadership in organizations*. Englewood Cliffs, NJ: Prentice Hall.

8

Communication ❖

LEARNING OBJECTIVES

Upon completion of this chapter, students should be able to do the following:

- Define the communication process
- Discuss the different organizational needs fulfilled by communication
- Discuss the different modes of interpersonal communication
- Describe the different types of communication channels
- Explain formal and informal methods of organizational communication
- Explain individual and organizational barriers to effective communication
- Discuss how to promote good communication

One of the most famous publicized cases reflecting the importance of communication was NASA's attempt at a Mars landing. In that instance, the landing module crashed because of miscommunication. One scientist was making calculations using the metric system, while another one was using the English system (yards versus meters), and this information never was communicated properly. Similarly, it is still believed that the 9/11 terrorist attack on the United States could have been avoided through proper and speedy communication of pertinent information among the different agencies of law enforcement. Weedon (2003) notes, "Of the lessons learned from the tragic events of that day, one of the most important is the need to effectively communicate and exchange data in a timely fashion" (p. 18). He goes on to say,

> The inability of state and local law enforcement, criminal justice and related agencies to communicate and share information on a timely basis is epidemic across the nation. The lack of interoperability among police agencies, fire departments, emergency medical services and the numerous other public safety agencies is a chronic problem. In addition, the effects of the inability to communicate and share vital data among criminal justice agencies are not just felt during national emergencies but rather, on a day-to-day basis. (p. 18)

Emphasizing the importance of good and speedy communication, the chief of the Los Angeles County Sheriff's Department notes, "Communication is perhaps the most essential element of effective law enforcement in the war on terror" (Bayless, 2004, p. 47). This was demonstrated most recently in solving the 2013 Boston Marathon bombing case that left three dead and hundreds injured. The incident took place at 2:50 p.m. on Monday, April 15, near the finish line of the Boston Marathon in which more than 23,000 participated, with many times more people cheering them along the 26.2 mile route (CNN news). The task of identifying the suspects was difficult, given the number of people at the sight and with absolutely no lead. After going through thousands of hours of video footage and photographs collected from the CCTV and public, and interrogating several people, by Thursday 5 p.m. (ET) the FBI released pictures of two male suspects being sought in connection with the Boston Marathon bombings. And within 24 hours of releasing the photographs, law enforcement agencies had one suspect shot dead and the other was apprehended. All this happened through good and speedy communication among the FBI, the Department of Homeland Security, the Massachusetts State Police, residents, and many other local organizations of Massachusetts.

In the day-to-day duties performed by law enforcement agencies, miscommunication or ineffective communication can result in grave situations with serious outcomes. Think of the importance of effective communication in a 911 emergency call between the caller and the receiver, and with the various officers responding to attend to the emergency. At each exchange of information between different entities, there is a possibility for service failure because of communication error. Unfortunately, when communication goes bad in criminal justice, the effects are devastating for the system and the public alike. Therefore, to enhance public and officer safety, information systems must be used that facilitate real-time communications among law enforcement, judicial, correctional, and related agencies. There is also a need to continue developing information-sharing standards within the justice community to enable easy dissemination of information via global websites (Weedon, 2003).

In simple words, communication is one of the most important management tools within criminal justice agencies, which, when conducted effectively, promotes high service quality. It has a major impact on the performance of individuals, groups, and various agencies that collectively maintain law and order in a society. The importance of communication can be gauged from the fact that managers and administrators spend at least 80% of their workday in communication with others (Daft & Marcic, 2004, p. 480; Mintzberg, 1973). The various forms of communication that managers may be involved in during their day-to-day activities include meetings, telephone calls, the Internet, and talking informally while walking around. The other 20% of the time is typically spent in doing desk work, most of which may involve communication in the form of writing. In this chapter, communication of all kinds by both an individual and an organization is examined. At the individual level, the interest is in understanding the interpersonal aspects of communication, including communication channels, persuasion, and listening skills that influence a manager's or an administrator's[1] ability

---

[1]We will be using the terms *manager* and *administrator* interchangeably because what a manager is to a company, an administrator is to a public organization.

to communicate effectively. At the organization level, this chapter will examine different forms of communication, namely, one-way, two-way, nonverbal, upward, downward, and horizontal communication.

CAREER HIGHLIGHT BOX
PARALEGALS AND LEGAL ASSISTANTS

Nature of the Work

Paralegals and legal assistants do a variety of tasks to support lawyers, including maintaining and organizing files, conducting legal research, and drafting documents. Paralegals and legal assistants typically do the following:

- Investigate the facts of a case
- Conduct research on relevant laws, regulations, and legal articles
- Organize and present the information
- Keep information related to cases or transactions in computer databases
- Write reports to help lawyers prepare for trials
- Draft correspondence and other documents, such as contracts and mortgages
- Get affidavits and other formal statements that may be used as evidence in court
- Help lawyers during trials

Paralegals and legal assistants help lawyers prepare for hearings, trials, and corporate meetings. However, their specific duties may vary depending on the size of the firm or organization. In smaller firms, paralegals duties tend to vary more. In addition to reviewing and organizing information, paralegals may prepare written reports that help lawyers determine how to handle their cases. If lawyers decide to file lawsuits on behalf of clients, paralegals may help prepare the legal arguments and draft documents to be filed with the court. In larger organizations, paralegals work mostly on a particular phase of a case, rather than handling a case from beginning to end. For example, a litigation paralegal might only review legal material for internal use, maintain reference files, conduct research for lawyers, and collect and organize evidence for hearings. Litigation paralegals often do not attend trials, but might prepare trial documents or draft settlement agreements.

Law firms increasingly use technology and computer software for managing documents and preparing for trials. Paralegals use computer software to draft and index documents and prepare presentations. In addition, paralegals must be familiar with electronic database management and be up to date on the latest software used for electronic discovery. Electronic discovery refers to all electronic materials that are related to a trial, such as emails, data, documents, accounting databases, and websites.

Paralegals can assume more responsibilities by specializing in areas such as litigation, personal injury, corporate law, criminal law, employee benefits, intellectual property, bankruptcy, immigration, family law, and real estate. In addition, experienced paralegals

(Continued)

(Continued)

may assume supervisory responsibilities, such as overseeing team projects or delegating work to other paralegals. Paralegal tasks may differ depending on the type of department or the size of the law firm they work for. The following are examples of types of paralegals:

Corporate paralegals often help lawyers prepare employee contracts, shareholder agreements, stock-option plans, and companies' annual financial reports. Corporate paralegals may monitor and review government regulations to ensure that the corporation is aware of new legal requirements.

Litigation paralegals maintain documents received from clients, conduct research for lawyers, and retrieve and organize evidence for use at depositions and trials.

Work environment. Paralegals and legal assistants work in law offices and law libraries. Occasionally, they travel to gather information and do other tasks. Paralegals who work for law firms, corporations, and government agencies usually work full time. Although most paralegals work year-round, some are temporarily employed during busy times of the year. Paralegals who work for law firms may work very long hours and overtime to meet deadlines.

Training, Other Qualifications, and Advancement

Many paralegals and legal assistants have an associate's degree or a certificate in paralegal studies. Most paralegals and legal assistants have an associate's degree in paralegal studies, or a bachelor's degree in another field and a certificate in paralegal studies. In some cases, employers may hire college graduates with a bachelor's degree but no legal experience or education and train them on the job.

Education and training. There are several paths to become a paralegal. Candidates can enroll in a community college paralegal program to earn an associate's degree. A small number of schools also offer bachelor's and master's degrees in paralegal studies. Those who already have a bachelor's degree in another subject can earn a certificate in paralegal studies. Finally, some employers hire entry-level paralegals without any experience or education in paralegal studies and train them on the job, though these jobs typically require a bachelor's degree.

Associate's and bachelor's degree programs in paralegal studies usually combine paralegal training, such as courses in legal research and the legal applications of computers, with other academic subjects. Most certificate programs provide this intensive paralegal training for people who already hold college degrees. Some certificate programs only take a few months to complete.

More than 1,000 colleges and universities offer formal paralegal training programs. However, only about 270 paralegal programs are approved by the American Bar Association (ABA).

Many paralegal training programs also offer an internship, in which students gain practical experience by working for several months in a private law firm, the office of a public defender or attorney general, a corporate legal department, a legal aid organization, or a government agency. Internship experience helps students improve their technical skills and can enhance their employment prospects.

Employers sometimes hire college graduates with no legal experience or education and train them on the job. In these cases, the new employee often has experience in a technical field that is useful to law firms, such as tax preparation or criminal justice.

In many cases, employers prefer candidates who have at least one year of experience in a law firm or other office setting. In addition, a technical understanding of a specific legal specialty can be helpful. For example, a personal-injury law firm may desire a paralegal with a background in nursing or health administration. Work experience in a law firm or other office setting is particularly important for people who do not have formal paralegal training.

Certification and other qualifications. Although not required by most employers, earning voluntary certification may help applicants get a paralegal job. Many national and local paralegal organizations offer voluntary paralegal certifications to students able to pass an exam. Other organizations offer voluntary paralegal certifications for paralegals who meet certain experience and education criteria. For more information about paralegal certifications, see the Contacts for More Info section.

Other important qualities:

Computer skills. Paralegals need to be familiar with using computers for legal research and litigation support. They also use computer programs for organizing and maintaining important documents.

Interpersonal skills. Paralegals spend most of their time working with clients or other professionals and must be able to develop good relationships. They must make clients feel comfortable sharing personal information related to their cases.

Organizational skills. Paralegals may be responsible for many cases at one time. They must adapt quickly to changing deadlines.

Research skills. Paralegals need good research and investigative skills to conduct legal research.

Speaking and writing skills. Paralegals must be able to document and present their research and related information to their supervising attorney.

Advancement. Paralegals usually are given more responsibilities and require less supervision as they gain work experience. Experienced paralegals may supervise and delegate assignments to other paralegals and clerical staff.

Employment

Paralegals and legal assistants held about 256,000 jobs in May 2010. Paralegals are found in all types of organizations, but most work for law firms, corporate legal departments, and government agencies. The following industries employed the most paralegals and legal assistants in 2010: Legal services—70%; State and local government, excluding education and hospitals—9%; Federal government—6%; Finance and insurance—4%.

(Continued)

(Continued)

Job Outlook

As employers try to reduce costs and increase the efficiency of legal services, they are expected to hire more paralegals and legal assistants. Following the cutbacks experienced during the recent recession, some law firms are rebuilding their support staff by hiring paralegals. Paralegals can be a less costly alternative to lawyers and perform a wider variety of duties, including tasks once done by lawyers. This will cause an increase in demand for paralegals and legal assistants.

Employment change. Employment of paralegals and legal assistants is expected to grow from 256,000 to 302,900, which is an 18 percent growth from 2010 to 2020, about as fast as the average for all occupations. In addition, paralegals' work is less likely to be offshored than that of other legal workers. Paralegals routinely file and store important documents and work with lawyers to gather documents for important transactions, hearings, and depositions. They frequently handle documents and take statements, which must be done in person.

Law firms will continue to be the largest employers of paralegals, but many large corporations are increasing their in-house legal departments to cut costs. For many companies, the high cost of lawyers and their support staff makes it much more economical to have an in-house legal department rather than to retain outside counsel. This will lead to an increase in the demand of legal workers in a variety of settings, such as finance and insurance firms, consulting firms, and health care providers.

However, demand for paralegals could be limited by law firms' workloads. When work is slow, lawyers may increase the number of hours they can bill a client by doing tasks that were previously delegated to paralegals. This may make a firm less likely to keep some paralegals on staff or hire new ones until the work load increases.

Job prospects. This occupation attracts many applicants, and competition for jobs will be strong. Experienced, formally trained paralegals should have the best job prospects. In addition, many firms will prefer paralegals with experience and specialization in high-demand practice areas.

Earnings

Earnings of paralegals and legal assistants vary greatly. Salaries depend on education, training, experience, the type and size of employer, and the geographic location of the job. In general, paralegals that work for large law firms or in large cities earn more than those who work for smaller firms or in smaller cities. The median annual wage of paralegals and legal assistants was $46,680 in May 2010. The median wage is the wage at which half the workers in an occupation earned more than that amount and half earned less. The lowest 10 percent earned less than $29,460, and the top 10 percent earned more than $74,870.

In addition to earning a salary, many paralegals receive bonuses, in part, to compensate them for sometimes having to work long hours. Paralegals also receive vacation, paid sick leave, a 401 savings plan, life insurance, personal paid time off, dental insurance, and reimbursement for continuing legal education.

SOURCE: From the *Occupational Outlook Handbook,* 2012–13 Edition, by the U.S. Department of Labor, Bureau of Labor Statistics. Available online at http://www.bls.gov/ooh.

Definition

Communication is defined as a process by which ideas, thoughts, and information are exchanged and understood between two or more entities. Reaching a common understanding means that people have a fairly accurate idea of what is being communicated to them; it does not imply that people have to agree with each other (Daft & Marcic, 2004).

To improve the quality of communication, it is important to understand the communication process (Daft & Marcic, 2004; Drafke & Kossen, 2002). A prerequisite for communication is the existence of at least two entities—a receiving and a sending entity. The *sender* is anyone who wishes to convey the information or idea to others. Once the information or idea has been decided, then the sender *encodes* the information or idea into symbols or language that he or she believes the receiver can understand. The result of encoding is a *message*. A message is said to be clear when it contains information that is easily understood. Therefore, vocabulary and knowledge play an important role in the sender's ability to encode (see Figure 8.1). The message is sent through a *channel,* which is a communication carrier such as a formal report, a telephone call, an e-mail message, or a face-to-face meeting. The *receiver* is the person or group for whom the information or idea is intended. On receiving the message, the receiver *decodes* the symbols or language to interpret the meaning of the message. This process of decoding may not always be fully successful because the receiver interprets the message based on previous experience, culture, thoughts, feelings, beliefs, and attitudes. Subsequently, the receiver responds to the sender with a return message, considered *feedback,* which lets the sender know whether the message was received as intended. The message is considered *one-way communication* if there is no feedback, but with the feedback it is considered a *two-way communication* (Lewis, Goodman, & Fandt, 2001). Based on observations, interviews, and records of police, Manning (1988) gives a descriptive rendition of communication among the police and between the police and the public. He examines the symbolic transformation of communication, discussing how communication is mediated by classification systems, technology, roles and tasks, and interpretations within the police force. A flow chart is presented by Manning (p. 51) to provide a visual representation of call processing in the communications center of the British Police Department.

Communication takes place within a setting defined as the *social context,* which has an impact on the other components of the communication process. For example, communication between a sergeant and an officer during their kids' soccer game is more informal compared to communication in the sergeant's office. There will be fewer interruptions during communication in the sergeant's office, but the officer may be less outspoken in the feedback given. Manning (1988) discusses how selected factors in addition to message content impact organizational communication in law enforcement. He argues,

> The police have evolved technologically sophisticated equipment to cope with increased citizen demand, but messages are received, interpreted, processed, transformed, and allocated for resolution within socially patterned relationships. Social relations, coding procedures, interpretative practices, and working rules, are derived in part from the occupational culture, shape, constrain, and pattern messages regardless of their informational content and form. (pp. 3–4)

Figure 8.1 Communication Process

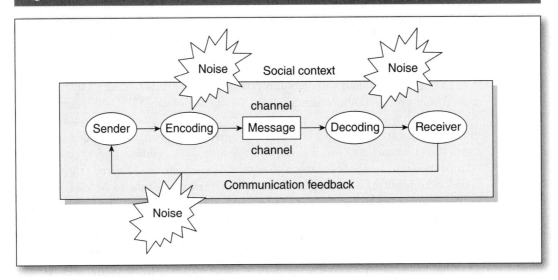

Manning (1988) makes the case that "meaning is socially constructed from the occasioned relevance of message content in an organizational structure through interpretative work" (pp. 3–4). The social context has become significantly important because of the increased diversity in the workforce within the United States.

Achieving high-quality communication is both complicated and difficult because there are innumerable opportunities for making an error in sending or receiving messages. Any internal or external interference or distraction in communicating the intended message is deemed *noise*. For example, poor handwriting, a poor telephone connection, a bad toner in the fax machine, and so forth may make communication unclear by introducing noise. Such noise can occur at any stage in the communication process. More discussion on the sources of noise and how to reduce them to promote effective communication is provided later in the chapter.

Organizational Needs Fulfilled by Communication

The act of communication is embedded in every management function. However, the three express purposes of communication are to provide information, motivate workers, and coordinate their efforts, with the intention of accomplishing organizational goals (Conger, 1998; Scott & Mitchell, 1976).

A basic function of communication is to *provide information* to the employees to help them perform their daily jobs effectively. For example,

Those in corrections want and need to know about the history of an individual entering an institution. Has the offender received medical treatment and vaccinations for potentially

contagious diseases? Does he or she have a history of violence toward police or other inmates? And, upon release, parole officers should be provided with the information they need to ensure that the offender continues to receive the treatment he or she needs in the community. (Weedon, 2003, p. 18)

The information exchange may also take the form of feedback, which is an assessment by managers or administrators and certain departments of the quality and quantity of work performed by workers and other departments. Typically, such knowledge is more important when a worker has just started a new job or when changes are made. When changes are initiated within an organization, clear communication of new tasks, goals, and responsibilities can help ensure that everyone understands what is expected of them to achieve organizational goals. In policing, for example, a formal memo may be distributed to all officers and then formally discussed during the shift staffing meetings to ensure everyone understands the change in policy or procedure. In the absence of proper communication from the supervisor or manager, a worker is left to gather information from coworkers, customers, clients, and others, which leads to service errors and compromises quality. Worker errors caused by a lack of proper information should be marked against the supervisor or manager who was responsible for getting the information to the worker instead of the worker who made the mistake.

Besides conveying information, communication is used to persuade, motivate, and influence people. Managers and administrators communicate with their employees to promote the vision of the organization and influence their behaviors to accomplish the vision. Managers communicate with employees to understand their needs and motivate them to work toward the accomplishment of organizational goals. As discussed in Chapter 6, motivation is a key determinant of individual and organizational performance. Poor communication is often blamed for unmotivated workers, leading to high absenteeism and turnover. The ability to persuade and influence has become more important in the current work environment, where the command-and-control method of managing is increasingly becoming outdated.

Growth in organizations introduces increasing diversification and specialization, making communication extremely vital for *coordinating* various tasks. By regularly communicating information about roles, rules, and norms to the group members, organizations can exert control over them. This coordination helps in the elimination of unnecessary duplication of effort and improves the overall efficiency and effectiveness. Often, it is seen that a lack of proper coordination in service and treatment programs results in wasteful actions and excess inventories. For example, failures of agencies to coordinate and communicate with one another may allow for one family to receive the same service from multiple agencies, resulting in duplication of services and resource waste. If better communication were used, the treatment providers could service more families while using fewer resources. Furthermore, communication allows the members of an organization to understand one another's personalities, attitudes, and values, which makes it easier to work together in achieving organizational goals. Open communication allows the groups to control the behavior of team members and prevent social loafing.

Press releases to the media perform another important function of communication that is unique to law enforcement agencies (see In the News 8.1). News media may be the primary sources of information for citizens to form perceptions of police legitimacy (Surette, 2001). Scholars have examined how news media affect attitudes toward police. Some studies report that such attitudes are positively influenced by consumption of mainstream news media (Escholz, Blackwell, Gertz, & Chiricos, 2002) and negatively impacted by consumption of nontraditional media such as political talk shows (Moy, Pfau, & Kahlor, 1999). In addition, "recent research on attitudes toward police has consistently found race to be a significant moderator of the effects of news media exposure" (Chermak, McGarrell, & Gruenewald, 2006, p. 263). The problem of poor relations between the police and minorities is not new. Following the bloody aftermath of the Democratic National Convention in Chicago in 1968, President Lyndon Johnson appointed the National Advisory Commission on Civil Disorders (also known as the Kerner Commission). The commission concluded that the police should be provided special training on ghetto problems and conditions to help improve police–minority relations (Barlow & Barlow, 1994). As the United States becomes more diverse with migration, multicultural skills become exceedingly important in managing police–minority relations. In the nearly five decades since the Kerner Commission, a great deal about minority relations and multicultural skills has been learned by communication researchers and trainers that can be applied in police training. This research emphasizes multicultural skill development that exposes officers to the influence of culture as a priority for police officers (Cornett-DeVito & McGlone, 2000). It emphasizes officers to communicate effectively with local residents in understanding what is important in each neighborhood and empowers officers to initiate creative responses to neighborhood problems (Lasley, 1994). In addition, U.S. law enforcement agencies are trying to increase minority representation, not only to make up for past deficiencies, but also to keep pace with the country's shifting demographics. For example, in 2000, racial and ethnic minorities made up 31% of the U.S. population, which increased to 36% in 2010 and is expected to be more than 50% by 2045 (U.S. Census Bureau, 2008). However, in 2007 only about one in four police officers was a member of a racial or ethnic minority group. These efforts to increase minority representation will allow for more cultural diversity in the police force and allow for better understanding of different cultures and more effective communication with the residents. This is a good step toward increasing police effectiveness and perceptions of police legitimacy in the communities they serve. Research shows that media's effects on attitudes toward police are dependent on race-specific communities (Doyle, 2003; Escholz et al., 2002; Weitzer & Tuch, 2004; Wortley, Macmillan, & Hagan, 1997). For example, Escholz et al. (2002) report that the reality show *COPS* produced a negative attitude toward police among African Americans because of their affinity with African American offenders. Conversely, white viewers were supportive of the police because of their affinity with the more dominant white police officers. One also needs to be mindful that the news media tend to sensationalize the events to capture viewers' attention and compete with other news media outlets. Therefore, law enforcement agencies should be extremely careful in press releases to media to ensure that the information is decoded by the receivers the way it was intended. Referring to the media releases on high-profile cases, Chermak et al. (2006) note,

> Police departments must be prepared to respond to such events because they have the potential to undermine any public relations and community policing efforts. Thus it is important for police departments to evaluate their relationship with media organizations and determine how best to use the media as a mechanism to communicate department goals and objectives, as well as make an effort to provide full accounts when crises occur. (p. 274)

Good understanding of communication at the organization level is important for smooth and effective functioning of criminal justice agencies. Alluding to the importance of communication in all aspects of criminal justice, Christensen (2006) notes, "No one in the corrections and law enforcement fields understand why incarceration is up 367% since 1980, and they refuse to agree on a course of action to reduce recidivism. The corrections field must adopt *better communication* if they intend to improve prison outcomes" (p. 51). Talking among themselves about how to improve treatment and rehabilitation could make a difference. Since police–community collaboration programs are also important in the reduction of recidivism, Arnold (2001) notes, "The law enforcement leaders must communicate their visions and expectations and provide the tools needed to achieve an objective, and hold their people accountable" (p. 150).

In the News 8.1
Formatting a Press Release

Every police department needs to have at least one person who knows how to send out press releases to the media. Many departments develop their own styles, but we have asked experts in public relations on their advice to create the best, most effective press releases.

Each press release should be on letterhead. Press releases that are posted on the Internet do not need to be a scanned version of the hard copy. The letterhead signals to the media where the press release came from, but if the release is on the police department's Web site, this information is obvious.

At the top of the press release include a date, name and contact information. Make sure to provide a phone number and e-mail address if applicable. The media need to be able to get a hold of this officer at the last minute so provide as much contact information as possible.

Under the contact information let the media know if the information is for immediate release or if it is to be held for a later release date. For example, if it is election time and the sheriff does not plan on running again, the department may notify the media but say, "embargoed for release until November 1." This will give the media enough time to go ahead and do a story and possibly interview the sheriff but hold the story until November 1. After the release date, give the press release a headline. Headlines can be bold, underlined, centered and slightly larger than the body of the press release.

(Continued)

(Continued)

The lead paragraph of the press release is where you will give the five Ws. "Every news story should contain the five Ws and an H: who, what, where, when, why and how," David Shank, president of Shank Public Relations Counselors, said.

The first and second paragraph is what Debbie Anglin, of Anglin Public Relations, calls the "so what?" She says to think like the newspaper reader would think. How would this story affect a reader; why should he read it? If the press release was about car safety seat checks, this would be the information that says how many children get hurt by improperly secured safety seats—information that would be important to a parent who was reading the story.

After all the hard facts and important information is given, now would be the time to provide a background paragraph. If the press release is about a safety program done by the department, explain how long this program has been running, how it got started, how it is funded, etc. This information is not vitally important to the story, so it does not go in the first paragraphs. When creating the press release keep in mind that different types of media require different things. Television stations and newspapers require pictures. Give the reporter some ideas for pictures. If the press release is about an officer retiring, invite the reporter to the retirement party. Not only will the retirement party give the reporter an opportunity to take pictures, but will give the reporter a chance to talk to other officers who know and care about the retiring officer.

If a press release is going to a radio station, think in sound bites. If an officer is diagnosed with cancer and fellow officers shave their heads in support, this is a feel-good kind of story and a radio station might want to talk to one of the officers and ask why he shaved his head. The interview is usually very short and can be done by phone, but adds a lot of depth to the story.

Don't send out press releases to every media contact; narrow it down to the appropriate editors. For example, the press release about the officers shaving their heads would be appropriate for a community editor but not a business editor.

If the police department sends a press release about ways to stay safe at Halloween and it doesn't run in a timely manner, feel free to call the editor. Maybe it just got overlooked or the editor needed more information but didn't have the chance to call. Ask if he got the press release and needs any additional information.

Keep the body text of the press release at 10 or 12 [point] size and the font in a standard style like Times New Roman. It is also a good idea to double space press releases and to not let them run past two pages. Editors want the information quickly; they don't want to have to read an entire book to find out about an upcoming event. Finally, at the end . . . type "\\\#\#" to signify the end of the press release.

SOURCE: From "Formatting a Press Release," by C. Whitehead, July 2004, *Law and Order, 52*(7), p. 20.

Interpersonal Communication

There are three modes of interpersonal communications, namely, verbal, written, and nonverbal, which may be used individually or in some combination for effective communication. In a study, Albert Mehrabian (1968) found that the relative weight in message interpretations is as follows: verbal impact, 7%; voice tone impact, 38%; and facial impact, 55%. The strong message of this research was that "it's not what you say but how you say it." Therefore, managers need to learn to use their nonverbal cues to complement and support their verbal and written messages. When the written, verbal, and nonverbal messages are contradictory, the receiver may be confused. Thus, it is extremely important for criminal justice professionals to ensure that the message being communicated through the use of different modes is consistent.

Oral or verbal communication. All forms of spoken information comprise oral communication. It is the most popular mode of communication among administrators, taking the form of face-to-face communication and telephone communication.

Written communication. Letters, memos, reports, policy manuals, and other documents comprise written communication. Though less preferred to oral communication, written communication is typically desired when evidence for later use is required (as is always the case in criminal justice). On a lighter side of written (mis)communication, one of the participants in a workshop narrated the following story. This human resource manager presented her half-yearly report on the employees' performance to her director, in which she had written "outstanding" next to the names of some of the employees. The director, without checking the contents of the report, congratulated these officers, which the manager found rather ridiculous. She had written "outstanding" across the names of the employees who were delinquent in filling out their half-yearly reports, but the director interpreted "outstanding" as meaning exceptional work had been accomplished by those employees. These miscommunications are of a greater concern in law enforcement services, where the demographics of officers are changing in line with the overall demographic changes in the United States. There has been an increase in people in the force whose first language is not English, which is the primary language of written communication in law enforcement agencies. Emphasizing the importance of written communication in law enforcement, Servino (1999) notes, "Judges and attorneys report that police officers' lack of written communication skills is a growing problem. Police administrators need to enforce minimum standards to ensure effective communication takes place" (p. 23). It is also important to note here that a police officer's written report does not stay with the police department but accompanies the case through court and into corrections as the offender moves through the process. For the case to be successfully processed, the officers have to convey their messages clearly so quality services can be provided at all levels of criminal justice.

Nonverbal communication. The act of communication can take place without talking or writing, but instead involving actions, gestures, symbols, and behaviors, which are termed *nonverbal* (Mehrabian, 1968; 1972). In addition, nonverbal communication may accompany verbal communication, generally through unconscious or subconscious cues. For example, movement of eyes, change of facial expressions, voice tone, mannerisms, posture, touch, and dress may reflect some forms of communication within the context in which verbal communication is taking place. Maximum potential for miscommunication through nonverbal cues happens in crosscultural communication. Gender differences can also contribute to nonverbal communication challenges, though these tend to be minor compared to cultural influences. Training in law enforcement often teaches officers to observe the body gestures and movements of individuals they question. According to Kiernan (2007), "The ability to read an emotion without benefit of a spoken or understood communication capability would seem an indisputable precept of training at all levels of law enforcement." She points out that "the law enforcement officers have limitless opportunities to apply this training in daily operational activity whether dealing with civil or criminal issues and are better prepared when confronted with a new form of adversary" (p. 47). At the same time, officers need to be careful of the nonverbal signals and messages they send to suspects. Pinizzotto and Davis (1999) reported on FBI research on various aspects of law enforcement safety related to the nonverbal communication cues that offenders perceive during their interaction with police officers. They concluded, "Law enforcement officers must remember that while they observe nonverbal messages from the individuals they question, these individuals also gather information from them. Subtle nuances that others would not view as weaknesses become opportunities for human predators to exploit. Law enforcement officers must protect themselves against such individuals who search for easy prey and strike with little or no warning" (p. 4).

Fitch and Means (2013) have proposed a very interesting IMPACT model of interpersonal communication, where each letter stands for one of the six principles of effective communication. (1) *Identify and manage emotions.* Most people think of themselves as rational human beings who make decisions based on logic and rationality. Yet when things go wrong the emotions kick in and the logic is thrown out of the window. People become unreasonable and uncooperative because the emotional brain (limbic system) has overridden the rational thinking areas of the brain. A well-trained officer should be trained to diffuse the emotions so that effective communication can take place. Empathizing with and acknowledging a person's concerns and feelings make the person feel that the officer is trying to help, which reduces emotional tension. This show of concern does not mean that the officer agrees that these concerns are legitimate. Subsequently, the officer should ask questions because it forces people to pause and think. The officer should paraphrase to check for understanding and to correct any confusion. (2) *Master the story.* Relying on internal attribution can be dangerous, as it encourages impulsive and rash conclusions and suppresses empathy, thus jeopardizing communication. However, seeing things from another person's perspective is important because it requires officers to suspend their assumptions and listen carefully to understand and master the story, which improves communication. (3) *Promote positive behavior.* People have an innate need to feel safe and control their lives. When people feel threatened or controlled, they act negatively by becoming aggressive. Officers can help people feel safe by reducing uncertainty by educating them about their decisions, actions, the rest of the process, and what to expect. The whole process can be intimidating for those who have never been exposed to the criminal justice system. Most people know little about the policies, procedures, and laws that most officers take for granted. In addition, officers should separate problems from people. Rather than questioning or attacking someone's motives or intent, which at best can only be a guess, the officer should focus on the person's objective conduct. For example, "Were you on your cell phone when you ran the stop sign and hit the car?" Such behavior from the officer will be more threatening to a person's self-esteem or sense of control, and is more likely to produce uncooperative behavior resulting in failed communication. (4) *Achieve rapport.* Instead of reacting impulsively to difficult situations, officers should provide a calming effect by not striking back to rude and uncooperative people. Such positive reinforcement will break down the barrier and allow for people to become more communicative with the officer. (5) *Control your response.* Officers should never lose control of their response, despite all distractions that may arise from uncooperative citizens. Very often, strong emotions may cloud the real issues, but an officer should be able to sift through these emotions and identify the issues and respond to them objectively. An officer needs to learn to respond to the issue.

Communication Channels

Among the different channels of communication are face-to-face, videoconferencing, telephone, e-mail, and memos or letter writing (Dunham, 1984; Lewis et al., 2001). The speed of the flow of communication through these channels can often be very slow, which makes it a critical factor in a service industry. Research has shown that each channel has a different capacity to convey information, often termed as *channel richness.* The hierarchy of channel richness is determined by three characteristics: (1) the ability to handle multiple cues simultaneously; (2) the ability to facilitate rapid, two-way feedback; and (3) the ability to establish a personal focus for the communication.

> *Face-to-face* is the richest medium of communication because it allows direct experience of multiple information cues, immediate feedback, and personal focus. Senders can provide instant clarification to any ambiguous information until a common understanding is reached.
>
> *Videoconferencing* is the next in richness because it does not provide all forms of nonverbal cues. Some of the cues get lost during the electronic focus of the camera.
>
> *Telephone conversations* are next in the richness hierarchy because they do not allow personal contact, and hence, most of the nonverbal cues are missing. However, both videoconferencing and the telephone allow the receiver to get instant clarification.
>
> *E-mail* has gained increasing popularity as a communication channel because of its low cost and convenience. However, e-mail messages lack both verbal and nonverbal cues, thus increasing the chances for misunderstandings.
>
> *Written letters* and *memos* can be personally focused, but they convey only the cues written on paper and are often slow to provide feedback; thus, they are lower in the channel richness hierarchy. The lowest on this hierarchy would be the impersonal written media, including fliers and bulletins, which are general in nature and do not focus on a single receiver, lack most cues, and do not permit feedback.

Though there is a channel richness hierarchy, it is important to understand that each communication channel has advantages and disadvantages, making them appropriate for different circumstances. For example, face-to-face communication is rich in context but may be very expensive in terms of cost and time to bring all parties together. On the other hand, e-mail is extremely inexpensive but does not have the ability to handle multiple cues simultaneously; does not facilitate rapid, two-way feedback; and is low in its ability to establish a personal focus for the communication.

As general advice to managers and administrators in choosing the appropriate communication medium, it is suggested that they must select a rich channel for effective communication of nonroutine and complicated messages. *Nonroutine communication* tends to concern new events and is generally ambiguous, involving greater potential for misunderstanding. Managers should use multiple communication media for important and complex messages, to ensure the full gist is understood by the receiver; for example, managers could use both formal announcements in staff meetings as well as memo distribution to all employees. In contrast, *routine communications* are typically embedded in some past context or experience that managers and administrators already agree on and understand, making them simpler. Therefore, routine messages can be efficiently communicated through a channel that is lower in richness. Think here of the police officer who uses 10 codes to communicate with the police dispatcher. When the communication is official and a permanent record needs to be maintained, written communication is more appropriate. Written communication of all events and interactions with the public or clients is mandatory in criminal justice, as noted in the common saying among criminal justice professionals, "If it's not in writing, it didn't happen." The key to this entire discussion is to select a channel to fit the message.

Organizational Communication

Communication within an organization can be effective when both the formal and informal organizational channels of communication are supportive. These channels can be supplemented by the managers with the use of informal channels to gather and disseminate information.

Formal Communication

The *formal communication network* is mirrored in the chain of command in an organization. The primary forms of communication flow are vertical (both downward and upward) and horizontal (Daft & Steers, 1986). To promote speedier exchange of information, learning organizations emphasize horizontal communication between workers across departments and levels. Electronic communication such as e-mail and instant messaging has made it easier for information to flow in all directions.

In *vertical communication*, there is an exchange of information between different levels in an organization. The communication flows upward or downward through the chain of command. Communication in corrections flows down the chain of command from the warden through the assistant wardens of operations and programs to the majors, lieutenants, sergeants, and so forth until reaching the correctional officers working with the inmates. Figure 8.2 illustrates the communication flow in the security division of a prison. The assistant warden of operations would also use downward communication with the various directors and other personnel under his or her command.

The messages and information sent by the senior management to their subordinates comprises *downward communication*. Since it is neither required nor possible for managers to communicate everything that happens within an organization, an important managerial decision is made regarding what information they need to communicate downward (Clampitt, DeKoch, & Cashman, 2000). To facilitate the day-to-day smooth functioning of the agency, downward communication in an organization typically would be composed of the following:

1. One of the important tasks of management is to communicate the big picture and information about specific targets and direction for lower levels as new strategies and goals are formulated. For example, police chiefs may want to communicate to all of their officers the big picture of the changed environment and the new initiatives to be taken to fight terrorism.

2. To facilitate implementation of modified goals and strategies, the management needs to communicate directives on how specific tasks should be done, along with the rationale for why these tasks need to occur.

3. At greater levels of specificity, the management needs to provide policies, rules, regulations, and benefits accompanying each task.

4. Management needs to provide directives on how the performance will be evaluated at the end of each task. This will form the feedback on the performance of individuals and, collectively, the performance of the departments.

5. To have workers attain their targets and fulfill the company's vision and mission, the management must communicate motivating statements to workers on a continuous basis. Sergeants have to ensure that their officers go home safely at the end of the day and continue to stay motivated to help fight crime.

The common methods of downward communication are through face-to-face addressing, speeches using the internal audio-visual media, messages in company newsletters or individual leaflets, e-mails, bulletin boards, and company manuals (London, 1999). All of these methods are typically one-way communications, as they do not encourage feedback. Another unfavorable factor that impacts this type of communication is the number of levels that the information needs to travel to reach all of the employees. Approximately 25% of information is typically lost each time it is passed from one person to the next (Lewis et al., 2001). Such information loss cannot be avoided in downward communication, though it can be reduced substantially by following the steps of effective communication described later.

Messages that flow from lower to higher levels in an organizational hierarchy are termed *upward communication*. Typically, such communication allows feedback on management initiatives or report progress, and permits employees to air their grievances (Frese, Teng, & Wijnen, 1999; Glauser, 1984; Love, 1998; Lurie, 1999), all of which is a reflection of a healthy and progressive organization.

Figure 8.2   Illustration of Downward Communication in a Correctional Facility

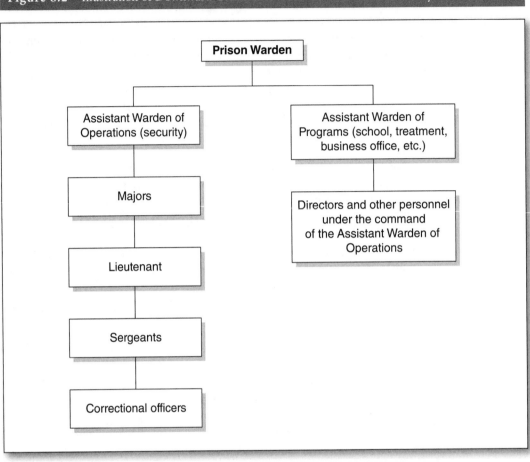

Organizations must facilitate upward communication, as it provides them an opportunity to benefit from ideas and inputs from people at all levels and gives them an understanding of the general environment at the lower level. Progressive organizations provide suggestion boxes, open-door policies, employee surveys, and opinion polls, as well as town hall kinds of face-to-face meetings between workers and upper management, to allow undistorted information to reach them. The upper-level managers are responsible for responding to messages from lower-level employees to let them know that their comments and suggestions are valued. In contrast, there are also organizations where managers are unprepared to hear employee problems, and all forms of upward communication airing grievances are quelled. The general environment is one of mistrust in such companies.

Interdependence between different functions and departments creates the need to communicate between peers and coworkers within and across departments, which is called *horizontal communication* (Daft & Marcic, 2004). The need for this form of lateral or diagonal exchange of messages may be driven by the need to coordinate activities, seek support of members, or simply share information among members within the same department or with members in other departments. Horizontal communication is greatly valued in learning organizations, which are based on little hierarchy and a culture that promotes participation and teamwork. The attention in these organizations is on problem solving and continuous modification of the process to promote flexibility and adaptability. Crossjurisdictional and crossdisciplinary events have become more significant in the law enforcement field in recent years. Within this changing context, Mulholland (2004) discusses the need to develop an effective means for real-time communication among various law-enforcing agencies at a crime scene. Bayless (2004) discusses the measures undertaken by Los Angeles to counter the threats of terrorism, which suggests the effective tactics of communicating among local, state, and federal operations. One of the most important elements of this communication strategy is the use of high-speed communication technology to rapidly contact people in times of crisis (Bayless, 2004). Universities around the United States have implemented emergency warning systems to alert faculty, staff, and students of potentially dangerous situations as a result of the recent school shootings on college campuses (Zalud, 2004). Emergency warnings are sent across e-mail systems, by cell phone, by text message, and through landline telephones to all affected parties. This real-time, horizontal communication pattern allows for better coordination of emergency services and a safer environment for the employees and students.

Communication in certain groups takes place in specific recurring patterns, which develops relationships among people over time, creating what are termed *communication networks* (George & Jones, 2002; Rogers & Rogers, 1976). If the members differ in ranking, then those with higher ranking are likely to dominate the communication network. The size of this formal or informal group will impact the effectiveness of communication within the network. Therefore, communication networks will be highly complex in a 15-member group, unlike in a 5-member group. There are special types of horizontal communications, which are classified as the wheel, the chain, the circle, and the all-channel network (George & Jones, 2002).

- The *wheel network* is a centralized network where team members do not communicate directly with one another but must report to one individual who is the sole sender of messages to other group members. Essentially, all information flows to and from this central member. Such networks are very effective when group members work independently, but group performance is determined by summing up the performance of the members of the group. For example, groups of sales representatives have little need to communicate directly with one another, but must communicate with the formal or informal leader of the group. These networks would work well in team sports such as swimming, track, or golf, where the coach communicates and coordinates with the entire team, and the team members can perform their tasks with minimal direct communication with the rest of the team. The wheel network can also be seen in prison systems. A central control booth regulates the entire prison building. All communication must pass through the person operating the control booth, whether it be a request to open a cell door or information concerning the movement of an inmate from one place to another. The officers in the correctional units operate independent of one another within each unit but are each dependent on the control booth to be in command of the facility. In another example, the dispatcher of the local sheriff's office performs wheel network communications. The sheriff's deputies work independent of one another while constantly maintaining contact with the dispatcher at a central location.

- A *chain network* is common when there is sequential task interdependence, which has no hierarchical implications. In such networks, there is a predetermined communication flow with members communicating with individuals on either side of them in the chain. One can see such networks on a company shop floor that has an assembly-line mode of manufacturing. Sometimes, chain networks may support hierarchical positioning within a group. For example, in a sit-down restaurant there is a network chain from the manager to the head chef, the sous chef, wait staff, busser, and cleaning people. Communication within this group essentially goes up and down the hierarchy. Likewise, in a juvenile facility, workers pass cases from one to another with little difficulty. Each worker has a specific task, which, once completed, leads the case to the next worker. The intake officer will perform the duties necessary to process a child into the facility. Once these duties are completed, the intake officer will pass the case to the court officer for preparation. The court officer handles the initial jurisdictional, adjudication, and disposition hearings. After disposition is ordered, the court officer will send the file to a probation officer who will ensure that the court's orders are carried out. If there is a need for institutionalization, the probation officer will communicate with the treatment provider and will monitor the case with a caseworker inside the treatment facility. All communication is done by phone and through record keeping in the child's case file.

- *Circle networks* occur within groups whose members are similar on some dimension, such as an area of expertise, location of offices, sitting arrangements during meetings, and the like. For example, within a university setting, the professors within a department who share similar expertise communicate with one another. These networks are fairly decentralized. Specialties in criminal justice operate in the same fashion. Those officers working in community-oriented policing communicate and coordinate with one another on programming, innovative ideas, and problems or concerns they discover in the area they patrol. Probation officers working with sex offenders hold staffing meetings as well as communicate informally about cases and potential treatment issues or possibilities on a regular basis. Circle networks work well in specialized units within criminal justice agencies.

- *All-channel networks* are least centralized and create the possibility for maximum participation of all members in the group. They are typically found in organizations or subgroups involved in complex work premised on reciprocal task interdependence, which requires every group member to communicate with every other group member. For example, within a hospital, the emergency room personnel would support an all-channel network; a new product team may support an all-channel network within a company; and a special operations task force, such as a special weapons and tactics (SWAT) team, would support an all-channel network in policing. These networks work well in team-oriented sports such as basketball, ice hockey, soccer, and football that require a high degree of member coordination.

No single network will prove effective in all situations. If the wheel network is overused because it is low in cost, where superiors instruct subordinates, then there may be dissatisfaction among the group members. These group members may have very low motivation to contribute to the group's overall effectiveness. Furthermore, teams should match the network type with their goals and tasks for high communication performance. If the problems are simple and the tasks require little member interdependence, then the wheel network will work best. An all-channel network in such a situation would be highly inefficient. Team members will feel bored with meetings and consider such meetings a waste of time. Moreover, all-channel networks have higher labor cost, as they involve all team members at all times.

Formal communication is generally slower. There is a strong belief among many (see In the News 2.2 in Chapter 2) that the 9/11 terrorist attacks on the United States could have been prevented if the information had flowed faster through the formal channels involving various law enforcement agencies. Despite the loosely connected information exchange, formalized communication networks play some crucial roles. In large organizations, they allow for better coordination of tasks that may be spread out among various agencies and functions. By reducing miscommunication, they cut down duplication of work and eliminate unnecessary waste. However, in the real world if one were to examine the communication in a large police department, one would find it hard to strictly match it with any of the methods described here. People are not typically segregated by cubicles or partitions. Normally, there are police officers of different ranks, complainants, and other staff interacting with one another in the hallway, seated, standing, or moving about in different directions. Therefore, the formal decision making follows the direction prescribed by these formal channels, but communication is a lot more loosely connected to social relationships. In addition, the rapidly changing information technology is altering information sharing and communication strategies.

Informal Communication

Information that flows outside the formally authorized channels and does not adhere to the hierarchy of authority is called *informal communication*. Such communication tends to connect everyone in the organization. Interpersonal social interactions are inevitable in the workplace, and these form the basis for informal communications. Two types of informal channels used in many organizations (Daft & Marcic, 2004) are described next.

Management by Wandering Around

Many executives mingle and talk directly with employees when they are walking through the company or across the shop floor, thus avoiding the vertical and horizontal chains of command (Peters & Waterman, 1982). By developing open communication with employees through such informal means, these executives learn more about their departments, divisions, and organizations. Most executives supplement the information gathered through formal channels with information from informal channels. In the working of large police departments, a lot of informal communication takes place in the hallways, at water coolers, in the washrooms, on the elevators, in the locker rooms, and so forth.

The Grapevine

Another form of informal communication takes place typically in person-to-person networks of employees, which are not officially endorsed by the organization (Davis & Newstrom, 1985). Also known as spontaneous communication, these channels are opportunistic and informal, and evolve from social relationships that develop within an organization. Close proximity, similarities in work activities, common interests, and shared values and social characteristics all promote informal communication among individuals. The grapevine cuts across all vertical and horizontal chains of command and links employees in all directions, irrespective of their formal position within the company. It disseminates information much faster than do the formal channels. Though the grapevine exists at all times, it can become a dominant communication channel when the formal channels are ineffective or closed. Typically, during greater uncertainty created by changes within an organization, sagging economic conditions, introduction of new technology, or changes in senior positions, the grapevine tends to be more active. Research shows that 80% of grapevine communication pertains to business-related subject matters, with 70% to 90% accuracy (Simmons, 1985). Using a survey to collect data from 22,000 shift workers in different industries, Ettorre (1997) discovered that 55% of workers get most of their information from the grapevine.

The very nature of the informal communication taking place among members results in certain distortion of information, based on individual understanding and renarrating it afterward. Such distorted information can create misunderstandings among employees. The grapevine can be harmful to an organization when wrong information is disseminated to group members. Moreover, the grapevine can be a deterrent to the enforcement of the supervisory authority because informal communication networks introduce their own set of power relations. The rumor mill can go into overdrive, creating difficult situations for administrators and the people they serve.

Barriers to Effective Communication

Since most people get into the act of communication without conscious thought or effort, they typically believe communication is simple. However, communication is complex, with innumerable opportunities for making an error in sending or receiving messages. Anything that interferes with a clear communication process is often termed *noise* or *barriers*. These barriers to effective communication may occur at various points in the process of communication and can be broadly classified as individual barriers and organizational barriers.

Individual barriers to communication. These barriers originate from the use of jargon, the use of incorrect channel or medium of communication, filtering and information distortion, a lack of feedback or inappropriate feedback, and poor listening (Daft & Marcic, 2004; George & Jones, 2002). The *use of jargon* may often cause miscommunication, especially when the message is received by someone outside of the profession. Similarly, semantics can often be confusing because of the diverse interpretations of the same word. It has been found that on average each word in the English language has 28 different definitions (Stoner & Freeman, 1989), which implies that the sender must be extremely careful to choose the words that will accurately encode the intended ideas. Errors in communication may occur because of the *use of an incorrect channel* or medium. Poor handwriting, a poor telephone connection, and so forth are all examples of bad channels or mediums. As discussed earlier, channels of communication can be placed on a hierarchy of richness. Great consideration should be given to choosing the appropriate channel of communication to match the nature of the message to reduce the chances of communication errors. *Filtering* occurs when the sender does not send the entire message. Part of the message may be withheld by the sender who thinks that the receiver does not need the entire information. Sometimes, the negative part of the information may be filtered because of the fear of unfavorable reaction. Other times, information distortion or alteration may be done deliberately by the senders to serve their interests at the expense of the organization's goals. Filtering may also occur when there are too many intermediaries through whom information has to travel. By the time the message reaches the intended receiver, it may be distorted. This distortion can be demonstrated by initiating a message that passes through several students. By the time it reaches back to the person who had initiated the message, it is completely different from what was originally said. Filtering and information distortion can be minimized by providing strict guidelines of communication, accompanied by good training so that workers know what, when, and how to communicate. Establishing trust along with efforts to solve problems and not punish people will also help reduce distortion of information. Organizations that have adopted the service quality philosophy in the workplace are more likely to encourage better communication. These organizations identify the root cause of the problem rather than dealing with only the symptom, and then try to improve the process. In such progressive, service-oriented organizations, workers know that when they communicate a problem to their superiors, they will not be punished, which discourages filtering and distortion of information. To promote good communication and eliminate as much noise as possible, managers should keep in mind the following tips:

- Unless the message is clear in the person's mind regarding what the person wants to say, chances are low that the sender will be able to communicate the idea effectively to others.
- Individuals should convey the idea or information in a very direct manner, encoding it in symbols or language that the receiver will understand. For example, use of jargon or specialized terminology can often confuse the message to a receiver outside the profession. *Policese* works well when police are communicating with one another. But unless a receiver is familiar with the specialized language of policing and with the 10 codes, the receiver is unlikely to understand what the police officer is communicating. Using nonverbal cues is another way to support the message.
- Choose the medium that is generally used to communicate with this group of people. However, keep in mind that more complicated and nonroutine messages should be communicated using a richer medium. Also, use informal channels to complement the gathering and dissemination of information.
- Always state the message in a manner that forces the receiver to provide feedback. Such feedback provides a good measure of how well the message was received and

interpreted by the receiver, suggesting that two-way communication is a significantly better form of communication than one-way.

- Adopting a service quality approach in the organization will promote a climate of trust and openness. It focuses on identifying the root cause and not acting on the symptom. Employees report symptoms; hence, they should not be punished but encouraged to help identify the root cause. Such an approach helps build trust, promotes communication, and improves the service delivery process.

- Be a good listener, and watch for nonverbal cues. Train subordinates to do the same. As an example, investigators are keen on watching for nonverbal cues when interrogating a suspect.

- Individuals from one culture should pay attention to culture differences when communicating with people from other cultures.

- As mentioned earlier, in the process of communication, feedback is important because it confirms that the message has been received and properly understood. Sometimes, feedback may not be provided because it may be making people feel uncomfortable, or it may be withheld deliberately by the receiver to serve personal interests at the expense of the organization's goals. In other instances, the receivers may be inconsistent in their verbal and nonverbal feedback. When the receiver either fails to provide feedback or provides an inappropriate or inconsistent feedback, it becomes uncertain whether the message was received the way it was intended by the sender, resulting in the breakdown of communication. Certain principles that need to be observed in providing effective feedback are as follows: (a) Feedback should be specific rather than general, including specific examples elaborating on what is being recommended. It should focus on things that the sender can control; (b) feedback should be given when the receiver appears ready to accept it; (c) do not provide feedback when the receiver is angry or upset; (d) feedback should focus on the behavior or act that can be changed rather than on the person; and (e) before sending the feedback, the sender should put himself or herself in the receiver's shoes to understand and experience the feedback the sender is about to provide.

- Research and experience show that employees and customers are important sources of information. Therefore, an important tool of managerial communication is *listening,* both to employees and to customers, which forms an important link in the communication process model. Listening involves the skill of grasping both the verbal and nonverbal components to interpret the message fully. Only then can the manager respond appropriately. It is found that about 75% of effective communication is listening, although most people spend only 30% to 40% of their time listening, which leads to many communication errors (Nichols, 1995). The following are guidelines to becoming an effective listener (Kiechel, 1987): (a) Do not concentrate on the response, but focus on what is being said by looking at the sender and not interrupting; (b) focus on understanding what is being heard and try to sense the sender's feelings; (c) look for both verbal and nonverbal content of messages and try to clarify when they are conflicting. Do not be afraid to ask questions to clarify and understand the message; (d) rephrase key points to ensure that the message was heard and understood in the way the sender intended; and (e) even though there may not be agreement with the sender's message, do not distract the sender by looking at a wristwatch, tapping fingers on a table, or the like.

Organizational barriers to communication. These barriers to communication are embedded in individual insensitivity to cultural diversity within a company and a general organizational culture of mistrust. Every organization is embedded in a culture. Within this overarching umbrella of organizational culture is the cultural diversity within an organization along with cultural sensitivity of the employees. Individuals are entrenched in language, religion, beliefs, and social values, all of which collectively define their culture. These cultural differences shape the filters that individuals use in their day-to-day communication. Encoding and decoding the sender's message or the receiver's feedback message can be potential sources for communication errors. The errors may occur because knowledge and culture act as filters that create noise when translating the symbols to meaning, causing the communication to break down. The greater the cultural differences are among employees, suppliers, and customers, the greater will be the challenges in crosscultural communication. Ethnocentrism, or the tendency to consider one's culture and its values as being superior to others, creates problems in communication. Therefore, the greater the difference between the cultures of the sender and the receiver, the greater is the probability of miscommunication. Most people have experienced the difficulty of communicating with people who do not speak the same language. Besides different languages, the linguistic style can introduce noise. Linguistic style is the person's way of speaking, including tone of voice, volume, speed, use of words, and so forth, all of which are sources of potential misunderstandings in crosscultural communication.

In the United States, immigration accounted for a major share of the increase in the labor force in the 1990s. The migrant workers are expected to provide a growing share of the workforce in the 21st century. By the year 2020, it is estimated that Asian Americans, African Americans, and Hispanics will comprise more than 35% of the U.S. population and will form 30% of the U.S. workforce. Also by the year 2020, it is estimated that women will comprise 50% of the U.S. workforce. The growing diversity of the U.S. population is bringing challenges for criminal justice agencies to be culturally sensitive in understanding, communicating with, and serving their diverse customer base effectively, as discussed in Chapter 4. Furthermore, in the 21st century, criminal justice agencies will have to learn to work with agencies in other parts of the world because the planning of terrorist activities may be done in one country or a nexus of countries. In this new world order, where society must deal with global terror, it is important for law enforcement agencies and other criminal justice organizations to learn the skills of communicating effectively with parallel agencies in other parts of the world. This growing interdependence means that criminal justice professionals will have to learn to cross lines of time, culture, and geography to be successful. Many criminal justice professionals today need to know a second and third language and develop crosscultural understanding. Firsthand learning about other cultures can be experienced by traveling and staying abroad, by inviting people from other countries to the policing or corrections agency to do joint training, or through formal training by experts from other cultures. The mind-set needed by criminal justice professionals is to expect the unexpected and be prepared for constant change.

Before engaging in work-related discussions, individuals have a need for social trust. In some companies, the organizational culture promotes trust and communication, while in many others it may stifle communication by creating distrust. A lack of trust causes defensive tactics among the communicating entities, motivating the receiver to spend much energy identifying the hidden meanings in the sender's message. Therefore, it is extremely important to nurture and reinforce trust and honesty in the workplace environment, which eases communication and reduces the likelihood of miscommunication. Managers who spend time walking around and directly communicating across different levels tend to foster greater trust among employees.

When the senior management is not careful in selecting and screening the information that needs to be shared with employees, it can cause information overload. Too much exchange of information can stifle communication by choking the channels and overloading the employees with more information than they can process. Such excess information leads to a failure to process some of the important information, processing information incorrectly, delaying the information processing, and lowering the quality of information processing.

On the other hand, when people are not informed about matters that have the potential to affect them personally, the grapevine as an informal communication channel takes root within the organization. Typically, the grapevine spreads information among members when they are not informed. Once started, the grapevine spreads rapidly and is hard to control, as noted earlier in the chapter. To prevent inaccurate information from spreading, organizations need to be in constant touch with their employees. They need to provide them with up-to-date, accurate information on issues important to workers and try to keep things more transparent and easily accessible. Agencies where information is deliberately withheld on the belief that "information is power" are most likely to have grapevines filling the void left by official information. However, when agencies are transparent and information can be easily accessed by any member of the organization, grapevines find it hard to establish roots.

Communication in a Learning Organization

In the past, organizational hierarchies were developed in part to move information up and down the system, working with the assumption that key ideas and decisions originated at the top and were channeled downward. Most for-profit companies today assume that ideas can emerge from everyone, and the role of the manager is to facilitate open channels of communication to allow ideas, information, and knowledge to flow throughout the organization. Criminal justice agencies have been slow to realize this but are making efforts to change the cumbersome communication channels found in the traditional organizational structures. In addition, an emphasis on knowledge management and information sharing has led to the flattening of organizational structures, resulting in greater empowerment and involvement of employees, which promotes open communication. In such progressive organizations, information travels throughout the company, cutting through the functional and hierarchical levels. This form of open communication is essential for building trust and commitment to promoting common goals between groups and teams that are important components of learning organizations. Feedback is an essential component of open communication because it helps individuals and the organization to learn and improve. Feedback can be received from supervisors, coworkers, customers, suppliers, members of partner organizations, and society. Furthermore, progressive criminal justice agencies have installed the latest information technology to allow fast movement of information within the organization. As discussed in In the News 8.2, information technology keeps everyone informed, allowing these agencies to provide rapid response to any emergency situation.

In the News 8.2
Communicating Through Crisis

Terrorism is no longer reserved for foreign countries. It is now a reality in the United States of America, spawned by the atrocities that occurred on September 11th. Nor is the threat of terrorism confined to New York or Washington, D.C. The threat spans coasts and traverses county lines.

As one of the largest metropolitan areas in the United States, Los Angeles has undertaken measures to prepare itself for this threat. These measures have included working on the state and federal level to reassess procedures and examining the effectiveness of current plans and operations. Self-assessment such as this has become commonplace in law enforcement agencies throughout America.

Yet, with all of these efforts and increased awareness, one constant overlaps all homeland security efforts. That constant is communication. Communication is perhaps the most essential element of effective law enforcement in the war on terror.

One of the most effective tactics for communicating in a crisis—such as a terrorist attack—utilizes technology known as high-speed communication. This technology enables law enforcement agencies to rapidly contact as many people as necessary in a time of crisis. Within minutes, important messages are delivered to neighborhoods, public officials, business districts and countless other individuals and groups. In essence, notification technology serves as a communication ladder, providing links between law enforcement officials and important target audiences from the ground up.

In the immediate aftermath of a terrorist incident, the police or sheriff's department is consumed with activity. A normally quiet precinct or department instantly becomes the communication hub for an entire city, potentially on the brink of chaos. In the early stages, gathering accurate information is critical. However, precisely interpreting that information and efficiently disseminating it to the public and private sectors is without a doubt the most important step in communicating during a crisis. Law enforcement command staff must take time to define their specific audiences and the messages that need to reach those individuals or groups.

The first task at hand is intelligence gathering: What has happened? Who has been affected? Where did the incident or attack take place? Are people or property still in danger? How much time is there? Being thorough on the front end, anticipating problems and targeting essential audiences will save time and energy. Once these questions have been asked and answered, officers can then begin the process of notifying the community at large.

The Technology

Given the unpredictable nature of terrorist attacks and the potential for significant loss of life and property damage, high-speed notification technology is one of law enforcement's greatest allies. A single dispatcher can reach literally thousands of people in a matter of minutes. It is proven technology: Law enforcement agencies, military bases, Fortune 500 companies and the highest levels of

(Continued)

(Continued)

national government have high-speed notification systems operational 24 hours a day. With this technology, recipients can receive time-sensitive, crucial messages on cell phones, by e-mail, pagers, fax and landline telephones.

The Los Angeles County Sheriff's Department utilizes a high-speed notification system developed by DCC (Dialogic Communications Corporation) called "The Communicator." The Los Angeles County Sheriff's Department has used it in numerous scenarios, such as bank robberies, child abductions/disappearances and severe weather conditions. However, after September 2001, the department began thinking of situations in which high-speed notification might be required to enhance communication in homeland security efforts.

Essentially, high-speed notification functions like a phone tree, without expending the time and energy of valuable human resources. The software is designed to retain an unlimited contact list, which should be updated consistently to ensure accuracy. The list can be manipulated from a single personal computer. Dispatchers pre-record, or record in real time, voice and text messages that can be distributed to a designated contact list with a click of the mouse. The message is sent with lightning speed, arriving via each contact's preferred form of communication in minutes.

Through an innovative GIS mapping interface, the high-speed notification software can alert any designated audience or targeted geographic area—a specific city street, a block of a downtown business district, or a tri-county area, for example. The mapping interface can be extremely beneficial when the threat may only occur in one specific area, or if different messages are required for different audiences in different locations.

Another important function, which pertains specifically to first responders, is the "status report" feature. This allows the dispatcher to know who has responded to his or her call for assistance and when they will arrive. "The Communicator" software may also be programmed to continue calling first responders until a designated number of contacts has been made. Once that threshold has been reached, the system discontinues calling. This avoids the problem of unneeded personnel arriving on the scene and confusing relief efforts.

Because databases can and should be built before an attack, law enforcement agencies can take pains up front to anticipate every possible audience they might need to reach. If this important step is taken, then in the event of an actual emergency, a dispatcher can record alerts and messages immediately after the scope of the attack has been determined and deliver it without hesitation to the appropriate recipients.

This proactive measure of pre-built databases brings up a particularly crucial point: Know your audiences. Discuss each audience internally in your agency one by one. How quickly will each one need to know that an attack has occurred? Who inside the agency should record the message? Will certain types of terrorist attacks make some citizens more vulnerable than others?

Once a specific group of contacts has been identified, spend time discussing the best way to communicate with each. For example, the technology could be used to alert thousands of people that the water supply has been contaminated or that a bomb has been detonated in a downtown shopping district. Thought should be given to how that message should be delivered to avoid a stampede of citizens into or out of the affected area. Also, prioritize the calls before a disaster occurs. If the water supply has been contaminated, should the water department or the affected neighborhoods be contacted first?

Following is a breakout of specific target groups that will likely appear on every law enforcement agency's contact database.

First-Response Teams

If public safety officials learned but one thing from September 11th, it was that response time and coordination among responders are truly the make-or-break factors. Firefighters, law enforcement officers and EMS units mobilized quickly and worked together in fluid precision. As a result, lives were saved.

First-response teams will generally be the first audience contacted in the event of a terrorist attack. These professionals are first on the scene, not only to provide medical attention and emergency response, but also to stabilize the inevitable panic that ensues following a violent episode. That is why it is so important to communicate with these men and women quickly and accurately.

With a high-speed notification system in place, these responders are better equipped to handle the situation once they arrive at the incident scene. Even a small amount of incident-specific information can greatly enhance their level of success. For example, if terrorists attacked a certain neighborhood by using a chemical weapon, the high-speed notification system would deliver a first-response message briefing teams about location, the toxicity of the substance and what HAZMAT equipment will be required to control the spread of the chemical.

High-speed notification systems also provide feedback features that record individual responses, such as fit-for-duty status and ETAs for assembling and rotating personnel. This can also be applied to a typical call-out procedure, whether summoning on-duty or off-duty personnel.

Cross-Jurisdictional

When terror strikes, it is not one agency's problem. Events of great magnitude require assistance at many levels of public safety, including local police departments and federal agencies. Because each of these groups has some degree of responsibility for the public, clear initial communication is an absolute must to avoid sending conflicting messages or premature information. In Los Angeles, for example, the sheriff's department along with the Los Angeles Police Department, the FBI and other public safety departments have formed the Terrorism Early Warning Task Force. This consortium consists of leaders from each law enforcement branch who have the authority to make decisions on behalf of their organization. The quick and accurate sharing of information is critical with this kind of structure.

High-speed notification can also be employed to alert law enforcement agencies on the outskirts of the disaster. This can potentially thwart massive traffic congestion or act as a call for more qualified manpower. In some cases, the notification may alert outlying officials that the perpetrators of an attack were seen leaving the scene in a specific vehicle. In any case, quick communication with surrounding jurisdictions could prove invaluable.

Government Officials

The goal of a terrorist attack is to create chaos. Chaos often occurs when appropriate groups are not aware of all of the facts and begin to speculate. It is important that they get reliable information, and quickly, in the event of an attack to minimize the spread of confusion.

Government officials (local, state and federal) have an extremely important role to play in the event of an attack of this nature. One, the public needs to know that leaders are in place and managing the crisis. Two, government officials can convincingly and authoritatively deliver messages that convey factual information to various audiences. When preparing for or responding to terrorist activity, government

(Continued)

(Continued)

officials have a responsibility to address and educate the public in a balanced and responsible manner. Using a high-speed notification system, law enforcement agencies can contact a wide range of important government officials and city leaders and immediately inform them of the situation's status. Communicating facts to these officials on a state and national level will allow them to knowledgeably address the public and the news media, which is critical to preventing rumor, panic and confusion.

Media

The news media play one of the most vital roles in our country when dealing with issues of terror and homeland security. Television, in particular, is where people turn to learn about an impending crisis or its aftermath. For that reason, law enforcement must communicate carefully with news outlets to ensure that facts are what is reported, not speculation. Keeping the media informed will help prevent unnecessary panic.

High-speed notification systems, such as "The Communicator," can provide the media with up-to-the-minute information with a built-in bulletin board feature. Through this automated system, reporters can simply call a designated number to receive recorded information about the situation at hand. Not only does this help communicate relevant facts to the media, but it also frees up valuable personnel who otherwise would be inundated with media inquiries. By utilizing high-speed notification, law enforcement agencies can enhance their ability to control the flow of information, ensuring that facts are being reported in a time frame that is considerate of journalists' deadlines.

General Public

Various messages may need to be delivered to the public in a terrorist attack, including evacuation procedures, status of survivors, shelter locations, existing threats and hospital availability. Most likely, the quantity of information that must reach different groups or people will seemingly expand with each passing hour.

An explosion occurs in a residential district, for example, and that explosion triggers a massive fire. The high-speed notification system would be activated. A qualified dispatcher would send a message informing residents in the immediate vicinity of the fire and of specific evacuation procedures, such as which route to take and which areas to avoid. The law enforcement agency would then use the GIS feature to deliver messages, moving out from the fire, to residents and business owners, until all segments of the general public that could potentially be affected by the blaze have been notified and given instructions.

Internal Considerations

As with all technology, it is important to have competent, trained individuals in place to operate it. As it relates to high-speed notification, the dispatcher or person operating the system must possess, above all else, great judgment and the ability to regroup in a moment's notice. Due to the quantity of information being processed, these dispatchers must have a complete understanding of the intelligence arena and the ability to decipher what is real or critical and what is not. Personnel using the high-speed notification technology must have access to technical support, should issues arise.

Once a person or team is in place, then it is time to plan the communication strategy, as discussed in this article—with attention to identifying key target audiences, managing contact data and pre-recording message scenarios. But most important, planning should include test call-outs. A system that remains idle and is only used when a disaster takes place is a system that is subject to error. Work out glitches and technical issues beforehand, then test it every month or use the technology for routine public information efforts, such as closed streets or utility problems.

Technology Website Available to Law Enforcement

The National Sheriffs' Association and the other premier law enforcement associations have come together in a collaborative effort to address the needs for technology standards. Sheriff Ted Kamatchus, NSA 3rd Vice President, and Sheriff Craig Webre, NSA 4th Vice President, represent NSA on the project. NSA Training Director Fred Wilson is the staff coordinator.

Through this collaborative effort, a website with information and links to help law enforcement agencies with technology issues has been developed: www.leitsc.org.

With the help of the U.S. Department of justice, NSA and other law enforcement associations are taking a probing look at how law enforcement agencies are operating with scarce or fewer resources. Surveys are being sent to selected sheriffs asking them to address the issues and solutions related to this matter. Sheriffs and chiefs will then be asked to attend a summit to share successes and promising practices. When the comments from the summit are recorded and tabulated, they will be included in a publication that will allow this information to be shared nationally.

Once the audiences are identified, individuals in charge of operating the high-speed notification system must input the data and maintain an accurate database. With new residents arriving into metropolitan areas daily and businesses opening and closing, managing the audience information is a step that cannot be overlooked when developing a communication plan for terrorist attacks. Stay in contact with neighborhood associations and chambers of commerce. Make your network proactive and visible to the public, so that people are educated about the importance of the notification technology.

Once a department has a high-speed notification system and communication strategy in place, it is vital that the individuals operating the technology continue to learn, master and incorporate new developing technologies and applications. For example, DCC offers interactive training workshops taught by experts in the high-speed notification field. Technology is always evolving, and it's important to learn and grow with it.

Conclusion

Terrorism is a very real threat to our society—today and for many years to come. As law enforcement agencies strengthen their homeland security programs in response to that threat, they must also understand the role of communication in controlling chaos and providing the general public with potentially life-saving instruction. And the ability to simultaneously send time-sensitive, critical messages to thousands of individuals and varied groups is an available resource that must be tapped.

SOURCE: From "Communicating Through Crisis," by K. Bayless, March 1, 2004, *Sheriff, 56*(2), pp. 47–50. *Sheriff* magazine published by National Sheriffs' Association.

As discussed in In the News 8.2, along with changes in organizational structure, there is a need to integrate information technology that allows high-speed communication. When terrorism or any other law-enforcement-related crisis occurs, multiple agencies need to be coordinated to provide a quick response. High-speed technology enables rapid collection and dissemination of information, facilitating the integration of activities of law enforcement officers, fire fighters, and EMS. At the time of the crisis, this can truly make a difference in managing the situation well versus managing in chaos. High-speed communication can also prepare law enforcement agencies to prevent a crisis from developing (for example, traffic congestion because of an accident). A variety of communication-related technologies such as the Global Positioning System (GPS), digital imaging of fingerprints, laptop computers, mobile radios, video cameras, night vision/electro-optics, and so forth are playing a significant role in reducing crime rates, apprehending criminals, and protecting society. Crime mapping using computers allows police to identify patterns and take appropriate actions to prevent future occurrences. Digital imaging of fingerprints instead of the traditional ink-and-paper method allows law enforcement agencies to transfer records electronically to the FBI's Integrated Automated Fingerprint Identification System (IAFIS). Cellular phones and mobile radios allow the officers to communicate with their headquarters from the crime scene, and to ask for any additional officers if needed. GPS software allows officers to pinpoint their exact location for the dispatcher, who can identify the shortest and fastest route to the crime scene. All in all, new and effective communication channels in criminal justice have made these agencies better and more efficient in carrying out their responsibilities.

Chapter Summary

- Communication is one of the most important elements of management within criminal justice agencies for providing a good quality of service.
- Communication is defined as a process by which ideas, thoughts, and information are exchanged and understood between two or more entities.
- In the communication process, the sender encodes the information and, using a channel, sends it to the receiver, who then decodes the message and follows it with a return message to the sender. The message is considered one-way communication if there is no feedback. If there is feedback, it is considered a two-way communication.
- Any internal or external interference or distraction in communicating the intended message is deemed noise, which can occur at any stage in the communication process.
- Though the act of communication is embedded in every management function, the three express purposes of communication are to provide information, motivate workers, and coordinate their efforts, with the intention of accomplishing organizational goals.
- There are three modes of interpersonal communications, namely, verbal, written, and nonverbal, which may be used individually or in some combination for effective communication. Managers must learn to use nonverbal cues to complement and support their verbal and written messages.

- The different channels of communication are face-to-face, videoconferencing, telephone, e-mail, and memo or letter writing. The hierarchy of channel richness is determined by three characteristics: (1) the ability to handle multiple cues simultaneously; (2) the ability to facilitate rapid, two-way feedback; and (3) the ability to establish a personal focus for the communication.

- Communication within an organization can be effective when both the formal and informal organizational channels of communication are supportive. Formal organizational communication can be categorized as vertical or horizontal. These channels can be supplemented by managers with the use of informal channels, such as the manager wandering around and the grapevine to gather and disseminate information.

- Anything that interferes with a clear communication process is often termed as noise or a barrier. Individual barriers originate from the use of jargon, use of incorrect channels or mediums of communication, filtering and information distortion, lack of feedback or inappropriate feedback, and poor listening. Organizational barriers to communication are embedded in individual insensitivity to cultural diversity within a company and a general organizational culture of mistrust.

- For-profit companies today assume that ideas can emerge from everyone. The role of the manager is to facilitate open channels of communication to allow ideas, information, and knowledge to flow throughout the organization. Although slow to adopt this concept, criminal justice agencies are moving toward this philosophy. Furthermore, an emphasis on knowledge management and information sharing has led to the flattening of organization structures, leading to greater empowerment and involvement of employees and promoting open communication.

Chapter Review Questions

1. Explain the process of communication. What are the important factors for effective communication?

2. What are the three modes of interpersonal communication? Explain the importance of these modes in law enforcement and criminal justice agencies.

3. What are the different channels of communication? Explain the channel richness hierarchy in law enforcement and criminal justice agencies.

4. Explain vertical and horizontal communications. How can you improve these communications within law enforcement and criminal justice agencies?

5. Explain individual and organizational barriers to effective communication. Explain how communication barriers might interrupt the duties of a police officer.

6. Describe how each of the following communication channels may be used in criminal justice: face-to-face, videoconferencing, telephone, e-mail, and memo or letter writing.

7. What is the difference between nonroutine communication and routine communication? Describe a scenario in which nonroutine communication may be used in a correctional facility. Now do the same with routine communication.

8. What is a communication network?

9. What are the communications challenges facing criminal justice?

CASE STUDY

Brady Johnson is a 6-foot, 2-inch white male who weighs approximately 260 pounds. He has openly admitted to having a drug problem. During previous prison stays, he attended Narcotics Anonymous meetings, although he claims that he sniffed heroine while in prison. He has been arrested many times for burglary, assault, robbery, and drug possession. In 2008, Johnson went to trial for attempted murder charges but was found not guilty. Eventually, he was imprisoned in the Viking Correctional Center after being convicted on burglary, assault, and possession charges. His sentence was four years. At best, he should be released in October 2012.

Recent DNA advancements linked Johnson to a sexual assault involving a 5-year-old female in Bardolph County. An indictment in that county was issued, and the judge in that case ordered him to be held without bond. However, after only 15 months in prison, Johnson was released from the Viking Correctional Center.

According to the prison, a record of the indictment was placed in Johnson's file by an office clerk but went unnoticed by releasing officers prior to his release. The releasing officers claim they were only provided his personal property information. They have stated that they did not have the opportunity to review his entire file. This is the second offender released after being indicted by the Bardolph County State's Attorney's Office. Two months ago, a four-time-convicted rapist was released as a result of miscommunication between the two agencies. Approximately two weeks after his release, he allegedly raped a woman at a bus stop. He is currently being held without bond as he awaits a trial in that incident.

Court records show that the Bardolph County prosecutors had difficulty communicating with the state prison officials about Johnson. The prison had failed on two previous occasions to bring him from the prison for hearings on the sexual assault charges. The district attorney's office had gone so far as to write a formal letter of complaint to the prison warden. The warden did not respond to the complaint, and as yet the correctional facility has not acknowledged receipt of the letter.

Questions for Review

1. What is/are the communication barrier(s) in this case? Why do you believe these occurred?

2. Who is at fault—the prison, the prosecutor's office, the process on which indictments and release procedures are based, or all of these? Are any other agencies at fault? If fault lies with the procedures, how can these be changed or enhanced to allow for better communication between the agencies?

3. Liability is always an issue in corrections. If Johnson harms someone else while free, who is liable? Why?

4. How could service quality be built into the responses of the prosecutor's office and the prison? Who are the customers that they serve?

Internet Resources

National District Attorneys Association—http://www.ndaa.org

National Youth Gang Center—http://www.iir.com/nygc

U.S. Office of Justice Programs, News Center— http://www.ojp.usdoj.gov/newsroom/newsroom

References and Suggested Readings

Adler, R. B., & Rodman, G. (1988). *Understanding human communications* (3rd ed.). New York, NY: Holt, Rinehart & Winston.

Aldag, R. J., & Kuzuhara, L. W. (2002). *Organizational behavior and management: An integrated skills approach.* Mason, OH: Thomson South-Western.

Andersen, P. A. (1999). *Nonverbal communication: Forms and functions.* Mountain View, CA: Mayfield.

Arnold, J. (2001, July). Leadership void or poor communication? *Law and Order, 49*(7).

Barlow, D., & Barlow, M. (1994). Cultural diversity training in criminal justice: A progressive or conservative reform? *Social Justice, 20,* 69–84.

Bayless, K. (2004, March 1). Communicating through crisis. *Sheriff, 56*(2).

Chermak, S., McGarrell, E., & Gruenewald, J. (2006). Media coverage of police misconduct and attitudes towards police. *Policing: An International Journal of Police Strategies and Management, 29*(2), 261–281.

Christensen, G. E. (2006, May/June). Fixing our system of corrections: Communicating to improve offender outcomes. *Community Corrections Report on Law and Corrections Practice, 13*(4).

Clampitt, P. G., DeKoch, R. J., & Cashman, T. (2000). A strategy for communicating about uncertainty. *Academy of Management Executive, 14*(4), 41–57.

Conger, J. A. (1998, May/June). The necessary art of persuasion. *Harvard Business Review,* 84–95.

Cornett-DeVito, M. M., & McGlone, E. L. (2000). Multicultural communication training for law enforcement officers: A case study. *Criminal Justice Policy Review, 11*(3), 234–253.

Daft, R. L., & Marcic, D. (2004). *Understanding management* (4th ed.). Mason, OH: Thomson South-Western.

Daft, R. L., & Steers, R. M. (1986). *Organizations: A micro/macro approach.* New York, NY: HarperCollins.

Davis, K., & Newstrom, J. W. (1985). *Human behavior at work: Organizational behavior* (7th ed.). New York, NY: McGraw-Hill.

Doyle, A. (2003). *Arresting images: Crime and policing in front of the television camera.* Toronto, Ontario, Canada: University of Toronto Press.

Drafke, M. W., & Kossen, S. (2002). *The human side of organizations* (8th ed.). Upper Saddle River, NJ: Prentice Hall.

Dunham, R. B. (1984). *Organizational behavior: People and processes in management.* Homewood, IL: Richard D. Irwin.

Escholz, S., Blackwell, B., Gertz, M., & Chiricos, T. (2002). Race and attitudes towards the police: Assessing the effect of watching reality police programs. *Journal of Criminal Justice, 30,* 327–341.

Ettorre, B. (1997, June). The unvarnished truth. *Management Review,* 54–57.

Fitch, B. D., & Means, R. (2013). The IMPACT principles: A model of interpersonal communication for law enforcement. *The Police Chief,* March.

Frese, M., Teng, E., & Wijnen, C. J. D. (1999, December). Helping to improve suggestion systems: Predictors of making suggestions in companies. *Journal of Organizational Behavior,* 1139–1155.

George, J. M., & Jones, G. R. (2002). *Organizational behavior* (3rd ed.). Upper Saddle River, NJ: Prentice Hall.

Glauser, M. J. (1984). Upward information flow in organizations: Review and conceptual analysis. *Human Relations, 37*(8), 613–643.

Harper, R. G., Weins, A. N., & Matarazzo, J. D. (1978). *Nonverbal communication: The state of the art.* New York, NY: Wiley.

Hellriegel, D., Slocum, J. W., Jr., & Woodman, R. W. (2001). *Organizational behavior* (9th ed.). Mason, OH: Thomson South-Western.

Kiechel, W. (1987, August 17). Learn how to listen. *Fortune,* 107–108.

Kiernan, K. (2007, July/August). Signals hidden in plain sight. *Crime and Justice International, 23*(99), 47.

Lasley, J. (1994). Ethnicity, gender, and police-community attitudes. *Social Science Quarterly, 75,* 85-97.

Lewis, P. S., Goodman, S. H., & Fandt, P. M. (2001). *Management: Challenges in the 21st century* (3rd ed.). Mason, OH: Thomson South-Western.

London, J. (1999, January). Bring your employee handbook into the millennium. *HR Focus, 76*(1), 6.

Love, T. (1998, May). Back to the old suggestion box. *Nation's Business.* Retrieved from http://findarticles .com/p/articles/mi_m1154/is_n5_v86/ai_n27524365/?tag=content;col1.

Lurie, M. I. (1999, November). The 8 essential steps in grievance processing. *Dispute Resolution Journal,* 61–65.

Manning, P. K. (1988). *Symbolic communication: Signifying calls and the police response.* Cambridge, MA: MIT Press.

Mehrabian, A. (1968, September). Communicating without words. *Psychology Today,* 53–55.

Mehrabian, A. (1972). *Nonverbal communication.* Chicago, IL: Aldine-Atherton.

Mintzberg, H. (1973). *The nature of managerial work.* Englewood Cliffs, NJ: Prentice Hall.

Moy, P., Pfau, M., & Kahlor, L. (1999). Media use and public confidence in democratic institutions. *Journal of Broadcasting and Electronic Media, 43,* 137–158.

Mulholland, D. J. (2004, July). Interagency communications during major events possible. *The Police Chief, 71*(7), 17.

Nichols, M. P. (1995). *The lost art of listening.* New York, NY: Guilford.

Peters, T. J., & Waterman, R. H., Jr. (1982). *In search of excellence.* New York, NY: Harper & Row.

Pinizzotto, A. J., & Davis, E. F. (1999, June). Offenders' perceptual shorthand: What messages are law enforcement officers sending to offenders? *FBI Law Enforcement Bulletin, 68*(6), 1–4.

Rogers, E. M., & Rogers, R. A. (1976). *Communication in organizations.* New York, NY: Free Press.

Scott, W. G., & Mitchell, T. R. (1976). *Organizational theory: A structural and behavioral analysis.* Homewood, IL: Richard D. Irwin.

Servino, C. (1999, May). Command English. *The Police Chief, 66*(5).

Simmons, D. B. (1985, November). The nature of the organizational grapevine. *Supervisory Management,* 39–42.

Stoner, J. A. F., & Freeman, R. E. (1989). *Management* (4th ed.). Englewood Cliffs, NJ: Prentice Hall.

Surette, R. (2001). Public information officers: The civilization of a criminal justice profession. *Journal of Criminal Justice, 29*(2), 107.

Tobias, L. L. (1989, December). Twenty-three ways to improve communication. *Training and Development Journal, 43*(12).

U.S. Census Bureau. (2008). Table 6. Percent of the projected population by race and Hispanic origin for the United States: 2010 to 2050. Retrieved from http://www.census.gov/population/www/projections/ summarytables.html.

Weedon, J. R. (2003, July). The importance of information sharing among agencies. *Corrections Today, 65*(4), 18.

Weitzer, R., & Tuch, S. A. (2004). Race and perceptions of police misconduct. *Social Problems, 51,* 305–325.

Whitehead, C. (2004, July). Formatting a press release. *Law and Order, 52*(7).

Wortley, S., Macmillan, R., & Hagan, J. (1997). Just deserts? The racial polarization of perceptions of criminal justice. *Law & Society Review, 31,* 637–676.

Zalud, B. (2004, May). Getting the word out. *Security, 41*(5).

Police
Administration

LEARNING OBJECTIVES

Upon completion of this chapter, students should be able to do the following:

- Discuss the history of policing
- Identify the tasks and responsibilities of police departments
- Explain potential problems in the current structure and design of police departments
- Describe how policing agencies are using open systems or service quality approaches

In the next five chapters, each component of the criminal justice system is described and connected to management and the organizational theory concepts discussed in the first portion of the textbook. The goal is to show how criminal justice agencies use management concepts to carry out their daily tasks and to demonstrate other ways in which the criminal justice system could make improvements to its current organizational strategies by incorporating service quality (open systems) approaches. We recommend that students keep organization and management theory in mind as they read these chapters.

The police are the gatekeepers of the criminal justice system. Whether an offender enters the criminal justice system is determined by the officer or officers working the scene of a crime. To clarify this concept, consider this example: If a person is stopped for speeding, the officer who makes the stop can choose to ticket the individual, issue a warning to slow down in the future, or release the person with no repercussions whatsoever. If a ticket is issued, the speeder may have to relinquish his or her driver's license, pay a fine, attend traffic court, and/or attend a seminar or class on driving defensively. The speeder is then considered officially "in the system," and the cost of his or her insurance may increase as a result of the ticket. If a warning is issued by the police officer, the speeder may find that a temporary mark is placed on his or her driving record, but the speeder is not required to go to court, pay a fine, or submit to any other sanction. This person has been excused from the system. Obviously, the person released without a ticket or a warning does not enter the criminal justice system at all. In this case, the police officer who handles the stop makes a discretionary decision regarding whether the offense is worthy of criminal justice involvement. The police officer essentially opens or closes the gates to the criminal justice system. This is a daily function of the police and is indicative of the types of decisions made by police officers at every crime scene.

In this chapter, a brief history of policing in the United States and the common tasks associated with law enforcement will be discussed. In addition, the traditional management style used in policing agencies will be identified. Finally, a review of how police departments have adopted an open system in specific areas of policing will be provided to the reader. Again, students are encouraged to consider the management and administrative concepts and theories introduced in Chapters 1 through 8 as they read this chapter and the remaining chapters on the various segments of the criminal justice system.

Brief History of Policing

Since colonial times in the United States, the public has been involved in assisting the police. In the early history of policing, able-bodied male citizens were called on to walk the borders of towns, protecting citizens as they slept. As *night watchmen,* their duties included controlling individuals who had the plague, preventing commercial fraud, calling out the time, providing weather reports, and enforcing licensing regulations (Miller, 2000; Rubinstein, 1973). Mostly, the watchmen's activities were reactive in nature. They responded to criminal activity when requested to do so by victims or witnesses (Monkkonen, 1981; Uchida, 1993). Watchmen, by and large, were not widely respected, were paid very little, and were subject to corruption and questionable methods in carrying out their duties. Other men were recruited into the sheriff's posse or elected as constables (Miller, 2000).

As cities grew larger and crime flourished, watchmen were viewed as inadequate in the protection of others. Boston and New York City are credited with adopting the first organized policing efforts in the early 1800s (Miller, 2000). Boston created small daytime patrols in 1838 but continued to use night watchmen until the 1850s. New York's policing efforts were organized into day and night patrols in 1845 and were centrally directed. New York had a large police force that walked regular beats and had the power to arrest without a warrant. This force was modeled after that created by Sir Robert Peel in London in 1829 (Cox, McCamey, & Scaramella, 2014; Uchida, 1993). Just as London's Metropolitan Police carried clubs rather than guns, American police originally did not carry revolvers. The police force was initially preventive in nature by being visible and uniformed to deter crime and disorder. Over time, however, U.S. police began to carry revolvers to equalize their confrontations with well-armed offenders (Miller, 2000). In areas where police forces were not available, citizens established vigilante groups, and private police forces (Wells Fargo in 1852,

Pinkertons in 1855, Brinks in 1859, and Burns in 1909) were used for the railroads and other industries (Cox et al., 2014; Fischer & Green, 1992).

Policing in America did not come without debate. Americans were reluctant to adopt police forces because of fear that it would lead to government suppression (Richardson, 1974). In addition, "Democratic ideology prompted [citizens] to fear an institution imported from monarchical Europe" (Miller, 2000, p. 30). Once adopted, citizens made sure that police forces were run by local political representatives to maintain as much control over them as possible. With growing disorder in the late 18th and early 19th centuries and increased immigration, the need for social order was amplified. As a result, more organized, visible, uniformed, and armed policing efforts were established, and policing functions such as order maintenance were adopted. The police became increasingly more responsible for traffic issues, finding lost children, helping with fires, moderating domestic disputes, and so forth outside of their traditional law enforcement function (Cox et al., 2014; Miller, 2000). One may consider this the first attempt by the police to become service-oriented.

The police also argued over their role and organization. "Battles over how they should be administered, how they should act on the beat, and what laws they should enforce were found in most American cities" (Miller, 2000, p. 30). Because of the political ties of police forces, promotion and hiring standards as well as controls over enforcement of the laws were easily manipulated by politics. One of the main themes in the literature on policing in the 19th century is the large-scale corruption that plagued police departments all across the country (Miller, 2000; Uchida, 1993). The upper and middle classes, who were often tied into political agendas and reform measures, enjoyed many benefits of having the police suppress the poorer classes. "Besides trying to reshape the police, reformers tried to control working-class and immigrant recreational habits by passing laws against gambling, prostitution, Sunday drinking in saloons or full prohibition of alcohol" (Miller, 2000, p. 31). As expected, these unenforceable laws allowed for increased opportunities for police corruption and increased tension between the police and the citizens these laws were aimed to control. The general consensus became that the police existed to protect the respectable people, namely, the upper and middle classes, from the others—immigrants, lower classes, blacks, and so forth. How the police did that was of no concern, as long as it did not disturb the daily comings and goings of those viewed as respectable citizens (Cox et al., 2014; Miller, 2000).

Even though technology was expected to improve the administration and efficiency of the police, it did not come without problems (as discussed in Chapter 4). Because of technological advances such as the car, those who had historically not been subjected to police authority found themselves ticketed for speeding and other related offenses (Cox et al., 2014; Mastrofski, 2007). Furthermore, newly developed methods of communication such as the telegraph, telephone, and two-way radio were expected to increase police response and their ability to provide law enforcement and order maintenance. But what really occurred was that technological advancements increased citizen *complaints* against the police, as the community's expectations of police performance grew, the ability of the police to handle the increased number of calls for service declined. The police found themselves in a situation where they could not respond adequately to service calls and found little time for law enforcement–related activities (Cox et al., 2014; Mastrofski, 2007). Police administrators also realized that just as technology can contribute to increased crime control, it can also contribute to increased criminal violations as offenders quickly become savvy at using technology to violate the law. Basically, the image of the police took a huge hit in the middle of the 20th century. The issues of police corruption, lack of professionalism, and public distrust were amplified by the inability of the police to provide the services expected (Cox et al., 2014; Mastrofski, 2007). Calls for police professionalism became commonplace.

Attempts at professionalizing the police have occurred since the 1900s. August Vollmer, who was the chief of police in Berkeley, California, was one of the first to call for removal of the police from direct political influence, and he supported college education and increased training of police officers. He worked with the Wickersham Commission, appointed by President Herbert Hoover in 1929, to survey police in America. He was also involved in police technology and was a strong supporter of police ethics. He established foundations for hiring and training police officers that are still models for today's police academies (Cox et al., 2014). O. W. Wilson, along with other reformers such as J. Edgar Hoover, V. A. Leonard, and William Parker, also initiated changes in the image of the police (Conser & Russell, 2000; Cox et al., 2014). Even though these attempts have contributed to the police being better educated, better trained, and better equipped than ever before (Cox et al., 2014), the police image is still negative, in most cases, in the beginning of the 21st century. As an example, an article written by a small-town police chief in 2001 noted that the biggest drawback to implementing community-oriented policing in that city was the department's image and the citizen perceptions of the police as unprofessional, unskilled, and incapable, much like Don Knotts's portrayal of Deputy Sheriff Barney Fife on *The Andy Griffith Show*. Residents viewed the police as ticket writers who knew, or cared, very little about the other functions of the police department (Stokes, 2001). Cases such as George Zimmerman and Trayvon Martin do not help the police repair their image when citizens challenge the professionalism of the police and their ability to do their jobs correctly, and claim that the police are still willing to protect some people while repressing others, such as minorities. In the News 9.1 discusses the tensions between the police and citizens in Sanford, Florida, before and after Trayvon Martin was killed. Unfortunately, these stories are not unique and have been continual problems for policing agencies throughout the country.

In The News 9.1
Police Chief in Florida Tries to Ease Old Tensions

Police Chief in Florida Tries to Ease Old Tensions

SANFORD, Fla.—Within days of becoming the police chief in this small city outside Orlando, Cecil E. Smith began to see clearly the scope of the challenges he faced.

There were grumblings within the Police Department's ranks: at least one supervisor said he did not want to work for a black man.

Out on the streets, some black residents voiced misgivings of a different sort. Chief Smith may be black, but he is a Northerner. How could he ever understand them?

"This has been a slave town forever," one resident said to Chief Smith in a low voice. "There are people who still feel white people are the devil. You're not from here. You don't understand."

Peering through his glasses, Chief Smith locked eyes with the man, he later recalled. "Enlighten me," he said, "so I can enlighten my people."

The department Chief Smith now leads and the city it serves are in the arduous stages of trying to integrate lessons drawn from the episode that brought infamy to Sanford 16 months ago. The fatal shooting of Trayvon Martin, an unarmed black teenager, by George Zimmerman, a volunteer neighborhood watchman, compelled many to assert that racial profiling and citizen vigilantism had taken place.

Sandford's Police Department became the focus of much of the rage. That the agency neither arrested nor charged Mr. Zimmerman, who claimed self-defense, was taken by some as proof of not only ineptness but also bias.

This seemed especially true after a special prosecutor, appointed by the governor, charged Mr. Zimmerman with second-degree murder more than six weeks after the shooting. Had Mr. Zimmerman, who is Hispanic, been black, many believed, he would not have been released on claims of self-defense. His trial began here with jury selection last week.

Since the shooting, city officials and religious leaders have labored to soothe tensions. The police chief who oversaw the Zimmerman case, Bill Lee, was fired. An interfaith coalition of ministers was formed. The city asked the Justice Department to review the Police Department's practices—the request was turned down, at least for now—and a panel of community leaders was assembled to assess relations between the public and the police.

But the biggest hurdle remains: decades of animus between black residents and the Police Department.

"The black community, they don't trust the Sanford police," said Turner Clayton Jr., the president of the Seminole County N.A.A.C.P. "They trust the Sheriff's Office and any other agency more."

Responsibility for mending relations has largely fallen on the shoulders of Chief Smith, 52, a balding, soft-spoken man of medium build from Chicago's West Side.

Before besting 75 other candidates for the job, which he began on April 1, Chief Smith spent his previous 26 years in law enforcement in Elgin, Ill., where he investigated drugs and gangs, worked in community relations and rose to deputy chief. His own family is a picture of diversity. He and his wife of 15 years, who is white, have parented five children between them, and one of his goddaughters is a lesbian.

After arriving in Sanford, Chief Smith deployed strategies he honed in Elgin. At community events, he doles out hugs. Every Thursday afternoon, he and a dozen or so officers go door to door in a different neighborhood—introducing themselves with smiles, pumping hands, scribbling down names and numbers, and asking if there are problems that the police can address.

This outreach has left residents both astounded and delighted. "I've been here 30 years, and I didn't know you did this," one woman said during an outing last week.

The chief has also been spotted in plain clothes late at night chatting with people in Goldsboro, a historic black neighborhood. "I saw him mingling with teenagers," said Cindy Philemon, who works in Goldsboro. "All I could do was smile. My heart was filled with joy. Before, it was like neglect."

(Continued)

(Continued)

But local black leaders say it is too early to deem Chief Smith's leadership a success, especially because the department remains more or less unchanged.

"Two months won't take away six decades—it just can't," said Kenneth Bentley, a community activist and educator. "At the end of the day, he's still chief over those officers that have the same mentality."

While the enmity toward the police is rooted in Sanford's segregationist past, black residents and leaders said it had been fueled by what they described as mistreatment and the agency's failure to thoroughly investigate the shooting deaths of many young black men—an assertion that the police dispute.

"The Trayvon Martin case just happened to bring it to a boiling point," said Velma Williams, the city's only black commissioner. "Those feelings have been there long before."

Chief Smith said he was addressing any hints of bias in his department. After learning of the supervisor who complained about his appointment, Chief Smith called a meeting. "I was informed someone didn't want to work for a black chief," he recalled telling the quiet room. "If you don't want to work for me, there's the door."

He recently appointed a longtime Sanford law enforcement officer, Darren Scott, who is black, as his deputy. Chief Smith is not the department's first black leader, but this is the first time people can recall two black men holding the department's top spots. Just over half of Chief Smith's officers are white men, and he is seeking more diversity in recruits.

City leaders, including Ms. Williams, insist that they have faith in the new chief. Mayor Jeff Triplett said, "This guy is highly focused on rebuilding that trust, doing what's right for the community." He added, "I don't see him stopping."

Restoring trust, the mayor said, "was the main crux of what we thought we needed to repair."

Still, critics questioned the staying power of the department's outreach efforts once the Zimmerman trial ends and the intense national attention drifts. Promises and efforts made before, they said, have all sputtered out.

At the very least, some residents say the aftermath of Mr. Martin's shooting forced city leaders to take a hard look at issues that many felt had gone unaddressed for too long.

"The untold story of Sanford would never have been told," said Mr. Bentley, the community activist, "if one person had let another person walk through the neighborhood."

SOURCE: "Police Chief In Florida Tries to Ease Old Tensions," by Cara Buckley, June 16, 2013, *The New York Times*. Retrieved July 3, 2013, from http://www.nytimes.com/2013/06/17/us/in-city-of-zimmerman-trial-police-chief-navigates-race-relations.html?pagewanted=all. A version of this article appeared in print on June 17, 2013, on page A9 of the New York edition with the headline: Police Chief In Florida Tries to Ease Old Tensions.

Besides increasing professionalism, modern police departments have attempted to change their image by recruiting and hiring more minority and female officers, providing sensitivity and diversity training, getting officers out of patrol cars and onto the streets, and developing positive relationships with community leaders (Cox et al., 2014; Miller, 2000). Problem-oriented policing and community-oriented policing have been widely used since the 1980s in efforts to improve relationships between citizens and the police. *Community-oriented policing* includes a variety of collaborative initiatives tailored to fit each community's needs. The goal is to alleviate the issues in the community that cause crime (Cox, 1996; Cox et al., 2014; Cox & Wade, 2002; Eck & Rosenbaum, 1994; Rosenbaum, 2000). Community policing officers are expected to form relationships with residents in the neighborhoods being policed, with other public service agencies, and with private service providers. They are given the opportunity to use nontraditional approaches to policing to deal with problems identified by citizens and service providers. Community policing officers are rewarded for being innovative and creative in resolving issues (Cox et al., 2014). A more detailed approach of community-oriented policing will be described later in this chapter, but for now, suffice it to say that this approach is basically the exact opposite of traditional policing practices, which emphasize a closed system that is reactive in nature and supports little or no innovation or challenge to authority. Police departments have also adopted problem-oriented policing strategies that are believed to be more effective long-term in reducing calls for service by solving the problem creating the call (Goldstein, 1990) and hotspot policing that requires half of the police force to concentrate their efforts in certain geographical areas that are identified as crime prone or increased risk. Furthermore, departments are using Compstat to allow middle managers in the police agency to make decisions on patrol and service responses as long as they meet the objectives set by upper-level administrators (Silverman, 1999; Mastrofski, 2007). Finally, *intelligence-led policing* relies heavily on data-driven policing strategies that identify and alleviate risks and patterns of crime associated with groups, individuals, and geographical locations (Cox et al., 2014).

Although this is an abbreviated version of the history of policing, the reader can use the material to identify the root causes of some of the problems facing the police today. For example, issues associated with professionalism can be traced to the early 1900s. Resolution to the problems brought about by trying to professionalize the policing industry has still not occurred, and the image of the police remains negative among certain populations. Nevertheless, being familiar with the history provides a contextual meaning with which to better understand the current ideas, situations, and reactions of police departments. By looking at the past, one can better relate to present-day and future events in policing.

Private Policing

Public police departments are not the only policing agencies in the United States. As mentioned previously, private policing agencies were created as early as the mid-1800s. Although in some cases, private policing forces began as vigilante efforts to rid towns or rural areas of criminals and other undesirables and to police areas where public police did not exist, there was also the creation of formal and organized establishments. "Private forces were usually created to combat labour unions in areas where police forces sympathized with strikers and refused to serve the employers" (Miller, 2000, p. 34). The Pinkerton National Detective Agency, Burns, Pennsylvania Coal and

Iron Police Force, and other private agencies supplied strikebreakers and guards to industries and did investigatory work for bankers and other upper-class citizens.

One of the biggest issues surrounding private police historically has been public criticism. Public officials complained that private sector agencies competed with the public police. Others questioned the methods employed by private police officers. Newspapers reported that private police officers engaged in outrageous tactics that involved threats to keep potential complainants from going to the public police (Joh, 2006). Courts also found the testimony of private detectives to be suspect unless it was corroborated by other witnesses.

According to Joh (2006), the height of public scrutiny occurred in 1892 in the Homestead Riot in Pennsylvania. Private Pinkerton guards were hired to quell the striking steelworkers. As the guards approached on river barges, the workers fired gunshots at them. The guards responded accordingly. In the end, three workers and seven guards were killed while many more were injured. The Pinkerton guards eventually surrendered to the workers and were beaten by the angry mob. State troopers had to occupy the factory for four days after the incident. The Homestead Riot led to congressional inquiries, although after investigations the House of Representatives reaffirmed that citizens had the right to protect private property and could use private resources to do so when the state failed to give adequate protection (Joh, 2006). Because of the riot and its resulting hearings, courts became more distrustful of private detectives, and private policing agencies partially turned away from strike and labor work as their sole means of income. Private policing agencies focused instead on professional jewelry and bank theft. Dealing with petty theft, patrolling rail yards, serving warrants, and protecting small businesses were also lucrative for private police. In addition, congressional investigations in the 1930s led the LaFollette Committee to state the following:

> Public police systems are established by law. They are paid from public treasuries and are expected to be responsive to the requirements of entire communities. They must perform their duties impartially, without regard to the economic, racial, or religious status or views of the individual members of the community. The final responsibility for the actions of the public police systems rests in elected representatives who are accountable to the electorate. . . . Private police systems, on the other hand, are created to meet the economic needs and desires of private interests. They are paid from private funds and act as the agents and servitors of their employers, who occupy their positions by virtue of their ownership of property or as appointed agents of stockholders or owners. . . . Private police systems, therefore, cannot be viewed as agencies of law and order. (Joh, 2006, p. 370)

Although no regulatory processes developed from the LaFollette Committee's statements, they did reinforce the negative perceptions of private policing agencies. Such agencies continued to exist, however, because there was a need for the protection of private property by citizens and industry. There was also the understanding that public police could not be everywhere all the time, so private police filled the void (Joh, 2006).

In the 1970s, the federal government sponsored a series of studies on private policing. They found that private police agencies had prospered in the United

States (Joh, 2006). In addition, the government suggested that private policing agencies could partner with public agencies in a number of areas to provide more complementary services to citizens and public and private industry (Kakalik & Wildhorn, 1971).

As a result of these studies, there has been an increased interest in public–private partnerships among policing agencies. Joint investigations and formal information-sharing networks have been set up and are currently used by private and public police to identify crime patterns and suspects of which each may be aware In addition, public attitudes toward private policing have changed as private police have become more common in business environments, schools, neighborhoods, and in technology security. The Bureau of Labor Statistics (2013) actually estimates that the private policing field will grow by 19% over the 2010–2020 period and will become more involved in providing services traditionally offered by public police. On a last note, it should be mentioned that since September 11, 2001, private policing has become even more important in the protection of U.S. infrastructures. Energy companies, banks, finance operations, transportations systems, shipping companies, Internet providers, and so on are privately owned, and many employ private police to protect them (Joh, 2006). With this in mind, private police may easily be the first in line to respond to potential terrorist attacks on these businesses. Despite the lack of formal regulatory processes in private policing, the industry has flourished and cemented itself as an indispensable segment of public security and as a central provider of protection services to the public and private interests. Chapter 13 provides a more in-depth study of private security and its role in servicing the public and private stakeholders.

Policing Agencies

The federal government has never created a single, formal policing agency; however, there are several federal agencies that resemble policing forces. U.S. Marshals originally policed the western territories until they became states. Marshals have the power to arrest people committing federal crimes in states or territories. The Secret Service, created during the U.S. Civil War, is a federal detective agency that concentrates on suppressing counterfeiting and protecting presidents and other U.S. dignitaries. The Bureau of Immigration and Naturalization polices the borders of the United States through teams of guards and other officials (Miller, 2000). The Federal Bureau of Investigation (FBI) was formed in 1908 under J. Edgar Hoover to control radicalism and wartime spying, and to investigate other federal crimes. The FBI is heavily involved in contemporary policing efforts through its training schools; crime labs; and its annual compilation of crime statistics, known as the *Uniform Crime Reports* (Miller, 2000). On occasion, the U.S. Army has acted as a federal police force in quieting riots and controlling crowds and protesters.

After the terrorist attacks of September 11, 2001, the federal government created the Department of Homeland Security by combining 22 federal agencies into one governmental department. Using the principles of the supply chain synergy model (described in Chapter 2), the agencies that traditionally handled law enforcement–type activities, such as the U.S. Secret Service, Coast Guard, Customs Service, and Immigration and Naturalization Service, were integrated into the new department. The federal government believed that this reorganization would strengthen communication among these agencies, which would help improve the quality of service provided to the citizens of the United States. Figure 9.1 shows the organizational chart of the Department of Homeland Security.

The U.S. Department of Homeland Security DHS claimed in its 2010 Quadrennial Homeland Security Review Report that the role of the department is much broader than just the prevention of terrorism. The DHS believed that the role encompasses "contributions from all Federal agencies, State, local, tribal and territorial governments, businesses, and nongovernmental organizations, as well as individuals, families, and communities. International partnerships are also essential to success" in protecting the American way of life and preventing future terrorist attacks (Department of Homeland Security, 2010, pp. 2–3). To do this, the DHS has clarified its goals as follows:

Table 9.1 Mission and Goals of Department of Homeland Security (Adapted)

Mission of Department of Homeland Security	Goals
1. Preventing Terrorism and Enhancing Security	• Goal 1.1: Prevent Terrorist Attacks • Goal 1.2: Prevent the Unauthorized Acquisition or Use of Chemical, Biological, Radiological, and Nuclear Materials and Capabilities • Goal 1: Manage Risks to Critical Infrastructure, Key Leadership, and Events
2. Securing and Managing Our Borders	• Goal 2.1: Effectively Control U.S. Air, Land, and Sea Borders • Goal 2.2: Safeguard Lawful Trade and Travel • Goal 2.3: Disrupt and Dismantle Transnational Criminal Organizations
3. Enforcing and Administering Our Immigration Laws	• Goal 3.1: Strengthen and Effectively Administer the Immigration System • Goal 3.2: Prevent Unlawful Immigration
4. Safeguarding and Securing Cyberspace	• Goal 4.1: Create a Safe, Secure, and Resilient Cyber Environment • Goal 4.2: Promote Cybersecurity Knowledge and Innovation

Mission of Department of Homeland Security	Goals
5. Ensuring Resilience to Disasters	• Goal 5.1: Mitigate Hazards • Goal 5.2: Enhance Preparedness • Goal 5.3: Ensure Effective Emergency Response • Goal 5.4: Rapidly Recover

SOURCE: Department of Homeland Security (2010). Quadrennial Homeland Security Review Report: A Strategic Framework for Homeland Security. Retrieved from http://www.dhs.gov/xlibrary/assets/qhsr_report.pdf.

To develop these goals and to comply with the open government plan implemented by President Barack Obama, the Department of Homeland Security used an open-systems input process in 2004 in the creation of its original strategic plan (the department continues to do this in the 2012–2016 strategic plan). Using the tenet of service quality that the public should be a part of the delivery process, the department involved stakeholders (citizens, governmental entities, and private businesses) by surveying them to determine the strengths and weaknesses of the department. Keeping the communication channels open, it used stakeholders' feedback to develop strategic goals and to identify performance measures that would motivate DHS employees to work toward accomplishing the goals. Since then, the DHS has modified the goals slightly by attempting to clarify them and to narrow the mission of the organization. But the agency continues to educate citizens and lower-level public protection agencies about what to expect and how to act in various circumstances.

States have created their own police forces to protect the citizens residing within their borders. Although the organization of these agencies differs from state to state, most states have a state police force that patrols state highways and roads. Some states have also developed state policing agencies that focus specifically on crime enforcement and investigation. In Georgia, for example, the Georgia Bureau of Investigation concentrates on criminal investigations, forensic laboratory services, and computerized criminal justice information, while the Georgia State Patrol is tasked with investigating traffic accidents and enforcing driving laws. State policing agencies often work on investigations with federal agencies and local policing agencies. Often, state police can be found providing training and other assistance to municipal policing officers. These agencies may have resources and special skills not found at the local law enforcement level. The Bureau of Justice Statistics (2011) estimates that approximately 61,000 police officers were employed by state policing agencies in 2008.

Although these agencies exist and are important in the overall functions of policing in America, law enforcement has, by and large, remained a local function carried out in thousands of cities across the United States (Miller, 2000). Approximately 60% of the 765,000 police officers in the United States are employed in city police departments,

Figure 9.1 One Team, One Mission, Securing Our Homeland

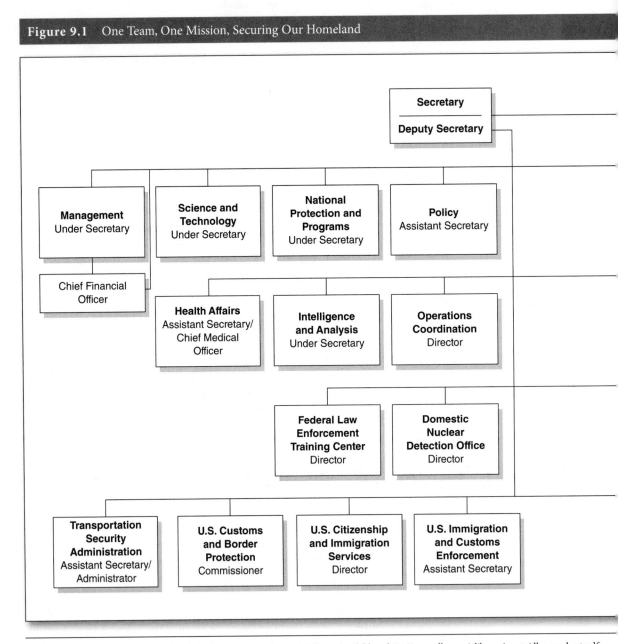

SOURCE: From *U.S. Department of Homeland Security Organizational Chart.* Available at http://www.dhs.gov/xlibrary/assets/dhs-orgchart.pdf.

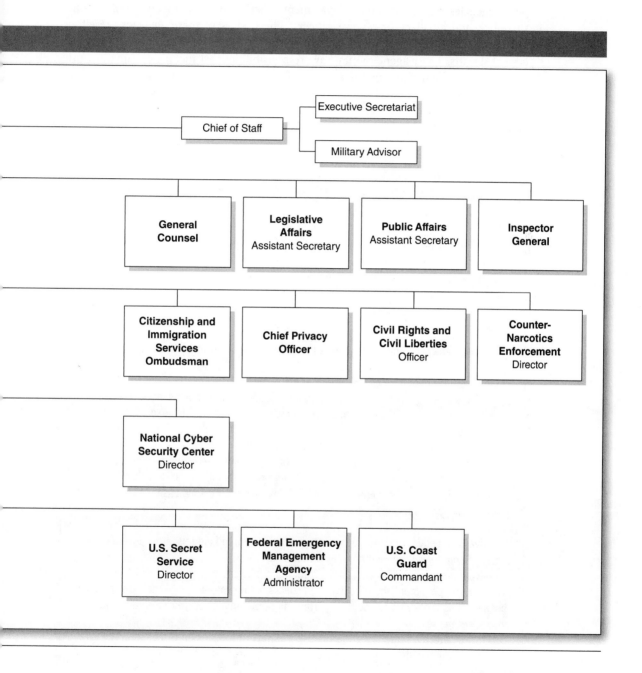

with another 24% employed by sheriff's offices (Bureau of Justice Statistics, 2011). Local police agencies include city police departments, sheriff's offices, university police, transit police, and auxiliary or reserve officers. The leaders of these agencies are either appointed by a city council, in the case of chiefs, or elected by the general public, in the case of sheriffs. These agencies may have responsibilities that include criminal investigations, routine and traffic patrol, security of courthouses, security of jails, transportation of prisoners, and serving papers. They provide a number of services to those working in criminal justice and the general public in addition to the traditional law enforcement duty.

CAREER HIGHLIGHT BOX
PRIVATE DETECTIVES AND INVESTIGATORS

Nature of the Work

Private detectives and investigators find facts and analyze information about legal, financial, and personal matters. They offer many services, including verifying people's backgrounds, tracing missing persons, investigating computer crimes, and protecting celebrities.

Duties

Private detectives and investigators typically do the following:

- Interview people to gather information
- Do various types of searches, using a computer or non-computerized records
- Conduct surveillance (looking for, following, or watching a person without that person noticing)
- Collect evidence to present in court
- Verify employment, income, and facts on a person's background
- Investigate computer crimes, such as identity theft and illegal downloads
- Help in cases of criminal and civil liability, missing-persons cases, and insurance claims and fraud

Private detectives and investigators typically work for individuals, attorneys, and businesses. Some have their own investigative agency.

Private detectives and investigators offer many services, based on clients' needs. They may perform pre-employment background checks or look into a charge that someone has been stealing money from a company. They might be hired to prove or disprove infidelity in a divorce case.

Private detectives and investigators use a variety of tools when researching the facts in a case. Much of their work is done with a computer, which allows them to quickly get information, such as records of a person's prior arrests, telephone numbers, social networking–site details, and emails.

They make phone calls to verify facts, such as a person's income and place of employment. They also interview people when conducting a background investigation.

Investigators may go undercover, pretending to be someone else to go unnoticed, to get information, or to observe a suspect.

Detectives also conduct surveillance when investigating a case. They may watch a site, such as the person's home or office, often from an inconspicuous location or a vehicle. Using photographic and video cameras, binoculars, and global positioning systems (GPS), detectives gather information on persons of interest. Surveillance can be time consuming.

Detectives and investigators must be mindful of the law when conducting investigations. They must have a good understanding of federal, state, and local laws, such as privacy laws, and other legal issues affecting their work.

However, as the legality of certain methods may be unclear, investigators and detectives must make use good judgment when deciding how to pursue a case. They must collect evidence properly, so that it can be used legally in court.

The following are examples of types of private detectives and investigators:

Computer forensic investigators specialize in recovering, analyzing, and presenting data from computers for use in investigations or as evidence. They may be able to recover deleted emails and documents.

Legal investigators help prepare criminal defenses, verify facts in civil law suits, locate witnesses, and serve legal documents. They often work for lawyers and law firms.

Corporate investigators conduct internal and external investigations for corporations. Internally, they may investigate drug use in the workplace or ensure that expense accounts are not abused. Externally, they may try to thwart criminal schemes, such as fraudulent billing by a supplier.

Financial investigators may be hired to develop confidential financial profiles of individuals and companies that are prospective parties to large financial transactions. These investigators often are certified public accountants (CPAs), who work closely with investment bankers and other accountants. For more information, see the profile on accountants and auditors. Investigators also might search for assets to recover damages awarded by a court in fraud and theft cases.

Store detectives, also known as *loss prevention agents*, catch people who try to steal merchandise or destroy store property.

Hotel detectives protect guests from theft of their belongings and preserve order in hotel restaurants and bars. They also may keep undesirable individuals, such as known thieves, off the premises.

Work environment. Private detectives and investigators held about 34,700 jobs in 2010.

(Continued)

(Continued)

Private detectives and investigators work in a wide variety of environments, depending on the case that they are working on. Some spend more time in their offices conducting computer searches and making phone calls. Others spend more time in the field, conducting interviews or doing surveillance.

Investigators generally work alone, but they may work with others while conducting surveillance or following a subject.

Some of the work involves confrontation, so the job can be stressful and dangerous. Some situations, such as certain bodyguard assignments for corporate or celebrity clients, call for the investigator to be armed. In most cases, however, a weapon is not necessary because private detectives and investigators' purpose is information gathering and not law enforcement or criminal apprehension.

Owners of investigative agencies have the added stress of having to deal with demanding and, sometimes, distraught clients.

Private detectives and investigators often work irregular hours because they need to conduct surveillance and to contact people outside of normal work hours. They may work early mornings, evenings, weekends, and holidays. In addition, they may have to work outdoors, or from a vehicle, in all kinds of weather.

Training, Other Qualifications, and Advancement

Private detectives and investigators usually have some college education. However, many jobs do not have formal education requirements, and private detectives and investigators learn on the job. Previous experience in investigative work can be beneficial. Private detectives and investigators need a license in most states.

Important Qualities

Communication skills. Detectives and investigators must be able to listen carefully and ask appropriate questions when interviewing a person of interest.

Honesty. Detectives and investigators must tell the truth to gain the trust of their clients and people they interview, as well as to establish credibility in a court of law.

Inquisitiveness. Private detectives and investigators must want to ask questions and to search for the truth.

Problem-solving skills. Detectives and investigators must be able to think on their feet and make quick decisions based on the information that they have at a given time.

Resourcefulness. Detectives and investigators must work persistently with whatever leads they have, no matter how limited, to determine the next step toward their goal. They sometimes need to figure out what a person of interest will do next.

Education and Training

Most private detectives and investigators learn on the job.

Although new investigators must learn how to gather information, additional training depends on the type of firm that hires them. For instance, at an insurance company, a new investigator will learn to recognize insurance fraud. Learning by doing, in which new investigators are put on cases and gain skills as they go, is a common approach. Corporate investigators hired by large companies, however, may receive formal training in business practices, management structure, and various finance-related topics.

Private detectives and investigators usually have some college education. Although some investigation jobs may not have specific education requirements, others require candidates to have a high school diploma.

Some jobs may require an associate's or bachelor's degree. Postsecondary courses in criminal justice and political science are helpful to aspiring private detectives and investigators.

Although previous work experience is generally required, some people enter the occupation directly after graduating from college with an associate's degree or bachelor's degree in criminal justice or police science.

Corporate investigators typically need a bachelor's degree. Coursework in finance, accounting, and business is often preferred. Because many financial investigators have an accountant's background, they typically have a bachelor's degree in accounting or a related field.

Many computer forensics investigators need a bachelor's degree in a related field, such as computer science or criminal justice. Many colleges and universities now offer certificate programs in computer forensics, and others offer a bachelor's or a master's degree. Because computer forensics specialists need both computer skills and investigative skills, extensive training may be required.

Many computer forensic investigators learn their trade while working for a law enforcement agency, where they are taught how to gather evidence and to spot computer-related crimes. Many people enter law enforcement to get this training and to establish a reputation before moving on to the private sector.

Because they work with changing technologies, computer forensic investigators never stop training. They must learn the latest methods of fraud detection and new software programs and operating systems by attending conferences and courses offered by software vendors and professional associations.

Work Experience

Private detectives and investigators typically have previous work experience. Some have worked for insurance or collections companies, as paralegals, in finance, or in accounting. Many investigators enter the field after serving in law enforcement, the military, or federal intelligence jobs. These people, who frequently are able to retire after 25 years of service, often become private detectives or investigators as a second career.

(Continued)

(Continued)

Licenses

Most states license private detectives and investigators. However, requirements vary by state. Some states have few requirements, and many others have stringent regulations.

In most states, detectives and investigators who carry handguns must meet additional requirements. Some states require an additional license to work as a bodyguard.

Because laws change, jobseekers should verify the licensing laws related to private investigators with the state and locality in which they want to work.

There are no licenses specifically for computer forensic investigators, but some states require them to be licensed private investigators. Even in states or localities where licensure is not required, having a private investigator license is useful, because it allows computer forensic investigators to do follow-up and related investigative work.

Certification

Some private detectives and investigators can get certification from a professional organization to demonstrate competency, which may help them to advance their careers. For investigators who specialize in negligence or criminal defense investigation, the National Association of Legal Investigators offers the Certified Legal Investigator certification. For investigators who specialize in security, ASIS International offers the Professional Certified Investigator certification.

Advancement

Most private detective agencies are small, with little room for advancement. Usually, there are no defined ranks or steps, so advancement takes the form of increases in salary and better assignments. Many detectives and investigators start their own firms after gaining a few years of experience. Corporate and legal investigators may rise to supervisor or manager of the security or investigations department.

Employment

Employment of private detectives and investigators is expected to grow 21 percent from 2010 to 2020, faster than the average for all occupations. Increased demand for private detectives and investigators will stem from heightened security concerns and the need to protect property and confidential information.

Technological advances have led to an increase in cybercrimes, such as identity theft and spamming. Internet scams, as well as various other types of financial and insurance fraud, create demand for investigative services.

Background checks will continue to be a source of work for many investigators, as both employers and personal contacts want to verify that people are credible. More individuals are investigating care facilities, such as childcare providers and hospitals.

Job Prospects

Competition is expected for most jobs, because private detective and investigator careers attract many qualified people, including relatively young retirees from law enforcement or military careers.

The best opportunities for jobseekers will be in entry-level jobs in detective agencies. People with related work experience, as well as those with interviewing and computer skills, may find more opportunities.

Earnings

The median annual wage of private detectives and investigators was $42,870 in May 2010. The median wage is the wage at which half the workers in an occupation earned more than that amount and half earned less. The lowest 10 percent earned less than $25,760, and the top 10 percent earned more than $74,970.

Private detectives and investigators often work irregular hours because they need to conduct surveillance and to contact people outside of normal work hours. They may work early mornings, evenings, weekends, and holidays. In addition, they may have to work outdoors, or from a vehicle, in all kinds of weather.

SOURCE: Bureau of Labor Statistics, U.S. Department of Labor, *Occupational Outlook Handbook, 2012–13 Edition*, Private Detectives and Investigators, on the Internet at http://www.bls.gov/ooh/protective-service/private-detectives-and-investigators.htm.

Police Functions

In 1977, the National Advisory Commission on Criminal Justice Standards and Goals identified 12 policing functions. According to the commission, the police are responsible for the following:

1. Maintenance of order

2. Enforcement of the law

3. Prevention of criminal activity

4. Detection of criminal activity

5. Apprehension of criminals

6. Participation in court proceedings

7. Protection of constitutional guarantees

8. Assistance to those who cannot care for themselves or who are in danger of physical harm

9. Control of traffic

10. Resolution of day-to-day conflicts among family, friends, and neighbors

11. Creation and maintenance of a feeling of security in the community

12. Promotion and preservation of civil order

After inspecting the goals, we propose grouping them into two primary functions, namely, agents of control and agents of support, which include three police tasks—crime-related tasks, order maintenance, and crime prevention. Crime-related tasks or law enforcement consists of enforcing laws, apprehending criminals, participating in court when necessary, protecting constitutional rights, and providing assistance to those who need protection. It could be argued that order maintenance functions include providing assistance to those who cannot help themselves, controlling traffic, resolving conflicts, creating a feeling of security, and promoting civil order (Cox et al., 2014). Crime prevention involves the detection of criminal activity as well as some of the tasks already mentioned. What develops from these three tasks is that police become agents of control by performing crime-related tasks and order maintenance, and they become agents of support through order-maintenance tasks and crime prevention.

Crime-related tasks correlate specifically to what most of society expects the police to be doing in their daily roles. The public believes the police spend their time making reports on criminal incidents, investigating acts of crime, apprehending offenders, making arrests, interviewing offenders, and booking offenders into jail. Community members also expect them to collect evidence, recover stolen property, provide reports to the prosecutor and the court, and participate as witnesses in cases that appear before judges or a jury (Cox et al., 2014; Meese, 1993). Although crime-related tasks are an important function of the police, the bulk of policing is spent maintaining order.

Order maintenance requires that the police use mediation and negotiation skills to resolve disputes between parties (Cox & Wade, 2002; Meese 1993). Usually, it involves a suggestion made by the officer to one or both of the parties with the goal of settling the dispute in a manner that restores peace to the situation. In the case of youths who may be hanging out on the corner, disturbing the individuals living near the area, the officer might suggest the youths move their group to the local park or community center instead of sitting on the corner. The officer will also discuss the situation with the neighbors, letting them know that there are few activities for the children to be involved in and that the group is only trying to socialize with each other in lawful ways. Realizing that both parties have to give and take in the situation, the police officer will come to a resolution that relieves the most tension and uses the least amount of official (law enforcement) action.

Crime prevention is the third task accomplished by police officers. Police officers provide programs designed to educate the public on crimes and criminal statutes, engage in deterrent patrol and traffic control, make building and housing security checks, and use informants and intelligence sources to identify criminals and criminal activity (Cox & Wade, 2002; Meese, 1993). Community policing efforts are also viewed as crime prevention tactics. As noted in Meese (1993), when the police deal with neighborhood disorder and decay, they lessen the conditions that allow crime to flourish. This provides the citizenry with greater satisfaction in the police, opening communication channels and forging relationships of collaboration and police–citizen cooperation.

These roles should be viewed as complementary rather than adversarial to the position of the police. All of these functions are carried out under the watchful eyes of the public, the media, and the police administration. Officers who work directly on the street report their activities to their field supervisors on a regular basis. The field supervisor will report to the shift commanders, who relay information to the deputy chiefs, and so it goes until it reaches the chief of police. No activity or function goes unreported, as the structure of the police department requires accountability and strict adherence to a chain of command. Next, the structure of police departments will be investigated further.

Organization and Structure of Police Departments

Police departments are municipal agencies that fall under the control of the mayor or city manager. The mayor influences the hiring or firing of the police chief and the activities of the department directly and indirectly. Police departments are formally structured under the chief of police. In the chain of command, there are usually two divisions of labor under the police chief. The first is the *operations division,* which performs line staff functions such as patrol, traffic enforcement, and juvenile investigations and detective work, among other tasks (Cox et al., 2014). The second division is the *administrative* or *staff services division,* which consists of record keeping, communications, training and education, and public relations. This division may include civilian employees as well as police officers. It is important to note here that the tasks mentioned may be divided differently in some departments, but most follow this format. Depending on the size of the agency, more or fewer divisions and employees may be involved in the chain of command (Cox et al., 2014).

Historically, the formal structure of the police department was modeled after a *paramilitary* format that stressed the use of orders and directives and used a rigid chain of command. There were three levels of management in the police structure: top management (chief, assistant chiefs), middle management (corporals, division sergeants), and lower management (sergeants). This structure distinguished the decision makers from the line staff in the department and supported uniform operations and the ability to move staff across positions (Batts, Smoot, & Scrivner, 2012). For the most part, this type of structure was resistant to change and failed to promote communication and interaction among the divisions, which is essential for superior service. In addition, despite the best efforts of reformers, the traditional structure did not allow police professionals to think for themselves, but expected them to blindly follow orders and regulations, which alienated officers from administrators and created an atmosphere of resentment (Uchida, 1993). When police union demands are added to this system, then one can identify the distinct disadvantages of the closed-system format in policing and the cumbersome processes that prevent the police from quickly responding to changing environmental factors. Due to the problems associated with traditional organizational structures, accompanied with the new expectations of police officers, technological advances (Batts et al., 2012), and because of ongoing research in policing, some police departments have made changes. Although the chain of command still exists and the use of rules, orders, and regulations is common, some aspects of policing have become more flexible and responsive to the needs of the public, other criminal justice agencies, and lower-level police officers. Some of these attempts are still in the experimental stages, while others have created new challenges—and problems—for the police department. At this point, we should mention that this textbook cannot cover all of the modifications taking place in policing; however, we will address some of the more popular innovations.

Policing Responses to Problems Associated With Traditional Organizational Structure

Batts et al. (2012) suggest that there is a new generation of police officers entering the police workforce. These officers are much more accepting of affirmative action, immigration, diversity in the workforce and community, and the appropriate scope of government. This generation is also more likely to be college-educated, oriented toward teamwork, collaborative, and independent in their thinking (Batts et al., 2012; Beck & Wade, 2004; Hicks & Hicks, 1999). But this generation may need help focusing on single issues and seeing projects through to the end. Additionally, this generation is seen as "placing a greater value on balancing work and family, experiencing comfort with questioning authority and challenging the traditional chain of command, demanding ongoing performance feedback, expecting transparency and timely outcome measures that show what is working, and relying on instant feedback from electronic communication and social networking" (Batts et al., 2012, p. 4). Harrison (2007) and Sullivan (2004) suggest that police leaders seek ways to bridge the gap between the expectations of the new generation of recruits and the traditional police structure. The traditional police organizational structure may have to adapt to these expectations (or force the new recruits to adapt) if it plans to recruit and keep qualified employees in policing.

Some policing agencies have implemented changes that are believed to better service the community as well as encourage new recruits and older officers working in the field. Mentoring programs where new officers are paired with seasoned officers allow for coaching and training. These programs also allow for seasoned officers to show the young recruits how their role in the organization contributes to the accomplishment of the overall organizational objectives and mission. The mentors can stress the importance of task completion and identify ways the new officers can accomplish personal goals while meeting organizational expectations (Batts et al., 2012). Another approach used with mentoring mirrors the "first-year experience" that college students have. New recruits are exposed to a lengthy training period at the front end of the system, which may include extensive training by the department or through statewide pre-academy orientations (Batts et al., 2012; Scrivner, 2010).

Specialization of services is another change. As the United States moves from an industrial nation to a service-oriented nation, service-related jobs have increased. In service fields, specialists are required much more than generalists (Sapp, 1992). As a result, law enforcement has responded with more training in diversity, technology, and investigations, among other areas. The development of divisions that specialize in specific areas, such as community policing, juvenile policing, and gangs, and inservice training offered early on in officers' careers in investigating with the use of technology to develop integrated services between investigators and technicians, are just two examples of how policing agencies have adapted to specializations.

Specialization brings with it the need for employees to have more education, creates greater expense as wages are expected to be higher, and holds the expectation of flexible management (also common expectations of the new generation). In addition, specialization can bring boredom and carelessness when it is too narrowly focused and does not allow for opportunities to work in numerous situations. Batts et al. (2012) suggest developing "renaissance" officers who are equipped with knowledge and experiences in a variety of specialties and creating different types of jobs, outside of the traditional patrol and investigation, to deter boredom. As pointed out by Sapp (1992), increased communication and personal contact are the keys to keeping professional and specialized staff happy. As expected, this has required a change in the vertical chains of communication and in the supervision, evaluation, training, and daily interactions of policing staff.

Specialization is not without its criticism, however. Braiden (1992) claims that specialization in policing has brought with it myriad disconnected law enforcement functions that do not allow officers to work with one another as they had in the past. Instead, officers in one specialty may be working the same or a similar case as officers in another specialty, but they do not share information because their specialties keep them apart (Braiden, 1992). In addition, specialties can become so focused that officers can do little or nothing else to contribute to the overall policing goals. In this case, reevaluation may be necessary. Another issue of concern with specialization is the ability of the department to provide adequate staff to support the specialties. What may happen, as pointed out by Jones (1980) and Loveday (2007), is that visible policing and patrol become less supported as more and more officers move into areas of interest, and the department as a whole becomes top-heavy with administration and others holding specialized positions.

A second approach to changing traditional policing structures has been increased *professionalization*:

> Like other professions, law enforcement faces the need to upgrade its operating procedures to address contemporary issues and insulate the profession from litigation arising from employee misconduct. In our rapidly changing society, law enforcement agencies are also facing the critical challenge of ensuring that their missions and practices are aligned with community needs. (Bowman, 2001, p. 27)

Furthermore, as law enforcement is called on to perform more diverse and complex services, police officers are expected to adopt higher standards of performance and ethics. By viewing themselves as professionals and specialists, police officers demand the right to make more decisions on their functions and activities. If not given these opportunities, resentment toward the management can occur, as mentioned earlier (Sapp, 1992). As a matter of fact, a study done in 2000 by Stanard and Associates reported that the biggest stressor for police officers is their administration (Fischer, 2003). Also, benefit and compensation packages are much more important to professionals and specialists. Police unions have actually reported that younger-generation officers are more demanding of time off versus overtime pay and more flexible work schedules (Rozas, 2008). Departments that have acknowledged the importance of professionalism and understand its consequences have adopted diverse job assignments, such as directed patrol strategies, split-force policing, and suspect-oriented policing, as well as bicycle patrols, boat patrols, foot patrols, and aircraft patrols (Cox et al., 2014), along with increased inservice training opportunities, educational support, flexible time work scheduling, and career ladders that allow for merit pay increases, recognition, and more than one method for promotion (Rozas, 2008). Scrivner (2010) also suggests that these agencies have changed discipline systems from a "days off" approach to a behavior-change approach, which is more appropriate for a professional workforce.

No discussion of professionalism is complete without mention of higher-education requirements in policing. Thinking of promotion, merit raises, and recognition, it may be assumed that the person receiving such accolades is performing at a high level of achievement. It may also be assumed that the person deserves the accolades because of knowledge or expertise acquired through education, which is the basis for most professional positions in society. Much has been written on whether the requirement of a college education is important—or, for that part, necessary—in performing police functions (see Dantzker, 1989; Kappeler, Sapp, & Carter, 1992; Mayo, 2006; Paoline & Terrill, 2007; Varricchio, 1998; and others). Reports claim that police officers with college degrees perform better overall on patrol, when handling stressful situations, in community policing, and in managing citizen issues (Dantzker, 1989). Others claim that sheer experience and on-the-job training in policing are sufficient to master the trade (Paoline & Terrill, 2007). Whether these arguments are valid is still up for debate, as empirical research is ongoing in this field. Although, as mentioned earlier, new-generation officers are more likely to be college educated, and they expect that their education will allow for advancement opportunities and autonomy.

However, there are pressing issues brought about in the debate, one of which is the increased costs of employing those with college educations. As expected, people with degrees require higher salaries and benefits packages than do those without higher education. In addition, they are more likely to challenge the status quo in the agency through creative and critical thinking and innovation. They are trained in college courses to look ahead and to anticipate and challenge issues. This is not conducive to the traditional policing organization. Another issue raised is that of burnout or boredom. Those with degrees may find the job monotonous and become frustrated. Other concerns (such as measuring police performance) are also evident in determining if higher education is an important variable to consider when selecting police officers.

Currently, most police departments only require high school diplomas or general education diplomas and choose to provide job training to their recruits. Even those requiring college training do not call for completed bachelor's degrees (60 college credit hours being the norm). In light of the many attempts to professionalize policing, it is interesting that policing agencies do not seem to buy into the education argument.

Accreditation is also a factor in professionalism. According to Cox and Wade (2002), the objectives of accreditation include developing standards on which agency performance can be measured and individual objective assessments of officers can be made. Accreditation has evolved from a decade of debate among law enforcement agencies seeking ways to professionalize and renew the image of policing (Bowman, 2001). Peace Officer Standards and Training (POST) boards located in individual states and the Commission on the Accreditation for Law Enforcement Agencies (CALEA) have created certification processes for new officers and established hundreds of standards by which to evaluate police agencies (Cox & Wade, 2002). While POST uses standardized written examinations, training, and education standards to ensure a minimum level of knowledge among police officers, CALEA focuses on professional criteria met at the agency level. When working with CALEA, departments voluntarily meet the standards of professionalism, which do the following:

- Require an agency to develop a comprehensive, well thought out, uniform set of written directives. This is one of the most successful methods for reaching administrative and operational goals, while also providing direction to personnel.
- Provide the necessary reports and analyses a CEO needs to make fact-based, informed management decisions.
- Require a preparedness program be put in place—so an agency is ready to address natural or man-made critical incidents.
- Are a means for developing or improving upon an agency's relationship with the community.
- Strengthen an agency's accountability, both within the agency and the community, through a continuum of standards that clearly define authority, performance, and responsibilities.
- Can limit an agency's liability and risk exposure because it demonstrates that internationally recognized standards for law enforcement have been met, as verified by a team of independent outside CALEA-trained assessors.
- Facilitates an agency's pursuit of professional excellence. (CALEA, 2010, n.p.)

Agencies that want to participate in accreditation work with outside assessors to determine which standards best apply to the agency and what they should be doing to meet the standards. It should be noted here that not all standards identified by CALEA would apply to every agency. CALEA's standards specify form, not function, in the police department. They are considered the means rather than the end results (Sykes, 1992).

The consequences of accreditation are far-reaching. Lateral moves between departments and transfers of officers from one department or state to another should be seamless if all of the officers received the same training. The overall management of training, performance, and supervision should also improve. In addition, the level of service provided to communities as tracked by the departments should show better results as the departments strive to meet service standards. Ethical expectations and understandings also improve with accreditation monitoring (Cox et al., 2014).

The unfortunate downside is the cost related to the accreditation process. It can cost $5,000 or more to begin accreditation, and $3,400 or more to maintain annual certification (CALEA, 2010). Cost varies by department size, which is based on the number of employees. The cost of accreditation has been burdensome for smaller departments, sheriff's departments, and states with limited funding for criminal justice. Considering the impact accreditation would have on small departments and on policing in general, this fact is troublesome. The majority of police departments in the United States are small, with some only employing a few full-time officers. Police agencies also, by and large, have limited resources. This means that most of the nation's law enforcement officers may not have the opportunity to work in nationally accredited agencies, potentially limiting the quality of police services to the community and coordination of law enforcement agencies involved in accreditation processes (Bowman, 2001). As a result, some states have chosen, because of costs or opposition, to create their own police accreditation organizations. In some cases these are modeled after CALEA, while in others they are not. New York, for instance, created its own autonomous accreditation process for agencies in that state to become accredited without associated fees. Florida, on the other hand, modeled its accreditation program after CALEA but used fewer standards and tailored them to Florida law enforcement agencies (Bowman, 2001).

The reason why accreditation is much sought after by policing agencies is threefold. First, it allows for highly coordinated efforts among policing agencies. Second, it provides agencies with an existing base of knowledge and research upon which to promote uniformity and reform. The third and final reason for agencies to seek accreditation is because it promotes professionalism by increasing the standards of performance and ethics. In doing so, it decreases an agency's vulnerability to litigation by requiring written policies and procedures developed from a set of nationally tested law enforcement standards (Bowman, 2001). For the general public, accreditation means the potential for more quality services and service delivery; and for the police officer, it means increased professionalism and advancement opportunities and decreased lawsuits.

As mentioned previously, the public's perception of the police and the policing industry's image can influence the cooperative relationship between the community and the police—and, in the long run, the services provided. The Office of Community Oriented Policing Services (2009) claims,

> Police departments must adhere to the principles of integrity and professionalism as cornerstones of community trust-building. Because officers occupy a position of trust and confidence in their communities and are afforded awesome authority to carry out their duties, any excessive use of that authority, abuse of power, or failure to fulfill their duties can erode public trust and reduce or destroy their credibility within the communities they serve. Every member of a police department must understand that he or she represents the entire agency, that personal conduct is his or her own responsibility, and that he or she will be held accountable for all conduct, whether positive or negative. (p. 7)

If there is a negative view of the police in the minds of citizens, then the public will be less willing to help in the pursuit of crime control. However, if the police can manage to promote responsibility and positive relationships with the public, the community becomes a valuable resource in maintaining social order. To promote active participation of the community, police departments are taking a more proactive stance on ethics and police corruption alongside the adoption of accreditation standards (Goergen, 2001).

Ethics is defined as doing the right thing. "It means more than simply acting within the scope of the law" (Cox, Campbell, & McCamey, 2002, p. 1). Unfortunately, this may not be as clearly understood by police officers as it should be. In a study by Allen, Mhlanga, and Khan (2006), police officers were surveyed to determine their responses to situations in which ethical conduct might be challenged. Questions where

> respondents indicated unethical or improper responses included situations in which their co-workers were involved, such as when co-workers were stealing merchandise from a mini-mart, engaging in illegal gambling during their off-duty hours, violating traffic laws, and using vulgar or profane language with public citizens. (pp. 23–24)

Amazingly, more than 80% of the respondents claimed to have attended an ethics course or training in the past. Yet, when asked, they were willing to turn the other cheek regarding the unethical behaviors of their fellow officers (Allen et al., 2006). Loyalty to the group is commendable until it becomes detrimental to the organization, the person, and the social order of society (Cox et al., 2002). Police departments are finally realizing the importance of enforcing ethical behaviors and the impact of unethical behavior on the policing image, and they are adopting a number of ways to encourage officers to act more ethically, aside from the traditional and well-known approach of internal affairs. Many of these approaches are agency-specific, although a few of the more prevalent practices will be discussed here. Ethics and ethical practices were also addressed in Chapter 5.

Doing away with the "don't ask, don't tell" policy among police officers and policing administrators is one way to increase integrity. "This approach, in which neither new recruits nor sworn officers are asked to openly discuss ethical violations or misconduct, appears to assume that if these issues are not addressed they don't exist. Nothing, of course, could be further from the truth" (Cox & Allen, 2005, p. 35). Ignoring the behavior does not make it go away. Instead, it fosters an environment of secrets and reinforces the *police subculture,* which consists of "the informal rules and regulations, tactics, and folklore passed on from one generation of police officers to another. It is both a result and a cause of police isolation from the larger society and police solidarity" (Cox, 1996, p. 165). The subculture is the foundation of the police mentality of "us against them." Police departments across the United States are encouraging officers to bring to light actions that may violate the ethical expectations of law enforcement, even though it means breaking down the police subculture. They have done so both verbally in staff meetings and personal meetings with officers as well as through the introduction of an agency code of ethics. The code of ethics binds the officers together in the pursuit of proper behaviors. It also obligates them to one another and to the agency. Having the code in place allows administrators to sanction those who violate the requirements. As noted in In the News 9.2, the Burlington Police Department in North Carolina has identified the following as its code of ethics, which parallels the code created by the International Association of Chiefs of Police (IACP).

In the News 9.2
Burlington Police Department Code of Ethics

All Sworn and Civilian personnel will abide by the Law Enforcement Code of Ethics published by the IACP.

Law Enforcement Code of Ethics

All law enforcement officers must be fully aware of the ethical responsibilities of their position and must strive constantly to live up to the highest possible standards of professional policing.

The International Association of Chiefs of Police believes it is important that police officers have clear advice and counsel available to assist them in performing their duties consistent with these standards, and has adopted the following ethical mandates as guidelines to meet these ends.

Primary Responsibilities of a Police Officer

A police officer acts as an official representative of government who is required and trusted to work within the law. The officer's powers and duties are conferred by statute. The fundamental duties of a police officer include serving the community; safeguarding lives and property; protecting the innocent; keeping the peace; and ensuring the rights of all to liberty, equality and justice.

Performance of the Duties of a Police Officer

A police officer shall perform all duties impartially, without favor or affection or ill will and without regard to status, sex, race, religion, political belief or aspiration. All citizens will be treated equally with courtesy, consideration and dignity.

Officers will never allow personal feelings, animosities or friendships to influence official conduct. Laws will be enforced appropriately and courteously and, in carrying out their responsibilities, officers will strive to obtain maximum cooperation from the public. They will conduct themselves in appearance and deportment in such a manner as to inspire confidence and respect for the position of public trust they hold.

Discretion

A police officer will use responsibly the discretion vested in the position and exercise it within the law. The principle of reasonableness will guide the officer's determinations and the officer will consider all surrounding circumstances in determining whether any legal action shall be taken.

Consistent and wise use of discretion, based on professional policing competence, will do much to preserve good relationships and retain the confidence of the public. There can be difficulty in choosing between conflicting courses of action. It is important to remember that a timely word of advice rather than arrest which may be correct in appropriate circumstances can be a more effective means of achieving a desired end.

Use of Force

A police officer will never employ unnecessary force or violence and will use only such force in the discharge of duty as is reasonable in all circumstances.

Force should be used only with the greatest restraint and only after discussion, negotiation and persuasion have been found to be inappropriate or ineffective. While the use of force is occasionally unavoidable, every police officer will refrain from applying the unnecessary infliction of pain or suffering and will never engage in cruel, degrading or inhuman treatment of any person.

Confidentiality

Whatever a police officer sees, hears or learns of, which is of a confidential nature, will be kept secret unless the performance of duty or legal provision requires otherwise.

Members of the public have a right to security and privacy, and information obtained about them must not be improperly divulged.

Integrity

A police officer will not engage in acts of corruption or bribery, nor will an officer condone such acts by other police officers.

The public demands that the integrity of police officers be above reproach. Police officers must, therefore, avoid any conduct that might compromise integrity and thus undercut the public confidence in a law enforcement agency. Officers will refuse to accept any gifts, presents, subscriptions, favors, gratuities or promises that could be interpreted as seeking to cause the officer to refrain from performing official responsibilities honestly and within the law. Police officers must not receive private or special advantage from their official status, Respect from the public cannot be bought; it can only be earned and cultivated.

Cooperation With Other Officers and Agencies

Police officers will cooperate with all legally authorized agencies and their representatives in the pursuit of justice.

An officer or agency may be one among many organizations that may provide law enforcement services to a jurisdiction. It is imperative that a police officer assist colleagues fully and completely with respect and consideration at all times.

(Continued)

(Continued)

Personal/Professional Capabilities

Police officers will be responsible for their own standard of professional performance and will take every reasonable opportunity to enhance and improve their level of knowledge and competence.

Through study and experience, a police officer can acquire the high level of knowledge and competence that is essential for the efficient and effective performance of duty. The acquisition of knowledge is a never-ending process of personal and professional development that should be pursued constantly.

Private Life

Police officers will behave in a manner that does not bring discredit to their agencies or themselves.

A police officer's character and conduct while off duty must always be exemplary, thus maintaining a position of respect in the community in which he or she lives and serves. The officer's personal behavior must be beyond reproach.

SOURCE: International Association of Chiefs of Police. Available online at http://ci.burlington.nc.us/index .asp?NID=1010.

Any officer who violates the code of ethics, or ignores the unethical behaviors of another, would be susceptible to sanctions.

Understanding that discretion does not inherently lead to unethical behavior is another key approach to promoting integrity in the workforce. Police officers have to be provided the ability to make decisions in carrying out their duties in the field; however, they should also understand that there are guidelines and parameters in exercising that discretion (Gleason, 2006). Police administrators must create an environment that encourages discretion within defined boundaries to increase ethical behaviors.

Training in ethics, both inservice and prior to employment, is also used to strengthen good behavior among police. Revisiting the issue of higher education, one can argue that colleges and universities play integral roles in shaping the principles of students enrolled in their courses. Taking the approach that ethics can be learned, universities promote morality through reinforcements provided in classroom lecture examples, situation-based curricula, guest speakers, and classes focused specifically on ethics. Police departments that have built college credits or degrees into their hiring criteria may have done so as a result of the benefits officers have gained from these classes. They can expect that those coming into the agency with higher education are better prepared to handle situations in which ethical decisions may come into play. Police departments can also view ethics training as risk management. As Gleason (2006, n.p.) suggested, police civil lawsuits often result from the following:

- Negligent hiring
- Failure to supervise

- Failure to train
- Negligent entrusting
- Negligent assigning
- Failure to discipline
- Negligent retaining
- Unnecessary or excessive force
- False arrests
- Negligent vehicle operation

[A] common thread [in this list] is the exercise of imprudent judgment that either creates the circumstances leading up to the ultimate failure or precipitates the action or inaction that directly causes the loss or injury.

Ethics training teaches officers to think before acting and reduces the chances that an officer will make a poor decision.

Constant reminding of what is ethical and unethical and what constitutes corruption is necessary. As pointed out by Allen et al. (2006), just because an officer attends a single class or seminar on ethical conduct does not mean that the officer is going to demonstrate good behavior, as conveyed by the 80% of respondents who would choose to ignore inappropriate behavior by a coworker. The actions expected must be reviewed, reviewed, and reviewed again. In addition, management has to constantly and consistently convey the message that corruption is not tolerated. Those departments that are taking ethical issues seriously provide reinforcements for doing the right thing, beginning at the socialization process and continuing through promotion.

Like in any business, ethical behavior in law enforcement must start at the top. Modeling the behavior expected of others is basic common sense for the policing administrator. The chief should not fix friends' or family members' traffic tickets, accept gratuities, lie, or take gifts for services, especially if these actions have been identified as improper behaviors for others (Allen et al., 2006). The view of the police administrator as the ethical leader has taken on a life of its own, as police departments strive to overcome the challenges created by traditional policing management practices. But by looking at corruption as an agency failure rather than an individual problem, the traditions, policies, and practices that fostered this type of behavior are being changed and eliminated (Murphy & Caplan, 1991). In the broader scope of service delivery, officers who practice ethical behaviors and agencies that promote ethical actions are better service providers.

Community Policing: The Opportunity to Provide Quality Services

Although police forces in the United States and abroad have implemented many strategies to reduce crime, community policing has had an impact on both organizational structure and community relations. Law enforcement departments have used the core community policing elements of community partnerships, problem solving, and organizational transformation to develop community-oriented policing initiatives, such as foot patrol, school resource officers, neighborhood watch programs, and others to become more proactive in their approach to the community. In turn, this has relaxed and worked to modify the rigid structures of police departments.

Community policing is a philosophy, not a tactic (Carter, 1992). "It is a proactive, decentralized approach to policing, designed to reduce crime, disorder, and fear of crime, while also responding to explicit needs and demands of the community" (Carter, 1992, p. 78). Since it involves adoption of a philosophy, it permeates all units, divisions, and levels of the policing organization. Community policing promotes innovative thinking and problem-solving activities (which fits well with new-generation and college-educated police officers) (Carter, 1992). It also allows officers working in this unit to make decisions on the best way to approach situations (within policy and procedural guidelines). In doing so, police officers are provided greater task autonomy and task significance. Ownership of the decision and the resulting actions belongs to the individual officer, allowing the officer to better identify with the work and the outcomes. Feedback to officers on the success of the activities and their approaches to building community relations comes from both the administration and the public being served.

It may be argued that community policing has resulted in the biggest change to police practices in recent years (Giacomazzi & Brody, 2004) and has most affected the way in which the police provide services. This is also the best place to see service quality initiatives at work in policing. Implementing community policing philosophies in a police department involves changing the structure of the police department to include a bilateral communication system and more elaborate hiring, training, and promotion practices (Oettmeier & Wycoff, 1994). Police departments also have to better incorporate input from the external environment (Dilulio, 1993; Oakes, 1995). Departments that actively engage in community policing, not just experiment in isolated programs that use community policing philosophies, must focus on strategic planning that involves all organizational employees and other key stakeholders. The strategic plan is a document that should cover a 5- to 10-year period and should explicitly identify the agency's activities, organizational goals, objectives, and action plans. In addition, it should provide performance measures for each of the objectives identified (Giacomazzi & Brody, 2004). For the strategic plan to be effective, all personnel must be involved in the planning and be widely versed in how to implement it (Office of Community Oriented Policing Services, 2012). Initially, such elaborate planning may likely burden the police department and appear less efficient than the traditional top-down approach used in police management (Cheurprakobkit, 2001; Crank & Langworthy, 1997; Schafer, 2001). But those departments that have engaged in long-term strategic planning in community policing are seeing greater benefits for both the organization and the citizens affected (Giacomazzi & Brody, 2004). They are also seeing more sustainable community policing programs.

Scholars such as Sparrow (1988), Denhardt (1995), and Oettmeier and Wycoff (1994) have noted that changes to key organizational elements, such as communication practices, quality circles that allow for participative management, rewards systems, and employee performance evaluations, promote the community policing values and goals and lead to community policing success. Under the community policing umbrella, officers have to be provided the autonomy to make decisions without constantly seeking permission from their superiors. Such an approach will create problem-solving partnerships that meet the community and strategic goals. Departments may also have to broaden their officer performance measures to include community satisfaction, less fear of crime, improved quality of life, and alleviation of problems. This information may come from community and partnership feedback rather than from arrest data and departmental statistics (Office of Community Oriented Policing Services, 2012). Police departments may also have to turn to innovative strategies in meeting the demands for police services while supporting community policing programs. In this case, Glensor and Peak (1996) recommend that police departments free up time for problem solving by police officers by taking offense reports over the phone or instituting a mail-in reporting system. Community policing actually encourages despecialization. "To achieve community policing goals, officers have to be able to handle multiple responsibilities and take a team approach to collaborative problem solving and partnering with the community" (Office of Community Oriented Policing, 2012, p. 9). Although this may appear contrary to the approaches discussed earlier in making police departments more professional and appealing to new-generation officers, it may not be as conflicting as it first appears. New-generation officers want autonomy in their positions, and they are more willing to forge relationships, partnerships, and collaborations. They also are more educated in and understanding of the issues confronting diverse populations. So even though they may lose the opportunity to develop some specialized skills, they may be better suited, and happier overall, working in a community policing environment that allows for flexibility in job performance and task completion.

The traditional police culture as well as resistance to change, trust issues, role ambiguity, conflict, power issues, and informal communications may all contribute to the failure of the implementation of community policing (Giacomazzi & Brody, 2004). A successful transition requires a redefining of the police culture to include the participation of other service providers and citizens in solving neighborhood problems. Unfortunately, this is contrary to the traditional idea that citizens should have little involvement in the police process, other than as witnesses, complainants, and victims (Giacomazzi & Brody, 2004; Thurman, Zhao, & Giacomazzi, 2001). Changing an organizational culture can be difficult; however, using the recruiting process along with other measures, such as modeling behaviors, rewarding behaviors, communicating expectations, and training, will promote an organizational climate that supports community policing as well as better service delivery.

As pointed out in the earlier chapters, "Effective organizations learn to connect to their environments in meaningful ways" (Giacomazzi & Brody, 2004, p. 40). In the case of implementing community policing, involving key stakeholders in the transition and planning processes allows for better police–community collaboration right from the beginning. Dilulio (1993) claims that community policing can only have a measurable positive impact if the police and key stakeholders actively assist, cooperate, and participate. Promoting a feeling of partnership between the police and citizens is the impetus for successful community policing execution.

When measuring the effectiveness of community policing, departments have to consider both the changes within the organization as well as the accomplishment of organizational goals. Ongoing assessments are important to ensure that the organizational changes necessary to implement effective community policing are taking place and that community members' ties to the police department remain strong by allowing their input into the performance evaluations. Although traditional measures of policing effectiveness, such as crime statistics, 911 responses, police response time, and so forth, are still suitable assessments in community policing, they should be supplemented with measurements that consider community partnerships, involvement, and problem-solving activities (Bureau of Justice Assistance, 1994).

The few evaluations of community policing programs that have occurred show inconsistent results. Some suggest that community policing is a sustainable approach to policing (Weisel & Eck, 2000), while others assert that police departments should move past community policing's failures and try something new (Kerlikowske, 2004). Cox and McCamey (2008) suggest the following:

> What we have learned [in community policing], among other things, is that in every facet of police work, we need to inform, discuss with, and value members of the community. If the network perspective [and the service quality approach, for that matter] of criminal justice is accepted, community policing would appear to be a step in the right direction because it recognizes the interrelationships among the police, other service agencies, and the public. (p. 145)

Crank, Kadleck, and Koski (2010) have also argued that Compstat and other data-driven approaches to policing, like intelligence-led policing, are the wave of the future. Heightened focus on terrorism-oriented policing has also taken priority over community policing initiatives in many departments. Lee (2010) found that police departments more focused on homeland security planning had fewer officers working in community policing.

The policing field is constantly evolving as the demands and expectations of the public and those employed as law enforcement providers increase. Although the traditional structure is still in place in most agencies, administrators are at least acknowledging its inherent disadvantages and making attempts to address those shortcomings. Doing away completely with a reliance on the rigid, policy-driven nature of the police department may not be the answer, since liability and other issues remain. However, as has been pointed out, police officers are better educated and better prepared than ever before, so some modernization of the structure is necessary to recruit and retain police officers and to allow those employed to better serve citizens.

In Chapter 3, customers were described as one of the participants in the service delivery process. These customers evaluate the quality of a service primarily by the quality of the human contact. The quality of law enforcement services is judged by the contacts with frontline police officers. Unlike physical resources, which depreciate when used, employees become more valuable with time and through proper training and experience. Management's challenge, therefore, is to harness an employee's latent cognitive energy and transform it into a competitive weapon (Sawhney, 2013). Progressive police departments may use any number of procedures to influence the quality and skills of new employees. Recruitment can be key in this process.

However, recruitment can provide only a partial solution, as new recruits may only form a small portion of the total workforce in a police department. Therefore, the importance of training in promoting ethical behavior and a motivated police workforce cannot be overstated. High-quality service providers require customer-focused behaviors and appropriate skills and abilities for performing the job. All of these develop from the creation of a positive work environment and through supervisors who act as coaches and mentors rather than administrators (Sawhney, 2013). Well-trained police officers can be innovative in making decisions and in advancing quality and customer satisfaction goals. It must be remembered, though, that a combination of the intangible nature of law enforcement services and the customer as a participant in the service delivery process brings the possibility of variation of service from customer to customer. Fitzsimmons and Fitzsimmons (2006) note, "A customer expects to be treated fairly and be given the same service that others receive. The development of standards and of employee training in proper procedures is the key to ensuring consistency in the service provided" (p. 25). Therefore, it is important for police departments to consider internal or external accreditation processes to ensure greater standardization of service delivery and to include the stakeholders in the process of police service delivery, which will ultimately improve the quality of law enforcement service as perceived by the customers. It is also important for officers to be well trained in the use and abuse of discretion. "Discretion, when properly exercised, makes the law more just" (Gleason, 2006, n.p.).

Chapter Summary

- Much has been written about the history of police in America. Their history can be traced back to early colonies that used night watchmen to protect the citizens while they slept. A growth in population and increased social disorder provided the impetus for organized policing in the early 1800s. Early police departments were modeled after the London Metropolitan Police, although they were tied directly into the political structure of cities.

- The organizational structure of policing has been debated since the first police force was created. Arguments over how police departments should be managed, the duties of the police, and their role in the enforcement of laws have plagued the profession. Police corruption has also been an issue.

- The negative policing image is probably one of the biggest issues facing law enforcement. Police corruption, historically and now, has led to poor relationships between society and police officers. In addition, the advent of technological advances has increased expectations from the community but decreased, in some cases, the ability of the police to respond adequately to the community's needs and demands. Professionalization, recruitment of minorities and women, and community-oriented policing initiatives have been used to improve the community's attitudes and perceptions of the police. Community policing is probably the best approach to instituting quality services for citizens.

- Private policing has been around as long as public policing. Private agencies were in demand in the mid-1800s to resolve labor union disputes. They also worked with private citizens to protect private property, in divorce cases, and to safeguard small businesses. Private police agencies are not regulated in the same fashion as public agencies. Today's private police are extremely important in the protection of U.S. infrastructures owned by private companies. Cooperation between private and public policing agencies has increased as a result of the terrorist attacks of September 11, 2001.

- The federal government has never identified a national police force; however, there are several federal agencies that perform traditional policing duties. The U.S. Department of Homeland Security combined several of the policing-based agencies at the federal level into one department.
- The police perform two primary functions—they act as agents of control and agents of support by performing crime-related activities, order maintenance, and crime prevention.
- A chief of police is the top administrator in a police department. There are three levels of management in police departments—top management, middle management, and lower-level management or first-line supervisors. Although the groupings may vary slightly, police departments are typically divided into operations divisions and administrative divisions.
- Police departments are structured in paramilitary formats that follow policies and procedures and promote rigid chains of command. This structure is resistant to change and fails to promote good communication channels. Unwieldy processes and procedures have been created as a result of the bureaucracy. Thus, police departments cannot quickly respond to changes in their environment.
- A new generation of workers is entering the workforce—including the field of policing. These workers are more likely to be college educated, willing to challenge authority and structure, willing to work as teams and in collaborations, willing to work with minorities and diverse populations, and more demanding of flexible work schedules and time off. The traditional policing organizational structure may have to adapt to meet the needs and demands of the new generation of officer or create ways to adapt the new-generation officer to the structure, such as mentoring and first-year experiences.
- To overcome the distinct disadvantages of the closed-system structure and to better serve the community, policing agencies have moved toward the following:

  o Mentoring programs
  o Specializations in services offered to the community and other agencies
  o Increased professionalism through the adoption of diverse job assignments, increased inservice training, and higher-education requirements
  o Compliance with widely accepted and tested accreditation standards
  o Development of policies and work environments that do not promote or tolerate police misconduct
  o Use of community-oriented policing programs

- Doing away completely with the traditional police management structure may not be a possibility because of the liability associated with the job. But as police officers become better educated and better prepared, increased flexibility by policing management and in the organizational structure will be necessary.

Chapter Review Questions

1. Describe how the history of policing has contributed to the negative image of the police officer in contemporary society.

2. How might public and private policing agencies work together against crime in today's society? Identify a cooperative program between two such agencies with which you are familiar.

3. In your opinion, how should police departments meet the needs and demands of the new-generation workforce?

4. Explain why accreditation is useful for a policing agency.

5. Relate community policing initiatives to the service quality approach addressed in Chapter 3.

CASE STUDY

Blake City has a population of 952,000 people. It is the geographical hub for the southern part of the state. The city, like many others, has experienced a declining revenue and tax base. For the past four years, the city has decreased funding to schools and social service agencies by more than $1.5 million. One of the hardest-hit areas has been parks and recreation, where more than 24 recreation centers have closed for afterschool activities and extracurricular sports. Citizens who reside in areas most affected by the closed recreation centers relied on the centers for afterschool care while they worked. The citizens have lobbied for more funding for parks and recreation, and there has been increased media attention to these issues.

You are the police chief of the Blake City Police Department. It has come to your attention through the local media that more than 18,000 court cases have been dismissed by judges in the past three years as a result of police officers failing to appear in court. The media reported that the dismissed cases could have resulted in more than $3 million in fines for the city, since most cases in the municipal court result in an average fine of $190.00.

This news has not set well in the community. With budget reductions, reduced services, and heightened stress, community members are demanding to know why officers are not following through on the cases. Additionally, there have been questions raised about the lax approach to punishing offenders, since some offenders have had multiple cases dismissed.

Questions for Review

1. What may possibly explain the failure-to-appear issue the department is facing?

2. Why haven't the courts or lower-level managers in the police department noticed the issue? Would this behavior have continued unnoticed if it hadn't been for the media?

3. As the police chief, how do you respond to the media? How do you respond to the citizens questioning the actions of the police?

4. Keeping quality service approaches in mind, how do you ensure that changes are made that will increase the positive view of the police department?

Internet Resources

Commission on the Accreditation for Law Enforcement Agencies (CALEA)—http://www.calea.org

Federal Bureau of Investigation—http://www.fbi.gov

Office of Community Oriented Policing Services (COPS)—http://www.cops.usdoj.gov

References and Suggested Readings

Allen, J. M., Mhlanga, B. M., & Khan, E. (2006). Education, training, and ethical dilemmas: Responses of criminal justice practitioners regarding professional and ethical issues. *Professional Issues in Criminal Justice: A Professional Journal, 1*(1), 3–28.

Auerbach, J. S. (1966). *Labor and liberty: The LaFollette Committee and the New Deal.* Indianapolis, IN: Bobbs-Merrill.

Batt, A. W., Smoot, S. M., & Scrivner, E. (2012). *Police leadership challenges in a changing world.* New Perspectives in Policing, National Institute of Justice. Retrieved from https://ncjrs.gov/pdffiles1/nij/238338.pdf.

Beck, J., & M. Wade. (2004). Got game: How the gamer generation is reshaping business forever. Boston, MA: Harvard Business School Press.

Bowman, D. (2001, February). An emerging alliance between the commission of accreditation for law enforcement agencies (CALEA) and the local law enforcement community. *Law Enforcement Executive Forum Journal, 1*(2), 27–38.

Braiden, C. R. (1992). Enriching traditional roles. In L. T. Hoover (Ed.), *Police management: Issues and perspectives* (pp. 87–116). Washington, DC: Police Executive Research Forum.

Bureau of Justice Assistance. (1994). *Understanding community policing: A framework for action.* Washington, DC: U.S. Department of Justice, Office of Justice Programs. Retrieved from http://www.ncjrs.gov/pdf files/commp.pdf.

Bureau of Justice Statistics. (2004). *State and local law enforcement statistics.* Washington, DC: U.S. Department of Justice, Office of Justice Programs.

Bureau of Justice Statistics. (2011). Census of state and local law enforcement agencies, 2008. Washington, DC: U.S. Department of Justice. Office of Justice Programs.

Bureau of Labor Statistics, U.S. Department of Labor. *Occupational outlook handbook, 2012–2013 edition,* Private Detectives and Investigators. Retrieved from http://www.bls.gov/ooh/protective-service/private-detectives-and-investigators.htm.

Carter, D. L. (1992). Community alliance. In L. T. Hoover (Ed.), *Police management: Issues and perspectives* (pp. 61–86). Washington, DC: Police Executive Research Forum.

Cheurprakobkit, S. (2001). Organizational impacts on community policing: Management issues and officers' perceptions. *Crime Prevention and Community Safety: An International Journal, 1*(1), 43–54.

Commission on Accreditation for Law Enforcement Agencies, Inc. (2010). *About CALEA.* Retrieved from http://www.calea.org/Online/AboutCALEA/Commission.htm.

Conser, J. A., & Russell, G. D. (2000). *Law enforcement in the United States.* Gaithersburg, MD: Aspen.

Cox, S. M. (1996). *Police: Practices, perspective, problems.* Boston, MA: Allyn & Bacon.

Cox, S. M., & Allen, J. M. (2005). Encouraging ethical practices in policing. *Law Enforcement Executive Forum, 5*(3), 35–41.

Cox, S. M., Campbell, T. G., & McCamey, W. P. (2002). Doing the right thing: Why a few police officers find it so difficult. *Illinois Law Enforcement Executive Forum, 2*(2), 1–7.

Cox, S. M., & McCamey, W. P. (2008). *Introduction to criminal justice: Exploring the network.* Durham, NC: Carolina Academic Press.

Cox, S. M., McCamey, W. P., & Scaramella, G. L. (2014). *Introduction to policing* (2nd ed.). Thousand Oaks, CA: Sage.

Cox, S. M., & Wade, J. (2002). *The criminal justice network: An introduction* (4th ed.). Boston, MA: McGraw-Hill.

Crank, J. P., Kadleck, C., & Koski, C.M. (2010). The USA: The next big thing. *Police Practice & Research, 11*(5), 405–442.

Crank, J., & Langworthy, R. (1997). Fragmented centralization and the organization of the police. *Policing and Society, 6*(3), 213–229.

Cunningham, W. C., Strauchs, J. J., & Van Meter, C. W. (1990). *The Hallcrest report II: Private security trends, 1970–2000.* Washington, DC: U.S. Department of Justice.

Dantzker, M. L. (1989). Identifying determinants of job satisfaction among police officers. *Journal of Police and Criminal Psychology, 10*(1), 47–56.

Denhardt, R. (1995). *Public administration: An action orientation* (2nd ed.). Belmont, CA: Wadsworth.

Department of Homeland Security. (2010, February). *Quadrennial homeland security review report: A strategic framework for homeland security.* Retrieved from http://www.dhs.gov/xlibrary/assets/qhsr_report.pdf.

Dilulio, J. J. (1993). *Rethinking the criminal justice system: Toward a new paradigm.* Washington, DC: U.S. Department of Justice.

Eck, J. E., & Rosenbaum, D. P. (1994). The new police order: Effectiveness, equity, and efficiency in community policing. In D. P. Rosenbaum (Ed.), *The challenge of community policing: Testing the promises* (pp. 3–23). Thousand Oaks, CA: Sage.

Fischer, R. (2003). The police executive: Training for leadership. In M. Palmiotto & M. Dantzker (Eds.), *Policing and training issues* (pp. 51–65). Upper Saddle River, NJ: Prentice Hall.

Fischer, R. J., & Green, G. (1992). *Introduction to security* (5th ed.). Boston, MA: Butterworth-Heinemann.

Fitzsimmons, J. A., & Fitzsimmons, M. J. (2006). *Service management: Operations, strategy, information technology* (5th ed.). Columbus, OH: McGraw-Hill/Irwin.

Giacomazzi, A. L., & Brody, D. C. (2004). The effectiveness of external assessments in facilitating organizational change in law enforcement. *Policing, 27*(1), 37–55.

Gleason, T. (2006). Ethics training for police. *The Police Chief, 73*(11).

Glensor, R. W., & Peak, K. (1996). Implementing change: Community-oriented policing and problem solving. *Law Enforcement Bulletin, 65*(7), 14–21.

Goergen, T. M. (2001). The public trust: A statement on ethics. *Illinois Law Enforcement Executive Forum, 1*(2), 1–3.

Goldstein, H. (1990). *Problem-oriented policing.* New York, NY: McGraw-Hill.

Harrison, B. (2007). Gamers, millennials, and generation next: Implications for policing. *Police Chief, 74*(10).

Hicks, R., & Hicks, K. (1999). *Boomers, Xers, and other strangers.* Wheaton, IL: Tyndale House.

Joh, E. (2006). The forgotten threat: Private policing and the state. *Indiana Journal of Global Legal Studies, 13*(2), 357–389.

Jones, J. E. (1981). The organizational universe. In J. E. Jones & J. W. Pfeiffer (Eds.), *The 1981 annual handbook for group facilitators.* San Diego, CA: University Associates, Inc.

Jones, M. (1980). *Organisational aspects of police behaviour.* Farnborough, Hampshire, England: Gower.

Kakalik, J. S., & Wildhorn, S. (1971). *Private police in the United States.* Washington, DC: U.S. Department of Justice.

Kappeler, V. E., Sapp, A. D., & Carter, D. L. (1992). Police officer higher education, citizen complaints, and departmental rule violations. *American Journal of the Police, 11*(2), 37–54.

Kerlikowske, R. G. (2004). The end of community policing: Remembering the lessons learned. *FBI Law Enforcement Bulletin, 73*(4), 6–11.

Lee, J. (2010). Policing after 9/11: Community policing in an age of homeland security. *Police Quarterly, 13*(4), 347–366.

Loveday, B. (2007). Workforce modernisation in the police service. *International Journal of Police Science and Management, 10*(2), 136–144.

Lurigo, A. J., & Rosenbaum, D. P. (1994). The impact of community policing on police personnel. In D. P. Rosenbaum (Ed.), *The challenge of community policing: Testing the promises* (pp. 147–163). Thousand Oaks, CA: Sage.

Lurigo, A. J., & Skogan, W. G. (2000). Winning the hearts and minds of police officers: An assessment of perceptions of community policing in Chicago. In R. W. Glensor, M. E. Correia, & K. J. Peak (Eds.), *Policing communities: Understanding crime and solving problems* (pp. 246–256). Los Angeles, CA: Roxbury.

Mastrofski, S. D. (2007). *Police organization and management issues for the next decade.* National Institute of Justice, Department of Justice, Washington, DC. Retrieved from https://www.ncjrs.gov/pdffiles1/nij/grants/218584.pdf.

Mayo, L. (2006). College education and policing. *The Police Chief, 73*(8). Retrieved from http://www.police chiefmagazine.org/magazine/index.cfm?fuseaction=display&article_id=955&issue_ id=82006.

Meese, E. (1993). Community policing and the police officer. *Perspectives on Policing, 15.* National Institute of Justice, Department of Justice, Washington, DC.

Miller, W. (2000). The good, the bad & the ugly: Policing America. *History Today, 50*(8), 29–35.

Monkkonen, E. H. (1981). *Police in urban America, 1860–1920.* Cambridge, England: Cambridge University Press.

Murphy, P. V., & Caplan, D. G. (1991). Fostering integrity. In R. Dunham & G. Alpert (Eds.), *Critical issues in policing* (pp. 304–324). Prospect Heights, IL: Waveland Press.

National Advisory Commission on Criminal Justice Standards and Goals. (1977). *Police chief executive.* Washington, DC: U.S. Government Printing Office.

Oakes, D. H. (1995). Rights and responsibilities. In A. Etzioni (Ed.), *Rights and the common good: The communitarian perspective.* New York, NY: St. Martin's Press.

Oettmeier, T., & Wycoff, M. A. (1994). *Evaluating patrol officer performance under community policing: The Houston experience.* Washington, DC: National Institute of Justice.

Office of Community Oriented Policing Services. (2009). Building trust between police and the citizens they serve: An internal affairs promising practices guide for local law enforcement. Retrieved from http://ric-zai-inc.com/Publications/cops-p170-pub.pdf.

Office of Community Oriented Policing Services. (2012). Community policing defined. Retrieved from http://ric-zai-inc.com/Publications/cops-p157-pub.pdf.

Paoline, E. A., & Terrill, W. (2007). Police education, experience, and the use of force. *Criminal Justice and Behavior, 34*(2), 179–196.

Richardson, J. F. (1974). *Urban police in the United States.* Port Washington, NY: Kennikat Press.

Rosenbaum, D. P. (2000). The changing role of the police. In R. W. Glensor, M. E. Correia, & K. J. Peak (Eds.), *Policing communities: Understanding crime and solving problems* (pp. 46–66). Los Angeles, CA: Roxbury.

Rozas, A. (2008). Random alcohol testing proposed for Chicago police officers who fire their weapons. *Chicago Tribune* (June 14). Retrieved from http://articles.chicagotribune.com/2008-06-14/news/0806130369_1_police-officers-departmental-guidelines-proposal.

Rubinstein, J. (1973). *City police.* New York, NY: Farrar, Straus and Giroux.

Sapp, A. D. (1992). Alternative futures. In L. T. Hoover (Ed.), *Police management: Issues and perspectives* (pp. 175–201). Washington, DC: Police Executive Research Forum.

Sawhney, R. (2013). Implementing labor flexibility: A missing link between acquired labor flexibility and plant performance. *Journal of Operations Management, 31*(1), 98–108.

Schafer, J. A. (2001). *The challenges of successful organizational change.* New York, NY: LFB Scholarly.

Scrivner, E. (2010). *Practitioner perspectives: Community policing in a democracy.* Washington, DC: U.S. Department of Justice, Office of Community Oriented Policing Services.

Silverman, E. B. (1999). NYPD battles crime: Innovative strategies in policing. Boston, MA: Northeastern University Press.

Sparrow, M. K. (1988). Implementing community policing. *Perspectives on Policing, 9* (NCJ 114217).

Stokes, R. (2001). Implementation of community-oriented policing in a small rural community. *Illinois Law Enforcement Executive Forum, 1*(2), 43–49.

Sullivan, B. 2004. Police supervision in the 21st century: Can traditional work standards and the contemporary employee coexist? *Police Chief, 71*(10).

Sykes, G. W. (1992). Stability amid change. In L. T. Hoover (Ed.), *Police management: Issues and perspectives* (pp. 159–174). Washington, DC: Police Executive Research Forum.

Thurman, Q. T., Zhao, J., & Giacomazzi, A. L. (2001). *Community policing in a community era: An introduction and exploration.* Los Angeles, CA: Roxbury.

Uchida, C. D. (1993). The development of the American police: An historical overview. In R. Dunham and G. Alpert (Eds.), *Critical issues in policing: Contemporary readings* (2nd ed., pp. 16–32). Prospect Heights, IL: Waveland Press.

U.S. Department of Homeland Security. (2008). *One team, one mission, securing our homeland: U.S. Department of Homeland Security Strategic Plan Fiscal Years 2008–2013.* Washington, DC: Author. Retrieved from http://www.dhs.gov/xlibrary/assets/DHS_StratPlan_FINAL_ spread.pdf.

Varricchio, D. (1998). Continuing education: Expanding opportunities for officers. *FBI Law Enforcement Bulletin, 67*(4), 10–14.

Weisel, D. L., & Eck, J. E. (2000). Toward a practical approach to organizational change. In R. W. Glensor, M. E. Corriea, & K. J. Peak (Eds.), *Policing communities: Understanding and solving problems* (pp. 257–271). Los Angeles, CA: Roxbury.

10

Courts

LEARNING OBJECTIVES

Upon completion of this chapter, students should be able to do the following:

- Discuss the organizational structure of the court systems in the United States
- Give examples of how the court system, problem-solving courts, and the juvenile justice system react to issues in their structure
- Talk about how court organizational structure affects not only what courts do but also the quality of their performance
- Analyze how technological advances enhance quality service in the judiciary

The chapters in this book have talked about managing organizations in general by providing theories of administration that are applied in both profit and non-profit organizations. They have also discussed the criminal justice system's various components. The courts are perhaps the most influential part of the system since the decisions they make impact how the police enforce the laws, how probation and parole officers enforce court conditions found in community corrections contracts, and how prisons incarcerate offenders. Judges are sometimes referred to as the most powerful people in the criminal justice system. When looking at the judges' impact on the goals and functions of other criminal justice agencies, this statement appears to have some merit.

In this chapter, the functions of both adult and juvenile courts and the managerial aspects of each will be discussed. Issues facing courts and the ways in which they are providing better access and meeting the needs of victims, offenders, and those working within the courts as well as societal needs will also be addressed.

The Court System

Courts are unique entities. They do not operate according to traditional business practices or organizational structures (although one could argue they most closely resemble a closed-system model). They are not limited by whom they allow in or by expected outcomes. Anyone having a grievance or controversy is entitled to and must be given access to the courts regardless of the person's race, religion, gender, or ability to pay. There is never one goal or outcome that is universally accepted as correct when cases are brought before the court. The court's pursuit of justice is broadly interpreted and applied. Justice for one person may not be viewed as justice for another, and decisions made in one case may not apply in another case. Courts may actually pursue a service—such as processing a case through court, as in the following example—even when a person does not wish to receive the service. For example, a domestic violence case may proceed to court even though the victim chooses not to pursue charges. The charges can be brought by the state (the prosecuting attorney) and pursued by the court without the voluntary participation of those it is trying to serve (the victim and society). Since there are many stakeholders of the criminal justice system, it is possible that the interest of the indirect consumers (in this case, society) may be stronger than the interest of the direct consumer (the victim of the domestic violence). It is assumed that the courts have a macrovision and can look broadly at the interest of society when making judgments in private matters. This is sometimes difficult to understand by those on the outside of the court system and raises questions about the effectiveness of the courts' administration and ability to accomplish goals, thus reflecting poor service quality in the minds of the general public. In this instance, it becomes extremely important for the courts to use proper communication channels to disseminate information that educates the public about the courts' decisions and their relation to law and order. Such education helps align the public's perception of service with what the courts deliver, thus reflecting higher service quality in the minds of the community.

Courts require some form of management to fulfill their function; but courts, based on operational and organizational mandates, are complicated. In most cases, they are self-governing and have multifaceted objectives, with few clearly defined outcomes or predetermined ends. The court uses input from past cases (known as precedent), prosecutors, legislation, the media, and defense counsel to determine outputs in its everyday activities. To understand how courts are managed and which policies or processes of administration result in best practices in courts, one must first become familiar with how courts operate, who and what resources are involved, and what results are permissible and expected.

The judicial system in the United States is both dual and hierarchical. The system is dual because there are federal and state courts, each having separate jurisdictions. The court system is hierarchical in that both the federal and state systems consist of two kinds of courts—trial courts and appellate courts. All cases are litigated first at the trial level, where factual determinations are made and legal issues are initially resolved. Then, the issues of law may be reviewed or challenged in a higher court, known as the appellate court. The appellate court's function is to ensure that the trial court's application of the law is consistent with the U.S. Constitution, the individual state constitutions, and existing laws. The appellate court decisions form the basis of law, and these courts are considered the final arbiter of conflicts regarding interpretation and application of the law.

Federal Court Organization

The legislative branch of the government plays a considerable role in court operations. According to the U.S. Constitution, Congress has the power to create federal courts and determine their jurisdiction. It is Congress—not the judiciary—that determines the types of cases heard in federal courts. Congress, with confirmation from the Senate, also determines how many judges are appointed and where they are assigned in federal courts. Finally, Congress approves the federal judiciary's budget (U.S. Courts, n.d.).

The U.S. government is designed to be a "checks and balances" system. The legislative, executive, and judicial branches are separate from one another, but the Constitution requires them to cooperate with one another. Congress, with a signature from the president of the United States, passes federal laws. The judicial branch has the authority to decide if those laws are constitutional and to resolve disputes regarding those laws (U.S. Courts, n.d.). It is the executive branch of government that enforces court decisions.

The managerial style of the federal court system is set up to promote judicial independence or *judicial autonomy* from the other branches of the government. Judges are commissioned to a specific federal court, appointed for life contingent on good behavior, and can be removed only through an impeachment process (see Article III of the U.S. Constitution). The security of lifetime employment of federal court judges reduces outside interference and the potential incentive to decide cases in favor of a particular side or political position. Critics of the court system have argued that politics, in particular, played a role in limiting judges' judicial independence (Tarr, 2007; See, 2007). What has occurred instead is a push for judicial accountability, meaning holding judges responsible for the decisions they make by questioning the judgments, applying legislative limits on decisions, and critically assessing the credentials of each judge recommended for court appointment or election.

In essence, this allows politics from the legislative branch to enter into the judicial system. Burbank (2008) claims that the concepts of judicial independence and judicial accountability, as they currently stand, are at odds with one another. Basically, the legislative branch wants to control the politics of judges, while judges want to decide on the constitutionality of the laws made by the legislative branch. The legislators put limitations on judges' decisions, while judges feel a necessary pressure to provide input into prospective laws and regulations before they have been passed. What occurs as a result is a conflict between governmental branch relationships, which may cause a disparity in the interests of different stakeholders. Burbank (2008) acknowledges that politics must play a role in the courts, albeit a limited one, so that judges can ensure fundamental rights to citizens (even if this means limiting judicial independence).

It is common knowledge that judges hold a leadership role in the courtroom. Their actions and decisions motivate the individuals who come before the courts and those who work within criminal justice, set policy, and make changes. Their approval or endorsement of programs, technology, procedures, and demeanor set the tone for the court and pave the way for improvements. Artis (2004) points out that lower-court judges' influence goes well beyond the courtroom and into how cases are plea-bargained or settled outside of court—and, for that matter, what types of cases come to court to begin with. Daly (1987; 1989) reported that interviews with judges in lower courts revealed that they use the offender's gender, familial status, and their own paternalistic views—in the cases of mothers—in deciding case outcomes. This, according to Daly, may be one reason why female offenders are given lighter sentences than male offenders, and may even contribute to decisions in child custody cases in civil courts (Artis, 2004).

Federal Court Design

At the federal level, the Administrative Office of the United States Courts handles the managerial and administrative functions of the federal courts. It is responsible for budgeting, docket control, and statistical analysis. The office may also assign cases to judges for hearing.

Federal courts have limited jurisdiction. They may only make decisions in certain types of cases as identified by the U.S. Constitution or enacted by Congress. Federal courts interpret and apply the law in both civil and criminal matters. In theory, federal courts do not create laws but instead establish policy.

The daily operation of the federal courts is decentralized, allowing each court to operate with a great deal of autonomy, consistent with the policies established at the regional (Circuit Court) and national (U.S. Supreme Court) levels. Included in the process of court management are the participants. Each individual court is responsible for supervising or controlling defendants, attorneys, witnesses, jurors, clerks, probation officers, interpreters, judges, magistrates, court reporters, and other personnel used by the court. Because so many different entities have to be integrated to ensure smooth functioning of the courts, it is important that the various elements of workplace design such as job design, training, goal setting, performance appraisal, pay, career development, and promotions are in place.

Theories of Judicial Decision Making

The traditional role of the courts was to resolve disputes and review decisions of lower-court judges. Judges have traditionally been viewed as rational actors who make decisions that are likely to lead them to their goals, and it has been assumed that judges want to make decisions that result in the best legal understanding (George & Yoon, 2008). Contemporary workloads, though, have forced judges to expand their pretrial roles in assisting with early resolution of issues through nonadjudicative processes,

rather than occupying court time with full-blown hearings. Consequently, two theories have evolved as to how courts exercise their formal powers and their informal influence. According to the *managerial theory,* the judges make decisions based on the volume of their workload. Thus, the growing docket and speedy trial issues override considerations of the law (George & Yoon, 2008). Such an approach may compromise the quality of service offered to the public. Alternatively, the *attitudinal theory* is premised on the belief that judges are political actors who make decisions that maximize their political preferences (Segal & Spaeth, 1993). Use of personal preferences and attitudes in deliberating may increase the variation in service, which can be construed as bad service quality by the public. The attitudinal theory requires agenda control by the judges or justices to determine which issues to address; when they will be addressed; and how the policies will be implemented, proactively or retroactively (Fallon, Meltzer, & Shapiro, 2003).

The managerial theory claims that district judges have expanded their pretrial roles to achieve early resolution of cases through nonadjudicative processes. According to this theory, courts are simply trying to stay on top of the workload as opposed to deciding cases on their merit. At the Circuit Court level, there are 179 judgeships authorized to handle appeals (Administrative Office of the U.S. Courts, 2006). The numbers of appeals filed can exceed more than 50,000 in a year, creating an almost impossible workload. Resnick (1982) asserts that district judges have relied on the Federal Rules of Civil Procedure to convince parties to end suits quickly rather than taking up the court's time in trial because it would be overwhelming for district court judges to try to hear all of the cases on their dockets. The managerial theory also explains the increased use of summary dispositions, decreased grants of en banc (when all members of the appellate court hear a single argument), and the increase in refusing oral arguments and authoring nonpublished opinions (George & Yoon, 2008).

The U.S. Supreme Court's selection process for *writ of certiorari* (also called a *cert petition*)—where the Supreme Court orders the record of a case from a lower court—reflects the ultimate embodiment of the attitudinal theory. The Supreme Court, although encumbered with a heavy caseload, is an atypical court. It manages the high volume of cert petitions received each year (averaging more than 7,000) by requesting briefings and only hearing oral arguments in 100 or fewer cases. Unlike the Circuit Court of Appeals, which must conduct judicial review of certain cases including criminal appeals, the Supreme Court has the discretion of denying cases for review. The Court controls its docket and agenda by selecting only cases the justices believe lack clarity in the law or when the law is nonexistent. Only on occasion does the Court take cases that will enhance or further the justices' ideological preferences and personal agendas (George & Yoon, 2008).

In principle, the issues confronting the Supreme Court should arise out of cases originally heard at the trial court level. In fact, Pacelle (1991) proclaimed that the Supreme Court should not become a proactive institution and that the justices must wait until they are presented with a case that matches their political priorities in appropriately framed legal arguments. In other words, appellate courts should be passive institutions, deciding only on issues others bring to them. Recently, researchers pointed to a trend or a tendency of the courts to settle and decide issues that fall more appropriately within the realm of other branches of the government. Some label this judicial activism the *judicialization of politics* (Tate & Vallinder, 1995), while others call it the *politicization of the judiciary process* (O'Connor, 2008). Tate and Vallinder (1995) believe that this is perhaps one of the biggest trends of the late 20th and early 21st centuries. The public seems to agree. In 2005 and 2006, surveys were conducted by the Princeton Survey Research Associates International for the Annenberg Public Policy Center of the University of Pennsylvania, where they found that 62% of respondents believed judges were legislating from their benches instead of interpreting the law, and that judges favored the wealthy and those with political influence. Another 75% of the respondents said that judges' rulings are influenced by their political ideology to a great or moderate extent (Jamieson, 2006). Former U.S. Supreme Court Justice Sandra Day O'Connor also agreed with this proposition in an article she wrote for *Parade* magazine in 2008. Justice O'Connor discussed the issues brought about by judges' election campaigns, many of which are supported by funds from special interest groups that may then expect judicial rulings favoring their views. According to O'Connor, the resolution to this problem is to develop groups of citizens that recommend potential judges to the governor. The governor then appoints a judicial official who after several years is subjected to a vote by the public on whether he or she should retain the judgeship. This allows for both appointment and electoral input without the political pressures resulting from the need for fundraising in partisan elections.

Dihn (2007) believes that politics shapes the environment in which judges operate. According to him, this may lead career-minded judges to tailor their rulings to conform to the views of the politically influential, particularly if they plan to seek promotion to higher and more prestigious courts (p. 943). Judges seeking higher positions know that presidents and senators appoint judges who have previous judicial experience and whose rulings are not seen as disagreeable to their politics.

> Such career judges thus will have an incentive to placate the officeholders who they anticipate would play a role in their future elevation (as well as the private opinion makers who would hold forth on their nominations). Career judges will have reason to decide cases based not just on their honest estimation of what the law actually requires, but also, at the margins, based on their sense of what outcomes the political elites may favor. (p. 943)

This threatens the quality of service provided to litigants or defendants who appear before courts hoping to be treated fairly, as well as to the American people, who look to courts for impartiality.

The attitudinal theory is further demonstrated through the significant power provided to the chief judge in each jurisdiction. The chief justice of the Supreme Court has the power to assign other justices to write opinions on case determinations if the chief is in the majority vote on the case (George & Yoon, 2008). This power allows for both formal and informal influence over the tone of the opinion. In addition, even though the chief only has one vote in a case, this vote takes precedence in case of a tie, enabling the chief to sway the legal outcome, which allows for the influence of political ideologies (George & Yoon, 2008).

State Court Organization

Structurally, the state court system is similar to the federal system in that there is a hierarchy of levels ranging from trial courts to appellate courts. But the variety of systems within the state court construct range from a unified trial court, like that used in Illinois (see Figure 10.1) and other states, to many different or segmented trial courts, as exemplified by the New York system (see Figure 10.2). The appellate system varies as well from a single appellate court of last resort (West Virginia and Washington, DC) to multiple appellate courts (Georgia and Indiana). The majority of states, however, have two appellate levels, an intermediary level and the court of last resort (also known as state supreme courts).

Although most state court systems provide general jurisdiction to their courts, many (40) of the state trial courts elect to manage their caseloads by subject matter jurisdiction, the amount in controversy, or the seriousness of the offense (misdemeanors versus felonies). Therefore, the courts are separated into those of limited and general jurisdiction. The limited jurisdiction courts include specialty courts, juvenile courts, traffic courts, small claims courts, and probate matters (Bureau of Justice Statistics, n.d.), the first two of which will be discussed next.

Specialty Courts

Although courts of general jurisdiction are efficient because they can more readily accommodate a variety of case types and can consolidate related matters into one issue, a trend is emerging in most states to create *specialty courts*. These courts, commonly referred to as *problem-solving courts,* are being created to address particular social issues such as drugs, truancy, teen crime, domestic violence, mental health, guns, and quality-of-life concerns. Although each of these courts addresses distinct social issues, they share some commonalities. They focus more on rehabilitation than punishment by putting forth that the "one size fits all" approach to traditional criminal justice is not working (Libby, 2009, p. 24). They shift the traditional role of the court from a strictly legal perspective to a more individualized therapeutic approach that emphasizes both the victim and the offender. Wolf (2007) suggests that specialized courts support a "belief that courts can and should play a role in trying to solve the problems that are fueling caseloads; a belief that outcomes—not just process and precedent—matter; and a recognition that the coercive power of courts can change people's behavior" (p. 1).

As described next, problem-solving courts are more service-oriented than the traditional court structure; they also allow for specialization of staff and services, a focus on clients and the community, enhanced communication networks, and collaboration. In addition, specialized courts can provide higher service quality by following the original tenets of the criminal justice system, which propagated justice through a more personalized and customized approach to reform offenders by focusing on their specific needs in the prevention of criminal behavior.

Judges and other personnel who work in specialized courts have the potential to become specialized in the area addressed by the court, which possibly leads to better outcomes. As these individuals experience greater training opportunities and updates

Figure 10.1 2005 Structure of the Illinois Court System and General Route of Appeal

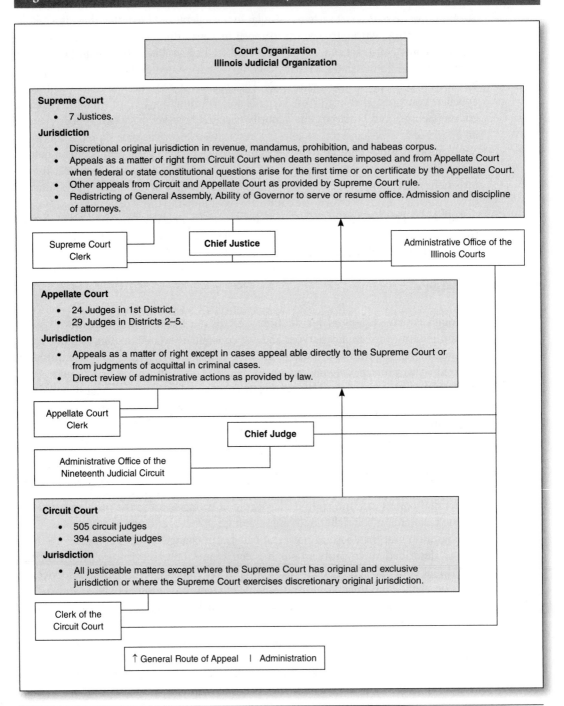

SOURCE: Nineteenth Judicial Court, State of Illinois, http://www.19thcircuitcourt.state.il.us/crtorg/ct_org05.htm.

on the latest best practices, they become better able to service the defendants coming before the court, and they are more likely to have better working relationships with service providers (Wolf, 2007).

Literature has begun to emerge focusing on the general value of problem-solving principles and ways these can be transferred to traditional courts. According to Wolf (2007), the six principles of problem-solving justice are these:

1. Enhanced Information

Better staff training (about complex issues such as domestic violence and drug addiction) combined with better information (about litigants, victims, and the community context of crime) can help improve the decision making of judges, attorneys, and other justice officials. High-quality information—gathered with the assistance of technology and shared in accordance with confidentiality laws—can help practitioners make more informed decisions about both treatment needs and the risks individual defendants pose to public safety, ensuring that offenders receive an appropriate level of supervision and services.

2. Community Engagement

Citizens and neighborhood groups have an important role to play in helping the justice system identify, prioritize, and solve local problems. Actively engaging citizens helps improve public trust in justice. Greater trust, in turn, helps people feel safer, fosters law-abiding behavior, and makes members of the public more willing to cooperate in the pursuit of justice (as witnesses, jury members, etc.).

3. Collaboration

Justice system leaders are uniquely positioned to engage a diverse range of people, government agencies, and community organizations in collaborative efforts to improve public safety. By bringing together the players in the justice system (e.g., judges, prosecutors, attorneys, probation officers, and court managers) and reaching out to the potential stakeholders beyond the courthouse (e.g., social service providers, victims' groups, schools, and the like), the justice agencies improve interagency communication. Furthermore, such an approach encourages greater trust between citizens and government and fosters new responses, including new diversion and sentencing options, when appropriate.

4. Individualized Justice

Using valid evidence-based risk and needs assessment instruments, the justice system can link offenders to individually tailored, community-based services (e.g., job training, drug treatment, safety planning, mental health counseling) where appropriate. In doing so (and by treating defendants with dignity and respect), the justice system can help reduce recidivism, improve community safety, and enhance confidence in the justice system. Links to services can also aid victims, improving their safety and helping to restore their lives.

5. Accountability

The justice system can send the message that all criminal behavior, even low-level quality-of-life crime, has an impact on community safety and has consequences. By insisting on regular and rigorous compliance monitoring, and clear consequences for noncompliance, the justice system can improve the accountability of offenders. It can also improve the accountability of service providers (i.e., probation officers, parole officers, and treatment providers) by requiring regular reports on their work with participants.

6. Outcomes

The active and ongoing collection and analysis of data—measuring outcomes and process, costs and benefits—are crucial tools for evaluating the effectiveness of operations and encouraging continuous improvement. Public dissemination of this information can be a valuable symbol of public accountability.

Miller and Johnson (2009) note that the earlier suggestions may be easier to say than to achieve. Their study found that problems facing these courts do not just include "tough to reform offenders" but also include "tough to reform agencies" that may be set in their ways of working with offenders and unwilling to change to meet the needs of offenders. Wolf (2007) suggests that practices used in problem-solving courts can easily be transitioned into traditional court structures. Either the traditional court can adopt the strategies used in the specialized court, or it can share in the resources of the specialized court (and vice versa). Wolf is not alone in his proposal. According to him, the Conference of Chief Justices and Conference of the State Court Administrators suggested the adoption of principles and methods used by problem-solving courts by the larger system of justice in 2000. In 2002, the American Bar Association (ABA) passed a resolution suggesting the same (p. 1).

Despite their popularity, problem-solving courts have raised concerns that they consume substantial court resources; that they alter the role of judges and defense attorneys; and that they change the adversarial process into a therapeutic one, thereby surrendering various constitutional rights of defendants. Libby (2009) points out that although the problem-solving courts and their courtroom space may be supported by governmental funds, the programs they use may not. This can lead to the judge needing to apply for private funding (through grants or foundations) or to solicit funds in other ways to support the alternative justice approach.

Of course, as discussed in Chapter 4, potential conflicts of interest can arise when administrators are involved in solicitation and fundraising (Libby, 2009). Dorf and Fagan (2003) explain that specialized courts put the judge in a nontraditional role, and one that may not be completely unbiased and impartial. As they expound in their article, in the traditional adversarial process, the judge understands that the state wants punishment and the defendant does not—they are both given a fair chance to explain their positions. However, in a specialized court, both the state and potentially the judge want treatment, regardless of the defendant's stance. In this case, the judge is really acting as a coercive agent for the state and not as an independent assessor (Dorf & Fagan, 2003; Nolan, 2003). This is a role with which judges may not be completely comfortable, since the traditional court emphasizes little judicial involvement outside of findings of law, guilt or innocence, and sentencing. Unlike traditional court, the judge in problem-solving courts is much more hands-on in the rehabilitative process. Another issue, also mentioned earlier, is the resistance to change faced by problem-solving courts. Miller and Johnson (2009) noted in their study that workers within the court resisted the measurement tools used by the court to gauge success and resisted their roles in the court. They also found that territorial jealousy was an issue among traditional service providers, such as mental health counselors and criminal justice workers, which defeated the team effort indicative of problem-solving courts. Finally, Miller and Johnson found separation between problem-solving courts and traditional courts, with judges in problem-solving courts not viewed as doing "real judging" and problem-solving courts not counting in overall state court performance measures. The future of these courts is uncertain and will only be determined through time and research on usage, success, intra- and interorganizational structures and conflicts, and budgetary considerations.

Juvenile Courts

In the early 19th century, juveniles were tried alongside adults. They also were incarcerated in adult prisons, as few other options were available for the rehabilitation of youth. In 1825, the Society for the Prevention of Juvenile Delinquency advocated the separation of juvenile and adult offenders (Snyder & Sickmund, 1999). The efforts of this group led to the building of several institutions called Houses of Refuge for youth. Many of the children housed in these institutions had not committed crimes but were status offenders or victims of abuse and neglect (Shepard, 1999). Houses of Refuge eventually gave way to reformatories, which still kept youthful offenders away from adults and attempted to protect children from adverse home situations; minimize court proceedings; provide indeterminate sentences so that a child could be held as long as necessary to accomplish reform; provide punishment when other options failed; and focus on education, vocational training, and religious schooling. Reformatories also used military drills, physical exercise, and supervision to teach sobriety, carefulness, and good sense (Shepard, 1999). Challenges to reformatories and Houses of Refuge ultimately led to the establishment of a separate juvenile justice court system in the United States.

The first family court system in America was instituted in Cook County, Illinois, in 1899. By 1945, all states had created separate juvenile justice systems, including courts, to process children who committed delinquent or criminal acts as well as children in need of care or protection from the state (Cox, Allen, Hanser, & Conrad, 2014). Contemporary juvenile courts have exclusive jurisdiction over matters concerning people under the statutorily defined age of adulthood (the age at which a person is considered an adult varies state to state, from 16 to 18 years of age). Juvenile courts handle cases that involve the commission of crimes or delinquent acts by children, the abuse and neglect of children, and adoption. They also deal with *status offenders*— those who commit acts that are considered criminal because of the person's age—such as truants, runaways, or those guilty of incorrigible conduct. Youth who appear in juvenile court have the same rights as those afforded to adults under the U.S. Constitution, with the exception of a right to trial by a jury of their peers—although some states offer jury trials to youth when defined as possible in the state's statutes.

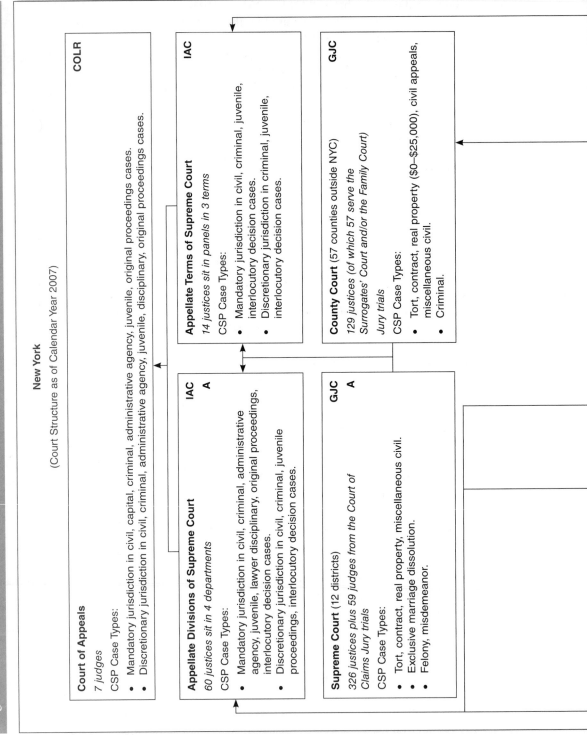

Figure 10.2 New York Court Structure, 2007

New York

(Court Structure as of Calendar Year 2007)

COLR

Court of Appeals

7 judges

CSP Case Types:

- Mandatory jurisdiction in civil, capital, criminal, administrative agency, juvenile, original proceedings cases.
- Discretionary jurisdiction in civil, criminal, administrative agency, juvenile, disciplinary, original proceedings cases.

IAC

Appellate Terms of Supreme Court

14 justices sit in panels in 3 terms

CSP Case Types:

- Mandatory jurisdiction in civil, criminal, juvenile, interlocutory decision cases.
- Discretionary jurisdiction in criminal, juvenile, interlocutory decision cases.

GJC

County Court (57 counties outside NYC)

129 justices (of which 57 serve the Surrogates' Court and/or the Family Court)

Jury trials

CSP Case Types:

- Tort, contract, real property ($0–$25,000), civil appeals, miscellaneous civil.
- Criminal.

IAC

A

Appellate Divisions of Supreme Court

60 justices sit in 4 departments

CSP Case Types:

- Mandatory jurisdiction in civil, criminal, administrative agency, juvenile, lawyer disciplinary, original proceedings, interlocutory decision cases.
- Discretionary jurisdiction in civil, criminal, juvenile proceedings, interlocutory decision cases.

GJC

A

Supreme Court (12 districts)

326 justices plus 59 judges from the Court of Claims Jury trials

CSP Case Types:

- Tort, contract, real property, miscellaneous civil.
- Exclusive marriage dissolution.
- Felony, misdemeanor.

Court of Claims (1 court)   LJC

86 justices (of which 59 act as Supreme Court justices)

No jury trials

CSP Case Types:
- Tort, contract, real property, involving the state.

Family Court (62 counties)   LJC

127 judges plus 51 judges from the County Court and 81 quasijudicial staff

No jury trials

CSP Case Types:
- Guardianship.
- Domestic relations.
- Exclusive domestic violence.
- Exclusive juvenile.

Criminal Court of the City of New York (1 court)   LJC

120 judges

Jury trials

CSP Case Types:
- Tort, contract, real property ($0–$25,000), small claims (up to $5,000), miscellaneous civil.

Surrogates' Court (62 counties)   LJC

31 surrogates plus 51 judges from the County Court

Jury trials in probate/estate

CSP Case Types:
- Probate/estate.
- Adoption.

District Court (Nassau and Suffolk counties)   LJC

50 judges

Jury trials except in traffic

CSP Case Types:
- Tort, contract, real property ($0–$15,000), small claims (up to $5,000).
- Felony, misdemeanor, preliminary hearings.
- Traffic infractions, ordinance violations.

Criminal Court of the City of New York (1 court)   LJC

107 judges

Jury trials for highest-level misdemeanor

CSP Case Types:
- Misdemeanor, preliminary hearings.
- Traffic infractions, ordinance violations.

City Court (61 courts)   LJC

158 judges

Jury trials for highest-level misdemeanor

CSP Case Types:
- Tort, contract, real property ($0–$15,000), small claims (up to $5,000).
- Felony, misdemeanor, preliminary hearings.
- Traffic infractions, ordinance violations.

Town and Village Justice Court (1,487 court)   Locally Funded   LJC

2,300 judges

Jury trials in most cases

CSP Case Types:
- Tort, contract, real property ($0–$3,000), small claims (up to $3,000).
- Misdemeanor, preliminary hearings.
- Traffic/other violations.

SOURCE: National Center for State Courts, Court Statistics Project, http://www.courtstatistics.org, 2010.

NOTE: COLR = Court of Last Resort; IAC = Intermediate Appellate Court; GJC = General Jurisdiction Court; LJC = Limited Jurisdiction Court; A = Appeal from Administrative Agency.

Juvenile courts operate from guidelines established in state juvenile court acts. These acts authorize the jurisdiction of juvenile courts, establish what types of cases will be heard in juvenile court, identify procedural guidelines for juvenile court, and define substantive law relative to juveniles (Cox et al., 2014). In addition, the age limits of juveniles who may appear in juvenile court and the nature of the acts over which the court has jurisdiction are also defined in the various states' juvenile court acts.

Juvenile courts are considered a formal court of law in the United States. They operate very similarly, in structure and procedure, to adult trial courts. Chief judicial judges supervise the court and its operations just as they do state courts, unless the state has instituted a state court administrator, in which case the court falls under the administrator's control. Appeals resulting from juvenile courts proceed to the appellate court level for review. As mentioned before, juvenile court has exclusive jurisdiction over matters involving children, although all states have provisions in their juvenile court acts that allow for juvenile offenders to be tried in adult courts under certain circumstances. In many states, statutes allow for the exclusion of some youth from juvenile court, regardless of their age, if they commit a certain offense (typically a serious or index crime). Other states allow for prosecutor discretion in determining whether the case warrants juvenile or adult court processing (Cox et al., 2014).

Goals of the Juvenile Court

The juvenile court system has perhaps historically been the best example of the service quality approach. At its core is the goal of providing individualized justice through treatment, reform, and rehabilitation to youth who come within its jurisdiction. The juvenile court uses wide discretion to accomplish this goal and typically works very hard to determine what is in the best interest of the child before making a ruling on disposition. Although confidentiality is a key element, the juvenile court relies on a number of parties to assist in determining how best to rehabilitate or protect the child. Parents, social service agencies, schools, community programs, probation officers, police, correctional institutions, and counselors work together to address the special needs of youth under the juvenile court's jurisdiction, making it one of the few entities in criminal justice to build on the interdependence of the various agencies involved.

Juvenile courts around the nation have implemented programs that specifically reach out to the various stakeholders in juvenile cases. Programs like restorative justice bring the victim, the offender, and representatives of the community together to resolve the criminal issue in a mutually beneficial way. *Restorative justice* views crime as an act against an individual, not the state, and strives to mend the harms done by the criminal act instead of just punishing the offender. The basic concepts of restorative justice—accountability, competency, and public safety—promote a belief that all parties to the offense must be involved in the justice process to the greatest extent possible to respond effectively to crime (Bazemore & Umbreit, 1997). In addition, in the juvenile justice context, restorative justice is concerned with making the process less formal; more neighborhood-friendly; and a shared responsibility among juvenile justice personnel, offenders, victims, and community members (Bazemore & Umbreit, 1997).

Restorative justice programs are offered at all levels of the criminal justice system. They can be concentrated during pre-adjudication activities, as are victim–offender mediation programs, or they can be used during the corrections phase, as are victim impact panels and victim impact classes, restitution, and community service. The most common programs under the restorative justice umbrella include victim–offender mediation, sentencing or peacemaking circles, family group conferencing, and reparative probation or boards (Center for Restorative Justice and Mediation, 1996). Victim impact classes/panels, community service, and restitution are all considered part of restorative justice practices.

Juvenile courts also continue to support diversionary tactics employed by the police, such as station adjustments, despite criticisms that these may violate the constitutional rights of youth by issuing punishments when there has been no formal court adjudication. *Station adjustments* allow the police to intervene and redirect youth while still holding them accountable for their actions. Juveniles who experience station adjustments are arrested and brought to a police station. Instead of going to juvenile court, the youth are required to complete one or more conditions (typically community service) as part of the station adjustment plan supervised by the arresting police officer (Cox et al., 2014). Those who do so are diverted from formal court proceedings. Those who do not complete the plan may be referred to juvenile court for processing. Although station adjustments are controversial, Illinois is one state that allows them. Police officers in Illinois may issue formal or informal station adjustments (as noted in Table 10.1). According to a study on whether Illinois officers adhere to the law regarding station adjustments and distinguish between formal and informal adjustments when issuing station adjustment plans, Lavery (2002) reports that of the 69 officers who responded to the survey, only 35 said they distinguish between formal and informal station adjustments. Of those distinguishing between the two types of adjustments, only 23 reported that they actually use written agreement forms to draw up plans, even though it is mandatory to do so in the legislation.

Regardless of whether the station adjustment is formal or informal, station adjustments are yet another way to reduce the interaction of youth with the court system and to provide them with services outside of correctional institutions or probation. The fact that youth can expunge station adjustments from their records and can refrain from receiving court sanctions is a service to the children and their futures (Cox et al., 2014). The juvenile courts, and the state legislators, clearly view this approach by law enforcement as a beneficial service to juvenile offenders.

Juvenile court personnel also support and participate in other programs sponsored by the police such as police–school liaison programs, Drug Abuse Resistance Education (D.A.R.E.), and other proactive delinquency diversion programs. Juvenile court makes referrals to *teen or peer courts,* sometimes facilitated by police departments, schools, or other community agencies. Teen courts have originated as a way to keep first-time or misdemeanant offenders who are willing to admit guilt out of the formal juvenile justice system. The courts are made up of teens under the age of 17 who process delinquency cases by acting as prosecutor, public defender, jury, bailiff, and clerk. An adult attorney acts as the judge to ensure fairness and legality of the proceedings (Cox et al., 2014). As noted in In the News 10.1, offenders who attend teen court are required to complete the sentence handed down by the teen jury. Those who do not abide by the sentencing guidelines are referred to the formal juvenile justice court for additional processing. Some juvenile court jurisdictions have also adopted drug courts, a form of problem-solving courts, to better meet the needs of youthful offenders. Drug courts use intensive therapeutic interventions to aid youth in stopping the abuse of drugs and alcohol. Recent research has raised some issues regarding drug courts, particularly with regard to graduation rates and offender characteristics. In a review of drug court literature, Stein, Deberard, and Homan (2013) found,

> One clear trend in the available studies was the dramatic difference in recidivism rates for adolescents who succeed in graduating from drug court, relative to those who do not. In addition, the review revealed that behavior patterns evidenced during drug court participation were most strongly associated with both the probability of graduating successfully from drug court and recidivism (e.g., few in-program arrests, citations, detentions, and referrals; greater length of time in program or amount of treatment; lower use of drug and alcohol use, few positive urine screens, greater school attendance). Unfortunately, nonwhite participants tend to have a lower probability of graduation from drug court and experience higher recidivism during and following the program. Available juvenile drug treatment court studies confirm a number of reputed adolescent risk factors associated with substance abuse, criminality, treatment failure, and recidivism among adolescents (e.g., higher levels of emotional and behavioral problems, higher levels and severity of pre-program substance abuse, male gender). (p. 159)

Table 10.1 Comparison of Formal and Informal Station Adjustments

	Informal Station Adjustment	**Formal Station Adjustment**
Necessary prerequisites	An informal station adjustment may be issued when there is probable cause to believe that a minor has committed an offense.	A formal station adjustment may be issued when there is probable cause to believe that a minor has committed an offense, the minor has admitted to the offense, and the minor and the minor's parents sign a written agreement form. The written agreement form is to include a description of the offense, the station adjustment conditions, the consequences if the minor fails to abide by the conditions, an acknowledgment that the police department's record of the formal station adjustment can be expunged, and an acknowledgment that the minor's admission of the offense can be used in future court hearings.

	Informal Station Adjustment	**Formal Station Adjustment**
Conditions that can be imposed	Informal station adjustment conditions include: (1) curfews, (2) restrictions from entering designated geographic areas, (3) restrictions from contacting specified persons, (4) school attendance, (5) up to 25 hours of community service, (6) community mediation, (7) teen court, and (8) pay restitution within 90 days.	Formal station adjustment conditions include: (1) curfews, (2) restrictions from entering designated geographic areas, (3) restrictions from contacting specified persons, (4) school attendance, (5) up to 25 hours of community service, (6) community mediation, (7) teen court, (8) restitution, (9) refraining from possessing a firearm, and (10) reporting to a police officer at designated times, including verification that the minor is at home during designated hours. Minors have up to 120 days to complete the formal station adjustment conditions.
Consequences for failing to abide by conditions	If a minor fails to abide by the conditions of an informal station adjustment, then the juvenile police officer may: (1) impose a formal station adjustment, or (2) refer the minor to court.	If a minor fails to abide by the conditions of a formal station adjustment, the juvenile police officer may: (1) give the minor a warning, (2) extend the time period of the formal station adjustment, (3) extend community service hours, (4) terminate the formal station adjustment and take no other action, or (5) terminate the formal station adjustment and refer the minor to court.

SOURCE: From "Police Use of Formal and Informal Station Adjustments for Juveniles in Illinois," by T. Lavery, 2002, *On Good Authority, 6(4)*, pp. 1–5. Available at http://www.icjia.state.il.us/public/pdf/oga/station%20adjust.pdf.

In the News 10.1
Jurors Join Teen Court—45 Students
Trained to Handle Alternative Youth Court System

DECATUR—LaTaija Johnson, one of more than 45 high school students who went through training Wednesday afternoon to become jurors for Macon County's Teen Court, asked a question worth repeating.

After learning during a mock hearing that a 16-year-old basketball player disagreed with the punishment his father gave him after he was arrested for possession of alcohol, the Eisenhower High School senior asked what consequences he thought would be better.

"That's a really good question," said Laura Kidd, an intern with the Teen Court program. "Could you say that again, that real loud please?"

LaTaija's question reflected the Teen Court philosophy, and so did the sentence the students discussed—one requiring the offender to help out with basketball at the local Boys & Girls Club and

(Continued)

(Continued)

perform additional community service at an agency serving individuals with substance abuse problems—a sentence that addressed his strengths and his weaknesses.

"Our job isn't to judge," said Barbara Stevens, a junior at Decatur Christian School. "Our job is to aid in the rebuilding process."

That was the main point of the four-hour training Wednesday afternoon at the Hope Academy Center of Richland Community College. The newest additions to the court's jury pool, who will begin serving next month, also represent Argenta-Oreana, Maroa-Forsyth and St. Teresa high schools.

Twelve teen jurors under the guidance of a local attorney convene Macon County's Teen Court twice a month at the Macon County Health Department to dispense restorative justice to mostly nonviolent juvenile offenders as an alternative to the juvenile court system.

Huston Mathias, another intern, told trainees that being a juror gave him a fresh perspective on his own problems. "I saw that my stuff wasn't so horrible," he said.

Shelleay Green, a senior at MacArthur High School, said she was impressed by how the process seeks to repair all the damage caused by an offender's behavior.

"It's not just the victim who gets hurt," she said. "It's anybody the crime negatively affects."

Jaron Adams, a junior at Eisenhower High School, said Teen Court works by giving juvenile offenders a second chance. "Teenagers can relate better to other teenagers, so it's really helping," he said.

SOURCE: From "Jurors Join Teen Court," by T. Churchill, May 29, 2008, *Herald & Review.* Copyright © 2008, *Herald & Review,* Decatur, IL.

In addition, juvenile courts have addressed issues of diversity and bias in their systems. A community-based program in Harrisburg, Pennsylvania, addressed minority overrepresentation in the juvenile justice system by decreasing rates of arrest and rearrest for clients and focusing on educational failure, dropouts, and truancy (Welsh, Jenkins, & Harris, 1999). City officials in Santa Cruz, California, also changed procedures, policies, practices, and programs that they identified as barriers to services for minorities to address overrepresentation in their jurisdiction. They now include objective decision-making techniques in weighing risks and needs, cultural sensitivity training, and decreased delays in detention releases and court appearances in their day-to-day practices (Dighton, 2003). Another approach is the Juvenile Detention Alternatives Initiative introduced by the Annie E. Casey Foundation. This initiative is currently operating in 110 local jurisdictions in 27 states and the District of Columbia. It has eight main goals: (1) collaboration between the actors and the agencies involved in the justice system; (2) collection and utilization of data to diagnose problems and impact of reforms; (3) admission screenings to identify which youth are in most need of detention and pose the most threat to society; (4) use of nonsecure alternatives to detention for those who would have been locked up in the past; (5) expediting cases through the juvenile system to reduce lengths of stay in detention; (6) flexibility in policies and practices to deal with "special" cases like probation violations; (7) attention to racial disparities in contact and incarceration; and (8) intensive monitoring of the conditions found in confinement (Annie E. Casey Foundation, 2009). The foundation has touted the success of this approach in its studies on the initiative. Whether these states continue their aggressive work toward changes and whether these approaches continue to work in lowering the number of incarcerated youth and minorities is yet to be seen.

Juvenile courts seek programs and agencies in the community to use in youth dispositions. Aside from the police, they work with a host of other agencies, such as YMCAs, mentoring programs, counseling agencies, child protection groups, and traditional and vocational schools, just to name a few, to encourage the reintegration of youth in society. Despite these measures and a very recent focus on incarceration initiatives, juvenile courts face their biggest challenge to date—becoming more and more similar to adult courts in sanctioning ideologies. While the court has become more formal through higher court rulings such as *In re Gault* (1967) and *Kent v. the United States* (1966), so has the approach to youthful offenders. "Today's juvenile court is so different from the original [juvenile] court and more similar to the [adult] criminal courts than at any prior in the past century" (Lindner, 2004, p. 151). Replicating the adult court's approach to harsher and more punitive sentences, the juvenile court system has become more control-oriented and less focused on rehabilitation, as a whole. State legislators have implemented statutes mirroring this approach that apply to offenders falling within the juvenile court's jurisdiction. Examples of the punitive ideology include increased use of mandatory waivers to adult criminal courts; use of determinate sentencing, which decreases flexibility in meeting the juvenile offenders' needs; and increased sanctions in the sentencing of youth based on public safety and individual accountability language in juvenile court acts (Lindner, 2004). Unfortunately, these changes have led to calls for the complete abolishment of the juvenile court system since there is little need to have a separate court for kids that operates exactly as the adult court.

We believe that the juvenile court will prevail despite the challenging environment. Its underlying approach to working with youth and to providing care and rehabilitation has a place in society, especially as the criminal justice system is expected to become more service-oriented than it was in the past. In addition, its goals are worthy, even when they are modified through legislation. More focus on services for offenders, victims, and the community may be the key in revitalizing the juvenile justice system. Restorative justice proponents seem to believe this is the case as they gain momentum with juvenile court acts. Paired with faith-based organizations, restorative justice programs appear to fit well with both the control and the rehabilitation models of juvenile court. This approach works well because offenders are required to make whole, or repair the damage to, those they harmed with the threat of additional punishment looming over them (Cox et al., 2014). As suggested in service quality literature, doing it right the first time costs less to society. Properly addressing the needs of offenders when they are young will reduce recidivism and help produce productive citizens, which provides a greater taxpaying workforce and reduces the cost to society by decreasing the number of adult offenders.

Perhaps prison overcrowding and technological changes (discussed in Chapter 4) will continue to encourage justice initiatives that rely on community-based approaches to rehabilitation and offender reintegration. This encourages the offenders to become more involved in the services they receive from the system and to become more proactive in their rehabilitation process. Offenders may not choose to take on this role willingly, which suggests that the system has to educate offenders in both their roles within the process and in how to be self-reliant customers of the services offered. When the system is actively involved in educating offenders and offenders take the roles of active customers, the system can provide greater opportunities for customization of services that better meet the individual needs of offenders.

State Court Management

State court management has faced myriad problems, especially since state courts are not standardized. In most states, courts are either managed by chief justices or court administrators. As mentioned before, chief justices have always been responsible for the administration of courts. This has resulted in a "variety of uncoordinated and inconsistent administrative practices" (Cox & McCamey, 2008, p. 208). Chief justices do not necessarily occupy their positions because of skills in management or administration, but instead are appointed to these positions because of seniority, in most cases. So there is no guarantee that they will manage the court effectively and efficiently.

To rectify some of these issues, all states have implemented state court administration offices. State court administrators assist judges in administrative and nonjudicial functions, such as record keeping, judicial training, research and planning, budget preparation, and so forth (Durham & Becker, 2012; Cox & McCamey, 2008). The creation of court administrators has resulted in a significant change in the administration of the courts. Court administrator offices, though, have not existed without resistance. Neubauer (2005) points out that judges may actually see the efforts of the court administrator as intruding, while other court employees, such as clerks and reporters, see them as threatening, since court administrators may control the hiring and firing of staff as well as the supervision and evaluation of personnel. Just as there is no guarantee that chief justices will be good leaders or effective managers, the same holds true with state court administrators. "Courts are complicated, difficult organizations to lead, let alone change" (Griller, 2008, p. 101), so agencies such as the National Center for State Courts are developing experimental curriculum modules for judges and court managers. The modules deal with general subjects such as team building, agenda setting, long-term planning, and organizational theory, as well as specific subjects such as court culture, case flow management, and organizational structure and decision making (Griller, 2008). The idea here is that leadership in courts cannot be assumed to exist but can be taught to those placed in charge.

The concept of unified court management through a state court administrator was first suggested by Roscoe Pound in a 1906 address to the American Bar Association (Pound, 1906). In this address, he suggested that performance could be measured if courts were simple, unified, and used science and business-like methods. In particular, he advocated for a reorganization of state courts through unification and simplification—with lines of authority filtering from the top to the bottom. He recommended judicial superintendents—not management by a chief judge—who would supervise and provide leadership in a unified court system. According to Pound, the superintendent could oversee calendars, assign cases and judges, and ensure that judicial power was fully and effectively employed. He proposed the use of courts of general jurisdiction with specialist judges to whom distinctive classes of litigation could be assigned as needed.

Pound (1906) also proposed improvements in court efficiency through Taylor's scientific management principles. Borrowing these concepts and applying them to the court system, Pound advocated that the courts should emphasize the system and its effectiveness before individuals. Furthermore, the system, through supervising managers, should identify the one best way to perform court tasks. He proposed that the practice of scientific management, like that used in a factory, was needed to solve the problems of the government and courts (Pound, 1940). Although initially there was little enthusiasm for his idea of a single statewide court system, his concept of court reform essentially came about in the form of state court administration offices.

One of the primary tasks of court managers (whether it is the chief justice or a court administrator) is to measure performance. In an effort to make court performance measurement more accessible, the National Center for State Courts introduced "CourTools" measures to better help the court identify if it is achieving its purpose (see www.ncsconline.org/D_Research/CourTools/tcmp_courtools.htm). Slayton (2008) states that a

> well-functioning court seeks to assess its flexibility in managing and adjusting judge and staff resources to ensure appropriate individual attention to cases and better respond to evolving customer needs. At the same time, a court wants to ensure appropriate controls are in place to achieve stable, predictable, and timely case processing. (p. 115)

In a time of increased scrutiny of the criminal justice system and of court systems and decisions, performance measures demonstrating efficiency and effectiveness can be very useful. CourTools, in particular, addresses service delivery in courts by focusing on how individuals are treated, how cases are handled, and how the court controls its operations. Focusing on three areas of service quality measurement, CourTools analyzes access and fairness by surveying individual satisfaction rates on timeliness, ability of the court to resolve the dispute, and perceptions of fairness; clearance rates by reviewing how the court keeps up with the current demands for service/caseloads; and time to disposition, which calculates the length of elapsed time between case filing and case resolution. CourTools also measures case management by reviewing cost per case, file security and integrity, satisfaction of court employees, and so forth (see Cour-Tools: http://www.courtools.org). All of these indicators provide courts with a way to collect and present evidence of their effectiveness and efficiency in servicing the needs and expectations of clients. In addition, the information gathered is important in showing accountability and in relationships with both society and other branches of the government.

To further improve the smooth functioning of the courts and to better manage budgets and resources, some courts use a weighted caseload to determine fiscal needs for court support staff. California was one of the first states to use weighted caseloads for judges, but has more recently moved away from this approach in favor of a simulation methodology and continuous data collection (Flango & Ostrum, 1996). A *weighted caseload* is the determination of the amount of time it takes to process a court's caseload from the filing of the initial paperwork until the disposition. In this approach, courts can objectively identify the amount of time and staff needed to process given types of cases. It is critical, though, that the weights be adjusted and updated to ensure that they accurately represent workload time. A number of states, including Nebraska, New Mexico, Washington, and Wisconsin, use weighted caseloads to measure future and present need for court support staff (Flango & Ostrum, 1996).

Massachusetts courts have also implemented a system similar to weighting by using metrics to measure timeliness and expedition on a statewide basis across all trial court departments. Collaboration between the legislature and the judiciary established a baseline for equitably allocating resources for staffing. Once created and implemented, the system greatly improved the court's ability to schedule trial dates with certainty and reduced backlog. Police, witness, and juror expenses and services were also more efficiently used (Monan & Keating, 2007). The court reports that it has decreased continuances by 22% and is trying cases on their first and second trial date 60% of the time (Oliver, 2008). Massachusetts has also developed and implemented a web-based system that collects, stores, and tracks data covering all court departments in all seven of the state trial courts. By using the CourTools' metric, Massachusetts is able to compare its progress with national benchmarks (Monan & Keating, 2007).

Aside from structural concerns, performance issues, budgetary matters, decreasing judicial independence, and delays in processing, courts at both the federal and state levels are facing concerns regarding complaints from the public on the environmental waste created by the court and consumer dissatisfaction with litigation. The federal judiciary offers a system run by the Administrative Office of the U.S. Courts (n.d.) that allows for electronic public access to case and docket information in federal courts. Other courts, in particular state systems, have also been investigating the use of electronic case processing, which will likely result in structural changes to the court. Utah courts are considering providing an increased proportion of their services over the telephone and Internet instead of at physical court locations using court personnel:

> Redesign of this sort may help improve service to the public while providing opportunities to save costs [by using less staff and time, and fewer resources, like paper]. Thus, in the longer term, the issue shifts away from current economic constraints toward desired service strategies. (*Report of the Access and Service Delivery Committee to the Minnesota Judicial Council,* 2008, p. 5)

Other states, such as Alabama, Arizona, California, Colorado, Connecticut, Delaware, New Jersey, New York, North Carolina, Ohio, Texas, Washington, and the District of Columbia, are using statewide e-filing systems for court documents. In 2005, New Jersey made e-filing mandatory (ABA, n.d.). Although e-filing should make the process faster and easier, there have been issues because of the heterogeneity of the state court systems. Unlike the federal system, where there is a master electronic platform for all e-filing, each of the states has its own rules for filing documents. Local jurisdictions also have their own rules for filing electronically. Yet another issue is that some states do not have any rules at all for e-filing (ABA, n.d.). As the ease of use continues to improve and more standardization of filing is established, it is likely that more state courts will accept, and potentially mandate, the technological innovation.

So, too, might the use of e-filing and software programs assist the litigants who go to court without legal counsel. Bladow and Johnson (2008) report that legal needs studies and court statistics show that 40% to 90% of all litigants represent themselves, primarily in civil matters such as eviction and divorce and in creditor issues. Having legal documents accessible on the web allows for self-represented litigants, those in the community, and those working in the court system to have better access to the court and to its documents, thus significantly improving the service quality. Information technology provides customers with ways of taking an active part in the judicial process. Arm's length transactions are becoming more common because they offer customer convenience and efficient criminal justice service delivery. Technology also meets the needs of a specific population, namely, those who choose to represent themselves in court. Thinking creatively about the nature of the service may identify even more convenient forms of delivery through an electronic medium as courts evolve.

CAREER HIGHLIGHT BOX
LAWYERS

Nature of the Work

Lawyers advise and represent individuals, businesses, or government agencies on legal issues or disputes.

Duties

Lawyers typically do the following:

- Advise and represent clients in courts, before government agencies, or in private legal matters
- Communicate with their clients and others
- Conduct research and analysis of legal problems
- Interpret laws, rulings, and regulations for individuals and businesses
- Present facts in writing or verbally to their clients or others and argue on their behalf
- Prepare and file legal documents, such as lawsuits, appeals, wills, contracts, and deeds

(Continued)

(Continued)

Lawyers, also called attorneys, act as both advocates and advisors.

As advocates, they represent one of the parties in criminal and civil trials by presenting evidence and arguing in court to support their client.

As advisors, lawyers counsel their clients about their legal rights and obligations and suggest courses of action in business and personal matters. All attorneys research the intent of laws and judicial decisions and apply the laws to the specific circumstances that their clients face.

To prepare for cases more efficiently, lawyers increasingly use the Internet, online legal databases, and virtual law libraries. Lawyers also often oversee the work of support staff, such as paralegals and legal assistants. For more information about legal support staff, see the profile on paralegals and legal assistants.

Lawyers may have different titles and different duties, depending on where they work.

Criminal law attorneys are also known as **prosecutors** or **defense attorneys**.

Prosecutors work for the government to file a lawsuit, or charge, against an individual or corporation accused of violating the law.

Defense attorneys work for either individuals or the government (as public defenders) to represent, or defend, the accused.

Government counsels commonly work in government agencies. They write and interpret laws and regulations and set up procedures to enforce them. Government counsels also write legal reviews on agencies' decisions. They argue civil and criminal cases on behalf of the government.

Corporate counsels, also called *in-house counsels*, are lawyers who work for corporations. They advise a corporation's executives about legal issues related to the corporation's business activities. These issues might involve patents, government regulations, contracts with other companies, property interests, taxes, or collective-bargaining agreements with unions.

Legal aid lawyers work for private, nonprofit organizations for disadvantaged people. They generally handle civil cases, such as those about leases, job discrimination, and wage disputes, rather than criminal cases.

Lawyers often specialize in a particular area. The following are some examples of types of lawyers:

Environmental lawyers deal with issues and regulations that are related to the environment. They might represent advocacy groups, waste disposal companies, or government agencies to make sure they comply with the relevant laws.

Tax lawyers handle a variety of tax-related issues for individuals and corporations. Tax lawyers may help clients navigate complex tax regulations so that they pay the appropriate tax on income, profits, property, and so on. For example, they might advise a corporation on how much tax it needs to pay from profits made in different states to comply with the Internal Revenue Service's (IRS) rules.

Intellectual property lawyers deal with the laws related to inventions, patents, trademarks, and creative works such as music, books, and movies. An intellectual property lawyer might advise a client about whether it is okay to use published material in the client's forthcoming book.

Family lawyers handle a variety of legal issues that pertain to the family. They may advise clients regarding divorce, child custody, and adoption proceedings.

Securities lawyers work on legal issues arising from the buying and sell of stocks, ensuring that all disclosure requirements are met. They may advise corporations that are interested in listing in the stock exchange through an initial public offering (IPO) or buying shares in another corporation.

Litigation lawyers handle all lawsuits and disputes between parties. These could be contract disputes, personal injury disputes, or real estate and property disputes. Litigation lawyers may specialize in a certain area, such as personal injury law, or may be a general lawyer for all types of disputes and lawsuits.

Some attorneys become teachers in law schools. For more information on law school professors, see the profile on postsecondary teachers.

Training, Other Qualifications, and Advancement

Formal requirements to become a lawyer usually include a 4-year college degree, 3 years of law school, and passing a written bar examination. However, some requirements vary by state.

Education

Becoming a lawyer usually takes 7 years of full-time study after high school—4 years of undergraduate study followed by 3 years of law school. Most states and jurisdictions require future lawyers to complete a juris doctor (J.D.) degree from a law school accredited by the American Bar Association (ABA). ABA accreditation signifies that the law school—particularly its curricula and faculty—meets certain standards.

A bachelor's degree is required for entry into most law schools, and courses in English, public speaking, government, history, economics, and mathematics are useful.

Many law schools, particularly those approved by the ABA, also require applicants to take the Law School Admission Test (LSAT), a test that measures applicants' aptitude for the study of law.

As of August 2011, ABA had approved 200 law schools; others were approved by state authorities only. Admission to law schools—especially the most prestigious ones—is competitive because the number of applicants greatly exceeds the number that can be admitted each year.

A J. D. degree program includes courses such as constitutional law, contracts, property law, civil procedure, and legal writing. Law students may choose specialized courses in areas such as tax, labor, or corporate law.

Law students often gain practical experience by participating in school-sponsored legal clinics, in a school's moot court competitions, in practice trials under the supervision of experienced lawyers and judges, and through research and writing on legal issues for a school's law journals.

(Continued)

Part-time or summer jobs in law firms, government agencies, and corporate legal departments also provide valuable experience. These experiences can help law students decide what kind of legal work they want to focus on in their careers. These experiences may also lead directly to a job after graduation.

Licenses

Becoming licensed as a lawyer is called being "admitted to the bar" and licensing exams are called "bar exams."

To practice law in any state, a person must be admitted to its bar under rules established by the jurisdiction's highest court. The requirements vary by individual states and jurisdictions. For more details on individual state and jurisdiction requirements, visit the National Conference of Bar Examiners.

Most states require that applicants graduate from an ABA-accredited law school, pass one or more written bar exams, and be found by an admitting board to have the character to represent and advise others. Lawyers who want to practice in more than one state must often take separate bar exams in each state.

Training

After graduation, lawyers must keep informed about legal developments that affect their practices. In 2011, 45 states required lawyers to participate in continuing legal education either every year or every 3 years.

Many law schools and state and local bar associations provide continuing legal education courses that help lawyers stay current with recent developments. Courses vary by state and are generally related to the practice of law, such as legal ethics, taxes and tax fraud, and health care. Some states allow lawyers to take their continuing education credits through online courses.

Advancement

Newly hired attorneys usually start as associates and work with more experienced lawyers or judges. After several years, some lawyers may be admitted to partnership and become partial owners of the firm they work for. Some lawyers go into practice for themselves or move to the legal department of a large corporation.

A few experienced lawyers may be nominated or elected to judgeships. Other lawyers may become full-time law school faculty or administrators. For more information about judges and law school faculty, see the profile on judges, mediators, and hearing officers, and the profile on postsecondary teachers.

Important Qualities

Analytical skills. Lawyers help their clients resolve problems or issues. As a result, they must be able to analyze large amounts of information, determine relevant facts, and propose viable solutions.

Interpersonal skills. Lawyers must win the respect and confidence of their clients by building a trusting relationship so that clients feel comfortable and share personal information related to their case.

Problem-solving skills. Lawyers must separate their emotions and prejudice from their clients' problems and objectively evaluate the matter. Therefore, good problem-solving skills are important for lawyers to prepare the best defense or recommendation.

Research skills. Preparing legal advice or representation for a client commonly requires substantial research. All lawyers need to be able to find what applicable laws and regulations apply to a specific matter.

Speaking skills. Lawyers are hired by their clients to speak on their behalf. Lawyers must be able to clearly present and explain evidence to a judge and jury.

Writing skills. Lawyers need to be precise and specific when preparing documents, such as wills, trusts, and powers of attorney.

Employment

Employment of lawyers is expected to grow by 10 percent from 2010 to 2020, about as fast as the average for all occupations. Demand for legal work will continue as individuals, businesses, and all levels of government will need legal services in many areas.

However, growth in demand for lawyers will be constrained as businesses increasingly use large accounting firms and paralegals to do some of the same tasks that lawyers do. For example, accounting firms may provide employee-benefit counseling, process documents, or handle various other services that law firms previously handled.

Lawyers will continue to be needed in the federal government to prosecute or defend civil cases on behalf of the United States, prosecute criminal cases brought by the federal government, and collect money owed to the federal government. However, budgetary constraints at all levels of government, including federal, will moderate employment growth.

Job Prospects

Competition should continue to be strong because more students are graduating from law school each year than there are jobs available. As in the past, some recent law school graduates who have been unable to find permanent positions are turning to the growing number of temporary staffing firms that place attorneys in short-term jobs. This service allows companies to hire lawyers "as-needed" and permits beginning lawyers to develop practical skills.

Job opportunities are typically affected by cyclical swings in the economy. During recessions, demand declines for some discretionary legal services, such as planning estates, drafting wills, and handling real estate transactions. Also, corporations are less

(Continued)

(Continued)

likely to litigate cases when declining sales and profits restrict their budgets. Some corporations and law firms may even cut staff to contain costs until business improves.

Because of the strong competition, a law graduate's willingness to relocate and work experience are becoming more important. However, to be licensed in another state, a lawyer may have to take an additional state bar examination.

Job Outlook

Lawyers held about 728,200 jobs in 2010. A majority of lawyers work in private or corporate legal offices. Some are employed in local, state and federal governments. About 22 percent of lawyers were self-employed in 2010.

The following industries employed the most lawyers in 2010:

Legal services	51%
Government	18
Finance and insurance	3
Management of companies and enterprises	2

Lawyers work mostly in offices. However, some travel to attend meetings with clients at various locations, such as homes, hospitals, or prisons. Some lawyers gather evidence; others appear before courts. Lawyers who represent clients in courts may face heavy pressure during trials.

Work Schedules

The majority of lawyers work full time, and many work long hours. Lawyers who are in private practice or those who work in large firms often work long hours conducting research and preparing or reviewing documents.

The median annual wage of lawyers was $112,760 in May 2010. The median wage is the wage at which half the workers in an occupation earned more than that amount and half earned less. The lowest 10 percent earned less than $54,130, and the top 10 percent earned more than $166,400.

Salaries of experienced lawyers vary widely according to the type, size, and location of their employer. Lawyers who own their own practices usually earn less than those who are partners in law firms.

The majority of lawyers work full time and many work long hours. Lawyers who are in private practice or those who work in large firms often work long hours conducting research and preparing or reviewing documents.

SOURCE: Bureau of Labor Statistics, U.S. Department of Labor, *Occupational Outlook Handbook, 2012–13 Edition*, Lawyers, on the Internet at http://www.bls.gov/ooh/legal/lawyers.htm.

A lack of access to the U.S. court system has been pointed to as one of the biggest issues in litigation complaints by academics and lawyers. Arguments that pursuing litigation is too expensive and that those who do choose to go to court are pushed toward conflict resolution strategies instead of jury trials have dominated the discussion on the reasons for the decline of litigation in the United States. In addition, analysts have claimed that declining jury trials weaken the judicial structure and lower the education of citizens in the court system traditionally gained through jury service. A last concern in this debate is that courts may be seen as unfair if most litigation is resolved through conflict resolution instead of in court (Henry, 2007). As Henry points out, the trend toward resolution practices by the courts, such as dispute resolution, conflict resolution, online resolution, and others, is not a disservice to the public. In his assessment, the public avoids litigation as much as possible anyway, and it is mainly practicing lawyers and legal academics who are most concerned with the lower number of litigation cases. Mediation and resolution programs assist the public just fine in resolving issues between parties. They are less costly and result in fewer delays in the process. More individuals actually have access to them as well, since they are offered in both the public and private arenas. Henry states, "It begins to appear that the consumer and the judiciary have taken a turn together toward a more pragmatic, more managed, and consumer-friendly system" (p. 964). Now, it is time for attorneys to catch up with the new paradigm and to become problem solvers while still serving the court.

Driven by information technology and capacity constraint, this new service development model could be called the "push theory" of service innovation. Within this new paradigm, an important consideration in providing legal services is the realization that the customer can play an active role in the service delivery process. As customer participation increases and as courts continue to seek the input of stakeholders in new innovations, the entire judicial process will likely be changed to facilitate greater customer involvement. For a smooth transition in adopting the emerging service development model, the traditionalists will have to let go of convention and realize the importance of moving ahead with new strategies and innovations available to serve society.

Within this new service delivery paradigm, an important consideration will be that the knowledge, experience, motivation, and honesty of the customers will directly impact the performance of the legal system. The combination of the intangible nature of legal service and the customer as a participant in the service delivery will result in increased variation of service from customer to customer. Such variation in service is not inherently bad unless the customer perceives this variation as a decline in service quality. As stated a number of times in this textbook, a customer expects to be treated fairly and to be given the same service that others receive. Greacen (2008) points out that the individuals, including court personnel and defendants, realize that not everyone wins in court. They expect there to be a losing party and a winning party, but they judge their experience in court on their perception of fairness of the trial process rather than the outcome of the court ruling. If participants in the court process believe that the judge conducted the hearing in a procedurally fair way, they have higher levels of satisfaction with the outcome (regardless of whether they won or lost). According to

Greacen, there is also evidence that individuals who perceive they are treated fairly during a court case have a higher likelihood of complying with a court order (p. 111).

In conclusion, "good people are doing good work in court systems hampered by a lack of good structure and good processes" (Durham & Becker, 2012, p. 7); but the efficient management of the third branch of government is a daunting task. Courts are not merely processing centers. There is a culture of independence and autonomy provided to a judge that develops as soon as a judge is elected or appointed and continues through the leadership and administrative process as judges make decisions that impact law, people, and other branches of government (Durham & Becker, 2012). The rules that apply in the management of businesses and other organizations may not be entirely appropriate for the judiciary, who has a more difficult time seeing it as a system; but certain practices hold true. Courts are accountable to the public for the effective management of judicial affairs. Inefficient or outdated expenses, activities, or methods shown to fail should be replaced by new ones that generate positive results or enhance the overall functioning of the system. Archaic practices should be replaced by approaches that are more modern, and enhanced technology should be employed to meet the needs of current situations and stakeholders. However, management change must not come at the expense or the exclusion of constitutional rights and equal access to the courts. Speedier service by the courts does not mean lower quality or reduced freedoms. The court must find a way to combine the traditional closed-system structure with an open-system approach to better serve its clientele.

Chapter Summary

- Courts in the United States are dual and hierarchical. There are federal and state courts that have separate jurisdictions over cases. State courts hear cases that involve state or local matters and violations of the law, while federal courts primarily handle cases that involve federal laws.
- The court system in the United States is hierarchical in that both the federal and state systems are composed of two kinds of courts—trial courts and appellate courts. All cases are litigated at the trial level and then the issues of law may be challenged in a higher court known as the appellate court. The U.S. Supreme Court is the court of last resort, meaning that it is the final appellate level in the American court system.
- Courts are designed to promote judicial autonomy by allowing the judicial system to be separate from the other two branches of government. Judges, who facilitate the system, are elected or appointed to positions within the courts. Those who serve at the federal level are appointed for life, contingent on good behavior. They can only be removed through impeachment. This allows for further independence from politics and pressures from special interest groups (although there is some evidence that the courts are not completely insulated from these issues).
- Each court system, at both the state and federal levels, is in charge of appointing a chief judge who manages the court by assigning judges to hear cases; controlling the budget; supervising other personnel, probation and pretrial officers; and performing other administrative duties. The chief judge can be highly influential in the outcomes of cases and in determining legislation. The chief judge may also work with a court administrator, if the state uses that organizational structure.
- Federal court management occurs through the Administrative Office of the U.S. Courts, which works to improve court efficiency and responsiveness.

- There are currently two theories on judicial decision making in the courts—managerial theory and attitudinal theory. Managerial theory proposes that judges make decisions based on the volume of their workload. Attitudinal theory is based on the belief that judges hear cases and make decisions based on their political preferences. This practice is called the judicialization of politics or the politicalization of the judiciary process. The U.S. Supreme Court has been viewed by some as participating in this trend.
- State court systems typically use unified trial courts or segmented trial courts. State court systems may have a single appellate court or many appellate courts. All states have a court of last resort known as the state supreme court.
- Unlike the federal system, state courts are not managed through a single, centralized method. State courts may be administered by a chief judge in each jurisdiction or through a centralized office of state court administrators. They measure success through performance measures, budgetary management, case processing, judicial independence, use of technology, and support for litigation decisions. Determining actual, tangible results for these issues, though, is difficult for state courts. Currently, state courts use CourTools, weighted caseloads, metrics for timeliness and expedition, web-based case management, earth-friendly practices, and resolution/mediation practices in litigation cases to efficiently manage the state judiciary.
- Specialized courts, known as problem-solving courts, are quickly becoming popular in all states. These courts address specific offender needs by focusing on services to meet those needs. Drug courts and mental health courts are popular versions of problem-solving courts. The courts have experienced some criticism because they operate differently and outside of traditional court structures; judges are more involved in fundraising for the programs offered, and are not seen as doing the traditional job of the judge in court. These courts have also shown mixed results with regard to success.
- Juvenile courts, which are part of the state system, have limited jurisdiction over issues involving people under the age of statutorily defined adulthood. State juvenile courts guide the everyday mission and scope of the various juvenile courts by clearly defining what cases are heard, procedural guidelines, substantive laws, age limitations of juveniles, and the nature of the acts over which juvenile court has jurisdiction. Juvenile courts have always focused on the particular needs and special concerns of the youth who fall within their jurisdiction. They have willingly worked with the community, other social service agencies, treatment providers, schools, and families in rehabilitating youth and resolving childhood issues. Contemporary juvenile courts use restorative justice programming, police-sponsored station adjustments, teen or peer courts, drug courts; and efforts to reduce minority overrepresentation to address stakeholder needs.

Chapter Review Questions

1. What is judicial autonomy or independence? What can be done to increase judicial autonomy? How does judicial autonomy impact service quality in the judicial system?

2. What are the two theories of judicial decision making? What are the primary differences between the two? How can we hold judges more accountable for their decision making?

3. What are the commonly held expectations of courts? What are the expectations of problem-solving courts? According to these, are courts effective? How can we measure court effectiveness?

4. How is the juvenile court system using service quality in the reform of youth? What about in the processing of youth in court?

5. Who are the stakeholders of the American judicial system? How can courts (at all levels) better meet the needs of stakeholders? Of victims? Of offenders? Of funding sources?

6. In your opinion, can we use a systems approach to courts? Why or why not? Do you consider courts open or closed systems? Why?

CASE STUDY

In September 2013, Margaret Barnes, a county probation officer, was called into Judge Vin's chambers and asked questions about a case scheduled for hearing that day. The judge asked the probation officer for a verbal summary of the case and a recommendation on disposition. The judge questioned Barnes about why she felt the disposition was appropriate. At the end of the conversation, the judge said, "Thanks. That saves me from having to read the file."

Later that afternoon, during the hearing, the judge appeared to be bored while both the prosecutor and the defense counsel presented the case. The judge put his feet up on the bench, his arms behind his head, and at several points during the procedure closed his eyes. An hour into the hearing, the judge leaned forward and said, "I've heard enough. This is my ruling." The judge then proceeded to repeat the recommendation given to him by Barnes earlier in the day.

About two months after the hearing, Barnes was called to a deposition investigating the judge's behavior in other cases. She was asked about her communications with the judge prior to or after court hearings. She admitted to ex parte conversations with the judge.

The judge was livid when he found out about the investigation (which was eventually dropped) and the individuals who had been deposed. He called Barnes into his office and fired her on the spot. He accused her of defamation of character and threatened to sue her. Barnes appealed her removal from the job to the county board, and the chief justice, and hired an attorney to represent her in a civil case of wrongful termination. Only one attorney in town would accept the case, and he said they wouldn't likely win. He also said that he had to be very careful in his representation of her since he appeared in front of this judge in other cases and he didn't want to jeopardize his clients' chances in those cases.

Questions for Review

1. Who are the stakeholders in this case?

2. Is there an ethical or legal issue presented in case? What is it? Who is at fault? Why? How does the legal or ethical issue hamper the quality of services received by the stakeholders you identified above?

3. How can judges ensure fundamental fairness in and outside of the courtroom? How do others (outsiders, victims, defendants, etc.) determine judicial fairness?

Internet Resources

California Court Structure—http://www.glenncourt.ca.gov/general_info/teachers/structure.html

Center for Court Innovation—http://www.courtinnovation.org

National Center for State Courts, Comparing State Courts—http://www.ncsc.org/Information-and-Resources/Comparing-state-courts.aspx

References and Suggested Readings

Administrative Office of the U.S. Courts. (2006). *Annual report of the director.* Retrieved from http://www .uscourts.gov/library/annualreports/2006/2006_annualreport.pdf.

Administrative Office of the U.S. Courts. (n.d.). *PACER Service Center.* Retrieved from http://pacer.psc .uscourts.gov/index.html.

American Bar Association. (n.d.). *ABA Legal Technology Resource Center electronic filing resource page.* Retrieved from http://www.abanet.org/tech/ltrc/research/efiling.

Annie E. Casey Foundation. (2009). Two decades of JDAI: A progress report. Retrieved from http://www .aecf.org/MajorInitiatives/~/media/Pubs/Initiatives/Juvenile%20Detention%20Alternatives%20 Initiative/TwoDecadesofJDAIFromDemonstrationProjecttoNat/JDAI_National_final_10_07_09.pdf.

Artis, J. E. (2004). Judging the best interests of the child: Judges' accounts of the Tender Years Doctrine. *Law & Society Review, 38*(4), 769–807.

Bazemore, G., & Umbreit, M. (1997). *Regional symposium training manual: A comparison of four restorative conferencing models.* Washington, DC: U.S. Department of Justice, Office of Justice Programs.

Bazemore, G., & Umbreit, M. (1999). Conferences, circles, boards, and mediations: Restorative justice and citizen involvement in the response to youth crime. Washington, DC: Office of Juvenile Justice and Delinquency Prevention.

Bladow, K., & Johnson, C. (2008). Online document assembly. In C. R. Flango, A. M. McDowell, C. F. Campbell, & N. B. Kauder (Eds.), *Future trends in state courts, 2008* (pp. 44–49). Washington, DC: National Center for State Courts. Retrieved from http://contentdm.ncsconline.org/cgi-bin/show file.exe?CISOROOT=/ctadmin&CISOPTR=1258.

Blakely v. Washington, 542 U.S. 296 (2004).

Breed v. Jones, 421 U.S. 519, 95 S.Ct. 1779 (1975).

Burbank, S. B. (2008). Judicial independence, judicial accountability, and interbranch relationships. *Daedalus, 137*(4), 16–27.

Bureau of Justice Statistics. (n.d.). *What are problem-solving courts?* Retrieved from http://www.ojp.usdoj .gov/BJA/evaluation/psi_courts.

Carr, C. (1998). *VORS program evaluation report.* Inglewood, CA: Centenela Valley Juvenile Diversion Project.

Cavan, R. S. (1969). *Juvenile delinquency: Development, treatment, control* (2nd ed.). Philadelphia, PA: J. B. Lippincott.

Center for Restorative Justice and Mediation. (1996). *Restorative justice: For victims, communities, and offenders. What is restorative justice?* St. Paul: School of Social Work, University of Minnesota.

Conference of State Court Administrators. (1999). *Position paper on problem-solving courts.* Arlington, VA: Government Relations Office. Retrieved from http://cosca.ncsc.dni.us/WhitePapers/Therapeutic Justice2-Aug-99.pdf.

Cox, S. M., Allen, J. M., Hanser, R. H., & Conrad, J. J. (2014). *Juvenile justice: A guide to theory, policy, and practice.* Thousand Oaks, CA: Sage.

Cox, S. M., & McCamey, W. (2008). *Introduction to criminal justice: Exploring the network* (5th ed.). Durham, NC: Carolina Academic Press.

Crimes and Criminal Procedure, 18 U.S.C. § 3602 (2004).

Daly, K. (1987). Structure and practice of familial-based justice in a criminal court. *Law & Society Review, 21,* 267–90.

Daly, K. (1989). Rethinking judicial paternalism: Gender, work-family relations, and sentencing. *Gender and Society, 3,* 9–36.

Davis, R. C., Tichane, M., & Grayson, D. (1980). *Mediation and arbitration as alternatives to prosecution in felony cases: An evaluation of the Brooklyn Dispute Resolution Center (first year).* New York, NY: VERA Institute of Justice.

Dighton, D. (2003, Summer). Minority overrepresentation in the criminal justice and juvenile justice systems. *The Compiler, 22,* 1–6.

Dihn, V. D. (2007). Threats to judicial independence, real and imagined. *Georgetown Law Journal, 95*(4), 929–944.

Dorf, M. C., & Fagan, J. A. (2003). Community courts and community justice. *American Law Review, 40*(4), 1501–1512.

Durham, C. M., & Becker, D. J. (2012). A case for court governance principles. National Center for State Courts. Retrieved from http://www.ncsc.org/Services-and-Experts/Court-leadership/~/media/Files/PDF/Services%20and%20Experts/Areas%20of%20expertise/Becker-Durham-A-Case-for-Court-Governance-Principles.ashx.

Fallon, R. H., Meltzer, D. J., & Shapiro, D. L. (2003). *Hart & Wechsler's the federal courts and the federal system* (5th ed.). New York, NY: Foundation Press.

Fercello, C., & Umbreit, M. (1998). *Client evaluation of family group conferencing in 12 sites in 1st Judicial District of Minnesota.* Unpublished manuscript, University of Minnesota.

Flango, C. R., McDowell, A. M., Campbell, C. F., & Kauder, N. B. (Eds.). (2008). *Future trends in state courts, 2008.* Washington, DC: National Center for State Courts. Retrieved from http://contentdm.ncsconline.org/cgi-bin/showfile.exe?CISOROOT=/ctadmin&CISOPTR=1258.

Flango, V. E., & Ostrum, B. J. (1996). *Assessing the need for judges and court support staff.* Washington, DC: National Center for State Courts. Retrieved from http://www.ncsconline.org/WC/Publications/Res_WorkLd_AssessNeedsJudges&StaffPub.pdf.

General Electric Co. v. Joiner, 522 U.S. 136 (1997).

George, T. E., & Yoon, A. H. (2008). Chief judges: The limits of attitudinal theory and possible paradox of managerial judging. *Vanderbilt Law Review, 61,* 1–61.

Giles, M., Walker, T., & Zorn, C. (2006). Setting a judicial agenda: The decision to grant en banc review in U.S. Courts of Appeals. *Journal of Politics, 68,* 852–866.

Greacen, J. M. (2008). The court administrator's perspective: Research on "procedural justice"—what are the implications of social science research findings for judges and courts? In C. R. Flango, A. M. McDowell, C. F. Campbell, & N. B. Kauder (Eds.), *Future trends in state courts, 2008.* Washington, DC: National Center for State Courts. Retrieved from http://contentdm.ncsconline.org/cgi-bin/showfile.exe?CISOROOT=/ctadmin&CISOPTR=1258.

Griller, G. M. (2008). New dimensions in court leadership. In C. R. Flango, A. M. McDowell, C. F. Campbell, & N. B. Kauder (Eds.), *Future trends in state courts, 2008.* Washington, DC: National Center for State Courts. Retrieved from http://contentdm.ncsconline.org/cgi-bin/showfile.exe?CISO ROOT=/ctadmin&CISOPTR=1258.

Henry, J. F. (2007). The courts at a crossroads: A consumer perspective of the judicial system. *Georgetown Law Journal, 95*(4), 945–964.

In re Gault, 387 U.S. 1, 87 S.Ct. 1428 (1967).

In re Holmes, 379 Pa. 599, 109 A 2d. 523 (1954), cert. denied, 348 U.S. 973, 75 S.Ct. 535 (1955).

In re Winship, 397 U.S. 358, 90 S.Ct. 1968 (1970).

Institute of Applied Research. (2004). *A cost-benefit analysis of the St. Louis City Adult Felony Drug Court.* St. Louis, MO: Author. Retrieved from http://www.iarstl.org/papers/SLFDCcostbenefit.pdf.

Jamieson, K. H. (2006). *Americans trust courts but also believed them biased, surveys find.* Retrieved from http://www.annenbergpublicpolicycenter.org/NewsDetails.aspx?myId=13.

Kent v. the United States, 383 U.S. 541, 86 S.Ct. 1045 (1966).

Koontz, H. (1914). *Toward a unified theory of management.* New York, NY: McGraw-Hill.

Krause, J. (2006, February). The force of e-filing: The move toward digital documents is slow, confusing—and inevitable. *ABA Journal: Law News Now.* Retrieved from http://www.abajournal.com/magazine/the_force_of_e_filing.

Lavery, T. (2002). Police use of formal and informal station adjustments for juveniles in Illinois. *On Good Authority, 6*(4), 1–5.

Levrant, S., Cullen, F. T., Fulton, B., & Wozniak, J. F. (1999). Reconsidering restorative justice: The corruption of benevolence revisited. *Crime & Delinquency, 45*(1), 3–27.

Libby, E. (2009). Watch what you ask for. *ABA Journal, 95*(4), 24.

Lindner, C. (2004, Spring). A century of revolutionary changes in the United States juvenile court systems. *Perspectives, 71*(3), 24–29.

Lowi, T. J. (1979). *The end of liberalism: The second republic of the United States.* New York, NY: Norton.

Marbury v. Madison, 1 Cranch 137, 170 (1802).

McKeiver v. Pennsylvania, 403 U.S. 528, 91 S.Ct (1971).

Miller, J., & Johnson, D. (2009). New approaches to criminal justice. Lanham, MD: Rowman & Littlefield.

Monan, J. D., & Keating, M. B. (2007, September 15). Efficient courts enhance access to justice. *Boston Globe.* Retrieved from http://www.boston.com/news/globe/editorial_opinion/oped/articles/2007/09/15/efficient_courts_enhance_access_to_justice.

Mooney, C. Z., & Mei-Hsien, L. (1995). Legislative morality in the American states: The case of pre-*Roe* abortion regulation reform. *American Journal of Political Science, 39*(3), 599–627.

National Victims Center. (1998). *Promising practices and strategies for victim services in corrections.* Retrieved from http://www.nicic.org/Library/015440.

Neubauer, D. W. (2005). *American courts and the criminal justice system* (8th ed.). Belmont, CA: Thomson Wadsworth.

New York State Bar Association, Committee on Court Structure and Judicial Selection. (2004). *Stated purpose.* Retrieved from http://www.nysba.org/AM/Template.cfm?Section=Special_Committee_ on_ Court_Structure_and_Judicial_Selection_Home&Template=/CM/HTMLDisplay.cfm& ContentID=5981.

New York State Governor's Office. (2007, April 26). *New York Governor Spitzer proposes sweeping court reforms; proposes streamlined court system; judicial selection reform; pay equity for judges.* Retrieved from http://www.ny.gov/governor/press/0426071_print.html.

New York State Unified Court System. (2008). *State of the judiciary: Structure of New York State courts.* Retrieved from http://www.courts.state.ny.us/admin/stateofjudiciary/stofjud8/struct.htm.

Niemeyer, M., & Shichor, D. (1996). A preliminary study of a large victim/offender reconciliation program. *Federal Probation, 60,* 30–34.

Nolan, J. L. (2003). Redefining criminal courts: Problem solving and the meaning of justice. *American Law Review, 40*(4), 1541–1566.

Nugent, W. R. (2001). Participation in victim–offender mediation and the reoffense: Successful replications? *Research on Social Work Practice, 11*(1), 5–23.

Nugent, W. R., & Paddock, J. (1995). The effect of victim–offender mediation on severity of reoffense. *Mediation Quarterly, 12,* 353–367.

O'Connor, S. D. (2008, February 24). How to save our courts. *Parade.*

Oliver, T. M. (2008). *Court reform continues in full swing five years after Monan Report ushers in new era.* Retrieved from http://www.massbar.org/for-attorneys/publications/lawyers-journal/2008/january/court-reform-continues-in-full-swing-five-years-after-monan-report-ushers-in-new-era.

Pacelle, R. L. (1991). *The transformation of the Supreme Court's agenda: From the New Deal to the Reagan administration.* Boulder, CO: Westview Press.

Pound, R. (1906). The causes of popular dissatisfaction with the administration of justice. *American Law Review, 40,* 729–749.

Pound, R. (1923). *Interpretations of legal history.* New York, NY: Macmillan.

Pound, R. (1940, April). Principles and outline of a modern unified court organization. *Journal of the American Judicature Society, 23,* 225–230.

Report of the Access and Service Delivery Committee to the Minnesota Judicial Council. (2008, July 17). Retrieved from http://www.courtsolutions.org/sites/S70/File/ASD%20Report%20without%20appen dices.pdf.

Resnick, J. (1982). Managerial judges. *Harvard Law Review, 96,* 377–379.

Roberts, L. (1998). *Victim offender mediation: An evaluation of the Pima County Juvenile Court Center's Victim Offender Mediation Program (VOMP)*. Langley, B.C., Canada: Frasier Area Community Justice Initiatives.

Roe v. Wade, 410 U.S. 113 (1973).

Roper v. Simmons, 543 U.S. 551 (2005).

Roy, S. (1993). Two types of juvenile restitution programs in two Midwestern counties. *Federal Probation, 57*, 48–53.

Schall v. Martin, 467 U.S. 253 (1984).

Schattschneider, E. E. (1960). *The semisovereign people: A realist's view of democracy in America.* New York, NY: Harcourt Brace.

Schneider, A. (1986). Restitution and recidivism rates of juvenile offenders: Results from four experimental studies. *Criminology, 24,* 533–552.

Schneider, P. (2000, October 26). Repairing the effects of crime; programs bring together victims and offenders. *Capital Times* (Madison, WI), p. 1B

Schubert, G. (1959). *Quantitative analysis of judicial behavior.* Glencoe, IL: Free Press.

See, H. (2007). An essay on judicial selection: A brief history. In K. Bybee (Ed.), *Bench press: The collision of courts, politics, and the media,*. Stanford, CA: Stanford University Press.

Segal, J. A., & Spaeth, H. J. (1993). *The Supreme Court and the attitudinal model.* New York, NY: Cambridge University Press.

Shepard, R. E., Jr. (1999). The juvenile court at 100 years: A look back. *Juvenile Justice, 6*(2), 13–21.

Shover, N., & Henderson, B. (1995). Repressive crime control and male persistent thieves. In H. D. Barlow (Ed.), *Crime and public policy: Putting theory to work.* Boulder, CO: Westview Press.

Slayton, D. (2008). Using performance measures to enhance fair and impartial courts: A practitioner's view. In C. R. Flango, A. M. McDowell, C. F. Campbell, & N. B. Kauder (Eds.), *Future trends in state courts, 2008* (pp. 115–118). Washington, DC: National Center for State Courts. Retrieved from http://con tentdm.ncsconline.org/cgi-bin/showfile.exe?CISOROOT=/ctadmin&CISOPTR=1258.

Snyder, H. N., & Sickmund, M. (1999, November). *Juvenile offenders and victims: 1999 national report.* Washington, DC: U.S. Department of Justice.

Stein, D. M., Deberard, S., & Homan, K. (2013). Predicting success and failure in juvenile drug treatment court: A meta-analytic review. *Journal of Substance Abuse Treatment, 44*(2), 159–168. doi:10.1016/j .jsat.2012.07.002

Stone, S., Helms, W., & Edgeworth, P. (1998). *Cobb County Juvenile Mediation Program evaluation.* Cobb County, GA: Juvenile Court Mediation Program.

Stotland, E. (1969). Exploratory investigations of empathy. In L. Berkowitz (Ed.), *Advances in experimental social psychology ,4,* 271–314. New York, NY: Academic Press.

Supreme Court of Florida. (n.d.). *2006–2007 annual report.* Tallahassee, FL: Office of the State Courts Administrator. Retrieved from http://www.flcourts.org/gen_public/pubs/bin/annual_report0607.pdf.

Tarr, G. A. (2007). Politicizing the process: The new process of state judicial elections. In K. Bybee (Ed.), *Bench press: The collision of courts, politics, and the media.* Stanford, CA: Stanford University Press.

Tate, C. N., & Vallinder, T. (1995). *The global expansion of judicial power.* New York, NY: New York University Press.

Ulmer, S. S. (1984). The Supreme Court's certiorari decisions: Conflict as a predictive variable. *American Political Science Review, 78*(4), 901–911.

Umbreit, M. (1996). *Information on research findings related to uniquely restorative justice interventions: Victim–offender mediation and family group conferencing.* Unpublished manuscript, University of Minnesota, St. Paul.

Umbreit, M. (1998). *Family group conferencing: Implications for crime victims.* Washington, DC: Office for Victims of Crime, U.S. Department of Justice.

Umbreit, M. (1999). *Victim–offender mediation and dialogue: Guidelines for victim sensitive practice.* Unpublished manuscript, University of Minnesota, St. Paul.

United States v. Booker, 543 U.S. 220 (2005).

U.S. Courts. (2001, April). Electronic access to bankruptcy courts boon to public. *The Third Branch.* Retrieved from http://www.uscourts.gov/ttb/sep02ttb/electronic.html.

U.S. Courts (n.d.). *Understanding the federal courts.* Washington, DC: Author. Retrieved from http://www .uscourts.gov/understand03.

Utah State Courts. (2008). *Utah drug courts.* Retrieved from http://www.utcourts.gov/drugcourts.

Walker, S. (1998a). *Popular justice: A history of American criminal justice* (2nd ed.). New York, NY: Oxford University Press.

Walker, S. (1998b). *Sense and nonsense about crime and drugs: A policy guide* (4th ed.). Belmont, CA: West/Wadsworth.

Welsh, W. N., Jenkins, P. H., & Harris, P. W. (1999). Reducing minority overrepresentation in juvenile justice: Results of community-based delinquency prevention in Harrisburg. *Journal of Research in Crime and Delinquency, 36,* 87–110.

Wilkinson, R. A. (1997). Back to basics. *Corrections Today, 59,* 6–7.

Wolf, R. V. (2007). *Don't reinvent the wheel: Lessons from problem-solving courts.* Washington, DC: Center for Court Innovation, Bureau of Justice Assistance. Retrieved from http://www.courtinnovation.org/_ uploads/documents/Dont%20Reinvent.pdf.

Wynne, J. (1996). Leeds mediation and reparation service: Ten years experience of victim-offender mediation. In B. Galaway & J. Hudson (Eds.), *Restorative justice: International perspectives* (pp. 443–461). Monsey, NY: Criminal Justice Press.

Younger v. Harris, 401 U.S. 37 (1971).

Zehr, H. (1990). *Changing lenses.* Scottsdale, PA: Herald Press.

Probation
and Parole

LEARNING OBJECTIVES

Upon completion of this chapter, students should be able to do the following:

- Discuss the history of probation and parole
- Identify management processes traditionally used in probation and parole agencies
- Explain how open-systems and service quality approaches have been used in probation and parole agencies
- Point out the issues probation and parole currently face
- State how additional service quality management techniques could enhance effectiveness through improved client services

Community-based corrections includes probation, parole, halfway houses, electronic monitoring, furloughs, work release, restorative justice, and other similar programs that are nonincarcerative in nature. These programs are designed to allow offenders to be in the community so that they can continue relationships with support systems such as family, friends, jobs, and so forth. The most well-known community corrections programs are probation and parole. They are widely used throughout the United States with offenders who are viewed as low risks to society as well as offenders who have paid their debt to society through an incarceration period. Although the total number of people under correctional supervision in the United States is declining, there were approximately 3,971,319 individuals on probation and 853,852 on parole at the end of 2011 (Glaze & Parks, 2012). Parole experienced its second year of increased numbers. "Males made up three-quarters (75%) of the adult probation population. Over half (54%) of probationers were white non-Hispanic, and nearly a third (31%) were black non-Hispanic. Nearly three-quarters (72%) were on active status and about 1 in 5 (18%) were being supervised for a violent offense. Fifty-three percent of probationers were being supervised for a felony offense in 2011, compared to 50% in 2010" (Marushak & Parks, 2012 p. 7). "Males continued to make up about 9 in 10 (89%) of the adult parole population. About 4 in 10 parolees were white non-Hispanic (41%) or black non-Hispanic (39%), and about 2 in 10 (18%) were Hispanic. Among parolees, 81% were on active supervision and 96% had a maximum sentence of one year or more. More than a quarter (28%) were being supervised for a violent offense" (Marushak & Parks, 2012, p. 9). These populations place unique demands on the criminal justice system, and the roles and duties of the individuals employed in the system have been tremendously altered by a changing probationer and parolee demographic.

Since most community corrections programs focus on offenders placed on probation or monitored on parole, this chapter will concentrate specifically on these two services. The beginning of the chapter will address the history of probation and parole services in the United States, along with their goals and functions. Next, the duties of probation and parole officers will be discussed. The structural design of probation and parole as well as the issues confronted will be analyzed. Finally, a discussion of what probation and parole agencies have done to overcome the issues and what they can do to resolve service quality complaints will be presented.

Probation

Probation is a court sentence that allows an offender to remain in the community while under the supervision of a representative appointed by the court, as long as the individual complies with court-ordered sanctions and conditions. In some cases, probation can be combined with a sentence of incarceration followed by community supervision (Murashak & Parks, 2012). *Probationers* are individuals who have been convicted of a crime but are sentenced to probation instead of being confined in an institution. *Probation officers* are court-appointed representatives who supervise probationers and ensure that they comply with court-ordered conditions while on probation. The use of probation is especially valuable as a less costly alternative to overcrowded prisons (McCarthy & McCarthy, 1991). It is used in both adult and juvenile courts as a means for promoting safety, helping offenders, and enforcing court orders. Like many other correctional alternatives, probation faces a number of issues, namely, failures to decrease restitution, underfunding, caseload management issues, and a lack of identified direction.

The word *probation* comes from the Latin term *probatio,* which means to test or to prove. The history of probation can be traced to suspended sentencing practices in England during the Middle Ages. Early American courts also allowed for judicial reprieves that granted judges the right to suspend sentences for offenders convicted of nonviolent or minor crimes (New York City Department of Probation, n.d.). Although these practices were allowable, they were not widely used, and most offenders who appeared in court were incarcerated. Probation in its current form began in 1841 when

John Augustus, a local businessman, requested that judges let him pay fines for and supervise offenders convicted of minor crimes. Once he had bailed the offenders out of jail, he would help them find employment and begin a reformed lifestyle. When the offenders were ordered to return to court, Augustus would accompany them and report to the judge on their behavioral changes. As a result of his efforts and the success he experienced with offenders, Massachusetts passed the first probation law in 1878 (Cox & McCamey, 2008).

Even with a formal probation system in place, probation as a sentencing practice did not become popular until after the first juvenile court was created in Chicago in 1899. Because of the more liberal treatment-oriented approach used with youth convicted of crimes, states saw probation as a better fit for juveniles who needed individualized, case-by-case sentencing. Once probation became widely used with youthful offenders, adult courts adopted the process as well. In 1925, the National Probation Act was passed, creating a federal probation system, and by 1956, all states provided some form of probation as a sentencing alternative in both adult and youth courts (Macallair, 2002). Currently, probation services are administered by municipal, county, state, and federal governments through either the judicial or executive branches. In some areas of the United States, probation services are combined with parole services (discussed in detail later in this chapter) under one executive office or through the county or state government. In this case, probation officers act as parole officers as well, by monitoring both types of cases.

Probation is very task-oriented in accomplishing its goals. One of the goals of probation is to protect the members of society by preventing additional crime. Probation addresses this goal through the *presentence investigation report (PSI)*. The judge can order the probation officer to write a PSI prior to the sentencing hearing for an offender. The report provides the court with a complete history of the offender including prior criminal acts, family and school involvement, psychological or medical issues, drug or alcohol use, employment history, and educational/vocational abilities, among other things. The report documents the facts of the crime and the offender's risk to society while providing a statement on the needs the offender has to be rehabilitated (Cohn & Ferriter, 1990). One objective of the report is to provide the judge with enough information to make an appropriate sentencing decision. The report is also aimed at facilitating the supervision and treatment of the offender once sentenced, since both correctional staff and probation officers rely on the report to identify programs and services that are of benefit to the offender. Furthermore, parole boards use the report when making decisions on the release of an offender from prison (Glueck, 1952). Most important is the fact that the presentence investigation report is the screening tool in determining the risk the offenders pose to the community if they are allowed to remain free in society. It is the information gathered for this report that helps in predicting if the offender is likely to commit an additional crime. Offenders viewed as suitable to remain in the community are recommended for probation, while those seen as dangerous to the community are identified as such in the report and sentenced to more secure placements. If the probation officer investigates and reports the information thoroughly and completely, and the judge uses the report in decision making, the presentence investigation is a good resource in the protection of society through the prevention of additional crimes (Cohn & Ferriter, 1990; Cox & McCamey, 2008).

A second goal in probation is to help offenders, which is accomplished through the supervision and management process. Probation officers are tasked with enforcing the conditions imposed by the court. They do this by supervising the probationers' behaviors and removing them from the community when they violate the stipulations of their probation. Aside from the supervision tasks, probation officers also act as referral agents by managing and identifying the needs of offenders and connecting them to service providers who can best address the issues faced by the offender (Cox & McCamey, 2008). For example, probation officers may refer probationers to drug counseling if they see that offenders are struggling with drug use. The hope is that counseling will assist the offenders to overcome the drug problem and successfully complete probation while remaining in good standing. Probation officers also provide other services to probationers on an as-needed basis, such as assisting them in getting employment, enrolling in school, finding a place to live, registering for public aid, working with social service agencies, and acting as role models for offenders. Probation officers may even defend probationers against inappropriate stigmatization and treatment from other agencies, the community, and the offender's family (Cox & McCamey, 2008). Essentially, the probation officer protects the rights and liberties of both society and the probationer.

From the viewpoint of the courts and much of society, the enforcement of court orders is of primary importance in the administration of probation (Storm, 1997). Probationers are required to meet certain conditions imposed by the court to remain on probation. Aside from being a law-abiding citizen, the probationer can also be required to maintain employment or attend school; submit to drug or alcohol testing and counseling; attend family or individual counseling; receive medical assistance; attend other programs or services seen as beneficial to the offender; break ties with known felons, other probationers, or parolees; meet curfew or home detention requirements; and so on. Other stipulations, considered *special conditions,* may also be applied on a case-by-case basis (Storm, 1997). For instance, a probationer convicted of drunk driving may be required to attend a victim impact panel sponsored by Mothers Against Drunk Driving (MADD). Other probationers may have to pay restitution to their victims and complete community service activities. Special conditions are attempts to individualize probation services so that they are advantageous to the offender and potentially reduce the likelihood that the probationer will recidivate.

Probationers who violate the court-imposed stipulations risk having their probation sentence revoked. There are two types of probation violations—technical and new offense (rearrest). Technical violations are usually minor in nature and address all of the conditions in the probation order aside from the commission of additional criminal acts. Accordingly, an offender who fails to attend school or get a job has committed a technical violation. An offender who fails a drug test or who refuses to attend individual counseling has also committed a technical violation. In these instances, the probation officer has the discretion to ask the court to revoke probation. It is important to note here, however, that the probation officer does not have to pursue revocation and, in most cases, relies on the seriousness of the violation in determining whether a revocation hearing is necessary (Cox, Allen, Hanser, & Conrad, 2014). Unless there is legislation or organizational policy stating otherwise, the most common approach to technical violations is a warning from the probation officer or extra meetings or phone calls between the offender and the officer. Repeated technical violations may result in the revocation of probation, since continued violations are most likely a sign that the probationer is not willing or able to comply with the court's orders. A rearrest or the commission of a new offense is seen as a serious violation of probation, since maintaining a law-abiding life is viewed as one of the most important conditions placed on a probationer. A probationer who commits a new criminal act is at the highest risk of having the probation sentence revoked (Cox et al., 2014). During revocation hearings, probationers who are determined to have violated the conditions of probation may be reprimanded and returned to probation supervision, have additional stipulations added to the probation contract, or have the probation revoked and be placed in a correctional institution or other secure facility. Ultimately, what occurs during a revocation hearing is the judge's decision. Parole, discussed next, is similar to probation and can also result in revocation.

Parole

Deriving from the French word *parole,* meaning word of honor, *parole* is the conditional release of a prisoner under the supervision of a parole officer after having served a period of incarceration (Petersilia, 2000). It includes those released under mandatory and discretionary release systems and postcustody conditional releases (Marushak & Parks, 2012). Most recently, parole is referred to as offender reentry or community transition (G. Hughes, 2007). However, the approach is the same, with the exception of greater emphasis on the parolee's transition to freedom, beginning in the prison and continuing through community-based support programs. *Parolees* are offenders being supervised on parole. Inmates can be released from incarceration by a parole board *(discretionary parole)* or according to the provisions of a mandate *(mandatory parole).* Under discretionary parole, a parole board (usually politically appointed) has the authority to conditionally release inmates based on statutory or administrative determination of eligibility. Their discretion may be limited by legislation. The parole board reviews the case and may interview the offender requesting release. A decision is then made, through majority vote, on the offender's suitability for reentry into the community. Mandatory parole occurs in jurisdictions where determinate sentences are used. In this case, inmates are conditionally released from prison after serving a minimum period of incarceration minus good time credits earned (Hughes, Wilson, & Beck, 2001). Like probationers, parolees must comply with conditions instituted by the supervising parole agency. Failure to comply can result in parole revocation and a return to prison.

Historically, parole was first used in Ireland and Australia, where it was granted as an award to inmates for good behavior, meritorious service, positive attitude changes, and accepting increasing responsibilities. Inmates who could demonstrate that they would perform well in free society were released early from their prison sentences. In the 1800s, prison administrator Sir Walter Crofton used "tickets of leave," which were positive marks based on work performance, behavior, and educational improvement, to determine which inmates qualified for early release in the Irish prison system (Petersilia, 2000, p. 36). He also implemented intermediate prisons where inmates could live and work while taking on more responsibilities than provided to those in other secure facilities. Those inmates released on parole were required to submit monthly reports to the police. The police inspector helped them find jobs and monitored their activities (Clear & Cole, 1997).

Modern-day parole in the United States is credited to Zebulon Brockway, who was the superintendent of the Elmira Reformatory in New York in the late 1800s and incorporated the ideas introduced by Crofton. Brockway used intermediate sentences, which allowed the prison to determine the length of time a prisoner was incarcerated, parole, and the earning of good-time credits in his program with youthful offenders. Brockway did not rely on the police to supervise parolees, but asked for community volunteers to supervise the inmates once released into society. Later, supervision was provided by volunteer prison societies that were interested in the welfare of newly released offenders (McCarthy & McCarthy, 1991). The concepts of indeterminate sentencing, a system for granting release from prison, postrelease supervision, and specific criteria for parole revocation were extremely popular in the early 1900s and were quickly adopted by all but three states (namely, Florida, Mississippi, and Virginia) (Clear & Cole, 1997). By 1942, those three states had implemented a parole system, as had the federal government.

In the first half of the 20th century, the use of parole gained popularity and the numbers of inmates released as a result of parole practices almost doubled (Petersilia, 2000). However, by 1977, some states began to apply more rigid determinate and mandatory sentences to specific offenses. Because of these sentences, parole boards became less important and, in some cases, the determination of when to parole was given to the judge who handled the case originally. Questions regarding the use of parole and whether it occurs because of good behavior and attitude changes by the offender or because of the sheer numbers of offenders waiting to enter prisons were raised by the public and politicians alike. Nevertheless, in those jurisdictions where parole boards continued to exist, they represented an important means for controlling prison overcrowding (Cox & Wade, 2002). Although opponents of parole argue that prison overcrowding is the primary reason for parole and question the decisions made by parole boards, supporters claim that the purpose of incarceration and release is to rehabilitate, not only to punish (Petersilia, 2000). Proponents point to the fact that parole boards consider a multitude of issues when deciding to parole, including institutional behavior, incarceration length, crime severity, criminal history, mental illness, and victim input (Caplan, 2007, p. 18). "Through the exercise of its discretion, parole boards can actually target more violent and dangerous offenders for longer periods of incarceration" (Petersilia, 2000, p. 1). As noted by Burke (1995), parole is a controlled privilege that is only earned by selected inmates.

However, when that privilege is eliminated and mandatory releases are put in place, all inmates, regardless of their violent tendencies, are entitled to be released.

Currently, many parole systems in the United States are either nonexistent or in a period of instability. At the federal level, parole was abolished in 1997. Federal inmates now serve a period of supervised release from incarceration after completing a determined period of time in prison. By 2000, discretionary parole was abolished in 16 states for all offenders, while 4 other states abolished discretionary parole for certain violent offenses and other crimes against persons (Hughes et al., 2001). Mandatory parole presently accounts for the majority of parole releases, with approximately 178,933 parolees released on mandatory parole compared to 144,530 released on discretionary parole in 2011 (Marushak & Parks, 2011, p. 19).

Because of the unpredictable and varying nature of parole in states that use it, it is difficult to identify specific objectives of parole systems. Parole was originally created to assist inmates in transitioning from prison to free society. It was believed that parole would promote offender reform rather than provide increased surveillance and punishments. Traditionally, parole officers would assist with job placement, counseling, dependency issues, integration into the family, and identification of support systems, among other things. However, enlarged caseloads along with punitive public attitudes have led to decreased services to parolees (Petersilia, 2000). According to Lynch (1998), safety and security are the biggest issues in parole today. This is evidenced in legislative decisions to allow parole officers to have arrest powers and the right to carry guns in the course of their duties. In addition, parole officers are seen more and more as law enforcement officers than as parole officers. It is not uncommon for states to require parole officers to complete police training courses prior to or immediately after being hired. California, for example, requires parole officers to complete four weeks at the police academy (Employment Development Department, 1998). Zero tolerance for parole violations has led to the job of parole officer being focused more on supervision and control than on service opportunities (Petersilia, 2000). It is rather ironic that at the time when offenders are at the greatest risk of recidivating, they may receive the least number of services. With the changing roles in parole management and changing focus of parole services, Holt (1998) claims that many parole agencies "are still struggling to contribute without a coherent conceptual basis of operation or a clear sense of purpose" (p. 39).

As with all areas of criminal justice, the number of services offenders receive varies according to the state and jurisdiction in which they are being supervised. Subsequently, it should be noted here that even though critics claim that parole in general does not seem to focus enough effort on its intended purpose, there are areas of the United States that are providing traditional service activities. States such as Kansas, Georgia, New Jersey, and Rhode Island have reworked their parole systems to include job development programs, detoxification services, and substance abuse treatment (Burke, 2004). Although this is good news, as mentioned earlier, these services are diminishing for a number of reasons. First, as the parole population increases and the needs of offenders multiply, parole officers have less time to provide conventional services outside of surveillance and control. In addition, as more mandatory conditions on offenders are imposed with greater frequency by releasing authorities, control and surveillance requirements intensify. Parolees are held accountable for more behaviors than ever before (Petersilia, 2000), including those involving restitution, curfew, community service, drug testing, and so forth. Some of these behaviors fall outside of the standard parolee conditions of getting a job, reporting changes in their residence, remaining in the jurisdiction, not committing additional crimes, reducing contacts with other offenders, submitting to searches by parole officers and the police, not carrying weapons, and so forth. According to Lucken (1997), an unintended consequence of increasing conditions on parolees, which are almost impossible to fulfill, is increased violations and returns to the correctional system.

Reductions in programs aimed at rehabilitation have also created problems in the brokering of services for parolees. As fewer and fewer spots are available in treatment programs, a smaller number of parolees are actually able to comply with their mandatory parole requirements. Perhaps most significant is that ideologically, and as pointed out earlier, parole has appeared to change its focus from a social services orientation to a law enforcement concentration. As Feeley and Simon (1992) argue, a systems analysis approach to danger management has been put into place in parole systems. Rather than focusing on rehabilitation, parole management uses control strategies to supervise, and in most cases confine, high-risk criminals. They contend that a new penology has emerged that simply strives to manage risk by use of actuarial methods rather than focusing on service quality, reintegration, and needs assessments. By and large, this puts parolees—and, in most cases, parole officers—in a difficult situation that almost inevitably leads to failure. It brings to light the problems that emerge when organizations make decisions without evaluating their capacity constraints, the needs of the customers, and the needs of the downstream organizations to which their output will become an input. Demanding more from the system where the capacity is limited does not help anybody, as is reflected in the current parole system.

In the News 11.1
This Time, Parolee Has a Plan—A Halfway House
to Help Him Stay Out of Prison

Paroled out of San Quentin at 8 a.m. Saturday, Ronald Eugene Williams hopped two buses and by 4:45 p.m. had rolled into the Greyhound-Amtrak station in Old Town Roseville.

From there, the nine-time convicted felon got a ride to an Auburn halfway house for drug addicts and alcoholics that he will call home for the next six months.

On Monday, he checked in with his new parole agent and shocked her world.

"I was pleasantly surprised," agent Magdalena Cardona said. "Because when you look at his bio and his track record, it's not good. But he had a really good attitude when he showed up."

So far, it's been a good week of parole for the 44-year-old Williams. Just 155 more weeks like it, and he'll become one of the lucky few parolees in California who overcome their past to create promise for their future.

(Continued)

(Continued)

With California struggling to fix a parole system where only three in 10 offenders complete their three years of supervised release without returning to prison, Williams represents a case study on whether the state can turn those numbers around.

Stacked against the backgrounds of the 370 parolees who walk out of California prisons every day, Williams' record is typical—and horrid.

It sports 31 arrests, nine felony convictions—most on drug or domestic violence charges—and 11 parole revocations.

He's addicted to methamphetamine and takes lithium for bipolar disorder.

He smoked pot at age 10 but says he didn't really go bad until his older brother raped and murdered a woman 28 years ago.

He has six children by five mothers.

He's also unguardedly optimistic about his re-entry into freedom.

"I'm pretty relaxed," Williams said Saturday morning at 6, one of 14 prisoners caged in the Receiving and Release office at San Quentin. "I have a plan. This is the first time I've ever paroled with a plan. It's a plan I know is going to work."

His ticket to drug treatment, at a cost of $90 a day to taxpayers, makes Williams think he can make it this time.

"I have a great chance," he said. "I'm just going to follow through."

'We'll leave the light on'

Williams claims he's been drug-free since he got picked up June 1, 2007, on a parolee-at-large warrant.

Big-eyed and confident, he boarded the van out of San Quentin wearing a saggy pair of jeans he bought from another inmate for $15. His state-issued T-shirt looked like it could have used a wash.

"Gentlemen, good luck," correctional officer Luis Medina told Williams and the rest when they walked out of the building. "We'll leave the light on for you."

Of the 13 other parolees, six had no place to go. Four were pretty sure they'd be able to get jobs. One had lined up enrollment in a trade school. One said he would live and work on a fishing boat in Crescent City. One has multiple sclerosis.

"I guess I have to parole homeless," said Darnell Duffy, 38, destination Fairfield. "Hopefully my uncle will let me live with him."

Williams has been in that boat before. Last time out in January, he lived in a motel for a while on his $200 gate money, then went "couch surfing" in friends' living rooms from North Highlands to Rancho Cordova.

Sober when he got out of the Sierra Conservation Center in Jamestown, he soon got reacquainted with the crank pipe.

"It took two weeks before I got high," he said.

'You saved the day'

To keep him from temptation this time, a nonprofit parolee assistance group called Friends Outside had arranged with the California Department of Corrections and Rehabilitation to drive him directly to Auburn.

The ride never showed, so Williams took the prison van with the other parolees to the San Rafael bus station. From there, he boarded a Golden Gate Transit bus to the Transbay Terminal in downtown San Francisco.

At the San Francisco Greyhound, one of Williams' fellow parolees asked him if he'd like to get a drink at a nearby bar. It was not yet noon. Williams declined.

He bought a new shirt at Walgreens on Mission Street, ate a sirloin bacon cheeseburger at Jack-in-the-Box around the corner and hung close to the station until the call came to board the bus to Sacramento.

He got his share of sideways glances on the streets, and even drew a "security check on (aisle) seven" on the intercom while he shopped at Walgreens.

He also hauled in one extraordinary act of kindness.

When a broken pay phone at the Roseville bus station wouldn't take his money, he couldn't call the people at the halfway house to come pick him up.

Rosemarie Ontiveros, 65, watched from a distance. She saw Williams with everything he owned in a cardboard box and knew what was going on.

She offered Williams her cell phone. "You saved the day," Williams told her.

Ontiveros said she's got a son of her own in prison, in Tehachapi. "He's supposed to get out in a year," she said.

Forty-five minutes later, Bob Murray pulled into the station in his SUV. He's the executive director of Health, Hope and Healing, a faith-based drug treatment provider with a couple of recovery homes in Placer County.

Murray shook hands with Williams and whisked him away to his facility on Meadow Glen Road. "He's in good shape for the shape he's in," Murray joked.

'One day at a time'

Williams has tried and failed a couple of times at recovery. He said he didn't know much about Health, Hope and Healing's game plan or what to expect there.

"I'm just going in open-minded," he said. "I really don't have anything on my mind except getting what they have to offer."

Over the next few days, Williams dug in for a month-long "blackout" period during which he can't talk to family and friends or anybody else. His agenda is to focus on where he is, why he's there and what it's going to take for him to straighten out his life.

One piece of bad news jolted Williams on his second day out: While he was in prison, his only sister died.

"We'll get him through this," Murray said. "It won't derail him from this program."

At the parole office on Monday, agent Cardona put a few special conditions on Williams' freedom that he must meet to stay out of prison.

He's subject to random drug tests. He has to enroll in a 52-week batterer's program (paid for by the state at $40 a day), stay away from the woman he repeatedly victimized over a period of 16 years and check in with a mental health counselor at the parole outpatient clinic.

Williams, who scored off the charts for his propensity for violence in the system's risk-needs assessment while he was imprisoned, has been placed on "high-control" supervision—the system's most severe.

Cardona declined to predict his outcome.

"I don't know," Cardona said. "It wouldn't be fair to predict that, but he's off to a good start. He has a good attitude. He has a good placement. All we can really do for him is take it one day at a time. Ultimately, it's going to be up to him to do the work."

The issues raised in the discussion on both probation and parole are demonstrated in In the News 11.1. As had previously occurred with Williams, even parolees released with reintegration plans are at great risk of failure. Those released without plans, such as the six mentioned in the article, have nothing going for them except recidivism. Parole officers, in this case, need to provide more services but are limited because of caseload sizes and case management approaches. (A more in-depth discussion of these problems will occur later in the chapter.) The parole officers not only impact the services provided to offenders in most need of assistance to fully reintegrate them into society, but also the community itself. If neither probation nor parole can accomplish its intended missions, then we must ask what benefits these programs are providing to the offenders relying on them to attain paths to productive citizenship and to the community that is relying on them for safety. One also has to wonder about the probation and parole officers who appear to be working in a field that lacks clarity. How can they successfully complete their jobs and provide the best service quality when their organizational goals are not clearly defined or the means to achieving the goals they believe they should meet are impossible to implement? These are important questions for the administration to consider in structuring the agency to provide a better working environment for the officers and to improve the service quality in meeting the needs of society and the probationer or parolee.

CAREER HIGHLIGHT BOX
CORRECTIONAL OFFICERS

Nature of the Work

Correctional officers are responsible for overseeing individuals who have been arrested and are awaiting trial or who have been sentenced to serve time in a jail, reformatory, or prison. Typically, offenders serving time at county jails are sentenced to a year or less. Those serving a year or more are usually in state or federal prisons.

Duties

Correctional officers typically do the following:

- Enforce rules and keep order within jails or prisons
- Supervise activities of inmates
- Aid in rehabilitation and counseling of offenders
- Inspect conditions within facilities to ensure that they meet established standards
- Search inmates for contraband items
- Report on inmate conduct

Inside the prison or jail, correctional officers enforce rules and regulations. They maintain security by preventing any disturbances, assaults, or escapes. Correctional officers supervise the daily activities of inmates, ensuring that inmates obey the rules and finish their work. Correctional officers also ensure that they know where all inmates are.

Officers must search inmates for contraband such as weapons or drugs, settle disputes between inmates, and enforce discipline. The officers enforce regulations through effective communication and the use of progressive sanctions, which involve punishments such as loss of privileges. Sanctions are progressive in that they start out small for a lesser or single offense but become more severe for more serious offenses or when repeat offenses occur. In addition, officers may aid inmates in their rehabilitation by scheduling work assignments, counseling, and educational opportunities.

Correctional officers periodically inspect facilities. They check cells and other areas for unsanitary conditions, contraband, signs of a security breach such as any tampering with window bars or doors, and any other evidence of violations of the rules. Officers also inspect mail and visitors for prohibited items. They write reports or fill out daily logs detailing inmate behavior and anything of note that occurred during their shift.

Correctional officers may have to restrain inmates in handcuffs and leg irons to escort them safely to and from cells and other areas and to see authorized visitors. Officers also escort prisoners between the institution and courtrooms, medical facilities, and other destinations.

Correctional officers cannot show favoritism and must report any inmate who violates the rules. If a crime is committed within their institution or an inmate escapes, they help the responsible law enforcement authorities investigate or search for the escapee.

Correctional officers have no responsibilities for law enforcement outside of their place of work. For information on other law enforcement occupations, see the profile on police and detectives. For information on counseling offenders outside of prisons, see the profile on probation officers and correctional treatment specialists.

Bailiffs, also known as marshals or court officers, are law enforcement officers who maintain safety and order in courtrooms. Their duties, which vary by location, include enforcing courtroom rules, assisting judges, guarding juries from outside contact, delivering court documents, and providing general security for courthouses.

Correctional officers held about 493,100 jobs in 2010. Ninety-five percent of correctional officers worked for federal, state, and local governments in May 2010. Most of the remainder were employed by private companies that provide correctional services to prisons and jails.

Working in a correctional institution can be stressful and dangerous. Every year, correctional officers are injured in confrontations with inmates. Correctional officers have one of the highest rates of nonfatal on-the-job injuries. Correctional officers may work indoors or outdoors. Some correctional institutions are well lighted, temperature controlled, and ventilated, but others are old, overcrowded, hot, and noisy.

Because offenders typically stay longer in state and federal prisons than in county jails, correctional officers in prisons come to know the people with whom they are dealing. They know what they need in terms of security and being taken care of. Therefore, state and federal prisons tend to be safer places to work than county jails.

(Continued)

(Continued)

Injuries

Correctional officers have a higher rate of injury and illness than the national average. They may face physical injury when conflicts with inmates occur. They may also be exposed to contagious diseases at work, although precautions are taken to avoid this possibility. The job demands that officers be alert and ready to react throughout their entire shift. The work can be stressful, and some officers experience anxiety.

Work Schedules

Correctional officers usually work 8 hours per day, 5 days per week, on rotating shifts. Some correctional facilities have longer shifts and more days off between scheduled workweeks. Because jail and prison security must be provided around the clock, officers work all hours of the day and night, weekends, and holidays. In addition, officers may be required to work paid overtime.

Training, Other Qualifications, and Advancement

Correctional officers go through a training academy and then are assigned to a facility for on-the-job training. Qualifications vary by agency, but all agencies require a high school diploma or equivalent. Some also require some college education or work experience.

Education

Correctional officers must have at least a high school diploma or equivalent. Some state and local corrections agencies require some college credits, but law enforcement or military experience may be substituted for this requirement. For employment in federal prisons, the Federal Bureau of Prisons requires entry-level correctional officers to have at least a bachelor's degree; 3 years of full-time experience in a field providing counseling, assistance, or supervision to individuals; or a combination of the two.

Training

Federal, state, and some local departments of corrections, as well as some private corrections companies, provide training for correctional officers based on guidelines established by the American Correctional Association (ACA). Some states have regional training academies that are available to local agencies. Academy trainees receive instruction in a number of subjects, including institutional policies, regulations, and operations, as well as custody and security procedures.

After formal academy instruction, state and local correctional agencies provide on-the-job training, including training on legal restrictions and interpersonal relations. Many systems also provide training in firearms proficiency and self-defense. Trainees typically receive several weeks or months of training in a job under the supervision of an experienced officer. However, on-the-job training varies widely from agency to agency.

New federal correctional officers must undergo 200 hours of formal training within the first year of employment, including 120 hours of specialized training at the U.S. Federal Bureau of Prisons residential training center. Experienced officers receive annual in-service training to keep up on new developments and procedures.

Correctional officers who are members of prison tactical response teams are trained to respond to disturbances, riots, hostage situations, and other potentially dangerous confrontations. Team members practice disarming prisoners, wielding weapons, and using other tactics to maintain the safety of inmates and officers alike.

Certification

Officers may complete a variety of certifications that provide additional resources for their daily work. These certifications also are a means to further the officers' careers because they may lead to promotions.

Advancement

Qualified officers may advance to the position of correctional sergeant, who is responsible for maintaining security and directing the activities of other officers. Qualified officers also can be promoted to supervisory or administrative positions, including warden. Officers sometimes transfer to related jobs, such as probation officer, parole officer, or correctional treatment specialist. For more information, see the profile on probation officers and correctional treatment specialists.

Important Qualities

Critical-thinking skills. Correctional officers must determine the best practical approach to solving a problem.

Good judgment. Officers must use both their training and common sense to quickly determine the best course of action and to take necessary steps to achieve a desired outcome.

Interpersonal skills. Correctional officers must be able to interact and effectively communicate with inmates and others to maintain order in correctional facilities and courtrooms.

Negotiation skills. Officers must be able to assist others in resolving differences to avoid conflict.

Physical strength. Correctional officers must have the strength to physically move or subdue inmates.

Self discipline. Correctional officers must control their emotions when confronted with hostile situations.

(Continued)

(Continued)

Writing skills. Officers must be able to understand and learn training materials and write reports regularly.

Correctional officers usually must be at least 18 to 21 years of age, must be a U.S. citizen or permanent resident, and must have no felony convictions. New applicants for federal corrections positions must be appointed before they are 37 years old.

Job Outlook

Employment of correctional officers is expected to grow by 5 percent from 2010 to 2020, slower than the average for all occupations.

Demand for correctional officers will come from population growth. However, because of budgetary constraints and a general downward trend in crime rates in recent years, demand will likely grow at a slower rate. Faced with growing costs for keeping people in prison, many state governments have moved toward laws requiring shorter prison terms and alternatives to prison. Community-based programs designed to rehabilitate offenders and limit their risk of repeated offenses while keeping the public safe may reduce prison rates.

Job Prospects

Some local and state corrections agencies experience high job turnover because of low salaries and shift work, as well as the stress that many correctional officers feel. The need to replace correctional officers who transfer to other occupations, retire, or leave the labor force, coupled with rising employment demand, should generate job openings.

Some employment opportunities also will come in the private sector as public authorities contract with private companies to provide and staff corrections facilities. Some state and federal corrections agencies use private prison services.

Earnings

The median annual wage of correctional officers and jailers was $39,040 in May 2010. The median wage is the wage at which half the workers in an occupation earned more than that amount and half earned less. The lowest 10 percent earned less than $26,040, and the top 10 percent earned more than $67,250.

The median annual wage in the public sector was $54,310 in the federal government, $38,690 in state government, and $38,980 in local government in May 2010. In the facilities support services industry, in which a relatively small number of officers employed by privately operated prisons is classified, the median annual wage was $30,460.

The median annual wage of bailiffs was $38,570 in May 2010. The lowest 10 percent earned less than $18,980, and the top 10 percent earned more than $66,400. The median annual wage of bailiffs employed by local governments was $34,490.

In addition to receiving typical benefits, correctional officers employed in the public sector usually are provided with uniforms or with a clothing allowance to buy their own uniforms. Many departments offer retirement benefits, although benefits vary. Unionized correctional officers often have slightly higher wages and benefits.

Correctional officers usually work 8 hours per day, 5 days per week, on rotating shifts. Some correctional facilities have longer shifts and more days off between scheduled workweeks. Because prison and jail security must be provided around the clock, officers work all hours of the day and night, weekends, and holidays. In addition, officers may be required to work paid overtime.

SOURCE: Bureau of Labor Statistics, U.S. Department of Labor, *Occupational Outlook Handbook, 2012–13 Edition*, Correctional Officers, on the Internet at http://www.bls.gov/ooh/protective-service/correctional-officers.htm.

Probation and Parole Officers

Probation and parole officers, for the most part, serve the same functions—they help and control offenders. They are hired to deal with offenders' problems by providing services and identifying resources for the offenders. They are also expected to monitor offenders' behaviors and ensure that the court's orders are met. This creates a dual role for officers in that they are part caseworkers and social work providers and part law enforcers and correctional officers (McCarthy & McCarthy, 1991). Most officers function in one role more often than the other, depending on their personality. For instance, one officer may be more of a caregiver and work predominantly on providing services and rehabilitative programming, while another officer may view the rules of the court as most important and spend little time on treatment. The caregiver officer would likely report fewer violations because of seeing the rules as less important than the offender's progress in treatment. The rule enforcer could possibly pursue more revocations since rule infractions are believed to be more important than reform. The divergence in service received by the offender because of the personality of the officer may be interpreted as a lack of consistent service quality. Reducing the discretion of the service providers is one approach to achieving consistent service quality; however, this may not work well in the probation and parole fields, where officers need the flexibility to work with offenders and provide treatment and assistance as offenders' needs arise. Instead, the best approach is to combine the dual roles as much as possible so that an adequate amount of time and attention is spent on rehabilitation while ensuring that the court's stipulations are followed. At the same time, the media could be used to educate the general public on how and why customized treatments suiting the needs of the offenders can be a better approach in rehabilitating them effectively so that the public does not see it as discrimination and inconsistent service quality.

Historically, probation and parole officers were expected to approach the job from a caseworker position. It was anticipated that the officer would develop a one-to-one relationship with the offender, which would be used to change the offender's behaviors. The probation and parole officer could rely on the information gained from the relationship to identify problems or concerns the offender needed addressed, and then could either work on those problems directly with the offender or indirectly by referring the offender to other resources (McCarthy & McCarthy, 1991). Today, it is not uncommon to see probation and parole officers spending less time in the field (at offenders' homes, jobs, schools, social functions) and more time in the office. Under this new style of case management, called *resource brokerage*, officers are brokering resources to offenders by referring clients to community resources that can meet the unique needs of each probationer or parolee. Although the probation and parole officer is the primary supervisor of the case, the actual services provided to and treatment of the offender are farmed out to other social service providers. This new arrangement allows the officer to operate with fewer skills in social work and treatment, and to spend a reduced amount of time on each case (McCarthy & McCarthy, 1991). Fortunately, through resource brokerage, the offender is provided an opportunity to interact with and develop relationships with several providers in the community, which may better assist in reintegration. Unfortunately, though, this approach goes against the fundamental goals of probation and parole and may allow for increased recidivism, since offenders spend very little time with the person charged with monitoring, and ultimately mentoring them.

Aside from monitoring and helping offenders, probation and parole officers diagnose needs and risks while supervising clients. The needs of an offender are determined through needs assessments and diagnoses. According to Holt (1998), these assessments are intended to do the following:

1. Provide an objective way of evaluating the offender's public risk and personal needs.

2. Allocate resources based on need.

3. Direct the agent's time by prioritizing cases.

4. Provide a management information system to evaluate the process. (p. 37)

The risk assessments are based on research embedded in predicting the likelihood offenders will recidivate. They contain checklist items that are assigned point values. The higher total points offenders earn, the greater the risk the offenders pose to the community and the greater their needs are for increased treatment and close supervision. An offender who scores high on the risk and needs assessment may be placed on intensive supervision, which could require daily contact between the supervising officer and the offender.

Diagnosis is the second factor in risk and needs assessments. Probation and parole officers may formally request a psychological assessment of an offender to determine the mental needs of the person or may informally determine psychological needs through observation of the offender. Although a staple in probation and parole supervision, issues have been raised with risk and needs assessments. Critics have pointed to the fact that violent offense recidivism cannot be predicted through statistical methods (Burke, Adams, & Ney, 1990). In addition, opponents claim that scores on the risk and needs assessments can be manipulated to modify workloads (Petersilia, 2000). Finally, Holt (1998) suggests that there is a low correlation between the scales and their actual ability to predict recidivism. According to him, they may be better suited for determining resource allocation than for predicting recidivism.

Supervision is the most active part of a probation and parole officer's job. The officer meets with and monitors the offender's successes and failures on probation and parole. The officer may spend months or years working with a single offender. As mentioned before, the amount of supervision given to a case may depend on the probation or parole officer's approach to the job and on the agency's determination of caseload management. If the agency expects that officers will act as caseworkers, the supervising officer may spend much more time with the offender. However, if resource brokerage is the accepted form of supervision, the officer may spend less time in the field with the client and more time on administrative duties.

Agencies may also determine supervision levels by creating generalized and specialized caseloads. Supervision levels will impact how often an officer interacts with an offender and the approach the officer takes in managing the case. Officers who monitor *generalized caseloads* may have some offenders who require minimum intervention and other offenders who need intensive supervision. In agencies that use *specialized caseloads,* offenders with a particular trait are matched with supervising officers with specialized skills who can best deal with those traits. For example, a specialized caseload may consist of all youthful offenders, those who have committed sex offenses, or those who need intensive supervision. An officer may even have a caseload in which every offender is sentenced to an electronic monitor. Specialized caseloads are used in agencies where there are enough resources to assign probation and parole officers to specific tasks, when there are probation and parole officers who have focused skills in certain areas of treatment, and when there are high numbers of offenders who need a specific type of assistance. In general, all probation and parole organizations offer some form of specialized caseloads to better meet the needs of their clients. Both risk and needs assessments and the use of specialized caseloads are known as evidence-based practices. *Evidence-based practices* rely on empirically based statistical measures; targeted interventions with higher-risk offenders and the use of technology, such as GPS monitoring systems; to reduce the incidents of crime and recidivism (Petersilia, 2000).

The Structure of Probation and Parole

Probation and parole services have traditionally relied on an open-systems approach to supervision. Officers work with the offender to input as much information into the case as possible to develop the best approach to rehabilitation for the client. The officer interviews many parties (e.g., family, friends, employers, school personnel, etc.) in creating the presentence investigation report and then uses that information to create a case plan for the probationer or parolee. Community services and outside treatment providers are relied on to provide assistance in the rehabilitation of the offender, and the case is reviewed periodically to ensure that the goals are being met and the offender is making progress toward reform. The review process, which also seeks information from those working with the offender, allows for a feedback loop where adjustments can be made as the case proceeds, just as would occur in an input/throughout/output open-systems process.

Probation officers and parole officers work independently of one another in their respective agencies. Although they may consult other probation and parole officers on particularly difficult cases or on unique situations, they operate for the most part as specialists requiring little micromanagement. The organizational structure varies from agency to agency—there may be highly formalized hierarchies in large urban areas, but overall it tends to be flat, with horizontal communication. Probation and parole officers may focus more on the means (i.e., services provided to offenders) used to achieve the organizational goals (i.e., lowered recidivism) than on the end results. The primary approach to accomplishing the goals involves finding the right services to reform a client and prevent additional crimes.

Issues Confronting Probation and Parole

Probation and parole are service-oriented professions. They attempt to work with offenders to identify their needs and risks as well as with the community to reintegrate probationers and parolees into society. As has been described earlier, their goals are to reduce recidivism, which protects society from crime and assist clients in complying with court orders and other stipulations imposed by parole boards. This, in turn, leads to successful rehabilitation. The goals are rather challenging, and recently probation and parole agencies have not been overly successful in reaching them. The Bureau of Justice Statistics reports that about 16% of all parolees were returned to incarceration in 2006. Concerns regarding the quality of supervision of probationers and parolees have been raised, as society takes note of increasing crimes committed by those under court or corrections supervision. Research on these issues has pointed to several explanations for why probation and parole have faced challenges in lowering recidivism rates.

One possible explanation is a lack of funding. Since 1985, prison populations have more than doubled, as have their budgets, staff, and facility space (Manhattan Institute for Policy Research, 1999). Much of the nation's and each states correctional budget is devoted to managing the prison systems. The state of Florida, for example, in 1999–2000 had a corrections budget of $1,586,325,436. Of this amount, 60.4% (amounting to $958,261,460) was spent on custody and control of inmates inside institutions, while only $247,947,210 (or 15.6%) was used for community supervision programs. The remaining budget went to administrative costs (4.5%), health services (14.7%), and offender work and training (4.8%) (Florida Department of Corrections, 2001). Florida is not alone. Texas spent approximately 15% of a $3,119,197,031 budget on community supervision in 2011. More than 74% percent of the budget was spent housing felons (Texas Department of Criminal Justice, 2011).

As pointed out in *Broken Windows Probation: The Next Step in Fighting Crime* (Manhattan Institute for Policy Research, 1999), the disparities in prison and probation/parole budgets are evident when one looks at per-offender spending amounts. The government spends between $20,000 to $50,000 to house an offender in prison, but only about $200 per year per probationer for supervision. A quick glance at probation and parole officer caseloads demonstrates the effect this disparity has on supervision since the average caseloads in probation and parole range from 90 to 100 clients for every officer. Texas reported 81,000 parole and mandatory offenders under supervision by 1,300 active parole officers in 2011—an average caseload of 62 to 1 (Texas Department of Criminal Justice, 2011). Some areas of the United States have even reported caseload sizes of 300 low-risk offenders to 1 officer. Even specialized caseloads such as those with sex offenders report 30 to 1 ratios throughout the United States (Florida Senate, 2007).

One has to question the quality of services a probationer or parolee receives when an officer is expected to assist 100 or more probationers each month with counseling, job placement, family issues, and so forth. If the officer works an average of 5 days, at 7.5 hours per day of duty with a half-hour off for lunch, then an officer has a maximum of 165 hours per month (22 days x 7.5 hours) to work on cases. Considering a very conservative estimate of 15% of time spent on traveling from case to case, and another 15% of time spent on paperwork in the office, around 115 hours are left to be allocated among 100 cases, implying about 69 minutes per case per month. In these 69 minutes, the officer has to read notes written on the client from the last meeting, meet the client, contact other pertinent agencies involved with the correctional process, and write notes about the progress on the case after the meeting. This breakdown of activities does not account for time lost due to other uncertainties that may arise in the officer–client meeting. However, the previous calculation clearly illustrates that the time spent by an officer adding value to clients is extremely small. In a qualitative study of probation and parole officers' feelings on caseload size and workload allocation, DeMichele and Payne (2007) report that officers felt like they were expected to supervise more offenders with fewer resources. The lack of funding allows for little emphasis on one-to-one supervision and creates massive caseloads. The resulting consequence is a policing supervision style instead of a social work approach. Since it is the supervision and service provider aspect that underlies the historical function of these programs, it is likely that role ambiguity and role conflict are exacerbated among probation and parole officers.

Another reason why probation and parole services may have altered their approach to case management can be explained by the changing demographics in offenders. Probation used to be reserved for offenders who were at low risk of recidivating and who did not pose a serious threat to society. Guidance, counseling, treatment, and assistance in finding jobs were usually all that were needed by these offenders. Parole was an earned privilege by offenders who provided evidence during their incarceration period that they were reformed and would not commit a future criminal offense. Although parole could alleviate prison overcrowding, inmates were actually judged on their success in completing rehabilitation programming while incarcerated before being released. Those who did not pursue reform while imprisoned were not released, unlike today's mandatory release processes where offenders are only required to serve a minimum number of years (regardless of behavior or rehabilitation) before being released.

Likewise, contemporary courts view probation and parole differently today, and current caseloads contain more felons than ever before. According to Taxman, Shepardson, and Byrne (2004), more than half of probationers on caseloads today are convicted felons. In those states not using parole, they either receive probation in lieu of incarceration or are granted probation after short periods of incarceration. Therefore, probation and parole caseloads are beginning to mirror prison populations.

> These offenders have more criminogenic needs, as they may be gang members, sex offenders, or domestic violence offenders. As a result, these offenders will require more officer time to provide adequate supervision, treatment, and enforcement of conditions, and hopefully behavior change. (DeMichele & Payne, 2007, p. 30)

As pointed out previously, it may be difficult for officers who manage these caseloads to find enough hours in the day or work week to focus on each offender individually, as was intended in the past.

A third explanation is the implementation of a "one size fits all" approach to probation and parole. Instead of honoring the intended focus of individualized justice brought forth by probation and parole, where each case was analyzed and then a determination was made as to what stipulations best met the offender's needs and risk level, courts and parole boards are now placing more and more rules on all offenders regardless of the situation. Such an approach limits the options available to an officer in customizing the correctional method to be adopted according to the needs of the client, thus compromising the quality of service delivered. As mentioned before, mandatory and specialized conditions have become so overbearing that compliance with all of them in a timely manner is nearly impossible.

Adair (2004) points out that as conditions placed on offenders increase, discretionary authority decreases among officers. What he terms the "formalization of supervision" (p. 51) results in a more formal, less individualized process that determines specific conditions of supervision. One example he provides is in the collection of fees. Because courts and parole boards are ordering offenders to pay restitution, probation and parole maintenance fees, court costs, and so forth, probation and parole officers are becoming bill collectors in charge of getting the fees from offenders on top of their traditional supervision tasks. In addition, court of appeals decisions have set requirements forcing judges to order precise payment timetables at the time of sentencing (Adair, 2004) instead of allowing probation and parole officers to collect the payments when it best meets the offender's schedule. The probation and parole officer working directly with the offender would know better than the sentencing judge as to when the offender could afford to make the payments because they know if the offender is making money. With the current arrangement, it does not matter if the offender can meet the payment schedule, and it forces officers to document violations by offenders who fail to make the payments. Since the decision is reserved for the court, "it sacrifices the decision-making of those in the best position to exercise it, and substitutes decision-making that cannot be as familiar with the needs of the individual offender" (Adair, 2004, p. 51). This creates the appearance that technical violations, such as not paying the fees associated with probation and parole, are more important than assessment and rehabilitation. Officers are forced to devote a part of their time and attention to tracking violations, which creates more paperwork and administrative duties and leaves less time for value-added activities that contribute to rehabilitating the client.

The amount of paperwork that probation and parole officers have to complete should not be ignored as an issue in supervision. Manually maintaining probation and parole files takes up a significant portion of an officer's time. Probation and parole officers are required to keep case notes on all contacts with the offender and any other parties involved in the case, as well as the progress, or nonprogress, of the offender. Officers are also required to provide copies of all treatment and case plan reports filed with the agency to the court, attorneys, other treatment providers, and community services programs that are working with the offender. In addition, officers who have clients on GPS tracking systems or electronic monitors must also track these offenders through computer automation and other programs. Using the technology and equipment required to monitor today's offenders can be time-consuming as well. In some cases, officers are not able to leave the office to work in the field because of the administrative duties that must be completed. What results is a system of case management from the office.

Harris, Clear, and Baird (1989) found that community corrections as a whole continues to support treatment ideologies. However, these agencies may be limited in their ability to actually carry out the service-oriented approach. DeMichele and Payne (2007) found, in the study mentioned previously on probation and parole officers' feelings toward their jobs, that respondents do not believe they can meet the needs of offenders with the limited community resources available. Aside from the lack of funding to pay for treatment, probation and parole officers encounter a limited number of spots in treatment programs for offenders. This means that even if the officer wants to provide services to the probationer or parolee, the officer often cannot do so because there are no treatment slots available for enrollment. Consequently, the offender is placed on a waiting list. Offenders in need of drug treatment, for example, may not be able to enroll in a program until a spot is available. This usually requires another offender to complete or drop out of the program. Langan (1994) reported that 32% of offenders required to seek drug counseling never received the ordered drug treatment while on probation. Although this may have partially been due to an unwillingness to attend the treatment, it could have also been related to a lack of openings in treatment programs. Offenders ordered to receive other types of treatment face the same issues. One of the authors of this book encountered this personally while working in the criminal justice field. At one point, a delinquent in need of sexual offender treatment was allowed to remain free on probation because there were no spaces available in the sexual treatment facility. Almost five months passed before the perpetrator was able to enter the program and begin treatment.

A good deal of the problems probation and parole are facing—such as funding, legislative mandates, and lack of treatment opportunities—are systemic and beyond the control of the two agencies. However, to accomplish their missions, they must determine how best to work with offenders while still meeting the rigid guidelines and expectations placed on them through courts and legislative rulings. The next section of this chapter will discuss adaptations made by probation and parole officers and their respective agencies to better meet the needs of their clients in spite of the uncertain and challenging environment.

Adaptations Made in Probation and Parole to Meet Client and Community Needs

To be successful within the confines of the judicial and legislative environments, probation and parole must address the wants and needs of both the public and the offenders they service. According to *Broken Windows Probation: The Next Step in Fighting Crime* (Manhattan Institute for Policy Research, 1999), the public wants to feel safe, a feeling they get when they know that violent and dangerous offenders are being controlled by the criminal justice system. The public also wants to know that offenders are being held accountable for their behaviors and are receiving the treatment or sanctions they need to behave in society. Clients on probation and parole want to be free members of society, and they want what they perceive everyone else has—material goods, jobs, money, homes, families, friends, and so forth. Probationers and parolees want the means to get these items, to function within society, and to not be underneath a continuous threat of incarceration. The job of probation and parole then becomes finding a middle ground. They have to create a paradigm that gives top priority to offender needs, offender accountability, community involvement, and public safety. How do they accomplish all of these goals simultaneously? The discussion that follows suggests activities that probation and parole agencies have practiced in the past that should be revisited, as well as some new practices that appear to be promising in providing quality services to probationers, parolees, and the community.

Barklage, Miller, and Bonham (2006) claim that improved delivery of service to the offender and the community is paramount in providing safety and holding the offender accountable. To effectively provide good service quality, they suggest that probation and parole officers be given the discretion to make changes to supervision guidelines on an as-needed basis:

> Because every change in circumstance cannot be anticipated at the time of sentencing, it is helpful if the conditions of supervision can be adjusted and modified, sometimes on very short notice, in order to meet a particular offender's needs or answer a particular concern in the community. (p. 37)

As probation or parole officers supervise offenders, they may notice behaviors that need treatment or that develop over the supervision period but were not considered in the original creation of the probation or parole contract. Under current judicial requirements, probation or parole officers must petition the court or parole board and a hearing must be held to request treatment prior to any therapy taking place, if it was not originally ordered. In this case, and in those in which immediate attention is needed, treatment is delayed and the professional training and judgment of the probation or parole officer are doubted. Since such tight restrictions have been placed on the officer's use of discretion, the only way around this issue is to order treatment to begin with, at the time of the sentencing hearing, if there is even a minute amount of evidence that it may be needed. However, Adair (2004) claims that this is unfair to the offender, who ultimately does not need treatment but must complete it before being successfully discharged from probation or parole, and to the community, which now has to pay for the wasteful use of limited resources. Had the officer been provided the opportunity and responsibility for identifying the offender's need as well as modifying the supervision contract after the sentencing hearing, both issues could have been avoided.

Although this has been common practice in the past and has been widely used in juvenile courts, Adair (2004) points out that this procedure has been limited in recent years through appeals courts' decisions and through formalization processes in probation and parole. This is in opposition to service quality approaches because the immediate needs of the offender and the community are not placed at the forefront, and "too much limitation of the community supervisor's discretion is obviously problematic, for it will render the agent unable to respond to changing conditions in an offender's circumstances" (Barklage et al., 2006, p. 40). Knowing clients is a significant advantage for an officer in customizing the service and individual treatment to probationers and parolees. Barklage et al. (2006) claim that since modifications to the court's order are sometimes necessary, there should be an implementation of guidelines to control adjustments. First, they put forward that supervising agencies should clearly document all instructions or modifications to probation and parole contracts, ensure that the client understands the instructions and modifications, provide acknowledgement forms to the client that allow for signature acceptance of the new condition, and inform the client that the new condition is temporary and can be formally reviewed by a judge at the request of the probationer or parolee. The client should also be given a statement of the evidence used by the officer to make the modification. It should be made clear to the probationer or parolee that failure to adhere to the new condition is considered a violation and may result in revocation. Modifications are viewed as temporary until or unless they are imposed by the court or parole board on a more permanent basis (Barklage et al., 2006). Since probationers and parolees conduct their transactions directly with the service provider—the probation or parole officer—most often in person, a well-trained officer with discretionary powers can best serve the interests of the client by customizing the services appropriately. Therefore, greater and not less discretionary power would fit best when servicing clients, along with superior training, to improve the service quality delivery. Moreover, such an approach allows the offenders to participate in their rehabilitation process by providing input in designing a program that would best serve their needs. This assists not only the direct client, the offender, but also the indirect client, the community, which is required to pay for fewer wasted services.

Another past practice that has been used in probation and parole focuses on offender violations. In the past, supervising officers were allowed to use discretion to determine if a violation of the contract necessitated a revocation. The approach was that of problem solving instead of punishing, and the result was reduced numbers of probationers and parolees entering correctional facilities. However, in today's society, stricter approaches to crime and violations, as well as harsher sentencing philosophies regarding criminal justice and probation and parole among the public, the courts, and lawmakers, have resulted in increased calls for revocation when offenders violate probation and parole contracts. The result is increasing numbers of probationers going into prison and parolees returning to prison. Although revocation and a return to prison may be necessary in some cases, in others it is not warranted. Swift and certain responses to violations are important, but using a blanket revocation approach to violations is inappropriate and ineffective, just as limiting a probation or parole officer's discretion in working with clients is a disservice to those being served. Instead of relying on sanctions to control offenders, Burke (2004) and others suggest that incentives and positive rewards for desired behaviors are more effective in reducing the number of clients violating the conditions imposed. Research has provided mixed results on using punishment as a negative reinforcement technique. Studies have shown that punishment may strengthen undesired behavior as a rebellion by an individual who is punished. It may also create a demotivating working environment, accompanied by hostility toward the superiors who handed down the punishment (Frimary & Poling, 1995)—or, in this case, between the clients and their probation or parole officers. With this in mind, it may be beneficial to return to increased discretion for probation and parole officers regarding violations and to add in a balanced approach to supervision that includes sanctions when necessary and reinforcements for desired behaviors.

To show how this would work, the state of Georgia can be used as an example. Georgia has implemented a behavior response and adjustment guide (see Figure 11.1). Under the state's plan, parole officers are directed to teach the offenders positive social behaviors by rewarding, through praise, certificates, awards, and so forth, behaviors they want repeated and responding to undesirable behaviors by extinguishing or changing them based on a focused level of response (Burke, 2004). In this scenario, a parole officer who has a client that commits a minor technical violation, such as not reporting to a meeting with the officer, can send a letter of reprimand to the offender, verbally warn the offender not to repeat the behavior, or increase the number of times the offender has to see the officer in the future, as well as several other options. The officer does not have to report a violation to the court and seek a revocation or modification of the conditions. However, if the officer has a client who has never missed a scheduled meeting with the parole officer within a specific time period, the supervising agent can reward the client with a verbal or written certificate of recognition. Rewards increase as good behavior continues and may include reduced reporting, early termination, recognition by upper administrators, donated gifts, and so forth. This behavior pattern is the basis for the reinforcement theory of motivation (i.e., people often repeat behavior that provides pleasure and avoid behavior that is

Figure 11.1 Georgia's New Policy on Violations and the Use of Reinforcement and Georgia's Behavior Response and Adjustment Guide (BRAG)

Georgia's New Policy on Violations and the Use of Reinforcement

SECTION 3.500. SANCTIONS VIOLATIONS AND DELINQUENT REPORTS (Policy 2.124, 2.104) (ACA 3–3168)

3.501. Releasee Behavior Releasee behavior is of central concern to the Board. Effective supervision directs the releasee in learning pro-social behaviors that increase public safety and reduce recidivism. The successful releasee meets the vision of success established by the Board. This vision of success includes, but is not limited to, a releasee who is law abiding , self-sufficient, stable in employment, supporting family and dependents, and abstaining from substance use and/or abuse. (Rev.03/03)

3.502. Responding to Releasee Behavior The skillful parole officer will understand the appropriate response to any behavior is a response designed to increase desirable behavior and decrease or extinguish the undesirable behavior. In determining the appropriateness of the response to the behavior, the behavior must first be defined and then recorded. Efforts should be taken to determine the situation or context in which the behavior occurred. The targeted behavior should be addressed utilizing reinforcers if the behavior was desirable or punishers to extinguish an undesired behavior. It is essential that the response to any behavior be done as close as possible to the occurrence of the behavior. (Rev.03/03)

3.502.1. Use of Reinforcement Scientific evidence suggests that it is four times more effective to reinforce desired behaviors than punishment or punishment alone. Studies also suggest that reinforcement of a behavior increases the frequency of that behavior in the future.This is consistent with the "swift" and "certain" tenets of Results Driven Supervision. The use of social reinforcers such as verbal praise, words of encouragement, and statements like "good job" or "keep up the good work" have a significant impact on influencing or reinforcing behavior. This type of positive reinforcement can be achieved with very little effort or time consideration. Parole officers should seek to utilize this type of reinforcement at every opportunity when interacting with the releasees. Other types of reinforcers are material reinforcers and preferred activity reinforcers. Material reinforcers consist of letters of recognition, statements of commendation, graduation certificates, and similar awards. Preferred activity reinforcers would include activities such as extended curfew hours, bimonthly or quarterly reporting and could culminate in a request to the Board for commutation of the releasee's sentence. When utilizing these reinforcers, it is essential that the releasee is aware that the reinforcer is a consequence of the desired behavior and the utilization of the reinforcers should be documented in FLOID. (Rev.03/03)

3.502. 2 Reinforcer Awards Criteria The following awards can be presented to the releasee upon meeting the listed requirements: (Rev.03/03)

Compliance Certificate. Certificate awarded at six-month intervals to the releasee who has exhibited desired behavior and has no violations.

Mr. (or Ms.) Clean Award. Certificate awarded at six-month intervals to the releasee who has no positive drug screens. The releasee must be on the substance abuse track.

(Continued)

Figure 11.1 (Continued)

Stability Award. Certificate awarded at six-month intervals to the releasee who has maintained stable employment and residence.

Lifestyle Commitment Award. Certificate awarded to the releasee who has documented involvement in prosocial activities, such as volunteer work, church affiliation, community service. The releasee should also have stable residence and employment.

3.502.3. Responding to Violations and Undesired Behaviors When responding to violations and undesired behaviors, the parole officer should keep in mind the Board's vision of success for the releasee. Therefore, the emphasis in responding to release behavior is to respond in a manner which will affect a behavioral change in the desired direction. The response might incorporate strategies for extinguishing (punishing) a behavior as well as strategies for changing it. It is important that the parole officer respond swiftly to all violations and undesired behaviors. The failure to respond to any undesired behavior effectively reinforces the behavior. This could lead to that behavior [repeating] or increasing. To deter violations from occurring, the parole officer should demonstrate that all detected violations will have a swift and appropriate response. Violation responses should be tailored to the severity of the violation and the risks posed by the releasee. A "focusing" guide is provided . . . to assist the officer in determining the proper targeting and level of response. Once the level is determined, the BRAG . . . can be applied. (Rev.03/03)

Georgia's Behavior Response and Adjustment Guide (BRAG)

Suggested Response	POSITIVE	BEHAVIOR	NEGATIVE	Suggested Response
Verbal Recognition	90 days clean		Positive drug test(s)	Specific issue hearing
Letter of Recognition	90 days employed		Program nonattendance	Outpatient program
Certificate of Completion	6 months stable residence	L	Failure to report	Self-help program
6-Month Compliance Certificate	Completed first school semester or 30 days regular GED attendance	O	EM violations (minor)	PO letter of reprimand
		W	Assessment not attended	PO verbal reprimand
	Outpatient program completion		Failure to support dependents	Increased screening
	30 days electronic monitoring (EM) violation-free		Unemployed (short period)	Increased reporting
	2 months perfect attendance at cognitive skills course		Special condition violation	Verbal warning
			Fee arrearage $60 or less	
			Technical violation—other	

Positive Behaviors	Criteria		Violations	Responses
1-Year Compliance Certificate Mr./Ms. Clean Award Letter of Recognition EM early termination Certificate of Completion Reduced reporting Chief recognition Decreased supervision level	12 months stability (employment and residence, few to no violations) 6 months clean 2 months perfect attendance at cognitive skills class Completed 1 year of school or 6 months of regular GED attendance 90 days EM violation-free Outpatient program completion Cognitive skills course completion	**M E D I U M**	Misdemeanor arrest Multiple positive drug tests Multiple program nonattendance EM violations (serious) Unemployed (lengthy) Assessments not attended (multiple) Sex offender violations (minor) Fee arrearage $100 or less	Administrative hearing In-house program Restart program EM extension Outpatient program Specific issue hearing Increased screening Increased reporting Verbal reprimand—Chief Restorative/community service work Increase supervision level
Commutation Request Donated Gift Certificate (GED/school graduation) Cognitive Skills Graduation Lifestyle Commitment Award Second Mr./Ms. Clean Award Reduced reporting	24 months stability Completed school or GED 12 months clean Volunteer work, church affiliation Prosocial activities	**H I G H**	Felony arrest Violent misdemeanor arrest or DUI Positive drug tests (critical) Program nonattendance (critical) Sex offender violation (serious) EM violations (critical) Possession of a weapon Absconding TRW issued Failure to attend administrative hearing Unemployed (critical) Fee arrearage over $100	Request revocation Short-term incarceration (local detention) Electronic monitoring In-house program Administrative hearing Outpatient program EM extension Whitworth detention

SOURCE: From *Parole Violations Revisited*, by P. Burke, 2004, Washington, DC: U.S. Department of Justice, National Institute of Corrections.

unpleasant) proposed by B. F. Skinner (1969) and discussed in detail in Chapter 6. Research is still ongoing on this approach to supervision, so time will tell if it is appropriate for offender monitoring.

A crucial component of probation and parole supervision success is the involvement of outside agencies. Community leaders, faith-based organizations, social service agencies, and special interest groups sponsor many of the treatment and rehabilitation programs as well as reintegration programs used by offenders. To provide superior service quality, the roles of these different organizations can be, and are, enhanced and coordinated. The President's Prisoner Reentry Initiative (PRI) has recognized the need for community collaboration in successful prisoner reentry. Faith-based organizations engage approximately 45 million volunteers across the United States and raise about $81 million annually to assist in paying for social needs. The federal government has seen this as a valuable resource for offender reentry and for those who remain incarcerated (Office of Justice Programs, 2011). In 2006 and 2007, the U.S. Department of Labor funded 30 grants to faith-based organizations to provide postrelease programming to offenders. The emphasis was on employment training and services as well as mentoring (Office of Justice Programs, n.d.). Services involving multiple agencies have significant management implications for ensuring quality in customized service offerings. While restorative justice initiatives have increased victim and community roles in probation programming and increased collaboration between schools and probation agencies with the addition of school-based probation programs, these projects remain few and far between. Alliances like the Serious Habitual Offender Comprehensive Action Program, initiated by Illinois police departments to allow for multidisciplinary interagency case management and information sharing, would also work well in probation and parole (Cox et al., 2014). By bringing policing, school, supervising, and prosecuting agencies together in monthly meetings to discuss those offenders who consistently violate the conditions of probation or parole, interventions could be identified and efforts to deal more appropriately with repeat violators could be cultivated.

Other efforts we suggest that are, in some cases, occurring in the field include revisiting and clarifying agency goals and mission statements. As suggested early on in this chapter, probation organizations have become overwhelmed by the numbers of offenders sentenced to this disposition, while parole agencies have faced attacks on their effectiveness because of essentially the same issue. Retooling their approach to supervision, as well as better identifying their purpose, is fundamental to overcoming, or at least coming to terms with, this matter. As pointed out in Chapter 1, effective organizations have clearly defined goals, missions, and objectives. Community corrections agencies have to ask themselves if the focus on violations is the most important task of supervision.

Historically, the answer has been no. Probation and parole agencies were created to protect the public but also to assist the offender. Perhaps public safety does not mean returning record numbers of offenders to prison, but modifying behaviors through prosocial collaborations with society—even if that means allowing for lesser sanctions when minor violations occur. Every time the courts place new conditions on the offenders, part of the productive capacity of the officers is lost in implementing these demands. A better strategy to enhance the delivery of service quality could be achieved by providing more thorough training to the officers in following proper procedures and empowering them with greater discretion to make sound decisions in the field when dealing with clients and the community at large. Applying business principles to both short- and long-term operations allows for increased accountability for clients as well as agencies.

This approach brings to light another concern—that of too many conditions on offenders. In their current form, probation and parole contracts set the offender up for failure by requiring so many conditions that the offender cannot comply, or after efforts to meet the terms the offender becomes overwhelmed and decides not to participate. No amount of community assistance will negate this issue. According to Burke (2004), it is crucial to focus on the importance of "crafting conditions of supervision that will assist in addressing risk and criminogenic needs and that take into account the availability of resources in the community" (p. 61) and the capability of the offender. In a true systems approach, the offender would be allowed to actively participate in the formulation and implementation of the contract. Who better to know what is or is not possible than the person being asked to complete the task? Such an open-systems approach gives a client a sense of responsibility and ownership toward designing the rehabilitation process, which can act as a positive reinforcement that encourages corrective behavior. In addition, it provides better service quality and satisfaction to the community, and a greater sense of achievement and motivation to both the officer and the client in resolving the case successfully. Of course, this is not to suggest that the plan only focus on the offenders' wants, but incorporating their input is a good way to ensure that offenders are invested in successfully completing the requirements (just as incorporating the input of agency staff in the organization's goals, mission, and objectives allows them to feel invested in the agency).

Rethinking the job duties of probation and parole officers regarding the collection of fees and modifying the day-to-day work schedules of officers are other approaches that may foster better supervision. First, business or accounting offices are better equipped to collect and process money than are probation and parole officers, and they should be used. Fortunately, some agencies have already adopted this practice, which relieves the supervising agent of bill collection activities and reduces the perceived pressure to file a violation against an offender because of late fees. Second, crime and recidivism is not an 8-to-5 occurrence, and the needs of probationers and parolees do not stop in the evenings or on the weekends. Thus, probation and parole officers may see increased results if they work during odd hours and on irregular work schedules. Market research should be conducted to determine the most appropriate working hours for supervising officers (Manhattan Institute for Policy Research, 1999). If officers are not scheduled to be in the office during traditional work times, the tendency to supervise from the office may well be reduced, and a return to caseworker approaches will be fostered instead of the current emphasis on policing functions.

On a last note, a study of four state parole systems and their parole violation and revocation processes identified the following suggestions for strengthening supervision practices:

- States should identify clear and consistent violation and revocation policies by providing training to line officers about when to initiate formal violation proceedings against technical violators;
- Agencies should use a systems approach to focus on offender reentry by addressing institutional corrections concerns as well as the supervising agency's concerns;
- States should pay attention to the conditions of supervision by providing constraints that are accomplishable with the resources available yet that remain focused on the offender's needs and risks to society;
- Agencies should be trained in and use a consistent and effective assessment tool in identifying the severity of violations and the risks posed by the offender to the community;
- States should put into place a range of immediate responses to violations that utilize other alternatives outside of revocation, and supervising agencies and officers should be trained on the policy;
- States should clearly identify the goals of supervision and revocation by including statements that emphasize assistance, reintegration, and reductions in recidivism;
- Agencies should form collaborative teams with individuals, groups, the community, and other organizations outside of the agency's boundaries;
- Agencies should use evidence-based practices to identify effective interventions that increase successful completion of the supervisory period;
- Agencies and states should identify incentives in supervision in order to change behaviors and increase responses that support prosocial conduct;
- Agencies and states should recognize the limits of compliance and surveillance-driven supervision by acknowledging that simply monitoring behavior does not instigate change, but has the opposite effect. (Burke, 2004, pp. 61–62)

Although the study's list applies primarily to parole, these initiatives could easily be incorporated into probation systems.

To deliver the highest-quality service, frontline officers need to be empowered, motivated, informed, competent, committed, and well trained. They must exhibit the skills to take responsibility; manage themselves; and respond to pressures from offenders, victims, and the community. Ideally, officers should have personality attributes that include flexibility, an ability to monitor and change behavior on the basis of situational cues, and empathy for offenders. Furthermore, it is important to understand that in this service delivery process, the input is the offender (client) for whom the service is being performed and value is being added. Because clients typically arrive at their own discretion and with unique demands on the service system, matching service capacity with demand is a challenge. Nevertheless, the client can act as a temporary employee, arriving just when needed to perform duties. However, for clients to be used productively, the service process needs to be redesigned to facilitate greater involvement of them. In addition, the client needs to be educated and trained to work as a coproducer in the identification and completion of services and programs. In the current system, which appears to be moving away from service approaches, the officers are already short on time and capacity; this requires a lot of thinking about how the system can be redesigned to educate clients to enable them to act as coproducers. In this chapter, the authors have attempted to provide numerous ideas regarding redesigning the parole and probation system as a starting point for further discussion in this area.

Chapter Summary

- Probation is a court sentence that allows an offender to remain in the community under the supervision of a probation officer or court-appointed representative. The probationer must comply with conditions imposed by the court to remain in the community and on probation.
- Probation is a task-oriented field. Probation officers write presentence investigation reports that determine a probationer's risk and needs to protect the public from additional offending. Probation officers also supervise, assist, and manage offenders by brokering services for them, monitoring behaviors and reporting violations of conditions to the court, counseling, acting as role models, and protecting the rights and liberties of probationers and the community.
- Probationers who violate the conditions of probation may face a revocation hearing where they can be sent to prison, receive another disposition, or have their probation conditions modified and be returned to probation supervision.
- Parole is very similar to probation, except that parolees are released from prison into the community either by parole boards (discretionary parole) or through mandatory release legislation. Parolees must also comply with conditions imposed by the parole board or a supervising agency. Parole has been a controversial disposition.
- Parole officers serve the same functions as probation officers—to help and control offenders while supporting reintegration.
- Probation and parole agencies have traditionally used an open-systems approach to the supervision of offenders. These agencies tend to have flat hierarchies, horizontal and vertical communication, close relationships with other agencies, and service-oriented approaches to working with clients.
- Probation and parole face a number of issues including fiscal crises; a changing demographic among clients; increased conditions and requirements from courts, legislators, and parole boards; large amounts of paperwork and administrative duties; decreased abilities in providing treatment and rehabilitative services to clients; and increased community hostility regarding violations of probation and parole conditions.
- Changes that can be made to probation and parole practices to better serve the client base and the community include increased discretion among officers in the modification of court-ordered or parole board–developed contracts; decreased requirements to seek revocation hearings for minor or technical violations; improved use of a balanced approach to supervision that uses sanctions and reinforcements for positive behaviors; more involvement of outside agencies and supportive collaborations; closer inspection of agency goals, values, and missions; more focused approaches to assigning conditions of probation and parole; use of collection agencies or business offices to collect fees associated with supervision; and modifications to geographical and work-hour assignments of probation and parole officers.
- As Burke (2004) observed in Kansas, Georgia, New Jersey, and Rhode Island, parole violations and revocation processes can be streamlined, modified, and revisited to better serve the community, the clients, and the supervising officers. The approaches used in these states could undoubtedly be workable in probation practices.

Chapter Review Questions

1. Explain how and why supervision efforts in probation and parole have changed over time. Are they more or less focused on client needs?

2. Investigate a probation agency online by finding a link to its organizational chart. Using the information on the chart, describe the organizational structure. Who is in charge? How many levels are there between line staff and the top administrator? Is this a horizontal or vertical hierarchy? What else do you notice about the agency's structure? In your opinion, would this agency use an open-systems or closed-system approach, and why?

3. Of the issues mentioned in the chapter, which do you think is the most crucial facing probation and parole agencies? Develop a plan for modification to address this issue. How did you build service quality approaches into your modification plan?

4. Describe a service quality approach in probation or parole.

CASE STUDY

You are the chief parole officer in a regional office with the Department of Corrections—the Adult Parole Division—in Grand Island, Nebraska. Your primary duties include the supervision of two other officers who assist in overseeing parolees in your assigned jurisdiction. The Nebraska parole program has been in existence since the early 1900s. According to the Adult Parole Administration Office, "Nebraska's parole officers play an extremely important role in the transition that an inmate makes when they are released into the community. The officer's goal is to assist each parolee in achieving a successful discharge from parole supervision and to become a responsible member of society" (Nebraska Department of Correctional Services, n.d.). Traditionally, parole officers have practiced caseworker approaches in supervision management of offenders. In 2005, the Parole Division in Nebraska handled 870 cases. There were 342 revocations that year. The numbers of both paroled inmates and revocations have increased since that time. Currently, parole officer caseloads throughout the state vary by geographical location and population within the jurisdiction. Your officers maintain generalized caseloads that include traditional adult offenders, juvenile offenders, sex offenders, intensive supervision offenders, and other special needs criminals. Their workloads range from 85–120 parolees.

Your office uses a state-mandated, automated case management software program to track offenders and to monitor the work performance of your parole officers. According to organizational policy, officers are required to log in to the automation system at least three times per day during the 5-day workweek. They can log in from home, work, their iPhones, or through public terminals. The parole officers must document contacts (phone, face-to-face, e-mail, etc.) with clients and treatment providers as well as court appearances, violations, and detentions or jail holdings of parolees. They also maintain a record of their comings and goings throughout the day. In case of an emergency, the automation program is used to determine the last known whereabouts of the officer or a specific parolee.

You receive monthly audit reports from the Nebraska Department of Correctional Services on work performance, parolee/parole officer contacts, treatment referrals, compliance statistics, fee collections, court dates and schedules, risk and needs assessments and reviews, and detention and jail holdings of parole violators. The report also specifies the number of violation reports filed by individual parole officers and revocation hearings held, and their results for all seven parole offices in the state. The performance of parole officers under your supervision is measured against other officers in the state. They are expected to meet statistically significant standards to be seen as satisfactorily doing their jobs.

Brooke Addison has been a top-performing parole officer. She has worked for the department for eight years. Her performance evaluations have always been superior, and audits of her work have shown high numbers of parolee/parole officer contacts, compliance statistics, collections of supervision and other fees, and completion of risk and needs reviews. Her colleagues in your office and in other regional offices get along well with her, and she has had only minor complaints from exparolees, which is not uncommon in this field of work. As her supervisor, you have not witnessed any inappropriate behaviors.

Several months ago, Officer Addison complained, in an informal conversation, that she felt as though parole officers were "spinning our wheels and getting absolutely nowhere." She stated that although she filed parole violations with the releasing authority, it did not seem that they were taken seriously by the parole board. In one specific incident, she claimed that a client had stolen a friend's rent money, bought and used crack cocaine, hid from the police when they were called to the residence, and had to be cornered by a police dog to be taken into custody. Addison filed a revocation request with the releasing authority, which was later denied even though the parole board believed the incident had occurred. The offender was placed on electronic monitoring. She also stated that several other offenders she was supervising had no place to live, no employment skills, and were "so addicted to drugs and alcohol that they cannot do anything else." At one point in the conversation, she said that sometimes she just wants to scream because she becomes so frustrated. According to her, "It doesn't matter what you do, they just won't listen. I feel like the clients don't care, the parole board doesn't care, everyone blames me when one of them commits another crime, and I'm starting to wonder why I care."

After this conversation, no other concerns were raised by Officer Addison, and she appeared to continue working at the level she had in the past. She has not had an increase in missed work days or asked to be reassigned to another office or jurisdiction. Her demeanor around the office is consistent with that of previous years. The audits of her monthly performance did not show a change in productivity.

However, last month's audit revealed that Officer Addison failed to log in to the automation system the required number of times each day. It also showed that she failed to document meetings, face-to-face or otherwise, with 47 of her 94 clients. The statistics showed higher-than-usual detentions and jail holdings for the month, yet she filed fewer violation reports than in previous months. To be in compliance with organizational policy, you had to confront her about the decrease in her performance in a one-to-one formal meeting.

During the required formal meeting with Officer Addison, she stated that she just was not motivated over the past month. She promised to increase her performance and stated that no other issues were bothering her. She said she was still happy with her job and wanted to assist parolees in any way she could.

(Continued)

(Continued)

This month's audit revealed still lower performance levels for Officer Addison. Although she logged in each day as required, she filed three times the amount of violation reports and twice the number of revocations as her usual average. She also had more detentions and jail holdings than normal. Her statistics in fee collections, treatment referrals, and parolee/parole officer contacts dropped. In one particular case, you noticed that a parolee committed a technical violation by failing to appear for treatment. Officer Addison detained the parolee and filed a revocation request instead of meeting with the offender, placing a violation report on file, and attempting to resolve the issue. According to the case file, the parolee has a family with three young children who rely on his income to live. You are required to hold another formal meeting with Officer Addison to address the changes in her work performance.

Questions for Review

1. What issues do you think are most crucial to address with Officer Addison in the second formal meeting?

2. Could officer burnout be a potential explanation for Officer Addison's changes in work performance? Could this be the result of a change in her approach to case management (surveillance and control versus caseworker)? What else can you identify as reasons for the difference in her work? What theory may have been a motivating factor for Officer Addison previously, and how might that have changed?

3. What recommendations would you make to Officer Addison and to the Nebraska Department of Correctional Services' main office regarding parole supervision or parole officer evaluation?

4. Are Officer Addison's clients being serviced in an effective manner? If so, how? If not, why not? If you do not believe they are, what would you recommend as alternatives to ensure better-quality service?

Internet Resources

American Probation and Parole Association—http://www.appa-net.org

Federal Probation and Pretrial Officers Association—http://www.fppoa.org

United States Department of Justice, U.S. Parole Commission—http://www.justice.gov/uspc

References and Suggested Readings

Adair, D. N. (2004). The incredible shrinking probation officer. *Federal Probation, 68*(3), 51–56.

Barklage, H., Miller, D., & Bonham, G., Jr. (2006). Probation conditions versus probation officer directives: Where the twain shall meet. *Federal Probation, 70*(3), 37–41.

Bureau of Justice Statistics (2013). *Recidivism.* Washington, DC. Retrieved from http://www.bjs.gov/index .cfm?ty=tp&tid=17.

Burke, P. (1995). *Abolishing parole: Why the emperor has no clothes.* Lexington, KY: American Probation and Parole Association.

Burke, P. (2004). *Parole violations revisited.* Washington, DC: U.S. Department of Justice, National Institute of Corrections.

Burke, P., Adams, L., & Ney, B. (1990). Policy for parole release and revocation: The National Institute of Corrections 1988–1989 Technical Assistance Project. Longmont, CO: National Institute of Corrections.

Caplan, J. M. (2007). What factors affect parole: A review of empirical research. *Federal Probation, 71*(1), 16–19.

Clear, T., & Cole, G. (1997). *American corrections.* Belmont, CA: Wadsworth.

Cohn, A., & Ferriter, M. (1990). The presentence investigation report: An old saw with new teeth. *Federal Probation, 54*(3), 15–26.

Cox, S. M., Allen, J. M., Hanser, R. H., & Conrad, J. J. (2014). *Juvenile justice: A guide to theory, policy, and practice* (6th ed.). Thousand Oaks, CA: Sage.

Cox, S. M., & McCamey, W. (2008). *Introduction to criminal justice: Exploring the network* (5th ed.). Durham, NC: Carolina Academic Press.

Cox, S. M., & Wade, W. (2002). *The criminal justice network: An introduction* (4th ed.). Boston, MA: McGraw-Hill.

DeMichele, M., & Payne, B. (2007). Probation and parole officers speak out—caseload and workload allocation. *Federal Probation, 71*(3), 30–35.

Employment Development Department. (1998). *Probation officers and parole agents.* Retrieved from http:// www.calmis.ca.gov/file/occguide/PROBOFF.HTM.

Feeley, M., & Simon, J. (1992). The new penology: Notes on the emerging strategy of corrections and its implications. *Criminology, 30*(4), 449–476.

Florida Department of Corrections. (2001). *Florida Department of Corrections 1999–2000 annual report.* Retrieved from http://www.dc.state.fl.us/pub/annual/9900/index.html.

Florida Senate. (2007, January). *Interim Project Report 2007-110: Convicted felons on probation and prevention of subsequent crimes.* Committee on Criminal Justice. Retrieved from http://www.flsenate .gov/data/Publications/2007/Senate/reports/interim_reports/pdf/2007-110cj.pdf.

Frimary, P., & Poling, A. (1995, Winter). Making life easier with effort: Basic findings and applied research on response effort. *Journal of Applied Behavioral Analysis, 28*(4), 583–590.

Glaze, L., & Parks, E. (2012). Correctional populations in the United States, 2011. Washington, DC: U.S. Department of Justice, Bureau of Justice Statistics. Retrieved from http://www.bjs.gov/content/pub/ pdf/cpus11.pdf.

Glueck, S. (1952). *Crime and corrections: Selected papers.* Cambridge, MA: Addison-Wesley.

Harris, P., Clear, T., & Baird, C. (1989). Have community supervision officers changed their attitudes toward their work? *Justice Quarterly, 6*(2), 233–246.

Holt, N. (1998). The current state of parole in America. In J. Petersilia (Ed.), *Community corrections: Probation, parole, and intermediate sanctions* (pp. 28–41). New York, NY: Oxford University Press.

Hughes, G. (2007). Parole boards are worth saving. *Corrections Today, 69*(4), 86–87.

Hughes, T. A., Wilson, D. J., & Beck, A. J. (2001). *Trends in state parole, 1999–2000.* Washington, DC: U.S. Department of Justice, Bureau of Justice Statistics.

Langan, P. (1994). Between prison and probation: Intermediate sanctions. *Science, 264,* 791–794.

Lucken, K. (1997). The dynamics of penal reform. *Crime, Law and Social Change, 26*(4), 367–384.

Lynch, M. (1998). Waste managers? The new penology, crime fighting, and parole agent identity. *Law & Society Review, 32*(4), 839–869.

Macallair, D. (2002). *The history of the presentence investigation report.* San Francisco, CA: Center on Juvenile and Criminal Justice. Retrieved from http://www.cjcj.org/files/the_history.pdf.

Manhattan Institute for Policy Research. (1999). *Broken windows probation: The next step in fighting crime.* New York, NY: Reinventing Probation Council. Retrieved from http://www.manhattan-institute.org/html/cr_7.htm.

Marushak, L. M., & Parks, E. (2012). Probation and parole in the United States, 2011. U.S. Department of Justice, Bureau of Justice Statistics. Retrieved from, http://www.bjs.gov/content/pub/pdf/ppus11.pdf.

McCarthy, B. R., & McCarthy, B. J., Jr. (1991). *Community-based corrections* (2nd ed.). Pacific Grove, CA: Brooks/Cole.

Nebraska Department of Correctional Services. (n.d.). *Adult parole supervision.* Retrieved from, http://www.corrections.state.ne.us/programs/adult_parole/index.html.

New York City Department of Probation. (n.d.). *A brief history of probation.* Retrieved from http://www.nyc.gov/html/prob/html/about/history.shtml.

Office of Justice Programs. (n.d.). *Learn about reentry.* Retrieved from http://www.reentry.gov/learn.html.

Office of Justice Programs. (2011). Fact sheet: Faith-based programs. U.S. Department of Justice, Washington, DC. Retrieved from http://www.ojp.usdoj.gov/newsroom/factsheets/ojpfs_faith-basedprog.html.

Petersilia, J. (1999). Parole and prisoner reentry in the United States. In M. Tonry & J. Petersilia (Eds.), *Prisons* (pp. 479–529). Chicago, IL: University of Chicago Press.

Petersilia, J. (2000). Parole and prisoner reentry in the United States. *Perspectives, 24*(3), 32–46.

Skinner, B. F. (1969). *Contingencies of reinforcement: A theoretical analysis.* East Norwalk, CT: Appleton-Century-Crofts.

Storm, J. (1997). What United States probation officers do. *Corrections Today, 69*(4), 13–19.

Taxman, F., Shepardson, E., & Byrne, J. (2004). *Tools of the trade: A guide to incorporating science into practice.* Washington, DC: U.S. Department of Justice, Bureau of Prisons, National Institute of Corrections. Retrieved from http://www.nicic.org/Library/020095.

Texas Department of Corrections. (2011). Texas Department of Corrections: Annual review. Retrieved from http://www.tdcj.state.tx.us/documents/Annual_Review_2011.pdf.

12

Prisons, Jails, and Detention Centers

❖

LEARNING OBJECTIVES

Upon completion of this chapter, students should be able to do the following:

- Explain the differences between prisons, jails, and detention centers
- Identify the development of correctional facilities
- Describe the managerial styles used in each type of facility
- Explain how the closed managerial system creates problems for jails, prisons, and detention centers
- Discuss potential management and structural changes that could occur as a result of improvements in service quality

I had no excuse for the hole I had dug for myself. Knowing that I was the one who chose to sell cocaine, there was no one but myself to blame for the problems I had created. Although, initially, I thought the sentence excessive, the more time I spent confined, the more I realized how common the feeling of self-pity was among the prisoners around me. Everyone complained as if they were victims of a corrupt legal system. They were incarcerated because of rats who had snitched them out. Or their prosecutors had a personal vendetta against them. They weren't guilty. It was as if I were one of the few people in the entire prison who [was] actually guilty.

—Michael Santos on his prison experience
from his book *About Prison*, 2004

A t age 23, Michael Santos was arrested for selling cocaine, convicted, and sentenced to 45 years in the federal prison system—many of those years in maximum-security prisons. In many ways, Santos is a rather typical prisoner. Drug charges have been the cause of a substantial growth in incarceration rates in the federal prison systems (Harrison & Beck, 2006b), with 47% of all federal inmates serving time for drug offenses in 2013 (Federal Bureau of Prisons, n.d.). In other ways, he is not so typical, having earned two college degrees and being a published author. According to the National Assessment of Adult Literacy (NAAL), only 43% of inmates in 2003 had a high school diploma upon entering prison, while about 20% earned a GED while in prison (Greenberg, Dunleavy, & Kutner, 2007, p. 6).

This chapter first examines the history of prisons, incarceration rates, types of institutions, and classification of inmates. The chapter then looks at legal aspects of staff recruitment, training, and retention. Management strategies such as motivation, discipline, leadership and planning/budgeting, as well as current issues affecting prison populations, are also addressed.

A Brief History of Prisons in the United States

Using the definition of a prison as a facility that holds criminal offenders, it is clear that prisons have always existed. *Bridewells* appeared in the 1500s as places to house the poor, but slowly turned into facilities to house debtors, criminals, beggars, and anyone else seen to be in need of structure and reform (Roth, 2005). According to Roth, Massachusetts Bay Colony had a prison in 1636. Smaller jails also began appearing and typically held inmates for less than a year because of the large labor shortage colonists confronted. Physical mutilation and a short stay were much more common than long sentences, so the offenders could quickly return to society. A former copper mine became the Newgate Prison in Connecticut, while pits dug into the ground served to incarcerate those in Maine (Roth, 2005). According to Friedman (1993), there was no penal theory underlying these approaches. They only strove to cause "so much dread that no sane person would want to be in one" (p. 78).

The *Walnut Street Jail* in Pennsylvania was one of the first major steps toward the era of mass prisons in the United States (Johnston, n.d.). Pennsylvania was a Quaker state, and the Quaker ideals of penance, retribution, rehabilitation, and deterrence were embedded in the operations of the jail built in 1790. The policy of solitary confinement and silence was designed to encourage bored prisoners to consult the Bible. Inmates were hooded to keep them from seeing others on those rare occasions when people would enter or leave the prison.

The building of the Cherry Hill or *Eastern State Penitentiary* in Philadelphia was *avant garde* compared to most facilities at that time. The technology available in 1820s and 1830s allowed for central heating, flushing toilets, and showers in these facilities, which were conveniences not found in other public buildings (Johnston, n.d.). Eastern State Penitentiary was finished in 1829 and tried to incorporate the same philosophy of solitary confinement as the earlier Walnut Street Jail. Unfortunately, the radial-design prison

quickly became overcrowded, and solitary confinement was no longer a possibility. Prisons as humane alternatives to torture and death gained popularity during this period.

The next approach to incarceration in the United States was the *Auburn system.* Thomas Eddy, who built the prison in Auburn, New York, believed in rehabilitation, not corporal punishment, as a means to reform prisoners (Roth, 2005). The Auburn system was unique in that it promoted silence as the key to reform. Prisoners were allowed to work, eat, and move about together, but they could not speak to one another. The Auburn system was economically better than the Pennsylvania style in that it could house inmates together as opposed to separate cells. The Auburn style flourished, and dozens more prisons were built that emulated the style. The *Elmira Reformatory,* also in New York, tried another approach that was gaining popularity outside of the United States. Influenced by Sir Walter Crofton's Irish system of earning "marks" for good behavior, Elmira embraced the concept of earning time off one's sentence. Zebulon Brockway became the first warden of Elmira and firmly agreed with the reformatory model. Since the belief was that youth were more likely to be rehabilitated, young men in Elmira were the first test cases for earning time off their sentences, known as good time (Roth, 2005). A rewards system was set up so that those inmates who were actively engaged in educational and vocational services and those who behaved in an acceptable manner would earn privileges. Inmates would move from one grade or level to another as they successfully accomplished what was required. While Elmira heralded in the birth of parole in the United States, it was not considered a success because of high rates of recidivism. Like the other prisons before it, Elmira was soon overcrowded and the system designed for its small population failed to work well when the population grew too large.

Incarceration Rates

Although incarceration rates have declined for the third straight year, prisons have been a popular sentence in the United States (Carson & Golinelli, 2013). The United States incarcerates more people than any other country in the world (Hartney, 2006) and spends approximately $70 billion a year on corrections (National Association for the Advancement of Colored People, 2013). Overcrowding is an issue in today's institutions as they struggle to find treatment and rehabilitative techniques that work with large numbers of incarcerated offenders. At the end of 2012, there were 1,571,013 people imprisoned in federal, state, and local facilities (Carson & Golinelli, 2013). These rates reflect the whole of the United States, but the rates differ based on location. For example, California has had the greatest rate of decline in incarceration, with 15,035 fewer prisoners incarcerated in 2012 than in 2011, while Louisiana and the federal prison system both had increases of more than 1,000 prisoners in 2012 compared to 2011 (Carson & Golinelli, 2013). Texas experienced the second-largest prison population decline in 2012 (down 5,852), followed by North Carolina (down 2,304); and Colorado, Arkansas, New York, Florida, and Virginia reported declines of more than 1,000 inmates during the same period (Carson & Golinelli, 2013).

Depending on the type of crime committed and the length of the sentence, offenders are housed in the most appropriate facility based on security level and offender needs, which are identified using a *classification system*. Such classification systems have been around for a long time, but not until 1976 in *Pugh v. Locke* did federal courts view the proper classification of offenders as a constitutional right (Craddock, 1996, p. 87). Classification systems are now engineered to ensure proper placement regarding security level, custody supervision, and housing. They are also used to make decisions on medical and mental health treatment and placement in educational, vocational, and work programs.

Some research (Bench & Allen, 2003) suggests that classification only serves to label inmates rather than reflect their characteristics. However, others feel that not all inmates have the same needs. Therefore, classifying inmates ensures that the facility meets the needs of the particular inmates as well as balances those needs with the safety of others (Woolredge, 2003), improving the quality of services offered. Although there are a number of ways to assess risks and needs of offenders, suffice it to say that those inmates with the greatest need for services are those receiving the most services. The inmates scoring highest on risk assessments are those sent to higher security level institutions or placed in higher security sections of other prisons.

Most inmates will be able to move from more restrictive settings to less restrictive housing as they improve their behavior and move closer to their date of release. Reevaluating classification scores makes it possible to give those needing the most services the attention they need while minimizing the opportunities for deviance for the offenders who require more security. The continuous reevaluation process allows the prisons to better match their resources with prisoner needs, resulting in improved capacity use. In addition, it allows for greater customization of service to satisfy different inmate needs, which improves service quality.

Correctional Facilities at the Federal Level

The Federal Bureau of Prisons (BOP) was created in 1930 to act as a centralized administrative office for federal prison facilities. Today, the BOP consists of 119 facilities, 6 regional offices, 2 staff training centers, 22 residential reentry management offices, and 1 central office that serves as the headquarters. Approximately 38,000 workers are employed in various positions to secure and treat almost 219,000 federal offenders (BOP, n.d.d).

Federal prisons have security levels based on perceived risk of violence or escape and type of crime (BOP, n.d.c). Minimum-security or *federal prison camps (FPCs)* have dorm-style housing, low inmate-to-staff ratio, and little or no perimeter fencing. Federal prison camps are work and program-oriented. Low security or *federal correctional institutions (FCIs)* are very similar to the federal prison camps, but have double rolls of fencing and a slightly higher inmate-to-staff ratio. Medium-security FCIs and USPSs have tighter external security, using electronic monitoring devices added to the double fencing around the perimeter. The dorm-style housing seen in FPCs and FCIs is replaced with cells, and internal security is much greater. High security or *U.S.*

penitentiaries (USPs) have the greatest external perimeter security, with reinforced walls, fencing, and guard towers. Internal security is very controlled, which necessitates the highest inmate-to-staff ratio (BOP, n.d.c). Similar to state institutions, the federal system features complexes that group multiple security levels in close proximity, known as *federal correctional complexes (FCCs)*. Finally, the federal prison system uses *administrative facilities* to house pretrial offenders, to contain extremely dangerous or violent offenders, to treat seriously ill offenders or those with chronic medical problems, and to secure offenders who are escape-prone. "Administrative facilities include Metropolitan Correctional Centers (MCCs), Metropolitan Detention Centers (MDCs), Federal Detention Centers (FDCs), and Federal Medical Centers (FMCs), as well as the Federal Transfer Center (FTC), the Medical Center for Federal Prisoners (MCFP), and the Administrative-Maximum (ADX) U.S. Penitentiary. Administrative facilities, except the ADX, are capable of holding inmates in all security categories" (BOP, n.d.c, para. 7). Currently, the federal system has one Secure Female Facility (SFF) designated to house female offenders.

Specialized Facilities at the Federal Level

Some federal offenders are placed at halfway houses, also known as *residential reentry centers* (RRCs). RRCs hold offenders accountable for their behavior, and expect offenders to secure full-time employment within days of transferring to the facility, to be responsible for their medical and mental health expenses, and to pay approximately 25% of their gross income for housing at the facility (BOP, n.d.c). Treatment is also offered, and the staff members at RRCs help offenders find housing, employment, and continued mental health or medical assistance before being released. An important component of RRCs is drug abuse treatment. Inmates placed in RRCs participate in more structured programming to prepare for reentry into the community.

The Federal Bureau of Prisons houses females in numerous institutions in a coed style, with the exception of the single SFF located in West Virginia (BOP, n.d.a). "The BOP provides female offenders with appropriate programs and services to meet their physical, social, and psychological needs. In 1993, for example, the BOP developed and implemented a new designation and classification system for female offenders to account for the fact that female offenders are less likely to be violent or attempt escape" (BOP, n.d.a, para. 1). Additionally, programming at facilities that house female offenders includes vocational skills such as data processing, painting, bricklaying, just to name a few, and "medical and social services related to pregnancy, birth control, child placement, and abortion" (BOP, n.d.a, para. 3). Glaze and Maruschak (2008) reported that an "estimated 809,800 prisoners of the 1,518,535 held in the nation's prisons at midyear 2007 were parents of minor children, or children under age 18" (p. 1). "Male (50%) and female (61%) inmates in state prison who reported no prior incarceration sentences were equally likely to be a parent as male (53%) and female (65%) inmates with 10 or more prior incarcerations. In federal prison, findings were similar for men while women with no prior incarceration sentences (54%) were less likely to be a mother than women who reported they had 10 or more prior incarcerations (81%)"

(Glaze and Maruschak, 2008, p. 4). Mothers in state prisons were three times more likely to report having lived in a single-parent household in the month before their arrest (Glaze & Maruschak, 2008). Concerns about the safety and well-being of their children are paramount among female inmates. Federal institutions struggle with maintaining ties between mothers and their children, similar to state facilities.

Although rare, some juveniles fall within federal jurisdiction (depending on several issues including the identity of the defendant or victim, type of crime, and where the crime was committed). "Historically, the federal juvenile population has consisted [predominately] of Native American males with an extensive history of drug and/or alcohol use/abuse, and violent behavior. These juveniles tend to be older in age, generally between 17 to 20 years of age, and are typically sentenced for sex-related offenses" (BOP, n.d.b, para. 6). Secure and nonsecure facilities are provided for juveniles at the federal level. Each sponsors a variety of mental health, educational, and vocational programs. Nonsecure facilities do not have perimeter fencing and provide more opportunities for interaction with the community. Secure facilities at the federal level strongly resemble other medium- and maximum-level facilities discussed in this chapter. As with state-operated juvenile facilities, reunification with the family is a goal of the BOP. Visitation with family is encouraged in all prison and jail facilities for youth.

Possibly the most unique facility in the federal system is the *Administrative Maximum* U.S. Penitentiary in Florence, Colorado, known as the "Alcatraz of the Rockies" (Schuster, 2007). Similar to the supermax state prisons, the administrative maximum facility houses the escape-prone and violent criminals. The idea behind the facility is to incapacitate the incorrigible offender by eliminating all opportunities for deviance (Briggs, Sundt, & Castellano, 2003). Leaving the cell is uncommon, and there is little or no human contact since there are no jobs or formalized programs in which inmates can participate.

Special and continuous training is necessary for correctional officers, staff, and treatment providers working within these institutions. In addition, continued focus on the types of inmates housed and their needs and risks is necessary. But development and continued operation of specialized institutions adds additional strain on federal budgets, staffing, and administrative upkeep, although it is much more easily handled at the federal level, where the majority of tax dollars are spent.

Correctional Facilities at the State Level

When inmates are sentenced, the jurisdiction and length of sentence are also considered in determining where they will be housed. A number of prisons are spread throughout each state, and they vary in security levels, much like the federal system. States customize their newly built prisons to their needs, and revisions occur on a continuous basis. Typical state facilities include secure housing units such as that found in California, super-maximum-security facilities, maximum-security facilities, medium-security facilities, and minimum-security facilities.

Secure housing units (SHUs) are designed to detain inmates whose conduct in other facilities endangered the safety of others or the security of the institution. Typically, these inmates have committed serious rule violations while housed in other facilities. Secure housing units have created controversy regarding their strict treatment of offenders, lengthy incarceration periods, and heightened control over every movement made within the facility. In 1997, about 30 states had some type of administrative segregation units or SHUs within the perimeter of maximum level prisons, or they created super-maximum-security prisons that stood alone (Briggs et al., 2003, p. 1341). *Super-maximum-security prisons* house extremely violent or dangerous inmates and those who are considered a high escape risk. The focus in "supermax" prisons is on control and custody.

Security around *maximum-security prisons* strongly resembles that of supermax prisons. Maximum-security prisons are tightly monitored and have the highest staff-to-inmate ratio. These institutions typically house dangerous offenders and those serving long sentences. Treatment is limited at most maximum-security facilities because the focus of such institutions is on retribution and incapacitation. At least one maximum level prison in states with capital punishment will hold death-row inmates.

The majority of inmates incarcerated in state facilities will be housed in medium-security facilities. *Medium-security prisons* usually resemble maximum-level institutions in that they have guards at the perimeter, high fencing, and concertina wire; however, there is much more freedom of inmate movement within the facilities. These centers house younger and less dangerous offenders and offer more opportunities for vocational training, treatment, and work programs (Illinois Department of Corrections [IDOC], 2012e). *Minimum-security prisons* house nonviolent and nontraditional inmates. Few inmates are housed in minimum-security facilities; generally, those who are housed there are participating in work and educational release programs. These facilities are used to promote family ties and reintegration as well as to provide better opportunities for inmates nearing release to reconnect with the outside world. The purpose for such a design is generated by the idea that normalcy in interactions is needed, since the inmate will soon reenter society.

Specialized Facilities at the State Level

Many states have created specialized medium-security facilities for mentally ill and developmentally delayed inmates. In these facilities, psychiatric units, testing, and treatment are provided. In addition, specialized work programs are regularly used. The goals are to provide the inmates with skills that will carry over once released.

Although not as popular nationwide, *adult transitional centers* have also been designed to allow offenders who are within a couple of years from supervised release to reintegrate gradually back into society. Inmates are provided opportunities to go into the community for a specified amount of time to work, receive education, get vocational training, or receive medical/psychological treatment (Georgia Department of Corrections, n.d.)

Women are also considered a special population in state facilities. States usually have one or more facilities for women at all security levels. Cocorrectional facilities are also common at the state level where both men and women are housed in the same institution (Maguire & Pastore, 1995). Often, these facilities resemble more a college campus with cottage-style housing than a penal institution. Maintaining positive relationships between inmates and children are a special concern for women's prisons. Regular visits, family days, and videoconferencing technology are used in some facilities to maintain family ties (Georgia Department of Corrections, n.d.).

Juveniles are another special population, and like the facilities for women, there are a number of facilities—detention (or jails) and prisons—based on differing security levels and special needs, created for youth. Cox, Allen, Hanser, and Conrad (2014) note that detention is most often brief, while prison stays are only used after all other community-based alternates are exhausted or if the juvenile poses a serious threat to society. Juvenile facilities mirror those used for adults, although access to treatment and education programs is greater. Like the adult system, there are negative aspects to incarcerating youth in correctional facilities. Juveniles become isolated from family and community, they receive control more often than treatment, and they are influenced negatively by other delinquent youth. Unlike the adult system, which uses a classification process to determine risks and needs of inmates, assignment to juvenile facilities is too often based on vacancies rather than matching juveniles to the most appropriate facility (Cox et al., 2014). Such an approach leads to a waste of precious resources without providing optimal benefits to the customer, which goes against the tenets of service quality.

Dealing with these special populations means additional training for staff and management. The basic ideas are to provide more services to those inmates closer to release and who have higher needs while still upholding the correctional objectives of retribution, specific and general deterrence, and rehabilitation. Each of these facilities must determine how best to accomplish these goals while meeting the needs of inmates. This is perhaps easier said than done, since there is no centralized authority governing state facilities and they have little control over who the court mandates to reside within the facilities. In some cases, they may be pursuing very different and conflicting goals from the court systems. Although *Turner v. Safley* (1987) limits the ability of judges to regulate the actions of prison administrators, this lack of coordination between the courts and correctional facilities adversely impacts the service quality offered. Promoting coordination and cooperation between different subsystems, known as a *supply chain* perspective, may perhaps accomplish more than when the subsystems are working in isolation. Problem-solving courts, mentioned in Chapter 10, and a return to a more treatment-oriented, community-based approach are ways of bridging the gap we have historically seen in these subsystems.

CAREER HIGHLIGHT BOX
SUBSTANCE ABUSE AND BEHAVIOR DISORDER COUNSELORS

Nature of the Work

Substance abuse and behavioral disorder counselors advise people who have alcoholism or other types of addiction, eating disorders, or other behavioral problems. They provide treatment and support to help the client recover from addiction or modify problem behaviors.

Duties

Substance abuse and behavioral disorder counselors typically do the following:

- Evaluate clients' mental and physical health, addiction or problem behavior, and openness to treatment
- Help clients develop treatment goals and plans
- Review and recommend treatment options with clients and their families
- Help clients develop skills and behaviors necessary to recover from their addiction or modify their behavior
- Work with clients to identify behaviors or situations that interfere with their recovery
- Teach families about addiction or behavior disorders and help them develop strategies to cope with those problems
- Refer clients to other resources or services, such as job placement services and support groups
- Develop and conduct outreach programs to help people learn about addictions and destructive behavior, and how to avoid them

Substance abuse and behavioral disorder counselors, also called addiction counselors, work with clients both one-on-one and in group sessions. Many incorporate the principles of 12-step programs, such as Alcoholics Anonymous, to guide their practice. They teach clients how to cope with stress and life's problems in ways that help them recover. Furthermore, they help clients rebuild professional relationships and, if necessary, reestablish their career. They also help clients improve their personal relationships and find ways to discuss their addiction or other problem with family and friends.

Many addiction counselors work with other health and mental health professionals, such as psychiatrists, social workers, doctors, and nurses. Some work in facilities that employ many types of health care and mental health professionals. In these settings, treatment professionals work in teams to develop treatment plans and coordinate care for patients. For more information, see the profiles on social workers, physicians and surgeons, and registered nurses.

Some counselors work with clients who have been ordered by a judge to receive treatment for addiction. Others work with specific populations, such as teenagers, veterans, or people with disabilities. Some specialize in crisis intervention; these counselors step in when someone is endangering their life or the lives of others. Other counselors specialize in noncrisis interventions, which encourage a person with addictions or other problems to get help. Noncrisis interventions often are performed at the request of friends and family.

Some substance abuse and behavioral disorder counselors work in private practice, where they work alone or with a group of counselors or other professionals. These counselors manage their practice as a business. This includes working with clients and insurance companies to receive payment for their services. In addition, they market their practice to bring in new clients.

(Continued)

(Continued)

Substance abuse and behavioral disorder counselors held about 85,500 jobs in 2010. The industries employing the most substance abuse and behavioral disorder counselors in 2010 were as follows:

Outpatient mental health and substance abuse centers	18%
Residential mental health and substance abuse facilities	16
Individual and family services	14
State and local government, excluding education and hospitals	12
Hospitals; state, local, and private	11

Substance abuse and behavioral disorder counselors work in a wide variety of settings, including mental health centers, prisons, probation or parole agencies, and juvenile detention facilities. They also work in halfway houses, detox centers, or in employee assistance programs (EAPs). EAPs are mental health programs provided by some companies to help employees deal with personal problems.

Some addiction counselors work in residential treatment centers, where clients live in the facility for a fixed period of time. Others work with clients in outpatient treatment centers. Some counselors work in private practice, where they may work alone or with a group of counselors or other professionals.

Although rewarding, the work of substance abuse and behavioral disorder counselors is often stressful. Many counselors have to deal with large workloads. They do not always have enough resources to meet the demand for their services. Also, they may have to intervene in crisis situations or work with agitated clients, which can be tense.

Work Schedules

Most substance abuse and behavioral disorder counselors work full time. In some settings, such as inpatient facilities, they may need to work evenings, nights, or weekends.

Training, Other Qualifications, and Advancement

Educational requirements range from a high school diploma to a master's degree, depending on the setting, type of work, state regulations, and level of responsibility.

Education

Requirements range from a high school diploma and certification to a master's degree. However, workers with more education are able to provide more services to their clients, such as private one-on-one counseling sessions, and they require less supervision than those with less education. Those interested should research their state's educational requirements.

Licenses and Certification

Substance abuse and behavioral disorder counselors in private practice must be licensed. Being licensed to work in this setting requires a master's degree and 2,000 to 3,000 hours of supervised clinical experience. In addition, counselors must pass a state-recognized exam and complete continuing education every year. Contact information for your state's regulating board can be found through the National Board for Certified Counselors.

The licensure or certification criteria for substance abuse and behavioral disorder counselors outside of private practice vary from state to state. For example, not all states require a specific degree, but many require applicants to pass an exam. Contact information for your state's licensing board can found through the Addiction Technology Transfer Center.

Training

Workers with less education, such as a high school diploma, may be required to go through a period of on-the-job training. Training prepares counselors how to respond to a crisis situation, and interact with families and people with addictions.

Important Qualities

Compassion. Counselors often work with people who are dealing with stressful and difficult situations, so they must be compassionate and empathize with their clients.

Listening skills. Good listening skills are essential for substance abuse and behavioral disorder counselors. They need to give their full attention to a client to be able to understand that client's problems and values.

Patience. Substance abuse and behavioral disorder counselors must be able to remain calm when working with all types of clients, including those who may be distressed or angry.

People skills. Counselors must be able to work with different types of people. They spend most of their time working directly with clients or other professionals and must be able to develop and nurture good relationships.

Speaking skills. Substance abuse and behavioral disorder counselors need to be able to communicate with clients effectively. They must express ideas and information in a way that their clients easily understand.

Employment

Employment of substance abuse and behavioral disorder counselors is expected to grow by 27 percent from 2010 to 2020, faster than the average for all occupations. Growth is expected as more people seek treatment for their addictions or other behaviors and drug offenders are increasingly sentenced to treatment rather than jail time.

(Continued)

(Continued)

In recent years, the criminal justice system has recognized that people committing crimes related to drugs are less likely to offend again if they get treatment for addiction. As a result, sentences for drug offenders often include treatment programs. This practice is expected to increase the use of substance abuse treatment programs and the demand for addiction counselors.

Also, over the projections period, more people are expected to seek treatment for problems with addiction or other problems. As the population grows, the number of individuals entering therapy is expected to increase as well. This is expected to cause a continued demand for counselors in mental health centers, halfway houses, and detox centers.

Employment of substance abuse and behavioral disorder counselors in residential mental health and substance abuse facilities is expected to grow by 44 percent from 2010 to 2020. As more individuals seek treatment, there will be an increase in demand for counseling services in residential facilities.

Employment growth from 2010 to 2020 for the industries employing the most substance abuse and behavioral disorder counselors is as follows:

Individual and family services	49%
Residential mental health and substance abuse facilities	44
Hospitals; state, local, and private	17
Outpatient mental health and substance abuse centers	16
State and local government, excluding education and hospitals	7

Job Prospects

Job prospects are excellent for substance abuse and behavioral disorder counselors, particularly for those with specialized training or education. Employers often have difficulty recruiting workers with the proper educational requirements and experience in working with addiction. In addition, many workers leave the field after a few years and need to be replaced. As result, those interested in entering this field should find favorable prospects.

Earnings

The median annual wage of substance abuse and behavioral disorder counselors was $38,120 in May 2010. The median wage is the wage at which half the workers in an occupation earned more than that amount and half earned less. The lowest 10 percent earned less than $24,690 and the top 10 percent earned more than $60,400.

In 2010, the median annual wages for substance abuse and behavioral disorder counselors in the industries employing the most substance abuse and behavioral disorder counselors were as follows:

Hospitals; state, local, and private	$45,160
Local government	44,280
Individual and family services	37,020
Outpatient mental health and substance abuse centers	35,670
Residential mental health and substance abuse facilities	33,570

Most substance abuse and behavioral disorder counselors work full time. In some settings, such as inpatient facilities, they may need to work evenings, nights, or weekends.

SOURCE: Bureau of Labor Statistics, U.S. Department of Labor, *Occupational Outlook Handbook, 2012–13 Edition*, Substance Abuse and Behavioral Disorder Counselors, on the Internet at http://www .bls.gov/ooh/community-and-social-service/substance-abuse-and-behavioral-disorder-counselors.htm.

Private Prisons

Private prisons are for-profit agencies that enter into a contract with public prison institutions to house and secure inmates. Some of the first prisons in the United States were private, but states soon took on the role of controlling inmate populations. In the 1980s, the Corrections Corporation of America (CCA) offered to take over the failing Tennessee prison system with a 99-year lease costing only $250 million (McDonald, Fournier, Russell-Einhourn, & Crawford, 1998, p. 4). While Tennessee refused the offer, other states saw the value of private prisons in comparison to their own cost-effectiveness. Contracting with private organizations to provide services for prisons was not a new phenomenon. Food services and counseling services that are required in the day-to-day management of prisons had long been handled by private contractors. The U.S. Immigration Service had even used private facilities to house immigrants awaiting hearings or deportation in 1979 (McDonald et al., 1998, p. 5). This opened the door for private security firms such as the CCA; Wackenhut, Inc.; and Corrections Services Corporation (formerly ESMOR) to begin running facilities across the United States. Although issues regarding the legality of these facilities were raised when the government began contracting with them, the issues took a backseat to more immediate problems such as overcrowded facilities and tight budgets (McDonald et al., 1998).

Saving money is not the major advantage of using private prisons since savings are modest at best and may even be questionable, as shown in In the News 12.1. Critics of prison privatization have argued that little cost savings exist when states partner with private prison firms. These arguments center on flawed studies by corrections corporations that have shown cost savings even though the methodologies of the studies were lacking. Critics also argue that studies on cost savings have looked at newer and less problematic facilities, rather than considering the types of buildings often used by public prisons, which were built many years ago and are in need of repair. The argument, here, is that private prisons will see costs increase as the buildings they own and operate deteriorate (Deckert & Wood, 2011). Finally, critics suggest that private companies are not really shouldering the full costs associated with building facilities as suggested in their studies on cost effectiveness. Private prison corporations may target poorer and less financially sophisticated communities with high unemployment rates as places to build prisons and jails. The private company then uses tax reductions and incentives from the local government, along with high-risk investments, to finance the costs of the facility. If the private prison later experiences a bankruptcy, it is the community, and ultimately the public, left holding the debt (Austin & Coventry, 2001; Deckert & Wood, 2011).

As with any controversy, there is another side to the argument. Some argue that a net savings exists when using private prisons. Research on labor costs in prisons suggests that up to two-thirds of prison budgets are spent on labor expenses. Private prison guards and staff generally make less in wages and benefits than those employed in public prisons. This may be, in part, because of the existence of unions in public facilities, but not in private prisons. Additionally, private prison administrators claim they have more flexibility in reducing overtime pay, providing incentives and promotions based on performance, and firing staff members who are not performing up to standards (Deckert & Wood, 2011). Private prison companies have also shown cost savings in the construction and maintenance of prisons. Typically, the cost of building and maintaining jails and prisons is paid by the public through tax dollars. But when a state partners with a private prison firm, the state may allow the company to build and maintain prisons and jails that best meet the company's needs and maximize technology and prison design (which lowers labor expenses for the company in the long run). This provides an upfront savings to taxpayers, who are no longer responsible for construction and building upkeep (Deckert & Wood, 2011). Another argument for net savings surrounds the government procurement systems. States and the federal government enter into contracts with vendors, which often last multiple years, by agreeing to purchase goods and services from only those companies. For the duration of the contract, public agencies must pay the agreed-on contractual rate regardless of the market value. This does not allow for flexibility in pricing or for price comparisons. Private prison administrators argue that they are part of the free market and can purchase goods and services at the least expensive rate. They also do not enter into long-term vendor contracts, so they are able to minimize costs for goods and services by shopping around for the best deal (Deckert & Wood, 2011). Most states choose to partner with private prisons to alleviate overcrowding (McDonald &

Patten, 2004). The Federal Bureau of Prisons in Washington, DC, and the states of Texas, Florida, Oklahoma, Louisiana, Tennessee, California, Mississippi, and Colorado house inmates in the 158 private prisons found in the United States (Camp & Gaes, 2001). In fact, CCA is the ninth-largest prison system in the United States, housing more than 80,000 inmates in more than 60 facilities (44 of which are company owned) with a total bed capacity of more than 90,000. "CCA currently partners with all three federal corrections agencies (The Federal Bureau of Prisons, the U.S. Marshals Service and Immigration and Customs Enforcement), 16 states, more than a dozen local municipalities, and Puerto Rico and the U.S. Virgin Islands" (Corrections Corporation of America, 2008, para. 3).

In the News 12.1
Police Chief Considers Absorbing Private Site

Backed into a corner by a budget crunch and severe overcrowding, Ohio prisons chief Terry J. Collins said yesterday that he is looking at taking over one of the state's two legally mandated private prisons.

"Every prison should be on the table," Collins told the Ohio Senate Finance Committee. "I think I have to look at if I can do it cheaper."

The state contracts for the operation of two private prisons: North Coast Correctional Treatment Facility, a 552-bed, minimum-security facility for alcohol and drug offenders in Grafton in Lorain County, and the Lake Erie Correctional Institution, a 1,380-bed, minimum- and medium-security prison in Conneaut in Ashtabula County.

Both are operated by Management & Training Corp., of Centerville, Utah.

A state law passed by majority Republicans in 1996 and signed by then-Gov. George V. Voinovich, a Republican, requires the Department of Rehabilitation and Correction to pay for two private prisons. It also requires that each prison show an annual savings of at least 5 percent compared with state operation.

Collins said yesterday that he thinks he might be able to save even more by combining the administration and operation of the North Coast facility with the adjacent, state-run Grafton Correctional Institution.

The House version of the state budget would open the door by allowing Collins to take a small part of the private-prison population, about 25 inmates imprisoned for multiple drunken-driving convictions.

Collins acknowledged that, if taking over the prison would be cost-effective, he would return to the legislature to get state law changed to say his department "may" instead of "must" contract for private prisons.

That prompted an immediate reaction from Sen. Bill Seitz, R-Cincinnati, who questioned Collins sharply about how he would run the private prison at lower cost because current law already requires a built-in 5 percent savings.

The animated conversation between Seitz and Collins continued in the hallway after the hearing.

(Continued)

(Continued)

Collins told committee members that he is "disappointed and frustrated" by House Democrats' decision to pull a sentencing-reform proposal out of the budget. The House version of the budget allocated $100,000 for the Council of State Governments to study reforms intended to reduce the prison population.

Sen. Ray Miller, D-Columbus, said studying reforms would "take a good idea and send it down a dark, deep hole never to be seen again."

Collins urged senators to reinstate the sentencing reform, including a provision granting inmates up to seven days per month in "earned credit" off their sentence if they are enrolled in specified programming.

The reforms are opposed by prosecutors across the state. They countered with a proposal to reduce mandatory sentences for drug crimes to provide an overcrowding relief valve.

Collins' proposal echoes an idea voiced eight years ago by the Ohio Civil Service Employees Association, the union representing prison guards and other employees. The union said in 2001 that the state could save $6 million annually by merging operations at North Coast with the Grafton prison.

SOURCE: From "Police Chief Considers Absorbing Private Site," by A. Johnson, April 30, 2009, *The Columbus Dispatch*. Copyright ©2009 The Dispatch Printing Co.

The issues created for management when choosing to contract with a private prison are enormous. Performance standards and accountability along with safety and security remain controversial issues surrounding private prisons. Contracts between states and private prison corporations specify objectives and performance indicators. States closely audit the facilities to ensure compliance and may actually require private facilities to meet performance measures that exceed those found in public prisons (Deckert & Wood, 2011; McDonald & Patten, 2004). In fact, private prisons may be specifically forbidden to overcrowd the facility, while public prisons are not inhibited in overcrowding. Additionally, private prisons in comparison to public facilities are more likely to seek and keep accreditation through the American Correctional Association, ensuring that they are meeting minimum quality standards seen by the discipline as necessary to the humane care and treatment of inmates (Dekert & Wood, 2011; Stephan, 2008). Not everyone agrees that private facilities perform better or are more accountable than public prisons, though. "Opponents of private prisons concede that public prisons have set the bar abysmally low in terms of their performance standards—particularly in terms of health care, rehabilitation programs, and the safety of staff and inmates" (Dekert & Wood, 2011, p. 228). In their arguments on the failures of private prisons to outperform public facilities, critics claim that private prisons are ill-equipped to provide mental health care and care for chronically ill inmates, such as those with HIV/AIDS, diabetes, cancer, and so forth (Dekert & Wood, 2011). Additionally, the Department of Justice (Stephan, 2005) found that private prisons provided fewer programs focused on education, treatment, work, psychological problems, HIV/AIDS, and sex offending. Critics argue that private facilities save money by not offering these programs and push the costs of these programs to taxpayers once the inmates are released because the inmates are still in need of these services (Dekert & Wood, 2011).

Others argue that there are systematic problems in maintaining a secure facility due, in part, to the very qualities that make them seem more economically feasible (Camp & Gaes, 2001). That is, labor expenses are less, and profits are higher, when prisons are understaffed, correctional officers are underpaid, and not enough of the budget is reserved for proper training. Companies such as CCA have been accused of forgoing proper staffing and training, which, at least in one case, resulted in a lawsuit and settlement for an inmate who was almost beaten to death by another inmate (see In The News 12.2). Opponents claim that there is such an intense desire to maintain the contract with the state that private prisons may actually not report staff-to-inmate or inmate-to-inmate violence that occurs in the facility for fear of losing profits (Dekert & Wood, 2011). But not all research on private prisons is negative; there is additional research demonstrating that private prisons outperform both state and federal prisons in lower rates of staff and inmate assaults (Lukemeyer & McCorkle, 2006). Private prisons on the whole appear to be significantly less likely to experience violence than federal prisons, alleviating inmate fears of attack and allowing for more opportunities to implement services and rehabilitation.

Contracts made with private facilities have to specify the exact guidelines the institution is to follow. However, difficulties arise in trying to identify for contractual reasons all of the situations that might occur within an institution, such as using deadly force or preventing escape and administrative disciplinary procedures. Furthermore, contracts have to specify that the due process rights of inmates are protected even in cases where they may violate the rules of the institution.

In The News 12.2
Idaho Inmates Settle Lawsuit Over Prison Violence

A potential class-action lawsuit against the nation's largest private prison company over allegations of violence at the Idaho Correctional Center has been settled in federal court.

The agreement between the inmates and Nashville, Tenn.-based Corrections Corporation of America was filed Tuesday in U.S. District Court in Boise.

In it, CCA doesn't acknowledge the allegations but agrees to increase staffing, investigate all assaults and make other sweeping changes at the lockup south of Boise. If the company fails to make the changes, the inmates can ask the courts to force CCA to comply.

The inmates, represented by the American Civil Liberties Union, sued last year on behalf of everyone incarcerated at the CCA-run state prison. They said the prison was so violent it was dubbed

(Continued)

(Continued)

"Gladiator School," and that guards used inmate-on-inmate violence as a management tool and then denied prisoners medical care as a way to cover up the assaults.

CCA has denied all the allegations as part of the settlement, but the agreement is governed under a section of the Prison Litigation Reform Act which only applies in cases in which prisoners' constitutional rights have been violated.

As part of a prepared statement written by the ACLU and approved by CCA, both sides said that rather spending time and resources trying to litigate allegations of past problems, the groups would work toward improving future conditions at the prison. Those steps include hiring three additional correctional officers, ensuring prison staffing meets state requirements and following standard operating procedures already set up by the Idaho Department of Correction.

The agreement came after both sides spent three days in federal mediation sessions last week. Federal oversight of the settlement will last for two years.

In the lawsuit, the inmates cited an Associated Press investigation that found the private prison had more cases of inmate-on-inmate violence than all other Idaho prisons combined.

"The unnecessary carnage and suffering that has resulted is shameful and inexcusable," the ACLU wrote in the lawsuit. "ICC not only condones prisoner violence, the entrenched culture of ICC promotes, facilitates, and encourages it."

While the prison is owned by the state, it is run for a profit by CCA under a contract with the Idaho Department of Correction. The inmates claimed the company made decisions based on profit rather than on "responsible administration of the prison."

The prisoners' lawsuit didn't ask for money, just changes in the way CCA runs the lockup.

Under the settlement, the company has agreed to leave more prison beds open so it can easily move threatened inmates to new cellblocks when necessary. It also agreed to report all assaults that appear to amount to aggravated battery to the Ada County sheriff's office, to increase the level of training given to guards and to discipline staffers who don't take appropriate measures to stop or prevent assaults.

"This settlement is in the best interest of our clients, CCA and the state of Idaho," ACLU senior attorney Stephen Pevar said in the prepared statement.

Idaho Department of Correction Director Brent Reinke said he was pleased with the settlement, because he thinks it will improve the sometimes adversarial relationship the state has had with CCA. Idaho has increased the number of employees it has monitoring operations at the private prison and in the past has fined CCA thousands of dollars for failing to meet contract requirements. Still, Idaho officials decided to renew CCA's contract to run the prison and the state has even added more than 600 beds to the lockup, making it the state's largest prison.

"We are working with the contractor, rather than against the contractor, which is huge—it's huge—when you can try to get things resolved," he said.

Reinke said he was also pleased that ICC warden Timothy Wengler was one of the CCA officials who signed the settlement agreement.

"I respect those in Tennessee (CCA's headquarters). But I really want to have a good manager here," Reinke said. "The fact that he's stepping up and has signed the agreement, well, his name is on the line now."

The Department of Correction was originally named as a defendant in the case, but the inmates agreed to drop the allegations against the agency after state officials agreed to enforce any of the court's actions.

Idaho officials will closely review the 18 key items listed in the settlement to make sure they comply with the contract between CCA and the state, Reinke said. If not, the contract may be adjusted to add the requirements.

CCA spokesman Steve Owen said his company is "turning a page and looking forward" and the settlement reflects "how pleased we are with the progress that's been made at the facility."

Any costs associated with the increased staffing, investigations and training aren't a concern, he said.

"I think we view all those things that are being done as positives," he said.

CCA has faced several lawsuits in Idaho over violence and assaults at the prison. Security cameras from the facility showed one attack, in which guards watched while an inmate named Hanni Elabed was beaten unconscious and then stomped in the head multiple times. The company reached an undisclosed settlement with Elabed, who was left with brain damage and likely permanent disabilities from the attack.

Many of the attacks listed in the ACLU lawsuit happened while former warden Phillip Valdez was leading the prison. CCA eventually reassigned Valdez to the assistant warden post at the Leavenworth Detention Center, a prison the company runs for the U.S. Marshals Service in Kansas.

Just last week, CCA reached a settlement with an inmate named Marlin Riggs, who was the lead plaintiff in the potential class-action lawsuit in Idaho until the court split the case into two lawsuits. He contended he warned guards that he was about to be attacked by other inmates but they refused to move to him to another unit or give him any other protection. Shortly after returning to his cellblock, Riggs was beaten so badly that bones in his face were broken and his blood was splattered across the walls and ceiling of his cell.

CCA's settlement with Riggs was sealed by the court.

SOURCE: From "Idaho Inmates Settle Lawsuit Over Prison Violence" by Rebecca Boone, *Blumberg Business Week*, The Associated Press, September 20, 2011. Retrieved from http://www.businessweek.com/ap/financialnews/D9PSH4DG0.htm.

Legal issues have risen, questioning whether the protection of inmates' rights lies with the state or whether these rights can be transferred to private prisons (Austin & Coventry, 2001). The U.S. Supreme Court has ruled that all inmates are entitled to federal constitutional and civil rights under 42 U.S.C., Section 1983 (which is part of the Civil Rights Act of 1871) (*Cooper v. Pate*, 1964). Under these rulings, prisoners in private state facilities can sue the private corporation for deprivation of constitutional rights (see *West v. Atkins*, 1988), but the Court has failed to extend this privilege to federal inmates housed in private facilities. Federal inmates can sue individual employees of private facilities but not the private corporation because correctional officers in private facilities are not entitled to the qualified immunity that their public counterparts enjoy (see *Correctional Services Corp. v. Malesko*, 2001; *Richardson v. McKnight*, 1997). In addition, federal inmates can sue individual employees of private facilities but not the private corporation for violations of constitutional rights, even though it is acting as a federal agent in carrying out duties that would have normally been performed by the federal government (see *Minneci v. Pollard*, 2011; *Richardson v. McKnight*, 1997). "Ethical arguments against the use of private prisons are myriad, and involve a host of moral, religious, and social justice platform[s]" and concerns about the political maneuvering of private prison corporations produce an additional set of arguments for and against these institutions (Dekert & Wood, 2011, quoted in Chambliss, 2011, p. 231). At any rate, and with all arguments for and against privatization aside, prison managers have to decide if private prisons offer a good alternative for housing inmates despite the various administrative issues that arise.

Centralization Versus Decentralization in Prisons and Prison Systems

In general, prisons have traditionally operated as single entities within a larger correctional system. McShane and Williams (1996) suggest that, historically, wardens were given full reign over how their prison was managed. This decentralized approach of having wardens make their own decisions often bred mismanagement and corruption. But a more centralized approach was not seen as ideal, either, since it could promote an adversarial relationship between the staff and the headquarters.

Over time, there has been a steady move to combine some centralized practices with the decentralized approach in prison management. Agencies such as the American Correctional Association started providing training and guidelines to correctional facilities and offered accreditation and guidelines for minimum treatment and care of inmates. Although these were not mandatory, they did provide for guidance and standardization among facilities, as wardens could more easily investigate what other facilities were doing. Centralized approaches, through the use of state offices or departments of corrections, have also been seen as a better means for distributing resources more equitably and for addressing legal concerns. This approach, though, has not been without its problems. McShane and Williams (1996) suggest that a return to traditional decentralization may be necessary for several reasons. To begin with, there has been a move toward smaller facilities catering to the needs of specialized populations. Mega-institutions are not as ideal to handle populations such as the elderly, HIV/AIDS patients, or those who are mentally ill. Grouping these specialized populations into smaller facilities allows their needs to be better attended to, and it enables the management and staff to be better trained. In turn, those working most closely with the inmates are in the best position to make decisions regarding their care, custody, and treatment.

Upper-level administrators employed in state departments of corrections are also showing interest in the concept of *unit management*. Unit teams, often staffed with a manager, caseworker, mental health professional, educational professional, secretary, and corrections counselor, have been given authority to handle self-contained units within larger facilities (McShane & Williams, 1996). McShane and Williams (1996) add that the increased liability of wardens has also been a factor in moving toward a decentralized approach in running prison systems. If the wardens can be held liable for decisions made in their facilities, then it makes sense that they would want to have more control and authority over policy and procedures in their facilities than administrators at the state or federal level. Finally, McShane and Williams argued that the increased competitiveness among units for resources influences the state departments to give the decision-making responsibilities to those having greater knowledge of the day-to-day operations and needs of those units. To counter many of the problems that arise from a centralized headquarters being impractical, alienating, and costly, many systems have adopted regional offices that manage a small number of prisons within a specific geographical area.

The objective in most states is to provide prison oversight without constraining facilities to the point that they become ineffective in accomplishing their goals. Prison oversight is a topic that has been studied with intensity in the last decade. In the case of prisons, oversight refers to the external mechanisms used to monitor prisons. Dietch (2010) argued that prison oversight is not a "one size fits all" approach, and that many mechanisms can be used by prison administrators and states to effectively monitor facilities, promote accountability and transparency in the prison system, and resolve problems facing prisons. Deitch (2010, p. 1440) claimed that prison oversight has seven distinct functions:

1. *Regulation* is a process used by government entities that license prison facilities and determine and enforce mandates and policies that apply to all prisons within a geographical area. "The key concepts at work here are 'enforcement authority' and 'control.'"

2. *Audit* is concerned with performance indicators, standards, and policies, and if the prison is being fiscally responsible. The audit could come from state-appointed representatives or from the American Correctional Association. "As a general matter, the auditing function is designed to give either prison administrators or those who regulate or accredit them some objective measures of how the agency is doing and/or whether tax monies are being well spent. The emphasis is on the audit as a management tool."

3. *Accreditation* is voluntary and costly, but the American Correctional Association or some other agencies provides the prison with a snapshot of their overall effectiveness in using best practices in the field of corrections. Accreditation practices have been more performance-based and more meaningful as an indicator of effectiveness than in past years.

4. *Investigations* are reactive in nature, whereas other oversight mechanisms are proactive. Even so, "This function can encompass everything from an ombudsman's investigation of a prisoner's complaint, to an inspector general's review of an excessive use of force claim, to an independent commission's review of agency operations in the wake of a series of complaints, to criminal prosecution of staff for official misconduct." Investigations are a critical component of accountability.

5. *Legal* allows for the use of courts and court-ordered corrective actions when wrongdoings are determined. "The legal function, like the investigation function, is

reactive in nature, though the ongoing supervision of the legal system is designed to fix an unacceptable set of conditions and not just punish wrongdoing."

6. *Reporting* supports the transparency goal. This mechanism allows those outside of the institution to "shine a light on the closed world of corrections." Reported findings may pressure changes in the treatment of inmates, policy changes in sentencing practices, and other administrative practices.

7. *Inspection and monitoring* "involves an entity outside of the corrections agency with the power and the mandate to routinely inspect all correctional institutions in a jurisdiction not just those with publicized problems and to report publicly on how people within each prison or jail facility are treated. More so than any other oversight function, the inspection/monitoring function is intended to be preventative in nature." Monitoring and inspection allows for a holistic review of prison practices, culture, and inmate housing and treatment.

As suggested by Dietch (2010), oversight is imperative, regardless of whether an institution or a prison system will operate as a closed or open structure. Although oversight should be used in both open and closed systems, in those organizations where closed systems are most often used, oversight becomes even more necessary to ensure accountability and transparency in the management and control of human beings. "Such transparency provides both a form of protection from harm and an assurance that rights will be vindicated. External oversight also benefits administrators by providing them with the objective feedback they need about their performance. Internal accountability measures and external forms of oversight are neither in competition nor mutually exclusive; they are designed to meet entirely different—but complementary— needs" (Deitch, 2010, p. 1440). So even closed-system organizations may want to consider the input that can be derived from oversight mechanisms. In conclusion, oversight is a multifaceted trait that is designed to provide the best environment for leadership and administration, resulting in improved service quality.

Organizational Structure of Prisons

The paramilitary structure is relatively similar for federal, state, and private prisons. Upper-level management differs slightly since federal and private prisons do not have to report to state governors. Depending on the size of the institution, the number of staff members and types of administration also vary. In most cases, the governor of a state allows a commissioner or department of corrections to administer the prison system with or without external oversight committees. Within each institution, there is another organizational structure, beginning with the warden. The position of warden is appointed by the governor or a state department of corrections director. McShane and Williams (1996) note that, historically, the appointment of a warden was often a way for a politician to pay back a political supporter, although this has changed significantly over the years. In 2001, Lambert and Regan suggested that the position of warden is generally filled by people who work their way up the organizational structure. Through observing biographies of current wardens, they concluded that wardens of today are well-educated and experienced. It is not unusual for wardens to have an undergraduate degree in the social sciences, while many hold graduate degrees in business administration. Deputy wardens are used in a number of prisons as well, and their duties are similar to those of the warden. The duties of wardens and deputy wardens require a good deal of knowledge about custody/security, programs, and administrative services. In a medium-sized prison, the organizational structure may include one deputy warden in charge of custody/security, one overseeing administrative services, and another in charge of programs/treatment.

Security and Custody in Prisons

The security or custody division is the operational branch of the penal facility. Internal and external security as well as inmate supervision are assignments given on the basis of rank. Many facilities have a captain, lieutenants, sergeants, and corporals, and at the lower end of the hierarchical ranks are operational line staff. Sergeants or corporals are generally the first line of staff supervisors.

Administrative Services in Prisons

The administrative services division is the support branch of the facility. This division is sometimes further split into staff support and facility maintenance.

This division encompasses everything necessary to keep the prison properly functioning such as heating, water, laundry, food preparation, fire protection, and so forth. This division also includes a catch-all grouping of various tasks that keep the business end of the facility running smoothly such as accounting, planning, recruitment of new officers, training, and the like. Administrative services may have a unique set of goals and objectives that can be in conflict with other divisions. At the same time, this division is dependent on other divisions to meet its objectives.

Program and Treatment Services in Prisons

There are numerous programs available in most prisons, and the program/treatment division often includes a plethora of responsibilities. Education, vocational training, prison industries or other work programs, counseling, casework, and other services providing inmate treatment are found under program or treatment services. In many of these positions, professional degrees are required. Because these areas require professionals from outside of corrections rather than sworn officers who progress through the ranks, they bring a variety of backgrounds to the institutions that do not consist of the typical paramilitary training found in other divisions.

Those employees working in the treatment programs may have trouble with the paramilitary structure of the prison, have trouble balancing their best clinical practice with limitations of time and environment, and experience ethical dilemmas resulting from dual role conflict (Cropsey, Wexler, Melnick, Taxman, & Young, 2007; Magaletta, Patry, Dietz, & Ax, 2007). These employees tend to face high stress and burnout from providing treatment and programming in a rigid environment. Researchers have cited perceptions of being in danger, close inmate contact, and a lack of perceived administrative support as reasons for burnout and stress (Garland, 2004) among prison treatment providers.

Correctional Facilities at the Local Level: Jails

Jails are typically the first contact an offender has with the correctional system. In some cases, offenders are held in jails for short periods and then released, never to experience the prison system. Throughout history, jails have been criticized because of the poor conditions within which inmates are housed. In the 1980s and 1990s, many jails were cited for failing to meet fire standards, health and sanitation standards, and various other issues (Cox & Wade, 2002). For the most part, jails have been limited in the amount of security they provide, the types of inmates they can hold, and the length of time an inmate is housed.

Today, jails are short-term facilities that serve many functions (Harrison & Beck, 2006a). In general, they hold all convicted inmates who are to serve sentences of less than one year. Jails still hold arrested suspects awaiting trial that cannot afford to pay a bail bond or who are not granted bail by the court. Jails also house people needing protective custody, those cited for contempt, and those who are material witnesses to a crime. In addition, jails temporarily hold juveniles or mentally ill people until they can be transferred to an appropriate facility. Probation, parole, or bail-bond violators; inmates waiting for transfer to a state or federal prison; and state and federal inmates who are transferred to the jail because of overcrowding in other prisons may also be found in local jails (Cox & Wade, 2002).

Most jails are relatively small, although those in major cities such as Los Angeles, New York, Chicago, and Dallas are rather sizeable. According to Minton (2013), at midyear 2012, there were 744,524 people in jails or supervised by jail administrators in the United States. Males accounted for 87% of the jail population in midyear 2012, and whites accounted for 46% of the total, blacks 37% of the total, and Hispanics represented 15% of inmates (Minton, 2013, p. 1). At midyear 2012, about 6 in 10 inmates were not convicted but were in jail waiting for court action on their cases (Minton, 2013, p. 1). Jails are usually financed and managed at the local or county level. Because of this, they remain fairly autonomous and fall victim, in some cases, to local politics. They are typically low priorities on the county budgets and are supervised by elected officials (the county sheriff, for example). Staff members directly supervising inmates often have little formal training or education. It is not uncommon for them to be underpaid and to experience extremely high inmate-to-staff ratios (Cox & Wade, 2002). These conditions, as well as overcrowding, inmate health conditions, and lack of training, contribute to other job characteristics that cause job stress, job dissatisfaction, and organizational commitment (Paoline & Lambert, 2012).

Jail Design

There is no distinctive jail design—all will have some variation—yet it is possible to have a general idea about how jails have been constructed during different periods. Smaller jails are found in rural areas and larger facilities in cities and metropolitan areas. Jails are sometimes attached to a courthouse or other municipal building, while others stand alone. Jails can also be classified as first generation, second generation, or third generation (Stinchcomb & Fox, 1999). These classifications progress as a result of the growing use of technology and greater understanding of effective supervision.

First-generation jails are similar to the type of jail viewed in many television shows, where the jailer or deputy walks down a catwalk past a series of cells. The problem with these older facilities is that the officers can only glance at what is going on in the cells when they stroll by (Stinchcomb & Fox, 1999). To counter the supervision problems of first-generation jails, the long corridors that only allowed for intermittent surveillance were replaced by hallways surrounding a control center. Officers in *second-generation jails* could view any cell at any time without a great deal of contact with the inmate (which creates the feeling of an impersonal atmosphere). Stinchcomb and Fox (1999) refer to this style of management as indirect or remote surveillance. *Third-generation jails* are an attempt to handle both the surveillance problems found in first-generation jails and the impersonal atmosphere of second-generation jails. The result is a management style of direct supervision. These facilities have grown in popularity, with one in five jails now using a direct supervision approach (Applegate & Paoline, 2007). The Corrections Center of Northwest Ohio (CCNO) is one example of how a change in jail architecture has also affected management (CCNO, 2009). At the CCNO, corrections officers spend their time in the housing units with the inmates rather than sitting at a control center and making observations. Improvements over the older-generation jails include the following:

Better inmate control. Officers on hand make it easier to assign privileges, provide leadership, and set standards for behavior.

Less tension and violence. It is easier to manage problems when officers are walking among the inmates, watching for situations that they can handle immediately before the problem escalates.

Lessened noise. The architecture (carpeted floors in open areas, solid construction, and acoustic tiles on walls and ceiling), paired with officer control, reduces noise in the facility.

Higher staff morale. Jobs are more satisfying when officers are given the authority to problem solve on their own, thus building leadership and management skills.

Reduced amount of idleness. Inmates are offered a number of opportunities for indoor and outdoor recreation, educational services, library visits, visitation with family or friends, and other programs, all supervised by staff.

More controlled movement. Officers are on hand to escort inmates to and from all activities at a scheduled time.

Additional information. Officers are equipped to answer inmates' questions about court, their commissary accounts, or to connect with case managers.

Increased privileges. Telephones and a limited number of computers are available to inmates earning those privileges. Direct supervision of the inmates reduces the likelihood that inmates will loan shark, barter, or trade.

Lowered costs. It costs less to maintain one larger facility than multiple smaller jails. Purchases can be made in bulk. CCNO holds primarily misdemeanants and lower-felony inmates; thus dorm-style rooms accommodate the majority of offenders rather than cells.

Reduced incidences of vandalism. The possibilities of vandalism are greatly reduced with officers present among the inmates. CCNO is also a nonsmoking facility and costs of cigarette burns and damage are eliminated.

Increased discipline. Segregation units are used when inmates exhibit poor behavior. Privileges are removed while constitutional rights are still protected. A 23-hour lockdown in segregation discourages inmates from breaking rules (CCNO, 2009).

Applegate and Paoline (2007) point out that research on jail design and its impact on employee motivation and job satisfaction is still in its infancy. Their findings of officers working in both single-jail facilities and new-generation jails found that neither supervision style improved officers' work perceptions. They argued that any attempt to implement direct supervision in a jail should consider how officers are supervised and the organization climate of the jail (Applegate & Paoline, 2007). A key to the success of any program used in an institution is good leadership, training, and connecting it to the organizational mission and culture.

Accreditation has also become popular in today's jail systems. Jails and other correctional institutions can achieve accredited status through the American Correctional Association. Just as in policing, accreditation can increase efficiency, training standards, and liability and accountability among jail staff. Today, more than 100 jails have been accredited. Parrish (2006) claims this is the benchmark for a successful jail because "it is good business practices that drive the design and operation of well-run facilities" (p. 6).

Organizational Structure of Jails

The organizational structure in jails often begins with an elected county sheriff who is also in charge of law enforcement functions in the county; however, a small number of jails have a county administrator or a board of administrators who heads the organization. Other cities have a board of commissioners who appoint a police chief and corrections director. In many ways, these appointed positions split the duties usually performed by the sheriff. While the police chief handles the law enforcement duties, the corrections director handles the jail administration duties. The jail administrator or assistant chief deputy is employed directly under the sheriff in the organizational structure. Like prisons, jails use a typical paramilitary structure with captains implementing policy over either the linear jail, the pretrial facility, the support section of the jail, or the direct-supervision jail.

Juvenile detention centers of today look and operate much like local jails. Private and public entities run the facilities, and they vary greatly in size, length of inmate stay, type of programs used, and costs. Some facilities incorporate behavior modification programs into the daily functions of the facility, while others operate pretty much as warehouses where few, if any, rehabilitation programs are used (Cox & Wade, 2002). Educational programs are the one mainstay throughout juvenile facilities. Although some states provide oversight, these institutions are difficult to inspect and control because they are managed at the local or county level by chief probation officers. Youth detention facilities experience overcrowding as children are awaiting court, serving minimal sentences in detention, or awaiting transfer to other facilities. Short stays in detention make it difficult for delinquents to work on educational assignments or to participate in treatment programming. The staff members are usually not required to have professional degrees or previous experience with delinquent youth.

As mentioned before, juvenile correctional centers are different from detention centers. Commitment to a juvenile prison is the least frequently employed disposition for youth and is reserved for those delinquents who have exhausted all other treatment and rehabilitation attempts, who have committed violent offenses against others, and who repeatedly appear in court for criminal violations. Youth sentenced to prison serve long sentences and are generally believed to be guaranteed a criminal career as an adult (Cox & Wade, 2002).

Issues Confronting Correctional Centers

Prisons, jails, and detention centers face many of the same managerial dilemmas as other organizations in criminal justice. Aside from the unique populations and structure they face each day, they are also confronted with issues in staff recruitment, training, and retention; motivation and discipline; budgeting and planning; overcrowding; accreditation; and quality-of-life concerns. In this portion of the chapter, these issues will be addressed, along with how they impact managerial and administrative decisions in correctional institutions.

Equal Employment Opportunity and Other Considerations for Management

Staff Recruitment, Training, and Retention

In earlier years, the standards for being a corrections officer were similar to those of a police officer—almost anyone willing to do the job for the low wages was qualified. The educated and achievement-oriented individuals had no incentive to apply. High rates of turnover and low qualification requirements ensured that vacated positions could be easily filled. With the exception of a few institutions, the standards, unfortunately, have not changed much in recent years, although it has become much more difficult to find willing applicants. The state of Kentucky has shown that standards can be raised as efficiency and effectiveness are emphasized in corrections. In Kentucky, drug use by staff is not tolerated and random drug testing is used; college education is emphasized for staff, and the department has been incorporating creative ways for the staff to get such an education (by using the Internet and through pay incentives); and the state has made its institutions smoke-free environments for both inmates and staff. The Kentucky Department of Corrections has also sought and received accreditation through the American Correctional Association (ACA) (Holcomb, 2006).

One of the problems in finding applicants is low visibility. Edwards (2007) notes that law enforcement is more visible on television and in the community, thus generating more interest. Outside of *Prison Break* and the older HBO series *Oz,* it is unusual to find any shows about prisons. The few there are do not provide a positive image of corrections officers. In addition, few law-abiding citizens go near prisons on a regular basis, so there is rarely a full understanding of the types of jobs available in penal institutions. Edwards suggests that this lack of visibility results in many citizens seeing correctional officer positions as the only opportunities available inside the facility. Those not wanting to be corrections officers do not apply.

Once a person expresses interest in the job, screening candidates becomes very important. Screening for good employees is usually determined through a process that includes a background check, written civil service exam, oral interviews, and a job-task analysis performed through an assessment center. Similar to policing, corrections facilities are looking for stable and reliable personnel. Formal educational requirements are not standard and vary from institution to institution, as mentioned before.

Training standards also vary by institution and facility level. The ACA recommends 40 hours of training for corrections officers before they receive a job assignment, and at least 120 hours of additional training within the first year (ACA, 1990, pp. 79–81). And training of staff at the state level varies greatly. State-level officers usually train at their state-sponsored training academies. The U.S. Bureau of Prisons requires 200 hours of training for new federal officers in federal institutions (CareerOverview, 2007).

Retention has long plagued corrections, with staff turnover being a constant issue. In 2000, almost 40 states had turnover rates of 20% or more (Lommel, 2004, p. 54) in corrections. Research shows that burnout is a major contributor to staff turnover. Gould, Watson, Price, and Valliant's (2013) research supported this assertion by finding that correctional officers in both adult and juvenile facilities experience increased levels of emotional exhaustion and depersonalization, which are related to burnout. Training employees to competence in many of the highly specialized areas of corrections is frustrating and expensive when employees leave. Parrish (2006) points out that it takes roughly 50% of a correctional officer's annual salary to recruit, train, and hire a new employee. Not only is the institution required to hire and retrain new employees, but the shortage of workers also creates more stress and lower morale for those who remain—thus impacting service quality. In addition, the staff must work with more inexperienced people and work longer hours if overtime is the only available remedy for the shortage of employees. Safety becomes a real concern in these cases.

McVey and McVey (2005) suggest that retention solutions require both external and internal strategies for success. Externally, corrections must compete with the private sector to attract employees. The private sector is better able to compete because it is often able to offer flexible work schedules, streamlined hiring processes, and competitive pay and compensation. Public corrections departments can only address these areas within governmental and legal limitations. Compensation is one example where private industry can simply compete more strongly by offering more money, when necessary. Public institutions are limited in the wages they can offer, but may benefit by highlighting their retirement plans and insurance packages in the hiring and retention process. Barring changes in governmental reform, public institutions may have to rely more heavily on internal strategies to retain employees.

While the paramilitary structure works well with corrections departments, McVey and McVey (2005) see no problems with allowing employees to move up in rank by actively seeking higher positions, rather than mechanically moving through the ranks as each position empties. They also suggest that leaders be identified among the newest hires and engaged in more decision-making activities. McVey and McVey recommend creating multilevel job classifications as ways to reward added skills and knowledge. Last, Lommel (2004) warns about ignoring the old adage that people leave bosses—not jobs. The quality of supervisors must be improved in correctional facilities. This can be accomplished through additional training of supervisors and by scrutinizing their abilities or simply getting rid of those who do not improve. Taking a long look at who should be promoted from within and not relying on the good ol' boy system for promotions and rewards is important as well. Active, participative management among those seen as potential leaders may make a difference in employee retention and motivation.

Addressing burnout among correctional officers is also important to retention. Prisoners have many resources available to them on how to deal with the stress of their living environment. Correctional officers, who experience similar situations as inmates in many cases, have very few resources (Gould et al., 2013). Providing peer support groups and psychological services to correctional officers who are feeling exhausted or depersonalized are two ways that facilities can alleviate the effects of burnout. Annual training for officers at all levels and experience can be used to identify the characteristics of burnout and to provide effective stress-management techniques. "Particularly, the use of social support (e.g., debriefing with coworkers, seeking advice or help from others), positive reframing (e.g., trying to see things in a more positive light, looking for something good in what happened), and planning (e.g., trying to come up [with] a strategy about what to do, thinking hard about what steps to take) should be reinforced, while the use of dysfunctional strategies, such as denial and substance abuse, should be discouraged" (Gould et al., 2013, p. 46). Following these suggestions will assist prison leadership in retaining employees and motivating them. Motivation of correctional staff is discussed in more detail next.

The importance of successful recruitment and training may be reflected in lower retention rates and better employee satisfaction. Officers who feel better prepared to handle the required tasks will have improved attitudes, making the daily operations run more smoothly (Lommel, 2004). Proper training also increases the safety of both inmates and staff and reduces the likelihood that correctional officers leave the job. After recruitment and training comes one of the most important areas for consideration by management—keeping the employee motivated and disciplined.

Employee Motivation and Discipline

According to a national survey by the Conference Board, it is not unusual to find employees of every age or income level who feel dissatisfied with their jobs (Kimball & Nink, 2006). While some are only motivated by the promise of a paycheck, others are unmotivated because they feel alienated by employers or do not identify with the mission of the agency. Low motivation has serious consequences for management, as it results in increased absenteeism and lowered psychological and physical well-being. In criminal justice, we are often most concerned with decreased motivation caused by job burnout. Keinan and Maslach-Pines (2007) found that prison staff had much higher levels of burnout than found in the general population, even higher than police officers. Other studies on correctional staff burnout have pointed to role stressors, in the form of role conflict, role ambiguity, role overload, and perceived dangerousness of the job as increasing the chances of burnout (Dignam, Barrera, & West, 1986; Drory & Shamir, 1988; Garland, 2004; Lambert, Hogan, Jiang, & Jenkins, 2009; Shamir & Drory, 1982; Whitehead, 1989).

In corrections, unmotivated employees can result in huge safety concerns, both for themselves and for inmates. Useem and Piehl (2006) found that lowered rates of violence, lowered rates of homicide, and smaller proportions of inmates in segregation in some facilities were the result of improved motivation through correctional leadership. Lambert, Hogan, Cheeseman, Jiang, and Khondaker (2012) also found in a study on the job characteristics model that job feedback and job autonomy were related to emotional burnout specifically for correctional staff. Their findings suggest that not knowing what is expected in carrying out the job because of a lack of feedback from the administration makes the job more difficult and increases negative feelings toward the job. Additionally, a lack of job autonomy creates a sense of frustration and strain as staff feel that they are "pawns in the workplace who have no say in job-related matters" (Lambert et al., 2012, p. 13). Kimball and Nink (2006) suggest the following ways for management to increase motivation of subordinates in corrections:

- Make clear expectations.
- Supply appropriate equipment and materials to perform jobs adequately.
- Provide opportunities for subordinates to do tasks they have been trained to perform.
- Recognize good work regularly—not just at times of performance reviews.

- Offer regular progress/performance reviews.
- Provide encouragement from both coworkers and management.
- Take opinions under consideration.
- Make the organizational mission seem important.
- Create an environment of coworkers who are committed to the quality of performance.
- Offer opportunities for advancement. (pp. 67–71)

The previous steps will help subordinates satisfy both their *intrinsic* and *extrinsic needs*. These steps are in line with the tenets prescribed in the various motivational theories discussed earlier in Chapter 6.

Although many other areas of job design need to be studied regarding correctional staff, research in this area demonstrates a necessity to focus on job design characteristics that enhance the chances for positive work outcomes while reducing the chances for negative work outcomes (Lambert et al., 2012).

Sometimes, supervisors need to correct the work-related behavior of their subordinates along with providing positive reinforcement to motivate them. Discipline should not be perceived by subordinates as punishment; rather, it should be seen as an opportunity to improve their performance. According to Archambeault and Archambeault (1982), discipline measures should be generally progressive: informal counseling, verbal warnings, written warnings, fines, suspension, demotion, and finally dismissal (p. 129). When discipline is used properly, employees should know where they stand regarding offenses, what type of improvement is expected, and the consequences if improvement is not made. The employee's immediate supervisor is best equipped to find problems with the employee's behavior or performance, as well as to discuss the problem with the subordinate (Bohlander & Snell, 2007). Failure on the part of management to document disciplinary problems can result in appeals that challenge management's corrective actions. Many of these problems can be resolved by disseminating the expectations, rules, and regulations for review periodically by all employees.

External Factors

As discussed in Chapter 4, there are many external factors affecting agencies in criminal justice. Bohlander and Snell (2007) suggest that organizations should analyze the external and internal factors affecting their core values to be the most effective. Along with those suggestions by Dietch (2010) discussed earlier, the external examination might include an assessment of how the organization is meeting or exceeding in the following areas: competition for employees, decisions by the unions, prison rights, economic factors, labor trends, incarceration trends, and the like.

Accreditation and changes in ACA standards may mean more record keeping and more training—all resulting in increased costs that must be allocated in budgets. Pay increases might be a factor affecting budgets if local competition for jobs is high or pay increases by unions are demanded. The general economic state of the region, state, or even the nation will affect the amount of money allotted to run corrections departments. In essence, more money will go into the budget when times are good and less when states or the federal government need to tighten the purse strings. Incarceration trends must also be watched. With more female inmates entering the system, a greater proportion of the budget may be directed to building more prisons for women and offering more treatment programs based on gender, such as parenting classes. Finally, courts have decided on certain rights of inmates that must be adhered to, or threats of federal takeover or inmate litigation might increase.

There are numerous rights afforded to prisoners in correctional facilities. Although some of these rights add to the expenses of the penal institutions, some of them do not. They can be maintained through policy and procedure as well as training of staff. For example, respectfully diverting one's attention while an inmate is undressed is a way of respecting the inmate's privacy and does not involve any expense. Addressing inmates by names rather than numbers can also be accomplished at no cost. A law library will cost more in the beginning, but keeping it up to date will be a lesser expense and offers a service to inmates who may need to continue their legal battles. In other cases, not allotting enough money in the budget to cover inmate costs affects the quality of life for inmates. For example, having too many inmates in programs designed for a small number reduces the value of the treatment. Not having enough medical staff to attend to the needs of the population can lead to serious illness and injuries that may spread throughout the facility. Inmates have the right to be free of violence from other prisoners, and not having enough staff to adequately protect inmates is another situation that distracts from the quality of life in the institution.

Internal Factors

Internal factors include the culture, competencies, and composition of the staff (Bohlander & Snell, 2007). What are the strengths and weaknesses of the employees? Are the attitudes and beliefs of employees in line with the mission? Will new employees be difficult to train? Does the staff fully understand inmate rights, sexual harassment guidelines, and other policies and procedures? A general assessment of the staff considers these questions, and the question of whether the inmate-to-staff ratio is one that promotes safety and security. Surveys can be conducted to determine where the staff needs to improve and where appropriate funds can be allocated for that improvement. The formulation and implementation of plans and policies can move forward after internal and external audits.

Clearly, the hands of managers in corrections are often tied by the state fiscal budget. Limitations on services offered in prisons are a direct result of political and social demands. There are serious consequences to not having funding that is appropriate to solve operational problems such as overcrowding and understaffing. It is not uncommon to see prisons dealing with overcrowding by releasing inmates early, privatizing services, using fewer staff to monitor incarcerated inmates, or cutting costs in housing and food. Not too long ago, one Kentucky jail was forced to free offenders to stay within its budget ("Kentucky Jail Frees 30 in Budget Squeeze," 2002), and Iowa made the decision to furlough officers and have a 20-day lockdown to save money ("Iowa Will Furlough Officers, Trim Care," 2002). We are also well aware of California's prison woes and the newly implemented California Public Safety Realignment initiative that plans to reduce the prison population through natural attrition and to place newly convicted, nonviolent, nonserious, nonsexual offenders in local jails under county jurisdiction (Carson & Sabol, 2012). Questions in these cases must be raised about the quality of service being offered to inmates as well as victims and society members.

California Public Safety Realignment

On May 23, 2011, the U.S. Supreme Court upheld the ruling by a lower three-judge court that the State of California must reduce its prison population to 137.5% of design capacity (approximately 110,000 prisoners) within two years to alleviate overcrowding. In response, the California State Legislature and governor enacted two laws—AB 109 and AB 117—to reduce the number of inmates housed in state prisons starting October 1, 2011.

The Public Safety Realignment (PSR) policy is designed to reduce the prison population through normal attrition of the existing population while placing new nonviolent, nonserious, nonsexual offenders under county jurisdiction for incarceration in local jail facilities. Inmates released from local jails will be placed under a county-directed post-release community supervision program (PRCS) instead of the state's parole system. The state is giving additional funding to the 58 counties in California to deal with the increased correctional population and responsibility, but each county must develop a plan for custody and post-custody that best serves the needs of the county.

Since California incarcerates more individuals than any other state except Texas (10.8% of the U.S. state prison population), changes in California's prison population will have national implications. In 2011, the sentenced U.S. state prison population decreased by 21,663 inmates. California contributed 15,188 inmates (70%) to the total decrease. On December 31, 2010, California reported a total jurisdictional population of 165,062. On the same day in 2011, the population was 149,569. Between 2010 and 2011, the number of sentenced female inmates in the California state prison population decreased at a faster rate (down 17.5%) than did males (down 8.7%).

A total of 96,669 inmates were admitted to California state prisons during 2011. Admissions during the first three quarters of 2011 accounted for 89% (about 86,000) of all state prison admissions, compared to 11% (about 10,600) during the fourth quarter (figure 2). Fourth quarter releases also declined from 25% in 2010 to 21% in 2011, and the types of release changed significantly. During the first three quarters of 2011, 98% of releases were conditional mandatory releases to parole, compared to 1.5% for unconditional releases due to expiration of prison sentences (not shown). In quarter 4, only 46% of releases were conditional, while 52% were unconditional without

FIGURE 2
Admissions and releases from the California Department of Corrections and Rehabilitation, by quarter, 2010–2011

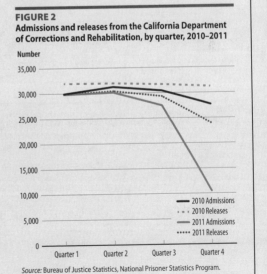

Source: Bureau of Justice Statistics, National Prisoner Statistics Program.

(Continued)

(Continued)

post-release stipulations. Overall, unconditional releases increased by 691% from 2010 to 2011, while conditional releases decreased 20% (table 3). All types of admissions to California state prisons decreased in 2011, with readmissions of parole violators down 22%.

The offense distribution of admissions to California state prisons changed after October 1, 2011 (table 4). The percentage of inmates admitted for violent offenses increased from 30% on September 30, 2011, to 41% on December 31, 2011. Decreases

in property and drug offenders contributed to the change.

BJS will continue to monitor the change in the California state prison population, including the demographic and criminal characteristics, as low-level offenders are diverted from state prison to incarceration in local facilities. The California Department of Corrections and Rehabilitation publishes weekly updates on the progress of PSR on their website: http://www.cdcr.ca.gov/Reports_Research/Offender_Information_Services_Branch/Population_Reports.html.

TABLE 3
Admissions, releases, and yearend sentenced population in California state prisons, December 31, 2000–2011

	Admissions			Releases			Yearend sentenced population		
Year	Total[a]	New court commitments	Parole violators[b]	Total[c]	Conditional[d]	Unconditional[e]	Total	Male	Female
2000	129,640	40,277	89,363	129,621	122,393	3,145	160,412	149,815	10,597
2001	126,895	37,923	88,972	129,982	122,887	3,522	157,295	147,758	9,537
2002	124,179	38,605	85,574	119,683	114,211	3,444	159,984	150,374	9,610
2003	125,312	43,413	81,899	118,646	112,445	3,110	162,678	152,385	10,293
2004	123,537	46,812	76,725	117,762	114,860	2,705	164,933	154,051	10,882
2005	129,559	48,597	80,962	121,730	119,485	2,030	168,982	157,704	11,278
2006	138,523	48,640	89,883	130,060	127,817	1,994	173,942	162,361	11,581
2007	139,608	46,980	92,628	135,920	133,776	1,925	172,856	161,551	11,305
2008	140,827	46,380	94,447	136,925	134,974	1,759	172,583	161,220	11,363
2009	129,705	44,926	84,779	128,869	126,841	1,796	170,131	159,396	10,735
2010	118,943	41,521	77,422	121,918	119,941	1,728	164,213	154,450	9,763
2011	96,669	36,376	60,293	109,467	95,541	13,676	149,025	140,972	8,053
Percent change									
Average annual, 2000–2010	-0.8%	0.3%	-1.3%	-0.6%	-0.2%	-5.4%	0.2%	0.3%	-0.7%
2010–2011	-18.7	-12.4	-22.1	-10.2	-20.3	691.4	-9.2	-8.7	-17.5

Note: Counts are based on prisoners with a sentence of more than 1 year.
[a]Excludes transfers, escapes, and those absent without leave (AWOL). Includes other conditional release violators, returns from appeal or bond, and other admissions.
[b]Includes all conditional release violators returned to prison for violations of conditions of release or for new crimes.
[c]Excludes transfers, escapes, and those absent without leave (AWOL). Includes other conditional release violators, returns from appeal or bond, and other admissions.
[d]Includes releases to probation, supervised mandatory releases, and other unspecified conditional releases.
[e]Includes expirations of sentence, communtations, and other unconditional releases.
Source: Bureau of Justice Statistics, National Prisoner Statistics Program, 2000–2011.

TABLE 4
Admissions of sentenced offenders to California state prisons, by quarter and offense type, 2010–2011

		Violent		Property		Drugs		Public-order	
Date of admission	Total[a,b,c]	Number	Percent	Number	Percent	Number	Percent	Number	Percent
Total admissions in 2010	117,674	35,639	30.3%	38,260	32.5%	29,105	24.7%	13,728	11.7%
Quarter 1	29,041	8,558	29.5	9,483	32.7	7,452	25.7	3,333	11.5
Quarter 2	30,521	9,144	30.0	9,954	32.6	7,654	25.1	3,499	11.5
Quarter 3	30,004	9,156	30.5	9,736	32.4	7,350	24.5	3,533	11.8
Quarter 4	28,108	8,781	31.2	9,087	32.3	6,649	23.7	3,363	12.0
Total admissions in 2011	95,814	30,538	31.9%	30,295	31.6%	22,058	23.0%	12,026	12.6%
Quarter 1	29,016	9,103	31.4	9,381	32.3	6,732	23.2	3,554	12.2
Quarter 2	29,431	9,159	31.1	9,324	31.7	7,018	23.8	3,690	12.5
Quarter 3	27,065	8,105	29.9	8,935	33.0	6,426	23.7	3,341	12.3
Quarter 4	10,302	4,171	40.5	2,655	25.8	1,882	18.3	1,441	14.0

[a]Counts are based on prisoners with a sentence of more than 1 year.
[b]Analysis based on National Corrections Reporting Program administrative data. These data may vary slightly from NPS data because of collection differences.
[c]Includes other and unspecified offenses.
Source: Bureau of Justice Statistics, National Corrections Reporting Program, 2010–2011.

Overcrowding leads to serious deprivation of inmate rights, an issue that spurs litigation as well as threats of a federal takeover (McShane, 1996). Mark Jones (cited in W. C. Jones, 2009) supports this statement in his claim that reducing meals and exceeding the capacities of prisons can result in prisoner unrest and increased violence and in federal court intervention. High inmate-to-staff ratios, lack of mental health or medical care, or programs too full to produce meaningful treatment or education are legitimate indications of deprivations in quality of life. Space and privacy are always conditions inmates are concerned about, and when too many inmates are housed together, tensions rise and chances of violence increase, not to mention administrators begin to see the types of problems in staff turnover, burnout, job dissatisfaction, and lowered motivation discussed earlier.

In the context of service quality, corrections is a process that is meant to add value to the offenders by enabling them to serve their punishment, receive treatment, and assimilate into society like regular citizens. Although recidivism is not the only indicator of effectiveness in corrections, we have to consider that 12% of parolees were returned to prison in 2011 (Maruschak & Parks, 2012), so there may be a potential service failure in corrections. To revisit a previous example, if an individual goes for a haircut that is not properly performed, the person may have to return to get the problem fixed. The hair stylist should not charge for the second visit to get the problem rectified. The stylist is losing time to fix the error that was committed when the stylist provided a poor service the first time. This extra time and the resources spent by the hair stylist in fixing the error are a loss of profit to the stylist. Taguchi and Clausing (1990) would define this loss of time and resources in fixing the problem as a loss to society; these resources could have been used for better purposes. Increased recidivism, likewise, can be interpreted as a loss to society. Thinking proactively about the design of modern prisons, jails, and detention centers that better serve the changing needs of society may result in reduced recidivism. Ross (2006) suggests the use of dormitory-style housing in lower-security facilities because it is less expensive and allows for more freedom, autonomy, and a personalized atmosphere for the inmate. This may allow inmates to feel less anxiety and frustration as they serve time in a facility. Although there are safety concerns with dormitories, Ross claims that most inmates can succeed in dormitory-style living arrangements. As pointed out previously, another approach to improved service quality in prisons is through staff recruitment, training, and retention. Finding ways to motivate correctional officers, who in turn can better serve their customers (the offenders), could lead to reduced recidivism. Accreditation standards support these changes. Of course, not all of the responsibility for recidivism lies in corrections. Community members are responsible for reintegrating offenders into the community by providing for their needs once they are released from prison. Failure on either side can lead to reinstitutionalization.

Chapter Summary

- Correctional institutions have existed as long as individuals have been deviant. Originally, they used torture and mutilation to change behaviors. Currently, inmates are, for the most part, protected inside correctional institutions. Deterrence, rehabilitation, retribution, and punishment are the goals of corrections.

- Incarceration rates have greatly increased, and overcrowding is one of the biggest issues facing prisons.
- Classification systems that assess the needs and risks of offenders are used in determining where an inmate should reside and which services the inmate should receive. Those with the highest needs and greatest risk reside in the securest facilities and receive the greatest number of services.
- Correctional institutions may be run by local governments, state governments, or the federal government. The institutions are classified as minimum-, medium-, and maximum-security levels. Super-maximum-security prisons house the most violent or dangerous offenders. Other correctional institutions include secure housing facilities, halfway houses, adult transitional facilities, administrative maximum facilities, and youth detention facilities. The trend today is toward specialized facilities that house inmates with mental or psychological needs, women, youth, and so on.
- All penal institutions have paramilitary structures with top-down communication. Hierarchies within the facilities are clearly defined, and policies and procedures are created by administrators and passed down to the line staff. Divisions within the institution include the administration, the security and custody division, and the program and treatment services division.
- Private prisons also exist in the United States. They typically contract bed space to state or federal governments to house inmates for whom there is no space in public facilities (because of overcrowding). Private companies can offer higher wages, faster hiring processes, and better employment packages to staff. However, retirement and benefits packages are generally not as good as those offered by the government.
- Jails are local institutions that house inmates for short periods of time. They have changed drastically over the years, as documented in discussions of first-, second-, and third-generation jails. Jails are also closed systems with paramilitary structures. They are plagued by high inmate turnover, overcrowding, and inmate health issues.
- Juvenile detention centers are similar to local jails. They house youth for short periods of time as they await trial or are being transferred to another facility. Both private and public youth detention centers vary in size and types of programs offered.
- Staff recruitment, training, burnout, and retention; motivation and discipline; budgeting and planning; and overcrowding are a few of the issues plaguing corrections institutions. Others include accreditation, diseases, and quality-of-life concerns.
- Accreditation, reducing overcrowding and recidivism, meeting new standards in structure, and motivating and training staff may be the best service quality approaches correctional facilities can take.

Chapter Review Questions

1. Identify five major issues facing U.S. prisons today.

2. Why might a state not want to use private prisons to house inmates? What managerial and administrative issues might a state face if inmates were placed in private prisons? How might service quality and delivery differ in a private prison as compared to a public prison?

3. You serve as a warden of a medium-security facility. Officer Corrick, who has worked in the facility for three years, comes to your office one day. He says that he's thinking about applying to a position in another career field. According to Corrick, he feels depressed and as though he isn't moving ahead in his career. Corrick is one of your best officers. Do you think this is an indication of officer burnout? What would you say to Corrick? How might you encourage Corrick to remain employed with the facility?

4. How can prisons better adapt the quality service approach to inmate management and officer training? How can they incorporate open-systems approaches in their facilities?

CASE STUDY

As the chief detention officer of Hope Youth Facility, you oversee approximately 450 delinquent youth and 82 staff members. The workforce includes detention correctional staff, programming staff, and educational staff. You have an assistant chief detention officer who works directly under you and supervises the majority of the custody and security staff. You focus your efforts primarily on the distributors and vendors and the training and education of employees.

You provided a training two weeks ago on relationships in the workplace. In the training you cautioned employees from developing romantic relationships with one another and with the youth under their control. You also provided a written policy to every administrator and officer working at the facility that forbids sexual and romantic contact with inmates.

Today, a young lady who has been employed with the center for about six months comes to your office. Currently, she works the evening shift on Friday, Saturday, and Sunday nights and attends college full-time during the week. The young lady says that she has information about a relationship between a correctional officer and a 16-year-old juvenile housed in the center. She felt that she had to disclose the information to you after attending the training you provided. The young lady proceeds to tell you a seasoned female correctional officer has been romantically and sexually involved with a male youth currently housed in the facility. According to her, the relationship began before the youth was incarcerated but has continued while the youth has been in the care of the facility. She claimed that she told the assistant chief detention officer a couple of months ago, who said he would handle it, but the relationship has continued. Once the conversation was finished, you immediately called the assistant chief detention officer. The assistant chief confirmed that he was aware of the relationship. He stated that he had intended to speak with the female correctional officer but had been busy with other disciplinary issues and "had let it slip through the cracks." He then made a joke about the fact that it was a female officer sexually involved with a male offender rather than the other way around. You were completely surprised by his nonchalant attitude and the inappropriateness of the joke. You told him to follow up immediately with the female correctional officer and that you wanted to see him and her in your office the next morning. You also planned a meeting with the incarcerated youth.

Questions for Review

1. What are the issues involved in this case? What liability do you have in the situation? What about the facility as a whole? The county? The state?

2. What could you have done differently in this case as an administrator responsible for children?

3. Was quality service delivered in this case? How can facilities ensure quality service when youth are a vulnerable population in prison facilities?

Internet Resources

Bureau of Justice Statistics—http://www.bjs.gov

Corrections Corporation of America (CCA)—http://cca.com

National Institute of Justice—http://nij.gov

References and Suggested Readings

Alabama: Ex-officer sues for inmate offenses. (2002, February 15). *Corrections Digest, 33*(7), 5.

Alabama needs 71% budget increase to avert federal control of prisons. (2002, December 13). *Corrections Digest, 33*(50), 1.

American Correctional Association. (1990). *Standards for adult correctional institutions.* Laurel, MD: Author.

Andrews, A. A., Bonta, J., & Hoge, R. (1990). Classification for effective rehabilitation: Rediscovering psychology. *Criminal Justice and Behavior, 17*(1), 19–52.

Applegate, B., & Paoline, E. (2007). Jail officers' perceptions of the work environment in traditional versus new generation facilities. *American Journal of Criminal Justice, 31*(2), 64–80. doi:10.1007/s12103-007-9005-z

Archambeault, W., & Archambeault, B. (1982). *Correctional supervisory management: Principles of organization, policy, and law.* Englewood Cliffs, NJ: Prentice Hall.

Austin, J., & Coventry, G. (2001). *Emerging issues on privatized prisons.* Washington, DC: U.S. Department of Justice, Bureau of Justice Statistics.

Baker, N., & Carrere, M. (2007). Unlocking the door to relationship-based corrections recruitment. *Corrections Today, 69*(1), 36–39.

Beck, A. J., & Hughes, T. A. (2005). *Sexual violence reported by correctional authorities, 2004.* Washington, DC: U.S. Department of Justice, Office of Justice Statistics.

Beiser, V. (2003, October 19). A necessary evil? *Los Angeles Times.* Retrieved from http://www.supermaxed.com/Beiser-Pelican.htm.

Bench, L. L., & Allen, T. D. (2003). Investigating the stigma of prison classification: An experimental design. *The Prison Journal, 83*(4), 367–382.

Berk, R. A., Ladd, H., Graziano, H., & Baek, J. (2003). A randomized experiment testing inmate classification systems. *Criminology and Public Policy, 2*(2), 213–215.

Bohlander, G., & Snell, S. (2007). *Managing human resources.* Mason, OH: Thompson South-Western.

Bonner, R., & Vandecreek, L. D. (2006). Ethical decision making for correctional mental health providers. *Criminal Justice and Behavior, 33*(4), 542–564.

Briggs, C. S., Sundt, J. L., & Castellano, T. C. (2003). The effect of super maximum security on aggregate levels of institutional violence. *Criminology, 41*(4), 1341–1377.

Briscoe, W., Forh, C., Haynes, V., & Wheeler, B. (2004). Minority recruitment for the 21st century. *Corrections Today, 66*(5), 128–130.

Camp, C. G., & Camp, G. M. (1997). *The corrections yearbook 1997.* South Salem, NY: Criminal Justice Institute.

Camp, S. C., & Gaes, G. G. (2001). *Growth and quality of the U.S. private prisons: Evidence from a national survey.* Washington, DC: Federal Bureau of Prisons, Office of Research.

Camp, S. D., & Langan, N. P. (2005). Perceptions about minority and female opportunities for job advancement: Are beliefs about equal opportunity fixed? *The Prison Journal, 85*(4), 399–419.

CareerOverview. (2007). *Correctional officer careers, jobs, and training information.* Retrieved from http://www.careeroverview.com/corrections-officer-careers.html.

Carson, E. A., & Golinelli, D. (2013). Prisoners in 2012—advance counts. U.S. Department of Justice. Bureau of Justice Statistics. Retrieved from http://www.bjs.gov/content/pub/pdf/p12ac.pdf.

Carson, E. A., & Sabol, W. J. (2012, December). Prisoners in 2011. U.S. Department of Justice, Office of Justice Programs. Retrieved from http://www.bjs.gov/content/pub/pdf/p11.pdf.

Chambliss, W. (2011). *Corrections: Key issues in crime and punishment.* Thousand Oaks, CA: Sage.

Champion, D. J. (1998). *Criminal justice in the United States* (2nd ed.). Chicago, IL: Nelson-Hall.

Christensen, G. E. (2006, May/June). Fixing our system of corrections: Communicating to improve offender outcomes. *Community Corrections Report on Law and Corrections Practice, 13*(4).

Chunn, G. C. (2003). Correctional women's issues: Items to remember in the future. *Corrections Today, 67*(6), 76–78.

Civil Rights Act, 42 U.S.C. § 1983 (1871).

Clark, M. T. (2004). New Jersey Supreme Court upholds $1.6 million harassment verdict. *Prison Legal News, 15*(5), 22.

Cooper v. Pate, 378 U.S. 546 (1964).

Correctional Services Corp v. Malesko, 534 U.S. 61 (2001).

Corrections Center of Northwest Ohio. (2009). *Welcome to the corrections center of northwest Ohio.* Retrieved from http://www.ccnoregionaljail.org/newgenerationjail.htm.

Corrections Corporation of America. (2008). About CCA. Retrieved from http://www.cca.com/about.

Cox, S. M., Allen, J. M., Hanser, R., & Conrad, J. (2014). *Juvenile justice: A guide to theory, policy and practice* (6th ed.). Thousand Oaks, CA: Sage.

Cox, S. M., & Wade, J. (2002). *The criminal justice network: An introduction* (4th ed.). Boston, MA: McGraw-Hill.

Craddock, A. (1996). Classification systems. In M. D. Shane (Ed.), *Encyclopedia of American prisons* (pp. 87–95). New York, NY: Garland.

Cropsey, K. L., Wexler, H. K., Melnick, G., Taxman, F. S., & Young, D. W. (2007). Specialized prisons and services: Results from a national survey. *The Prison Journal, 87*(3), 58–85.

Deckert, A., & Wood, W. R. (2011). Prison privatization and contract facilities. In W. J. Chambliss (Ed.), *Corrections: Key issues in crime and punishment.* Thousand Oaks, CA: Sage.

Deitch, M. (2010). Distinguishing the various functions of effective prison oversight. *Pace Law Review, 30*(5), 1438–1445.

Denton County Sheriff's Office. (2007a). *Jail administration.* Retrieved from http://sheriff.dentoncounty .com/main.asp?Dept=54&Link=510.

Denton County Sheriff's Office. (2007b). *Sheriff.* Retrieved from http://sheriff.dentoncounty.com/main .asp?Dept=54.

Dignam, J., Barrera, M., & West, S. (1986). Occupational stress, social support, and burnout among correctional officers. *American Journal of Community Psychology, 14*, 177–193.

Drory, A., & Shamir, B. (1988). Effects of organizational and life variables on job satisfaction and burnout. *Group and Organization Studies, 13*, 441–455.

Edwards, C. R. (2007). Developing student interest in corrections: A role for universities and correctional organizations. *Corrections Today, 69*(1), 40–43.

Egger, D. (2006, May 4). Moussaoui headed for "Alcatraz of the Rockies." Washingtonpost.com. Retrieved from http://www.msnbc.msn.com/id/12636492.

Ertel, K. (2005). Warden's consensual affair created hostile prison workplace. *Trial, 41*(10), 78.

Federal Bureau of Prisons. (n.d.a). *Female offender programs.* Retrieved from http://www.bop.gov/inmate_ programs/female.jsp.

Federal Bureau of Prisons. (n.d.b). *Juveniles in the Bureau.* Retrieved from http://www.bop.gov/inmate_ programs/juveniles.jsp.

Federal Bureau of Prisons. (n.d.c). *Prison types and general information.* Retrieved from http://www.bop .gov/locations/institutions/index.jsp.

Federal Bureau of Prisons. (n.d.d). *Quick facts about the Bureau of Prisons.* Retrieved from http://www.bop .gov/about/index.jsp.

Federal Bureau of Prisons. (n.d.e). *Prison types and general information.* Retrieved from http://www.bop .gov/locations/institutions/index.jsp.

Florida nurses net $1 million for sexual harassment by prisoners. (2007). *Prison Legal News, 18*(8), 26.

Friedman, L. M. (1993). *Crime and punishment in American history.* New York, NY: Basic Books.

Garland, B. (2004). The impact of administrative support on prison treatment staff burnout: An exploratory study. *The Prison Journal, 84*(4), 452–471.

Georgia Department of Corrections. (n.d.). Transitional centers. Retrieved from http://www.dcor.state.ga .us/Divisions/Corrections/Transitional.html.

Glaze, L. E., & Maruschak, L. M. (2008). Parents in prison and their minor children. Bureau of Justice Statistics Special Report, U.S. Department of Justice, Office of Justice Statistics. Retrieved from, http://bjs.gov/content/pub/pdf/pptmc.pdf.

Gould, D. D., Watson, S. L., Price, S. R., & Valliant, P. M. (2013). The relationship between burnout and coping in adult and young offender center correctional officers: An exploratory investigation. *Psychological Services, 10*(1), 37–47. doi:10.1037/a0029655

Greenberg, E., Dunleavy, E., & Kutner, M. (2007). *Literacy behind bars: Results from the 2003 National Assessment of Adult Literacy Prison Survey.* Washington, DC: U.S. Department of Education, National Center for Education Sciences.

Hansen, R. D. (2002). Inmate suicide in prisons: An analysis of legal liability under 42 USC section 1983. *The Prison Journal, 82*(12), 459–477.

Harrison, P. M., & Beck, A. J. (2006a). *Prison and jail inmates at midyear, 2005.* Washington, DC: U.S. Department of Justice, Bureau of Justice Statistics.

Harrison, P. M., & Beck, A. J. (2006b). *Prisoners in 2005.* Washington, DC: U.S. Department of Justice, Bureau of Justice Statistics.

Hartney, C. (2006). U.S. rates of incarceration: A global perspective. *Fact Sheet, Research from the National Council on Crime and Delinquency.* Retrieved from http://www.nccd-crc.org/nccd/pubs/2006nov_factsheet_incarceration.pdf.

Holcomb, D. (2006). The Kentucky DOC stands out among others. *Corrections Today, 68*(3), 14–15.

Holsinger, A. M., Lowenkamp, C. T., & Latessa, E. L. (2006). Predicting institutional misconduct using the youth level of service/care case management. *American Journal of Criminal Justice, 30*(2), 267–286.

Illinois Department of Corrections. (2012a). *Decatur Correctional Center.* Retrieved from http://www2.illinois.gov/idoc/facilities/Pages/decaturcorrectionalcenter.aspx.

Illinois Department of Corrections. (2012b). *Dixon Correctional Center.* Retrieved from http://www2.illinois.gov/idoc/facilities/Pages/dixoncorrectionalcenter.aspx.

Illinois Department of Corrections. (2012c). *Menard Correctional Center.* Retrieved from http://www2.illinois.gov/idoc/facilities/Pages/menardcorrectionalcenter.aspx

Illinois Department of Corrections. (2012d). *Pinckneyville Correctional Center.* Retrieved from www2.illinois.gov/idoc/facilities/Pages/pinckneyvillecorrectionalcenter.aspx.

Illinois Department of Corrections. (2012e). *Vienna Correctional Center.* Retrieved from http://www2.illinois.gov/idoc/facilities/Pages/pinckneyvillecorrectionalcenter.aspx.

Iowa will furlough officers, trim care. (2002, July 19). *Corrections Digest, 33*(29), 2.

Johnston, N. (n.d.). *Prison reform in Pennsylvania.* Philadelphia, PA: The Pennsylvania Prison Society. Retrieved from http://www.prisonsociety.org/about/history.shtml.

Jones, W. C. (2009, July 10). Budget cuts in Georgia prisons. *The Florida Times-Union.* Retrieved from http://jacksonville.com/news/georgia/2009-07-0/story/budget_cuts_in_georgia_prisons.

Keinan, G., & Maslach-Pines, A. (2007). Stress and burnout among prison personnel: Sources, outcomes, and intervention strategies. *Criminal Justice and Behavior, 34*, 380–398.

Kentucky jail frees 30 in budget squeeze. (2002, October 4). *Corrections Digest, 33*(39), 3.

Kerle, K. (2002). Recruitment and retention. *American Jails, 16*(3), 5.

Kimball, L. S., & Nink, C. E. (2006). How to improve employee motivation, commitment, productivity, well-being, and safety. *Corrections Today, 68*(3), 66–71.

Lachance-McCullough, M. L., & Tesoriero, J. M. (1996). AIDS. In M. D. Shane (Ed.), *Encyclopedia of American prisons* (pp. 12–20). New York, NY: Garland.

Lambert, E., Hogan, N. L., Cheeseman, K., Shanhe, D., Jiang, S., & Khondaker, M. I. (2012). Is the job burning me out? An exploratory test of the job characteristics model on the emotional burnout of prison staff. *The Prison Journal, 92*(1), 3–23. doi:10.1177/0032885511428794

Lambert, E., Hogan, N., Jiang, S., & Jenkins, M. (2009). I am fried: The issues of stressors and burnout among correctional staff. *Corrections Compendium, 34*(2), 16–23.

Lambert, S., & Regan, D. (2001). *Great jobs for criminal justice majors.* New York, NY: McGraw-Hill.

Langan, P., & Levin, D. (2002). *Recidivism of prisoners released in 1994* (Bureau of Justice Statistics Special Report). U.S. Department of Justice. Retrieved from http://www.ojp .usdoj.gov/bjs/pub/pdf/rpr94.pdf.

Lenz, N. (2002). "Luxuries" in prison: The relationship between amenity funding and public support. *Crime & Delinquency, 48*(4), 499–525.

Lommel, J. (2004). Turning around turnover. *Corrections Today, 66*(5), 54–58.

Lukemeyer, A., & McCorkle, R. C. (2006). Privatization of prisons. *American Review of Public Administration, 36*(2), 189–206.

Magaletta, P. R., Patry, M. W., Dietz, E. F., & Ax, R. K. (2007). What is correctional about clinical practice in corrections? *Criminal Justice and Behavior, 34*(1), 7–21.

Maguire, K., & Pastore, A. L. (1995). *Bureau of Justice Statistics sourcebook of criminal justice statistics, 1994.* Albany, NY: Hindelang Criminal Justice Research Center.

Maruschak, L. M., & Parks, E. (2012). Probation and parole in the United States, 2011. U.S. Department of Justice. Office of Justice Programs. Bureau of Justice Statistics. Retrieved from http://www.bjs.gov/content/pub/pdf/ppus11.pdf.

McCampbell, S. W. (2006). Recruiting and retaining jail employees: Money isn't the long-term solution. *American Jails, 20*(2), 9.

McDevitt, D. S. (1999a). Commonsense leaders. *Law and Order, 47*(8), 95–97.

McDevitt, D. S. (1999b). Ineffective management strategies and why managers use them. *Law and Order, 47*(7), 143–146.

McDonald, D., Fournier, E., Russell-Einhourn, M., & Crawford, S. (1998). *Private prisons in the United States: Executive summary.* Cambridge, MA: Abt Associates Inc.

McDonald, D., & Patten, C. (2004). *Governments' management of private prisons.* National Institute of Justice. Retrieved from https://www.ncjrs.gov/pdffiles1/nij/grants/203968.pdf.

McKinley, J. C. (2007, December 31). In prison, toddlers serve time with Mom. The *New York Times.* Retrieved from http://www.nytimes.com/2007/12/31/world/americas/31mexico.html.

McShane, M. D. (1996). Crowding. In M. D. Shane (Ed.), *Encyclopedia of American prisons* (pp. 134–137). New York, NY: Garland.

McShane, M. D., & Williams, F. P. (1996). Administration. In M. D. Shane (Ed.), *Encyclopedia of American prisons* (pp. 4–8). New York, NY: Garland.

McVey, C. C., & McVey, R. T. (2005). Responding to today's workforce: Attracting, retaining, and developing the new generation of workers. *Corrections Today, 67*(7), 80–84.

Michigan Civil Service Commission. (2007). *Job specification: Deputy prison warden.* Retrieved from http://www.michigan.gov/documents/DeputyPrisonWarden_12528_7.pdf.

Minneci v. Pollard, 132 S. Ct. 617–2012

Minton, T. D. (2013, May). Jail inmates at midyear 2012—Statistical tables. U.S. Department of Justice, Bureau of Justice Statistics. Retrieved from http://www.bjs.gov/content/pub/pdf/jim12st.pdf.

Mumola, C. J. (2000). *Bureau of Justice Statistics special report: Incarcerated parents and their children.* Washington, DC: U.S. Department of Justice, Office of Justice Statistics.

National Association for the Advancement of Colored People. (2013). Criminal justice fact sheet. Retrieved from http://www.naacp.org/pages/criminal-justice-fact-sheet.

Nebraska Department of Correctional Services. (n.d.). *Administrative regulation number 116.01: Department of correctional services state of Nebraska: Inmate rights.* Retrieved from http://www.corrections.state .ne.us/policies/files/ar116.01.pdf.

Nevada seeks emergency modular units to avert federal intervention. (2007, February 23). *Corrections Digest, 38*(8), 1.

Officer wins harassment case. (1999, April 6). *Corrections Digest, 30*(23), 4–6.

$1.18 million in Santa Clara County sexual assault/harassment suit. (2001). *Prison Legal News, 12*(3), 30.

Paoline, E., & Lambert, E. (2012). The issue of control in jail: The effects of professionalism, detainee control, and administrative support on job stress, job satisfaction, and organizational commitment among jail staff. *American Journal of Criminal Justice, 37*(2), 179–199. doi:10.1007/s12103-011-9128-0

Parrish, D. (2006). Jails are not what they used to be. *Corrections Today, 68*(1), 6.

Pollock, J. M. (2002). Parenting programs in women's prisons. *Women & Criminal Justice, 14*(1), 131–154.

Rader, N. (2005). Surrendering solidarity: Considering the relationship among female corrections officers. *Women and Criminal Justice, 16*(3), 27–42.

Rampant sexual favoritism by California prison warden is actionable under hostile work environment theory. (2006). *Prison Legal News, 17*(6), 18.

Richardson v. McKnight, 521 U.S. 410 (1997).

Ross, C. (2006). Building a better prison. *Consulting-Specifying Engineer, 39*(4), 30–36.

Roth, M. P. (2005). Crime and punishment: A history of the criminal justice system. Belmont, CA: Thomson Wadsworth.

Sabol, W. J., Couture, H., & Harrison, P. (2007). *Prisoners in 2006.* Washington, DC: U.S. Department of Justice, Office of Justice Statistics.

Sabol, W. J., Minton, T. D., & Harrison, P. M. (2007). Prison and jail inmates at midyear 2006. *Bureau of Justice Statistics Bulletin.* Retrieved from http://www.ojp.usdoj.gov/bjs/pub/pdf/pjim06.pdf.

Sanders, W. B. (1974). Some early beginnings of the children's court movement in England. In F. L. Faust & P. J. Brantingham (Eds.), *Juvenile justice philosophy* (pp. 72–117). St. Paul, MN: West.

Santos, M. G. (2004). *About prison.* Belmont, CA: Thomson Wadsworth.

Schuster, H. (Producer). (2007, October 14). *60 Minutes* [television broadcast]. New York, NY: CBS.

Sexual harassment case settled. (1999). *Corrections Digest, 30*(51), 4.

Shamir, B., & Drory, A. (1982). Occupational tedium among prison officers. *Criminal Justice and Behavior, 9,* 79–99.

Stephan, J. (2008). *Census of state and federal correctional facilities, 2005.* U.S. Department of Justice, Bureau of Justice Statistics. Retrieved from http://www.bjs.gov/content/pub/pdf/csfcf05.pdf.

Stinchcomb, J. B. (2007). Strategic guidelines for development in the 21st century work force. *Corrections Today, 69*(1), 72–74.

Stinchcomb, J. B., & Fox, V. B. (1999). *Introduction to corrections.* Upper Saddle River, NJ: Prentice Hall.

Taguchi, G., & Clausing, D. (1990, January/February). Robust quality. *Harvard Business Review, 68*(1), 65–76.

Thomas, M. (2007, November). Black and minority ethnic prison officers' experience within HM prison service. *Prison Service Journal, 174,* 27–31.

Turner v. Safley, 482 US 78 - 1987.

U.S. Department of Justice. (2004). *Data collections for the Prison Rape Elimination Act of 2003.* Washington, DC: Author. Retrieved from http://www.ojp.usdoj.gov/bjs/pub/pdf/dcprea03.pdf.

U.S. Equal Employment Opportunity Commission. (2008a). *Policy guidance on current issues of sexual harassment.* Retrieved from http://www.eeoc.gov/policy/docs/currentissues.html.

U.S. Equal Employment Opportunity Commission. (2008b). *Sexual harassment.* Retrieved from http://www.eeoc.gov/types/sexual_harassment.html.

Useem, B., & Piehl, A. M. (2006). Prison buildup and disorder. *Punishment & Society, 8*(1), 87–115.

Ward, D. A., & Werlich, T. G. (2003). Alcatraz and Marion: Evaluating super-maximum custody. *Punishment & Society, 5*(1), 53–75.

West v. Atkins, 108 S Ct 2250 (1988).

Whitehead, J. (1989). *Burnout in probation and corrections.* New York, NY: Praeger.

Woolredge, J. (2003). Keeping pace with evolving prison populations for effective management. *Criminology & Public Policy, 2*(2), 253.

13

Security Management*

LEARNING OBJECTIVES

Upon completion of this chapter, students should be able to do the following:

- Discuss the development of private security
- Understand the relationship between law enforcement and security organizations as well as the issues between the two agencies
- Know the various organizational types of security—contract, inhouse, etc.
- Understand the problems associated with the professionalization of the security industry
- Identify how the quality service approach is used in the security industry

Although this text is primarily focused on public, nonprofit organizations in the criminal justice system and the services they provide, the security industry is extremely important and influential in the everyday activities of criminal justice personnel. Most people know very little about the private policing industry, yet it is three times larger than the public policing sector and the largest provider of policing services in the United States (Joh, 2004, p. 49). The security industry traditionally consists of for-profit organizations and historically has operated separately from the criminal

---

*This chapter is, in part, a summary of printed material found in the following resource: *Introduction to Security* (9th ed.), by R. Fischer, E. Halibozek, and D. Walters, 2012, Waltham, MA: Elsevier. The information has been reprinted with permission from the publisher. A special thanks is given to Robert Fischer for his writing of the majority of the chapter.

justice system. The security industry has been a response to, and a reflection of, a changing society, mirroring not only its social structure but also its economic conditions, its perception of law and crime, and its morality. Thus, security remains a field of both tradition and dramatic change. One such change occurred after the terrorist attacks on September 11, 2001. Since the nation's critical infrastructures—such as electricity, water, and banking—rely on private agencies for protection, private security companies have become more involved with the federal government and the various components of the criminal justice system in the fight against crime and terrorism. Now, there are partnerships in information sharing and management and, in light of the currently failing economy, in securing economic, social, and business structures. Companies in the United States rely on private security for a wide range of functions, such as protecting employees and property, conducting investigations and preemployment screening, providing information technology security, and protecting intellectual property and sensitive corporate information (Strom, Berzofsky, Shook-Sa, Barrick, Daye, Horstmann, & Kinney, 2010). The introduction of high-tech systems and computers has also changed the nature of the job of the 21st-century security professional. Strom et al. (2010, pp. 2–3) reported that a 2009 American Society of Industrial Security (ASIS) symposium identified 18 core elements of security:

1. Physical security

2. Personnel security

3. Information systems security

4. Investigations

5. Loss prevention

6. Risk management

7. Legal aspects

8. Emergency and contingency planning

9. Fire protection

10. Crisis management

11. Disaster management

12. Counterterrorism

13. Competitive intelligence

14. Executive protection

15. Violence in the workplace

16. Crime prevention

17. Crime prevention through environmental design (CPTED)

18. Security architecture and engineering

As the events on September 11, 2001, and the ongoing work performed by security personnel bring to light, security today must be directed toward modern problems.

This chapter will briefly discuss the history of the security industry (although it is best covered in a full introduction to security text), the problems facing the industry, and the aftermath of September 11, 2001. The cooperative endeavors of private security agencies in working with public entities will also be addressed, as will the managerial approaches used in the security field.

Development of Private Security

The development of police and security forces occurred as a response to public pressure. Because of the slow development of public state and federal law enforcement agencies and the steady escalation of crime in an increasingly urban and industrialized society, what might be considered the first professional private security responses occurred in the second half of the 19th century.

In the 1850s, Allan Pinkerton, a "copper" (police officers were identified by the copper badges they wore) from Scotland, who eventually became the Chicago Police Department's first detective, established the first private security operation in the United States, known as Pinkerton. Pinkerton's North West Police Agency, formed in 1855, provided security and conducted investigations of crimes for various railroads. Two years later, the Pinkerton Protection Patrol began to offer a private watchman service for railroad yards and industrial concerns. President Lincoln recognized Pinkerton's organizational skills and hired the agency to perform intelligence duties during the U.S. Civil War (Levine, 1963). This may well be considered the first collaborative project between private and public law enforcement agencies.

Also in the 1850s, Henry Wells and William Fargo were partners in the American Express Company, which was chartered to operate a freight service east of the Mississippi River. By 1852, they had expanded their operating charter westward as Wells Fargo and Company.

Washington Perry Brink in Chicago founded Brinks, Inc., in 1859, as a freight and package delivery service. More than 30 years later, in 1891, he transported his first payroll, which was the beginning of armored car and courier services. By 1900, Brinks had a fleet of 85 wagons in the field (Kakalik & Wildhorn, 1971). Adams Express was founded by Alvin Adams in 1840 as an independent postal express service. By 1854, it was a limited stock company with a number of entities. Adams Express specialized more in packages containing valuables than in letters (Hahn, 1990). Brinks, Wells Fargo, and Adams Express were the first major firms to offer security for the transportation of valuables and money.

William J. Burns, a former Secret Service investigator and head of the Bureau of Investigation (forerunner of the Federal Bureau of Investigation [FBI]), started the William J. Burns Detective Agency in 1909. It became the sole investigating agency for the American Bankers' Association and grew to become the second-largest (after Pinkerton) contract guard and investigative service in the United States (Cunningham,

Strauchs, & Van Meter, 1990). For all intents and purposes, Pinkerton and Burns were the only national investigative bodies concerned with nonspecialized crimes in the country until the advent of the FBI, making private security forces even more invaluable.

Basically starting in the 1870s, only private agencies provided contract security services to industrial facilities across the country. In many cases, particularly around the end of the 19th century and during the Great Depression of the 1930s, the services were, to say the least, controversial. Both the Battle of Homestead in 1892, during which workers striking at that plant were shot and beaten by security forces (mentioned in Chapter 9), and the strikes in the automobile industry in the mid-1930s are examples of excesses from overzealous security operatives in relatively recent history. With few exceptions, proprietary, or inhouse, security forces hardly existed before the defense-related "plant protection" boom of the early 1940s.

By 1955, security took a major leap forward with the formation of the American Society for Industrial Security (ASIS). Today, the organization is the *American Society for Industrial Security International,* reflecting the global emphasis on security operations for private industries. For most practitioners, 1955 signifies the beginning of the modern age of security. Before 1955, there were no professional organizations of significance, no certifications, no college programs, and no cohesive body to advance the interests of the field.

It should be noted, though, that the impetus for modern private security effectively began in the 1940s with the creation of the federal Industrial Security Program (today named the Defense Industrial Security Program [DISP]), considered a subordinate command within the Department of Defense. Today, the National Industrial Security Program (NISP) is the nominal authority in the United States for managing the needs of private industry to access classified information. The *National Industrial Security Program's Operating Manual* (NISPOM/DoD 5220.22-M) currently consists of 11 chapters and 3 appendices, totaling 141 pages. The most recent (2006) revisions include the Intelligence Reform and Terrorism Prevention Act of 2004 and other changes taking effect since September 11, 2001 (see http://www.fas.org).

Today's changed climate of increased security services came as businesses undertook expanded operations that needed more protection. Retail establishments, hotels, restaurants, theaters, warehouses, trucking companies, industrial companies, hospitals, and other institutions and services were growing and facing a serious need to protect their property and personnel. Security officers were traditionally the first line of defense, but it was not long before that this important function was being overchallenged by the increasing complexity of fraud, arson, burglary, and other areas in which more sophisticated criminal practices began to prevail. Security consulting agencies and private investigation firms were created in growing numbers to handle these special types of cases. From among these, another large contractor emerged and joined the field alongside Pinkerton (now part of Securitas), Burns (a subsidiary of Borg Warner [Wells Fargo]), and Brinks. In 1954, George R. Wackenhut formed the Wackenhut Corporation (now known as G4S Secure Solutions) with three other former FBI agents. Baker Industries and Guardsmark have also joined the providers along with many regional firms located throughout the United States. The largest of all security providers in the 21st century is now Securitas Security Services USA, Inc.

Issues and Growth of Private Security

Anti–Vietnam War protests created an additional demand for security industries in the 1970s. Currently, the threat of terrorism against U.S. businesses throughout the world and the kidnapping by extremist groups of executives assigned outside the United States have also increased the need for expanded security services. Of final concern has been an increase in drugs and violence in the workplace and the terrorist attacks of September 11, 2001, on the World Trade Center and Pentagon (Cunningham et al., 1990). Each of these problems has shaped the security industry as seen today and has dramatically increased expenditures in the security field. Expenditures in private security exceeded $100 billion annually in 2000 (www.ilj.org), up from $66 billion in 1998 (Fischer, Halibozek, & Green, 2008). These expenditures continue to grow, with spending on home and security at $35 billion in 2001 and $69.1 billion in 2011 (Dancs, 2012). Security services employed more than 1 million officers in 2009 (U.S. Department of Labor, Bureau of Labor Statistics, 2012). According to Zalud (2002) of *Security* magazine, after the September 11, 2001, attack on the World Trade Center, 13% of respondents to the magazine's annual security survey indicated adding inhouse staff or hiring more security officers through an outside contract service as important endeavors. Obviously, the respondents followed through on these goals, since a 2005 employment trends report stated that 4,000 companies reported that 56.5% of security was handled by inhouse staff while 34.5% was handled by outside contractors, private firms, or other agencies (American Society for Industrial Security [ASIS] Foundation, 2005). With this growth have come profits, problems, and increasing needs for professionalism and quality services approaches.

Crime Trends and Security

According to a 2002 Brookings Institution report, the Enron and WorldCom scandals alone cost the U.S. economy approximately $37 billion to $42 billion off the gross domestic product during the first year. A 2002 joint conference of the National White Collar Crime Center and the Coalition for the Prevention of Economic Crime ("Funny Money," 2002) identified the following as the most serious of economic crime problems:

- Money laundering
- Identity fraud
- E-commerce crime
- Insurance crime
- Victim services
- Terrorism

The conclusion of the conference was that the amount of "dirty money" worldwide tops $3 trillion ("Funny Money," 2002) and is a problem for businesses and governments alike. Figures on business losses as a result of white-collar crimes and corporate crimes vary greatly because satisfactory measures of many crimes against business and industry have not yet been found and because much of the internal crime occurring is never reported to the police. It is instead handled through internal disciplinary action to avoid the bad publicity and management embarrassment that could result from exposing the business's lack of security controls. Nevertheless, such questions still exist as to why crimes against businesses are escalating. Security concerns remain rather constant for employee theft, property crime, and issues related to human safety. The newest problems revolve around fraud, computer crime, workplace violence, and terrorism. Governments, especially in developing countries, are finding that radical groups can easily create shell companies to launder money. These countries do not have the resources or the training and skills to track and stop the illegal activity. Consequently, they have to reach out to more sophisticated countries for assistance. If assistance is not provided, and as the crimes continue, the criminal groups become more willing to resort to violence to protect their profits and are more dangerous to the communities where they reside. As noted in In the News 13.1, President Alpha Conde of Guinea realizes the issues facing his country as a result of dirty money and needs the assistance of public and private security agencies in identifying criminal activity and working together to reduce it. He has requested the assistance of the Federal Bureau of Investigation (FBI) in the United States as well as help from other countries involved in the G8 (Canada, France, Germany, Italy, Japan, Russia, the USA, and the UK).

In the News 13.1
Help Us Follow the Dirty Money, Guinea Asks G8

(Reuters)—Guinea, one of Africa's poorest nations despite abundant natural resources, has urged the G8 to back its battle with corruption by helping trace shell companies used to hide crooked deals and track dirty money flows.

The resulting increased prosperity, President Alpha Conde said, would help stem growing radicalism in a region already threatened by unrest in Mali that has placed Guinea and its neighbours at risk of becoming conduits for drugs and guns.

Guinea has long been one of Africa's "geological scandals": the West African country has rich reserves of iron ore, gold, bauxite and other minerals, but little has been tapped and half its 10 million people live in poverty.

Speaking ahead of an annual G8 meeting expected to put the resources industry and transparency high on the agenda, Conde said Guinea needed logistical support from U.S., British and other governments and law enforcement agencies.

"Mining companies are . . . British, American, Canadian, Australian, and London's City and New York are the centres of capitalism. If we want to fight for transparency, we need the support of the G8," Conde told Reuters in London, before a discussion on transparency including other African leaders and British Prime Minister David Cameron on Saturday.

"There is no corruption without corrupters."

He also said Guinea might have to postpone a long-awaited parliamentary election scheduled for June 30 after opposition parties refused to register candidates.

A former Sorbonne law professor, Conde came to power in 2010 after half a century in opposition, promising to end decades of corruption and mismanagement. He has been supported by a raft of high-profile international advisers, including philanthropist George Soros and former British Prime Minister Tony Blair.

"We have limited means. We cannot follow shell companies in tax havens, so we need these big countries to help us find all the proof for payments and corruption," Conde said, adding Guinea's laws allowed it to annul corruptly obtained licences.

"Also, sometimes, firms tell us they made 10 of profit. If they say 10 in Guinea and 100 in England, we can pursue that."

Shell companies have frequently been blamed as tools in corrupt resources deals across Africa. Transparency activists say they are widely used to hide the ultimate beneficiaries, whether government officials or profiteering intermediaries.

As part of Conde's overhaul of the mining sector, Guinea is reviewing mining contracts, scrapping as many as 800 that had been lying fallow and scrutinizing those signed during what the government says was an era of opaque deals.

These include the license for the northern half of its giant Simandou iron ore deposit held by BSG Resources, the mining arm of Israeli billionaire Beny Steinmetz's business empire, and partner Vale (VALE5.SA).

The original concession, secured by BSGR just before the death of then-President Lansana Conte, has come under scrutiny. In April, FBI agents arrested a BSGR representative on charges of obstructing a criminal investigation, tampering with a witness and destroying records. BSGR has denied wrongdoing.

Conde declined to comment on the outcome of the review but welcomed the FBI's support.

"I believe in presuming innocence until guilt is proven," he said. "But it is very important that the FBI and the U.S. judicial system was able to obtain this evidence—we would never have been able to."

The Steinmetz case has generated much media interest and remains controversial for Guinea, whose critics say it suits the interests of the country's advisers. But Conde says the advice of international banks, law firms and others was indispensable.

"Negotiating without it would have been (like) heading straight for the slaughterhouse," he said.

Conde, a longtime advocate of African cooperation, called for greater regional collaboration on the infrastructure needed for tapping mineral resources, but also on security, describing as "embarrassing" France's intervention in the Malian crisis.

Among his major concerns, Conde said, was the flow of guns and drugs that once went through the Sahara but now transiting countries such as his own, blaming the Western military action in Libya in particular for spreading weapons across the region.

"It is not about asking for help, because this concerns the G8," he said. "It is in our common interest that the Sahara does not become another Afghanistan, as much for terrorism as for drug trafficking."

Conde said increased radicalism was a function of poverty and high youth unemployment, but acknowledged that he was also concerned by the rise of hardline Islamist preachers.

"All of our countries are under threat. Why? Because al Qaeda is not just Tuaregs and Arabs. They are Malians, Ivorians, Senegalese, Guineans."

(Additional reporting by Matthew Tostevin; Editing by Alistair Lyon)

Source: From 'Help Us Follow the Dirty Money, Guinea Asks G8,' by Clara Ferreira-Marques, June 15, 2013, Reuters. Retrieved from August 9, 2013, from http://www.reuters.com/article/2013/06/15/us-g8-guinea-idUSBRE95E0 AL20130615

As the brief history of security indicated, there is always an intimate link between the need for security, cultural and social changes, and crime. It could be argued that a variety of causes, both social and economic, are behind the influx of crimes against businesses. Among them are an erosion of family and religious restraints, the trend toward permissiveness, the increasing anonymity of business at every level of commerce, the decline in feelings of worker loyalty toward the company, and a general decline in morality accompanied by the pervasive attitude that there is no such thing as right and wrong but rather only what feels good. In addition, the rapidly changing technology of business and personal lives is often far ahead of security measures used to protect personal and business intellectual property. The dominance of the computer and related technology in business has improved worldwide business efficiency, but not without a price. The Internet, while providing the path for information transfer, has also provided unheard-of opportunities to steal or manipulate intellectual property.

The changes in attitudes, personal values, and technology have created a new problem for security managers—that of employee theft and malfeasance. As noted in In the News 13.2, in 1990, McDonnell Douglas Corporation fired 150 employees who allegedly used interest-free company loans intended for the purchase of computers to buy stereo equipment and other luxury items. A data-processing employee reportedly processed the $4,000 loans by printing phony invoices for computers. Although this may seem surprising, these problems are dwarfed by the troubles created by corrupt accounting practices at Arthur Andersen, WorldCom, and Enron.

In the News 13.2
McDonnell Douglas Fires 150 for Misuse of Company Loans

McDonnell Douglas Corp. fired more than 150 employees who allegedly used interest-free company loans intended for personal computers to buy stereos or big-screen televisions or simply for extra cash.

The workers received loans of up to $4,000 each under the company's loan program but never bought computers, company spokesman Don Hanson said Friday.

A data processing employee reportedly processed the loans by printing phony invoices for computer sales, then took a $1,000 kickback. Loan applicants would then pay back the loan in interest-free paycheck deductions.

Some workers at the Long Beach plant used the money to buy big-screen televisions and stereo systems, the *Long Beach Press-Telegram* reported.

In another scheme, employees would buy a $4,000 computer, submit the invoice for a loan, then sell the computer back to the retailer.

The program began in 1984 to allow people to shop for the best computer bargain and get the loan for the amount of the sale.

In 2001, a natural gas pipeline company called Enron filed for bankruptcy protection after revealing that it had overstated its profits by almost $600 million and had hidden more than $500 million in debt. At the time, this was the biggest corporate bankruptcy to date, and thousands of investors and company employees lost billions of dollars in investments and retirement funds (Kobrak, 2009). In the wake of the Enron scandal, the government passed the Sarbanes-Oxley Act of 2002 to combat corruption in public companies. This regulation has aided corporations' chief security officers (CSOs) by minimizing scandal and requiring greater financial disclosures, better scrutiny by corporate boards and their audit committees, and tighter overall accounting controls. Oversight by SEC regulators, coupled with weaker internal control mechanisms, clearly define white-collar crimes as being prevalent and a security challenge that cannot be overlooked.

It is far beyond the scope of this chapter to attempt to analyze or even to catalog all of the factors involved in the trend toward increasing crime in businesses. What is important here is to make a clear note of the fact of such increases—and of their impact on society's attempts to protect itself through the increased use of private security. Of more significance is the realization that public law enforcement systems by themselves cannot adequately control or prevent crime (Cunningham et al., 1990). In spite of their steady growth, both in costs and in numbers of personnel, public law enforcement agencies have increasingly been compelled to be reactive and to concentrate more of their activities on the maintenance of public order and the apprehension of criminals. Even community-oriented policing rests on the need for a cooperative approach to law enforcement.

But today, the sheer volume of crime and its cost, along with budget cutbacks in the public sector, have overstrained public law enforcement agencies. As discussed in Chapter 4, there is never enough funding for all of the police-oriented programs and services expected by society. The approximately 500,000 local law enforcement personnel in this country cannot possibly provide protection for all those who need it (Cunningham et al., 1990); thus, there is an increasing call for private security companies and cooperative measures between public and private organizations. The Institute for Law and Justice, authors of the 1990 *Hallcrest II Report,* indicated that by 2000 there would be more than 1.9 million people employed in private security, with total expenditures for its products and services estimated at $100 billion (Cunningham et al., 1990). This compares with police protection expenditures for federal, state, and local governments of only $45 billion. However, it must be noted that this gap has narrowed as government agencies have responded to the events of September 11, 2001, with more than 1 million security agents employed in 2009 and 641,590 public police officers in 2009 (Strom, Berzofsky, Shook-Sa, Barrick, Daye, Horstmann, & Kinney, 2010).

Growing Pains and Government Involvement

Inevitably, the explosive growth of the security industry in the second half of the 20th century has not been without its problems, leading to rising concern for the quality of selection, training, and performance of security personnel. The hijackings that led to the destruction of the World Trade Center in 2001 were blamed on poorly trained private-contract security screeners at U.S. airports and governmental intelligence agencies. Whether the blame is fair may be debatable because screeners were not looking for box cutters or other implements used by the hijackers; nor had they been trained to do so. Within months, the U.S. government had established federal control over this segment of security to increase standards, training, and professionalism. Even within the industry itself, there has been growing pressure for improved standards, higher pay, and greater professionalism, just as in the public sector. ASIS has developed industry standards that are regularly being discussed by representatives in the security industry and federal government.

Considering the importance of private security personnel in the anticrime effort and their quasi–law enforcement functions, it is ironic that they receive so little training in comparison to their public sector contemporaries. Unlike public sector police agencies, private security firm training requirements are often tied to licensure and certification by states. State requirements can vary widely (Strom et al., 2010). According to a 2005 study by Associated Criminal Justice & Security Consultants (2006), many security officers, on average, receive fewer than 8 hours of prejob training. Another study found that 65% of private security personnel received no training before beginning their job assignments (Kakalik & Wildhorn, 1971), and Nemeth (2004) noted that even though almost 50% of private security guards reported that they carry firearms, fewer than 20% reported that they had received firearms training. Basic public sector police training is 720 hours prior to licensing or certification. To complicate these figures, it should be mentioned that security officer training is often completed through an orientation video. On the other side of the spectrum, there are contract and proprietary security operations that provide very good training programs. Some contract security companies such as Wackenhut have client contracts established that provide from 40 to 120 hours of prepost assignment training requirements, dependent on the designated officer's position. This does not include on-the-job training (OJT). Additionally, an increasing number of states are intensifying their training requirements for licensure and certification (Bureau of Labor Statistics, 2009; Dempsey, 2008; Dempsey & Forst, 2008). "The number of programs is growing and the offerings include both continuing education programs and college majors with special focus on security. In the United States, college degree programs in private security increased from 5 in 1970 to 46 in 1990" (Strom et al., 2010, pp. 6–11).

Differences in pay and training are evidenced in how a security officer is classified. *Contract security officers* usually work for a private security company that "contracts" its employees to other businesses. *Proprietary security officers* are hired directly by a business and are generally better trained and better paid than their contract counterparts. Many officers—no matter whether they are contract or proprietary—are underpaid, undertrained, undersupervised, and unregulated. By and large, however, security managers have somewhat overlooked the values of maximizing training opportunities and requirements. This may be related to why those outside of the security industry, namely, the public and public police, have thought of security officers in a negative light. Viewing security officers as night watchmen, guards, or door monitors is not uncommon.

Minimal standards do exist in some places, but there is still a reluctance to train, educate, and adequately compensate the security forces. Business considerations in making a product for profit can make it difficult for companies to see the need to pay for costly security programs. Thus, they often opt for the lowest-priced solution, no matter whether it affords real protection. Fortunately, this kind of thinking is undergoing a change as industry realizes that the adage "you get what you pay for" very definitely applies to the quality of security. This realization should in turn add pressure to the security industry to upgrade the position of its security officers. Current standards, codes of ethics, and educational courses that are supported by industry participation assist in the increased accountability and professionalism of the private security field.

The issue of mandatory training was debated during the 1990s. The Gore Bill, introduced in 1991 by then-Senator Al Gore (D-TN), recommended minimum training for all security personnel without setting a minimum standard. The Sundquist Bill, introduced in 1993 by Representative Don Sundquist (R-TN), spelled out specific training requirements, adding to the 1991 senate bill. The Sundquist Bill recommended 16 hours of training for unarmed officers and 40 hours for armed personnel. Also in 1993, Representative Matthew Martinez (D-CA) reintroduced a bill mandating 12 hours of training for unarmed security personnel and 27 hours for armed officers. What is obvious here is that the federal government started to take an active interest in setting minimum standards for the security profession. (For a discussion of these bills, see the April 1994 article, "Why Is Security Officer Training Legislation Needed?" by John Chuvala III, CPP, and Robert J. Fischer, *Security Management*.) It is important to note that no federal legislation regulating private security was passed until 2002 following the World Trade Center disaster. With the support of ASIS, the Private Security Officer Employment Standards Act of 2002 was passed, allowing all security employers access to federal employment background checks through the National Crime Information Center. A 2004 law, titled the Private Security Officer Employment Authorization Act, included in Section 6402 of the Intelligence Reform and Terrorism Prevention Act of 2004, also "provided authority for states to perform fingerprint-based checks of state and national criminal history records to screen prospective and current private security officers. The checks performed under the Act are not mandatory, however, and employers may decline to participate or may allow employment while the results of the check are pending" (Strom et al., 2010, pp. 6–8). Another interesting note about the 2004 act is that states can decline to participate if the governor of a state issues an order to that effect. Why a state would not want to allow private security firms access to FBI-maintained criminal databases is unclear since these records would clearly provide a more exhaustive background check than would single-state criminal background checks.

Today, private security is still moving toward a new professionalism. In defining the desired professionalism, most authorities often cite the need for a code of ethics and for credentials including education and training, experience, and membership in a professional society. This continuing thrust toward professionalism is observable in the proliferation of active private security professional organizations and associations.

It also finds its voice in the library of professional security literature—magazines, Internet sites, and books—and in the increased development of college-level courses and degree programs in security, as mentioned earlier.

The Aftermath of September 11, 2001

There are few events that create a lasting impression. However, no one of age will likely forget where he or she was the morning of September 11, 2001. This is a day that changed life in the United States and throughout the world. Security began an evolution that will continue for many years. The most telling change in the United States was the eventual creation of the Department of Homeland Security.

Then-President George W. Bush made a commitment to the American people and others in the world to fight a war on terrorism. On January 24, 2003, Tom Ridge was sworn in as the first Secretary of the Department of Homeland Security (DHS). The cabinet-level department merged 22 federal agencies with more than 180,000 employees. To put this landmark move into perspective, the establishment of the department is the largest reorganization of the U.S. federal government since the creation of the Department of Defense in 1947. Creating a new governmental department is not as easy as it appears, and ongoing problems with the administration of this vast bureaucracy are apparent. Recent disappointment with the Federal Emergency Management Agency's handling of emergency aid in New Orleans after Hurricane Katrina, which hit the coast of Louisiana in 2005, killing an estimated 1,800 people and causing $81 billion in damages (U.S. Department of Health and Human Services, n.d.), is just one symptom of a greater problem of handling a large organization. The DHS continues to evolve and, now more than ever, includes the public in its mission. Janet Napolitano, the current Secretary of the Department of Homeland Security, launched a public awareness campaign called, "If you see something, say something" and revised the mission of the agency to include responses to terror threats and natural disasters. Inclusion of the public has not stopped there. The establishment and maintenance of the original Homeland Security Advisory System (HSAS)—now called the National Terrorism Advisory System (NTAS)—designed to provide the American public with an ongoing color indication of the level of potential terrorist threat against the nation was another example, although it has since been retired. The significance of these moves cannot be overstated. The security industry, which for the most part operated independent of federal control, has undergone dramatic changes as a result. For example, the federal government, with the creation of the Transportation Security Administration, has taken over the security of American airports, traditionally patrolled by private contract and proprietary services. The hand of the federal involvement is also visible in other transportation fields such as maritime activities and trucking. This has created a unique situation where public law enforcement is expected to work hand-in-hand with private security providers that remain a constant in these industries. These relationships have become well-established, with a report by the Law Enforcement–Private Security Consortium identifying more than 450 public law enforcement–private security partnerships in

2006. Often called *partnerships,* public policing agencies and private companies or proprietary police are engaging in primarily three forms of cooperation (Joh, 2004). In the first case, public policing agencies are showing more willingness to enter into joint investigations with private police by providing personnel, administrative, and technical resources. Second, some partnerships are engaged in active information sharing on crime patterns and suspects. In the third type of partnership, private policing groups act as public police officers when hired by districts and private businesses that are in close geographical proximity to one another. In this case, the district decides to apply special taxes to its members to pay for a private policing firm. The private police work with the public police in that area (Joh, 2004, pp. 71–72). Partnerships, although not regulated or monitored by the government, have benefited private agencies. According to Joh, "A more subtle effect of public support has been the increased legitimacy of private policing, and a greater willingness by public police to cooperate with them, whether or not they are engaged in formal partnerships" (p. 72).

Although partnerships are more common today than ever before, the roles of the private security industry and public policing allow for complementary and competing interests. However, even though the roles of the two groups are similar (in fact, overlapping in many areas), they are not identical. Most contact between public and private agencies is spontaneous and cooperative, but far too often the contact is negative, to the detriment of both groups.

Fischer, Halibozek, and Green (2008) claim the relationship between the two groups continues to be strained (although personal contacts may be warm) because of several key issues:

1. Lack of mutual respect

2. Lack of communication

3. Lack of law enforcement knowledge of private security

4. Perceived competition

5. Lack of standards for private security personnel

6. Perceived corruption of police

7. Jurisdictional conflict, especially when private problems (e.g., corporate theft or arson) are involved

8. Confusion of identity and the issues flowing from it, such as arming and training of private police

9. Mutual image and communications problems

10. Provision of services in borderline or overlapping areas of responsibility and interest (e.g., provision of security during strikes, traffic control, and shared use of municipal and private fire-fighting personnel)

11. Moonlighting policies for public police and issues stemming from these policies

12. Difference in legal powers, which can lead to concerns about abuse of power, and so on (e.g., police officers working off duty may now be private citizens subject to rules of citizen's arrest)

13. False alarm rates (police resent responding to false alarms), which in some communities are more than 90%

Historically, public police have often accused the private sector of mishandling cases, breaking the law to make cases, being poorly trained, and generally being composed of those who could not meet the standards for police officers. The private security sector often views the public sector as being self-centered and arrogant. Moreover, public law enforcement officers often moonlight, thereby taking work away from the private security sector. Even today, the private sector is still considered by public police as only somewhat effective in reducing direct-dollar crime loss, and its contributions to reducing the volume of crime, apprehending criminal suspects, and maintaining order are judged ineffective. Public law enforcement has given private security low ratings in 10 areas, including quality of personnel, training, and knowledge of legal authority. The feelings about the lack of training may be justified, as addressed previously (Associated Criminal Justice & Security Consultants, 2006).

The employment of police officers as private security personnel during their off-duty hours has also caused much criticism. Some say that moonlighting police are only "hired guns" and that such police officers take jobs away from security firms. Opponents claim that decreased productivity, fatigue, and stress are also increased in those officers that moonlight for security firms (Brunet, 2008; Strom et al., 2010). Other problems include the question of who is liable for the officer's actions—the public agency that employs the officer full time or the private security firm employing the officer in a part-time capacity. Is the employer of the off-duty officer liable, or does the liability stay with the police department that trained the officer? In *West v. Atkins* (1988), the U.S. Supreme Court held that "A police officer will be deemed to be acting under the color of law when he is acting in his official capacity or while exercising his responsibilities pursuant to state law." To determine liability several criteria may be used to decide if the officer was acting in the color of the law, to include whether the department has a policy requiring officers to be on duty at all times, if the officer displayed a department-issued badge, if the officer identified himself or herself as a police officer, whether the officer carried a department-issued weapon, and if the officer placed the individual under arrest. Since not all states are willing to create legislation addressing the issue of moonlighting, this can often be a tricky situation for administrators.

Another source of conflict is the high rate of false alarms. While improved technology has reduced the number of false alarms, there are still problems associated with the human element, "critter infringement," and the occasional electronic failure. When an alarm sounds, an alarm company employee may respond or the police department may be called. In some jurisdictions, police report that 10% to 12% of all calls for police service are from false alarms. Some police departments have reacted to this high rate by fining alarm companies or businesses and even delaying their response pending internal confirmation of an actual intrusion.

Yet much of the conflict between private and public agencies is the result of misconception. There is a general misunderstanding of the roles played by the respective agencies. Perhaps this is understandable because even within their own areas, police and private security officers often fail to understand the common goals of the other agencies. In partnerships, there is also the issue that the objectives shared by each agency involved are the same and serve the same establishment. This may not be the case, as public police attempt to identify and apprehend offenders and private security attempts to prevent crime in the first place. In addition, the private agency is more focused on protecting the interests of their particular client than in protecting the general public—which is the charge of public police.

There are three primary misconceptions standing in the way of police and private security working well together. The first misconception is that working together for a common goal is difficult to achieve, although police departments and private security agencies are beginning to work together, at times unknowingly. The idea that only the public police protect public property is the second misconception. The federal government has more than 10,000 contract security officers patrolling federal offices and buildings. In many cities, police departments have privatized certain police functions such as prisoner transport (Strom et al., 2010) and turned to private agencies to protect courts, city buildings, airports, and museums. A third misconception is that the private security sector is only concerned with crime prevention and deterrence rather than with investigation and apprehension. Although prevention is a key objective for private security, in reality, store detectives in many major cities make more arrests each year than do local police officers. In addition, certain types of crime are no longer investigated by local police departments but have instead become the job of private security personnel; these include credit card fraud, single bogus checks, and some thefts. The growing problems of drugs and violence in the workplace have also added to security's role in law enforcement. Cooperation between private security and public law enforcement is vital in dealing with growing domestic problems and the threat of terrorism.

Obviously, some degree of complementary activity already exists, but the question must be asked as to what can be done to improve the perceptions that the two areas have of each other and foster cooperative efforts between them. As is happening in some public police–private sector partnerships, the formation of joint private and public sector task forces to study responses to terrorism and major crime issues and strategy development is important. Joint seminars on terrorism and business crime have also been developed to help the two areas better understand their respective roles, and these could be used more often by each sector. Data files from both sectors should also be more freely exchanged (as is proposed in information-sharing partnerships). Private security personnel are often not allowed access to information on criminal cases even as a follow-up on data originally entered by them. Joh (2004) found that private agencies may also not share information with public agencies unless it benefits them in some way to do so. In what she calls "passive non-cooperation" (p. 85), private policing agencies may deliberately withhold information from the public police, even though it could assist in a case. Cooperation between the two agencies, according to Joh, is most likely to occur when it best meets the needs of a particular agency or, in the case of the private security agency, when it best meets the client's interests to do so. This points to the inherent difference in accountability between these two industries—with security agencies being accountable to their clients (not the people they police) and public agencies being accountable to the people they police (the community).

In all honesty, just how effective private security can be depends to a large degree on whether public law enforcement and private sector professionals are able to form a close partnership. The *Hallcrest II Report* recommends the following:

1. Upgrading private security. Statewide regulatory statutes are needed for background checks, training, codes of ethics, and licensing.

2. Increasing police knowledge of private security.

3. Expanding interaction. Joint task forces are needed, and both groups should share investigative information and specialized equipment.

4. Experimenting with the transfer of police functions. (Cunningham & Taylor, 1985)

To continue these partnerships and to strengthen future relationships, both private security and public enforcement may wish to consider the recommendations made by the 2004 National Policy Summit project supported by the U.S. Department of Justice, Office of Community Oriented Policing Services (COPS) (Security–Police Information Network, 2007). This joint partnering effort involved the International Association of Chiefs of Police (IACP) and the Security Industry Association (SIA), ASIS International, the National Association of Security Companies (NASC), and the International Security Management Association (ISMA). The organizations formed working groups during the summit and suggested the following (the first four are national-level recommendations, which require long-term efforts, while the fifth recommendation relates to local and regional efforts):

1. Leaders of the major law enforcement and private security organizations should make a formal commitment to cooperation.

2. The Department of Homeland Security (DHS) and/or Department of Justice (DOJ) should fund research and training on relevant legislation, private security, and law enforcement–private security cooperation.

3. The DHS and/or DOJ should create an advisory council composed of nationally prominent law enforcement and private security professionals to oversee day-to-day implementation issues of law enforcement–private security partnerships.

4. The DHS and/or DOJ, along with relevant membership organizations, should convene key practitioners to move this agenda forward.

5. Local partnerships should set priorities and address key problems as identified by the summit. Recommendations to address these problems include the following actions:

   - Improve joint response to critical incidents
   - Coordinate infrastructure protection
   - Improve communications and data interoperability

- Bolster information and intelligence sharing
- Prevent and investigate high-tech crime
- Devise responses to workplace violence

Execution of these recommendations should benefit all concerned. Law enforcement agencies will be better able to carry out their traditional crime-fighting duties and their additional homeland security duties by using the many private security resources in the community. Public–private cooperation is an important aspect—indeed, a potent technique—of community policing. Private security organizations will be better able to carry out their mission of protecting their companies' or clients' people, property, and information, while at the same time serving the homeland security objectives of their communities. The nation as a whole will benefit from the heightened effectiveness of law enforcement agencies and private security organizations (Olhausen Research, Inc., 2004).

Forming partnerships is just one more issue that management in both public and private sectors face, as discussed throughout this book. Overcoming the issues discussed will not be easy and will raise additional concerns of legal liability that both agencies will have to address.

Management Approaches

Security practices and procedures cover a broad spectrum of activities designed to eliminate or reduce the full range of potential hazards (loss, damage, or injury). In addition to these basic loss-prevention functions, security services in some situations might also provide armored car and armed courier service, bodyguard protection, management consulting, security consulting, and other specific types of protection. Many firms, particularly the smaller ones, specialize in specific types of services offered to a client. The larger the firm, the more likely it is to provide a full range of security services. These services may be proprietary, or inhouse, or they may be contract security services. In practice, it is common to find a combination of both services being used. This combination of proprietary and contract security is referred to as a *hybrid security system*.

Kenneth Fauth (quoted in Bottom & Kostanoski, 1983) pointed out more than 30 years ago that a systems approach to security was important, as businesses used loss prevention and security departments more and more. In that insightful comment, Fauth, former director of security and loss prevention at Spiegel, Inc., suggests clearly that security and loss prevention has evolved well beyond the officer at the gate. Though that thought is still vital, today's business assets comprise an almost infinite variety of protection needs. Moreover, security increasingly includes protection against contingencies that might prevent normal company operation from continuing and from making a profit. As the concept of risk management is further integrated into a comprehensive loss-prevention program, the security function focuses less and less on enforcement and more on anticipating and preventing loss through proactive programming. Such challenges indisputably require high-level security management and an increasingly well-credentialed group of security professionals.

The systems approach, as outlined by C. West Churchman in 1968, is the process of focusing on central objectives rather than on attempting to solve individual problems within an organization. By concentrating on the central objectives, the management team can address specific problems that will prevent the accomplishment of the central objectives. As noted earlier, these central objectives in security for the 21st century include protection from terrorism and control of economic crimes, as well as continuing to combat traditional security problems and focusing on specific client needs. In today's climate, this means integrated security systems where problems are approached from a team perspective. Public law enforcement at local, state, and federal levels, along with security interaction and operations, have to work together, sharing intelligence to control these problems and reestablish a sense of security in the world's citizens.

Security officer services, whether proprietary or contract, are still in demand today despite the growth in the use of technology. People and companies turn to security officers because psychologically they feel that technology or hardware may not be enough. As noted previously, in the aftermath of the September 11, 2001, terrorist attacks, security staffs have increased. Although some proprietary firms are relying more on technology to reduce security-cost overhead, three basic trends in security services are becoming apparent. First, the increased number of legal problems associated with inappropriate actions of officers and public outrage may eventually force states to regulate training and standards. However, based on the June 2005 report by Associated Criminal Justice & Security Consultants (2006), standards for security have not changed much, legally or otherwise, since 2001. There have been several federal attempts to pass legislation mandating minimum standards for security personnel, but they have yet to be successful. Second, as the field grows, it will continue to attract better-qualified individuals. The 2012 ASIS Annual Salary Survey indicated that 32% of the 1,400 respondents held a master's degree. Finally, although there was an initial push to disarm security personnel, it appears to have changed. This endeavor was true until the destruction of the World Trade Center. Since that time, the presence of armed security personnel in some venues appears to be increasing.

Contract Versus Proprietary Services

Contract and proprietary security services have been mentioned in this chapter, but there is a need to make a clear distinction between the two types of operations. *Proprietary security operations* are those that are inhouse, or controlled entirely by the company establishing security for its operations. The company—for example, Jones Distributing—hires a chief security officer (CSO) and all of the necessary support personnel and equipment to operate a security department. *Contract security services,* on the other hand, are those operations provided by a professional security company that contracts its services to another company. In this case, Jones Distributing would contract with Fischer Security Services for specific security services. In most cases, there would not be a CSO employed directly by Jones. Rather, the contract manager would work for Fischer Security Services. As noted earlier, the latest trend is to have a combination of proprietary and contract operations—hybrid security systems.

Researchers in the 1990s perceived more rapid growth in contract security services than in proprietary security. Although many firms are considering contract services, some existing proprietary security operations are converting to hybrids with proprietary management and contractual line services. *Security* magazine reported in 1990 that the trend would be toward increased use of contract employees, products, and services, causing the employee numbers in the contract area to double by the year 2000 (Zalud, 1990). This prediction was at least partially accurate in the new millennium. Several of the largest firms adopted contract security services to replace their proprietary systems. However, the change has not been a clear departure from company control to contract. At least three Fortune 500 companies have made the move to hybrid systems using proprietary oversight, contract officers, and increased reliance on electronic advancements to replace outdated equipment and officers, and ASIS (2005) reported that more than 56.5% of all security services remain in an inhouse security department or as company personnel.

Whether a company decides to use proprietary services or contract services is best answered by the manager of the firm or organization contemplating security services. That decision will rest on the particular characteristics of the company. These characteristics will include the location to be protected, the size of the force required, its mission, the length of time the officers will be needed, and the quality of personnel required. Ultimately, businesses may decide that the best approach in their case is a hybrid system.

CAREER HIGHLIGHT BOX
SECURITY GUARDS AND GAMING SURVEILLANCE OFFICERS

Nature of the Work

Security guards and gaming surveillance officers patrol and inspect property against fire, theft, vandalism, terrorism, and illegal activity. They monitor people and buildings in an effort to prevent crime.

Duties

Security guards and gaming surveillance officers typically do the following:

- Protect and enforce laws on an employer's property
- Monitor alarms and closed-circuit TV cameras
- Control access for employees, visitors, and outside contractors
- Conduct security checks over a specified area
- Write comprehensive reports outlining what they observed while on patrol
- Interview witnesses for later court testimony
- Detain criminal violators

(Continued)

(Continued)

Guards must remain alert, looking for anything out of the ordinary throughout their shift. In an emergency, guards may call for assistance from police, fire, or ambulance services. Some security guards may be armed.

A security guard's job responsibilities vary from one employer to another. In retail stores, guards protect people, records, merchandise, money, and equipment. They may work with undercover store detectives to prevent theft by customers or employees, detain shoplifting suspects until the police arrive, or patrol parking lots.

In office buildings, banks, hotels, and hospitals, guards maintain order and protect the organization's customers, staff, and property. Guards who work in museums or art galleries protect paintings and exhibits by watching people and inspecting packages entering and leaving the building. In factories, government buildings, and military bases, security guards protect information and products and check the credentials of people and vehicles entering and leaving the premises.

Guards working at universities, in parks, and at sports stadiums do crowd control, supervise parking and seating, and direct traffic. Security guards stationed at the entrance to bars and nightclubs keep under-age people from entering, collect cover charges at the door, and maintain order among customers.

Guards who work as transportation security screeners protect people, transportation equipment, and freight at airports, train stations, and other transportation facilities.

The following are examples of types of security guards and gaming surveillance officers:

Security guards, also called *security officers,* protect property, enforce laws on the property, deter criminal activity, and deal with other problems. Some guards are assigned a stationary position from which they may monitor alarms or surveillance cameras. Other guards may be assigned a patrol area where they conduct security checks.

Transportation security screeners, many of whom are Transportation Security Administration (TSA) officers, work at air, sea, and rail terminals and other transportation facilities, protecting people, freight, property, and equipment. They use metal detectors, x-ray machines, and other equipment to screen passengers and visitors for weapons and explosives, ensure that nothing is stolen while a vehicle is being loaded or unloaded, and watch for fires and criminals. Some officers work with dogs, which alert them to the presence of dangerous materials, such as bombs.

Armored car guards protect money and valuables during transit. They pick up money or other valuables from businesses and transport them to another location. These guards usually wear bulletproof vests and carry firearms, because transporting money between the truck and the business can be extremely hazardous.

Gaming surveillance officers, also known as *surveillance agents* and *gaming investigators,* act as security agents for casino employees, managers, and patrons. Using audio and video equipment in an observation room, they watch casino operations for irregular activities, such as cheating or theft, and monitor compliance with rules, regulations, and laws. They maintain and organize recordings from security cameras, which are sometimes used as evidence in police investigations. In addition, surveillance agents occasionally leave the observation room and walk the casino floor.

Security guards and gaming surveillance officers held about 1.1 million jobs in 2010. Security guards work in a wide variety of environments, including public buildings, retail stores, and office buildings. Guards who serve as transportation security screeners work in air, sea, and rail terminals and other transportation facilities. Gaming surveillance officers do most of their work in casino observation rooms, using audio and video equipment.

The following industries employed the most security guards and gaming surveillance officers in 2010:

Investigation and security services	53%
Government	9
Educational services; state, local, and private	6
Accommodation and food services	5
Hospitals; state, local, and private	4

In 2010, most gaming surveillance officers worked in gaming industries, casino hotels, and local governments. They are employed only in those states, and on those Indian reservations, where gambling is legal.

Transportation security screeners are employed by the federal government.

Most security guards and gaming surveillance officers spend considerable time on their feet, either assigned to a specific post or patrolling buildings and grounds. Some may sit for long hours behind a counter or in a guardhouse at the entrance to a gated facility or community.

Guards who work during the day may have a great deal of contact with other employees and the public.

Although the work can be routine, it can also be hazardous, particularly when an altercation occurs.

Injuries

Gaming surveillance officers have one of the highest rates of injury and illness of any occupation, and security guards have a higher rate than the national average. The work usually is routine, but these jobs can be hazardous. Guards must be constantly alert for threats to themselves and the property they are protecting.

(Continued)

(Continued)

Work Schedules

Security guards and gaming surveillance officers provide surveillance around the clock by working shifts of 8 hours or longer with rotating schedules. Some security guards choose to work part time while others may take on a second job.

Training, Other Qualifications, and Advancement

Most security guard jobs require an applicant to have a high school diploma or GED. Gaming surveillance officers sometimes need additional coursework beyond a high school diploma. Most states require guards to be licensed.

Important Qualities

Communication skills. Security guards must be able to speak with members of the public, suspected offenders, and law enforcement officers.

Decision-making skills. Guards must be able to quickly determine the best course of action when a dangerous situation arises.

Honesty. Guards must be honest because they are trusted to protect confidential information or expensive equipment.

Observation skills. Guards must be alert and aware of their surroundings, able to quickly recognize anything out of the ordinary.

Physical strength. Guards must be strong enough to deal with offenders and to handle emergency situations.

Education and Training

Unarmed guards generally need to have a high school diploma or GED, although some jobs may not have any specific educational requirement. For armed guards, employers usually prefer people who are high school graduates or who have some coursework in criminal justice.

Some employers prefer to hire security guards with some higher education, such as a police science or criminal justice degree. Programs and courses that focus specifically on security guards also are available at some postsecondary schools.

Many employers give newly hired guards instruction before they start the job and provide on-the-job training. The amount of training guards receive varies. Training covers numerous topics, such as emergency procedures, detention of suspected criminals, and communication skills.

ASIS International has written voluntary guidelines that recommend minimum criteria for selecting and training private security officers. The guidelines recommend that security guards receive preassignment training in accordance with all applicable legal requirements, 8–16 hours of on-the-job training, and 8 hours of annual training. This may include training in protection, public relations, report writing, deterring crises, first aid, and specialized training related to the guard's assignment. The guidelines also recommend that security guards be required to pass one or more written or performance exams.

In addition, the guidelines recommend annual firearms training for armed officers as required by the state in which they work. Training is more rigorous for armed guards because their employers are legally responsible for any use of force. Armed guards may be periodically tested in the use of firearms.

Transportation security screeners who work for the TSA must have a high school diploma, a GED, or 1 year of related work experience. They must be at least 18 years old and a U.S. citizen. TSA screeners must pass a background check, drug testing, and a physical exam. Candidates who meet these requirements must complete both classroom and on-the-job training before passing a certification exam. Ongoing training is usually required.

Gaming surveillance officers and investigators usually need some training beyond high school, but not necessarily a bachelor's degree. Several educational institutions offer certification programs. Classroom training generally is conducted in a casino-like atmosphere and includes the use of surveillance camera equipment. Employers may prefer individuals with casino experience or investigation experience. Technical skills and experience with computers also is a plus.

Licenses

Most states require that guards be licensed. To be licensed as a guard, individuals must usually be at least 18 years old, pass a background check, and complete classroom training. However, licensing requirements vary from state to state.

Drug testing is often required and may be ongoing and random. Many jobs also require a driver's license. An increasing number of states are making ongoing training a legal requirement for keeping a license.

Guards who carry weapons must be licensed by the appropriate government authority. Armed guard positions also have more stringent background checks and entry requirements than those of unarmed guards. Rigorous hiring and screening programs, including background, criminal record, and fingerprint checks, are typical for armed guards.

Certification

In addition to being licensed, some security guards may choose to become certified. ASIS International offers the Certified Protection Professional certification for security workers who want a transferable validation of their knowledge and skills.

Advancement

Because many people do not stay long in this occupation, opportunities for advancement are good for those who make a career in security.

(Continued)

(Continued)

Some guards may advance to positions of supervisor or security manager. Guards with postsecondary education or with related certifications may be preferred. Armed security guards have a greater potential for advancement and enjoy higher earnings.

Guards with management skills may open their own contract security guard agencies. Guards also can move to an organization that needs higher levels of security, which may result in more prestige or higher pay.

Job Outlook

Employment of security guards is expected to grow by 19 percent from 2010 to 2020, about as fast as the average for all occupations.

Security guards will be needed to protect both people and property. This occupation is expected to add 195,000, a large number of jobs, over the 2010–2020 decade. Concern about crime, vandalism, and terrorism continue to increase the need for security. Demand should be strong in the private sector as private security firms take over some of the work police officers used to do.

Employment of transportation security screeners is expected to grow by 10 percent, about as fast as the average for all occupations. Demand for TSA screeners, who work for the federal government, will stem from transportation security concerns.

Employment of gaming surveillance officers is expected to grow by 9 percent, slower than the average for all occupations. As gambling continues to be legalized in more states and casinos grow in number, gaming surveillance officers will see additional job openings.

Technological advances will continue to create demand for casino security guards who have knowledge of computers and video surveillance equipment.

Job Prospects

Job opportunities for security guards will stem from growing demand for various forms of security.

Additional opportunities will be due to turnover. Although many people are attracted to part time positions because of the limited training requirements, there will be more competition for higher paying positions that require more training.

Those with related work experience, such as a background in law enforcement, and those with computer and technology skills should find the best job prospects.

Earnings

The median annual wage of security guards and gaming surveillance officers was $24,380 in May 2010. The median wage is the wage at which half the workers in an occupation earned more than that amount and half earned less. The lowest 10 percent earned $17,210, and the top 10 percent earned more than $41,680.

The median annual wages for security guard and gaming surveillance officer occupations in May 2010 were as follows:

- $37,070 for transportation security screeners
- $30,680 for gaming surveillance officers and gaming investigators
- $23,920 for security guards

Security guards and gaming surveillance officers provide surveillance around the clock by working shifts of 8 hours or longer with rotating schedules. Some security guards choose to work part time while others may take on a second job.

SOURCE: Bureau of Labor Statistics, U.S. Department of Labor, *Occupational Outlook Handbook, 2012–13 Edition*, Security Guards and Gaming Surveillance Officers, on the Internet at http://www.bls.gov/ooh/protective-service/security-guards.htm.

Differences in Private Security and Public Law Enforcement

Although public and private police might, in certain circumstances, perform the same functions for the same individuals or organizations, they are inherently different in their objectives. A law enforcement officer might be assigned to protect a threatened individual; a private bodyguard frequently is hired to perform the same protective function. Public police commonly perform patrol functions, which include checking the external premises of stores or manufacturing facilities. But patrol is also one of the major activities of private security. The activity itself, then, is not always a differentiating factor. As discussed earlier, private security functions are essentially client-oriented; public law enforcement functions are societal or community-oriented.

Public policing is a localized, highly decentralized industry (although each individual department may rely on a centralized structure). Much of the public policing organization's objectives and work revolve around "its leadership, local politics, the professional culture of the police, and the outlook of the community that the department serves" (Joh, 2004, p. 60). Here lies a major difference between public and private agencies. Although social and cultural belief systems from the larger society may influence private agencies, the organizations, by and large, have a client-driven focus, as mentioned previously, according to Shearing & Stenning (cited in Joh, 2004). It is the specific client (the business, corporation, district, and so forth) that hired the private policing agency that determines the objectives of the security firm. So, unlike public criminal justice agencies, the private firm is focused only on pleasing one client (not providing many services to many stakeholders). As Joh (2004) points out, what a business defines as deviant or inappropriate behavior that requires a response by the security agency may not be based solely on morality or the law but on what the client views as important (p. 62).

Joh (2004) and Shearing and Stenning (cited in Joh) point out that private agencies may pursue the client's goals in one of four ways. First, private police focus on loss instead of crime. They are primarily hired to protect property and for asset protection; thus, they are engaged in many more activities outside of crime control. Second, private police are more concerned with prevention of deviance instead of detection and apprehension of criminals. They "are concerned not so much with the punishment of individual wrongdoers but the disruption of routine activity (e.g., a smoothly functioning workplace), policing efforts focus heavily on surveillance" (Joh, 2004, p. 62). However, as discussed earlier, the intensity of this focus has changed in recent years. A third method is through using means to control crime or deviance that do not involve the public criminal justice system. When prevention fails and an employee engages in behaviors that result in a loss to the corporation, measures such as firing, banning, or fining the employee may be used by the business and enforced by the private policing agency. This is, basically, a way to resolve issues without bringing unneeded, or unwanted, attention to the corporation that may alarm the general public and disposes of issues that the business does not feel warrant public or criminal justice prosecution, according to Shearing and Stenning (cited in Joh, 2004). Joh suggests that some businesses will tolerate various forms of deviance because they do not want to invest the time or loss of resources into the pursuit of prosecution or the involvement of the public criminal justice system. Finally, as corporations have moved into larger and larger spaces and opened their spaces to the public, private policing agencies have taken on the responsibility of policing and controlling these areas. Malls and large corporate campuses are examples of massive private properties.

Another key distinction is the possession and exercise of police powers—that is, the power of arrest. The vast majority of private security personnel have no police powers. In some jurisdictions, "special officer" status is granted, in most cases by statute or ordinance, which includes limited power of arrest in specified areas or premises. The limitations on the exercise of special police powers and the fact that their activities are client-oriented and client-controlled (as opposed to being directed primarily by public law enforcement agencies) make it reasonable to include such personnel as part of the private security industry. (This discussion omits the situation of the law enforcement officer who is moonlighting as a part-time private security officer because police powers in that situation derive from the public rather than the private role.)

In the final remarks for this chapter, it should be noted that security and loss-prevention functions and law enforcement, while diverse, have a common goal. The definition of security has been debated, but the bottom line is clear. Security services protect both private and public places; law enforcement protects both public and private property. The difference is found in their primary goals. Law enforcement agencies are charged with the protection of government interests, representing the people; whereas private security is charged with protecting a specific interest, whether public or private.

The old distinction between public law enforcement and private security will continue to exist. However, the story is different when considering the relationship between contract and proprietary security. As businesses continue to evolve, it appears that hybrid systems will become a dominant organizational scheme for many businesses establishing security operations.

Finally, all people concerned with security, whether federal government agencies, state law enforcement organizations, local law enforcement, or private security, will need to learn to work together to focus resources needed to successfully combat threats created by the potential for terrorist attacks and cybercrimes.

Chapter Summary

- Private security services were created as a response to public pressure for actions that public policing could not provide. Pinkerton, Wells and Fargo, Brink, and Burns were able to address the needs of businesses and private citizens in ways that public agencies were unable to by providing protection and transportation of goods and services. Wackenhut, Inc., Securitas, and regional firms have also joined the industry as major contributors of security services globally.
- The 1950s development of professional organizations in security, such as ASIS International, increased the professionalism, training, and expectations of the security industry.
- Contemporary security agencies protect retail establishments, hotels, restaurants, theaters, warehouses, trucking companies, industrial companies, hospitals, and other institutional and service agencies. Security officers also participate in investigations of business fraud, arson, burglary, and other areas. Collaboration between the security industry and public policing agencies has increased, although much work still needs to be done.
- The need for private security in industry is linked to social, cultural, and financial changes in the larger society. As demands on public law enforcement agencies have grown, community members and even the federal government have turned to private security to assist in anticrime and antiterrorism efforts.
- Security personnel may be employed as contract security officers or proprietary security officers. Contract security officers work for a private security company that "contracts" their employees to other businesses. Proprietary security officers are hired directly by a business to provide security for the company. They are usually better trained, better paid, and more likely to remain with the company than contract security officers. Whether a company chooses to hire contract officers from a security agency or employ their own proprietary security personnel may depend on the characteristics of the company. Companies may even choose to combine the two types of security services by using a hybrid system.
- Currently, there are no mandatory state or federal training guidelines for security officers. Proprietary officers receive more training than contract officers, but even for them, there are no minimum standards. Governmental efforts to set minimum criteria for training have failed. However, the push for professionalism in security has led to the development of a code of ethics, as well as a drive for educational requirements and minimum training standards. There has also been a demand for membership in a professional organization such as ASIS and for federal employment background checks.
- The systems approach to management is typically used in security. This allows for the creation of central objectives on which the company can focus. The management team can then address specific problems that prevent the accomplishment of the central objectives. In today's environment, the systems approach allows for integrated security systems using a team method (collaboration with public agencies) to share intelligence and focus on anticrime and antiterrorist efforts.
- At times, the public police and the security industry have been competitive and at other times collaborative. Conflicts between the two groups stem primarily from misconceptions of the roles played by each agency. Notwithstanding those issues, however, the two agencies have collaborated on issues related to

terrorism and business crimes. They also work together to protect public property, such as courthouses and federal offices, and to free up time in the public sector from crime prevention to allow more focus on violent crimes and crime responses.

- To continue collaborative efforts between public policing agencies and private security agencies, the respective groups may wish to focus on making formal commitments to one another to cooperate, applying for funding opportunities that promote collaborative projects, creating advisory councils that provide for representation from both disciplines, and working with the DOJ and DHS on setting priorities and focusing on key problems that move the two groups into more complementary positions.

Chapter Review Questions

1. Why was the development of private security necessary in the United States? What services do private security agencies provide that cannot be provided by public law enforcement agencies?

2. Historically, what was the nature of the relationship between public law enforcement agencies and private security agencies? As the climate has changed in the United States, how has this relationship changed? What changes do you foresee in the future?

3. What is contract security? What is proprietary or inhouse security? What is a hybrid system? Using the management and administrative concepts you have learned, determine how a company would decide which security system was right for it?

4. Why is the systems approach to management the best approach for the security industry? Would another managerial approach work as well? If so, name the approach and describe it.

5. Do security firms use service quality? If so, how? If not, what should they do to focus on providing better services? How might collaborations between the public and private sector provide better-quality services to the public and private businesses?

CASE STUDY

Jenjeev Security Company is a contract-based company that hires security guards to firms, corporations, and other businesses for a variety of security services. It has been in business since 1934 and currently employs a president, 2 vice presidents, 9 regional directors, and 275 security officers, as well as 30 to 40 secretarial and bookkeeping staff members throughout the United States. Jenjeev prides itself on consistent customer service, employees that are free of criminal backgrounds, and a 60-hour training program for all security employees, provided by the U.S. Department of Justice. In the last 40 years, Jenjeev Security Company has been incident free—meaning that no employees have been arrested or charged with a criminal act while working at the company. Jenjeev has also never been indicted or investigated for any wrongdoing. Currently, Jenjeev Security holds $5 million a year in federal security contracts. Many of the companies that work with Jenjeev have long-term and continuing contracts with the business, while others are repeat customers.

In August 2011, Jenjeev was contracted to provide 11 officers as bodyguards for a white supremacist leader and his group on a speaking tour across America. All 11 officers sent to the job had worked with Jenjeev for at least one year. Because of the nature of the client's message and his ties to a neo-Nazi prison gang called the Aryan Brotherhood, the bodyguards were armed and told to remain close to the group they were guarding at all times.

After one specific speaking engagement in New York City, the supremacist leader and his group were attempting to exit the building while a large crowd was gathered outside. During this attempt, the crowd became aggressive in its efforts to get close to the group members. The crowd was yelling, pushing, and throwing items such as beer cans and bottles at the leader and his group. From within the agitated crowd, one of the bodyguards claimed he heard gunshots. He yelled for the other guards to "get down" and drew his weapon, causing other bodyguards to draw their weapons and to move the clients more quickly to safety. When three loud bangs were heard, seven bodyguards opened fired into the crowded parking lot. During the shootings, four people were killed, and five more were injured, most of whom were African Americans. Several other injuries occurred as the crowd of people starting fighting among themselves. Public law enforcement agents were called in to regain peace and to arrest those accountable for the activities.

To date, no security officers have been arrested as the state and local police try to investigate the incident and to determine blame for the shootings. Approximately 30 crowd members consisting of whites and African Americans have faced prosecution for assault. Others are still being investigated.

The fallout of the event has led to increased racial tensions. African American leaders have called for governmental intervention to prevent additional incidents and for the arrest of the Jenjeev security guards. They have claimed that the race of the security guards and the propaganda of the speaker's message prompted the perception that black crowd members were dangerous and carrying weapons, which influenced the guards to overreact. African American leaders have also proposed that the lack of arrests of Jenjeev security guards is the government's way of supporting white America and is apparent racism. They point to the federal security contracts as evidence that the federal government is actively involved in continued bigotry. White supremacists have used the incident to push their agenda forward by blaming the black crowd members for the shooting. They have suggested that African Americans are a serious threat to the general public and "are just waiting to kill white Americans any chance they get."

The media have scrutinized the use of private security agencies to guard individuals who are likely to entice violence, such as a white supremacist. Questions have been raised about the dual roles of private security and public policing and how the two can better work together to prevent these types of occurrences again. Questions have also been raised about the training of the bodyguards and the minimum standards of training for armed security guards. The public has appeared shocked that private security officers do not need a minimum number of training hours to qualify as a security professional and to carry a firearm in public.

Jenjeev Security Company has been adamant that its guards acted appropriately to save their lives and the lives of their clients. It has stated that the bodyguards acted in "good faith" and were ambushed as they attempted to leave the crowded parking lot. The company is not a target in the investigation. It has offered to cooperate with the local police and federal government in the ongoing investigation. So far, the federal government has not opened an investigation into the event or pulled its contracts with Jenjeev Security, although this may occur in the future if there is continued pressure from the public and the media.

(Continued)

(Continued)

The security guards in question have each hired attorneys (which some believe are being paid by the security company) and have not spoken publicly about the incident.

Questions for Review

1. In your opinion, what factors may have led up to the shooting (i.e., lack of training, etc.)? Is Jenjeev Security Company at fault in this situation? Why or why not?

2. Should the federal government intervene in the investigations? Should the federal government intervene in the private security industry? Why or why not?

3. How could the public and private policing forces have worked together to prevent this occurrence? Is there anything that could have been done differently in this case on behalf of the respective agencies?

4. Does service quality have a role in this case? If so, what role does it play? Was service quality provided in this case? Could it have been performed better? How?

Internet Resources

ASIS International—http://www.asisonline.org

Securitas Security Services USA, Inc.—http://www.securitas.com/us/en

Security magazine—http://www.securitymagazine.com

References and Suggested Readings

Anderson, T. (2003, January). A year of reassessment: The ASIS annual employment survey looks at how 9-11 affected corporate security functions, staffing, budgets, and policies (Progress report). *Security Management.*

ASIS Foundation. (2005). *The ASIS Foundation security report: Scope and emerging trends: Executive summary.* Retrieved from http://www.asisonline.org/foundation/trendsinsecuritystudy.pdf.

ASIS Foundation. (2009). Compendium of the ASIS Academic/Practitioner Symposium, 1997–2008. In Strom, K., Berzofsky, M., Shook-Sa, B., Barrick, K., Daye, C, Horstmann, N., & Kinney, S. (2010). *The private security industry: A review of the definitions, available data sources, and paths moving forward.* Retrieved from, https://www.ncjrs.gov/pdffiles1/bjs/grants/232781.pdf.

ASIS International. (2006, February 7). *Workplace security legislation supported by ASIS international implemented by Department of Justice* [Press release]. Retrieved from http://www.asison line.org/newsroom/pressReleases/020706workplace.doc.

ASIS International. (2012). *Survey: Security execs get 2 percent salary bump.* Retrieved from http://www.securityinfowatch.com.

Associated Criminal Justice & Security Consultants. (2006, June). *Evaluation of basic training programs in law enforcement, security, and corrections for academic credit.* Unpublished manuscript, Kaplan University.

Bottom, N. R., & Kostanoski, J. (1983). *Security and loss control.* New York, NY: Macmillan.

Brookings Institution. (2002, July 25). *Brookings study details economic cost of recent corporate crises.* Washington, DC: Author. Retrieved from http://www.brookings.edu/comm/news/20020725graham.htm.

Brunet, J. R. (2008). Blurring the line between public and private sectors: The case of police officers' off-duty employment. *Public Personnel Management, 37*(2), 161–174. In Strom, K., Berzofsky, M., Shook-Sa, B., Barrick, K., Daye, C, Horstmann, N., & Kinney, S. (2010). *The private security industry: A review of the definitions, available data sources, and paths moving forward.* Retrieved from https://www.ncjrs.gov/pdffiles1/bjs/grants/232781.pdf.

Bureau of Labor Statistics (BLS). (2009). *Police and detectives. Occupational outlook handbook, 2010–2011 Edition.* Retrieved from http://www.bls.gov/oco/ocos160.htm.

Churchman, C. W. (1968). *The systems approach.* New York, NY: Delacorte Press.

Cunningham, W., Strauchs, J. J., & Van Meter, C. W. (1990). *The Hallcrest report II: Private security trends 1970–2000.* Boston, MA: Butterworth-Heinemann.

Cunningham, W., & Taylor, T. H. (1985). *Private security and police in America: The Hallcrest report.* Portland, OR: Chancellor Press.

Dalton, D. (1994, September). Looking for the quality-oriented contractor. *Security Technology & Design.*

Dancs, A. (2012). *Homeland Security: Spending since 9/11.* Retrieved from http://costofwar.com/publications/2011/ten-years-after-911/top-ten-security-spending-numbers-you-need-know.

Dempsey, J. S. (2008). *Introduction to private security.* Belmont, CA: Thomson Wadsworth.

Dempsey, J. S., & Forst, L. S. (2008). *An introduction to policing* (4th ed., pp. 62–63). Belmont, CA: Thomson/Wadsworth.

Fischer, R., Halibozek, E., & Green, G. (2008). *Introduction to security* (8th ed.). Boston, MA: Butterworth-Heinemann.

Freedonia Group. (2000, October). *Security services—Private companies report.* Cleveland, OH: Author. Retrieved from http://www.freedoniagroup.com/Security-Services.html.

Funny money. (2002, May 3). *Global Agenda.*

Hahn, C. (1990). *Adams' express and independent mail.* Retrieved from http://www.pennypost.org/PDF%20files/Adams%20Express%20by%20Hahn%201990.pdf.

Harne, E. G. (1996, March). Partnering with security providers. *Security Management.*

Hybrid staffing grows as contract replaces proprietary. (1996, April). *Security,* 86.

Joh, E. (2004). The paradox of private policing. *Journal of Criminal Law and Criminology, 95*(1), 49–131.

Kakalik, J. S., & Wildhorn, S. (1971). *Private police in the United States: Findings and recommendations* (RAND Report R-869-DOJ). Santa Monica, CA: The RAND Corporation.

Kobrak, C. (2009). Innovation corrupted: The origins and legacy of Enron's collapse. *Business History Review, 83*(1), 173–177.

Law Enforcement–Private Security Consortium. (2009). *Operation partnership: Trends and practices in law enforcement and private security collaborations.* Washington, DC: U.S. Department of Justice, Office of Community Oriented Policing Services.

Levine, S. A. (1963). Allan Pinkerton: America's first private eye. New York, NY: Dodd, Mead.

National Advisory Committee on Criminal Justice Standards and Goals. (1976). *Private security: Report of the Task Force on Private Security.* Washington, DC: U.S. Department of Justice, Law Enforcement Assistance Administration (LEAA).

Nemeth, C. J. (2004). *Private security and the law.* New York, NY: Elsevier.

Olhausen Research, Inc. (2004). *National policy summit: Private security/public policing.* Retrieved from http://www.cops.usdoj.gov/files/RIC/Publications/national_policy_summit.pdf.

150 scheming employees fired. (1990, May 27). *Peoria Journal Star.*

Security–Police Information Network. (2007). *Study of law enforcement-private security partnerships* (Project funded by the COPS Office). Washington, DC: U. S. Department of Justice. Retrieved from http://www.cops.usdoj.gov/files/RIC/Publications/connors-27.pdf.

Serb, T. J. (1983, November). How to select a guard company. *Security World,* 33.

Shearing, C. D., & Stenning, P. C. (1984). *Private security and private justice: The challenge of the 80s.* Quebec, Ont., Canada: Institute for Research on Public Policy.

Shearing, C. D., & Stenning, P. C. (1987). Say cheese! The Disney order that is not so Mickey Mouse. In C. D. Shearing & P. C. Stenning (Eds.), *Private policing* (pp. 317–323). Newbury Park, CA: Sage.

Siatt, W., & Matteson, S. (1982, January). Special report: Trends in security. *Security World, 25.*

Strom, K., Berzofsky, M., Shook-Sa, B., Barrick, K., Daye, C, Horstmann, N., & Kinney, S. (2010). *The private security industry: A review of the definitions, available data sources, and paths moving forward.* Retrieved from https://www.ncjrs.gov/pdffiles1/bjs/grants/232781.pdf.

U.S. Department of Defense. (2006, February 28). *National Industrial Security Program operating manual.* Retrieved from http://www.fas.org/sgp/library/nispom.htm.

U.S. Department of Health and Human Services. (n.d.). *Hurricane Katrina.* Retrieved from http://www.hhs .gov/disasters/emergency/naturaldisasters/hurricanes/katrina/index.html.

U.S. Department of Labor, Bureau of Labor Statistics. (2012, May). *Occupational employment and wages.* Washington, DC: Author.

West v. Atkins, 487 U.S. 42, 50 (1988).

Zalud, B. (1990, September). What's happening to security? *Security, 42.*

Zalud, B. (2002, January). 2002 industry forecast study security yin-yang: Terror push, recession. *Security.* Retrieved from http://www.securitymagazine.com/articles/2002-industry-forecast-study-br-security-yin-yang-terror-push-recession-drag-1.

14

Measuring Organizational Effectiveness and Service Quality

LEARNING OBJECTIVES

Upon completion of this chapter, students should be able to do the following:

- Define customer (market) orientation theory
- Define the quality function deployment technique
- Identify the three service matrices and their interlink
- Define the six stages of a matrix
- Identify different parts of a house of quality
- Define the dual functions of law enforcement agencies
- Define the internal and external measures of performance
- Apply the quality function deployment (QFD)
- Define its relative importance in QFD
- Calculate relative and absolute importance

(Continued)

(Continued)

- Calculate the correlation matrix in the roof of the house
- Calculate target specifications for service measures in the basement of the house
- Explain what is carried from the first to the second matrix
- Explain what is carried from the second to the third matrix
- Explain the advantages and disadvantages of QFD
- Differentiate between front office and back office
- Explain a process flowchart
- Explain different kinds of poka-yoke

Criminal justice agencies provide important services that not only ensure public safety, but also play a critical role in providing a stable environment for investment and economic growth in any nation, thus leading to prosperity. However, little is known about their service quality, which may be because of sparse public debate about criminal justice activities amplified by the problems in assessing the values of the services provided. Though that traditionally, criminal justice organizations did not have competitors, they are now finding, more and more private agencies are taking on public services, thus putting competitive pressure to improve their service delivery. Not only are criminal justice organizations being held to higher standards by citizens, they are also being asked by citizens, both at the local and national level, to justify their expenditures and activities, which are predominantly paid through tax dollars. To improve service delivery, as discussed throughout this book, criminal justice agencies have to recognize the customers and accept them as an integral part of the service process while designing the service delivery system. Supporting this viewpoint, Moore and Stephens (1991) argue that trying to fight crime without first developing relationships with the community is a fruitless exercise. Therefore, the principal objective of this chapter is to help students redesign/modify criminal justice services with the objective of placing the customer at the center of the organization's activities.

Application of Customer Orientation Theory to Enhance Service Quality

Drummond, Ensor, Laing, and Richardson (2000) applied the *customer (market) orientation theory,* which places the customer at the center of the organization's activities, to examine police service strategies in the New York Police Department (NYPD). The NYPD, which "presided over one of the worst crime rates in America coupled with a police force exhibiting poor morale and corruption" (p. 583), achieved a total transformation as a result of the efforts made. Drummond et al. found a "three stage turnaround process to enhance service quality and highlight the importance of market orientation in counteracting the concept of unwilling/reluctant customers" (p. 571). According to their findings, the improvement of service quality in the NYPD resulted from various factors, which can be grouped into the following areas:

Customer focus. The organization's culture placed importance on being customer focused and pursued formal programs for enhancement. It developed a deeper understanding of who its customers were, which established the overall role those departments/functional groups would play in external customer service. In addition, internal customer/supplier interfaces were improved to enhance internal service delivery (a supply chain approach was used, as presented in Chapter 3). The senior management in the NYPD viewed law enforcement as a service profession and implemented a service delivery program including courtesy, professionalism, and respect (CPR). Drummond et al. (2000) found that the CPR program was compliance tested via officers posing as members of the public, with duty officers being rewarded or rebuked. In Chapter 3, an extended discussion on recognizing the different customers of criminal justice services was provided, which is a prerequisite to improving the customer focus of the services offered.

Communication. The researchers found that the NYPD had a streamlined information flow system and a "high degree of awareness among staff as to how briefings would take place and how they could provide feedback to senior management" (Drummond et al., 2000, p. 581). In return, the senior managers emphasized the importance of communication with their staff to get their support for the program. Effective communication was evident in vertical (top-down and bottom-up) and horizontal (across functional areas) communication. The NYPD enhanced vertical communication through round-table sessions, bringing the commissioner into regular contact with patrol-level officers. COMPSTAT (a comparative statistics program used by police departments to collect and analyze crime data and set standards for policing accountability aimed at lowering criminal activity) was used to achieve lateral flows of communication, forcing patrol officers to cooperate, as it required them to talk to one another. External communication was also considered an extremely important function, as it was used to inform and secure feedback from customer groups in a two-way process. The NYPD used surveys/polls in the New York media relating to law enforcement issues to gather citizen feedback as a substitute for the high-cost strategy of conducting citizen surveys themselves. Communication was considered a learning process for the NYPD and for educating people about its role. The NYPD regularly invited community representatives into command centers to explain major initiatives prior to their implementation. In Chapter 8, an extended discussion was presented on how organizations—specifically, different agencies in the criminal justice system—can improve their communication process, which is an important component in improving customer satisfaction.

Leadership. Drummond et al. (2000) found strong leadership was evident in the NYPD in the form of a clearly communicated vision and a problem-solving approach that challenged the existing assumptions. The leadership style was supportive and facilitative and not autocratic or aggressive. In Chapter 7, an extensive discussion was provided on how organizations—especially the branches of the criminal justice system—can provide a supportive leadership role, which is important for improving customer satisfaction.

Motivation and morale. Employees were actively involved in giving suggestions and in the designing of the service process and improvements targeted at increasing customer focus. Employee empowerment was prevalent within the context of strong management control systems, which provided a basis for planning, problem solving, and learning. Collective team spirit was enhanced by the active support of senior management. In addition, greater internal customer/supplier interface allowed greater involvement, which not only streamlined processes but also provided higher staff morale. The behavioral shift in leadership style allowed for greater staff motivation. In Chapter 6, an extensive discussion was presented on various motivational theories to increase staff morale and enthusiasm, which is crucial to improving customer satisfaction.

The findings illustrating the NYPD turnaround process strengthen the conviction of the authors that the knowledge provided in this book can be used productively to bring customer orientation to the various branches of the criminal justice system at the national, state, and local levels. The first step in improving a service delivery process is identifying the customers and recognizing their importance—also called a customer focus—which is the primary theme presented in Chapters 1 through 3. In Chapter 4, the pressures forcing criminal justice agencies to become more customer-oriented were presented. In Chapters 5 through 8, the management principles of leadership, communication, motivation, and ethics, integrated with the principles of service quality, were presented—the application of which are demonstrated in the case of the NYPD service quality turnaround. In Chapters 9 through 13, the functional knowledge of criminal justice agencies was presented to help the reader integrate the service quality principles in these areas. In this last chapter, a hands-on tool is provided to incorporate the voice of the customer in designing/modifying criminal justice services to improve the delivery of service quality. This technique, called the *quality function deployment,* translates the voice of the customer or customer needs (the *whats*) into the day-to-day management activities within an organization (the *hows*) through a set of matrices.

Understanding the Dual Role of Criminal Justice Services

The criminal justice system is an example of a complex service environment that consists of demanding customers with diverse needs. Typically, criminal justice is committed to upholding the law and keeping the peace, preventing crime and keeping people safe, detecting and apprehending criminals, making arrests, punishing offenders, and assisting citizens in distress (Guy, 1992). The range of activities is very wide, and can be classified in two broad functions, namely, *agents of control* and *agents of support.* Crime statistics do not provide an accurate picture of the order maintenance functions performed by the police (Furstenberg & Wellford, 1973). As discussed in Chapter 9, by most estimates, only 25% of the police workload is directly related to crimes or law enforcement activities. Much greater time is spent on activities that can be only indirectly related to crime, such as responding to automatic alarms that may not be functioning properly, undertaking crime prevention initiatives, patrolling traffic accidents that may not involve criminal behavior, and performing social services such as assisting the elderly (Guy, 1992). Similarly, the other branches of the criminal justice system play this dual function in society, providing both control and support. For example, a probation officer not only provides control over the activities of the probationer, but also gives support to the individual to reintegrate into society. Likewise, courts not only deliberate cases that restrict the independence of the defendant, but they also have to think of the process of support so that the offender can return to society. In addition, the courts are deliberating on other issues that focus on the changing needs of society and have nothing to do with crime.

Recognizing the dual nature of the functions played by criminal justice agencies is a useful starting point. Police act as both an *agent of control* (referred to as the law enforcement and order maintenance roles in Chapter 9) and an *agent of support* (referred to as the order maintenance and crime prevention duties in Chapter 9) (Woolpert, 1980). Historically, the control function has been given more importance and greater media coverage, though in fact the supportive function forms the bulk of police work (Whitehouse, 1973; Woolpert, 1980). Therefore, police services need to be examined from these two viewpoints—one regarding services that are required to respond directly to public demands, and the other dealing with services required for community problem solving. A framework recognizing these two areas will facilitate the setting of appropriate service standards and the allocation of sufficient resources to meet the targets; otherwise, there may be tension because the support and control functions can be conflicting, at times. Substantiating this point, Butler (1992) gives an example of a community seeking to increase foot patrols to solve community problems. Involving more foot patrols will lead to diversion of resources from response services, which will in turn decrease the quality of response service. If this is not clearly communicated to the community, there may be a negative reaction to the police. The earlier argument also applies to other branches of the criminal justice system. The reader is encouraged to refer to Chapters 9 through 13 for a detailed discussion on the purpose and key functions of the various other branches of the criminal justice system.

Internal Versus External Measures

Often, criminal justice agencies operate under conflicting demands placed by different interest groups. Consequently, they must constantly reassess priorities to match the demands of pressure groups. In addition, they need a multiple-indicators approach to evaluate services; however, more inflexibility enters the system each time a detailed performance measure is instituted in criminal justice agencies, which subsequently increases the possibility of goal distortion and data manipulation. Therefore, there is a need to institute measures that drive efficient and effective agencies at the operational level, introducing the notion of management competence (Rogerson, 1995).

Performance assessment can be established on internal or external targets. *Internal measures* of service quality are associated with certain service functions or as indicators of progress toward a mission derived and monitored by administrators. These performance assessments are often implemented as a series of specific performance measures (Kelley & Swindell, 2002). In contrast, *external measures* of service effectiveness come from citizens, usually through *satisfaction surveys*. These two types of performance indicators are often characterized as *hard* and *soft measures* (Brudney & England, 1982).

The internal measures are typically quantitative in nature, thus bringing objectivity into the interpretation. For example, the police have relied on crime statistics as an indication of how well they are carrying out their duties. Rogerson (1995) lists some of the more obvious examples of quantitative measures of police performance currently in use:

- Total crimes per 1,000 population
- Number of burglary detections per 1,000 officers
- Burglaries of dwellings per 1,000 dwellings
- Number of detections for violent crime per 100 officers
- Violent crimes per 1,000 population
- Percentage of 911 calls answered within target times
- Percentage of calls requiring immediate police response attended within target times
- Numbers of persons arrested/reported for notifiable offenses prosecuted
- Net expenditure per head of population on police (p. 27)

Scholars (Grasso & Epstein, 1987; Rogerson, 1995) have argued that emphasis on such quantitative performance measures can result in goal distortion; manipulation of results; and a short-run, microlevel orientation. To illustrate such distortion in police services, Rogerson (1995) gives an example:

> To measure police activity against criminals, the number of intelligence reports may be monitored. The number of such reports would almost certainly increase, as low-grade information, of little operational use, is duly submitted on the requisite forms. Individual patrolling officers will also be gently nudged by the persuasive, hidden hand of numerical performance targets towards achieving the figures. (p. 26)

The ever-popular quota in ticket writing probably comes to mind. Under this approach, driving violation tickets would be issued to drivers by police officers in some towns for an act that would defy all logic, simply to meet the quantitative targets set by the agency.

Besides the temptation of distorting the numbers to suit the targets, the quantitative data suffer from other limitations. For example, national performance data are derived from averaging millions of police–public interactions, and it would not be prudent to use such data to create performance targets for the police officers working in local communities (Rogerson, 1995). Number and types of crimes committed in a community may be more of a reflection of its diverse demographics and economic problems, which may not resonate with the national averages. Furthermore, such objective statistics may be confounded by other factors, such as the propensity of the public to report crimes and the integrity of the police in recording those crimes. The traditional quantitative indicators often "neglect the enormous amount of social support they [police] give to people who desperately need help" (Rogerson, 1995, p. 28). It is a general belief that both the police and the public would benefit if the criteria for evaluating police performance were broadened to include support activities, such as returning stray pets to their owners, mediating family quarrels, removing illegally parked cars, and so forth (Rogerson, 1995). Scholars believe that quantitative performance measures cannot become "a substitute for full and proper police accountability to the general public. Accountability cannot be reduced to monitoring numbers. Accountability is about explanation, and this can only really be meaningful to the general public at a local level" (Rogerson, 1995, p. 28). Customer satisfaction should be an important part of performance accountability in a market system. Therefore, external measures of service effectiveness should be typically collected at the local level from citizens through satisfaction surveys.

Using QFD: Incorporating the Voice of the Customer in Improving Service Quality

Integrating External and Internal Measures

Most scholars, however, believe that it is important to integrate *objective/hard measures* with *subjective/soft measures,* thus incorporating the *voice of the customers* (which is external) into the design of the service process (which is internal). More than four decades ago, Ostrom (1973) recommended developing multiple indicators of service quality, including citizen perceptions and establishing relationships among indicators. In other words, there is a need to identify and develop internal performance measures that connect well with external measures provided by citizen evaluations. Kelly and Swindell (2002) found that in the existing evaluative system used by police, not much of a relationship existed between internal measures and several citizen satisfaction (external) measures. One obvious reason explaining this lack of relationship may be that internal measures are calculated typically at the national level, whereas external measures from citizen surveys are adopted at local neighborhood levels. Another important reason for this lack of correlation may be because of a comparability issue between administrative and citizen evaluations of service quality. Park (1984) has explained this lack of congruence between the types of things that departments measure and those that citizens notice. Typically, internal measures are based in inputs, efficiencies, and outputs, but external performance measures are outcome based. For example, public opinion surveys reveal the fear that people have about crime in their cities and neighborhoods. Fear of crime is real, but it is hard to measure. Therefore, it is important to understand the indicators of people's safety to develop realistic internal targets to fight crime. In other words, delivering quality services requires the determination of what the customer wants (external measures) and then responding through day-to-day management initiatives (internal measures).

One systematic tool for making a link between the customer needs and the day-to-day management initiatives is called *quality function deployment* (QFD) (Akao, 1990; Hauser & Clausing, 1988), also referred to as the *house of quality*. QFD is a powerful tool that allows the integration of both the service provider and the customer (various stakeholders who are direct and indirect customers). It is a structured methodology that was developed during the late 1960s in Japan by Yoji Akao and first applied at Mitsubishi Kobe Shipyards in 1972 to increase customer satisfaction. The technique was subsequently adapted to other manufacturing industries. In applying this technique to a service environment, the reader has to be mindful of the various characteristics that distinguish a service from a product, a detailed discussion on which was presented in Chapter 3. Furthermore, the complexities are magnified when the QFD is adapted to public services such as criminal justice because of the nature of the customers, the decision makers, and the complex environment surrounding public services.

In a service environment, QFD uses a set of three matrices to interlink external and internal measures, thus providing an interface between customer needs and day-to-day management techniques adopted at the frontline worker level (Ermer & Kniper, 1998). This technique allows the incorporation of the voice of the customer into the service process design, which improves service quality. To make the discussion more manageable to be covered in a single chapter, this discussion is limited to the law enforcement field, recognizing that different branches of the criminal justice system may have different requirements on performance and feedback. Here, the discussion is kept very general, but students are encouraged to mimic the steps and apply them to other agencies in criminal justice. First, a discussion is presented on the different subparts of a house of quality and how to construct it. Subsequently, the nature of the interface between the three matrices comprising service quality is described. To help the reader better assimilate these concepts, a QFD is constructed for law enforcement service using a hypothetical example presented in the Appendix at the end of this chapter.

Subparts of a House of Quality

Each matrix can be viewed as a set of six stages (see Figure 14.1), providing a systematic hierarchical framework (Han, Chen, Ebrahimpour, & Sodhi, 2001). The same six stages need to be followed in constructing the second and third matrix. The *first stage* is called the *voice of the customer,* and it is composed of three steps. The first step is to develop critical customer requirements, which are extremely important since they are the driving force in the QFD. These features form the primary service bundle attributes desired by the target customers. Therefore, the organization should objectively determine the group or groups that best describe its current or desired customer base. Using a variety of methods, the wants of the customer groups are determined. Some of the methods used for collecting this information (the whats) are interviews, questionnaires, town hall meetings, articles written in the local press, and reports presented in the local media. It is extremely critical for law enforcement

Figure 14.1 Subparts of a QFD Model

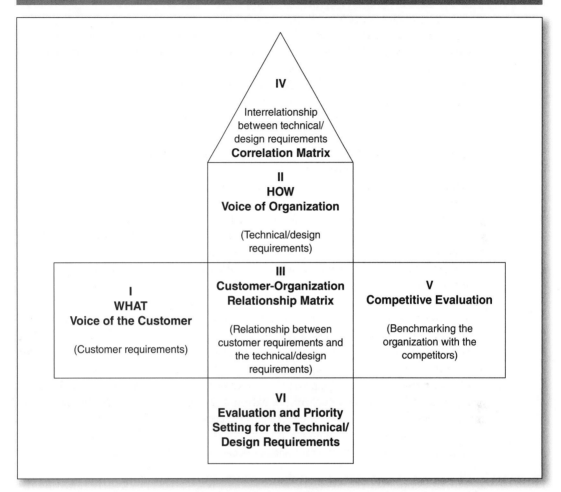

departments to use terms, phrases, and language that the customers understand if interviews and questionnaires are used. This means that the use of *police-ese* should be avoided in all communications with the public when collecting information. Law enforcement agencies also have to be careful that bias does not occur in customer response because of a fear of retaliation from the police for negative feedback. Often, a third party can be used to collect the information on behalf of the law enforcement agency to prevent any bias.

Typically, there will be too many customer requirements. These will be phrases used by customers to describe the service and service characteristics. To make them manageable, the second step in this stage is that customer requirements are systematically grouped or bundled to represent an overall customer concern. The QFD team will group this information using varying techniques ranging from intuition to sophisticated statistical techniques (Motwani, Kumar, & Mohamed, 1996). The outcome is customer requirements, which are then presented as the *rows of the matrix*.

Not all customer requirements are equally important. Therefore, after consolidating the "whats," as a third step, the QFD team should determine the priority that is to be allocated to each of the customer requirements. The objective here is to develop a better understanding of which customer requirements should receive greater attention in later service design efforts and the target levels that need to be set for them in the second stage. In setting these priorities, the QFD team will not only examine the collected data but will also work closely with customers to determine the priorities and factor in the customer-complaint data. More advanced statistical techniques can also be used that allow customers to state their preferences. These weightings are displayed next to the customer attribute in the *relative importance column*. The weightings are represented in terms of percentages, with the entire list totaling 100%. Sometimes, the weightings can be allocated on the basis of simple classifications of customer requirements. The customer requirement classified as very important can be weighted as 9, the customer requirement classified as being of medium importance can be weighted as 5, and the customer requirement classified as less important can be weighted as 1. There is no hard-and-fast rule on this weighting scheme; the QFD team members simply have to come to a consensus on the weights they would like to attach to each category.

In the *second stage,* the *service measures/characteristics* (the hows) are introduced. The QFD team describes the service measures/characteristics that identify how the service will be delivered to customers when they interact with the service provider. QFD teams should walk through the various steps at which the customer can potentially interact with the service provider and identify relevant measures to capture each interaction. These items that form the external service characteristics should be precise. Far more numbers of service measures/characteristics (hows) will be identified during the brainstorming session, but not all of them will be selected for implementation. Each measure/characteristic that is selected for implementation forms a *column in the matrix*.

In the *third stage,* the *relationship matrix* is created. The QFD team fills the *main body of the matrix* by indicating how much each service measure/characteristic (how) correlates to each customer requirement (what). The QFD team seeks consensus on these evaluations based on expert opinion, customer responses, and tabulated data from statistical studies under controlled experiments (Hauser & Clausing, 1988). These relationships are typically described on a scale anchored as strong (= 9 points), medium (= 5 points), weak (= 1 point), and no relationship (= 0 points). The direction of the relationships is represented by a positive or a negative sign.

Next, the *absolute importance* is calculated for each service measure, which provides a method for determining which service measures have the largest effect on meeting customer requirements. The above numerical values calculated in the third stage are multiplied with a relative importance rating (calculated in Step 3 of Stage 1 and given in the relative importance column) to calculate an absolute importance value for each service measure. The mathematical representation of calculating the absolute importance rating of each service measure is determined as follows (Han et al., 2001):

$$D_j = \Sigma_i A_i R_{ij} \text{ for } i = 1, \ldots \ldots n; \text{ and } j = 1, \ldots \ldots m$$

where

D_j = importance weight of the jth service measure

A_i = importance weight of the ith customer requirement

R_{ij} = relationship value between the ith customer requirement and the jth service measure

n = number of customer requirements

m = number of service measures

In the *fourth stage,* a *correlation matrix* between the service measures/characteristics is created, which is presented in the *roof of the house.* Here, the relationships between the service measures are identified. These relationships are typically described on a scale anchored as strong (= 9 points), medium (= 5 points), weak (= 1 point), and no relationship (= 0 points). The direction of the relationships is represented by a positive or a negative sign. A positive correlation is where one service measure supports another service measure. Alternatively, a negative correlation exists when one service measure adversely impacts another service measure. Information provided in the fourth stage helps the organization decide which service measures should be developed together (obviously, the ones with a high positive correlation). The information presented in the correlation matrix also informs the organization of which service measures will be negatively impacted by other service measures and, hence, to keep a close watch on them.

In the *fifth stage,* a *competitive analysis* is performed. The main objective here is to gauge whether meeting the perceived needs will yield a competitive advantage. In this exercise, a simple question is asked—namely, How good is this policing agency when compared to other law enforcement agencies located in a similar demographical location *in fulfilling the given customer requirements?* Here, it is important to choose another agency for comparison that faces similar demands so that the comparison is between apples and apples. There may not be any direct competition in the area of law enforcement; but such an analysis with agencies at other geographical locations can provide an advantage of greater funds and grant money. The comparison can also identify opportunities for improvement, which has positive implications for customer satisfaction. This comparison allows the organization to set realistic target levels for each of the customer requirements that the organization hopes to achieve. Because of limited resources, trade-offs have to be made between different customer requirements based on the comparison with the competition. The competitive analysis is represented on the *far-right side of the matrix.*

In the *sixth stage,* a *comparative analysis of the service measures/characteristics* is performed, which becomes the basis for setting the targets for service measures. The QFD team assesses and compares the organization's service measures/characteristics to those of the competition. In this exercise, a simple question is asked—namely, how good is this policing agency at *fulfilling a particular service measure* when compared to another law enforcement agency located in a similar demographical location? It is important to choose an agency that faces similar demands. These *comparisons with the competition* are represented in the *subbasement of the house.* These comparisons, along with the industry norms, then become the basis for specifying target values that the organization aims to achieve in order to improve. At this time, the organization can also explore the projected cost of enhancing the service measures to the target specification. It is prudent to brainstorm other organizational constraints such as technical difficulty and the amount of time that may be required to implement the target specifications of each service measure. At this point, if the QFD team members are not satisfied with any of the outcomes, they can go back and make changes to any of the previous stages. These service measure targets are typically presented in the *basement of the house.*

Interface Between Matrices

Traditionally, QFD has been presented in a manufacturing environment as a structured methodology that provided a chain-like interface between four matrices. This set of matrices translated customer requirements into product design and manufacturing process requirements, thus providing for increased customer satisfaction. However, in a service environment, such as law enforcement, *QFD uses three matrices.* It provides a chain-like interface between these different matrices, representing customer needs and service measures, design and process characteristics, and day-to-day quality management techniques adopted at the frontline worker level. This integration between matrices results in day-to-day consistency in meeting or exceeding customer requirements (Ermer & Kniper, 1998).

The *first matrix* presents the relationship between customer requirements (rows) and service measures/characteristics (columns) (Ermer & Kniper, 1998). The five broad dimensions typically representing customer requirements (the whats) are reliability, responsiveness, assurance, tangibles, and empathy (Parsuraman, Zeithaml, & Berry, 1985; 1988). The service measures/characteristics (the hows) can be broadly divided into (1) impact/outcome measures, which are associated with the outcome of the service; and (2) those involved with the service process, which are associated with the experience that customers have when they go through the service delivery process. For example, when a customer goes to a restaurant, the service is delivered on two fronts. The first is *outcome-based,* which is the quality/taste of the food. The second is *process-based,* which is the entire experience provided to the customers in the restaurant, beginning from the time they walked in, to the time they walked out. In law enforcement, an example of outcome-based measures would typically be the statistics collected on various types of crimes in a county. When the outcome-based statistics are declining, it provides greater satisfaction to the customer. On the other hand, the process-based measures would be composed of items such as, "How fast did the police respond to a 911 call?" or, "How did the officers interact once they were at the crime scene?" These measures will meet customer requirements as the customer goes through the process with law enforcement officers. Therefore, the first matrix identifies a set of service measures/characteristics (hows) delivered by the organization to satisfy the customers' desires (whats).

The *second matrix* takes the service measures/characteristics (the hows) from the first matrix and treats them as whats. In other words, the service measures/characteristics are what the organization wants to deliver (rows). Next, a set of *service design elements* (hows) are identified (columns) that can deliver these *service measures/characteristics* (whats). In simple words, Matrix 2 is providing an answer to the question, How should the service be designed (that is, what service design elements should be included) to optimally provide for the service measures/characteristics (derived from Matrix 1)? To answer this question, one has to do introspection within the organization to identify the specific service design elements. These service design elements relate to structural issues such as service capacity, facility design, technology, and location, as well as managerial issues such as service culture, including ethics and leadership, workforce selection and training, workforce motivation and empowerment, quality management, and information management.

The *third matrix* takes the service design elements (the hows) from the second matrix and treats them as whats. In other words, the service design elements are what the organization wants to deliver (rows). Next, a set of *day-to-day management techniques* are identified (hows) that can deliver these service design elements (columns). In simple words, Matrix 3 is providing an answer to the question of how the day-to-day service should be managed to ensure that the service design elements are consistently met. Some of the general daily management techniques (hows) that apply to most service settings include the number of hours in maintenance of equipment, numbers of hours of continuous education, and so forth.

What is carried from Matrix 1 to Matrix 2? The most important service measures/ *characteristics* (*hows*) based on their relative rank are carried into Matrix 2, where they become *whats*. Those service measures/*characteristics* that are ranked lower may either be dropped from further consideration or may be developed at a later time once the important service measures/*characteristics* are under control (Ermer & Kniper, 1998). However, common sense should not be given up in choosing which service measures/ *characteristics* to carry over and which to give up. The absolute importance of each service measure/*characteristic* in Matrix 1 is transferred to Matrix 2, where it becomes the relative importance column. Here, the choice is either to transfer the normalized scores or transfer them in their absolute form. There is no one best method. Typically, the use of normalized scores is preferred because the absolute score can soon become a gigantic number as it translates through the matrices. Subsequently, the absolute importance in Matrix 2 for each service design *element* is calculated, which shows how important each of *them is* in ensuring consistent service measures/*characteristics*. The absolute importance for each service design *element* appears at the bottom of Matrix 2. The normalized scores for absolute importance appear in the row directly below the absolute importance row, which can also be treated as relative rank.

What is carried from Matrix 2 to Matrix 3? The service design *elements* (*hows*) are carried over from Matrix 2 to Matrix 3, where they become *whats*. The normalized score for absolute importance of each service design *element* in Matrix 2 is transferred to Matrix 3 and becomes the relative importance column. Subsequently, the absolute importance in Matrix 3 for each management technique is calculated, which shows how important each of these techniques is in ensuring consistent service quality. The absolute importance for each *management* technique appears at the bottom of Matrix 3. The normalized scores for absolute importance appear in the row directly below the absolute importance row, which can also be treated as relative rank.

It should be noted here that the voice of the customer is introduced as customer requirements into the first matrix and then carried through the second and the third matrices by developing linkages between inputs and outputs of different phases of development. The earlier concepts are applied in constructing a QFD for a law enforcement service using an armchair example (Lilley & Hinduja, 2006; Ostrom, Parks, Percy, & Whitaker, 1979; Selen & Schepers, 2001; Sung, 2006) that is presented in the Appendix, which students are now encouraged to read. The purpose of this exercise is to provide the reader a better perspective on how these matrices are constructed. The reader is reminded that there would be far more entries in each of the matrices when constructed using a real-life example.

Advantages

When the house of quality is complete, the QFD team can then examine and use it to achieve service realization that will allow the criminal justice agency to enjoy improved resource use and provide greater customer and employee satisfaction. QFD enables an organization (the service provider) to focus proactively on customer requirements early in the design stage. It is a process that helps organizations make trade-offs between what the customer desires and what the organization can afford to provide. Moreover, it helps in evaluating customer requirements, which often may conflict with each other. For example, choosing to focus on pleasant demeanor and flexibility can be effective, but may come at the expense of other customer requirements such as speed and efficiency. However, careful planning through the use of QFD formally recognizes the existence of such a trade-off, allowing the planners to make informed choices and preventing service failures. The process of going through the trade-offs provides a comprehensive knowledge of the interrelatedness of the different functions within an organization and the corresponding impact on service performance (Stuart & Tax, 1996). It allows all the players to see the supply chain synergy between different functions, and forces them to communicate effectively across these functions and agencies to bring superior service quality. Moreover, these trade-offs call into application the leadership qualities of criminal justice officers and managers. In addition, use of QFD will build credibility for the criminal justice agency among citizens as they see their needs are being fulfilled. In addition, QFD team members obtain a collective understanding of the customer needs, which builds team awareness throughout the organization since the QFD members come from a variety of positions in the agency (Motwani et al., 1996). The team building promoted by QFD also allows for easier implementation of changes, as everyone takes ownership of the required modifications. Finally, the whole exercise creates documentation, which is very useful for improving service quality.

Disadvantages

Administrators are faced with asking the question of how accurate is the information available from the citizens submitting their responses. A major problem with these measures is that different people may use dissimilar evaluative criteria in responding to the survey questions. It is often asked whether citizens can really rate services with which they may have had very little or no interaction. Could the responses be influenced by race, gender, economic status, or rural/urban location? What about gossip and hearsay regarding police services? If the QFD is not constructed and applied properly, it may increase work without producing much benefit for the customer (Akao, 1990). Bias can be introduced into any stage of the QFD implementation and erroneous conclusions can be made (Griffin & Hauser, 1993). Since serial matrices are drawn, errors introduced at one stage can carry through the successive stages (Suttler, 1994). Furthermore, the QFD is an information-intensive exercise that requires good communication and statistical application, which if not provided can lead to failures and uninformed decisions. Of course, when done properly, citizen surveys can provide useful information about the overall service quality, but scientific methodology and education must be applied in the collection and analysis of the data.

CAREER HIGHLIGHT BOX
POLICE, FIRE, AND AMBULANCE DISPATCHERS

Nature of the Work

Police, fire, and ambulance dispatchers, also called 9-1-1 operators or public safety telecommunicators, answer emergency and non-emergency calls. They take information from the caller and send the appropriate type and number of units. Police, fire and ambulance dispatchers typically do the following:

- Answer 9-1-1 telephone calls
- Determine, from the caller, the type of emergency and its location
- Decide the appropriate emergency response based on agency policies and procedures
- Relay information to the appropriate emergency or non-emergency service agency or agencies

(Continued)

(Continued)

- Coordinate sending emergency response personnel
- Give over-the-phone medical help and other instructions before emergency personnel get to the scene
- Monitor and track the status of police, fire, and ambulance units on assignment
- Synchronize responses with other area communication centers
- Keep detailed records about calls

Dispatchers answer calls for service when someone needs help from police, fire fighters, emergency services, or a combination of the three. They take both emergency and non-emergency calls. Dispatchers must stay calm while collecting vital information from callers to determine the severity of a situation. They then give the appropriate first responder agencies information about the call. Some dispatchers only take calls. Others only use radios to send appropriate personnel. Many dispatchers do both tasks.

Dispatchers keep detailed records about the calls that they take. They may use a computer system to log important facts, such as the name and location of the caller. They may also use crime databases, maps, and weather reports, when helping emergency response teams. Dispatchers may monitor alarm systems, alerting law enforcement or fire personnel when a crime or fire occurs. In some situations, dispatchers must work with people in other jurisdictions to share information or to transfer calls.

Dispatchers must often give instructions on what to do before responders arrive. Some dispatchers are trained to give medical help over the phone, For example, they might help someone give first aid until emergency medical services get to the scene. (A separate statement on emergency medical technicians and paramedics appears elsewhere in the Handbook.)

Work environment. The work of dispatchers can be very hectic when many calls come in at the same time. The job of public safety dispatchers is particularly stressful because a slow or an improper response to a call can result in serious injury or further harm. Also, callers who are anxious or afraid may become excited and be unable to provide needed information; some may even become abusive. Despite provocations, dispatchers must remain calm, objective, and in control of the situation.

Dispatchers sit for long periods, using telephones, computers, and two-way radios. Much of their time is spent at video display terminals, viewing monitors and observing traffic patterns. As a result of working for long stretches with computers and other electronic equipment, dispatchers can experience significant eyestrain and back discomfort. Generally, dispatchers work a 40-hour week; however, rotating shifts and compressed work schedules are common. Most dispatchers work 8- to 12-hour shifts, but some agencies choose to use 24-hour shifts. Dispatchers often have to work weekends, holidays, and overtime, as emergency calls can come in at any time.

Training, Qualifications, and Advancement

Most police, fire, and ambulance dispatchers have a high school diploma or GED. Additional requirements vary. Many states require dispatchers to become certified. The important qualities desired in dispatchers are:

Ability to multitask. Responding to an emergency over the phone can be stressful. Dispatchers must stay calm to simultaneously answer calls, collect vital information, coordinate responders, and assist callers.

Empathy. People who call 9-1-1 are often in distress. Dispatchers must be willing and able to help callers with a wide variety of needs. They must be calm, polite, and sympathetic, while also quickly getting information.

Leadership skills. Dispatchers work with law enforcement, emergency response teams, and civilians in emergency situations. They must be able to efficiently communicate the nature of the emergency and coordinate the appropriate response.

Listening skills. When answering an emergency call or handling radio communications, a dispatcher must listen carefully. Some callers might have trouble speaking because of anxiety or stress. Dispatchers must be able to record the call accurately.

Problem-solving skills. Dispatchers must be able to choose wisely between tasks that are competing for their attention. They must be able to quickly determine the appropriate action when people call for help.

Education and training: The typical entry-level education is a high school diploma or a GED. However, some employers may not specify any educational requirements. Others prefer to hire dispatchers who have a related 2- or 4-year degree in a subject such as criminal justice, computer science, or communications.

Most dispatcher jobs require an applicant to complete an interview as well as to pass a written exam and a typing test. In addition, applicants may need to pass a background check, lie detector and drug tests, as well as tests for hearing and vision. Most states require a dispatcher to be a U.S. citizen, and some jobs require a driver's license. Both computer skills and customer service skills can be helpful, as is the ability to speak a second language.

Other qualifications. Training requirements vary by state. Some states require dispatchers to be certified. Several states require 40 hours or more of initial training. Some require continuing education every 2 to 3 years. Other states do not mandate any specific training, leaving individual agencies to conduct their own courses.

Some agencies have their own programs for certifying dispatchers; others use training from a professional association. The Association of Public-Safety Communications Officials (APCO), the National Emergency Number Association (NENA), and the National Academies of Emergency Dispatch (NAED) have established a number of recommended standards and best practices that agencies may use as a guideline for their own training programs.

Training is usually conducted in both a classroom setting and on the job, and is often followed by a probationary period of about 1 year. However, this may vary by agency as there is no national standard of how training is conducted or the length of probation.

Training covers a wide variety of topics, such as local geography, agency protocols, and standard procedures. Dispatchers are also taught how to use specialized equipment,

(Continued)

(Continued)

such as a 2-way radio and computer-aided dispatch (CAD) software. They receive training to prepare for specific types of incidents, such as a child abduction or a suicidal caller. Some dispatchers receive emergency medical dispatcher (EMD) training, which enables them to give medical assistance over the phone.

Certification and advancement. Dispatchers may choose to pursue additional certifications, such as NENA's emergency number professional (ENP) or APCO's Registered Public-Safety Leader (RPL) to prove their leadership skills and knowledge of the profession.

Dispatchers can become senior dispatchers or supervisors before going on to administrative positions, in which they may focus on a specific area, such as training or policy and procedures. Additional education and related work experience may be helpful in advancing to management level positions. Technology skills also may be helpful in becoming a supervisor.

Employment

Police, fire, and ambulance dispatchers held 100,100 jobs in 2010. It is expected to add 11,700 more new jobs between 2010 and 2020. Therefore, the total employment is expected to be 111,800 in 2020.

Job Outlook

The prevalence of cellular phones has increased the number of calls that dispatchers receive. This trend is likely to continue in the future, as new technologies, such as text messages and videos, will be used to communicate with dispatchers.

Employment change. Employment of police, fire, and ambulance dispatchers is expected to grow by 12 percent from 2010 to 2020, about as fast as average for all occupations. A larger and older population is likely to mean more emergency calls; and, therefore, a need for more dispatchers.

Job prospects. Favorable opportunities are expected, largely due to job openings arising from the need to replace workers who transfer to other occupations or who leave the occupation. The technology and equipment dispatchers use continues to evolve, creating a demand for workers with related technical skills. Job prospects will be best for those with customer service and computer skills.

Earnings

The median annual wage of police, fire, and ambulance dispatchers was $35,370 in May 2010. The median wage is the wage at which half the workers in an occupation earned more than that amount, and half earned less. The lowest 10 percent earned $22,310, and the top 10 percent earned more than $54,350. Most dispatchers work 8- to 12-hour shifts, but some agencies choose to use 24-hour shifts. Dispatchers often have to work weekends, holidays, and overtime, as emergency calls can come in at any time.

SOURCE: From the *Occupational Outlook Handbook,* 2012–13 Edition, by the U.S. Department of Labor, Bureau of Labor Statistics. Available online at http://www.bls.gov/ooh.

Designing Customer-Oriented Criminal Justice Services

Having learned how to incorporate the voice of the customer in service delivery processes, it is necessary to examine how to design this "customer-focused" system. The very first consideration in the design of a customer-focused service is to decide how the customer will interact with the organization, which introduces the *front office versus back office* concept. The *front office* of any service is the physical location where the service provider interacts with the customer and the service delivery takes place. The ground crew that checks passengers into airlines and the flight crew that services passengers during the flight are considered the front office of the airlines. Similarly, the area where a defendant interacts with the judge in a courtroom is the front office. Greater customer contact will require larger front-office space. On the other hand, the *back office* supports the activities of the front office, and is generally prevented from engaging in customer interactions. For example, the back office of an airline takes care of the luggage and other safety-related matters. In a courthouse, the court reporter who transcribes court activities or court clerks who handle the court's schedule are considered the back office; the control room from where the entire prison is monitored is the back office; law enforcement officers retrieving information from their computers or from dispatchers for verification are in the back office. Typically, customers are not allowed in the back office, which restricts their involvement. If a company decides to have limited customer involvement, then it typically transfers most activities to the back office and has a smaller front office. Courts that are allowing the use of the Internet to access court records and to file court documents are enlarging their front office—the customer is more involved in the activities that have traditionally taken place in the back office.

Some companies have used customer involvement to their advantage in the service delivery process. McDonald's, for example, has customers pick up their food, throw away their trash, and clear their tables. In this case, the customer is responsible for a portion of the service offered by McDonald's. Similarly, grocery stores that have customers bag their groceries are essentially using customers as temporary employees who arrive at work just in time to provide the services when they are needed. Obviously, such clever use of the customer to provide part of the services means a reduction in the cost of the service delivery, a part of which may be passed back to the customer in the form of reduced prices. The grocery chain Aldi's, for example, has lower grocery prices in part because customers load the items they buy into their grocery sacks. The important point here is that the service design had to be modified by Aldi's to include the customer in the service delivery. In the criminal justice system, the use of offenders in cleaning gang paraphernalia from buildings, involvement of communities in juries, volunteer cops, and neighborhood watch programs, to mention a few, are examples of clever uses of stakeholders in the service delivery. This reduces the cost of criminal justice administration. Similarly, prisons use convicts in cooking, cleaning, and in farming land and tending livestock used to feed inmates. According to the story presented in In the News 14.1, California prison factories generate $150 million in sales each year. This is a prime example of how effective and efficient use of customers can reduce the administrative cost of the criminal justice system and simultaneously provide better-quality service.

In the News 14.1
California Prison Factories Generate $150 Million in Sales Each Year, New UC Berkeley Report Finds

BERKELEY—If you think prison inmates only make license plates, you're behind the times.

A report released this month by an economist at the University of California, Berkeley found California prison factories and farms are responsible for over $150 million in direct sales annually in the state. Prison products today range from silk-screened clothing in Tehachapi to fine-ground optics in Vacaville.

The report is the first comprehensive study of the economic impact of the California Prison Industry Authority, the largest prison work program in any state. The organization employs about 7,000 inmates in 23 prisons from Del Norte to San Diego County, said report author George Goldman, a cooperative extension economist in the Department of Agriculture and Resource Economics at the UC Berkeley College of Natural Resources.

Prison work programs in California are voluntary, and inmates line up for a chance to work, even though they are paid on average only 57 cents per hour. The pay scale ranges from 30 cents to 95 cents per hour.

Goldman's study shows a positive economic impact on the state from prison work programs and also indicates what would happen if they did not exist. "If you wipe out the California Prison Industry Authority, you'd lose $62 million in personal income in the state," said Goldman. Additionally, 560 jobs would disappear, not counting those held by convicts and state civil service staff.

Goldman found prison labor is also healthy for the private sector. Prison programs produce goods that in many cases would otherwise come from outside the state while employing the private sector to supply raw materials. Biggest prison products are food, with $33 million in sales annually; fabrics, $32 million; paper and wood products, $30 million; and metal products, $22 million.

A main goal of prison work programs is to provide "a positive outlet to help inmates productively use their time and energies," said Frank Losco, spokesperson for the Prison Industry Authority. Another goal is to instill good work habits, including appropriate job behavior and time management.

Although the prison programs are self-supporting, "it's not trivial to set up one of these factories," said Goldman. "And the factories cannot be as efficient as the commercial sector, what with the extra costs of security, prison shutdowns and so forth."

In California, only government agencies are allowed to purchase prison products, unlike other states such as Nevada, where convicts make cars for retail sale, and Oregon, where jeans are produced. In fact, Oregon's jeans—labeled "Prison Blues"—proved so popular last year that prison factories couldn't keep up with demand.

In California, however, the prisons themselves are their own best customers. The California Department of Corrections purchases about half of what the prisons make, choosing from a Prison Industry Authority catalog.

Goldman has done economic surveys for many industries, but this is the first time he has studied prison work programs in depth, and even he was surprised at the breadth of items produced.

Prison goods and services include farm and dairy products, such as eggs, prunes and almonds; meat cutting; coffee roasting; manufacturing of furniture, shoes and clothing; dental and optical services; and much more, including a knitting mill run by the California Men's Colony in San Luis Obispo.

"I thought like everyone else, vaguely, that prisoners make license plates," said Goldman. "I didn't even know if they still did that.... I had no idea they made mattresses at San Quentin or still ran prison farms. They do make more than $10 million worth of license plates each year."

Compared to other California industries, prison production weighs in with about the same economic impact as book binding ($138 million), pulp mills ($133 million), chewing gum manufacturing ($142 million), or a single moderately successful Steven Spielberg film, said Goldman. That's small change compared to California's blockbuster industries such as agriculture, said Goldman, but "it's still a good thing and has a positive impact on the state."

SOURCE: From "California Prison Factories Generate $150 Million in Sales Each Year, New UC Berkeley Report Finds," by K. Scalise, June 25, 1998, University of California, Berkeley, Public Affairs Office, News Release. Available online at http://berkeley.edu/news/media/releases/98legacy/06-25-1998.html.

If the service delivery takes place at the service provider's facility, then attention to *facility design* is important because the customer's perception of quality may be influenced by the surroundings. Attention to layout, noise, furnishings, and so forth can influence the customer's impression of the service. Take the example of a luxury hotel, where the surroundings (color, decor, flower arrangements, etc.) lend to the general environment of pleasure. In another example, students may consider the classroom interaction in their impressions of their learning experience. To facilitate greater involvement of students in class discussion, the classroom has to be designed so that each student can interact face-to-face with the rest of the class. Classrooms that allow for students to move around, to swivel in their chairs to face others, and to see the person who is speaking may provide better surroundings for learning and involvement. Students have often commented to the authors that they get more involved in class discussions when the instructor can walk up within 10 feet of their seat and directly engage them. However, not all classrooms are designed in such a manner as to allow instructors to interact with their students within such close proximity, thus affecting the student's learning experience. Similar issues arise in designing a prison. It may be asked, How do the layout and furnishings in a prison impact the safety of the prisoners? Does the layout of the prison adequately separate the dangerous prisoners from the rest? Does the layout permit closed-circuit monitoring of prisoners at all times? Such questions are only raised if the prisoners are considered customers in the criminal justice system. Having a facility that supports inmate feelings of safety and security, and does not just consider traditional security measures, may improve the perception inmates have of the services they are receiving.

Unlike a product, a service cannot be inspected before delivery. For example, the improper use of force and foul language during an interrogation by a law enforcement officer would be termed a bad quality of service. However, by the time the inappropriate behavior of the officer is reported, the act has already been committed, and bad service has been delivered. The *simultaneous production and consumption* of services puts an added pressure on the service manager because it eliminates many opportunities for quality control. Therefore, quality control measures need to be installed within the service design and delivery process, supplemented with rigorous training of the officers, to prevent bad service occurrences. As has been pointed out in other chapters, training should be provided regularly in the criminal justice system to address the changing needs of society and to better tailor services to those needs.

For greater effectiveness, the training regimen should be designed in relation to the performance measures, which in turn should be aligned with the objectives of the organization to make them more responsive to the communities they serve. Currently, when police officers answer service calls relating to order maintenance, the appreciation they receive is primarily from the citizens who are served. However, the officers' reputations in the department and their promotions are largely determined by their performance in crime-related activities (Furstenberg & Wellford, 1973). Consequently, patrol officers soon start viewing service calls (for example, checking doors and windows on closed businesses, mediating family quarrels, removing illegally parked cars, and other mundane tasks) as a distraction from their real work, leading "to a disregard for the average consumer of police service" (Furstenberg & Wellford, 1973, p. 394). This cultivates police antipathy toward support activities, which leads to further social isolation. To counteract this process, involving consumers in police service evaluation, instead of relying solely on performance evaluations from immediate supervisors, may have a powerful impact on how the police are trained and how they deliver their services.

Furthermore, service is a *perishable* commodity, which if not consumed at the time of its offering cannot be inventoried for later use. For example, a county sheriff cannot tell officers to work longer hours on a given night to make up for a night when there were no calls and hence no work. A service manager or administrator has three basic options to tackle variable demands and a time-perishable capacity (Fitzsimmons & Fitzsimmons, 2006):

1. Managers can try to smooth demand by doing the following:

   - *Using reservations or appointments.* This provides more control to the service provider and helps to handle demand. For example, typically a doctor's clinic requires a patient to call ahead of time to make an appointment, unless it is an emergency. This gives the doctor's staff control over the arrival of the patients so that the demand for the doctor's services is spread evenly throughout the day. In some criminal justice services, this option may work well. For example, in a prison the recreation time or mealtime for inmates can be spread out so that not too much pressure is put on the security services at any given time. Probation offices and courts can also control how many cases will be handled on a given day and within a particular time frame. But in certain other areas such as policing, this option may not work since it is not possible to ask offenders or victims to schedule appointments to commit crimes or to interact with law enforcement.

   - *Using price incentives.* This allows the service provider to motivate the customers to shift their demand to different times of the day, resulting in greater demand uniformity. For example, telephone companies encourage customers to shift their calls to off-peak time by offering discounted rates on weekends and evenings. The customers who are price sensitive—generally, the ones making social calls—shift their demand to off-peak times, resulting in more evenness of demand throughout the day. Similarly, airlines provide discounted airline tickets for red-eye flights to shift some of the demand from peak time to off–peak time. The length of the visiting time for families of inmates can be used as an incentive to spread the demand throughout the day in a prison. For example, families that visit the prison during lean times of the day (morning hours) may spend a longer time with the prisoners.

2. Managers can adjust service capacity by doing the following:

- *Using part-time help during peak demand hours*. Students, for example, often do part-time jobs during peak hours in grocery stores or other retail outlets, which helps meet the increased demand for services. This option is exercised by the police force, and in some cases other criminal justice agencies, by calling in volunteer and auxiliary officers to help monitor traffic during parades and other celebrations in various cities.
- *Using cross-trained workers*. In grocery stores, the workers usually staffing the back office, for example, are called to help in attending customers when the checkout lines get long. This option is also used by policing agencies when officers doing back-office administrative work are stationed on the streets during big events, such as parades.
- *Scheduling work shifts to vary workforce in accordance with expected demand*. For example, more people work during early morning and evening shifts in grocery stores. Similar trends are followed in scheduling law enforcement officers and others, such as correctional officers, for different shifts and days of the week.
- *Increasing the customer self-service content*. Walmart, for example, has self-service checkout lanes, which customers can use if they do not want to wait in a line to be assisted by a checkout operator. Urban policing agencies have implemented computers to take nonemergency crime reports over the telephone. In Houston, Texas, for example, a person can report a burglary to their vehicle or stolen merchandise through computer prompts on the telephone. A police report is later sent via mail to the person, notifying the victim of the status of the case. The customer (the victim) does not have to wait for the police to show up at the scene before filing a report on the crime.

3. Managers can allow customers to wait longer:

- This option has the benefit of pushing up the use of service capacity. However, the downside is the risk of losing dissatisfied customers to a competitor. This option is typically unavailable in most areas of criminal justice, and especially law enforcement, due to the nature of the service. Victims of crimes cannot be expected to wait for lengthy periods while law enforcement works on other cases.

The *intangibility and heterogeneity* characteristics of service present complex situations. The intangibility characteristic of a service creates a problem for the customers because they are not able to see, feel, or test the performance before purchase. Consequently, customers make judgments of the service quality based on their perceptions that may be rooted in a number of indicators. For example, an impression of the quality of service received at a restaurant may be formed on the basis of cleanliness observed when a customer walks into the restaurant. The intangibility characteristic of service has important implications for the criminal justice system. For example, the fairness of a judge is dependent on the public's perception of the procedural processes used and decisions made by the judge (Burke & Lebed, 2007).

The customers' involvement in the service delivery process, along with the intangible nature of services, results in a large variation of service from customer to customer—thus introducing heterogeneity in services. Therefore, law enforcement services are closely monitored by various governmental and nongovernmental interest groups for fairness of treatment. Developing clear and detailed guidelines and standards, followed by good employee training in following proper procedures, is necessary for higher consistency in providing law enforcement services.

It is important to note that variation in service is not inherently bad, unless the customer perceives the variation to be a reflection of bad quality. Typically, when a service is delivered in the presence of other customers, the expectations of being treated fairly and being given the same service that others receive are higher. For example, in a retail store, customers' expectations of fairness in service received are influenced by what they see as the treatment given to other customers. On the other hand, if there is a customer–service provider interaction in the absence of other customers, then it is harder for the customer to make comparisons of fairness in service delivery. A doctor's interaction with a patient is typically removed from the presence of other patients. In such a case, the comparison of fairness is based on the perceptions formed from earlier experiences and the general awareness of the service that a customer may acquire. Expectations of service by customers can be shaped by providing them proper information. In profit-based companies, information dissemination is done through various advertising media. Similarly, law enforcement agencies can educate the various stakeholders to shape their opinions about the services offered. Very often, there is little clarity as to what to expect from law enforcement agencies in different circumstances. This void of formal information from law enforcement agencies allows informal communication channels to operate, which introduces large variations in the perception by customers about the quality of services to be expected from policing agencies. Such variations in expectations make it harder for law enforcement agencies to satisfy different stakeholders. Policing agencies and other criminal justice agencies can work to rectify this issue by fully using websites to advertise their services and programs. They can also provide information to customers by speaking at public forums, such as community clubs, schools, and city council meetings. Criminal justice agencies can also turn to the media, just as for-profit agencies do, and use public information campaigns to disseminate materials on services and programs offered. Customers have to play the role of a coproducer (refer to Chapter 3), so service quality will improve as information dissemination by criminal justice agencies educates their customers.

Tools to Build Quality in the Criminal Justice Service Delivery Process

One universal message propagated in the literature on quality is that it cannot be *inspected* into a product or service, but needs to be built into the process of making the product or delivering the service. If an error is caught through inspection, it can be rectified, but quality demands that the error should not have occurred in the first place. To introduce quality into the process, the service delivery system must be examined.

Total quality management (TQM). This is an approach to attaining excellence by infusing quality values throughout all activities and the workforce. Instead of solely relying on the quality control department to inspect and maintain quality, TQM supports the notion that all workers should be trained to infuse quality into everything they do. The concept is simple and uses a supply chain relationship between workers. Think of a car being manufactured on an assembly line, where a worker does a task and then passes the product to the next worker in line. Note that here the first worker is the supplier and the second worker is the customer. If the second worker, acting as a customer, is well trained about quality within his or her immediate domain, then he or she can check to ensure that the first worker has done good-quality work. When the second worker passes the product to the third worker, then the second worker acts as the supplier and the third worker is the customer. If this chain-like relationship is maintained, then everyone gets involved in infusing quality into the car. This notion of involving everyone is far more powerful in infusing quality than if the task of inspection was assigned solely to the quality control department. However, involving organization-wide participation in quality control requires a major shift in the mindset of the workforce and managers, necessitating greater involvement and empowerment of the workforce.

One way to involve workers is through the use of *quality circles (QC)*. The concept was first developed by Kaoru Ishikawa of the University of Tokyo in the early 1960s (Evans & Lindsay, 2005). It is a tool that allows group decision making, thus keeping the workforce motivated by signaling to them that their input is valuable in the efficient running of the organization. Typically, QC is a team of 6 to 12 workers and supervisors who meet regularly to discuss work-related issues with the express goal of improving service quality and productivity. The membership is voluntary. Whetten and Cameron (2002) provide the following important elements that need to be in place for the quality circles to be successful:

- Good employee–management relations are essential for the trust to emerge between members of the QC.
- Commitment of top management to the QC is important so that everyone in the organization takes them seriously and cooperates with them.
- A participative leadership style should be used by QC leaders so that members are more forthcoming in sharing their ideas. In an authoritarian leadership, the members may become unresponsive or leave the QC because it is voluntary. In addition, many nonassertive people may not participate in the QC, despite having valid ideas for improvement.
- The goals of the QC should be clearly stated so that there is no confusion due to ambiguity and so that different QCs do not digress into each other's territory. It is also important to clarify the relationship between the QCs and the quality control department. Otherwise, there could be unnecessary redundancy or threat felt by them.
- The program should be well publicized throughout the organization so that there is less resistance in sharing information and there is improved and open communication.

- QC programs should be customized to the local circumstances of the organization and not simply transplanted from another successful operation elsewhere.
- Management should recognize good ideas emerging from QCs and implement them for improving the quality and the productivity of the organization. If recognition is not given or the good ideas are not implemented, then the members of the QC will lose faith in the notion that the management is truly interested in involving them, which will result in QCs becoming defunct.

QCs not only provide valuable input to the improvement of service quality, but they can also help in developing present and future managers and leaders. Whetten and Cameron (2002) found that typically "the supervisors who were QC leaders were significantly more self-confident, knowledgeable, and poised than other supervisors who were attending the regular training program" (p. 520).

Statistical process control (SPC). There is a widespread agreement among practitioners that what gets recognized gets measured and what gets measured gets done. Typically, there are four stages to this process of recognizing and measuring: (1) An organization defines its purpose and identifies its key functions, (2) performance targets in the key functions are set, (3) performance measures are designed and measured for each of the identified functions, and (4) from the measurements a feedback loop is established for continuous improvement. To keep service in control, typically a feedback loop is required where the customers provide input on their experiences in the form of a survey questionnaire. The input is then compared to a service standard. Any deviation from the standard is communicated back to the system for adjustments. It must be realized that monitoring the customers after they have received the final service may be too late to avoid the loss of future sales (in the case of criminal justice, the negative perception toward the system), especially if a service failure has occurred. This difficulty in controlling service quality may be addressed by focusing on the delivery process itself and by employing a technique borrowed from manufacturing called *statistical process control (SPC).* This technique allows the organization to proactively determine that the service delivery process is working properly, thus minimizing the risk of service failure. Exposing the students to statistical process control is beyond the scope of this book, but students are encouraged to read a standard text on quality to acquire deeper knowledge of this topic.

Process flowchart. Another technique that can be used to correct the service delivery process is the *process flowchart.* It is used to examine the underlying sequence of operations and activities involved in the delivery of a particular service. Each activity is classified according to its nature, and the classification symbols are connected to provide the flowchart. Time and distance traveled by employee and customer and the time associated with activities such as delays, inspections, travel, and operations are typically measured. The resulting flowchart provides a diagrammatic representation of the *service blueprint,* which acts as a visual aid to identify opportunities for improvement in process efficiency. Unnecessary activities are removed, while other activities are modified and sometimes combined to bring greater efficiency while reducing cost.

A criminal justice agency should construct a process flowchart underlying the sequence of operations and activities to identify actions that need to be eliminated or modified to make the delivery of services more efficient.

Poka-yoke. Shigeo Shingo (1986) believed that most manufacturing errors occur not because employees are incompetent, but because of a lapse of attention caused by several interruptions throughout the day. He advocated the adoption of *poka-yoke* methods, which are foolproof devices and routines to be used by factory employees to achieve high quality without costly inspection. These poka-yokes are built into the manufacturing process to prevent errors from occurring, even when the operator loses focus because of interruptions. For example, if a board is placed incorrectly for drilling a hole, the machine that drills the holes will not operate because of a poka-yoke that uses an infrared beam to ensure that the board is placed correctly. The concept of poka-yoke can be adopted into services. A service can fail either because of an error committed by the service provider or because of the customer, who is an active player in the service delivery. In other words, service errors can originate from both the server and the customer; therefore, poka-yokes are needed for both the service provider and the customer to prevent errors from occurring.

Service provider errors can be categorized into three areas: tasks/activities, treatment of customer, and tangibles (Fitzsimmons & Fitzsimmons, 2006). An example of a *task poka-yoke* would be the use of premeasured milkshakes for small, medium, and large settings at McDonald's. Presettings allow for the same amount of serving per shake size, which rules out server error. Law enforcement officers are able to use *fact sheets* when documenting traffic accidents. These forms provide predetermined questions and answer spaces for officers to record all of the important information necessary to file the accident report. This greatly reduces the chance that an officer will fail to record pertinent information on the accident because of interruptions or other distractions. An example of a *treatment poka-yoke* would be a box on the customer check-in form that requires the front-office staff to enter the customer's eye color to ensure that they make eye contact when greeting the customer. Similar requirements can be introduced for police officers, which will make them appear more friendly and courteous. An example of a *tangible poka-yoke* would be the automatic feature of capitalizing the letter after the use of a period in Microsoft Word. As a criminal justice example, driver's licenses in some states are coded on the back with magnetic bars that police officers can scan into computers (much like credit cards) to automatically retrieve a driver's information to prevent errors due to manual recording.

For the customers as well, the errors fall into three categories: preparation, encounter, and resolution (Fitzsimmons & Fitzsimmons, 2006). An example of a *preparation poka-yoke* can be found on the form provided at the time a customer buys an airline ticket, which informs passengers of items that they cannot have in carry-on luggage due to safety regulations. Similarly, states supply their criminal codes on the Internet or on hard copy, which informs customers (members of society) of what is illegal and the resulting punishments. Those who drive are reminded of driving laws, such as speed limits, through signs posted on the roads, highways, and interstates. An example of an *encounter poka-yoke* would be the frames at airports and train stations that passengers use to determine if their carry-on luggage meets the allowable size requirements. Police departments commonly place speed detectors along highways and at entrances into cities that flash the drivers' speed as they pass. Even though a police officer is not present, the drivers are reminded of the maximum speed limit and provided with their speed during the encounter. The *resolution poka-yoke* is meant to shape the behavior of the customers as they exit the service. For example, Microsoft Word automatically generates a message asking if the document has been saved before exiting the program. As discussed in Chapter 11, probation and parole services as well as correctional institutions focus on shaping future behaviors throughout the service process and as customers exit the service. Police departments also provide to youthful offenders programs like station adjustments, which are aimed at stopping further delinquency. In this situation, officers are shaping the behavior of the children by releasing them without additional court involvement.

Poka-yokes can be incorporated into the physical design of criminal justice services to prevent server and customer errors. Such clever checks play an important role in services, where it is difficult for management to intervene in the service process to appraise and correct quality once it has started.

Service quality is a separate course in itself, and there is much literature on the subject. However, in this chapter, students have been exposed to some of the basic concepts, with the caveat that students who are more interested in the topic should examine the original sources.

Chapter Summary

- Criminal justice organizations are increasingly being asked, at all levels, to justify their expenditures and activities.
- The most important behavioral change that is required to improve service quality in the criminal justice system is the recognition that criminal justice agencies are in the business of providing various services that are consumed by diverse customers. They need to accept the importance of the customer in the entire service delivery system. The New York Police Department achieved a total transformation when it adopted customer orientation in its redesigned service delivery process.
- There is wide agreement among practitioners that what gets recognized gets measured and what gets measured gets done. Typically, there are four stages to this process of recognizing and measuring: (1) an organization defines its purpose and identifies its key functions, (2) performance targets in the key functions are set, (3) performance measures are designed and measured, and (4) a feedback loop is established for continuous improvement.
- The technique of quality function deployment (QFD) allows for the incorporation of the voice of the customer into the service process design.
- Law enforcement agencies play a dual function of control and support by acting as agents of control and agents of support. Crime-related tasks or law enforcement, order maintenance, and crime prevention fall within the two primary functions.
- Performance assessment can best be established by integrating the internal and external measures of performance. Such integration through the use of QFD allows an organization to incorporate the voice of the customer into the design of the service delivery process.

- QFD uses three matrices. It provides a chain-like interface between the different matrices. The first matrix presents the relationship between customer desires and service measures/characteristics. In the second matrix, the service measures/characteristics derived from the first matrix are treated as whats. In the second matrix, there is the identification of the service design elements (hows) that can deliver the whats. In the third matrix, the service design elements from the second matrix are treated as whats. Also in the third matrix, there is the identification of the daily management techniques that need to be adopted by the people who provide the service.
- The voice of the customer is introduced into the first matrix and then carried through the second and third matrices by developing linkages between inputs and outputs of different phases of development.
- Each matrix can be viewed as a set of six stages, providing a systematic hierarchical framework to fill the six parts of the house of quality.
- Once an organization has decided to incorporate the voice of the customer in the service delivery process, it has to think about how much contact to allow with the customer, which introduces the front office versus back office concept. The front office of any service is the physical location where the service provider interacts with the customer and the service delivery takes place. The back office supports the activities of the front office, and is generally removed from customer interactions. Through proper design, organizations can use customer involvement in the service delivery process to their advantage.
- If the service delivery takes place at the service provider's facility, then attention to facility design is important because the customer's perception of quality may be influenced by the surroundings.
- The simultaneous production and consumption of services puts an added pressure on the service manager because it eliminates many opportunities for quality control. Unlike a product, a service cannot be inspected before delivery. Therefore, quality control measures need to be installed within the service design and delivery process, supplemented with rigorous training to prevent bad service occurrences.
- A service is a perishable commodity, which if not consumed at the time of its offering cannot be inventoried for later use. Service managers or administrators have three basic options to tackle variable demand and a time-perishable capacity. They can try to smooth demand, adjust capacity, or allow customers to wait longer.
- The customers' involvement in the service delivery process, along with the intangible nature of services, results in a large variation of service from customer to customer. Educating customers on what to expect from services is important in shaping their expectations. One universal message propagated in the literature on quality is that quality cannot be *inspected* into a product or service, but needs to be built into the process of creating the product or delivering the service.
- Quality control tools such as total quality management, statistical process control, process flowchart, and poka-yoke can be used to improve service delivery quality in the criminal justice system.

Chapter Review Questions

1. Why is measuring service quality in the criminal justice system so difficult? Why is it important to incorporate the voice of the customer in designing a service?

2. What do you understand about internal and external performance measures? Why is it important for both of these kinds of measures to be integrated to improve the quality of service delivery? Identify internal and external performance measures for the law enforcement agency in your town.

3. Identify and explain the six stages involved in designing a house of quality. Design a house of quality for a law enforcement agency of your choice.

4. Incorporating the concept of front office versus back office, suggest at least five ways to improve the service in a criminal justice agency.

5. Since services face a time-perishable capacity, suggest at least five ways to smooth and improve capacity use in a criminal justice agency.

6. Draw a process flowchart for the law enforcement agency in your hometown.

7. What are poka-yokes? Suggest at least 10 poka-yokes to reduce errors and improve service delivery in the criminal justice field.

CASE STUDY

Parkway is a midsized suburb of Fort Lauderdale, Florida. According to the latest census data, the population is roughly 190,765. Many families with young and teenage children and immigrants from across the globe currently reside in the various subdivisions throughout the city. Demographically, males make up about 59.7% of the population and females are 40.3%. The median income is $42,433 a year with housing/condo values in the $205,000 to $300,000 range. Monthly rent averages $1,088. Blue-collar jobs (such as construction, waste management, and food services) are the most common positions held by men living in Parkway. Female residents are employed most often in health care, finance, insurance, and education positions. Approximately 18% of the residents live in poverty.

The racial makeup of Parkway is white non-Hispanic (57%), black (20.5%), Hispanic (17.1%), other races (3.5%), two or more races (3.3%), Asian Indian (1.2%), and Chinese (0.8%). A little less than half (48.9%) of the population is foreign born. The unemployment rate is approximately 4.7%. In comparison to Florida state statistics, Parkway's black race population percentage is significantly above the state average, its Hispanic race population percentage is also above the state average, the median age is below the state average, and the foreign-born population percentage is significantly above the state average.

Crime rates have been increasing over the last six years in Parkway despite efforts by the police department and city government. Last year, there were 4 murders, 38 rapes, 177 robberies, 280 assaults, 690 burglaries, 3,451 thefts, 570 motor vehicle thefts, and 19 arsons reported by the Parkway Police Department to the Federal Bureau of Investigation's (FBI) Uniform Crime Report. Other crimes also occurred in the jurisdiction, although they were not reported to the FBI. The Parkway Police Department currently employs 272 full-time workers. One hundred and seventy of these are street-level officers. Budget constraints make it impossible right now to employ more officers or to increase patrol efforts.

Parkway Police Department is a CALEA-accredited agency. The department has held accreditation since 2005. It is due for reevaluation this year by a team of assessors from CALEA. The evaluators will arrive to examine the department's policies, procedures, management, operations, and support services by the end of the year.

With this in mind, the Parkway Police Department has been gathering information to share with the evaluators. Part of the evaluation process includes input from residents regarding the police department and its services. To meet this requirement, the department sent surveys to city residents on their views of public safety issues and services the public believes the department is not providing. Residents were asked to share any perceived department shortcomings in the survey.

Results from the survey indicated citywide concern over the increasing crime rates. Satisfaction with the Parkway Police Department declined since the last accreditation review in 2005. Survey questions asking about potential community problems indicated that crime was ranked as a problem, drug problems increased in rating from 13% to 20%, and the public's sense of safety from violent crime declined from 90% to 72%. The public's sense of safety from property crime declined from 80% to 64%. The quality of police services was ranked as average to below average by 91% of the residents who responded to the survey. In 2005, the survey indicated good or excellent quality in police services by approximately the same percentage of residents. When compared to similar communities that also rank their police departments, the Parkway Police Department is below average in ranking.

During traffic stops, the Parkway patrol officers provide comment cards to stopped motorists to encourage telephone calls if the motorists feel they were not treated properly. Of the more than 30,000 cards distributed over the last three years, only about 5,000 were returned. The issues identified in the comments on the cards were resolved quickly and satisfactorily according to those involved. Knowing this, the police chief and city government are somewhat surprised by the results of the citizen satisfaction survey and the lowered ranking of quality of policing services.

The CALEA evaluators will use the survey information and comment cards, as well as other documents provided by the city and department, to determine if reaccreditation status will be awarded at their conference in March.

Questions for Review

1. What are possible explanations for the lowered rankings of the Parkway Police Department by citizens?

2. Using service quality concepts, what can be done to improve the Parkway Police Department's citizen satisfaction scores? What else should the Parkway Police Department do to improve the quality of service (within the budgetary confines)? Why didn't the Parkway Police Department chief and city council know about the declining image of the department prior to the survey? Why are these results a surprise?

3. If the Parkway Police Department placed the customer (specifically, the citizens) in the center of its organizational activities, how would customer focus, communication, leadership, motivation, and morale come into play?

4. What poka-yokes could the Parkway Police Department implement to reduce service errors?

Internet Resources

National Archive of Criminal Justice Data—http://www.icpsr.umich.edu/NACJD

National Criminal Justice Reference Service—http://www.ncjrs.gov

Sourcebook of Criminal Justice Statistics Online—http://www.albany.edu/sourcebook

References and Suggested Readings

Akao, Y. (1990). *QFD: Integrating customer requirement into product design.* Cambridge, MA: Productivity Press.

Brudney, J. L., & England, R. E. (1982). Urban policy making and subjective service evaluations: Are they compatible? *Public Administration Review, 42*(2), 127–135.

Burke, K., & Leben, S. (2007, September 26). *Procedural fairness: A key ingredient in public satisfaction.* A White Paper of the American Judges Association. Retrieved from http://aja.ncsc.dni.us/htdocs/AJAWhitePaper9-26-07.pdf.

Butler, A. J. P. (1992, January–March). Developing quality assurance in police services. *Public Money & Management,* 23–27.

Drummond, G., Ensor, J., Laing, A., & Richardson, N. (2000). Market orientation applied to police service strategies. *International Journal of Public Sector Management, 13*(7), 571–587.

Ermer, D. S., & Kniper, M. K. (1998). Delighting the customer: Quality function deployment for quality service design. *Total Quality Management, 9*(4&5), S86–S91.

Evans, J. R., & Lindsay, W. M. (2005). *The management and control of quality.* Mason, OH: Thomson South-Western.

Fitzsimmons, J. A., & Fitzsimmons, M. J. (2006). *Service management: Operations, strategy, information technology* (5th ed.). Boston, MA: McGraw-Hill/Irwin.

Furstenberg, F. F., Jr., & Wellford, C. F. (1973). Calling the police: The evaluation of police service. *Law & Society Review, 7*(3), 393–406.

Grasso, A. J., & Epstein, I. (1987). Management by measurement: Organizational dilemmas and opportunities. *Administration in Social Work, 11*(3), 89–100.

Griffin, A., & Hauser, J. R. (1993). The voice of the customer. *Marketing Science, 12*(1), 1–27.

Guy, B. (1992, January–March). Value for money in the police service. *Public Money & Management,* 41–45.

Han, S. B., Chen, S. K., Ebrahimpour, M., & Sodhi, M. S. (2001). A conceptual QFD planning model. *International Journal of Quality and Reliability Management, 18*(8), 796–812.

Hauser, J. R., & Clausing, D. (1988, May/June). The house of quality. *Harvard Business Review,* 63–73.

Kelley, J., & Swindell, D. (2002, September/October). A multiple indicator approach to municipal service evaluation: Correlating performance measurement and citizen satisfaction across jurisdictions. *Public Administration Review, 62*(5), 610–620.

Lilley, D., & Hinduja, S. (2006). Organizational values and police officer evaluation: A content comparison between traditional and community policing agencies. *Police Quarterly, 9*(4), 486–513.

Moore, M. H., & Stephens, D. W. (1991). *Beyond command and control: The strategic management of police departments.* Washington, DC: Police Executive Research Forum.

Motwani, J., Kumar, A., & Mohamed, Z. (1996). Implementing QFD for improving quality in education: An example. *Journal of Professional Services Marketing, 14*(2), 149–159.

Ostrom, E. (1973). The need for multiple indicators in measuring the output of public agencies. *Police Studies Journal, 2*(1), 85–91.

Ostrom, E., Parks, R. B., Percy, S. L., & Whitaker, G. P. (1979). Evaluating police organization. *Public Productivity Review, 3*(3), 3–27.

Park, R. B. (1984). Linking objective and subjective measures of performance. *Public Administration Review, 44*(2), 118–127.

Parsuraman, A., Zeithaml, V. A., & Berry, L. L. (1985, Fall). A conceptual model of service quality and its implications for future research. *Journal of Marketing, 49,* 41–50.

Parsuraman, A., Zeithaml, V. A., & Berry, L. L. (1988). SERVQUAL: A multiple-item scale for measuring consumer perceptions of service quality. *Journal of Retailing, 64*(1), 12–40.

Rogerson, P. (1995, October–December). Performance measurement and policing: Police service or law enforcement agency? *Public Money & Management,* 25–30.

Selen, W. J., & Schepers, J. (2001). Design of quality service systems in the public sector: Use of quality function deployment in police services. *Total Quality Management, 12*(5), 677–687.

Shingo, S. (1986). Zero quality control: Source inspection and the poka-yoke system. Stamford, CT: Productivity Press.

Stuart, F. I., & Tax, S. S. (1996). Planning for service quality: An integrative approach. *International Journal of Service Industry Management, 7*(4), 58–77.

Sung, H. E. (2006). Police effectiveness and democracy: Shape and direction of the relationship. *Policing: An International Journal of Police Strategies and Management, 29*(2), 347–367.

Suttler, G. (1994). Why bother using VOC? *Center for Quality of Management Journal, 3*(2), 5–6.

Whetten, D. A., & Cameron, K. S. (2002). *Developing management skills.* Upper Saddle River, NJ: Prentice Hall.

Whitehouse, J. (1973). Historical perspectives on the police community service function. *Journal of Police Science and Administration, 1*, 87–92.

Woolpert, S. (1980). Humanizing law enforcement: A new paradigm. *Journal of Humanistic Psychology, 20*, 67–80.

Appendix

Constructing QFD for Law Enforcement Services in Happymore

What do citizens of Happymore County (fictional name) want from their local law enforcement agency? Using multiple methods such as administering a questionnaire and interviews with experts and citizens, data are collected on what the citizens expect from the law enforcement agency in Happymore County. The numerous citizen responses are carefully examined and found to represent five broad categories, namely, assurance of security, responsiveness, reliability, and empathy from the law enforcement agency, and tangibles that make the agency look professional (discussed in Chapter 3). These five categories represent the voice of the customer in Matrix 1 (Figure 14.2). Next, the QFD team assigns relative importance to each of these five categories based on the data they have collected along with their knowledge of the discipline. The QFD team finds that the customers' most important requirement is the assurance of security, to which they assign a weight of 9. Next in importance is responsiveness, which is assigned a weight of 7. The least important requirement is tangibles, to which a weight of 1 is assigned.

Next, the QFD team identifies the service measures/characteristics that are outcome-based and those that are process-based. Outcome-based measures inform the customer about the success or failure of the service, which subsequently impacts the perception of the customer, whereas the process-based measures draw on the experience that customers encounter when they come in contact with a law enforcement service. Outcome-based service measures define the outcome of law enforcement services in terms of criminality, traffic problems, and public nuisance. Process-based service measures capture the essence of the various steps that customers may face in the service delivery process when they contact the law enforcement agency.

Next, the QFD team establishes the relationship between the service measures and the customer requirements, thus filling the main body of the matrix. The basic question to ask here is how a service measure correlates with a customer requirement. The relationships are represented as strong (9 points), medium (5 points), low (1 point), and no relationship (0). For example, a customer's requirement on "safety" will be strongly impacted by the service measure on "theft" within the county, thus getting 9 points. According to the QFD team, the data on theft do not impact any other customer requirement. For further clarity, take another service measure, say, "911 calls are responded to immediately." The

QFD team believes that the speed with which the 911 calls are responded to will *strongly* impact customers' perception of how safe people feel (9 points), it will *strongly* impact the customers' perception of the responsiveness of the law enforcement service (9 points), and it will have a *medium* impact on the customers' perception of whether the law enforcement service is dependable (5 points). The QFD team believes that the measure "911 calls are responded to immediately" does not impact the customers' perception about empathy and tangibles. In this fashion, the QFD team develops the rest of the matrix, establishing the relationships between the various service measures and the customer requirements.

Next, the absolute importance of each service measure is calculated, which is derived by adding the products of the strength of the relationships between the service measure and customer requirement and the relative importance of the customer requirement. For example, the absolute importance for "911 calls are responded to immediately" is 169. This score is derived by taking the impact of "911 calls are responded to immediately" on "assurance" (9 points) multiplied by the relative importance of "assurance" (9 points), plus the impact of "911 calls are responded to immediately" on "responsiveness" (9 points) multiplied by the relative importance of "responsiveness" (7 points), plus the impact of "911 calls are responded to immediately" on "reliability" (5 points) multiplied by the relative importance of "reliability" (5 points). In this fashion, the QFD team calculates the rest of the absolute importance entries. Subsequently, these absolute scores are normalized on a scale from 1 to 9 that is presented in the row below.

After that, the QFD team uses experts and citizens to evaluate how well Happymore County has performed on each of the five customer requirements as compared to Cheermore, another county with similar demographics. The comparison is done on a scale from 1 to 5, where 1 means poor and 5 means excellent. According to the information collected, Cheermore is rated 3 and Happymore is rated 4 on "assurance." These ratings imply that customers and experts feel that Happymore County is doing better than Cheermore County in fulfilling the customer requirement of "assurance." However, Happymore County has to improve because it is not rated 5. Similarly, comparisons for empathy, reliability, dependability, and tangibles are given. In the far-right column of Matrix 1 (Figure 14.2), the first number represents the rating for Cheermore County and the second number represents Happymore County.

Next, the QFD team compares the performance of Happymore County with Cheermore County on each of the service measures, using a 5-point scale with 1 meaning poor and 5 meaning excellent. This comparison appears in the basement of the house of quality (bottom row of Figure 14.2). The first number represents the rating for Cheermore County and the second number represents Happymore County. According to the comparison, Cheermore County is rated 3 and Happymore County is rated 4 on "theft." These ratings mean that the QFD team believes that Happymore County is doing better on its control of theft as compared to Cheermore County. However, Happymore County has to improve its performance on theft control because it is not rated 5. Similarly, comparisons for other service measures are performed.

Last, a correlation matrix between all of the service measures is provided in the roof of the matrix (Figure 14.2). The relationships are represented as strong (star), medium (circle), low (triangle), and no relationship. For example, "cases of theft" and "911 calls are responded to immediately" are highly correlated as shown by the star. In

Figure 14.2 Matrix 1: Relationship Between Customer Requirements and Service Measures

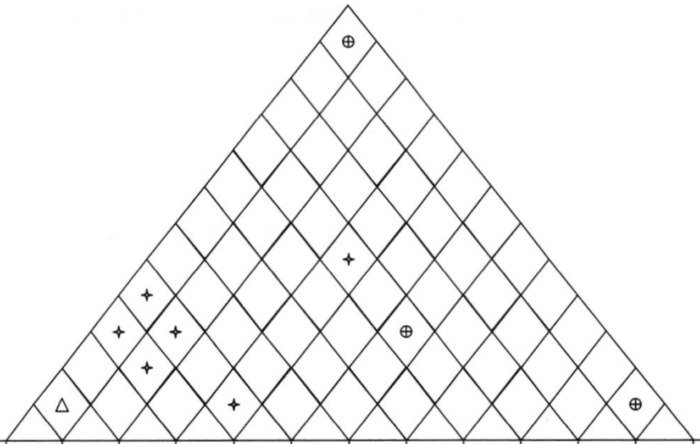

	Relative importance	Cases of theft (housebreak, shoplifting, etc.)	Cases of violent crimes	Cases of traffic accidents	911 calls responded to immediately	Officers can be reached easily	Officers are polite, respectful, friendly	Officers demonstrate good knowledge	Officers are fair in their treatment	Officers work well as a team	Officers take precautions in gun safety	Reports filed by officers are accurate	Records are easily available	Comparison with Cheermore County
Assurance: I want to feel safe and protected	9	9	9	9	9	9		1	9	5		9	9	3,4
Empathy: I want officers to show a caring attitude towards me	3						9						5	4,4
Responsiveness: I want officers to respond fast when called for assistance	7				9	9				5			5	5,4
Reliability: I want officers to perform service honestly, dependably, and accurately	5				5	5	5	9	9			9	9	3,4
Tangibles: I want officers and their equipment to be in perfect working conditions	1					1		1			1		9	5,3
Absolute importance		81	81	81	169	185	52	55	126	80	1	126	185	
Normalized score		4	4	4	8	9	3	3	6	4		6	9	
Comparison with Cheermore County		3,4	3,4	3,4	5,4	5,4	4,5	4,5	4,4	3,5	5,5	3,4	4,4	

a similar fashion, the QFD team completes the rest of the relationships in the roof of the house. A right angle drawn from the center of a cell will help identify the two service measures whose relationship is being represented. The reader is reminded that not all relationships are illustrated here, as this is an example used simply to demonstrate how relationships are represented in the roof of the house.

From Matrix 1 (Figure 14.2), the service measures (hows) are carried into Matrix 2 (Figure 14.3), where they become whats. The normalized absolute importance score of each service measure in Matrix 1 is transferred to Matrix 2, where they become relative importance scores. Also note that one of the items has been dropped based on the low absolute score. This item is "officers take precautions in gun safety."

Subsequently, the QFD team identifies the service design elements (hows) in the delivery-of-service measures (whats). These service design elements are capacity, facility design, technology, location, service culture including ethics and leadership, workforce selection and training, workforce motivation and empowerment, quality management, and information management. *Size and capacity* are important, as too little capacity may lead to poor service. *Facility design* indicates layout of the facility, how the back office and front office are designed to allow for effective communication and minimize unnecessary movement of the officers. *Process technology* is how the work is done and the choice of the technology that is used to provide service. *Location* is an important factor for a high-contact service such as law enforcement. The facility should be located by taking into account the demographics, distance from the school district, distance from the problem neighborhoods, and distance from heavy-traffic areas to allow for ease of driving to the crime location, and so on. *Service culture* is embedded in the leadership, and ethics will guide the service encounters. *Workforce selection and training* will provide for the skills required to perform the service. *Workforce empowerment and motivation* is important to the officers' attitudes and willingness. Decisions about how *quality* will be defined, measured, and monitored within the organization will critically impact service standards because of intangibility of the services and their simultaneous production and consumption (as discussed in Chapter 3). *Information management* including data collection, speed of data retrieval, and so forth can significantly impact the support that officers need from their office when they are in the field.

Next, the QFD team repeats the exercise of establishing the relationships between service measures (whats) and service design elements (hows), thus filling the main body of the matrix. The relationships are categorized as strong (9 points), medium (5 points), and low (1 point).

Then, the QFD team calculates the absolute importance for each service design element, which is derived by adding the products of the relative importance of the service measure and the strength of the relationships between the service measure and service design element. For example, "facility size and capacity" has an absolute importance score of 145. This score is derived by adding the strength of the relationship between "facility size and capacity" and all four entries in that column (Figure 14.3) multiplied by the relative importance of each entry. Therefore, it is $\{(5 \times 4) + (5 \times 4) + (5 \times 4) + (5 \times 9) + (5 \times 8)\}$. In this fashion, the QFD team calculates the rest of the absolute importance entries. The normalized scores are then provided in the row below the absolute scores, on a scale from 1 to 9.

Figure 14.3 Matrix 2: Relationship Between Service Measures and Service Design Elements

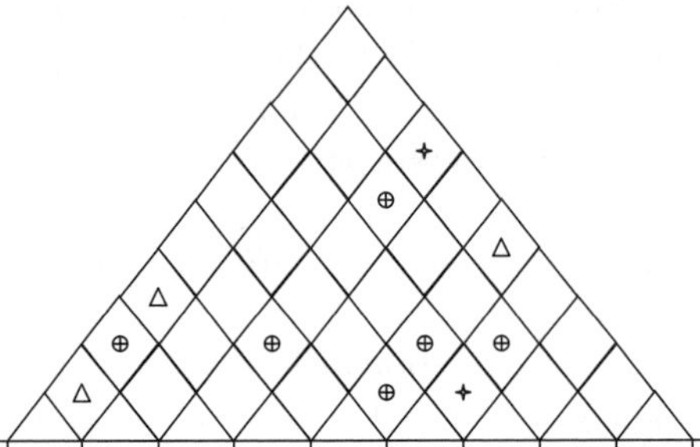

	Relative importance	Facility size and capacity	Facility design—layout (front vs. back office)	Technology and equipment	Location	Service culture (leadership, ethics)	Workforce—selection, training	Workforce—motivation, empowerment	Quality—measurement and monitoring	Information management—data collection	Comparison with Cheermore County
Cases of theft	4	5		5	9	5	9	9	5	5	3,4
Cases of violent crimes	4	5		5	9	5	9	9	5	5	3,4
Cases of traffic accidents	4	5		5	9	5	9	9	5	5	3,4
911 calls are responded to immediately	8	5	9	9	9	9	5	5	9	5	5,4
Officers can be reached easily	9	5	9	5	9	9	1	1	1		5,4
Officers are polite, respectful, friendly	3					9	9	5	1		4,5
Officers demonstrate good knowledge	3			5		5	9		9		4,4
Officers are fair in their treatment	6					9	9		1	5	3,5
Officers work well as a team	4		5			9	9	5			5,5
Reports filed by officers are accurate	6					5	9		9		3,4
Records are easily accessible	9		1				5		5	9	4,4
Absolute importance		145	182	192	261	375	400	192	276	211	
Normalized score		2	3	3	6	8	9	3	6	4	
Comparison with Cheermore County		3,5	4,5	5,4	4,4	4,5	4,4	4,5	3,5	5,4	

Next, the QFD team uses experts and citizens to evaluate how well Happymore County has performed on delivering each of the service measures/characteristics as compared to Cheermore County. Just as in Matrix 1, the comparison is done on a scale from 1 to 5, where 1 means poor and 5 means excellent (see right-hand side of Figure 14.3). The first number represents the rating for Cheermore County and the second number represents Happymore County.

Then, the QFD team compares the performance of Happymore County with Cheermore County on each of the service design elements, using the same 5-point scale. This comparison appears in the basement of the house of quality (see bottom of Figure 14.3). As before, the first number represents the rating for Cheermore County and the second number represents Happymore County.

Finally, a correlation matrix between all of the service design elements is provided in the roof of the matrix. As in Matrix 1, the relationships are represented as strong (star), medium (circle), low (triangle), and no relationship. A right angle drawn from the center of a cell will help identify the two service measures whose relationship is being represented by that cell. The reader is reminded that the roof does not explain all relationships, but is used for explaining how the relationships are captured in the roof of the house.

From Matrix 2 (Figure 14.3) the service design elements (hows) are carried into Matrix 3 (Figure 14.4), where they become whats. The normalized absolute importance score of each service design element in Matrix 2 is transferred to Matrix 3, where they become relative importance scores.

After that, the QFD team identifies the day-to-day management activities (hows) used to deliver the service design elements (whats). Subsequently, the QFD team establishes the relationships between service design elements and the day-to-day management activities in the main body of the matrix. The relationships are categorized as strong (9 points), medium (5 points), and low (1 point).

Next, the QFD team calculates the absolute importance for each of the day-to-day management activities, which is derived by adding the products of the relative importance of the service design element and the strength of the relationships between the day-to-day management activities and the service design element.

Then, the QFD team uses experts and citizens to evaluate how well Happymore County has performed on delivering each of the service design elements as compared to Cheermore County. As before, the comparison is done on a scale from 1 to 5, where 1 means poor and 5 means excellent. The first number represents the rating for Cheermore County and the second number represents Happymore County (see right-hand side of Figure 14.4).

Next, the QFD team compares the performance of Happymore with Cheermore Counties on each of the day-to-day management activities, using the same 5-point scale as earlier. This comparison appears in the basement of the house of quality. As before, the first number represents the rating for Cheermore County and the second number represents Happymore County (see at the bottom of Figure 14.4).

Finally, a correlation matrix between all of the day-to-day management activities is provided in the roof of the matrix. As in the other matrices, relationships are represented as strong (star), medium (circle), low (triangle), and no relationship. The reader is reminded that the roof does not explain all of the relationships, but is used for explaining how the relationships are captured in the roof of the house.

Figure 14.4   Matrix 3: Relationship Between Service Design Elements and Daily Management Activities

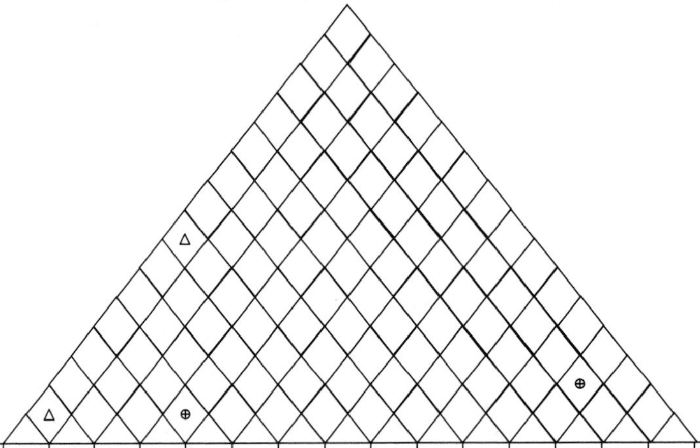

	Relative importance	Provide prevention talks to selected target groups	Maintain regular contact with business owners	Participate in safety forums/boards	Conduct day and night patrols	Exercise prevention by physical presence	Revisit victims	Conduct follow-up phone calls to assess the quality of service	Do extra shifts to manage work	Do technology upgrades twice a year	Leader shares problems with subordinates as a group, obtaining suggestions	Regularly visit target shooting range	Mandatory to spend one day a month in upgrading skills	Meet fitness goals every year	Visit in-training classes regularly	Regularly recertify officers in the use of force (handcuffing, chemicalspray, raids, etc.)	Comparison with Cheermore County
Facility size and capacity	2								7	7	5		7	5	5		3,5
Facility design–layout and communication	3				3	3			3	7	3						4,5
Technology and equipment	3			5					5	9		5	5		5		5,4
Location	6					3											4,4
Service culture (leadership, ethics)	8	7	7	7	7	7	7	7		3	7	3	5	5	5	5	4,5
Workforce—selection, training	9	7	7	7	7	7	7	7	5	5	7	7	7	7	7	7	4,4
Workforce—motivation, empowerment	3	7	7	7	7	7	7	7	5	5	7		7	7	7	7	4,5
Quality—measurementand monitoring	6	7	7	7	7	7	7	7		3	3		5	5	5	5	3,5
Information management	4	5	7	5	5	3	5	1		7							5,4
Absolute importance		202	210	202	226	221	202	186	98	192	177	102	183	164	179	154	
Comparison with Cheermore County		4,4	4,5	3,5	3,3	4,5	4,5	4,4	3,3	5,5	3,4	5,4	3,4	2,3	4,4	4,5	

Index

About the Authors

Jennifer M. Allen is a professor and department head of criminal justice at the University of North Georgia. She holds a Master of Science degree in administration and a doctorate in sociology. Prior to entering academia in 2008, she worked with delinquent juveniles and those victimized by abuse and neglect. Dr. Allen has published in the areas of restorative justice, juvenile delinquency and justice, youth programming, and policing administration and ethics. She teaches courses in juvenile justice, criminology, research methods, administration of criminal justice, family violence, corrections, and introduction to criminal justice at the graduate and undergraduate levels. She is also a coauthor of *Juvenile Justice: A Guide to Theory, Policy, and Practice* (Sage, 2014, 8th ed.), with Steven Cox, Robert Hanser, and John Conrad.

Rajeev Sawhney is a professor at Western Illinois University (WIU) in the Department of Management and Marketing. He holds a master's in economics, an MBA, and a doctorate in operations and supply chain management. Since 1999, Dr. Sawhney has been teaching at WIU in the areas of service operations management, quality management, strategic management, and supply chain management. During this period, he has been inducted multiple times into *Who's Who in the World, Who's Who Among America's Teachers, Who's Who in Science and Engineering,* and *Who's Who in Higher Business Education.* Dr. Sawhney has published several articles, a few of which have appeared in the *Journal of Operations Management*, the leading journal in the operations management discipline. He has also collaborated with Dr. Michiel R. Leenders in designing the Business Condition Index for the Purchasing Managers Association of Canada, which is now published monthly by leading Canadian newspapers. Dr. Sawhney serves as a consultant/researcher to Fortune 500 companies and nonprofit organizations. During this tenure, he has traveled extensively within and outside the United States, to Mexico, Canada, Asia, and Europe, to conduct workshops. Before moving to academics, Dr. Sawhney was a director with the Industry Ministry in India.